Dictionary of Medieval Knighthood and Chivalry

Dictionary of Medieval Knighthood and Chivalry

People, Places, and Events

BRADFORD B. BROUGHTON

Illustrations by Megan Broughton Blumbergs

Greenwood Press
New York • Westport, Connecticut • London

Library of Congress Cataloging-in-Publication Data

Broughton, Bradford B., 1926–
   Dictionary of medieval knighthood and chivalry : people, places,
and events / Bradford B. Broughton ; illustrations by Megan
Broughton Blumbergs.
      p.   cm.
   Bibliography: p.
   Includes index.
   ISBN 0–313–25347–1 (lib. bdg. : alk. paper)
   1. Knights and knighthood—Dictionaries.   2. Chivalry—
Dictionaries.   3. Knights and knighthood—England—Dictionaries.
4. Knights and knighthood—France—Dictionaries.   5. France—
Civilization—Medieval period, 987–1515.   6. England—Civilization—
Medieval period, 1066–1485.   I. Title.
CR4505.B76   1988
929.7'03'21—dc19   87–18163

British Library Cataloguing in Publication Data is available.

Library of Congress Catalog Card Number: 87–18163
ISBN: 0–313–25347–1

First published in 1988

Greenwood Press, Inc.
88 Post Road West, Westport, Connecticut 06881

Printed in the United States of America

∞

The paper used in this book complies with the
Permanent Paper Standard issued by the National
Information Standards Organization (Z39.48–1984).

10 9 8 7 6 5 4 3 2 1

To my grandchildren,

Kristoffer Brandon Blumbergs

Rebecca Ashley Blumbergs

Myles James Broughton

Isabelle Ashley Broughton

with all the loving affection this *medieval* grandfather

can bestow

Contents

Acknowledgments

My thanks and appreciation again go especially to my chairman, Dr. Mary Lay of the Technical Communications department and to the dean of Liberal Studies at Clarkson University, Owen E. Brady III, for their support, both psychic and financial, and their encouragement, both oral and sabbatical. Friends in the department also earned their share of credit in this undertaking for their uplifting comments and advice when the stack of notes still to be written up was enormous and the end was nowhere in sight: David Craig, Bill Karis, and Herb Smith. Special thanks again go to Dennis Horn for continually teaching me new ways to make the computer sing such lovely time-saving melodies. Without that support, this work could never have been written. My thanks again go to the staff at the Trinity College library in Dublin, especially the staff of its Lecky Library. Once again they helped me immeasurably during my return to Ireland for final notes and information for this volume. Particular expressions of appreciation go to Sean Breen, Tony Bohan, and all the rest.

To my son, Thaddeus and his family, I gratefully extend my thanks for their unflagging interest and moral encouragement, and to my fantastically gifted daughter, Megan, for making beautiful camera-ready sense of my scrawled genealogical charts.

Finally, and certainly the one person most responsible for the appearance of this work, I again delightedly praise and humbly thank June, my devoted and encouraging wife of thirty-seven years for editing copy and checking proof, but most particularly for her incredible and long-suffering patience as she agreed for two years that I could let slide some "house-things" to work on *the book*.

Abbreviations

PSTS - Publications of the Scottish Text Society, Edinburgh, 1884 ff.
PSuQ - *Philologische Studien und Quellen,* Wolfgang Binder, Hugo Moser,
        and Karl Stockmann, editors, Bielefeld, W. Germany, 1956
        ff.
RB - *Romanische Bibliothek. Hrsg. von Wendelin Foerster,* Halle,
        1888 ff.
Rdp - *Romans des douze pairs.*
Rolls Series - *Rerum Britannicarum medii aevi scriptores,* Published by
        the Authority of the Lords Commissioners of her Majesty's
        Treasury, under the Direction of the Master of the Rolls,
        London, 1857-1891.
SATF - *Société des Anciens Textes Franâais,* Paris: Firmin-Didot, 1875
        ff.; currently: Paris: Editions A. & J. Picard.
SEDES - *Société d'Edition D'Enseignment Superieur,* Paris, 5,
        Place de la Sorbonne.
ShF - *Société de l'histoire de France,* Paris.
Stevenson - Joseph Stevenson, *Church Historians of England,* London:
        Seeleys, 1851-1877.
STS - Scottish Text Society, 27 George Square, Edinburgh, Scotland,
        1884 ff.
UNCSRLL - North Carolina Studies in Romance Languages and Literature,
        University of North Carolina, Chapel Hill, NC, 1940 ff.
ZfdG - *Zeitschrift für deutsche Geisteswissengeschaft.*
ZfdP - *Zeitschrift für deutsche Philologie. Begr. von Hopfner u.*
        Zacher. Hrsg. von P. Merker und W. Stammler, Hanover, 1869;
        currently: Werner Besch, Hugo Moser, *et al*, editors,
        Bonn-Ippendorf, W. Germany.
ZrP - *Zeitschrift für romanische Philologie. Begr. von Gustav Grober;*
        Hrsg. von Alphons Hilka, Halle, 1876 ff.; currently: Karl
        Baldinger, editor, Heidelberg-Ziegelhausen, W. Germany.

Introduction

*In the course of the twelfth century, knights in the Anglo-Norman
and Angevin dominions as elsewhere became more aristocratic,
more exclusive [and] fewer....Some [reasons] may lie in constant
overseas campaigning, though that did not deter Duke William's
knights in 1066....In the great days of Norman expansion as many
knights as possible were needed and there were opportunities on
every hand. In the twelfth century demand diminished, and the en-
dless source of fiefs to reward and breed knights dried up, as
earlier generations became established in England and Wales and
southern Scotland and Ireland, in Italy, and Sicily and Antioch.
There was no soaring cost, save via inflation, of a knight's
equipment in the twelfth century to explain it....The expense of
knighthood is not confined to the sheer cost of horses, armor,
and weapons and the maintenance of all three....Far greater was
the cost of professionalism. By this I mean that mounted warfare
required a life-time dedication from an early age, in order especially to acquire the horsemanship necessary to manage those
great stallion warhorses in the heat and noise of battle, to deliver from the brute's heaving back all those accurate sword
strokes which the chansons endlessly admire, above all to take
part effectively in the shock-tactic of the charge....For all
this it was necessary to be released from, and elevated above,
the sordid necessity of earning a livelihood by any other means;
and the answer was the household and the fief. The result was
not only the knight, and the superb fighting machine of trained
and disciplined man and horse, but also the pride of professionalism, the happy warrior, and the elan of the elite.*

[R. A. Brown, "Status of the Norman Knight" in *War and
Government in the Middle Ages,* ed. John Gillingham, and J.
C. Holt, New York: Barnes and Noble, 1984, pp. 31-32.]

That quotation sets the stage effectively for this second
volume on medieval knighthood. It confirms that a knight was an important figure in the early medieval scheme of things, but his role
decreased in importance through time. Just how important he was and

how relatively unimportant he became will be left to the reader to discover through these pages.

A glance at the Topical List of Entries in the Table of Contents for this *Dictionary of Medieval Knighthood and Chivalry: People, Places and Events* reveals the scope of this work. Under People, it includes Rulers, Earls and Dukes, *Comtes*, Knights, Churchmen, Women, People, Individuals, Authors, and Fictional Characters. Under Places, it includes Castles and Places. Under Events, it includes Battles, Treaties, Books, Romances and *Lais*, *Chansons de geste*, Legal Terms, and Literary Terms. It even includes a section of Miscellaneous for those items not readily categorized.

This volume, which is a companion to *Dictionary of Medieval Knighthood and Chivalry: Concepts and Terms* (1986), identifies the names of many medieval European knights of all levels of nobility, fictional and real, with whom a reader might come into contact. It focuses on the "important" people, insofar as that term can be classified, for all medieval knights were important, but some were more important than others. It centers on the English and French knights with occasional side glances at major figures in Italy, Germany, Spain and the Low Countries.

No work like this can include the complete English, French and German peerage. Rather, space limitations and rigorous editing have limited the inclusion to entries whose names may be encountered as readers prowl through historical and fictional works dealing with or set in the Middle Ages. Included, therefore, have been the major earldoms of England, as well as some of the more famous knights who were not earls, but whose names are remembered even today. Most of the few earls who existed in England before William's arrival died or fled the countryside, and were replaced by the new monarch. However, those men were not necessarily "true-blue" supporters of their new king all the time, and as personal needs motivated, they occasionally rebelled against him. They have been identified here. For example, one of the biggest supporters of the king of England, but one of his biggest problem earls, was Robert of Bellême, (see Bellême-Montgomery), a cruel, greedy and merciless Norman. A few biographical lines about him make his actions a bit more understandable. A second and more famous example was Piers Gaveston,* a strange man who seemingly wielded a hypnotic influence over King Edward II of England. Readers, furthermore, will meet such well-known villains as Kings John* and Stephen* of England about whom they may wish to learn more.

Additionally, this work does not attempt to identify all the geographical locations or battles fought in Europe nor include every castle erected during the period, nor every romance, *lai** or *chanson de geste** written during the five hundred years spanned. Rather, the entries detailed were chosen because of their strategic and jurisdictional importance for the knighthood of England, France, and other European political entities. For example, one would find the actions of Simon de Montfort* and his followers in England during the Baron's War* of 1264-1265 difficult to understand unless the Provisions of Oxford* were provided.

On the literary or fictional side, readers frequently ask themselves did King Arthur* really exist? Who were the vassals of the king of France, the *douzepeers,** and why did the king choose them as he did? Many knights stride through literature. Who were they and what were the stories in which they appeared? A reader should find the answers to many of these questions in this work. And, insofar as I could, I have identified the most recent editions of literary works I cite here: *chansons de geste,* romances and *lais.* Just as this work was going to press, I learned of the recent appearance of the monumental work of André Moisan to which I call the reader's attention. Regrettably, I have not been able to examine and refer to his much needed work which just appeared late in 1986: *Répertoire des noms propres de personnes et de lieux cités dans les chansons de geste françaises et les oeuvres étrangère dérivées,* Geneva: Libraire Droz. Its 3,410 pages in five volumes replaced the highly valuable work of E. Langlois (Bibliog. 128) by offering five times as many entries as its predecessor, thus making identifications of French literary figures incredibly easy.

This work is intended to help the uninitiated reader understand more easily the development and growth of chivalry and knighthood in a world centuries removed from our own, a world peopled by characters who hold incredible fascination for the modern reader and student perhaps because they are so far removed and different. Set up alphabetically to provide a brief biography of some of the major historical knights and other personages of note, descriptions of major literary knightly characters and the works in which they appear, identifications of castles and other places of geographical interest and accounts of major battles in the period called "medieval" falling roughly between 1050 and 1400, this work is intended primarily as a reference work. For practically all of the entries included, reference is made to a major work or two on that subject, listed alphabetically in the Bibliography. Frequent cross-references are made to entries in the companion volume, Concepts and Terms, through the frequent use of the cross symbol (+). The asterisk (*) indicates cross references to this present volume. Although chivalry and knighthood existed also in Germany, Italy and other European countries, this work focuses primarily on the people, places and events in France and England, but includes some names from those other countries which a knight-errant might be expected to meet or visit on his continental peregrinations.

The figures in this work begin with Duke William of Normandy who brought the concept of knighthood with his invasion forces to the shores of England in 1066. Before that time, the Anglo-Saxon thanes+ were the important figures of the country, but they were not knights. William's mounted forces brought with them the idea of knights fighting on horseback instead of riding to an engagement and dismounting before beginning battle. The word *chivalry*+ comes from the French *chevalier,* meaning a mounted warrior. Seeing such figures ride around the countryside, the native English people called them *cnihts,*+ the Anglo-Saxon word for servant, because they appeared to serve their overlords in military and political matters. Their role in England grew when, to control the newly conquered land, William erected a new type of fortress called castle,+ and needed men to garrison it: knight-warriors serving a castellan-overlord.

As continuous warfare was the way of life for these knights, their love of battle, their hatred of restraint, and a sense of arrogant superiority became deeply ingrained in their natures, especially the French nobles on both sides of the English Channel. These men held a monopoly on the military profession. They trained for war, they bred for battle, they lived in warfare. To be an effective fighter, a man was required to have a horse, armor and weapons, all of which were expensive, and far beyond the reach of the serf or peasant. And to wield those materials effectively, a man had to have the leisure to practice their use continuously. This man, the *miles* or knight,+ was master of 11th-century France and England, and so long as he and his class, the nobles, held a monopoly on the military, rebellion was impossible. The lower classes had only the short bow as a weapon, and this was ineffective against the armor of the knight. Thus, until the non-noble class had money, leisure, and cheap effective weapons, the aristocracy was secure in its lofty place in society.

All this had emerged from the void in central political power left by the disintegration of the Roman Empire. Such a gap was filled by a series of contractual relationships between men based on land tenure. Weaker men took refuge under the protection of stronger men who by virtue of their wealth and position could offer protection. This resulted in a pyramidal structure of society in which every man was subordinated to another, every man was the vassal of another, setting up a huge structure of military and ecclesiastical land-holding aristocracy. Each warrior in essence became an independent lord with his own vassals, subsequently owing service to the king. The lord bestowed on those beneath him a fief or benefice, that is, a grant of land in return for service and support and other feudal obligations. Such an arrangement soon became hereditary.

Even though on a visit to Normandy in the mid-11th century, King Edward the Confessor* had promised the Anglo-Saxon throne to Duke William on his death, Saxon Earl Godwine's* son, Harold,* was elected to it by the Anglo-Saxon Witan on Edward's death in 1066. Duke William, however, was determined to have what he felt rightfully was his--the English throne--and he won it at the battle of Hastings* on October 14, 1066. Over the next four years, he established a powerful feudal monarchy, keeping 40 percent of the countryside for his own royal demesne, and imposing feudal demands on English barons, bishops and abbots. As a result, a French-speaking feudal aristocracy was established to control the Norman feudalism on English soil. Little changed among the people on the Anglo-Saxon shires and hundreds during this period, even under such tyrannical rulers as William's favorite second son, and successor, William II.*

This red-haired William II, Rufus as he was known, reigned with violence, cruelty, and injustice. His death at the hands of Walter Tirel* in 1100 brought his brother Henry I,* William the Conqueror's third son, to the throne. Ending his quarrel with his oldest brother, Robert II,* Curthose, Duke of Normandy (see Robert II), and by so doing, bringing that French dominion under the control of the English crown, Henry I did much to unite the England of the Anglo-Saxons with the England of the Normans by such means as instituting itinerant justices and circuit courts. He even married Matilda,* a princess of the Anglo-Saxon house of Wessex. The White Ship disaster,* however, deprived him of his only legitimate son, the Lord Prince William,* in 1120, and thus on his death in 1135, the crown passed to Stephen of Blois,* grandson of the Conqueror. That act began a period of anarchy as Henry's daughter, Matilda FitzEmpress,* sought to claim the throne for herself. To that end, she brought her second husband, Geoffrey of Anjou,* with her to England to fight for the crown for their son, Henry Plantagenet,* of Anjou. By 1153, young Henry had gained all of Normandy and forced the then childless King Stephen to recognize him as heir to the throne. Before he ascended the throne in 1154, Henry had married the divorced wife of King Louis VII* of France, Eleanor,* heiress to the duchy of Aquitaine,* and thereby he acquired control over that huge section of France. By adding this to his holdings in Normandy and Maine, Henry controlled an enormous portion of France.

Once in power in 1154, Henry II restored and developed the machinery of government which his grandfather namesake had created. He originated the English jury system, enlarged the jurisdiction of the royal courts and developed the common law. He altered the military system, replacing the feudal levy with a paid professional body of soldiers who stood ready to go and fight at any time, and he revived the concept of liability for military service of all freeholders in England--the concept of the Anglo-Saxon *fyrd*.+ Additionally, he tried to control the church by exercising control over ecclesiastical courts and by insisting that "criminous clerks" be tried by lay courts. After his close friend and colleague, Thomas à Becket,* had been apppointed to the archbishopric* of Canterbury, Becket changed from being a king's man to one who defended ecclesiastical liberties vehemently, enraging Henry and arousing his enmity, leading to Becket's murder in Canterbury cathedral in 1170. In the years following, Henry fought a continuing series of battles with his rebellious sons, young Henry,* Richard,* Geoffrey* and John,* who wanted autonomy in their own dominions while their father still lived.   After the death of young Henry in 1173, the three surviving sons joined with the French monarch, Philip II,* Augustus, son of Louis VII by his third wife, to force their father to grant their wishes. That union finally destroyed an aging Henry, and he died in 1189, naming Richard as his heir.

King Philip had ascended the French throne in 1180 at the age of 15, a descendant of the Capetian* line of French kings begun by Hugh Capet in 987.   The first four Capetian kings, Hugh* (987-996), Robert* (996-1031), Henry I* (1031-1060), and Philip I* (1060-1108), did little more than just keep the monarchy alive, and establish hereditary succession. Their resources consisted entirely of the Ile de France.* The duchy of Normandy,* founded by Duke Rollo in 911, was, however, outside their province. Under strong dukes, Normandy became the most powerful vassal of the French kings. Duke William II* enlarged its holdings by invading England as William the Conqueror. King Louis VI,* the Fat (1108-1137), increased the French royal domain by consolidating the royal authority in the Ile de France by overthrowing small vassals, supporting towns and the church against baronial opposition, and with the able assistance of his chief minister, Abbe Suger, abbot of Saint Denis,* awakening some national spirit in the north of France. His son, Louis VII, though able and energetic, was not the statesman his father was. His participation with his wife, Eleanor of Aquitaine, on the disastrous second crusade+ to the Holy Land lost considerable prestige for the royal house. Further loss occurred when Eleanor sought and was granted permission to divorce him in order to resume her duchy of Aquitaine.   Shortly thereafter, she married Prince Henry of England, taking Aquitaine with her as her marriage portion. As a result, Louis was overshadowed by his vassal Henry by the fact that Henry held fiefs for more than one-third of all France.

Philip II, also, was a different king than his father. He fought steadily to rid France of all English control by undermining the position of the English kings in France, and repeatedly intriguing against Henry II, Richard (1189-1199) and John (1199-1216). Finally in 1204, through a series of blunders and misgovernment by John of England, Philip obtained control of all the fiefs+ in France held by the English king except Gascony* and Poitou.* By his scheming and maneuvering, Philip earned the enmity of many continental nobles. In addition to the countless plotting of John to recover the lost land, Philip had to contend with the count of Flanders,* and Otto IV,* Holy Roman Emperor. The climax came at the battle of Bouvines* in 1214. That battle marked the end of the war between John and Philip which had begun in Normandy in 1202, and the end of the dispute between Frederick II* of Hohenstaufen and Otto IV of Brunswick over the crown of the Holy Roman Empire. Philip and his ally Frederick decisively defeated John, Otto and the count of Flanders. That victory allowed Philip to complete his takeover of Normandy, Anjou and Touraine, and to create for John such domestic difficulties at home in England that on his return he was confronted with a rebellion of the barons and was compelled to issue the *Magna Carta*+ in 1215. Additionally, Philip actively supported Simon de Montfort's actions as leader of the northern French forces against Languedoc+ in the Albigensian+ crusade in the southern portion of his country. This resulted in extending Capetian authority upon southern France. In his 43 years on the throne, Philip II increased considerably the royal domain, forced the barons and nobles to obey the crown, and created officials similar to the itinerant justices appointed by Henry II in England to govern the royal domains.

His successor, Louis VIII,* died after only three years, leaving a child king, Louis IX,* to rule under the regency of the queen, Blanche of Castile.* This child matured to become one of France's greatest monarchs, known better as Saint Louis. He possessed a rare combination of kingly talents and deep piety, and established a widespread European reputation for justice. He took up the cross as a crusader in 1144, and carried it all the rest of his life; he was canonized shortly after his death. He continued and refined his grandfather's system of royal officials to control the seneschals and bailiffs, and in a move that dealt a severe blow to the political independence of the feudal barons, insisted that appeal to the *curia regis** must be allowed from all feudal courts when certain issues were involved. At the time of his death, the French feudal lords had been reduced in power to obedience to the monarch, the country was becoming unified in spirit of patriotism and nationality, and Roman law was superseding feudal law throughout.

Thirteenth century England saw the troubled reign of Richard's successor, John, end in 1215 with the *Magna Carta*, a feudal document that lay down the principle of limited, contractual monarchy. John's death in 1216 left his nine-year-old son, Henry III,* as king to rule for fifty-six years. He proved to be a poor king, for he was subservient to the papacy, and allowed papal exploitation of England; he supported extravagantly such foreign enterprises as seeking the Sicilian crown for his son, aiding his brother Richard* of Cornwall in his efforts to gain the crown of the Holy Roman Empire, and patronizing several large groups of foreign relatives and favorites of his French wife. From the turmoil in his reign emerged the beginning of the English Parliament. The leader of the baronial opposition to the king was Simon de Montfort, son of the leader of the Albigensian crusade in France. In 1258 he demanded of the king the Provisions of Oxford* which included a reaffirmation of the *Magna Carta,* the dismissal of foreign favorites, the resistance of papal taxation, and the appointment of a permanent Great Council to control the crown. In the civil war that followed, the king was defeated and captured, and Montfort became virtual dictator of England. In 1265, to support his regime, he summoned a Great Council, now coming to be called a parliament, which included two knights from each shire, and two burgesses for the more important towns, as well as bishops, abbots and barons. Simon was overthrown and killed in the battle of Evesham* in that same year by forces of the king led by the king's eldest son, Edward,* who became the real ruler of the country for the rest of his father's reign. Edward I, coming to the throne in 1272, reigned until 1307; he well understood the significance of Simon de Montfort's tactics and policy, and followed much of it by summoning in 1295 the Model Parliament.

Under Edward I, England conquered Wales* in 1284, sought unsuccessfully to rule Ireland, and forced an alliance between Scotland and France when Edward claimed an ancient right of suzerainty over the Scots, but his efforts were defeated by Scottish resistance led by William Wallace* and Robert Bruce.* His son, Edward II* (1307-1327), was a weak and incompetent king who had continual troubles with the barons and Parliament. His forces were defeated by the Scots at Bannock Burn* in 1314, and he was deposed by Parliament and secretly murdered in 1327. His son, Edward III* (1327-1377), followed him, and reigned for fifty years.

Philip III,* the Bold, succeeded his father, Louis IX, on the throne of France in 1270, and was in turn succeeded by his more famous son, Philip IV,* the Fair, who reigned from 1285 to 1314. Three of his well-known actions were supporting the claims of a Frenchman, Clement V, to the papal throne and packing the College of Cardinals with French clergy; moving the papacy to Avignon; and attacking the Knights Templar.+ This latter group, fat with wealth and no longer involved in the crusades, held great privileges in France. In 1307, Philip ordered them seized and prosecuted. Under torture some of their leaders confessed the charges were true, and Pope Clement V condemned the Order from Avignon. All their moveable wealth was confiscated by Philip and their lands were given to the Hospitallers. Philip's sons followed successively to the throne but none left a male heir, so in 1328, the throne went to Philip VI* of the house of Valois* who battled the English over the French throne for a hundred years.

This strife, called the Hundred Years War,* stemmed from the French King Philip IV's eagerness to break the feudal grip of England on Aquitaine in the southeast corner of France because their presence there blocked unification of France under the French crown. He and Edward I were at war between 1294 and 1303 with no appreciable change in the situation. As an additional strain on this relationship between the two countries, later Edward III claimed the French throne. He was grandson of Philip IV, the Fair, through his mother, Isabelle,* Philip's daughter, and had challenged the succession of Philip VI of Valois in 1328. Invoking Salic law, the French excluded him from the throne, and he reluctantly did homage to the new Valois king for his French fiefs in 1329. Eight years later he repudiated that homage and declared himself king of France. Between 1337 and 1360 several battles occurred, but nothing important until 1346 when the English demolished the French at Crecy.* That victory was due to the superior effectiveness of the English longbow+ over the French feudal cavalry charge: the longbowmen were superior to mounted feudal knights. From there the English marched north and captured Calais* which they held for over two hundred years. A truce in the war followed the incursion of the Black Death,+ the plague which swept across Europe in 1348 and 1349, killing perhaps one-third of the population. In 1355, the Prince of Wales,* Edward, the Black Prince,* began another campaign in Aquitaine, and won another tremendous victory over the French at the battle of Poitiers* in 1356, in which the longbow again proved to be superior, and the French lost their king, John II,* and two of his sons as prisoners to the English. This resulted in a truce in 1357, for France in defeat was falling into collapse. The resultant Treaty of Bretigny* in 1360 ceded Calais and nearly all of Aquitaine to Edward III in full sovereignty, and no longer as fiefs of the French king, in return for which Edward abandoned all claims to the French crown. Charles V,* the Wise, new French king after the death of the captured John II in 1358, repudiated that Treaty of Bretigny by re-asserting claims of sovereignty over Aquitaine. This time, the French were well prepared to fight, for they had an extremely able leader in Bertrand du Guesclin* who cleverly allowed the English to exhaust themselves by running all over the countryside, and then launched a French offensive. By 1374, the English held only a few ports in France, and Charles was contemplating an invasion of England. His plans were stopped by a truce mediated by the papacy in 1375.

The Black Prince died in 1376, a year before his father, Edward III, so on the death of the aged monarch, the crown passed to his young grandson, Richard II.* In turmoil over the defeats in France, financial disorder of the government, and baronial attempts to enforce old manorial services on the peasantry, the peasants revolted in 1381. Even though they were unsuccessful, they obtained considerable advantage from their revolt, because the ancient holds exerted by serfdom over them were broken forever.

That, then, was the political panorama in which knighthood and chivalry developed in France and England and reached their zenith around the end of the 14th century.

Dictionary of Names, Places, and Events

A

Abagha, Mongol khan* of Persia and Mesopotamia; great-grandson of Jenghiz (Genghis) Khan.* He married the daughter of the eastern emperor Michael Paleologus of Constantinople, and became the protector, friend, and ally of Bohemond VI, lord of Antioch and Tripoli. (Bibliog. 184)

Abbasid, dynasty of Muslim caliphs+ who reigned in Bagdad from 750 to 1258. They were a Shi'ite sect who claimed descent from Abbas, an uncle of Mohammed. (Bibliog. 98)

Abbeville, French city on the River Somme, 12 miles from its mouth on the English Channel. Here in 1259, King Henry III* of England signed a treaty with King Louis IX* of France by which the province of Guienne* was ceded to the English. (Bibliog. 68, 184)

Aberfraw, kings of. See North Wales.

Abergavenny ("Over Gwent"), castle+ and demesne+ situated on the river Gavenny (Gwent). Although the lords of Abergavenny owed their title to William I* (1066- 1087), its best known holder was William Beauchamp, fourth son of Thomas, earl of Warwick.* He served in France under Sir John Chandos* with great distinction and was nominated by Edward III* as a Knight of the Garter* in 1375. In 1383, he was captain of Calais,* and in 1399, was appointed justiciar of South Wales and Pembroke.* (Bibliog. 47)

Absalon, archbishop of Lund, Denmark. After studying in Paris, he travelled widely before returning to Denmark in 1157. He was eloquent, learned, uncommonly strong, and was such a renowned warrior at sea and on land that he was held in high esteem by Danish King Waldemar I, the Great. Acting on his avowed principle that "both swords, the spiritual and the temporal, were entrusted to the clergy," he used his abilities as a statesman and warrior constantly to help Waldemar achieve the independence and consolidation of his country. (Bibliog. 68)

Abulfeda, (Abu l-Fida), (Emad ed-Din) (1273-1331), Arabic historian and geographer who fought against the crusaders from the age of 12 when in 1285 he joined the assault against a stronghold of the Hospitallers,+ and later at the sieges of Tripoli and Acre. In 1312, he became prince with the title of Malik us-Salih, and in 1320 received the hereditary title of sultan. His *Abridgement of the History of the Human Race* in the form of annals from the Creation up to 1328 gave insight into the Saracen Empire. This work was translated into Latin by Dobelius, professor of Arabic at Salerno, in 1610. (*Recueil des Historiens des Croisades, Historiens Orientaux* I, Paris, 1872) (Bibliog. 68)

Abu Shama (1203-1267), Arab philologist, teacher, and industrious anthropologist. His work, *Book of the Two Gardens*, concerning the dynasties of Saladin* and Nureddin provided valuable material, including numerous documents from the Sultan's chancellery. (Bibliog. 83)

Accalon of Gaul, paramour and champion of Morgan la Fée* in Arthurian legend. Morgan stole Excaliber* and its scabbard from Arthur,* and gave them to Accalon, who used them in his first fight against Arthur. Arthur was in danger of losing the fight until he recovered both the sword and its scabbard with the help of the Lady of the Lake, Niniane,* and killed Accalon. (in *Gawain,* *Ywain,* *Le Morholts, Suite de Merlin**) (Bibliog. 145)

Achaea, name, collectively, for the political entities on the Peloponnesian peninsula after the fall of the Byzantine* Empire and the sack of Constantinople by crusaders+ in 1204. (Bibliog. 100)

Acheflour, sister of Arthur* in *Perceval of Galles,* and mother of Perceval.* (Bibliog. 1, 2)

Ackerman, Francis (c. 1335-1387), Flemish soldier and diplomat. Born in Ghent,* he came to prominence in the struggles of the burghers of that town against Louis II de Mâle, count of Flanders.* He largely persuaded Philip von Artevelde to become first captain of the city of Ghent in 1382, and then with some troops he scoured the surrounding countryside for provisions which saved Ghent from being starved into submission. He was made admiral of the Flemish fleet, and visited England to obtain the help of Richard II.* He was instrumental in securing the peace treaty between Ghent and Philip the Bold,* duke of

Burgundy,* in 1385. He was murdered by Duke Philip's men in 1387. (Bibliog. 68)

Acre, ancient port city in Palestine,* which, after conquest by the crusaders+ in 1104, became a provincial harbor of importance second only to Caesarea and Tyre. Conquered in 1104 by the crusaders, it became the main harbor of the Latin kingdom of Jerusalem and a major port for East-West trade. Saladin* conquered it in 1187, but Richard I* reconquered it in 1192, after which it became the capital of the new **crusader** kingdom. By 1250, Acre had been fortified by Louis IX* but shortly after his return to France it began to decline economically when a new trade route to the East was opened through the Black Sea. Following its capture by the Mamluk Sultan in 1291, the city diminished in importance. (Bibliog. 98)

Acton Burnell castle,+ small manor in Shropshire owned in the 12th century by the Burnell family. Its most famous member, Robert Burnell, began his career as a clerk to Prince Edward,* later King Edward I, and by 1270 served as the prince's representative in England during Edward's absence on a crusade.+ When Edward ascended the throne in 1272, Robert was appointed chancellor, and in 1274 he was elected bishop of Bath and Wells. Edward tried unsuccessfully to have him elected archbishop* of Canterbury. (Bibliog. 247)

Adela of Blois (fl. 1160), third wife of Louis VII* of France, who finally bore him the son and heir he wanted—the child who became King Philip II.* She had four brothers of importance: Thibaut, count of Blois*; Henry, count of Champagne*; William, archbishop of Rheims; and Stephen, count of Sancerre. (Bibliog. 123)

Adenet le Roi, Flemish minstrel+ and poet whose name meant "little Adam"; he wrote between 1260 and 1282. He was educated as a minstrel by Henry III of Brabant,* a poet himself, and in 1269, he went to Flanders and became "roi des ménestrels" (president of the musicians guild) at the court of Gui de Dampierre. Seeking to revive interest in the *chansons de geste*,* he wrote versions of three old legends which he titled *Enfances Ogier*,* *Berta aus grans piés*,* and *Bueve de Commarchis*. He also wrote *Cléomadès*,* a romance. (Bibliog. 106)

Adhemar (d. 1098), bishop of Le Puy; early crusader.+ One of the first churchmen to respond in 1095 to Pope Urban II's fervent plea for a crusade, Adhemar, as a papal representative, was responsible for much of the highly effective organization surrounding the first crusade. He possessed the military skill and the tact necessary to unite the various highly independent leaders. He came from a noble Valentinois family, was a good horseman, and was well versed in the use of arms as he defended his church with vigor from the violent attacks of his neighboring lords. A fighting bishop, Adhemar marched at the head of his own contingent of crusaders, and led his men into battle, most notably at the battle of Antioch.* He died of plague at Antioch in 1098. (Bibliog. 199, 201)

Adhemar de Chabannes (c. 988-1034), descendant of a noble Limousin family, he studied at the cathedral of Limoges, and was a monk at Angoulême. His *Chronicle*, written in 1028, contained the best source for material of the 10th and early 11th century for the history of Aquitaine.* In this work he recorded the famous apochryphal conversation between King Hugh Capet,* and King Robert the Pious whose arrogant demand, "Who made you a count?" was answered by the Count Audebert de Perigord: "Who made you kings?" He died on a pilgrimage to Jerusalem. (Bibliog. 98, 178)

Adhemar (fl. 1195), viscount of Limoges, perpetual rebel against King Richard I* of England. By the end of Richard's life, he had entered into an alliance with Philip II,* Augustus of France against Richard. Richard accused him of refusing to relinquish to him, as rightful overlord, a treasure trove reportedly unearthed at Chalus in the Limousin. While besieging Adhemar's castle on March 26, 1199, Richard received the fatal neck wound from which he died on April 6. (Bibliog. 7, 27)

admiral, amiral, originally meaning a prince or *emir** (or *amir*) under the sultan, the term grew to mean any Saracen lord or chieftain, and then ultimately came to mean a commander of a fleet of ships. The first English admiral was William de Leybourne,* appointed by Edward I* in 1286 under the title of *Admiral de la mer du Roy d'Angleterre*. In France, Florent de Varenne may have been the first French admiral, appointed in 1270, but the infamous Enguerrand IV, de Coucy,* was more generally credited as being the first, having been appointed in 1284. (Bibliog. 68)

Admiralty, High Court of, English court of law in which the authority of the lord high admiral* was exercised in his judicial capacity. From early on, these powerful men were to judge in a summary way all matters relating to merchants and mariners which happened on the high seas, according to the Laws of Oléron,* so called because they were enacted in that place. (Bibliog. 68)

Adrian IV (Nicholas Breakspeare) (c. 1100-1159), the only English pope (1154-1159). Although he often supported Louis VII* of France against Henry II* of England, he was believed to be the pope who gave the king of England authority over Ireland when, in 1155, John of Salisbury* went to Rome on the king's behalf and obtained from Adrian the famous bull+ *Laudabiliter+* which sanctioned the plan of conquest of that country, as well as an emerald ring "by which investiture of the right to rule over Ireland might be made." This bull later was believed to have been a forgery. (Bibliog. 98)

Aelenge, Stonehenge,* the location at which Hengest* consulted with the British. (Bibliog. 129)

Aelroth, Saracen king Marsile's* nephew in the *Song of Roland,*￼ who asked for the right of striking the first blow against Charlemagne's* *douzepeers** at Rencesvals.* He suggested to his uncle that twelve Saracen knights be selected to oppose the *douzepeers.* He was killed by Roland. (Bibliog. 210)

Agenais, border area between the Garonne and Dordogne rivers in southern France; French King Charles IV* kept it in retaliation when Edward II* (1307-1327) refused to pay homage to the French king after the earl of Kent, the English governor of Guyenne, had been forced to surrender during the war of Saint-Sardos. (Bibliog. 203)

Aggstein, castle+ perched on a narrow ridge 1,000 feet above the Danube River in Austria* as one of the many castles guarding the Danube frontier. It was captured and levelled by the dukes of Austria in 1231 and again in 1296. (Bibliog. 30)

Aglovale, Perceval's* brother who accompanied Gawain* in search of Lancelot.* According to Malory's version, Lancelot accidentally killed him in the abduction of Guenevere.* (Bibliog. 145)

Agolant, Saracen killed at Aspremont by Roland in *Mainet,* Aquin,* Fouque de Candie,* Girard de Roussillon.** He was an African king, and father of Almont in *Orlando furioso,* but his name used to refer to pagan people in the *chansons de geste** of *Roland,* Aliscans,* Chevalerie Vivien.** (Bibliog. 8, 128, 210)

Agravain, second son of King Lot* of Lothian* and Orkney (according to

Malory*), and brother of Gawain*; knighted by King Arthur.* Often called *"li Orgueilleus"* (The Proud), he was handsome and an excellent fighter, but he had a suspicious, envious, and evil disposition, and was totally without compassion or pity. When he discovered that Lancelot,* whom he hated, had resumed his love affair with Guenevere,* Agravain denounced him to Arthur, and schemed to obtain proof of the guilty pair's secret. He was killed by Lancelot in the fight near the stake at which Guenevere was about to be burnt. (Bibliog. 1)

Aigues-Mortes, city of southern France near Nîmes, which was built and fortified by King Louis IX,* and served as his port of embarkation for both of his crusades+ in 1246 and 1270. This city was completely surrounded by fortifications in the form of a parallelogram 596 yards long by 149 yards broad, and consisted of crenellated+ walls 25 to 36 feet high, dominated at intervals by towers. (Bibliog. 68, 195)

Aimeri de Narbonne, chanson de geste* by Bertrand de Bar-sur-Aube* between 1190 and 1217. It centered on Aymeri, son of Hernaut de Beaulande, count of Narbonne. As a youth he accompanied Charlemagne* after the slaughter at Rencesvals,* and because he was the only warrior courageous enough to besiege Narbonne,* Charlemagne bestowed it on him as a fief after he captured it. Then he went to Pavia to seek the hand of Hermenjart, daughter of Desier,* and was aided there by Girart de Vienne. On his return with his bride, he was forced to reconquer his fief from the Saracens. (ed. Louis Demaison, 2 vols., Paris: *SATF,* 1887; tr. modern French by C. Chacornac, Paris, 1931) (Bibliog. 106)

Aiol et Mirabel, 12th-century *chanson de geste** included as a part of the *Geste de Saint-Gille.* In this work, Elie de St. Gille and his wife, Avisse, were exiled from the court of King Louis because of the evil plottings of the traitor, Macaire de Lauzanne. Their son was named Aiol after an episode in his youth in which he, like Hercules, killed a serpent: hence the name Aiol, a shortened form of the word *anguillolus,* meaning "eel-like, a slippery one." As a young man, Aiol joined the king's service as an unknown, distinguished himself with renown, and was restored his father's fiefs. (ed. Jacques Normand and Gaston Raynaud, Paris: *SATF,* 1877) (Bibliog. 106)

aires. See Brehon law.

Aix la Chapelle, town between the Rhine and the Meuse rivers known for its hot springs; it became the location of Charlemagne's* favorite palace. After being crowned Holy Roman Emperor on Christmas Day, A.D. 800, Charlemagne made Aix the real capital of the Carolingian Empire. Louis I,* the Pious* was crowned there in 814. Later, after the Emperor Frederick I,* Barbarossa declared Charlemagne to be a saint in 1164, pilgrims flocked to its church. (Bibliog. 98)

Akershus, massive royal palace and fortress in Oslo, Norway, begun by King Haakon V Magnusson around 1300 and not completed until the end of that century. (Bibliog. 30)

Albemarle, name by which Aumale* (Aumarle) became better known in the 1600's when the earls of Aumale became known as the earls of Albemarle. (Bibliog. 47)

Alberich de Pisançon, author of an early 12th century work on Alexander* the great which survived only in a 105-line fragment containing the description of Alexander's boyhood education. Written in the Franco-Provençal language, the fragment was translated into Middle High German* by a priest named Lamprecht.* (Bibliog. 106)

Albert I, the Bear (c. 1100-1170), margrave+ of Brandenburg. He inherited valuable estates from his father, Otto the Rich, count of Ballenstedt, and from his mother, the daughter of the duke of Saxony.* Campaigning for three years in Italy against the Wends, he secured their district from Pribislaus, duke of Brandenburg,* with whom he had made an arrangement when that duke died. Taking the title margrave of Brandenburg in 1150 on the duke's death, he pressed his warfare against the Wends, extended the area of his mark, and did much for the spread of Christianity. (Bibliog. 68)

Albini. See Arundel.

Albion, most ancient name for the British Isles, though generally restricted to England. Probably Celtic in origin, it was used by the Romans as reference to the chalk cliffs of Dover. (Bibliog. 68)

Albuquerque, Spanish castle+ built by order of Alfonso Sanches, son of King Dinis of Portugal (1279-1325). Situated on a huge pinnacle of rock commanding a wide sweep of country, this fortress was besieged many times during the conflict between Castile and Portugal in the 14th century, including a lengthy siege by King Pedro the Cruel (see Peter IV) in 1354. (Bibliog. 30)

Alcala de Guadaira, ridge-top castle+ of Moorish design near Seville, Spain, with a triple enciente+ of stone and a sun-dried mortar mixed with pebble aggregate to form an extremely hard building material. Two lofty square towers overlooked two large baileys.+ Its tallest eastern tower was linked to the main enciente only by a high bridge; it commanded the main enciente and the bridge approach with its barbican+ and three gateways. (Bibliog. 30)

Aldolf, earl of Gloucester* who in Arthurian legend defeated Hengest* in battle and later slew him. (Bibliog. 1)

Alein, the Rich Fisher, in Arthurian legend, the twelfth son of Bron,* who was designated the second Keeper of the Grail;* he performed the miracle of feeding a multitude with one fish. (Bibliog. 1)

Alençon, counts and dukes of, strong Norman family which began in the 10th century when Yves, lord of Bellême, possessed and fortified the town of Alençon on the Sarthe River in northwestern France. His successors became involved in the wars of the kings of England in Normandy, alternately were deprived of and repossessed their domains. Mabille (Mabel) Talvas, countess of Alençon and heiress of the family, married Roger of Montgomery* (see Bellême-Montgomery) and from them descended a second house of Alençon which became extinct when Robert II* became king of France and the county of Alençon was joined to the royal domain. Successively it was granted as appanage+ to Peter, son of Louis IX,* in 1268 and to Charles,* count of Valois, brother of Philip IV,* the Fair, in 1293. A third house of Alençon sprang from Charles, second son of the count of Valois, who died at the battle of Crécy* in 1346. This countship was raised to a peerage in 1367 and a dukedom in 1414. (Bibliog. 68, 164)

Alemaigne, Alemain, Almayne, Amlain, Almagne, names for Germany in the French verse romances; they were derived from the Germanic tribe of Alemanni. They also were the names for the kingdom of Cheldric in *Brut,** the empire of which Fenice's father was ruler in *Cligés,** and of which Henris was ruler in *Claris et Laris.** (Bibliog. 198)

Alexander I, the Fierce (c. 1078-1124), king of Scotland (1107-1124). He was the fourth son of Malcolm Canmore by his wife Margaret, grandniece of Edward the Confessor.* On the death of his brother Edgar I in 1107, he succeeded to the Scottish throne, but inherited only a portion of its possessions; the districts south of the Forth and Clyde were created into an earldom for his younger brother, David. When he ruthlessly suppressed a rebellion in the northern part of his possessions he earned the title of "the fierce," yet he founded bishoprics and abbeys including the abbey of Scone.+ He was succeeded by his brother David I.* (Bibliog. 159)

Alexander II (1198-1249), king of Scotland (1214-1249). Son of William* the Lion of Scotland,* he joined the barons of England against King John* in his second year on the throne, and even led an army into England in support of their cause. He helped with the pacification after John's death, and married John's daughter Joanna in 1221, thus becoming brother-in-law to the English king, Henry III.* Henry's threatened invasion of Scotland in 1243 broke friendly relations between the two countries, but Alexander's prompt actions in anticipation and the English barons' reluctance to participate in such a war compelled the two countries to make peace the next year. He died trying to secure for Scotland the Western Isles which owed their allegiance to the king of Norway.* (Bibliog. 68, 176)

Alexander III (1241-1285), king of Scotland (1249-1285). Son of Alexander II,* he succeeded his father to the throne in 1249. During his minority two rival parties struggled for control: one led by Walter Comyn,* earl of Mentieth, and the other by Alan Durward, the justiciar.+ When Alexander married Henry III's* daughter, Margaret, in 1251, the English king demanded that the Scots render homage to England, but Alexander refused. On reaching his majority in 1262, Alexander resumed the project in which his father had died thirteen years previously—the attempt to gather the Western Isles for Scotland. First, he sent formal claim of the Isles to King Haakon of Norway; Haakon not only rejected the claims but sailed to invade the isles. Pausing off Arran, Haakon opened negotiations with Alexander who sought to delay any action until late autumn storms would make Haakon's position perilous. Haakon finally decided to attack, but a severe storm so badly damaged his fleet that the resultant battle of Largs was indecisive. Frustrated, Haakon sailed back to Norway but died en route. Alexander thus was able to obtain the Isle of Man, and the Western Isles for a money payment, but Orkney and Shetland remained in Norse hands. After his three children died, he realized that he would have to take steps about his successor. He convinced the Scottish parliament to recognize as heir presumptive* his granddaughter Margaret, the Maid of Norway, in 1284, and the next year married a second time in hopes of producing a male heir. Unfortunately, such hopes were dashed when he fell from the back of his horse in the dark while riding to visit his new queen, and he died in 1285. Margaret's death on her way to Scotland brought on the competition for the vacant throne which Edward I* finally resolved by choosing John Baliol* in 1292. (Bibliog. 68, 176)

Alexander III (c. 1105-1181), pope (1159-1181). Born Ronaldo Bandinelli, a scion of an aristocratic family in Sienna, Italy, he studied canon law and was a famous teacher at Bologna University. He became a cardinal in 1150, and one of the mainstays of Pope Adrian IV.* Although he was elected pope in 1159 on the death of Adrian IV, he was blocked by Emperor Frederick I,* Barbarossa, who pushed a minority candidate onto the papal throne. Alexander thereupon fled to France where he received the support of King Henry II* of England and King Louis VII* of France. After being defeated at the battle of Legnano,* Frederick submitted to the pope's will. His dispute with Henry II was resolved in his favor after the assassination of Becket* in 1170 forced Henry to submit to a humiliating penance. Only in 1177 was he able to resolve the differences and ascend the papal throne. (Bibliog. 68, 98, 199)

Alexander Jaroslawitz Nevsky (1219-1263), prince of Novgorod, saint and grand duke of Wladimir. He added the name Nevsky after his small forces defeated the Swedish, Danish and Livonian knights on the Neva River (hence his name) near St. Petersburg on July 15, 1240, again in 1241, and 1242. (Bibliog. 68)

Alexander the Great, legends of. Alexander the Great (356-323 B.C.) was the son of King Philip of Macedon. At age 14, he was placed under the tutelage of Aristotle; at 16 he suppressed a rebellion while his father was absent; at 20, he ascended the throne made vacant the previous year by the assassination of his father. For the next thirteen years, until his death from fever at the age of 33, he concentrated his energies on stabilizing Greece and on conquering the rest of the world. He became the subject of numerous stories and legends, many of which carried over into the medieval world. (Bibliog. 63, 202)

Alexander, late 14th or early 15th century English work in prose, in which queen Talyfride, queen of the Amazons, told Alexander that because they were women, he would not be respected if he defeated them, thereby cleverly persuading him to accept a tribute from them in place of a battle. Other events in the work described the life of Alexander from his taming his great steed, Bucephalus, through his conquests, including his great battles with Darius near the river Gracus, his marriage to Darius' daughter, Roxana, and his visits with the Gymnosophists where he saw many strange beasts and people. It ended with an account of his death by poison at the age of 33 and his burial at Alexandria. (ed. J. S. Westlake, London: *EETS OS* 143, 1913) (Bibliog. 202)

Alexander, half-completed Middle High German* courtly epic by Rudolf von Ems* of over 21,000 lines that related Alexander's adventures as far as the expedition to the River Oxus. Alexander was depicted as an ideal ruler: brave, just, humane, generous. (ed. V. Junk, Stuttgart: *BLV,* #272 and #274, 1928) (Bibliog. 86)

Alexander and Dindimus, also known as *Alexander B,* this was an alliterative Middle English* romance from the early 14th century that detailed events in Alexander's life after he had killed Perseus, king of India, and had continued to Oxydracca, the land of the Gymnosophists.* (See Prester John in volume 1.) There he saw such marvels as disappearing trees being guarded by birds that spit deadly fire. When he found that the River Ganges was impassable for his army until July and August, he began to exchange messages across the river to the king of the land on the far shore, Dindimus. These two exchanged five letters which described, among other things, Alexander's astonishment at the misery and pain of Dindimus' subjects who never ploughed, hunted, or fished, who lived frugally, and who died at a fixed age; they avoided lusts, ate fruits, drank only milk and water, spoke truthfully, and never made war. Totally lost in trying to understand such a way of life, Alexander wrote, "You are beasts; we are men. We work hard and earn our pleasures." Before he turned homeward, Alexander erected a marble pillar to mark this furthest eastward spot he had reached. (ed. W. W. Skeat, London: *EETS ES* 31, 1878; repr. 1973) (Bibliog. 211)

Alexanderlied, 1) early Middle High German* poem translated from the work by Alberich de Pisançon* by pfaffe Lamprecht*; this work united two barely compatible components: Alexander as an admirable hero with many knightly virtues used as an example of the futility of worldly ambition and the vanity of things temporal. (ed. F. Maurer, Darmstadt, 1964) (Bibliog. 86); 2) second version by Ulrich von Etzenbach. (ed. W. Toisher, Stuttgart: *BLV,* #183, 1888) (Bibliog. 197)

Alexandre, Roman d', Old French epic by Alexander de Bernai in 12 syllable verse which gave its name to the verse form, alexandrine. Originally, the story was an adaptation by Alberich de Pisançon,* and continued by a poet named Lambert le Tort of a tale about the death of

Darius, and of Alexander's vengeance against the murderers, of his expeditions into India and to the Pillars of Hercules, of his trip in an airship and capture of Babylon, and finally of the plot of Antipater and Divinuspater against him. After an unknown arranger added a poem by Eustace known as the *Foraging of Gaza*, Alexander of Paris (de Bernai) revised the entire work into four divisions: a section that narrated the birth and childhood of Alexander and his youth up to the war with Darius, a section giving the foraging of Gaza, the longest portion including the work by Lambert on many marvels, and finally, the death of Alexander and the division of his empire among his twelve peers. (ed. H. Michelant, Stuttgart: *BLV*, 1846) (Bibliog. 106, 231)

Alexiad, history of Byzantium during the time of the crusades+ written by Anna Comnena* which explained the actions of the crusaders from the Byzantine point of view. (ed. B. Lieb, *Collection Byzantine de l'Association Guillaume Bude*, Paris, 1937-1945) (Bibliog. 195)

Alexius Comnenus (1048-1118), nephew of Isaac Comnenus, the most distinguished member of the Comnenus family. Ascending the throne as emperor of Byzantium* in 1081, he was one of the greatest statesmen of his time. He contended with participants of the first crusade,* who assembled in Constantinople* in 1096, by obtaining their allegiance and promises of help in recovering some of the Byzantine dominions in Asia before he would allow them to pass through on their way to fight the Seljuks. His life was recorded in detail by his daughter, Anna Comnena.* (Bibliog. 195)

Alfred the Great (849-899), king of Wessex (West Saxons) (871-899). His brother Aethelred shared the government with him from 866, leaving him free to fight the Danes. He stopped them in 871, but two attempts made within the next eight years proved fruitless, and the area was overrun by invaders. He reorganized his army and after he defeated the Danes in 878, England became divided between the independent Anglo-Saxon part dominated by Wessex, and the Danelaw,+ the Danish territory northwest of the road between London and Chester. To protect his country, Alfred built a strong system of defense-based fortifications, a fleet, and on compulsory military service for all free men of the kingdom. These measures proved successful when the Danes again tried to invade in 893. He established at his court a school for the sons of nobility; he patronized scholarship; he encouraged translation of works of philosophy and theology from Latin into Anglo-Saxon, and he wrote books himself on history and geography. (Bibliog. 98)

Algalife (Arabic: *Al Khalifa* for "successor" [of Mohammed]), caliph,+ uncle of Marsile* and ruler of Ethiopia.* As a member of Marsile's council, he interceded to protect Ganelon,* stayed at the front of the fighting at Rencesvals* after Marsile's flight, and was killed by Oliver, in the *Song of Roland.* (Bibliog. 210)

Al Hakim (996-1021), insane Fatamid caliph+ who founded one of the most bizarre sects of the Ismailians. See Fatamids.

Alhambra, castle+ and palace built between 1249 and 1354 for the Moorish monarchs of Granada in southern Spain, occupying a hilly terrace on the southern border of the city of Granada. This terrace, 2,430 feet long by 674 feet wide, and covering an area of about 35 acres, was enclosed by a strongly fortified wall with thirteen towers. Its name came from the Arabic word, *alhambra* meaning brick red and probably was derived from the color of the sun-dried bricks of fine gravel and clay from which the outer walls were made. Its enciente+ with towers incorporating part of the Alcazaba or palace of Granada had one of the strongest gates, the Justice Gate of 1348, which had a vaulted passage turning through three right angles. See castle gate.+ (Bibliog. 30, 68)

Alia-Aenor. See Eleanor of Aquitaine.

Alisaunder, Middle English* romance, also known as *Alexander A*, which skipped over Alexander's birth and early childhood, and began in his later youth when he drowned Nectanebus for treachery, and tamed the wild horse Bucephalus. See also *Kyng Alisaunder.* (ed. W. W. Skeat, London: *EETS ES* #1, London, 1867) (Bibliog. 202)

Aliscans, chanson de geste of the *Garin de Monglane* cycle written about 1165; it gave a new version of the theme of the *Chanson de Guillaume.* Aliscans was the name of the cemetery in France near Arles in which Guillaume fought beside Vivien. After all his men had been killed by Saracens, Guillaume fled on Baucent toward his home in Orange, but returned to the battlefield to tend the dying Vivien. After he finally escaped by disguising himself in Saracen armor, he was refused admission to Orange because he was not recognized in the alien attire. Before he could reveal his identity, he again was forced to flee as the Saracens under Tiebaut, former husband of Guillaume's wife, Guiborc,* besieged Orange. Guillaume sought help from King Louis, who finally agreed to send 200,000 men to help only after Guillaume's sister, Louis' wife Blancheflor,* begged him to do so.

When this army reached Orange, they found it had been burned and the women were locked in the donjon for safety from the Saracens. Guillaume had to show his face before his wife would recognize him and allow him into the desolated city. (ed. J. Frappier, *Les Chansons de Geste de Cycle de Guillaume d'Orange*, Paris: *SEDES*, 1955, I) (Bibliog. 106)

Allington castle,+ fortress in Kent given by William the Conqueror* to his half-brother, Bishop Odo.* Its original wooden structure was replaced in stone by Gundulf, the mason employed by the Conqueror to build the Tower of London. (Bibliog. 247)

Almayne, Almain, Almagne. See Alemaigne.

Almoravides, family of Muslim princes who reigned in Africa and in Spain between 1073 and 1147. Their name was derived from the sect of *Al-Morabethun* ("dedicated to the service of God") which arose mid-11th century among a poor tribe of Berbers in the Atlas Mountains on the African shores of the Atlantic Ocean. Under their leader Yussef, they spread from the Ebro and Tagus rivers in Spain to the frontiers of Sudan in eastern Africa. (Bibliog. 68)

Alnwick castle.+ Located in Northumberland* near Newcastle, this castle was built by Ivo de Vesci around 1100. It began as a motte and bailey+ structure, was fortified with stone in the 12th century, and was rebuilt by the Percy family after they obtained it in the 14th century. Here, William the Lion,* king of Scotland, was captured in 1174 as his forces aided the rebellious sons of King Henry II* of England. (Bibliog. 30, 247)

Alp Arsalan, Mohammed Ben Daoud (1029-1072), second sultan of the Seljuk dynasty in Persia, and great-grandson of Seljuk, founder of the dynasty. In 1063, he became sole ruler of Persia from the Oxus to the Tigris rivers. Ably assisted by Nizam al-Mulik, his vizier* and one of the most eminent of Muslim statesmen, he ruled well. Supporting him on the throne were 1,200 princes or sons of princes, and 200,000 soldiers. He invaded the Roman Empire through Constantinople in 1068, and after four bloody encounters, he defeated the emperor, Romanus Diogenes, near Malazkurd in a rout with terrible slaughter. Capturing the emperor, Romanus, he set a ransom+ of one million pieces of gold and an annual tribute of 3,000 pieces of gold, and intermarriage between the two families. The emperor agreed, but was unable to fulfill the terms of the treaty, so the war resumed. (Bibliog. 68)

Alpharts Tod, anonymous Middle High German* poem which emerged from the Dietrich* legend about 1250. Alphart, one of Dietrich's warriors and nephew of Hildebrand rode against the forces of Ermanrich, and subdued the warriors Witege and his companion Heime, two traitorous warriors who had deserted Dietrich. Alphart was treacherously attacked suddenly by both warriors and fell after heroic resistance. (ed. E. Martin, *Deutsches Heldenbuch*, Berlin: Weidmann, II, 1967) (Bibliog. 86)

Alsace, province in northeastern France between the Rhine River and the Vosges Mountains. Originally part of the middle kingdom assigned to Lothair by the Treaty of Verdun* in A.D. 843, it became part of the Holy Roman Empire between 870 and 1648. It became united with the duchy of Swabia* in 925, and subsequently was divided into feudal principalities which were controlled chiefly by the bishop of Strassburg and the Hapsburg family in the 14th century. (Bibliog. 239)

Amadas et Ydoine, French romance written about 1220, intending to ex-alt "fine and loyal love," it related how Amadas, seneschal of Burgundy, won the love of Ydoine, the duke's daughter, but before she would become his, she sent him off to seek worldly fame and prowess. However, before he could set out on this goal, he went mad with grief and frustration when he learned that she was to be married to the count of Nevers* while he was away. Although this marriage took place, it never was consummated. On a pilgrimage to Rome, Ydoine at Lucca discovered the deranged Amadas, and aided him to recover his wits, but then she was carried off by a discourteous and boorish knight. Amadas found her as she seemed to be dying, and she made him promise to have masses said for her soul. Just then, however, the discourteous knight reappeared, and confessed to Amadas that he had placed an enchanted ring on her finger which caused her to simulate death. When Amadas re-moved the ring she awoke and the two lovers returned to Burgundy where the count of Nevers divorced her and allowed the two to be united in marriage. (ed. J. R. Reinhard, Durham, NC, 1927) (Bibliog. 106)

Amadeus V, the Great (1249-1323), count of Savoy. He was such a diplomat and arbiter that he was made a prince of the Holy Roman Empire in 1310 by Emperor Henry VIII. When the Turks tried to take Rhodes from the Hospitallers,+ he acquired a great deal of renown by leading a relief expedition. As a result, he chose as his arms+ a Maltese cross+ with the letters F. E. R. T. (*Fortitudo ejus Rhodium tenuit).* He died in 1323 at Avignon trying to persuade Pope John XXII to preach a crusade.+ (Bibliog. 68)

Amadeus VI (1334-1383), count of Savoy, the so-called "Green Count" from the occasion of his knighthood at age 19 when he appeared in a series of tournaments wearing green plumes, a green silk tunic over his armor, green caparisons+ on his horse, and followed by eleven knights all in green, each led into the lists by a lady in green leading her champion's horse by a green cord. Later, while he was in Paris for the marriage of his niece, his extravagance led him to buy jeweled necklaces, table knives, boots, shoes, plumes and straw hats, and to give the French king a "chapel" of rubies and large pearls costing 1,000 florins.+ He also gave to the poet Guillaume de Machaut three gold francs for a metrical romance the poet had given him. As the count of the territory controlling the passes through the Alps between France and Italy, he was seventeenth of his dynasty, the brother-in-law of the queen of France, the founder of two orders of chivalry, and the leader of a crusade+ which had expelled the Turks from Gallipoli in 1365, and restored the emperor of Byzantium to his throne. Even though he hated mercenaries,+ calling them scoundrels and nobodies, he still used them, even going so far as to bribe them to betray their previous contracts. Then, in 1371, against the marquis of Saluzzo in Piedmont, Amadeus engaged the feared and brutal Anachino Baumgarten with his German-Hungarian company of 1,200 lances (see White Company), 600 brigandi and 300 archers. In 1382, when he supported the invasion into Lombardy of Charles III, the duke of Anjou,* his equipment included an enormous green pavilion+ ornamented with twelve shields bearing the arms of Savoy in red and white, an emerald surcoat embroidered with the red-and-white device, twelve saddle and bridle sets all in green, and four others ornamented with "Hungarian ribbon knots" for his immediate retinue, and green hoods, shoes, and tunics for his pages. (Bibliog. 223)

Amadis de Gaula, title of one of the earliest (c. 1325) and most influential romances of chivalry written on the Iberian peninsula (including Spain and Portugal). In it, Amadis personified all of the chivalric virtues: devotion to one woman, loyalty to his overlord, hatred of the infidel, defense of the oppressed, and pursuit of justice. Obviously, Amadas was modeled on Lancelot.* (ed. Edwin Place, Madrid, 1959) (Bibliog. 237)

Amazonia, land of women near Albania, partly in Asia and partly in Europe, this woman's country was called Amazonia after the widows of the Goths who were slain when leaving Scythia. These women donned their husbands' armor and weapons and avenged their husbands' deaths by killing all the young males and old men and children, and took away all the women. They had two queens, Lampeta and Marsepia, one to travel with the army and fight, and the other to remain and govern. Although they conquered a great part of Asia they chose their husbands from countries nearby, and would bear children by them; sons they would slay or send to their fathers who had been sent back to their homes; daughters they saved and taught to hunt and shoot. When these young girls were seven, their breasts would be burnt off so as not to interfere with shooting a bow. Hercules and Achilles were daunted by their ferocity, but Alexander was so amazed by it that he didn't attempt to conquer them with force, but rather with friendship and love, and thereby he made them subjects of his empire. (Bibliog. 18)

Ambroise, Ambrose (fl. 1190), Norman jongleur from Evreux, this poet described events of the third crusade+ as he witnessed them accompanying King Richard I,* Coeur de Lion, between 1190 and 1192. His *Estoire de la Guerre Sainte* was written in 12,332 octosyllables of monorhymed *laisses*. Even though he wrote with naive liveliness, and showed prejudice against the Saracens, the French and all other enemies of his master, his work was the chief source of information about the crusade of Richard I and its events between 1190 and 1192. (tr. Merton J. Hubert, *Crusade of Richard Lion-Heart by Ambroise*, New York, 1941; and Edward Stone, *Three Old French Chronicles of the Crusades*, Seattle, WA: University of Washington, 1939) (Bibliog. 106)

Amiens, Guy of (d. c. 1075), author of a poem on the battle of Hastings,* *De bello Hastingensi carmen auctore Widone*, which gave valuable information on the battle itself and on England for about 4 months afterward. (ed. C. Morton and H. Muntz, London: Oxford, 1972) (Bibliog. 99)

amiral. See admiral.

Amis et Amiles, chanson de geste* written in Anglo-Norman late in the 12th century, was the basis of the Middle English* story, *Amys and Amiloun*,* written at the end of the 13th century. A Latin prose version, *Vita Sanctorum Amici et Amelii*, written in the 12th century was adapted into Old French prose as *Li Amiitiez de Ami et Amile* in the 13th century. A similar German version was found in Hartmann von Aue's* *Der Arme Heinrich*,* written around 1200. In *Chevalier Ogier*,* these two were killed by Ogier and buried by Charlemagne. (ed. Peter Dembowski, Paris, *CFMA* #97, 1969) (Bibliog. 106)

Amr, Amir, Amhar, King Arthur's* son by Guenevere* as claimed in the *Mabinogion* and in Nennius. (Bibliog. 96)

Amys and Amiloun, Middle English* metrical romance that drew upon the qualities a late 14th century ideal knight. Two noble foster brothers, knights of Lombardy, were so bound in friendship that by means of their incredible resemblance to each other, Amiloun could take Amis' place in a trial by combat* and win by deception. For that deception, however, he was afflicted with leprosy but left before his plight was revealed. After much searching, Amis finally found his friend in a pitiable state, and, told that only blood from innocent babes would cure him, Amis willingly sacrificed his own children. Because God, however, could not allow such a sacrifice to occur, when Amis and his wife went to grieve over the bodies of their supposedly dead children, they found that the babes were only asleep. See *Amis et Amiles.* (ed. MacEdward Leach, London: *EETS ES,* 1937; tr. B. B. Broughton, *Middle English Metrical Romances,* New York: E. P. Dutton, 1966) (Bibliog. 28)

Andlau, Alsatian castle+ built around the middle of the 14th century, and presented to Bishop Berthold de Buchek by the knight Rodolphe Andlau, who recovered it as a fief+ a little later. In 1376, the Strassbourgians launched a punitive expedition against Rodolphe at the castle to avenge the soldiers he had killed earlier. (Bibliog. 196)

Andrea da Barberino, Florentine *cantastorie* of the late 14th century, he was the author of *Guerrino il Meschino* and *I reali di Francia.** (ed. G. Gambarin and G. Vandelli, Bari, 1947) (Bibliog. 245)

Andreas Capellanus (Andrew the Chaplain), Latin writer of the 12th century. He was born probably in France but nothing is known of his family or his education before he arrived in 1170 at the court of the counts of Champagne where he served as one of the chaplains to Marie, countess of Champagne. While there, he wrote the treatise Art of Courtly Love,* (*De arte honeste amandi*) which supposedly reflected the life and manners of the knightly society in France of his time. Written as a codification of the whole concept of *amor fin,* or "courtly love," Andreas made it a parody of Ovid's *Ars amatoria.* See *Art of Courtly Love.* (tr. and ed. J. J. Parry, Seattle, WA: University of Washington, 1941) (Bibliog. 5)

Andred, Tristan's* cousin who spied on his intrigue with Isolde. He played the same role at King Mark's* court as Mordred* did at Arthur's*: spying, ambushing, and being generally disagreeable. He was said to be responsible for Tristan's death, and was slain in revenge. (Bibliog. 1, 84, 117)

Angers, capital city of the province of Anjou* in northwestern France, it was rebuilt and made capital of their county by the counts of Anjou after being sacked and burned by the Normans in the 9th century. Its castle on the east bank of the Maine River was taken by the French under Philip II,* Augustus, in the 13th century as a forward location against Brittany. Later, between 1232 and 1238, Louis IX* surrounded it with a new wall in the form of an irregular pentagon with seventeen round towers reaching 40 to 60 meters in height; its perimeter stretched to 952 meters; its drum towers rising high above the curtain wall+ were capped with conical towers. Its striped walls were created by alternating rows of slate and black shale with rows of sandstone and granite. It was one of the most important fortresses of the time. (Bibliog. 4, 98, 196)

Angleterre, Engleterre, French name for England, specifically for King Arthur's kingdom (in *Brut**), but often used loosely by French and Anglo-Norman writers to mean the entire realm of Britain. (Bibliog. 242)

Angoulême, city in western France on the Charente River, northeast of Bordeaux. It was the center of the countship held by the Lúsignan family from 1220, and was ceded to England by the Treaty of Bretigny* in 1360, but was restored to France by King Charles V* in 1373. Its first count in 916 was Guillaume I, Taillefer. (Bibliog. 100, 239)

Angoumois, county in France, the center of which was Angoulême*; ceded to England by the Treaty of Bretigny* in 1360, it was restored to France in 1373. (Bibliog. 239)

Angus, one of the seven original mormaerships or earldoms of Scotland which more or less represented the seven provinces of the Pictish kingdom, afterwards called Alban, into which the country north of the Firth of Forth and the Firth of Clyde was divided before the 9th century. Those divisions were Angus (the name of the oldest brother) along with Mearns; Athole with Gowrey; Caithness* with Sutherland; Fife with Fothreve; Mar with Buchan; Moray (Muref, Moreb); and Stratherne with Menteith. The ruler of each of these districts bore the title of *ri* (king) but all were inferior to the *ardri* (supreme king). By the 10th century, each ruler was styled *mormaer (mormaor)* or great maer, the great steward of a province. During the reign of

Alexander I,* around 1114, the mormaer was called earl, or *come* (count). When King David I* (1124-1153) ascended the throne, his object was to feudalize the whole kingdom by introducing the feudal system of Norman England into Scotland, and adapting her institutions to feudal forms. To accomplish this, he placed the leading dignitaries of the kingdom in the position of crown vassals, based not on territorial districts but upon the relation to the tribes who peopled it, and the leader to hold an earldom of the crown in chief, as barons held their baronies in chief from the king.+ This process was carried on by his successors. During the reign of Malcolm IV (1153-1165), the seven earls of Scotland were Angus, Athole, Fife, Mar, Stratherne, and Buchan together with Dunbar from the Lothian.* In the 12th century six new earls were created: Menteith, Garioch, Lennox, Ross, Carrick, Caithness. By 1297, the seven earls had changed names to become Buchan, Menteith, Straherene, Lennox, Ross, Athole and Mar. In company with John Comyn, they suffered disaster on their invasion of England, and after that no mention of these seven earls as being of Scotland was made. Maud, daughter and heiress of John Comyn, became earl of Angus about 1240, and married Gilbert de Umfreville of Northumberland. (Bibliog. 47, 176)

Anhalt, section of the duchy of Saxony* which in the 12th century came under the rule of Albert* the Bear, margrave of Brandenburg.* Albert was descended from Albert, count of Ballenstedt, whose son Esico (d. 1059) probably was the first to bear the title of count of Anhalt. Esico's grandson, Otto the Rich, count of Ballenstedt, was the father of Albert the Bear, by whom Anhalt was united with Brandenburg. When Albert died in 1170, his son Bernard, who received the title of duke of Saxony in 1180, became count of Anhalt. Bernard died in 1212, and Anhalt, separated from Saxony, passed to his son Henry who took the title of prince in 1218. On his death in 1252, his three sons partitioned the principality and founded Aschersleben, Bernburg, and Zerbst. (Bibliog. 68)

Anjou, county in western France on the banks of the Loire, it was bounded on the north by Maine* which separated it from Normandy,* on the east by Lorraine, on the south by Poitou,* and on the west by Brittany.* It was created as a fief by the Capetian* kings and controlled by Count Fulk III Nera (987-1040), and his successors. It became English under King Henry II,* who inherited it from his father, Duke Geoffrey of Anjou,* in 1151; but was returned to France when it was stripped from King John* by the French king, Philip II,* Augustus, in 1204. Subsequently, it was inherited in 1264 by Prince Charles I,* who became king of Naples and Sicily; then it became a duchy in 1297, and came into royal control under Philip IV in 1328; between 1350 and 1480, it was controlled by the dukes of Anjou. Some of its notable counts, viscounts and dukes were:

  958 - Geoffrey I,* Grisgonelle (Greytunic)
  987 - Fulk III, the Black
1040 - Geoffrey II, Martel
1060 - Geoffrey III, the Bearded
1069 - Fulk IV, the Sullen, brother
1109 - Fulk V, king of Jerusalem
1129 - Geoffrey V, Plantagenet,* count of Anjou
1151 - Henry II, king of England
1189 - Richard, king of England
1199 - John, king of England
1202 - Philip II, Augustus, by sequestration
1264 - Charles I of France, eighth son of Louis VIII
1285 - Charles II of France, king of Naples
1290 - Marguerite of Anjou and Charles of Valois
1325 - Reunion to the crown by Philip
1356 - Louis I of France, son of Jean of Valois, and king of Naples
1384 - Louis II of France, son of Jean of Valois, and king of Naples
(Bibliog. 68, 100, 239)

Anna, Enna, daughter of Uther Pendragon* and Igerne,* the younger sister of Arthur,* the wife of King Lot* of Orkney,* and the mother of Gawain* in Arthurian legend. (Bibliog. 1, 117)

Anna Comnena (1083-1148), Byzantine empress and daughter of Alexius I Comnenus,* she became a nun and wrote history. Her book, the *Alexiad,* was one of the most important sources for the history of the crusades,+ for it gave the Byzantine reaction to the first crusade+ and to the establishment of the Latin kingdom of Jerusalem in the late 11th and early 12th centuries. Despite her deep interest in military questions, and her pride in her father's military successes, she considered war a shameful thing, a last resort when all else had failed, indeed a shameful confession of failure. (Bibliog. 68, 195)

Annales Cambriae, chronicle covering the period A.D. 444-954, with continuations to 1288. This was one of the best authorities for early Welsh history. (tr. A. W. Wade-Evans, *Nennius' History of Britons,* London, 1938) (Bibliog. 99)

Annales regni Scotiae, chronicle composed largely in French at St. Albans early in the 14th century. This work concerns itself primarily with the succession to the Scottish crown. (ed. and tr. Henry T. Riley, London: *Rolls Series,* 1865) (Bibliog. 99)

Annales Stanliensis (1204-1214), chronicle, begun, at least, in Stanley Abbey about the middle of the 13th century, by an author who sympathized with the barons in their conflicts with King John and King Henry III. (ed. R. Howlett, *Chronicles of the Reigns of Stephen, Henry II and Richard I,* ii, 506-558, London: *Rolls Series,* 1885) (Bibliog. 99)

Annowre, sorcerer who loved King Arthur* and who enticed him to her tower in the Forest Perilous. There when he would not make love to her, she plotted his death. Nimue (see Niniane) learned of Arthur's plight, and sought the help of Lancelot* or Tristan* to aid their king. Tristan arrived just in time to see two strange knights about to behead Arthur. He killed them, and released Arthur, who ran down the fleeing Annowre and smote off her head. (Bibliog. 117, 145)

Anseis, surnamed *li fiers* (the fierce), he was the seneschal of Heudon de Longres in the *chansons de geste.** He lived at the chateau of Vimer and was one of the *douzepeers** of Charlemagne* killed by Saracens* at Rencesvals* in the *Song of Roland.** (Bibliog. 210)

Anseis de Carthage, lengthy *chanson de geste** from the early 13th century that related how after he became king of Spain under Charlemagne,* Anseis impregnated the daughter of Ysoré l'Esclavon. Ysoré, enraged, converted from Christianity to paganism out of his hatred for Anseis' foul action, and then summoned Saracens* to help him defeat Anseis. Anseis, however, thwarted that plan by summoning Charlemagne to help him, and in the subsequent battle, the pagans were defeated. Anseis then married Gaudesse, daughter of Marsile.* (ed. Johann. Alton, Tubingen: *BLV,* CXCIV, 1892) (Bibliog. 106)

Anseis de Metz, fourth branch of the cycle of Lorraines which comprised *Hervis de Mes, Garin le Loherenc,** and *Gerbert de Mes.** This *chanson de geste** from the early years of the 12th century dealt with the vengeance wreaked upon Girart by Frontin's relatives. (ed. Hermann J. Green, Paris, 1939) (Bibliog. 21, 106)

Antioch, battle of (June 28, 1098), one of the most famous battles of the first crusade.+ Deciding to engage the besieging Muslims in battle, the crusaders in Antioch on June 28 arranged their forces in six divisions: 1) French and Flemish led by Hugh of Vermandois and Robert of Flanders; 2) Lorrainers led by Godfrey of Bouillon*; 3) Normans of Normandy under Duke Robert II*; 4) Raymond of Toulouse's* army under Bishop Adhemar*; 5) and 6) Italians and Normans of Sicily under Bohemond* and Tancred.* They marched out across the fortified bridge and wheeled up the bank to the right. Battle standards+ were flying, and morale was high although many of the crusading knights were on foot for the lack of horses. Kerbogha+ chose not to attack as they emerged, but to wait for the full crusaders' force to appear and then to crush them at once. However, the sight of their full array caused him to hesitate, and to offer a truce which the crusaders rejected. He then tried to lure them into dividing their forces, but his attempts were ignored. (See tactics.+) Through a rain of Muslim arrows the Franks advanced resolutely. Kerbogha then attacked their left flank, but Bohemond, anticipating that action, had created a seventh division to protect their flank and thereby thwarted that attack. As the Franks marched on steadily, the attacking forces wavered, and the heretofore resolute emirs panicked and began to desert Kerbogha. To counter the panic, Kerbogha set fire to the grass in front of his lines to stop the crusaders, but the solid cavalry mass extinguished the flames by their advance and soon closed to begin fierce hand-to-hand fighting which inflicted heavy losses. At this, the whole Muslim army fled. Keeping the crusaders closely restrained, the Christian leaders had their forces follow the fleeing Muslims closely, killing great numbers of exhausted stragglers, leaving the Christian peasants in the countryside to finish off the rest of the laggards. A defeated and disillusioned Kerbogha eventually reached Mosul, but this defeat had destroyed forever his prestige and power. (Bibliog. 195, 201)

Antioche, Chanson d', epic poem based on the events witnessed by Richard le Pélerin, a poet from Artois who was a participant on the first crusade.+ This "historic" poem was lost, but a reworking of it by Graindor de Douai,* written between 1180 and 1200, survived. It narrated the ill-fated expedition of Peter the Hermit (1097) (see crusades in volume 1) and the activities of Godfrey of Bouillon,* including the capture of Antioch, up to the entry of his army into Palestine. (ed. Paulin Paris, Paris, 1848) Basically a history, this work contained two "legendary" poems added by Graindor in which the role of marvellous events was stressed: *Les Chetifs** and *Chanson de Jerusalem.** These three poems together constituted the first cycle of the crusades. In the 13th century was added an introductory poem to explain the fairyland origins of Godfrey of Bouillon: *Le Chevalier au Cygne et Enfances Godefroi.** In the 14th century, the second cycle was completed by the poems *Baudouin de Sebourc, Bâtard de Bouillon,** and *Saladin.* (ed. Suzanne Duparc-Quoic, *Le Cycle de la Croisade,* Paris, 1955) (Bibliog. 135)

Antipodes, land on the other side of the earth. See Ethiopia. (Bibliog. 248)

Antor, father of Kay,* and foster father of King Arthur* in Arthurian legend; he assisted Merlin* in revealing that Igerne* was Arthur's mother. (Bibliog. 241)

Antwerp, city in Flanders* which was absorbed into the Holy Roman Empire and was made a marquessate by the Emperor Henry II in 1008, and as such was bestowed on Godfrey of Bouillon* in 1076. (Bibliog. 68)

Apostolic Majesty, title borne by the kings of Hungary.* About A. D. 1000 it was conferred by Pope Sylvester II upon St. Stephen (975-1038), the first Christian king of Hungary, in return for his zealous efforts to convert heathens. (Bibliog. 68)

Appleby castle,+ one of the principal border fortresses in Westmoreland* in the north of England. It was surrendered by King Malcolm of Scotland in 1157, and granted by Henry II* to Hugh de Morville but was forfeited by him for his role in the rebellion of young King Henry in 1173. (Bibliog. 104, 247)

Appolonius of Tyre, Middle English* metrical romance composed about 1380. The original poem was lost, and only the final 144 lines survived in a 15th century fragment. This story related the adventures of a young man, Appolonius, seeking fame and fortune. Arriving at the domain of an incestuous king who stated that he would permit his daughter to marry only the man who could answer the king's riddle, Appolonius deduced but dared not reveal the answer because it would expose the king's guilty incestuous secret. He left for another land, married a princess there, fathered a daughter who was falsely reported to have died at birth along with her mother. Subsequent events re-united the family and the guilty were punished. (ed. J. O. Halliwell-Phillips, *A New Boke about Shakespeare and Stratford on Avon,* London, 1850) (Bibliog. 202)

Apulia, region of southern Italy along the southeastern seacoast. It became part of the kingdom of Sicily between 1130 and 1282, and of the kingdom of Naples* after 1282. Its prominent dukes were Robert Guiscard* (1075), Roger Borsa (1085), and Roger II* (1127). (Bibliog. 100)

Aquin, chanson de geste of the cycle of the king, composed during the last half of the 12th century. Also known as *La Conquête de la Bretaigne*, but surviving only in a manuscript of the 15th century in the Ile de France* dialect. In this work, Aquin, a Saracen, seized Brittany during one of Charlemagne's* prolonged absences from France, and held it for 30 years. Then, after he threatened to invade more territory, including Paris and the Ile de France, the Bretons called upon Charlemagne for help. Responding at once, he overcame the Saracen strongholds and drove Aquin back toward Spain. (ed. F. Jouin des Longrais, Nantes: Société des Bibliophiles bretons, 1880) (Bibliog. 106)

Aquitaine, Guienne (Guyenne), Gascony, three names for basically the same huge region in southwestern France lying between the Pyrenees Mountains which served as a border with Spain, and the south and west of the Loire River. In the 12th century, it simply was the "empire" of the counts of Poitou,* built up much the same way as the empire of the counts of Anjou. Between 850 and 950, three lines of counts had established in turn a hegemony in what then was called Aquitaine, and had called themselves duke and sometimes duke of Aquitaine as a decorative mark of their hegemony. First it had been the counts of Auvergne,* then the counts of Poitou, and then briefly the counts of Toulouse,* and then again finally and permanently, the counts of Poitou. From 987, the title "duke of Aquitaine" was official in that it was recognized by the chancery of the king of France, but this duchy consisted simply of Poitou together with other counties which the family of the counts of Poitou had acquired or inherited (e.g. Limousin and Auvergne), and with others over which they established suzerainty (e.g., Perigord and Angoulême*). The alternate title of count of Poitou persisted through Richard I* into the 13th century. By the middle of the 11th century, dukes of Aquitaine acquired the duchy of Gascony* through purchase, inheritance, and warfare. Nonetheless, the dukes of Aquitaine saw no reason to move from their chief residence of Poitiers. It had become a powerful feudal duchy which passed to Capetian control when Eleanor of Aquitaine* married King Louis VII* in 1137, but later passed to the English Plantagenets* when she married Henry of Anjou* in 1152. He was duke of Normandy when he married her and so he became duke of Aquitaine as well. Thus by annexing the empire of the counts of Poitou to the empire of the counts of Anjou, Henry had created an immense accession of prestige. Henry II's* title both as king of England and duke of Aquitaine, as it had been since he married Eleanor, was *Dux Aquitanie*. Half a century later, after King John and Henry III had lost Poitou in the 13th century, and with it most of the earlier duchy of Aquitaine, it was natural for both English and French to speak of what was left as "Gascony," and this reference continued even after Henry II's duchy had been reconstructed to some extent in accordance with the Treaty of Paris in 1255. The name *Guyenne* was simply a corruption, a variant of the name Aquitaine. Aquitaine was converted into a principality in 1362 for Edward,* Duke of Cornwall (the Black Prince*), but was confiscated by the king of France in May 1370. Despite that, John of Gaunt,* who resigned his title of king of Castile and León, was created duke of Aquitaine for his life by his father, becoming duke of Aquitaine and Lancaster. The title passed to his grandson, Henry, son and heir apparent* of Henry IV, who, on the death of his grandfather in 1399, was made duke of Lancaster, and was granted the titles of Prince of Wales, dukes of Aquitaine, of Lancaster and of Cornwall, and earl of Chester. When he ascended the throne as Henry V, all his honours became merged with the crown. Some of its dukes included:

1087 - Guillaume IX (see William IX)
1127 - Guillaume X, count of Poitou and Limousin
1137 - Eleanor*
1169 - Richard I,* of England
1196 - Otto of Brunswick
1199 - John,* of England
1216 - Henry III,* of England
1272 - Edward I,* of England
1307 - Edward II,* of England
1327 - Edward III,* of England
1362 - Edward, the Black Prince, of England
1377 - Richard II,* of England
1399 - Henry IV,* of England
(Bibliog. 47, 130, 131, 239)

Arabic historians. Important for their accounts of history from the Arabic (Saracen) viewpoint were the following authors: Abu Shama,* Baha ad-Din,* Ibn al-Athir,* Ibn al-Qalanisi,* Ibn Wasil,* Imad ad-Din,* Kamal ad-Din,* Manaqib Rashid ad-Din,* Sibt Ibn al-Jauzi, Usama ibn Munqidh.* (Bibliog. 83)

Araby,Mount of, mountain peak in Wales more commonly known as Mount Snowdon where King Arthur* slew the giant Ritho in Arthurian legend. (Bibliog. 1, 145)

Aragon, Arragon, territory in Spain bounded on the north by the Pyrenees, and including the districts of Sorbarbe, Aragon and Ribagorza. About 1035, Sancho III the Great, ruler of the newly established kingdom of Navarre which included those three districts, bequeathed them to his sons, Gonzalez and Ramiro. Ramiro soon got rid of Gonzales and united those three districts into a single kingdom which grew in size and power to rival Castile with whom it shared the chief role in the struggle against the Moors. At the height of its power under James I (1213-1276), it included Valencia, Catalonia, the Balearic Islands and a large portion of Montpellier in France; his successor, Peter III (1276-1285), added Sicily to the dominions. (Bibliog. 68)

l'Archanz. See *Guillaume, Chanson de.*

Archbishop Turpin, one of Charlemagne's *douzepeers.** See Turpin, Archbishop.

Archbishop of Canterbury, ranking first among English bishops, the archbishop was styled Primate and Metropolitan of all England, and the first peer of the realm, and having precedence+ over all dukes not of the royal blood, and all great officers of state. He was styled His Grace in common speech, and wrote himself *Divina Providentia,* whereas other bishops style themselves *Divina Permissione.* At coronations he placed the crown on the king's head, and abroad, he sat at the pope's right foot. Among archbishops of Canterbury from 1184 to 1397 were:

Baldwin - 1184-1190
Hubert Walter - 1193-1205
Stephen Langton - 1206-1228
Edmund Rich - 1233-1240, canonized 1246
Boniface of Savoy* - 1241-1270
Simon Mepham - 1327-1333
Thomas Bradwardine - 1349-1366
William Wittlesey - 1368-1375
Simon Sudbury - 1375-1381, beheaded by rebels
William Courtney - 1381-1397
(Bibliog. 164)

Archbishops of York, some between 1189 and 1340 included:

Geoffrey* - 1189-1212
Simon Langton - (1215)
Walter de Gray - 1215-1255
Godfrey Ludham - 1258-1265
William Giffard - 1266-1279
William Wickware - 1279-1285
William Melton - 1316-1340
(Bibliog 70, 164)

Archpirate. See Eustace, the monk.

Archpriest. See Arnaut de Cervole.

Ardant, evil knight known as the Knight of the Dragon (Chevalier au Dragon) in Arthurian legend, because his shield contained a dragon's head which emitted flames. In his war against Arthur,* he fought with Perceval* who cut off his hand, and then plunged his sword into the dragon's mouth, whereupon the shield's head turned its flames back against its wounded owner and burnt him to ashes. (in *Perlesvaus**)
(Bibliog. 241)

ardri. See Angus.

Ariosto (1474-1533), Italian author of *Orlando furioso*. In 1504 he undertook to finish the epic *Orlando innamorato* which Boiardo* had left incomplete. Whereas Boiardo had had Orlando (Roland) motivated by love, Ariosto changed the direction of his work and had his hero driven to furious madness by jealousy, hence the title, "furioso." (ed. and tr. Guido Waldman, Oxford, 1974) (Bibliog. 8)

Arles, kingdom of, originally a city on the Rhône where the river divided to form its delta. After the fall of the Roman Empire, it passed to the control of the Visigoths and rapidly declined in importance. Plundered in 730 by the Saracens,* it was rebuilt to become a kingdom in 933 by the union of the old kingdoms of Provence or Cisjuran Burgundy and Burgundy Transjuran, and then bequeathed by its last sovereign, Rudolph III, to the emperor Conrad II. It comprised the countship of Burgundy,* the Lyonnais, and the territory bounded by the Mediterranean, the Rhône River and the Alps. Only after the 12th century was the title of Arles applied to this district when Arles itself became a free city, governed by consuls and *podestats** after the model of the Italian republic. In 1251 it submitted to Charles of Anjou* and from then was tied to the fortunes of Provence. (Bibliog. 68, 79)

Arme Heinrich, Der, German version of the *Amys and Amiloun** story by Hartmann von Aue.* (Eng. tr. Margaret Richey, *Hartmann von Aue: Selections,* New York, 1962) (Bibliog. 197)

Armonica, North Wales,* which Geoffrey of Monmouth* often confused with Armorica,* hence placing some of the actions of King Arthur* in Brittany instead of in northern Wales where they made more geographical sense. (Bibliog. 96)

Armorica, ancient name meaning "on the sea" in the Breton language, for the old French province of Brittany.* (Bibliog. 79)

Arnaut de Cervole (fl. 1350), notorious French free booter.* Called the "Archpriest" because he once held a clerical benefice, he had been wounded and captured in Poitiers,* and on paying his ransom, returned to France in 1357 to lead a free company* calling itself *Societa dell' acquisito.* Receiving support and assistance from a lord of Provence named Raimond des Baux, Arnaut's band grew into an army of 2,000, and its leader, the "Archpriest" into one of the greatest evildoers of his time. Evidence of his power was shown by the actions of Pope Innocent VI at Avignon who negotiated for security in advance of Arnaut's anticipated sweep through that section of the country. He was invited to the papal palace, treated as though he were royalty, ate with the pope and cardinals, and received a pardon for all his sins and a gift of 40,000 ecus+ to leave the area untouched. (Bibliog. 223)

Arques-la-Bataille, castle+ built by William of Arques on the French coast of the English Channel in 1038. Seated on a semicircular promontory, it commanded an important route from Dieppe to Rouen. Besieged and destroyed by William the Conqueror* in 1052, it was rebuilt later by Henry I* of England as a rectangular donjon+ surrounded by a wall with small turrets. It became the last castle to surrender to Geoffrey, count of Anjou* (1129-1151) when he conquered Normandy.* It was retaken by Philip II,* Augustus (1170-1223), and even though it withstood a siege by Richard I* (1189-1199), he recovered it by treaty. Then, in 1202, it was again besieged by Philip Augustus but without success. Two years later he had much better luck at Chateau Gailiard.* (Bibliog. 30, 196)

Arsouf, battle of (September 7, 1191). Richard I* and Saladin* fought an important battle in 1191 near this small town in Palestine which the crusaders+ had fortified to make an important harbor. Earlier that year, King Philip II,* Augustus, had returned to France from the Holy Land, leaving the crusaders under the primary generalship of King Richard I. After they captured Acre,* the crusaders needed a base from which to attack Jerusalem. Deciding on Arsouf, they marched from Acre to Jaffa* along the coast road, and were harassed by Saladin's army all the way, but most intensively between Caesarea and the Salt River. The Frankish horsemen were arranged in three divisions, with the main battle standard+ in the midst; the outer defenses were provided by armed men on foot: half marched between the knights and the Muslims, and the other half between the knights and the seashore. Unable to penetrate this efficient outer guard, the Muslims relied on their usual tactic of provoking the Christians into a premature charge, but the Christians resisted this challenge. On the next day, the Saracens intensified their harassing tactics. Using closer combat and frequent feints and charges, they forced the Franks to fight back; some of the Frankish knights even left the unit to attack. On the whole, however, the Christian host became even more compact and impregnable than before. This led to the battle of Arsouf.

On September 7, Saladin, seeing his enemy nearing Jaffa, urged his men to greater exertions. To counter this expected action, however, Richard organized his line of march more elaborately. But both sides used their usual tactics: the Muslims continued to provoke and weaken by archery to which they added charges and fighting at close quarters, particularly against the rear of the column. Despite these assaults, the Franks continued to withstand the attacks. In the rear formation particularly, the Hospitallers+ were violently impatient with the orders which forbade them to attack, but only to endure. For hours they marched and persisted; footsoldiers and archers fought off the repeated Muslin attacks magnificently. There came the time, however, when the Franks had to react: they charged because knights naturally took part in the fighting when the enemy forces pressed too closely on the column; they charged normally when the enemy was so heavily committed that he could not avoid taking the full impact of the charge; and they charged because there was a limit to the restraint which the individual knights could endure. At Arsouf, all three came into play. Richard ordered the footsoldiers to open their ranks, and the mounted onslaught to sweep into the Muslin forces on a massive scale. However, the charging knights did not push their pursuit too far from the main forces for fear of being lured into an ambush. This maneuver relieved the pressure on the marching army but only briefly. On the next day, Saladin rallied his men, and by the second day he again was ready for battle, and on the third, he once more was harassing the march of the crusaders just as before. (Bibliog. 37, 195, 201)

Art of Courtly Love (De arte honeste amandi), work by Andreas Capellanus* (Andrew the Chaplain), drawn up for Countess Marie of Champagne* between 1174 and 1186 to explain a supposedly new approach to the relationship between the sexes. Addressing his remarks as advice to a certain Walter, Andreas expounded first on love: what it was, what its effects were, who was subjected to it, and how it could be acquired. Then he gave eight model dialogues between men and women delineating all possible social conditions: noble+ to noble, noble to bourgeois, etc. Clergy should not love, but of course, they would; nuns should have nothing to do with it; true love could not be bought, and peasants and prostitutes were incapable of true love. He continued with reputed decisions in courts of love presided over by his patroness, Marie of Champagne joined by the countesses of Narbonne, of Flanders, and the queen of England, Eleanor of Aquitaine. He provided the 31 rules which were expected to govern the courtly lover. Among the more curious rules were:

1. Marriage is no real excuse for not loving.
2. He who is not jealous cannot love.
5. That which a lover takes against the will of his beloved has no relish.
11. It is not proper to love any woman whom one would be ashamed to seek to marry.
12. A true lover does not desire to embrace in love anyone except his beloved.
13. When made public love rarely endures.
15. Every lover regularly turns pale in the presence of his beloved.
24. Every act of a lover ends in the thought of his beloved.
26. Love can deny nothing to love.
27. A lover can never have enough of the solaces of his beloved.
31. Nothing forbids one woman from being loved by two men or one man by two women.

(ed. and tr. J. J. Parry, Seattle, WA: Washington University, 1946) (Bibliog. 5)

Of Arthour and Merlin, Middle English* romance written in the middle of the 13th century, and derived from French sources. It extended from the death of King Constans to the defeat of Rion immediately after the betrothal of Arthur* and Guenevere.* This work was filled with detailed accounts of single combats and of general mêlées. (ed. O. D. Macrae-Gibson, London: *EETS OS* #268, 1973, 1978) (Bibliog. 165)

Arthur, duke of Brittany (1187-1203), son of Geoffrey, duke of Brittany, and Constance, daughter of Conan V, previous duke of Brittany; and nephew of King Richard I.* In 1199, after the death of Richard, a party of nobility supported Arthur's claim to the English throne, but his uncle, John,* succeeded to it instead. Arthur's claim was supported in 1201 by Philip II,* Augustus of France who, as suzerain,+ recognized him as legal heir of the Angevin+ dominions in France; additionally, Arthur was betrothed to Philip's daughter, Marie of France. Betraying the homage he had offered King John, Arthur did homage to the king of France for Brittany,* Anjou,* Maine,* Touraine, and Poitou* in July 1202. For that, he was entrusted with a campaign in Poitou while Philip himself began a campaign in Normandy.* Such a coalition failed, however, when on August 1, 1202, John captured Arthur and imprisoned him, and from the moment when he was taken to the Tower of Rouen, he disappeared. About 1210, one of John's accomplices and the guardian of young Arthur, William de Briouse, confessed that on April 3, 1203, John had killed his nephew with his own hand because he was afraid he would escape and become a strong claimant for the English throne. Blaming him for Arthur's disappearance, the nobility deserted John. In 1216, when Prince Louis (VIII)* of France invaded England at the invitations of the barons in rebellion against John, his agents tried to gain credence for the story that John had been condemned to death by his peers in the court of the king of France as Arthur's murderer. This was an outright lie, but as a result of severance of the feudal bond between John and Philip in April 1202, a year before Arthur's mysterious disappearance in Rouen, Philip was justified in disinheriting his vassal, the English king. After this Philip II was able to conquer Normandy and Anjou with little opposition. See also Richmond. (Bibliog. 92, 162, 178)

Arthur, King, legendary king of England. A composite of his legends revealed that he died in A. D. 542 after a reign of twenty-two years. He was the son of Uther Pendragon* and Igerne,* the brother of Anna,* and half-brother of Morgan la Fée,* Morgawse,* Belisent,* Hermesent, and Acheflour.* Elevated to the throne of England by Merlin's* efforts, he first subdued the eleven rebellious vassals who also were fighting the Saxon (Saracen) invaders. He aided Leodegran* against his enemy, Rion, and married Leodegran's daughter, Guenevere.* He became father of Mordred* by his half-sister Morgawse, and of Borre le Cure

Hardy by Lysanor. His armies made many conquests on the Continent until he controlled a great empire. His knights embarked on the Grail* quest which was accomplished 454 years after the passion of Christ. This was followed by the war against the Romans in which Arthur slew Lucius, king of the Romans. Arthur was summoned home either from this Roman campaign (in Layamon*) or from his siege against Lancelot (in Malory* and others) to confront Mordred, who had seized his crown and his wife, Guenevere. Arthur met his death in slaying Mordred, although some accounts stated that he was taken to Avalon* to be healed and there awaited the summons to return when needed. Legends about Arthur appeared in almost every European language and as chronicle, pseudo-history, romance, epic, saga, ballad, and folktale. He probably was an historical figure in the early 6th century Britain who was celebrated for his exploits against the Saxon invaders.

His famous twelve battles cited by both Nennius and Geoffrey of Monmouth,* were, first, at the mouth of the River Glein (unknown location); then four fought alongside the River Dubglas (location unknown); then one in the Innius area (location unknown); then at the River Bassus—probably Bass Rock in the Firth of Forth, meaning that Arthur would have had to defend the entrance to the Firth of Forth. Then at "Cat Coit Celidon"—in the Celidon Wood which seems to have been Glasgow; then in Fort Guinnion—probably the Roman Binchester, twenty miles south of the Hadrian's Wall; then in the city of the Legion, probably not Chester but a newly constituted capital city of the Romans, Carlisle*; then on the banks of the River Tribruit probably near Stirling or Carlisle; then on Mount Agned at Edinburgh; and finally, the most famous one of all on Mount Badon which probably was at Mount Dunbarton or Dunbarton Rock.

By 600, he had appeared in a Welsh poem, "Gododdin," as a famous fighter; by 1100 he had become the hero of many fabulous adventures, the chief of a band of warriors who had supernatural attributes. Having a language similar to the Welsh, Cornishmen and Bretons helped spread Arthur's fame through their stories. Bretons played the major role in spreading his fame on the continent because, by being bilingual (French and Celtic), they were welcomed at the courts of the French and Breton nobles. Thus, Arthur's fame went wherever the French language went. Geoffrey of Monmouth compiled a Latin prose work, *Historia regum Brittaniae,** which gave further impetus to the stories. He was followed by Wace,* Layamon, and Chrétien de Troyes'* romances among many others. A recent work by Geoffrey Ashe (Bibliog.   12) identified Arthur with an historical figure of Riothamus in the late 5th century; Norma Goodrich (Bibliog. 96) proved his reality as an historical figure. (Bibliog. 10, 12, 96, 202)

Arthur, short Middle English* metrical romance from the second half of the 14th century. It gave a brief account of Arthur's entire life: his begetting and birth, coronation, establishment of the Round Table*, conquest of the Romans, Mordred's* treachery, and Arthur's* death, transportation to Avalon* and burial; it also contained a long list of his vassals. (ed. F. J. Furnivall, London: *EETS OS* 2, 1865, repr. 1965) (Bibliog. 10, 63)

Arthur and Gorlagon, medieval Latin Arthurian romance concerning Arthur's quest with Kay* and Walwein (Gawain)* to find out the secret of feminine psychology which his queen taunted him about not knowing. (ed. J. D. Bruce, *Hesperia,* Baltimore, 1913) (Bibliog. 10)

Artois, region in northern France bordering on the Strait of Dover, Flanders* and Picardy.* It was given as a dowry to Isabelle of Hainaut* on her marriage to King Philip II,* Augustus of France; it was inherited by Louis VIII* who made it part of the royal domain in 1222; it was returned to the count of Flanders in 1382, and two years later passed to the dukes of Burgundy* who held it until 1477. (Bibliog. 239)

Arundel, Thomas, bishop of Ely (1378-1388); archbishop* of York (1388-1396); archbishop of Canterbury (1396-1397, and 1399-1414); chancellor+ of England (1386-1389 and 1391-1396). He was the leader of the political faction opposing King Richard II.* (Bibliog. 153)

Arundel, ancient town, castle and earldom in Sussex* County, England. Roger de Montgomery, lord of Alençon in Normandy,* having remained regent in Normandy during the invasion of England, came to England at Christmas 1067 and was made earl, receiving from King William I* large grants of about one-third of the county of Sussex, including the city of Chichester and the castle of Arundel. In addition to being called the earl of Chichester, and sometimes the earl of Sussex, he frequently was called the earl of Arundel. In 1070 another earldom was conferred upon him: the whole of Shropshire with palatine+ authority together wih the castles of Shrewsbury, and so he was more commonly known as the earl of Shrewsbury.* He was the *Comus Rogerus* (Count Roger) of the *Domesday* survey. This honour+ was forfeited to the crown in 1102. In 1138, when William d'Aubigny (de Albeney or d'Albini), the *pincerna Regis* (chief butler for the king), married the queen dowager Adeliz (widow of Henry I*), the castle and honour of Arundel were settled upon him, making him the earl of Arundel. Though not a supporter of King Stephen,* he was influential in arranging the treaty of 1153 whereby the crown continued with King Stephen for life and then passed to Henry, the son of the Empress Matilda* (Maud). This has led some to assume that William became earl of Arundel by right of his marriage to Adeliz, for shortly after his marriage he was styled variously as earl of Chichester, earl of Sussex, earl of Arundel, and Earl William d'Aubigny. He probably had been created earl by King Stephen (1135-1154) just after his escape from custody. After his wife's death in 1151, William sought and received from Henry II* (1154-1189) confirmation of his earldom. His grandson, the sixth earl, William d'Aubigny, earl of Sussex and earl of Arundel, was a favorite of King John,* and accompanied him to talk with the rebelling barons at Runneymede* in 1215. A man to choose the winning side, he momentarily switched his allegiance to Prince Louis (VIII)* of France in 1216, but returned to John after the Royalist victory over the French at Lincoln* in 1217. Shortly thereafter he was appointed justiciar* by the young King Henry III* who restored to him his forfeited possessions. He died on a crusade in 1218.

Over a century later, Edmund,* earl of Kent, sixth son of Edward I,* was granted the honour and castle of Arundel in 1327. Despite his being beheaded for treason in 1330, his widow retained his honour and estate at Arundel, and passed them to her son, Richard FitzAlan. He was made justiciar for North Wales for life in 1334, governor of Carnarvon castle in 1339, and then sheriff of Shropshire for life in 1345. He took a distinguished part in the wars with France, serving as Admiral of the West in 1340-1341 and 1345-1347, commanding the second division at the battle of Crécy* in 1346, and participating in the fall of Calais* in 1347. Born about 1313, he married in 1320 Isabel, the daughter of Hugh le Despenser,* the Younger. Twenty-four years later, in 1344, he obtained a papal annulment of that marrriage on the ground that he was a minor at the time and never willingly had consented to that match. The resulting papal mandate stated that on the petition of Richard, earl of Arundel, and Isabel, daughter of Hugh le Despenser, who at the respective ages of 7 and 8, not by mutual consent but by fear of their relations, contracted espousals, and on coming to years of puberty expressly renounced them, but were forced by blows of the parents to cohabit, so that a son was born. This mandate annulled their marriage because they had lived apart constantly, and had provided for their son, so that they were free to marry others. What really happened was that this powerful earl desired to get rid of the woman to whom he had been married as a child, and who, since her father's attainder (arrest and conviction for treason) and execution, had ceased to be of any importance, so that he might marry the woman with whom he then was living. His son by his second wife, Richard FitzAlan, earl of Arundel and earl of Surrey, was the bearer of the crown at the coronation of Richard II,* and was made Admiral of the West and South in 1377 and subsequently of all England in 1386 when he was made a Knight of the Garter.* He distinguished himself in the French wars, gaining a brilliant victory over the French, Flemish and Spanish fleets off Margate in March 1387, and was made governor of Brest in 1388. Together with the duke of Gloucester,* he took a major part in activities against the king who in 1388 was entirely in that duke's power. In 1394, he received a pardon for all political offenses, but in 1397 was treacherously seized, tried at Westminister, and beheaded. The vacant earldom was granted to John Holand, duke of Exeter, Knight of the Garter, in 1398, but a year later he, too, was degraded and beheaded whereby all his honours and estates were forfeit to the crown. See also Mowbray. (Bibliog. 47, 66, 101)

Ascalon, battle of (August 14, 1099), major battle in the open field north of the city of Ascalon in the Holy Land between the twenty thousand men of the Fatimid* ruler of Egypt, El-Mustali Abul-Kasim Hamed under El-Afdal, and the crusaders+ under Duke Godfrey de Bouillon,* Raymond of Toulouse* and Robert Curthose of Normandy.* El-Afdal's forces consisted of black Sudanese infantrymen armed with bows and iron maces, and Moorish and Bedouin light horse, partly mailed troopers of the caliph's+ regular army who were armed with spears but not with bows like the Turks. Approaching Ascalon in nine columns, each leader in command of three columns, the crusaders caught El-Afdal by surprise, for he had not expected them to be so near. These nine corps were formed in a broad line with Robert of Normandy's three columns in the center, Raymond of Toulouse's three stationed between Robert and the Mediterranean Sea, and Godfrey's three off to the left toward the hills. In each corps, the infantry were in front and the cavalry in the rear. When the crusaders came into range, the Sudanese opened fire, falling to one knee to shoot as was their custom. Simultaneously, as the whole Saracen army began to make a horrible noise of trumpets and kettle-drums to dismay and distract the Christians, the Bedouin light horse rode out to the right to encircle the enemy. Godfrey easily stopped the encircling movement by riding down the light horsemen with his heavily armed cavalry as the main line of crusaders advanced and the Christian cavalry charged the Sudanese bowmen before they had time to discharge their bows more than once. All along the line, the bowmen were forced to retreat into the Egyptian cavalry, forcing the entire army into confusion, and then into panicked retreat. Some Egyptians fled into the town of Ascalon;

others, including El-Afdal, into the sea to swim to their fleet off shore; still others hid in the orchards or climbed trees in a sycamore grove to hide in the upper branches, and were burned to death. The booty+ was immense. Robert of Normandy bought the vizier's banner+ for 20 silver marks from the Norman who had captured it; the vizier's sword was sold by its finder for 60 bezants+; bullion and precious jewels were found in abundance in the Egyptian luggage, and a vast amount of armaments and animals fell into the crusaders' hands. However, petty squabbling among the crusader leaders created such a division in their ranks that they failed to capture the town of Ascalon. This battle had, however, destroyed the Egyptian army, and led to the crusaders becoming so contemptuous of Egyptians that they neglected even the most common precautions against Egyptian forces, and would attack them even if on unfavorable ground and outnumbered ten to one. Their attitude was changed at the battle of Ramelah* a few years later when Baldwin suffered disastrously at Egyptian hands. (Bibliog. 166, 195)

Ashby de la Zouch castle,+ manor in Leicestershire owned by Hugh de Grentmeisnil after the Norman conquest. In the 12th century, it became the property of Robert de Beaumont (see Combat of the Thirty), later earl of Leicester. About 1160, it went to Alan la Zouch, a Breton, who built a stone hall and solar at the manor. In 1314, a Shropshire family named Mortimer inherited the manor and took the name of Zouch. Its huge tower-house of sandstone ashlar,+ and known as the Hastings Tower along the large curtain work, measured 48 by 41 feet with walls over 8 feet thick which rose some 90 feet. (Bibliog. 247)

Asphaltus Lake, Dead Sea. This body of water in the Near East had no life: no fish in it nor fowl on its shores; nothing with life could drown in it, for if submerged, it soon would emerge unharmed; it cast up black clots of glue on its shores; apple trees which grew along its shore would produce fruit which was green until ripe, but then when cut open would contain only ashes. (Bibliog. 18)

*Aspremont, Chanson d', chanson de geste** from the last decade of the 12th century. In this unusually long work (11,376 lines), a Saracen king, Agolant,* sent a message of defiance to Charlemagne* from Italy. In anger, Charlemagne sought to slay the messenger, Balant, who delivered the infuriating message, but he was prevented from doing so by the intercession of Duke Naimes.* However, Charlemagne still reacted angrily to the defiance, and set out for Calabria with his army. With them was a young untried fighter named Roland, age 15. Centering around this young hero and his actions, the poem went on to relate how he saved Charlemagne's life, and won his famous sword, Durandal,+ and his marvellous horse, Veillantif.+ After much fighting, the Christians celebrated their victory at their main camp of Aspremont, hence the title of the work. One opinion about its composition stated that it was written about 1188 as propaganda for the third crusade. (ed. Louis Brandin, 2nd ed., Paris: *CFMA,* 1923,1924, 2 vols.; tr. modern French, Louis Brandin, Paris, 1925) (Bibliog. 106)

Asti, large city in Italy in the province of Alessandria (Piedmont) on the River Janaro. It was famous as a great commercial city and as one of the most powerful republics in northern Italy. It opposed Frederick I* in 1155, but was captured and burnt by him. In 1348 it fell to the Visconti* and thus passed to the control of France. (Bibliog. 68)

Athelstan (924-940), grandson of King Alfred the Great.* On the death of his father, Edward the Elder in 925, he was elected and was crowned king of the Mercians and West Saxons in Surrey.* Despite the active opposition of the nobles, England prospered under his reign until his death in 940. (Bibliog. 68)

Athelstan, Middle English* metrical romance composed between 1355 and 1380. It recounted a tale of the time of King Athelstan* (924-940). Athelstan and his wife were accused of plotting to murder his father, the king, and of murdering his brother, Prince Ethelwald. The accused had to prove their innocence by the ordeal of fire. (ed. A. McI. Trounce, London: *EETS OS* #224, 1951, repr. 1957) (Bibliog. 63)

Athis und Prophilias, anonymous Middle High German* story from the 13th century which combined the friendship theme and the curing of leprosy by innocent blood. (See *Amys and Amiloun, Der Arme Heinrich* and *Engelhard.)* (ed. Sr. M. Chrysostom Truka, *Roman d'Athis et Prophilias,* Wayne State Dissertation, 1974 [DAI:34:7250A]) (Bibliog.

L'Atre Périlleux (The Perilous Cemetery), Norman Arthurian romance written about 1250 and centering on the exploits of Gauvain (Gawain*). In this, Arthur's maiden cup-bearer was abducted by a red knight, Escanor, whose strength increased until noon and then waned. First Keu (Kay)* pursued him, but he was unhorsed and wounded; then Gauvain (Gawain) set out after him and met three damsels who were mourning the death of a knight at the hands of three villainous knights who thought they were killing Gauvain. Without identifying himself, he promised to avenge the victim. Spending the night in a cemetery, he learned of a damsel imprisoned in a tomb by a devil. He beheaded the fiend and on the next day caught and killed Escanor. He forced a faithless knight, Espinogre, to return to his lover, and he overcame the knights who claimed to have killed him. (ed. B. Boledge, Paris: *CFMA,* 1936) (Bibliog. 10)

*Auberi le Bourguignon, chanson de geste** from the 13th century. In it, Auberi, the son of Bazin, duke of Burgundy, who had been made a prisoner, was robbed of his inheritance by his uncle and cousins. He entered the service of King Ouri of Bavaria where he became famous. Avoiding traps constantly set by assassins, he ended by marrying the widow of the duke of Burgundy. Historically Ouri probably was Count Udalrich who was killed in 955 in a battle against the Hungarians. (ed. W. Benary, Halle, 1931) (Bibliog. 106)

Auberon, Roman d', poetical work serving as a prologue to the Turin manuscript of *Huon de Bordeaux.** This work introduced Auberon into the Charlemagne* cycle of *chansons de geste.** It was filled with extravagant fancies and included such diverse figures as Judas Maccabeus; Julius Caesar; King Arthur,* and his sister, the fairy, Morgue; and Auberon's twin brother. All were connected by birth or marriage. (ed. Jean Subrenat, Geneva, 1973; Bernice Waddell, Dissertation, University of North Carolina at Chapel Hill, 1973 [DAI 34:2584A]) (Bibliog. 63)

Aubigny. See Arundel.

Aubrey de Vere. See Oxford.

d'Audrehem, Marshal. See Du Guesclin, Bertrand.

Aue, Hartmann von. See Hartmann von Aue.

Augsberg, city of Germany, principal seat of commerce of southern Germany, capital of Swabia and Neuberg in Bavaria.* In 1276, it was raised to the rank of free imperial city. (Bibliog. 68)

Aumale, Aumerle (Albemarle), town in Normandy where the family of its first *comte,* Stephen, the son of a disinherited count of Champagne, were made earls of Yorkshire by King Stephen.* They chose to retain the name Aumale, feeling that their dignity was not augmented by the acquisition of a title taken from a Saxon ealdorman or earl. After the capture of the town of Aumale by King Philip II,* Augustus, in 1204,

the counts of Aumale retained the title although their connection with
Aumale itself ceased. The name was changed to Albemarle in the 1660's.
Its earls and dukes were:

1097 - Stephen, son of Odo, earl of Blois and lord of Holderness
1136 - William le Gros, son of Stephen; married Cecily, daughter of
           William, son of Duncan, son of Malcolm king of Scots
1180 - William de Mandeville, earl of Essex; married Hawise,
           daughter of William le Gros
1189 - William de Fortibus (or de Forts), second husband of Hawise
1196 - Baldwin de Bethune, third husband of Hawise
1212 - William de Fortibus, son of William, second husband of Hawise
1241 - William de Fortibus, died 1260 without issue
1356 - Thomas of Woodstock, duke of Gloucester; married Eleanor,
           daughter of Humphrey de Bohun, earl of Hereford and Essex
1398 - Edward Plantagenet, lord admiral, slain at Agincourt
(Bibliog. 47, 101)

Aungervyle, Richard, also known as Richard de Bury, an Oxford-educated
Benedictine monk who was tutor to the Prince of Wales,* later Edward
III,* in whom he inspired a love of books. Aungervyle later became
bishop of Durham,* and then lord high chancellor+ and treasurer of
England. He was involved in the sordid intrigues which preceded the
deposition of Edward II* from the throne, and he supplied Queen
Isabella* and Mortimer* in Paris with money in 1325 from the revenues
of Guyenne,* of which province he was treasurer. He even had to hide
in Paris from the officers sent by Edward II to apprehend him. On
Edward III's accession, his services were rewarded with rapid promo-
tion. Sent on embassies throughout Europe, he became acquainted with
most of the eminent men of the time. At Oxford for the use of
students, he founded a library which he furnished with the best collection of books in England at the time. (Bibliog. 68)

Aunters [Adventures] of Arthur at the Tarne Wathelan, 14th century
Middle English* romance in the northern dialect, this work contained
two chief incidents: the appearance of her mother's specter to Queen
Guenevere* who foretold the events which closed Arthur's* reign, and
the deaths of Gawain* and the other knights. Then it detailed the
fight between Gawain and a Scottish knight, Sir Galoran, who came to
claim the land which Arthur had taken from him and given to Gawain.
(ed. Ralph Hanna, Manchester, England: Manchester University, 1974)
(Bibliog. 63)

Auray, battle of (September 29, 1364), conflict between Charles of Blois* and John de Montfort* for the duchy of Brittany.* It and Cocherel* (May 16, 1364) were the last battles in France before a period of peace began during the Hundred Years War.* Auray was a battle fought out almost entirely by free companies.* Half the army of Charles was composed of French free companies, and four-fifths of Montfort's army were English mercenaries.+ At Auray on the rocky Breton coast, both sides dismounted and fought on foot. Montfort's forces were led by Sir John Chandos,* who adopted tactics he had learned under King Edward III* and Prince Edward*: taking a defensive position on a slope to await the attack by superior numbers of enemy forces. Chandos was short of archers; he had about 1,000 archers to 1,800 men-at-arms, but they did not decide that battle. Heavily armored to protect themselves against arrows, Charles' men dismounted and marched in serried ranks, carrying their shields before them. When the *mêlée*+ began, the archers cast aside their bows and fought with ax and sword as they had done at Poitiers* a decade earlier. Chandos tactically used his reserve of 200 lances under Sir Hugh Calveley* to strengthen various weak points in the line, but never to become so entangled that it couldn't pull out to strengthen a different weak point. Calveley had ordered his men to remove their cuissarts+ (leg pieces) to allow them greater freedom of movement in the now-heavier armor. In this battle, after Charles of Blois had been killed, and du Guesclin* taken prisoner, the succession of John de Montfort to the duchy of Brittany was assured, even though it remained a French fief. See also Clisson, Olivier de.(Bibliog. 153, 166)

Aurelius Ambrosias, king of England, son of King Constantine,* and brother of Constans and Uther.* To escape the treachery of King Vortiger, he and Uther were raised in Brittany. Merlin* aided him to achieve the throne; he was victorious over the Saxons, and died by poison given him by Appas. (Bibliog. 129, 202)

Austria, country in central Europe. Beginning as a margraviate+ founded by Charlemagne* near the end of the 8th century along the south bank of the Danube River east of the River Enns, it was called *Ostreich,* "eastern country," from its position relative to the rest of Germany. In August 955, Otto* the Great, German king and emperor, defeated the Magyars at Lechfeld,* freed Bavaria* from their invading presence, and refounded the east mark for the defense of his kingdom. In 976 his son, Otto II, entrusted the government of this mark, soon to be known as Austria, to his son Leopold, a member of the family of Babenberg. Leopold and his descendants ruled Austria until the extinction of the family in 1246. It was ruled by margraves+ down to the year 1156 when the territory west of the Enns was added to it, and it was raised to a duchy+ by Emperor Frederick I.* Its first duke was Henry Jasomirgot who went on the second crusade.+ After Henry's death, Emperor Frederick II* declared Austria and Styria as part of the empire, and it came under the control of the Hapsburgs.* More territory made it an archduchy+ in 1453. Some of its most famous and important dukes were:

1136 - Henry II Jasomirgot, first duke of Austria
1177 - Leopold VI, brother of Henry II
1194 - Leopold VII
1246 - Frederick II
1251 - Ottokar, king of Bohemia in 1253
1273 - Rudolph I of Hapsburg, afterward emperor
(Bibliog. 68, 79, 100)

Auvergne, section of south-central France. As part of Aquitaine,* it passed in 1152 to England when Eleanor* of Aquitaine married Henry II* of England. Divided by feudal lordships, it passed in part to the French crown in 1204, and another section, the duchy of Auvergne, passed to the dukes of Bourbon* in 1416. (Bibliog. 100, 200)

Avalon, Isle of, said to be the ancient name for Glastonbury* where Arthur was taken for his wounds to be healed. It was associated with Gryngamor and the sword, Caliburn+ or Excaliber.* It also has been identified with the Isle of Man in the Irish Sea. (Bibliog. 1, 96)

Avowing of King Arthur, Sir Gawain, Sir Kay, and Sir Bawdeyn of Bretan, Middle English* romance which related an incident near Carlisle.* Arthur* was hunting with the three knights, and all four undertook separate vows: Arthur to capture single-handed a ferocious bear; Gawain to watch all night at Tarn Wadling; Kay to fight all who oppose him; and Bawdeyn (Baldwin) never to be jealous of his wife or any fair woman, never to refuse food to any man, and not to fear any threat of death. Arthur won his bear but Kay* was unhorsed by a knight carrying off a beautiful maiden. Gawain,* however, defeated this knight. Kay then taunted the defeated knight cruelly, while Gawain, mindful of the claims of chivalry, was considerate and kind toward his fallen foe. Bawdeyn overthrew the five knights sent against him by the jealous Kay. (ed. R. Dahood, [critical edition], Dissertation, Stanford University, 1971 [DAI 31:4113A]). (Bibliog. 211)

Aye d'Avignon, *chanson de geste** from the end of the 12th century. It consisted of two parts: the original work (verses 1-2283) and a continuation (verses 2284-4136). In part I, Charlemagne* gave Aye, heiress to the fief of Avignon, in marriage to Garnier de Nanteuil. This marriage was opposed by Berengier,* a son of Ganelon* who wanted her and her fief for himself. He tried unsuccessfully to ruin Garnier, but then captured Aye when her husband was gone, and fled to Aigremore where Aye was taken from him by King Ganor, a Saracen, who had fallen in love with her himself. Ganor sent Berengier to Ganelon's good friend, Marsile,* in Spain. He killed Berengier in a fight between the men of Ganor and Marsile, and then took Aye back to Avignon after she had been a captive for three years. A son, Gui, was born to Aye and Garnier. In part II, Ganor, dressed as a pilgrim, came to Avignon and stole Gui. In trying to regain his son, Garnier once again ran afoul of the race of Ganelon, for his own brothers-in-law were on the side of the enemy. He captured them and was taking them to Charlemagne when he was attacked and killed. Ganor took an army to avenge Garnier, provided he might marry Aye in payment. After the traitors were punished, Ganor became a Christian and married Aye. (ed. S. J. Borg, Geneva: Droz, 1967) This story was continued in *Gui de Nanteuil.** (ed. Eddison C. Tatham, Dissertation, Arizona University, 1967 [DA 28:1061A, 1967]) (Bibliog. 10)

Aymer of Valence (d. 1260), bishop of Winchester. He was half-brother of King Henry III of England; his mother was Isabelle of Angoulême,* second wife of King John, and his father was Hugh of Lusignan, count of La Marche, whom Isabelle married in 1220 after John's death. Their children went to England in 1247 to obtain court preferment. In 1250, by putting strong pressure on the electors, Henry III obtained the see of Winchester for Aymer. He was totally unsuitable for that position: he was illiterate, ignorant of the English language, and completely secular in his lifestyle. That appointment and his subsequent activities as bishop brought down the wrath of the populace on the king for such appointments to foreign favorites. After he and his brothers repudiated the new constitution drawn up by the barons at the Parliament of 1258 (see Provisions of Oxford), he was pursued to Winchester, besieged and forced to leave England. As he had never been consecrated as bishop, the chapter elected a new bishop. Aymer complained to the pope who backed him, and was on his way back to England to exert his new authority when he died in Paris in 1260. (Bibliog. 68)

Aymeri de Narbonne. See *Aimeri de Narbonne.*

B

Bademagus, nephew of King Uriens of Gore in Arthurian legend. He left Arthur's* court in anger because Sir Tor had been chosen instead of himself to fill a vacant seat at the Round Table.* As he set out on the Grail* quest, he was struck down by an angelic knight for trying to take the adventurous shield reserved for Galahad.* (Bibliog. 117)

Badlesmere, Bartolomew of (1275-1322), English knight from Chilham castle in Kent, who fought in the Scottish wars of 1303 and 1304, and became governor of Bristol castle in 1307. He was made Lord Badlesmere in 1309 after being summoned to Parliament. In 1314, he was made governor of all the castles in Yorkshire and Westmoreland* which had been seized from Robert de Clifford*; he also became steward of the king's household. However, despite these honors from King Edward II,* he joined the rebellious forces of Thomas of Lancaster,* and after their defeat at the battle of Boroughbridge* in March 1322, he was hanged as a traitor at Canterbury in April 1322. On the death of his son, Giles, in 1338, the barony became extinct. (Bibliog. 47)

Baha ad-Din, Boha ed-din, Beha ed-Din (1145-1234), Arabian historian better known in the East as Ibn Seddad, he became a teacher at Mosul and was summoned by Saladin* to enter his service in 1188, and remained with him until Saladin's death. He served as a judge for the army, a judge of Jerusalem, and an ambassador for his leader. His biography of the great Saracen leader provided excellent historical and biographical information: *Sultanly Anecdotes and Josephly Virtues* (Joseph was Saladin's personal name). (text: *Recueil des Historiens des Croisades, Historiens Orientaux*, III, Paris, 1884; tr. C. W. Wilson and C. R. Conder, *Life of Saladin*, London: *PPTS,* The Library #13, 1897; repr. New York: AMS Press, 1971) (Bibliog.83)

Baker, Geoffrey le (d. 1358-1360), author of a chronicle begun in 1341 at the request of his patron, Sir Thomas de la More. This work, Chronicon *Galfridi le Baker de Swynebroke* (1303-1356), provided valuable firsthand information for events after 1341. (ed. E. M. Thompson, Oxford, 1889) (Bibliog. 99)

Balan, knight who helped his brother, Balin the Savage* capture King Rions for King Arthur,* and to win King Arthur's war against Lot, Rions, Nero and others in rebellion. (Bibliog. 117)

Baldwin, count of Flanders (1171-1205), one of the leaders of the fourth crusade.+ Young, gallant, pious, and virtuous, and one of the few who interpreted and observed his crusading vows strictly, he was the most popular leader with the crusaders. After the imperial crown of the new Latin empire of Constantinople had been offered and refused by Henry Dandalo, doge of Venice, it was offered to and accepted by him in 1204. A year later, he, Dandalo and the count of Blois marched to besiege Hadrianople where they were opposed by a larger force of the king of Bulgaria. These crusaders fought desperately, but were defeated, the count of Blois slain and Baldwin captured. Treated well as a valuable hostage at first, he then was mutilated by the king of Bulgaria in a rage over the loss of another city: his hands and feet were severed, and he was thrown into a ravine where he died three days later. (Bibliog. 68, 195)

Baldwin of Boulogne (1058-1118), king of Jerusalem. Totally different from his brother, Godfrey of Bouillon,* Baldwin had been destined for the church, so he had no family estate. Being trained at the great school at Reims gave him the taste for culture, but not being a churchman at heart, he soon left the church to serve under his brother in Lorraine. Taller than his brother, he had dark hair and a fair complexion, was haughty, cold, imperious, and so loved pomp and luxury that he refused to endure lengthy hardships. In short, he loved the pleasures of life. Thus, when he realized that his homeland offered no real future for him, he took his wife and children to the East where he established a kingdom for himself as Baldwin I, first king of the Latin kingdom of Jerusalem. (Bibliog. 195)

Baldwin II, count of Edessa (1100-1118) and king of Jerusalem (1118-1131). Originally known as Baldwin de Burg, son of Count Hugh of Rethel, he was nephew of Godfrey de Bouillon* and Baldwin I* (see Baldwin of Boulogne). After the capture of Jerusalem, he served with Bohemund in Antioch,* but when in 1118 he was on his way to spend Easter at Jerusalem and heard of the death of Baldwin I, and he went to Jerusalem to become king chiefly by the influence of the patriarch Arnulf, and extended the kingdom of Jerusalem to its widest limits.

His death in 1131 ended the first generation of the founders of the crusader state; his successors all were born in the Holy Land. (Bibliog. 68)

Baldwin III (1130-1162), king of Jerusalem (1143-1162). Eldest son of Fulk of Jerusalem and Melisinda, daughter of Baldwin II,* he became king in 1143 under the regency of his mother which lasted until 1152. In the inevitable struggle between the young king and his mother who had ruled with wisdom and vigor during the regency, she was unwilling to lay aside the reins of power. Baldwin, however, planned a coronation as a sign of his power, but was dissuaded, and chose instead to proclaim his authority by wearing his crown publicly in the Church of the Sepulchre. He spent most of his reign fighting against Nureddin to keep his territories. He died in 1162 without male heir, and was succeeded by his brother Almanric I. (Bibliog. 68, 195)

Baligant, Saracen *emir** of Babylon in the *chanson de geste** the *Song of Roland,** who was summoned by Marsile* to help him rid Spain of Charlemagne.* Landing at Saragossa, he marshaled his forces to ride out against the Christian forces of Charlemagne. He caught up with them just as they were leaving the battlefield after burying the fallen *douzepeers** and the two huge opposing forces hurled themselves into battle. Its outcome was decided by the duel between the two leaders, and naturally Charlemagne was the victor. (Bibliog. 210)

Baliol, John de (d. 1269), English baron and regent of Scotland after whom Baliol College at Oxford was named. Son of Hugh Baliol of Bernard's Castle in Durham, he served Henry III* in the contest with de Montfort* and the revolted barons. His son John Baliol* was a competitor with Bruce for the throne of Scotland. (Bibliog. 68, 176)

Baliol (Balliol), John (1240-1314), son of John de Baliol,* sometime regent of Scotland. By right of his descent from King David I* through his mother, he was crowned king of Scotland at Scone in 1292, having been awarded the crown by King Edward I.* He lost his English barony of Bywell which was given to John of Brittany, earl of Richmond,* nephew of Edward I. He abdicated the Scottish throne in 1296 and fled to France. His son and heir, Edward Balliol, was a prisoner in the Tower of London at the time of his father's death, and even though he was crowned king of Scotland in 1332, he did not succeed to the barony of Bywell which had been forfeited. (Bibliog. 47)

Balin, the Savage, brother of Balan.* Also called the "Knight of the

Two Swords" in Arthurian legend, Balin beheaded a Lady of the Lake,*
slew Lanceor, son of the king of Ireland, and Garlon, the invisible
knight, and gave a Dolorous Stroke* to Pellam.* He was killed by his
brother in a duel. (Bibliog. 145)

Bamburgh castle,+ citadel in Northumberland* standing near the coast
of the North Sea. Once the center of the kingdom of Berenicia, it took
its name from Queen Bebba, the queen of King Ethelfrith. When the area
was fortified, it was known as Bebbanburgh (Bebba's burh*). Recognizing its strategic importance in the rugged northland, William I* left
it untouched. It became a royal fortress in 1095 when King William II*
took it by force from Robert Mowbray, earl of Northampton. When Robert
escaped from the castle in his attempt to get help during William II's
siege, he was captured and paraded in front of the castle, and a
message was sent his wife, who still was stoutly defending the castle,
saying that unless she surrendered, her husband's eyes would be gouged
out. She yielded. Later Henry I* retained it, but Stephen* bestowed it
on Henry, earl of Huntingdon,* son of King David* of Scotland. It was
recovered for the crown by Henry II* in 1157 who chose to strengthen
it, and add a new keep between 1164 and 1170 at a cost of £4. It continued to play a defensive role throughout the entire medieval period.
(Bibliog. 104, 247)

Ban, king of Benwick, brother of Bors, father of Lancelot du Lak,* and
a natural son, Ector de Marys, in Arthurian legend. He helped Arthur*
fight the rebellious vassals and King Ryons. (Bibliog. 145)

Banastre, Adam, English rebel who reacted to the conflict between
Thomas of Lancaster* and King Edward II* by convincing other unhappy
military tenants of Earl Thomas' household to become outlaws with him.
On October 8, 1315, he and his followers moved south from their home
at Shevington to attack Liverpool castle, to plunder Holand's*
brother's home at Newton, and to storm Holton castle. Others in the
group went north and carried away arms stored at Clitheroe castle for
the Scottish wars. The sheriff of Lancaster gathered a force against
them and on November 4 defeated them in a battle lasting less than an
hour. Adam and his brother escaped, but were betrayed, captured and
beheaded; their fellow conspirators were treated equally severely.
(Bibliog. 125)

Banbury castle,+ fortress in Oxfordshire within a two-acre moated enclosure built in 1125 as a stronghold for the bishops of Lincoln.
(Bibliog. 247)

Bannock Burn, battle of (June 23-24, 1314), fight between the English army led by King Edward II* and the Scottish army led by King Robert* the Bruce to determine the fate of Stirling* castle, and to destroy the Scots army which was besieging it. This battle secured the independence of Scotland and established Bruce upon the Scottish throne. After capturing and dismantling Perth in 1313, Robert turned to besiege Stirling. Stirling's governor, Sir Philip de Mowbray, made an agreement with Edward Bruce, Robert's brother, to hand over the fortress on Midsummer's Day,+ June 24, 1314, if the siege had not been relieved by the arrival of an adequate English army within three leagues of the castle's gates. Mowbray raced to England and the king with the news. By May 26, 1314, King Edward II approached the March of Scotland with a force estimated between 6,000 and 6,500 men, mainly infantry, including the earl of Gloucester* and Hertford, the earl of Hereford* and Essex,* the earl of Pembroke,* and many lesser knights. Facing this group was Robert's smaller force, estimated around 5,000 men organized in four oblong formations called shiltrons* (or schiltroms) for the battle. Each shiltron was an oblong of men, many rows deep, walled in by their shields, and when attacked presenting in all directions an armed hedge of 18-foot pikes. When halted, the flank files and rearmost ranks faced outwards and the foremost ranks on each face knelt, planting their pikes in the ground between their knees. Formed this way, each shiltron, ready to bristle with pikes in any direction of an attack, moved across the battlefield slowly and steadily, immune from any surprise attack delivered by English heavy cavalry armed with the shorter 12-foot lance. Robert arranged his men into "battles"+ of a shiltron each. On the thousand-yard carse (plow land) bordering a river—between the Bannock Burn and the River Forth in a peat-covered area and dotted with mud-bottomed pools, the English army encamped. King Robert's forces lay a mile or so away in the King's Park, a broad woodland expanse in front of Stirling castle.

On Sunday afternoon, June 23, when King Edward II ordered Lord Clifford, Warden of the Scottish Marches, with 300 men to contact the castle, Robert ordered Randolph's battle to stop him. Arrogantly, the English charged the slowly advancing shiltron, but unable to penetrate the 18-foot pikes, they were cut to pieces. When they could not dent the formation, the English hurled maces, knives, swords, and spears against their foes. At the approach of the second shiltron of Douglas, the English broke and fled. Uneasy and unsure of their enemy's actions during the night, the English were kept cramped in formation and got no rest. Robert recognized the strategic importance of the English error in locating their encampment. While attacking, Robert's flanks would be protected by the river and the burn, and as they pressed back the front, the English would be forced into an ever-shrinking area, and would lose considerable mobility. Robert feared the Welsh and English bowmen could break up his shiltrons before they could close with the battles of Edward's army, and thus could offer the mailed horsemen the chance to charge and disperse his broken formations. Before he could solve that plight, his planning received a fortuitous but ill-advised interruption. A hot argument between the earls of Gloucester and Hereford about who would lead the foremost portion of the English van resulted in Gloucester's couching his lance and charging the gleaming hedge of pikes, alone. Rider and horse both were brought down before they could close, and both were slain. Bruce had so surprised the English by his advance that morning that Gloucester had not dressed in his surcoat with the famous Gloucester insignia of three ruddy chevrons+ on a gold field. Because the Scots had not recognized this head of a great family, they missed the chance to collect a large sum of ransom money. When the rest of the van saw Gloucester fall, they charged the shiltron on all sides, effectively cutting off any chance of the English archers softening it before the attack.   Moving slowly and steadily, the four shiltrons of the Scottish army pushed further and further into the English forces, compressing them more and more, and rendering more and more men unable to fight because of lack of room, and making the English archers unable to locate targets. At this point, Robert ordered his light cavalry to attack the formation of archers, and force them to scatter back into the compressing English encampment. Robert then chose this moment to order his "small folk,"* the late-comers to his encampment, to join the battle. When the English saw yet another group of between 2,000 and 2,500 men appear, their morale sank. King Edward realized that his only recourse was to flee, and with a small group of knights he raced toward Stirling castle a mile and a half away. The remainder of the English forces scattered, and the Scots pursued to try to finish them off. No accurate figures were available on the losses on both sides, but the English lost between 30 and 35 percent of their knights—an extraordinarily high percentage. (Bibliog. 20)

Baños de la Encina, castle built in Granada by the Caliph Hakam II in 967-968 to guard the Guadalquiver River. Its single enciente had 15 square towers and a double horseshoe gateway of ashlar.+ It was captured by the Christians before 1212. (Bibliog. 30)

Bar, county and duchy (959-1480) on the Meuse River in northeastern France. Originally part of Lotharingia,* it was granted independence from the dukes of Lotharingia in 959. In the 11th century, its counts were involved in matters at the French court, and were connected by marriage to the counts of Troyes-Champagne. Henry I, count of Champagne, inherited it and became a vassal of the Holy Roman Emperor for its eastern portion. In 1301, the western portion was annexed to the crown of France along with Champagne, and became a duchy in 1335. (Bibliog. 90, 92)

Barbour, John (c. 1316-1395), archdeacon of Aberdeen, and clerk of audit of the king's household who, in 1375-1376, wrote *The Bruce*, a 14,000-line English verse account of the life and deeds of Robert Bruce II,* for which he received a gift of £10 in 1377, and a lifetime pension of 20 shillings. The theme of this work was the freedom and liberation of Scotland from the dominion of a foreign people; it became a national epic which gave an account of the Scottish war of independence, and narrated the deeds of King Bruce of Scotland. This age of Robert the Bruce was the age of Scottish chivalry, and the figure of the Bruce was presented as the perfect model of a valiant knight, especially at the battle of Bannock Burn.* (ed. W. W. Skeat, London: *EETS ES* #11, 1870; #55, 1889; repr. 1968) (Bibliog. 63)

Barcelona, county of, province south of the Pyrenees Mountains which in Carolingian times was known as the Spanish March; it lay between Toulouse,* Aragon,* Gascony* and the Mediterranean Sea. (Bibliog. 162, 200)

Barnard castle,+ stronghold on the left bank of the Tees River in County Durham begun late in the 11th century by Barnard, son of Guy de Baliol. Its ramparts and ditch enclosed a rectangular bailey+ of about six acres. After a visit by King John* in 1216, it was besieged by Alexander of Scotland, but not taken. In 1292, when its owner, John Baliol* was crowned king of Scotland, it was forfeited to the English King Edward I.* Anthony Bek,* bishop of Durham, claimed the castle from the Baliol family between 1296 and 1301, but the king once again claimed it and finally bestowed it on Guy de Beauchamp, earl of Warwick.* (Bibliog. 247)

Barons' War (1263-1265), conflict between King Henry III* and the angry English barons led by Simon de Montfort,* earl of Leicester, which began on April 4, 1264, when King Henry led his army from Oxford to Northampton and ended on September 16, 1265, when peace was proclaimed at Winchester. Dissatisfied with the king's repeated infractions of the Provisions of Oxford* (1258), and his favoritism of foreigners, particularly his brothers-in-law, Montfort relied on two strategic districts for support: Wales, whose leader, Llewelyn, was exposed constantly to the attacks from the ultra-Royalist Marcher* barons. And secondly, Kent and Surrey where important ports, especially the Cinque Ports* so vital for foreign aid to the king, were held by loyal adherents of Montfort. Even though it harbored many royalists, London largely supported Montfort, also. In May 1263, after Montfort tried unsuccessfully to convince the king to adhere to and carry out the Provisions of Oxford, he moved from Oxford at the head of a force of young barons, secured the territory around the Severn River, and by July, he entered London. Both sides agreed to the arbitration of King Louis IX* of France.

In January 1264, after Louis decided against the barons, the unrest began anew. In April, four members of the Montfort family were captured at Northampton. The king continued his victorious march to Nottingham. Simon, meanwhile, not dissuaded by the capture of members of his family, marched on Rochester. King Henry and his son, Prince Edward,* marched quickly south to relieve Rochester and protect that district so vital to communication with their friends in France. Simon retired to London. The king and Edward tried to recover the Cinque Ports but at Sandwich, Dover, and other ports, were coldly refused admission and were forced to fall back on the royalist refuge of the Lewes Priory in May 1264. Aided by Londoners, Montfort tried unsuccessfully to secure an understanding with Henry III, and failing that, Montfort marched to Lewes,* captured both the king and the prince, and took over the government of England. Although both men were released under severe conditions within a year, Prince Edward immediately sought to reestablish royalist supremacy, and within a few months took up arms against his recent captor. Marching west quickly, he and his forces captured bridges across the Severn River to keep Simon and his forces in Wales. From Hereford, Simon tried to break through to Bristol but was prevented from doing so by the prince's rapid movements. His son, Simon the Younger, set out from London to attack Edward's flanks, sacked Winchester* on the way through, and moved through Oxford to Kenilworth, his paternal home. In August, Edward, aided by Warenne* and knights from abroad, surprised and captured many of Young Simon's knights, and thus placed himself between the two Montforts. By this diversion to Kenilworth, Edward allowed the elder Simon to cross the Severn and take a position near Evesham. Edward feigning a movement northward, turned suddenly to confront the rebels at Evesham. Simon the Younger was unable to get help to his beleaguered father, and in the resultant slaughter at the battle of Evesham* on August 14, 1265, the elder Simon and many of his barons were killed. That ended the Barons' War, and the

Dictum of Kenilworth* was formulated to help restore the peace. (Bibliog. 184)

Barton, Harry. See Lovelich, Henry.

Basin, chanson de geste* of the Charlemagne* cycle also known as *Charles et Elegast*, this work dealt with the youth of Charlemagne. By the title *Basin*, this work survived only in the *Karlamagnus Saga,** the Norse prose collection of Old French epics dealing with Charlemagne, written about 1300. Its two stock traitor figures, Rainfroi and Helpri, also appeared in two other poems about Charlemagne's youth, *Mainet,** and *Berta aus grans piés.** (ed. G. G. Kloeke, *Karel und Elegast*, Leiden, 1948) (Bibliog. 106)

Basin de Gennes, thief and famous magician in French epic poetry: in *Renaut de Montauban* (see *Four Sons of Aymon*), *Maugis*, and *Elie de Saint Gille.** (Bibliog. 135)

Basset, Ralph (fl. 1130), prominent justiciar in England under King Henry I* along with his son Richard Basset. Ralph was in the king's service soon after Henry's accession in 1100. (Bibliog. 120)

Basset, Ralph (c. 1290-1343), Lord Basset of Drayton; knighted with the Prince of Wales* in 1306, he was made a banneret+ in 1341. He became constable of Dover castle* in 1326, warden of the Cinque Ports,* and seneschal+ of Gascony,* and subsequently was appointed steward of the duchy of Aquitaine,* and in that position, defied the king of France. He married Joan, daughter of John de Grey, Lord Grey of Wilton. His grandson, Ralph, Lord Basset of Drayton (1335-1390), joined the army of the Black Prince* at Bordeaux in 1356. He distinguished himself in various wars with France, and was a deponent in the Scrope-Grosvenor controversy. (Bibliog. 47)

Bataille Loquifer, chanson de geste* of the Guillaume d'Orange cycle written by Graindor de Brie living in Norman Sicily in the 13th century. It contained a mixture of giants, fairies, Arthurian knights and the Devil himself; its hero, Rainouart, engaged Loquifer (Lucifer) in single combat, and fairies eventually took him to Avalon.* (ed. Monica Barnett, London: University of London, 1958) (Bibliog. 106)

Bâtard de Bouillon, chanson de geste* of the 14th century that continued the adventures of Baldwin (Baudouin)* the Third, king of Jerusalem, which were begun in *Baudouin de Sebourc.* (ed. R. F. Cook,

Textes littéraire français 187, Geneva: Droz, 1972) (Bibliog. 106)

battle, strategy of. Medieval battles were rare events, deliberately
so. Whenever possible, famous and clever warriors avoided direct confrontation with an enemy which a battle demanded. Instead they used
strategy to win their goals without committing their forces to
hand-to-hand fighting. Richard I* learned about battles firsthand at
age 15 when he joined his brothers in their rebellious attack on their
father, Henry II,* in eastern Normandy in 1173. Yet he fought only
three "battles" in the remaining twenty-five years of his life: early
in his career when he defeated a force of Brabançons in 1176, at
Arsouf* in 1191, and at Jaffa* in 1192. Not once did he go after
Saladin's army to confront and destroy it. Philip II,* Augustus, of
France fought only one: at Bouvines* in 1214, a battle which he tried
desperately to avoid and then fought only because it was inevitable.
Henry II never fought a single battle in his entire life. Some rulers
issued orders not to engage in battle: Charles V after Poitiers,*
Louis XI after Montlhery, and Charles VII during most of his reign all
issued orders specifically forbidding attack. Those kings were
successful rulers who regularly mustered troops and led them to war,
but who did not fight battles. These successful leaders were following
the sound tactical advice of the late Roman writer Vegetius whose
De re Militari was probably the best book ever written on medieval
warfare. His advice about battles quite simply was, "Don't." Should
one's army heavily outnumber one's enemy and their morale was poor,
their supplies short and they were tired and poorly led, perhaps then
one might attack; but battle was to be considered only as the last resort. (ed. R. Dybosky and Z. M. Arend, *Knyghthode and Bataile*, New
York, 1935)

What, then, were the disadvantages of battle? If one's goal
was to win and hold territory, and this meant capturing and holding
strongpoints, then victory in battle was advantageous, as it was for
Saladin at Hattin* in 1187, and for William the Conqueror at Hastings*
in 1066, for both knew that they probably would never have so large an
army at their disposal again. Normally, though, battle was a desperately chancy business because a few moments of panic could easily
undo months of planning. Further, a king or prince committing his
cause to battle recognized that he was putting himself into personal
jeopardy since the surest way to win a battle was to capture or kill
the opposing commander. In a well-planned campaign, other means could
be used to obtain the rewards of victory which did not involve the
penalties of defeat. These other means basically were to capture
one's opponent's strongpoints after ravaging the countryside to de-

prive him of supplies, and then to besiege his castles. That is how Charlemagne,* Edward III* and the Black Prince* operated. This strategy was advocated by Vegetius: "the main and principal point in war is to secure plenty of provisions for oneself and to destroy the enemy by famine. Famine is more terrible than the sword." The principal duties of a commander, then, were to avoid open battle, and to see that his troops were kept reasonably fit and well supplied with women.* (Bibliog. 91)

battle of the Standard (August 22, 1138). Battle at Northallerton between the invading Scottish forces and those of King Stephen* of England. It was known as the battle of the Standard, for the English carried in the midst of their forces a wagon displaying the consecrated banners of the archbishop's three minster churches: St. Peter of York, St. John of Beverly, and St. Wilfred of Ripon. Nearly all the important northern barons, except the earl of Chester, responded to the general alarm of the Scottish invasion of Northumberland by King David* to secure it as an earldom for his son. This battle was remembered primarily for the tactics used by the English yeomen. Being expert in the use of the longbow,+ they sent such a shower of arrows into the charging ranks of the Scots, armed only with sword and buckler, that they not only prevented the first rank of attackers from reaching the ranks of the English, but also forced the other ranks of the Scots into confusion and defeat. (Bibliog. 166)

Baudemagus, governor of the fortress which Lancelot* stormed to rescue Guenevere* in Chrétien de Troyes,* *Lancelot.** He was the father of Meleagant,* nephew of King Urien* of Gorre,* and was slain by Gawain.* (Bibliog. 96, 145)

Baudouin (Baldwin), brother of Roland,* and nephew of Charlemagne* in the *chanson de geste,** the *Chanson de Roland,** and in the *Chanson des Saisnes,** but not the same as Baldwin, the bastard son of Ogier and Mahaut, daughter of the chatelain of Saint-Omer in *Ogier,** or as Baldwin of Beauvais, crusader and brother of King Ernoul of Nimegue; or as the historical Baldwin of Boulogne,* brother of Godfrey of Bouillon,* who succeeded Godfrey to the throne of the kingdom of Jerusalem after the first crusade+ whose adventures were related in *le Roman de Baudouin de Sebourc,* the comic-heroic *chanson de geste* of the 14th century. These adventures were continued in *Bâtard de Bouillon.** (ed. Louis-Napoléon Boca, Valenciennes: B. Henry, 1841) (Bibliog. 106, 121, 128)

Bavaria, kingdom of southern Germany consisting of two portions: Bavaria proper and the palatinate+ of the Rhine. It was one of the great duchies of the Holy Roman Empire. After the death of Charlemagne,* Bavaria was governed by one of his grandsons whose successors bore the title of margrave,+ or lord of the marches.+ In 920, the ruling margrave was raised to the rank of duke. Bavarian East Mark (march)* became the separate duchy of Austria* in 1156, and was taken from Saxony by Frederick I*, Barbarossa in 1180 and given to the house of Wittelsbach. Later, in the 13th century, it was divided into Upper and Lower Bavaria. (Bibliog. 79, 100)

Bayonne, port city in southwestern France on the Nive River which the English captured in 1199 and held for centuries. (Bibliog. 200)

Beadous, French romance by Robert de Blois which had Gawain's* son as the hero. (Bibliog. 231)

Beatrix. See *Chevalier au Cygne.*

Beauchamp, John (1319-1388), the first English baron created by letters patent+: Baron of Kidderminster. In 1387, he was made steward of the king's household which led to his being created Lord Beauchamp. When sent in 1353 to rescue Saintonge, he won a remarkable victory against an attack by the French under King John II (1350-1364), and another remarkable victory at Saintes, capturing two marshals of France among many other important prisoners which allowed the English to make a fortune in ransoms.+ A few months after being summoned to Parliament, he was impeached by the "merciless" Parliament* (1388), beheaded on Tower Hill and his honors forfeited. (Bibliog. 35, 47)

Beaufort, name given to the four illegitimate children of John of Gaunt* and Kathryn de Swynford, wife of Sir Hugh de Swynford: John, created earl of Somerset and marquess of Dorset; Henry, afterwards bishop of Winchester and cardinal; Thomas, made duke of Exeter and chancellor; and Joan, who married Ralph Neville, first earl of Westmoreland. In 1396, some years after the birth of the children, John married Catherine, and in 1397, King Richard II* declared them to be legitimate. In 1407 that action was reaffirmed by their half-brother, King Henry IV,* but on that occasion, he expressly excluded them from any claim to the succession to the throne. (Bibliog. 47, 68)

Beaufort, crusader castle+ in the Holy Land which, by reason of its location atop a sheer rock face, and a rock-cut ditch and a curtain wall+ which incorporated a massive square keep,+ was so impregnable that it held out against Saladin* for a year, and was overcome only by starvation in 1190. Holding it for seventy years, the Muslims sold it in 1260 to the Knights Templar,+ but recovered it by bombardment in 1268. (Bibliog. 30)

Beaumanoir, Jean de (d. 1366), French knight from the castle of Josselin* who entered the service of Joan of Penthièvre, duchess of Brittany,* and distinguished himself in 1351 in the Combat of the Thirty* against the pro-English forces in Brittany. His conduct in this battle led him to be celebrated as a model of perfect chivalry.+ (Bibliog. 98)

Beaumanoir, Philippe de (c. 1250-1296), also known as Philippe de Remi, sire de Beaumanoir, he was a lyric poet who also was bailiff+ at Senlis and later at Clermont in 1280, and presided at several assizes+ at various towns. Unusually so, his *Coutumes de Beauvaisis* in poetry was considered one of the best works on old French law. He also was the author of two romances quite different in nature: *La Manekine** and *Jehan et Blonde.** (Bibliog. 68, 231)

Beaumaris, last of King Edward I's* Welsh castles+ undertaken by the great castle builder, Master James,+ but the Welsh submission to the English in 1296 caused work on it to be stopped before its completion. (Bibliog. 30)

Beaumayns, epithet given to Gareth,* youngest son of King Lot* of Orkney,* in Arthurian legend. (Bibliog. 145)

Beaumont, Henry (d. 1340), Lord Beaumont and earl of Buchan. He was the younger son of John de Brienne, king of Jerusalem and emperor of Constantinople, by Berengaria,* daughter of Alphonso IX of León who also was the father of Ferdinand II, king of Castile and León, and of Eleanor, first wife of Edward I* and mother of Edward II.* Thus as second cousin of King Edward II, he was called *consanguineus Regis*, and his sister, Isabel de Vesci, sometimes was called "kinswoman of Queen Eleanor." Knighted in 1308, he was appointed joint warden of Scotland (south of Forth). After 1339, he also was known as earl of Buchan by his marriage to the heiress of John Comyn, earl of Buchan. He fought on the side of the King Edward II at the battle of Boroughbridge,* and later was made constable of England. However, Beaumont turned against King Edward II and prevented his escape which led shortly thereafter to the Edward's murder at Berkeley castle.* For this, Beaumont was given Loughborough castle in 1334, was made constable of the army in 1336 and justiciar of Scotland in 1338. (Bibliog. 47)

Beaumont, Robert de. See Leicester.

Becket, Thomas à (1118-1170), archbishop of Canterbury,* martyred in 1170. By 1154, he had risen to become the archdeacon of Canterbury, and in the following year, Henry II* made him chancellor.+ Then, seeking to control the church in England by controlling the archbishop, King Henry appointed Becket to the post, but he soon found that Becket refused to accede to the king's wishes, especially about taxation of the clergy. After the king went over Thomas' head and promulgated the Constitutions of Clarendon+ in 1166, Thomas broke openly with him, and to escape the king's wrath, fled to France. A reconciliation brought Thomas back to England in 1170, but their conflict erupted again almost immediately when Thomas excommunicated the bishops who had assisted the archbishop of York in crowning Prince Henry* as heir to the throne because that was a right jealously guarded by the archbishop of Canterbury. In a black rage, the king incited four knights, William de Tracy,* Hugh de Morville, Reginald FitzUrse, and Richard le Breton, to assassinate Thomas at Canterbury on December 29, 1170. The murdered prelate became a martyr overnight, and was canonized in 1173. His tomb at Canterbury attracted pilgrims from all over Europe. Many biographies of Thomas were written shortly after his death, among them works by Alan of Tewkesbury, Benedict of Peterborough,* Herbert of Bosham, John of Salisbury,* William FitzStephen, and William, monk of Canterbury. (Bibliog. 63)

Bedevere, earl of Normandy and brother of Lucan in Arthurian legend. In Layamon's* account, he died in the Roman war; in Malory's,* he survived the Roman war, was the last knight left alive with the king in Arthur's final battle, and was the knight of the Round Table* who obeyed Arthur's dying command to throw Excaliber* into the water. (Bibliog. 129, 145, 202)

Bedford, earl of. See Enguerrand de Coucy VII.

Bedford castle,+ fortress held by the Beauchamp family throughout the 12th century by what they felt was their hereditary right. This was the castle of a family who joined the barons against King John,* but was captured in 1215 by Faulkes de Breauté* who made it his capital for nine years. When he was called upon by the new king, Henry III,* to surrender it in 1224, Faulkes refused, and was besieged for two months. After he surrendered, it was demolished. (Bibliog. 104)

Beeston castle,+ citadel in Cheshire commanding one of three gaps in the hills surrounding Chester.* It was begun in 1225 by Ranulph, seventh earl of Chester, who wanted to preserve his own freedom of action and to defy the king himself if necessary. Ranulph died seven years later, and when his family line came to an end on the death of his son, John, in 1237, the castle reverted to the king and was allowed to fall into ruin. (Bibliog. 104)

Beha ed-Din. See Baha ad-Din.

Bek, Anthony (d. 1310), bishop of Durham. Third son of Walter Bek, lord of Eresby in Lincolnshire, he became bishop of Durham in 1286 when as a young man he attracted the attention of King Edward I.* He combined secular and political interests, thereby becoming one of the most magnificent lords in England.   Besides an income from his bishopric, he had enormous wealth and took great delight in displaying it. His ordinary retinue, for example, consisted of 140 knights. Once just to show off, he paid 40 shillings for 40 herrings that could have been purchased for 4 pence. Famed for his chastity, he delighted in the outdoor life of hounds, hawks and horses. About 1300, he and the king fell out over his suspension of a prior named Richard. Bek was threatened with deprivation of his office, and left England to see Pope Boniface VII without the king's permission. The king seized his episcopal see in his absence. Bek obtained the pope's approval for his action, and on his return to England, he convinced the king to restore him to his see. In 1309, he sold an estate entrusted to his care. When challenged by the king, he could not account satisfactorily for that action, but died in 1310 before the king could take action against him. (Bibliog. 58)

"Bel amie, si est de nus: ne vus sanz mei, ne mei sanz vus." (Fr. "Dearest love, this is how we must be: never you without me, never me without you.") This was the essence of the Tristan* and Isolde story which Tristan engraved at the request of the queen, as related by Marie de France* in the lay *La Chievrefueil.** (Bibliog. 147)

Bel Chevalier (Bel Mauvais), cowardly knight in Arthurian legend, who originally refrained from performing knightly deeds for fear of losing his good looks. Once he had proved his courage, however, he was re-named from Bel Mauvais to Beau Hardi by Perceval.* (in Manessier,

Continuation of Perceval) (Bibliog. 242)

Le Bel Inconnu or Guinglain (The Fair Unknown), medieval French verse romance by Renaud de Beaujeu which told the history of Gawain's* son, Guinglain. A damsel and her dwarf arrived at King Arthur's* court seeking a champion who would deliver her mistress, the daughter of the king of Wales from two enchanters, who had turned her into a dragon.* To her surprise and disgust, the damsel's request was assigned to a young and nameless knight (Guinglain), and despite her scornful treatment of him on the trip, he accompanied her all the way to the city of Sinadon where he defeated the enchanters, removed the spell on the Blonde Esmerée by kissing her while she was in dragon form, and then married her.   (ed. G. Perrie Williams, Paris, *CFMA,* 1929) (Bibliog. 10)

Bel Repaire, Blancheflor's* besieged castle and its surrounding district which Clamadeau had laid waste, in Chrétien de Troyes'* *Perceval.** (Bibliog. 242)

Belesme, Robert of. See Bellême-Montgomery; Shrewsbury.

Belisent, daughter of Igerne* and Hoel, duke of Cornwall, in Arthurian legend. She married Lot* of Orkney* and became Gawain's* mother. (Bibliog. 202)

Bellême-Montgomery, powerful early English family with roots in France.   William of Bellême (d. c. 1028) constructed a huge lordship around Bellême-Alençon-Domfront* with castles in all three locations, partly in Normandy,* in France,* and in Maine.* Because it controlled many of the important routes between Normandy and Anjou,* it had great strategic potential.   By 1070 Roger II Montgomery, who had married Bellême's granddaughter, Mabel, had attached himself to Duke William* of Normandy long before he crossed the Channel. In fact, Roger was assigned to remain behind and help William's wife, the Duchess Mathilda with the government in Normandy. He journeyed to England with William in 1067, and was rewarded for his loyal service with estates in Arundel* and Chichester* and later the earldom of Shrewsbury.* In 1069, Shrewsbury was attacked and burned by a body of Welsh and discontented English led by Edric the Wild. After the fortress was rebuilt, it was awarded to Roger in 1072. He was appointed earl in 1074 and ordered to close the Welsh March from Chester to Hereford. In 1074, under the leadership of Earl Ralph of Norfolk (East Anglia) and Earl Roger of Hereford, and with the help and connivance of Earl

Waltheof (see Huntingdon), a conspiracy arose to drive out the Conqueror and divide England on a French feudal basis. The king's men had no trouble defeating them during his absence on the continent; Ralph fled the country; Roger was imprisoned, and Waltheof was executed. Earl Roger of Shrewsbury established himself firmly by that move. With the strong leadership of nearby areas thereby removed, he soon crossed the border of Wales, constructed a castle which he named Montgomery after his Norman home, and from there established control as far west in Wales* as Pembroke* before he died at Shrewsbury in 1094. By the time of his death, the Shrewsbury group of holdings had grown considerably by annexing territory in Wales and had formed a new stronghold to which Roger gave his name: Montgomery. He and Mabel had a large family; the eldest son, Roger of Bellême, inherited the Bellême lands after his mother's murder in 1079, and his father's lands in Normandy when he died in 1094. The English lands went to the second son, Hugh, but after he was killed in Wales in 1098, these English holdings were claimed by Robert, archenemy of Henry I,* from the border land of Perche.

Sometimes called Talvas because his maternal grandfather was named William Talvas, he was an enormously powerful baron, controlling land from the estuary of the Somme River in France through southern and western Normandy, southern and western England to North Wales. A tall, strong, daring soldier who was covetous of others' lands, he was clever as a military engineer, but was basically cruel. He frequently refused ransoms of valuable prisoners so he could torture them, and he did not hesitate to impale both men and women who fell into his hands. Supposedly, he blinded his grandson for some annoyance by the child's father. He was called Robert the Devil, but that name was transferred to the father of William the Conqueror.* He married Agnes, daughter and heir of Guy, count of Ponthieu, who bore him a son he named William Talvas after his grandfather. He warred constantly on his neighbors in Perche and Nonant, Normandy, blinding and maiming captives. On the death of his father in 1094, Robert inherited all the Norman estates, his brother Hugh obtaining the English holdings. On Hugh's death in 1098, Robert claimed the English holdings, and the English earldoms of Arundel,* and Shrewsbury,* but William II* made him pay £2,000 in relief+ for them. By that inheritance, Robert became the most powerful lord owing homage to the English king. On his Welsh lands, he bred stallions he imported from Spain. He was in Normandy when King William II died, so he hastened to England to pay homage to Henry I and to receive confirmation of his holdings, but he became Henry's archfoe. On the return in 1101 of Duke Robert Curthose of Normandy (see Robert II), Bellême and his brothers Arnulf and Roger began plotting against the English king. On the death in 1101 of his father-in-law, Robert succeeded to the county of Ponthieu, and hence became a member of a higher political rank than he ever had known before. Being a *comte*, he was allowed to deal with princes as one of their own rank because his new geographical position made him uniquely valuable to England, to France, and to Normandy.

King Henry knew that Robert was an unfaithful vassal, for he had spies report Robert's actions constantly. By 1102, Henry had a huge list of complaints against Bellême, and summoned him to court to answer them. He was fortifying his English castles when Henry surprised him by accusing him of forty-five acts of treason against the king of England and the duke of Normandy. When Bellême refused to appear to answer these accusations, the king ordered him either to appear or to be outlawed. Again Bellême flatly refused and made alliances with the Welsh and Irish. At this, Henry besieged Arundel. Bellême could not go to its assistance, so he agreed for Arundel to surrender if he could leave England safely. Then after Henry captured Tickhill* and besieged Shropshire, Bellême appealed desperately for help from the Welsh, the Irish and the Norse, but no help came from any of them. Thus with the support of the English host+ against this worst Norman baron, Henry finally forced Bellême to surrender and for him and his brothers to leave England, promising never to return. However, once he was back in Normandy, his cruelties grew worse. He supported Duke Robert Curthose at the battle of Tinchebrai,* but fled to save himself. He went to the king of France for assistance, and was sent by him to England as an ambassador in 1112. Despite his official role for the king of France, King Henry seized him, tried him before the English court, and imprisoned him for the remainder of his life; his date of death was unrecorded. His son, William Talvas, and his descendants continued as counts of Poitou and lords of Alençon but their power in England was gone. (Bibliog. 47, 58, 66, 130)

Benedict, abbot of Peterborough (d. 1193), supposed author of a work detailing the reigns of Kings Henry II* and Richard I,* *Gestis Regis Henri Secundi,** in which, among many other interesting points, the author reported that Richard gave King Arthur's* sword, Caliburn,+ to Tancred* of Sicily on his way through that country to the Holy Land in 1190. Benedict also was credited with a life of Thomas à Becket* which survived only in fragments incorporated into the *Quadrilogus*. (Bibliog. 27, 68)

Benevento, battle of (February 26, 1266), crucial conflict between the house of Hohenstaufen* and the papacy. Manfred, bastard son of Emperor

Frederick II,* still held the kingdom of the Two Sicilies after thirteen years (1254-1265) of papal attempts to oust him. Pope Clement IV enlisted the aid of Charles of Anjou,* the unscrupulous brother of King Louis IX* of France, by offering him the crown of the Two Sicilies if he could overthrow Manfred of Hohenstaufen. Leading an army estimated at 6,000 armed horsemen, 600 horse-arbalesters,+ and 20,000 men-at-arms, Charles marched to meet Manfred's forces on a plain beside the Calore River near Benevento. Manfred's forces consisted of his 1,200 German mercenary horsemen armed with new plate armor just coming into use, Saracen horsemen and footsoldiers, Sicilian Muslims, mercenary horsemen from Lombardy and Tuscany, and his own barons from the Two Sicilies. Charles drew up his forces on the plain in three successive corps of cavalry, and just before the battle, he ordered two footsoldiers behind each of his men-at-arms to aid any overthrown or dismounted horsemen, and to kill any enemy horsemen who were overthrown. This battle opened with a skirmish between Charles' infantry and the Saracen footmen of Manfred, but it had little effect. Then as the German cavalry rode slowly out at a trot to meet the Provençal knights and sergeants of Charles' first line, they had the advantage by being heavier men on heavier horses wearing impenetrable armor. Charles then sent out his French and Italian knights to join the contact, but the Germans held out, and were overcoming their enemy. Then a French knight spotted that every time these metal-clad German riders lifted their arms to strike a sword blow, they exposed an undefended opening at their armpits. Charles' men soon spread the cry, "à l'estoc" ("give the point"), to stab the German forces under their arms with their shorter and sharper swords. This had the desired effect, and the Germans soon were defeated. Of his 3,600 men, Manfred lost 3,000, including his own life. (Bibliog. 166)

Benevento, Treaty of (1156). King Roger II* of Sicily was succeeded in 1154 by his son, William I, frequently called "The Bad." Brought up to distrust nobles, William continually deprived them of power, and surrounded himself with his father's old and faithful servants. Shortly after he ascended the throne in 1154, when Italy was invaded by the Emperor Frederick Barbarossa,* William feared an alliance between the emperor and the eastern emperor of Byzantium, Manuel I, Comnenus.* His fears proved well founded, for soon thereafter, Manuel invaded southern Italy with the support of the Pope, Adrian IV*, and his troops proved quite successful. Quickly losing their impetus, however, Manuel's troops began to lose badly, and at the battle of Brindisi in 1156, William's forces soundly defeated them. Following this defeat,

William became merciless to the Sicilian rebels, followers of Robert, count of Loribello, who had supported the Greek invaders; he had captives hanged, blinded or thrown into the sea. Terrified by such actions, the towns recently captured by the Greeks offered no opposition as William recaptured the territory. As a result of this and the withdrawal of the Greek forces, Pope Adrian IV had to agree to William's demands at the Treaty of Benevento: he granted to William the kingdom of Sicily, the duchy of Apulia, and the principality of Capua with Naples, Amalfi, and Salerno. In return, William took the oath of homage and agreed to pay a tribute of 600 *schifati* for Apulia and Calabria. This treaty confirmed in favor of the king of Sicily all the privileges granted by Pope Urban II to Count Roger; Adrian IV further had to recognize all the Norman conquests in the Mediterranean. This broke the link between the papacy and the Germanic Empire, and henceforth, the popes had to seek support from the Norman kingdom of Sicily. (Bibliog. 38)

Benoît de Sainte-Maure, 12th-century *trouvère*+ attached to the court of Henry II* of England. To Benoît, Henry II referred the unfinished poem of the history of the dukes of Normandy by the Anglo-Norman poet Wace.* He earlier had written a *Roman de Troie* * about 1160 which converted the characters of Dares'* and Dictys'* classical stories into heroes of romance. (Bibliog. 68, 202)

Benwick, city and kingdom of Lancelot's* father in Arthurian legend which some scholars believed to be in Brittany,* and others in Burgundy,* and most recently, to be the city of Berwick in Scotland. See also Ban. (Bibliog. 1, 96, 117, 145)

Bercilak (Bertilak) de Hautdesert, Green Knight who involved Gawain* in the beheading game in the English Arthurian alliterative romance, *Sir Gawain and the Green Knight.* * (Bibliog. 206)

Berengaria of Navarre, daughter of King Sancho the Wise of Navarre. She married King Richard I* of England in Cyprus on his way to the third crusade,+ but they had no children. (Bibliog. 27, 92, 163)

Berengier, Berangier, Berenger, character in the *chansons de geste.* * As a relative of the traitor Ganelon,* he appeared in different roles: he was Ganelon's father in *Gaydon,* *Parise la Duchesse,* * and *Renaut de Montauban* (see *Four Sons of Aymon)* but he was Ganelon's son in *Aye d'Avignon,* * his brother in *Gaufrey,* * and his nephew in *Gui de Nanteuil.* * That name, however, was given to forty other characters in various other *chansons de geste*. (Bibliog. 128)

Berg, s'Heerenberg, seigneury, later a county in northern Netherlands. Formerly a duchy on the Rhine east of Cologne, it became a countship in 1108 and a duchy in 1380. (Bibliog. 100)

Berkeley, lords of. Roger, provost of the manor of Berkeley by Earl William FitzOsbern* to whom it had been granted at the Conquest, took the name of de Berkeley from his residence. He called himself William I de Berkeley. One of his illegitimate sons, Roger de Berkeley, who called himself William II, began building the castle+ of Berkeley around 1131. His son Roger de Berkeley completed the castle, but soon thereafter suffered badly at the hands of Walter, son of Miles, earl of Hereford during the wars between King Stephen* and Empress Matilda.* He died without issue, and the castle and honour were given by Henry of Anjou,* before he became Henry II,* to Robert FitzHarding, a rich and powerful merchant of Bristol. His son, Maurice FitzRobert FitzHarding, otherwise known as de Berkeley (1120-1190), received a confirmation of the grant of Berkeley from King Henry II in 1155, and again in 1189 from Queen Eleanor,* regent for her son Richard I.* He enlarged the castle of Berkeley which thereafter became the chief seat of and gave the name to the family. His son, Robert de Berkeley, called Robert the Rebellious (1165-1220), sided with the rebellious barons against King John,* was pardoned in 1214, rebelled again and was excommunicated, though restored in the first year of the reign of Henry III* (1216) for a fine of £966. His grandson, Maurice de Berkeley (1218-1281), even though fighting for the English king Henry III in France and in Wales, joined the barons against the king in 1264, and was present at the *Dictum of Kenilworth** in 1267.

His son, Thomas de Berkeley (1245-1321), fought at the battle of Evesham* though under age at the time, and for nearly every year for the remaining fifty years of his life fought against the Welsh, the Scots or the French. In 1297, he was made vice-constable of England, fought at the bloody battle of Falkirk* in 1298, the siege of Caerlaverock* in 1300, and after being captured at the battle of Bannock Burn* in 1314, paid a large sum for his own ransom. His son and heir, Thomas, Lord Berkeley, was knighted in 1322, fought at Boroughbridge* in 1322, and was captured, but was released from imprisonment in October 1326, and in April 1327 was made joint custodian of the deposed King Edward II,* whom he "courteously received" at Berkeley castle. However, he was ordered immediately to surrender the king to his fellow custodians to be murdered. In 1330, he was tried by a jury of twelve knights of Edward III* as an accessory to the murder of the king, but was acquitted, for Sir John Mautravers* and Sir Thomas Gurnay, custodians of Berkeley castle, were in fact guilty of that horrible murder. His son, Maurice (1330-1368), was commander in Gascony* in 1355, and distinguished himself at the battle of Poitiers* in September 1356 where he was severely wounded and taken prisoner. He died at Berkeley castle in 1368, never having fully recovered from his wounds from Poitiers. (Bibliog. 47)

Berkeley castle,+ Gloucestershire fortress built first by William FitzOsbern,* earl of Hereford and close friend of William the Conqueror.* Its shell keep+ in the shape of an irregular circle was flanked by one square and three circular towers, and was approached by an external staircase. Henry II* granted the castle and keep to Robert FitzHarding whom he created as baron of Berkeley. The third baron of Berkeley was made custodian of the deposed King Edward II,* but was forced to surrender the prisoner to John Mautravers* and Thomas Gurnay who murdered the king in 1327 in the room above the external staircase, known as Edward II Tower. (Bibliog. 30, 247)

Berkhamstead, honour+ and castle in Hertfordshire where the defeated Anglo-Saxon leaders submitted to the victorious Duke William* after the battle of Hastings* in 1066. Its earthworks were 45 feet high with a diameter of 60 feet at the top and 180 feet at the base, and its ob-long bailey+ measured 450 feet by 300 feet. William bestowed it upon Robert,* count of Mortain,* his half-brother. In 1104, Robert's son, William Clito,* was dispossessed of the lands for joining the rebellion against Henry I,* and the castle was given to Henry's chancellor, Ranulph.* Thomas à Becket* lived there for about seven years between 1155 and 1162. It withstood a heavy siege by Prince Louis* of France in 1216, enduring a fortnight's constant hammering by mangonels+ and other engines of fire before surrendering. It remained under crown control until it was granted in 1227 to Richard, earl of Cornwall,* brother of Henry III,* who made it one of his principal residences, dying there in 1272. He was succeeded by his son Edmund, upon whose death in 1300, the castle again reverted to the crown until 1336 when it was granted by King Edward III* to Edward the Black Prince* when he was made duke of Cornwall, and it remained as part of the lands belonging to the duchy of Cornwall. (Bibliog. 104, 247)

Bernardo del Carpio, legendary figure of French origin who in Spanish epic became a Leónese noble defecting from a sovereign who allied himself with an invader, Charlemagne.* A lost epic about him (c. 1200) apparently set out to provide a Leónese reply to the extravagant claims of the opening lines of the *Song of Roland** that Charlemagne and his Franks had liberated much of Spain from Moorish occupation. According to the surviving ballads on Bernardo, the childless Alfonso II disinherited his nephew and heir, Bernardo, because he was illegitimate. Bernardo responded by swearing that his parents had been married in secret. To prevent Bernardo from inheriting the realm, Alfonso planned to bestow it on Charlemagne and this, naturally, led to the conflict between Bernardo and Roland at Rencesvals.* (Bibliog. 237)

Bernard of Clairvaux (Saint Bernard) (1090-1153), one of the most important religious figures in the whole Middle Ages. Born to a noble family in Burgundy,* he founded a Cistercian monastery at Clairvaux in 1115 where he remained until his death. He became active in forming church policy, in which role he came into open opposition to King Louis VI.* In 1128, the Templars+ asked him to write their code of discipline which resulted in *de laude novae militae (In Praise of the New Knighthood)*. This work opposed secular chivalry+ and praised the idealism of the religious knights who had turned their back on their private interests in order to fight infidels.   After one of his pupils became Pope Eugenius II, Bernard wrote *De consideratione (On Consideration)* which argued that the pope should rule the Christian world while kings and nobles should fight the infidels. He thus became the spiritual leader of the second crusade, preaching for the fulfillment of the duty to protect the Holy Land and the Holy Sepulchre. (Bibliog. 111)

Bernart de Brubant, son of Aimeri de Narbonne, father of Bertran de Narbonne,* and brother to Guillaume d'Orange in the *chanson de geste,** *Aimeri de Narbonne.** (Bibliog. 128)

Bernart de Naisil, one of the foulest of the traitors who populated the French *chansons de geste.** He was brother to Hardré* and uncle of Fromont* in *Garin le Loherenc.** He belonged to the Bordelais who fought continual bloody feuds with the Lorrainers. Bernart, for example, shot an arrow from a window into the back of his enemy, Begue, as he was leaving the castle after a reconciliation had taken place. (Bibliog. 52)

Béroul, Norman poet who wrote a version of the Tristan* legend about 1191.   The surviving fragment of his 4,485-line version in Norman dialect began in the middle of the scene in which King Mark* spied on the lovers, Tristan and Isolde, from the tree, and ended with

Tristan's withdrawal to Brittany. (tr. A. S. Frederick, London: Penguin, 1970) (Bibliog. 10)

Berry, John, duke of (1340-1416), third son of King John II* of France, he was created count of Poitiers in 1356, and although he was made the king's lieutenant for southern France, the real power of that office was held by John of Armagnac whose daughter Jeanne, John married in 1360. When he lost his southern possessions by the Treaty of Bretigny,* he was compensated by the fiefs+ of Auvergne* and Berry, and was made a peer of France. He was held in England as a hostage for the ransom of his father as part of that treaty, and after his return to France in 1367 he became far more interested in his luxurious and artistic tastes than in fighting against the English. He died in 1416 in Paris leaving a vast treasury of jewelry, objects of art, and especially illuminated manuscripts. (Bibliog. 68)

Berta aus grans piés ("Big-foot Bertha"), *chanson de geste** by Adenet le Roi* in the late 13th century. Berta was a Hungarian princess betrothed to Pepin of France. Being persuaded by her attendants that Pepin would be too much for her on her wedding night, Berta allowed the daughter of one of her handmaids, Aliste, to substitute for her in the wedding bed. The next morning, as Berta tried to take the place of the handmaid in the sleeping king's bed, Aliste slipped a knife in her hand, screamed, and accused Berta of trying to kill her, the true queen. Berta was carried to the woods to be killed, but was spared and took refuge in the house of a prosperous peasant, Simon. After Queen Blancheflor of Hungary came for to visit her daughter the queen, and discovered the deception, the evil handmaid was burnt at the stake; Aliste, the false Berta, was sent to a convent; and all the court sought the true Berta. Eventually Pepin found her by chance, and only after her mother recognized her did Berta admit her true identity, and allow herself to be restored as queen. (ed. Urban T. Holmes, *Berte aus grans Piés*, Chapel Hill, NC: *UNCSRRL,* 1946) (Bibliog. 88, 106)

Berte, Berta, mother of Charlemagne.* Her actual name was Berta, daughter of the count of Laon, but tradition transformed her into "Berta aus grans piés" ("Big-foot Berta"), daughter of the king of Hungary. She appeared as the wife of Pepin and mother of Charlemagne in *Berte aus grans piés,** *Girart de Vienne,** *Gui de Nanteuil,** and *Renart de Montauban* (see *Four Sons of Aymon).* This also was the name of Charlemagne's sister, the mother of Roland, and wife first of Milon and then of Ganelon in *Roland,** *Berte e Milone,** *Orlandino.* (Bibliog. 88, 106, 128)

Berte e Milone, Franco-Italian romance written probably at the end of the 12th century in rhymed decasyllables. With *Orlandino*, these two formed the *Enfances Roland*. (ed. M. A. Mussafia, *Romania*, XIV, 1885, pp. 177-192) (Bibliog. 88)

Berthold von Holle, Middle High German* writer from Brunswick* who wrote during the middle of the 13th century; his *Crane** related the deeds of three knightly companions in service of the emperor. (Bibliog. 235)

Bertrand de Bar-sur-Aube, native of Champagne,* and the author of two *chansons de geste** between 1190 and 1217: *Aimeri de Narbonne** and *Girart de Vienne.** His classification of the French series of *chansons de geste* into three cycles: of the king (Charlemagne),* *Döon de Mayence,** and *Garin de Monglane,** usually was used to denote the "family" to which a particular *chanson* belonged. (Bibliog. 106)

Berwick-upon-Tweed castle,+ fortress in a strategic commercial center in southern Scotland at the crossing place of the Tweed River which Edward I* captured in 1296, and strengthened by raising its walls and keep. Robert Bruce* captured it in 1318, and after he decided to garrison the castle instead of destroying it, he raised the walls. By 1333, King Edward III* decided to recapture it. Its fate was settled by the battle of Halidon Hill* and on July 20, 1333, after a siege of three months, it once more became a frontier fortress controlled by the English. (Bibliog. 104)

Besançon, French province and city on the River Doubs east of Dijon. The city was well protected by strong fortifications and a citadel perched on an impregnable rock 410 feet above the river. In the 12th century, it passed with the rest of Franche-Comte to the German Empire and was made a free city under Frederick I.* In 1284, Pope Martin IV granted to Philip III* of France the right to levy a tithe on church property not only in the kingdom of France but also in the kingdom of Arles of which it was a part. (Bibliog. 68)

Bethune, Conan de (c. 1150-1224), French *trouvère+* from Arras who went to the court of Champagne about 1180 where he met Marie de France,* countess of Champagne. Much of his early poetry was stimulated by her as he spent time at her court, but his work generally focussed on the third crusade+ on which he participated between 1190 and 1192. He participated a second time in the fourth crusade and the capture of Constantinople, being the first to plant the crusaders' flag on the ramparts of the beleaguered city. He held high office in the new city, and died about 1224. (Bibliog. 68)

Bevis of Hampton*, *Bueves de Haumtone, popular tale preserved in Anglo-Norman, French, Norse, Welsh, Middle English,* Italian, and Irish from an original written around 1200. This told the story of Guy of Hampton's murder by Döon de Mayence (or Sir Murdour), at the instigation of Guy's wife, the daughter of the king of Scotland. After Guy's death, Bevis was sold into slavery, and was taken to the court of Ermyn, a Saracen king who, taking a fancy to him, educated, knighted, and promoted him to chamberlain+; and after making him his champion, he gave Bevis the sword Morglay and the swift horse Arundel. He even offered to Bevis his daughter, Josayn, but the offer was rejected. Sent to Bradmond, king of Damascus, he was cast into a dungeon inhabited by two man-eating dragons. Bevis slew the dragons, but was kept in the prison for seven years before escaping to find Josayn. He found Josayn married to someone else, however, and the two of them craftily got her away from her husband, and fled to a cave. One day while Bevis was away hunting, Josayn and her servant were attacked by two lions; the servant was killed and eaten, but the lions lay down to sleep and put their heads into Josayn's lap, indicating her chastity and virginity to Bevis. After many more adventures, Bevis and Josayn settled down to rule the land of Josayn's dead husband. (ed. E. Kölbing, London: *EETS ES* #46, #48, #65, 1886-1888) (Bibliog. 211)

biadh. See Brehon law.

Bigod, family name of the earls of Norfolk. This Norman family rose to prominence in England after the Conquest. Their name was thought to be derived from the French name for Normans, *"bigoz e drashiers,"* combining an oath commonly used, *"bi got,"* and *"drashiers,"* meaning beer-drinkers. Roger le Bigod, the first earl of Norfolk, was a Norman knight who earned the favor of King William I* by revealing the treachery of William, count of Mortain.* Roger's son Roger served the English kings well as dapifer+ (steward) to William II* and Henry I;* his eldest son, William, died in the White Ship* disaster. His next son, Hugh, obtained the family estates and matured during the conflicts between King Stephen* and the Empress Matilda,* becoming a master of desertion, treachery and rebellion. On the death of Henry I, Hugh raced to the archbishop of Canterbury and swore that Henry on his deathbed had named Stephen of Blois as his successor because he had had a bad quarrel with his daughter Matilda. Stephen's prompt arrival settled the matter for the archbishop and he became king with the archbishop's blessing. Hugh was rewarded with the earldom of Norfolk. Shortly thereafter, the barons rebelled, Hugh with them, and seized and held Norwich. King Stephen recovered Norwich, but spared Hugh for his rebellion. Then to reveal his true nature, Hugh in 1140 sided with Matilda, but a short time later in 1141 was beside Stephen at the battle of Lincoln. By 1148, he was solidly in control of his estates in Norfolk, so he sided with Archbishop Theobald against King Stephen. Five years later when Henry of Anjou* landed in England, Hugh threw in with him. Henry, as Henry II,* spent the first few years of his reign breaking the enormous power and subduing the barons, including Hugh. Thus it was not surprising to find that in 1173, when young Henry* rebelled in league with the English barons, the kings of France and of Scotland, Hugh was with him. On his death in 1177, his castles were siezed by the king. He was succeeded by his son Roger, the second earl of Norfolk, who tried unsuccessfully to obtain his family estates from King Henry II. He succeeded in getting them back from Richard I,* however, along with the stewardship of the royal household. He supported Richard's authority against Prince John* during Richard's absence on the crusade, accompanied Chancellor Longchamp* to Germany to negotiate for Richard I's release from German prison, and helped carry the canopy at Richard's second coronation. He remained in good favor with King John generally, but joined with the barons in the *Magna Carta Libertatum*+ in 1215 and was one of the twenty-four barons* chosen as executors of that *Magna Carta.* For this, his lands suffered cruelly under King John's troops. On the accession of Henry III,* however, he regained favor, and claimed his hereditary right to the stewardship of the King's household until his death in 1221.

His son, Hugh, became the third earl, married Matilda, daughter of William Marshal (see Pembroke) through whom, after the death of her five brothers, the office of marshal passed to her son Roger, fourth earl of Norfolk, who became earl marshal through his mother in 1246. He was a stubborn man. In 1249, when the count of Guines passed through England, Roger ordered his arrest in retaliation to a road tax which he had had to pay when travelling through the count's territory on his way to Lyons. He subesquently played an important role in the Provisions of Oxford* (1258), being one of the twelve barons chosen to represent the barons, and subsequently being chosen one of the council to advise the king. Dissension among the barons, however, sent him to side with King Henry against Simon de Montfort* a few years later during the Barons' War.* He died in 1270, and was succeeded by his son Roger. This Roger, also a stubborn baron, along with the earl of Hereford,* refused the direct order of King Edward I* to accompany the English army to Gascony as constable and marshal, but offered to serve beside the king at Flanders. Despite all the king's threats, these two men refused to obey, and thus were deprived of their offices. In response, they appeared in London at the head of an armed force, and compelled the king to relent. With the earl of Hereford he served at Falkirk,* where he commanded the first division, but he opposed a winter campaign and went home. On his death in 1306, his earldom and his marshalcy reverted to the crown and were granted to Thomas "of Brotherton," fifth son of Edward I. William Marshal had his daughter, Matilda, marry into the family; their son inherited Chepstow* castle+ which William had fortified and made almost invincible. With this castle went the title of earl marshal* of England to which William's father, Gilbert, had won the hereditary rights by judicial combat.+ (Bibliog. 47, 58, 90)

Billung, duke of, Saxon duke who formed a German march* which took in the lands reaching from the Elbe River to the strait that divided the island of Rugen from the mainland. (Bibliog. 79)

*Bisclavret, lai** by Marie de France* that told of a werewolf and his faithless wife, but mentioned no names or historical setting. Its title derived from the Breton "*bliez lauret*," which meant "speaking wolf"; the term "werewolf" came from the Franconian "*wari-wulf*" ("*wari*" = man) to Old English "werewulf." This story was imitated by a lai from the first half of the 13th century, *Melion*, but the scene had shifted to King Arthur's court. (tr. E. Mason, *Lays of Marie de France*, London, 1966) (Bibliog. 106, 147)

bishops, English, church officials who contributed greatly to the English government, frequently serving in official capacities. For example, Odo,* bishop of Bayeux, half-brother of William the Conqueror,* fought beside his brother at Hastings,* and was made earl of Kent, serving as a valuable minister in William's government. Later, he was banished from England to Normandy where he played a large role in politics until his death on the first crusade+ in 1097. See also Bek, Anthony. Bishops were almost always nominated by the king, and the priests in the chapters they were to control were practically never allowed to choose their own candidates. In making his choices, the king rarely used the criteria of holiness of life or of learning. Ordinarily, he used the office to reward faithful clerks of his household who had earned his gratitude and favor by their administrative abilities, by their service on diplomatic missions, and by their performance at the Exchequer* and in the courts. To such men, the king gave the office as a reward, and expected such services to continue. The selection by Richard I* of his half-brother Geoffrey* as archbishop of York* also revealed the problems that arose in the entire selection process of English church officials of that high position. England's church was divided into two provinces: one ruled by the archbishop* of Canterbury as Primate of All England; the other by the archbishop of York as Primate of England. Under the archbishop of Canterbury were the dioceses of Bath and Wells, Bristol, Chichester, Coventry and Litchfield, Ely, Exeter, Gloucester, Hereford, Lincoln, London, Norwich, Oxford, Peterborough, Rochester, Salisbury, Westminster, Winchester (Winton), and Worcester. Under the archbishop of York were Carlisle, Chester, Durham, Hexam, Man. Also under Canterbury were the Welsh dioceses of St. David's, Llandaff, Bangor, and St. Asaph. Ireland had the dioceses of Armagh (for Ulster), Dublin (for Leinster), Cashel (for Munster) and Tuam (for Connaught). (Bibliog. 79, 164)

Biterolf und Dietlieb, Middle High German* epic poem written in the second half of the 13th century by a poet from the Austrian province of Styria. Biterolf was king of Toledo; Dietlieb, his son. Biterolf left home to seek adventures, and ended up in King Etzel's court. When he was grown, Dietlieb set out to find his father. Among others, he fought the Burgundians at Worms, and finally found his way to Etzel's court. There he fought with his father without recognizing him until Dietrich intervened and mediated. After this, they all went to Worms where a series of single combats took place, including an inconclusive fight between Siegfried* and Dietlieb; finally, however, their dispute was settled peacefully. Throughout this poem, these two figures were portrayed as symbols of chivalric ideals. (ed. O. Janicke, *Deutsches Heldenbuch*, Berlin: Weidmann, I, 1963) (Bibliog. 235)

Blachernes, large palace built in the 11th century by the Byzantine emperor, Manuel Comnenos* along the shore in Constantinople.* (Bibliog. 50, 201)

Black Agnes. See Dunbar,Patrick.

Black Dog of Arden. Guy de Beauchamp. See Warwick.

Blaise, Merlin's* master in the Arthurian story of *Arthour and Merlin*; he lived in Northumbria and was a chronicler of Arthur's* reign. (Bibliog. 202)

Blancandrin et Orgueilleuse d'Amour, roman d'aventure of the 13th century, thought to have been written by a poet who called himself Mestre Requis. It related how its hero, Blancandrin, like Perceval,* was reared in solitude, and learned about knights and arms through pictures. Stealing his father's arms, he rode off to seek adventures. He became infatuated with the damsel, Orgueilleuse, and snatched a kiss from her unexpectedly. She hated him for this intrusion, but he finally overcame her aversion through prowess and cleverly manipulating her jealousy. (ed. Franklin Sweetser, Geneva, 1965) (Bibliog. 106, 231)

Blancemal, fairy; one of Gawain's* innumerable women friends, the mother of Guinglain in *Le Bel Inconnu.** (Bibliog. 242)

Blancheflor, name frequently given to women in the *chansons de geste.** Four such uses were 1) as wife of Charlemagne in *Aye d'Avignon** and *Macaire**; 2) as queen of Hungary and mother of Queen Berta in *Berta au grans piés**; 3) as daughter of Aimeri de Narbonne and wife of King Louis in *Hugues Capet,** and in *Aliscans**; 4) as daughter of Thierry, king of Maurienne in *Garin le Loherenc.** (Bibliog. 128)

Blanche Nef. See White Ship.

Blanche of Castile (1188-1252), queen of France as the wife of King Louis VIII (1223-1226)*; her mother, Eleanor of England,* was the daughter of Henry II* and Eleanor of Aquitaine.* On the death of King John in 1216, Louis claimed the English throne in her right, and invaded England unsuccessfully in pursuit of that claim. To support that claim, she established herself at Calais and organized two fleets, one under Eustace, the monk,* and one under Robert of Courtenay. In 1223, when her husband became king of France, Blanche concentrated on the education of her children, but when Louis died in 1226, she served as regent for her minor son, Louis IX,* and ran the government of France until he came of age in 1234. Among her accomplishments as regent were the settlement of the Albigensian+ problem, and the negotiation of the withdrawal of Henry III* to England in 1230. She resumed her role as regent during Louis IX's absence on his crusade in 1247, ruling until her death five years later. (Bibliog. 38)

Blois, city on the Loire River in north central France, between Tours and Orléans. The counts+ of Blois of the house of the Theobalds (Thibaud) began with Theobald I, the Cheat, who became count about 940. He was succeeded about 975 by his son Eudes I (Odo). In time the counts of Blois became one of the most powerful feudal powers in

France, ruling the counties of Tours, Troyes, and Meaux in Champagne*
at the same time. His younger son Eudes II, one of the most warlike of
the barons of his time, united his considerable domains from his
ancestors with those of Stephen I, count of Troyes. He was followed by
his son, Theobald III, who was defeated by the Angevins in 1044, and
was forced to yield the town of Tours and its dependencies to the
count of Anjou. In 1089, his eldest son, Stephen Henry, who had
married Adela, daughter of King William I of England, participated in
the first crusade+ and died in captivity in the Holy Land at the hands
of the Saracens.* His son, Theobald IV, the Great, succeeded him, and
united the countship of Troyes with his domains in 1128. In 1135, on
the death of his maternal uncle Henry I of England, he was called to
Normandy by the barons of that duchy, but renounced his claim when he
learned that his younger brother, Stephen, had been proclaimed king of
England. The power of these counts soon waned, however, as the pressures of ruling a divided area proved too much for one person, and
they lost Tours to the counts of Anjou. Thus, after the death of
Thibaud IV in 1151, their dominions were divided between the county of
Champagne bestowed on the senior member of the family, and the county
of Blois-Chartres which started its own dynasty. In 1391, the last
count of Blois sold his fief to Louis, duc d'Orléans. (Bibliog. 68,
79, 100, 239)

Blondel of Nêsle, twelfth century troubadour who joined the English
court and became a close confidant and friend and fellow poet of King
Richard I,* Coeur de Lion.* A legend related by the *ménestrel de
Reims** described how Richard had been captured on his return from the
third crusade,+ and had been secreted in the isolated castle of
Trifels by the German emperor. His friend, Blondel, sought him out by
wandering throughout the German Empire as an entertainer.+ Blondel
would sing a song known only to himself and his benefactor, Richard.
On the day that he heard their song repeated from high in a castle
keep,+ he knew that his search was over, and he hurried back to
England to report his discovery. Such a story was historically in-
accurate, but was widely accepted as the historical version of the
location of Richard's cell. (Bibliog. 27)

Blütezeit (Ger. "golden age"), period in medieval German literature
between 1180 and 1230 during which the four great literary masters
were active: Hartmann von Aue,* Wolfram von Eschenbach,* Walter von
der Vogelweide,* and Gottfried von Strassburg.* See *hofisches epos.*
(Bibliog. 86)

Bodel, Jean (c. 1170-1210), French poet who wrote lyric poetry, epic poetry and drama. Around 1200, he wrote the *Chanson des Saisnes** in which he mingled historical sagas with older traditions. Here Charlemagne's* struggles with Guiteclin, the Saxon king, reflected the historical battles of Charlemagne against the Saxons and their duke, Widukind. Bodel's account of how Charlemagne led his army into the field against the Saxons after the battle of Rencesvals* and Roland's* death agreed with historic tradition. (Bibliog. 231)

Bodiam castle,+ fortress near Hastings in Sussex built by Sir Edward Dallingrigge in 1385 as protection for that part of Sussex against the French raids on that section of the English countryside. It had no keep, but enclosed living quarters within its strong outer curtain wall.+ (Bibliog. 247)

Bohemia, part of the great Moravian Empire in the 9th century, but after its destruction by the Magyars in the 10th century, it became a duchy in the Holy Roman Empire.+ As such, it held dominion over Moravia and much of Hungary, Silesia and Krakow, but it was forced in 1041 to yield its Polish conquests to the Roman emperor, Henry III.* By the 12th century, it had been elevated in rank to an electorate and hereditary kingdom within the Roman Empire. It achieved its highest point under Ottokar II (1253-1278), who conquered Styria from Hungary, but who subsequently was defeated by the Emperor Rudolf of Hapsburg in 1278. (Bibliog. 79, 100)

Bohemond I of Taranto (1050-1111), prince of Antioch, and by far the most able of the leaders of the first crusade,+ and most proficient to establish a Latin princedom in Syria. He had joined the crusaders as the leader of the Italian Normans, and he and his Norman knights played an important role in the capture of Antioch.* He had enlisted Muslim* troops in his army, and probably learned to speak Arabic to be able to converse with the natives among his troops. Additionally, he was experienced in Muslim warfare, and showed a resourcefulness and military ability unequalled by any other leader. He had worked out the measures to counteract the Turkish tactics,+ not merely as exercises in theory, but in practical field tests as well. He succeeded even in those encounters in which he and his forces were encumbered by unarmed pilgrims who possessed little discipline, organization, or military training. Undoubtedly and unquestionably, he was one of the foremost military commanders of the time. (Bibliog. 37, 195, 201)

de Bohun, family of. Norman family who had settled and prospered in

England after the Norman Conquest. One of the earliest figures was
Henry de Bohun, who became first earl of Hereford* of the Bohun line
in 1199. He was the grandson of Margaret, daughter of Miles, earl of
Gloucester and Hereford, lord constable; and he married Maud, daughter
of Geoffrey FitzPiers, earl of Essex. He died at Boroughbridge in
1220. His son, Humphrey de Bohun, lord constable, succeeded to the
title as sixth earl of Hereford in 1220. After the death of his
mother's brother, William de Mandeville, Humphrey (d. 1275), sixth
earl of Hereford, was created the seventh earl of Essex. He served as
sheriff of Kent for three years, 1229-1232, and took part in the
king's French expeditions but retired in disgust with other barons at
King Henry III's partiality to the French. In 1250, he took the cross
and went to the Holy Land. He spoke out in defense of Simon de
Montfort* in 1252, was with the barons in their redress of grievances
in 1258, and had a share in the settlement of the government under the
Provisions of Oxford* in 1258, as one of the commissioners. In the
divisions which split the barons' confederation, however, he sided
with the king against Simon de Montfort, and was taken prisoner at the
battle of Evesham* in August 1265. He stood high in the king's favor
after that battle, for he was one of the arbitrators who worked with
the remnants of Montfort's party by the *Dictum of Kenilworth.**

His great-grandson, also named Humphrey(1276-1322), the fourth
earl of Hereford and the third earl of Essex, married Elizabeth, the
daughter of Edward I,* in 1302. This Humphrey took a leading part in a
tournament in 1307 when he fought against the king's favorite, Piers
Gaveston.* In 1307, he went north to oppose Robert Bruce.* In 1310, he
was one of the twenty-one Ordainers* appointed to reform the
government and the king's household. The ordinances banishing Gaveston
which they presented were accepted by the king in 1311, but in only
three months, the king recalled the exiled Gaveston. At this, Hereford
(de Bohun) joined with Thomas, earl of Lancaster, and other barons,
and took up arms, besieged, captured, and beheaded Gaveston. The king
was powerless to do anything, so he pardoned the barons. In 1314 the
war against Scotland was renewed, and Hereford was captured at the
battle of Bannock Burn,* and was exchanged for the wife of Robert
Bruce who long had been a captive in England. As feelings arose
against the king's new favorites, the Despensers,* Hereford appeared
at London in 1322 at the head of an army denouncing these new
favorites of the king. At this Edward II took to the field and defeated them at the battle of Boroughbridge* in March 1322. Hereford
(de Bohun) was killed in this battle. His son, William de Bohun, earl
of Northampton, was sent with 15,000 men by Edward III* to harass the
lands of the count of Flanders in 1337. Even though he proved un-

successful at the job, he later was made constable of England. In 1342, he led an invading force that landed in France near Brest and forced Charles of Blois* to abandon his blockade of that town, and then he laid siege to Morlaix. There on September 30, 1342, against a French relieving army seven or eight times as large as his own, Bohun won the first English victory on the continent since the days of Richard I.* (Bibliog. 35, 58, 70, 203)

Boiardo, Matteo Maria (1441-1494), Italian author of the unfinished epic *Orlando innamorato*. Its hero was the Carolingian hero Roland,* who no longer was primarily a fighting knight, but instead had become the exemplar of an Arthurian romance hero. (Bibliog. 245)

Bokhara, country and khanate* of central Asia in Turkistan. Known by ancient people as Sogdiana, this area was too far from Rome to be brought under Roman dominion, but it was involved in various bloody revolutions in Asia. Late in the 9th century, it was conquered by Ismael, first sovereign of the Sassanean dynasty whose successors held it until Malek Shah, third shah of the Seljuk* dynasty conquered it. In 1216, it was subdued by Mahomet Shah Kharezm who held it until Jenghiz (Genghis) Khan* conquered and destroyed it in 1220. It recovered somewhat under the rule of Octai Khan, Genghis' son, who was benevolent and humane, and that prosperity was maintained until Tamerlane* swept through in 1400, destroying everything in his path. (Bibliog. 68)

Bologna, province in northern Italy. On the crusades,+ the Bolognese took an active part, and in the dispute between the Ghibellines* and the Guelphs,* they sided with the Guelphs. They had to defend themselves against Emperor Frederick II* in 1240. Control of the province passed from one powerful family to another over the years until Pope Julius II incorporated it into the Papal States in the 15th century. (Bibliog. 68)

Bolton, castle+ in North Yorkshire built by Richard, lord Scrope, under a license granted in 1379. Similar in design to Bodiam,* its towers were rectangular instead of round. (Bibliog. 30)

Bon Chevalier, title by which Galahad,* the Grail Knight, generally was known in Arthurian legend. (Bibliog. 241)

Bonaguil, French castle+ in Aquitaine* built in the 13th century on a rocky promontory between two valleys. It had strong rounded towers, a

13-foot thick wall and a pentagonal keep. (Bibliog. 30)

la bone dame. See *Die Gute Frau.*

La Bone Florence of Rome, Middle English* romance in twelve-line stanzas from the late 14th century. It detailed the story of Florence, daughter of Otes, emperor of Rome, and her trials and tribulations with the men who wooed her: Miles and Esmere, sons of the king of Hungary, and Garcy, aged emperor of Constantinople. False accusations, treachery, imprisonment, being sold to a mariner—all happened to Florence before she made her accusers confess publicly all their sins against her, and she finally married Esmere, the man she really loved. (ed. Carol Heffernan, New York, 1973) (Bibliog. 202)

Boniface VIII, pope (1294-1303). Even though he favored his own family and relatives, and enlarged their holdings, he tried to restore to the papacy a large role in political affairs of Europe, and to renew interest in the crusades. His efforts to bring peace to the continent through papal arbitration merely embroiled him deeper in the conflicts: he was at odds with Charles II* of Anjou-Naples, and Philip IV,* the Fair, of France. In 1301 when his close friend, Bernard Saisset, bishop of Pamiers, was arrested by the French on the charge of treason, Boniface protested to King Philip about the matter of clerical immunity. His last letter to the French king on this matter, his bull *Unam Sanctam,* not only threatened the French monarch but also stated the principle that the authority of the Church was higher than that of the State and that every Christian should be subject to the apostolic authority of the pope. Philip summoned his Estates General who in 1303 announced support for the French king's position on the supremacy of sovereignty; Boniface was accused of heresy, and a delegation was sent to face him with that charge. Headed by William de Nogaret, Philip's influential counsellor, this delegation was met by Boniface's arrogant threat of excommunication. Nogaret took him prisoner at Agnoni, but he was rescued by the townspeople after only three days. The strain of the event was too much for him to endure, however, and he died shortly thereafter in Rome on October 11, 1303, a broken man. (Bibliog. 199)

Boniface of Savoy (d. 1270), archbishop* of Canterbury (1241-1270), who was elevated to that high position because he was the uncle of Eleanor of Provence, queen of Henry III* of England. He was a worldly-minded man, experienced in church affairs, with a good mind and a clear understanding of ecclesiastical principles. He was, also, a man of violent temper and frequently absented himself from his diocese. Even though he sided with the king in the Barons' War,* he did little to support that monarch by his actions. (Bibliog. 184)

Book of the Ordre of Chyualry. William Caxton's* translation and printed version of a French version of Ramon Lull's *Le Libre de l'Ordre de Cauayleria.*+ Its chapters explained the important elements of a knight's+ life: the Office of a Knight, Examination of a Squire,+ Ordination of a Knight,+ Significance of a Knight's Arms,+ Customs of a Knight, and the Honor Due to a Knight. (ed. A. T. P. Byles, London: *EETS OS* 168, 1926; repr. 1971) (Bibliog. 43)

Bordeaux, one of the wealthiest cities in France located on the Garonne River in Guienne.* (Bibliog. 68)

Bordelais, Bordelese, French family in the Lotharingian cycle* of *chansons de geste** who became bitterly angry and jealous when Bègue of the Lotharingian (Lorraine) family was invested with the duchy of Gascony and was betrothed to the daughter of the king of Moriane (or Arles*). This family included Hardré,* count+ palatine+; his brother Lancelin de Verdun; and Lancelin's son, Fromont.* In the first hostile encounter between these two families, Hardre was killed, and a long war ensued. Later Bègue was accidentally killed by a Bordelese hunter, and another war began. (Bibliog. 231)

Borel, earl of Le Mans in Arthurian legend; he had fought in the Roman war on Arthur's side, and was rewarded with Le Mans as a result. (Bibliog. 232)

Boroughbridge, battle of (March 16, 1322), combat between the Lancastrian rebels and the forces of King Edward II.* Highly upset at the favoritism shown by the king toward the Despensers,* father and son, the barons, led by Thomas,* earl of Lancaster, procured their banishment in 1321. But the king recalled them from exile in the following year, and waged war against the barons on their behalf. Pursued by the king's forces, the rebels under Thomas left Pontefract* castle where Lancaster hoped to make a stand, and headed north to secure help from the Scots. They reached only Boroughbridge on the south bank of the River Ure, for, at the north end of its narrow wooden bridge, stood the king's forces of the earl of Cumberland and Westmoreland led by Sir Andrew Harcla,* a capable veteran of the Scottish wars. Harcla had arranged all his dismounted knights and men-at-arms with some supporting pikemen along the north bank of the river. Facing this opposition, the Lancastrain force divided, one band under the earl of Hereford* (Bohun) and Robert de Clifford* concentrating on the bridge, and the other under Lancaster making for a nearby ford. Neither achieved any gain. Hereford was killed on the bridge by a Welsh pikeman who had hidden beneath the bridge, Clifford was severely wounded, and the remainder of their discouraged troops made no move to cross it. Lancaster's force was discouraged from crossing by the volley of arrows from Harcla's archers, and so he withdrew and sought an armistice. Some of his men deserted during the night, but the arrival of the sheriff of York cut off that avenue of escape, so Thomas of Lancaster surrendered the next morning along with Mowbray, Clifford and his other captains. Taken to Pontefract, the rebels were faced by the king who recounted in detail Lancaster's actions: his warlike array, his banners+ flying in open revolt, the actual conflict, and his capture. Such facts could not be disputed, nor explained away. On the morning of March 22, 1322, Lancaster was led out of the castle in penitential attire, and was beheaded before a jeering crowd. The rest of the leaders also were executed. Besides Lancaster, the dead included Humphrey de Bohun,* earl of Hereford; John Clifford, banneret,+ and John Mowbray, banneret, hanged at York; Henry Teyes, banneret, hanged at London; William Touchet, banneret, hanged and drawn. Roger Mortimer of Chircke, died in the Tower of London prison; Roger Mortimer,* earl of March, was imprisoned but escaped from the Tower of London in 1323 to France and the support of Queen Isabelle.* Harcla was rewarded with the earldom of Carlisle for his staunch defense of the bridge at Boroughbridge; shortly thereafter, however, he was degraded+ for treason. (Bibliog. 47, 153)

borough custom, English custom by which general lands descended to the youngest sons to the exclusion of all other children; in direct opposition to primogeniture,+ it applied where lands were held in socage.+ (Bibliog. 68)

Borre, King Arthur's* son by his lover, Lysanor; he became a good knight and a companion of the Round Table.* (Bibliog. 117)

Bouillon, small duchy centering in a castle of Bouillon near the French frontier with Belgium. Until the 11th century, the lords of Bouillon were vassals of the dukes of Lower Lotharingia*; under Emperor Henry IV,* they became direct vassals of the emperor. In 1093, Henry created the duchy+ of Bouillon on behalf of his faithful vassal, Godfrey de Bouillon,* who, three years later, pledged it to the bishop of Liège in Belgium when he left on the first crusade.+ (Bibliog. 30)

Boulogne, fortified port on the northern seacoast of France on the shores of the English Channel at the mouth of the River Liane. Charlemagne* had a castle built there to defend the coast from Norman invaders, but with the decline of the Carolingian Empire, Boulogne fell under the suzerainty+ of the counts of Flanders. From the year 965, it belonged to the house of Ponthieu. One of Boulogne's counts, Godfrey, one of the leaders of the first crusade,+ became the first king of Jerusalem. The town grew to become one of the major ports connecting France and England. Stephen of Blois,* who became king of England in 1335, had married Mahaut, daughter and heiress of Eustace, count of Boulogne. The fief+ of Boulogne eventually passed to Robert VI, count of Auvergne. Some of its other counts were:

1046 - Eustache I
1049 - Eustache II
1090 - Godfrey
1095 - Eustache III, aux Grenons
1125 - Mahaut de Boulogne, married Stephen de Blois
1150 - Eustache IV
1153 - Guillaume II, his brother
1159 - Marie, his sister, married Matthew of Alsace
1173 - Ida of Alsace, married four times;
1216 - Mahaut de Dammartin, married Philip Heurepel, son
            of Philip II,* Augustus
1269 - Marie, widow of Emperor Otto IV.*
(Bibliog. 98, 100)

Bourbon, name of the noble family of France from which many European kings emerged. It took its name from Bourbon d'Archambault, the chief town of the rich district of Bourbonnais in the center of France, which in the 10th century was one of the three great baronies of the kingdom. The Archambault family enlarged their holdings by gradually nibbling away territory from their neighbors: Berry, Nivernais, Auvergne.* Recognizing the growing strength of this family, the Capetians made them allies. Adhemar was invested with the barony in the 9th century to become its first baron. Mathilda, heiress of the first house of Bourbon, brought this lordship to the family of Dampierre by her marriage in 1196 to Guy de Dampierre, marshal of Champagne (d. 1215). In 1272, Beatrix, heiress of Bourbonnais, the daughter of Agnes of Bourbon-Dampierre and John of Burgundy, took her domains in Bourbonnais to the French royal house by marrying Robert de Clermont, sixth son of Louis IX.* Their eldest son. Louis I, became duc de Bourbon by letters patent+ in 1327 because all the older branches of the family had died out. Some of its other sires, barons and dukes were:

 980 - Archambaud I
1034 - Archambaud II
1078 - Archambaud III
1104 - Archambaud IV
1105 - Aimon II, brother of Archambaud III
1116 - Archambaud V, brother
1171 - Mahaut I, married (1) Gautier de Vienne; (2) Guy II de
        Dampierre
1215 - Archambaud VI, de Dampierre
1242 - Archambaud VII
1249 - Mahaut II, de Dampierre, married Eudes de Bourgogne
1262 - Agnes, sister of Mahaut, married Jean de Bourgogne
1287 - Beatrice de Bourgogne, married Robert de France, comte de
        Clermont
1310 - Louis I, first duc de Bourbon
1342 - Pierre I
1356 - Louis II
1410 - Jean I
(Bibliog. 68, 100, 196)

Bourbonnais. See Bourbon.

Bouvines, battle of (July 27, 1214), decisive battle between King John* of England and King Philip II,* Augustus, of France in the war which had begun twelve years earlier. Had the French lost, John of England would have won back the Anjevin and Norman dominions, the counts of Flanders would have been free of their French overlord, and the emperor would have been free of French influence in the borderlands between their two countries. It also was the decisive battle by which Frederick II* of Hohenstaufen* triumphed in his claim to the imperial crown over Otto IV* of Brunswick. The French used to their advantage their position on this battlefield in Flanders and followed the tactics+ basically found on the tournament field+ to defeat the English. John had decided to create a diversion to the Loire which would draw Philip's forces to the south and distract his attention, while the emperor and the princes of the Netherlands massed on the Flemish frontier to make a sudden dash to Paris.

    By this involvement of the French forces in Poitou* or Anjou* to the south, the allies would find comparatively little resistance in the north, and would be able to overrun all of northern France. John

embarked on his plan in February 1214 with mercenaries because he realized that his English baronage could not be trusted to support his
plan. He overran Poitou in March and crossed the Loire into Anjou in
April, expecting King Philip to move against him. Philip did as expected, but then had his son Prince Louis march toward Chinon* to cut
John's line of retreat to Aquitaine. John's allies, however, were not
ready for their part of this operation. Otto had marched to the
Netherlands in March, but had delayed to collect German troops, to
negotiate with the princes of the Low Countries, and to celebrate the
marriage of his daughter to Henry of Brabant. Only by June was he ready to move forward again, and he arrived in Brabant in July. Philip
had watched the growing forces in Brabant with apprehension, and
finally summoned all the available levies+ of the French.

Seizing the initiative, Philip chose a good field position on
the plains east of Bouvines to meet the massing enemy. The imperial
army of English, Brabantine, German, and Flemish formed facing
Bouvines with their 6,500 heavy cavalry in the wings, and the 40,000
infantry massed at the center supported by the emperor himself with
the cavalry corps. Philip similarly formed his forces of 7,000 cavalry
and 35,000 infantry exactly opposite the enemy, with himself and the
cavalry reserve and the Oriflamme+ in the rear behind the
footsoldiers. This battle opened with a cavalry charge on the French
right highlighted by individual feats of knightly gallantry, followed
by fighting between the two massed infantries. On the left wing, the
French forces defeated and captured William Longsword,* earl of
Salisbury; on the right wing, they defeated the Flemish horsemen. In
the center, they overran the infantry of the emperor, and began to encircle with cavalry the imperial forces in which the emperor fought.
The battle ended with the stand of Reginald of Boulogne, one of
Philip's rebellious barons, who formed a ring of 700 Brabançon pikemen
like the later shiltrons+ at Bannock Burn,* and repulsed every attack
by the French cavalry. This band of hardy warriors finally was overrun
and defeated by a charging band of 3,000 men at arms. As a result of
this defeat, King John lost Normandy,+ Anjou,+ and Touraine to the
French, and returned home to such difficulties with his barons in
England that he was forced a year later to issue the *Magna Carta
Libertatum*.+ This loss also cost Otto, King John's nephew, the imperial throne, and elevated on it Philip's ally, Frederick II, who had
come from Sicily to inherit his father's position. By this action, the
imperial throne once again became dependent upon Italian politics.
(Bibliog. 166)

Bowes castle,+ originally a possession of the honour+ of Richmond,* this Yorkshire castle came into the hands of Henry II* when Earl Conan died in 1171 without a male heir. Henry immediately strengthened it to become an important defense position against a Scottish invasion by building a keep 82 feet by 60 feet and 50 feet high. Two years later, William of Scotland* invaded and besieged the castle but his siege was lifted by the approach of the army of Archbishop Geoffrey* of York.* The fortress remained in the hands of the crown until Henry III* granted it to Peter, duke of Brittany, in 1233. (Bibliog. 104, 247)

Brabant, Brubant, ancient province in Belgium bordered by Limbourg and Liège on the east, Antwerp on the north, Namur and Hainault on the south, and Flanders on the west. When, in 1190, the duchy of Lower Lorraine split into a number of feudal states, the counts of Hainault, Namur, Luxemburg and Limburg asserted their independence, and the rest of the duchy united with the margraviate+ of Antwerp and were conferred in 1106 upon Godfrey the Bearded, count+ of Louvain* and Brussels; he was the first to assume the title of count of Brabant, which his great-grandson Henry I, the Warrior (1190-1235), exchanged for the title of duke.+ This duchy passed in regular succession to Henry II, the Magnanimous (1235-1248), and Henry III, the Debonnaire (d. 1261), but his heir was supplanted by a younger brother, John I, the Victorious, who added the district of Limbourg to his possessions by the battle of Woeringen in 1288, in which he killed his competitor, Henry of Luxembourg, with his own hand. (Bibliog. 68, 79)

Bracton, Henry of (d. 1268), English legal writer who held several ecclesiastical offices before becoming chancellor+ of the cathedral church at Exeter. Later, Henry II* appointed him as chief justiciar+ in 1265. He had been in the king's service, presumably as a law clerk to William Raleigh by 1240, and justice in eyre+ from 1244. He was the author of the most important law book in medieval England, *De Legibus et consuetudinibus Angliae libre quinque.* This work concerned jurisprudence and the principles of law, not procedure and the techniques of the court. It was the first comprehensive exposition of English law; its main structure was systemized English law built on about 2,000 cases taken from the plea rolls. (ed. George Woodbine, New Haven, CT, 1915-1940; repr. and tr. Samuel Thorne, Cambridge, MA: Harvard, 1968) (Bibliog. 98, 181)

Braganza, Portuguese castle+ rebuilt in the 14th century on the site of an earlier fortification which Sancho I had erected in 1180. (Bibliog. 30)

Bramber castle,+ fortress on the banks of the Adur River in Sussex which served as the home of the de Braose* family from the time of William I* until it was seized by King John* when he outlawed William de Braose in 1208. Henry III* returned it to them early in his reign. It fell into the hands of the dukes of Norfolk in the 14th century. (Bibliog.104)

Bramimonde, wife of the pagan King Marsile*; queen of all Spain, she gave Ganelon two pins for his wife. She surrendered Saragossa to Charlemagne* after the battle of Rencesvals* in the *Song of Roland.** (Bibliog. 210)

Brandenburg, name of a margraviate+ in Germany which later became the province of Prussia. The Slavic Wends who lived in that area were un-conquerable by Charlemagne,* but finally were defeated in 1134 by Albert the Bear who established order, planted German colonists, and laid the basis for expansion through cooperation with the Teutonic knights.+ (Bibliog. 100)

Brangane,Brangain,Bregnvein, Isolde's* maidservant who accompanied her from Ireland to Cornwall. She did not guard the love potion given to her by Isolde's mother in Ireland closely enough to prevent its accidental consumption by Tristan and Isolde, leading to the love com-plications in *Tristan* and in Malory's *Morte D'Arthur.** She married Kaherdin. (Bibliog. 97, 145)

de Braose baronies in Wales, Philip de Braose, lord of Bramber in Sussex, who conquered Radnor and Builth, died between 1134 and 1155. His son, William de Braose, by marriage to Bertha, co-heiress to the barony of Miles of Gloucester, added the lordships of Brecon and Abergavenny* to his family's estates in Wales; he died around 1192. His son, William de Braose, lord of Radnor, Brecknock, and Limerick, spent the early part of his life fighting the Welsh in Radnorshire. He was held in high favor by King John,* and was even granted the custody of Prince Arthur,* but in 1207, he and the king quarreled, probably over money, and in 1208 when John accused the whole family of dis-loyalty, William fled to Ireland. After a number of futile efforts to reconcile himself with the king, William was outlawed in 1210 and died in 1211. His wife and son were said to have been starved to death on King John's orders. His grandson, William de Braose, was executed by Llywelyn the Great* of Gwynedd 1230, leaving four daughters, all minors. After that execution, the English crown took control of the estates and granted the lordship of Builth in 1254 to the Lord

Edward*; the remainder of the estate went to the husbands of the other three daughters: 1) Maud (d. 1301), married to Roger de Mortimer* of Wigmore (d. 1282) who thereby gained the lordship of Radnor; 2) Isabel (Haverfordwest), married to David, son of Llywelyn the Great who died in 1246; 3) Eleanor married to Humphrey de Bohun* the Younger (d. 1265) to whom she took the lordship of Brecon; and 4) Eve, married to William de Cantilupe (Cantelou) (d. 1254) to whom she took the lordship of Abergavenny. (Bibliog. 68, 70)

Breauté, Faulkes de (d. 1226), Norman of illegitimate birth who came to England as a foreign mercenary captain, and became a famous military adventurer. After King John* appointed him sheriff of Glamorgan about 1211, he became the most tenacious ruthless, courageous and active of all John's sheriffs. Those and other attributes made him popular with John: he was an able man, but also godless and unscrupulous. John considered him to be chief of his counsellors and made him sheriff of Oxfordshire. After the changes in sheriffs demanded in the *Magna Carta Libertatum+* had been forced upon him, John acted cautiously; the changes he made were to his own advantage, although they gave the appearance of complying with the baron's demands. He dismissed sheriffs whom he thought might be rebellious, but kept those of proven loyalty such as William Brewer,* Nicolaa de la Haye,* and Faulkes de Breauté. When war broke out in the fall of 1215 between the barons and King John, Faulkes was appointed one of the leaders of the army which John left to watch London and to cut off the barons' supplies while he marched north. Wasting the eastern counties, the royal forces under Faulkes destroyed the castles and estates of the barons, and set fire to the suburbs of London.

Delighted with Faulkes' success in these tasks, just before he died, King John gave him as his wife the widow of Baldwin, earl of Aumale,* son of William de Reviers, earl of Devon,* and the custody of the castles+ of Windsor,* Oxford, Northampton, Bedford and Cambridge. He also obtained a manor in Surrey which stood on 100 acres of arable and meadow land stretching to the Thames; he called it "Faulkes Hall" which became "Vauxhall." Assembling a force of men as brutal as himself, including the earl of Chester,* Ralph de Blundevill, he assaulted and captured Worcester for the king, and after its stout resistance, plundered the abbey and tortured its citizens to give up their wealth. Yet in the *Magna Carta*, his name appeared twice: first, in the list of alien disturbers of the peace whom the king swore to banish from the kingdom, and at the same time, as one of the twenty-four guardians of the *Magna Carta Libertatum* provisions. In 1217, he attacked St. Albans, and sacked the town. Then he sacked the abbey, and demanded 100 marks from the abbot, ordering it to be delivered at once or he would sack and burn the town and the monastery. With the money he marched off, taking captives with him. That night, he dreamed that a huge stone fell on him from the abbey and mashed him to a powder. After his wife suggested that he should return the money and beg forgiveness from the abbot and the monks, he and his men returned to the abbey and bared their backs to be lashed by each monk. Then he strode to the abbot and remarked, "My wife has made me do this for a dream, but if you want me to restore what I took from you, I will not listen to you," and he stalked out. At the siege of Lincoln in spring of that year, 1217, he and his men secretly entered the castle, and from the bulwarks of the castle vigorously fought the forces of Prince Louis* of France by hurling projectiles on them. Then he dashed out into the street, in the thick of the fighting, was captured and rescued. Then, once the king's forces entered the city to trap the Frenchmen between them and Faulkes' men, the invaders were slaughtered.

With the fame from this adventure, he grew even more powerful. He became sheriff of six counties, had many large estates, and was named an executor of the late king John's will. But he aroused the enmity of Hubert de Burgh,* the justiciar,+ with his continuous brutalities. Finally in June 1224, he was accused of 45 acts of wrongful disseisin,+ and was adjudged to lie at the king's mercy+ and to pay a huge fine. He fled to Bedford* castle, seized one of the justices who laid that sentence upon him, and refused to release him. For that, he was excommunicated. He fled to Wales, leaving his brother, William, in charge of defending the castle at Bedford against the king's siege. To King Henry III's* demand for the release of the judge, Faulkes replied with the essence of feudal anarchy when he announced that for this above all, he and the garrison were not bound to the king by homage and fealty. The king, realizing that his country could not have peace so long as a man like Faulkes was in a position to defy the law, swore by the soul of his father (King John) that he would hang the garrison. Finally surrendering on August 14, William and 80 of the defenders were hanged by the king; Faulkes was captured in a church. He threw himself at the feet of the king and begged for mercy, reminding him of the services he had done for the king over the years. Declaring all his possessions forfeit, the king placed him in the custody of the bishop of London. When they heard his case, the nobles at Westminster decided that Faulkes should not suffer loss of life or limb, but should be banished from England forever, and he was given letters of conduct to quit the realm as quickly as possible. The earl of Warenne* was ordered to take him to the seacoast, and having put him aboard a ship, to commit him to the winds and the sails. Because of his damage to the French over the years, the king of France was tempted to hang him, but did not do so because Faulkes wore the crusader's cross. He then went to Rome to enlist the pope's aid in recovering his lands and his wife with her dower, but he died suddenly in France in 1226 on his way back from Rome, possibly poisoned, some say by his enemy, Hubert de Burgh. (Bibliog. 47, 58, 94)

Bredbeddle, green knight who, in *Grene Knight*, appeared at Arthur's court to issue his challenge. He became one of Arthur's companions and was able to conjure up the fiend, Burlow-Beanie,* in *King Arthur and King Cornwall.** (Bibliog. 1)

Brehon law, from the Gaelic *breitheam*, "judge," this was the law of Ireland before the Conquest. This series of laws governed the society under the old manorial system when the land was "folk-land" rather than "boc (book)-land"+ and comprised commons of tillage as well as pasture. Its social unit comprised several families and households numerous enough to occupy a *crich* (quasi-manor) within which existed a court and a complete system of primary social organizations. The *crich* formed a portion of the *tuath* (quasi-barony), one or more of which formed the *mor tuath*, or petty kingdom equivalent to a county or several counties governed by a *ri* or *regulus* who bore allegiance through superior *reguli* to the monarch. The upper classes were *aires*. To be eligible to become an *aire*, a freeman had to have a certain amount of wealth in cattle, a certain assortment of agricultural and household goods, and a house of certain dimensions ranging from 17 to 27 feet in length and containing a certain number of compartments. Built of timber and wattle, these houses were surrounded by open spaces of prescribed extents for each class. The lower limit was the distance to which the owner seated in his doorway could throw an object of given weight; multiples of that distance determined the space for higher classes. Serfs and slaves were designated as *ernaans*, but they could become *fuidhirs* or tenants of separate lands of nobles who called themselves *gaidel* or *gael*, and claimed a different descent. Besides these tenants were dependents called *ceiles* who stood just below the *flaths* or lords to whom they owed homage. The *ceiles* were attached to their lords by commendations+ of cattle which they used in their own tribal lands. Food-rents, or *biadh*, corresponding to the English *farm*,+ were supplied both at the residences of chiefs and at the tables of tenants. As coined money was practically unknown, the unit of value was the cow. (Bibliog. 68)

Bremûle (Brenville), battle of (August 20, 1119). King Henry I* of England spent much of his seventeen-year reign fighting Louis VI* in Normandy until the death in 1128 of William Clito,* his nephew. By 1119, however, Henry had the upper hand, and this was confirmed by the battle at Bremûle in the Vexin.* In 1106, Henry had captured his older brother, Robert Curthose, and thus had removed him from any further consideration, depriving him of his duchy of Normandy, and taking possession of the castle at Gisors.* Integral to the Norman part of the Vexin, this castle commanded the road from Rouen to Paris, and Henry and Louis had agreed previously that such a strategic location should be kept neutral. Louis protested Henry's violation of this agreement, and in 1109, offered to fight him in single combat to prove his right to it. Henry refused, and the two began a war that lasted twenty years. By April 1119, Louis felt he was ready for a showdown because he had captured Les Andelys (see Chateau Gailiard), and offered battle to Henry on the nearby plain at Bremûle. The resultant battle was disastrous for Louis; his troops panicked at the size and discipline of Henry's forces, and fled the field, carrying Louis in their flight, leaving both his war horse and his banner behind in their panic. (Bibliog. 37, 166)

Brennus, name given in history to two kings or chiefs of the Celtic Gauls, and probably not a name, but a title from the Cymric word *brehin* for king. The first Brennus crossed into Italy at the head of a large tribe of Gauls and ravaged Etruria in 391 B.C.; the second invaded Thrace in 280 B.C. (Bibliog. 68)

Brenville. See Bremûle.

Bretagne, Brittany* in the *chansons de geste.*

Bretigny, Treaty of, (May 8, 1360), peace pact signed between the French and the English that marked the end of twenty years active war, and basically signalled also the end of the first stage of the Hundred Years War.* After the devastating defeat of the French at both Crécy* and Poitiers,* both kingdoms were exhausted. Meeting in the small village of Bretigny, a league's distance from Chartres on May 1, 1369, the Black Prince* and the dauphin* hammered out an agreement within a week. Covering a maze of legal and territorial details in 39 articles and 5 letters of confirmation, this treaty reduced King John II's* ransom to three million gold ecus (see coinage+) (roughly £500,000) while the English reduced their territorial demands to those of the Treaty of London*: Guienne* was to be in full sovereignty, as were the Limousin, Poitou, the Angoumois, the Saintonge, Ponthieu and many other districts. Basically, in return for this concession of Guienne and Calais to the king of England free of homage, plus the transfer of other territories, towns, ports and castles between the Loire and the Pyrenees, and in the region of Calais representing about one third of France, King Edward III* renounced the crown of France and all territorial claims not granted in the treaty.

To ensure fulfillment, an earlier provision was renewed. Forty hostages representing the greatest men in the French realm were insisted upon. Heading the list were the four royal French princes: the king's two sons Louis and Jean (future dukes of Anjou and of Berry), his brother, the duke of Orléans, and the dauphin's brother-in-law, Louis II, duke of Bourbon. King John II was returned as far as Calais where he would remain until the first payment of 600,000 ecus+ on his ransom, and a preliminary transfer of territories was made. He then would be freed along with ten of his fellow prisoners, and replaced by forty other hostages: four from Paris and two from each of eighteen other towns. The remainder of the ransom was to be paid in six installments of 400,000 ecus at six-month intervals, and as the sovereignty of towns and castles was transferred, one-fifth of the remaining hostages were to be released. By October 1360, when the first 400,000 gold ecus, two-thirds of the first installment of the ransom, had been delivered, Edward allowed John II to go home, though he had to leave his three sons as hostages. One of John's sons, the duke of Anjou, broke his parole to rejoin his beautiful young wife, and refused to return. The chivalrous John II thereupon returned voluntarily to his London prison in 1364. His chivalrous act was so royally regarded that he was wined and dined extensively, but these banquets proved to be too much for him, and he died on April 8, 1364, at age 44. (Bibliog. 203, 223)

Breton *lais (lays)*, short narrative poems in French which in their subject matter frequently displayed a marked resemblance to episodes in Arthurian romances+; others dealt with Arthurian characters or were localized at Arthur's* court but did not imitate episodes from the romances. The majority of these bore no relation to longer works about Arthur and his knights of the Round Table.* They were written between the mid-12th century and the mid-14th centuries. The most famous were the works of Marie de France,* and the *Lai du Cor** by Robert Biket. (ed. T. Rumble, *Breton Lays in Middle English*, Detroit, 1965) (Bibliog. 10, 147)

Brewer, William (d. 1227), English sheriff who served the crown faithfully, competently, and ruthlessly for 50 years under kings Henry II,* Richard,* John,* and Henry III* until he died in 1227. Richard used him as an itinerant justice,+ a justice in eyre,+ and as an ambassador to the French court where he was instrumental in drawing up the terms for the release of Richard from captivity. On Richard's second absence abroad, Brewer was one of four justices appointed to guard the realm. John used him as sheriff+ in 11 different shires. John's trust and respect for him was made evident by his many grants to Brewer of lands, manors, boroughs, fisheries, fairs, and markets, and gifts of timber and permission to fortify three castles+ if he so desired. When Brewer's eldest son was captured while defending John's lands in Normandy,* John loaned him 2,000 marks+ to pay the ransom,+ and then 700 more when the original amount was not enough, on the stipulation that Brewer should sit at the Exchequer* for a fortnight each year to see that the Royal Seal was not abused. Additionally, King John often sent him on distasteful errands. He was sent with a strong military force to control Hampshire, Wiltshire, and Sussex when William Marshall, the earl of Pembroke* who had extensive holdings in those shires,+ had fallen from the king's grace. He also acted as intermediary between the king and the pope, showing that he was an experienced diplomat who had the king's confidence. Naturally, however, Brewer was hated widely, for as sheriff who was responsible for the revenues from six or more shires, he was a petty tyrant who employed efficient and ruthless undersheriffs or bailiffs.+ (Bibliog. 94)

Brian of the Isles, lord of the castle+ of Pendragon, he was an enemy of King Arthur*; he captured and imprisoned many knights and ladies until they all were rescued by Lancelot's* forcing Brian to yield or be killed. (Bibliog. 117)

Bridgnorth castle,+ pre-Conquest castle in Shropshire guarding the Severn River between Shrewsbury* and Worcester.* Rebuilt by Robert de Bellême (see Belleme-Montgomery) between 1098 and 1101, it was taken into the king's hands when Robert rebelled in 1102, and was kept in royal hands until the reign of King Stephen* when it fell into the hands of Roger de Mortimer* who surrendered it to Henry II* after a brief siege. It was maintained under the reigns of Richard,* John,* and Henry III,* but was let decay thereafter. (Bibliog. 104)

Brisane, Brisen, enchantress who came to King Pellam* and offered to arrange matters so that his daughter Elaine* would lie with Lancelot* and become pregnant with Galahad.* Later she accompanied Elaine to Arthur's* court to celebrate the king's victory over Claudas of

France. (Bibliog. 117)

Bristol castle,+ massive bulwark in Somerset during the reign of King Stephen* which was the stronghold of Robert, earl of Gloucester,* brother and champion of Empress Matilda.* When Henry II* ascended the throne, the castle was held by Earl Robert's son, William. Though Henry coveted the castle, he waited until Robert sided with his son, young Henry in the rebellion of 1173-1174 before he forced William to yield it. After that, it became one of the chief royal fortresses of England, ranking with those of Nottingham,* Newcastle, and Winchester* as a major fortress and political prison, and as a center of local administration. It was one of the castles handed over to the Lord Edward,* the heir apparent,* on his marriage to Eleanor of Castile in 1254. Later, after the Despensers'* fall, Queen Isabelle* had her son Edward III grant her the castle until her fall in 1330, when it was given to Queen Philippa, her son's wife. (Bibliog. 104)

Brittany, province in northwestern France lying mostly between the English Channel and the Gulf of Biscay. Originally it was known as Armorica,* but the immigration of Celtic Britons who had been expelled from Britain by the Anglo-Saxons in the 6th century caused the name to be changed to Britannia Minor, "The Lesser Britain." In the 11th century, the counts of Rennes became dukes of Brittany, and then became vassals of the dukes of Normandy.* Internal dissension between the houses of Nantes and Rennes forced the dukes of Brittany to seek foreign assistance. Duke Conan IV turned to Henry II* of England, but in order to obtain the aid he needed, he had to pay homage+ to Henry and to marry his daughter to Henry's third son, Geoffrey,* who was proclaimed heir to the duchy. On Conan's death in 1171, Geoffrey became duke of Brittany and the county was included in the vast territories of the Angevin Empire. When Geoffrey died in 1196, his son Arthur,* named for the legendary English monarch, became duke, and was nominated as heir to the English throne by a part of the nobility who opposed the claim of the deceased King Richard's brother, John.* The resultant dissension caused the French king, Philip II,* Augustus, to intervene. Then the murder of Arthur by the English king, John, in 1203 brought a new dynasty to power when, in 1213, the title of duke passed to the Capetian* prince, Peter of Dreux, through his marriage to Arthur's sister, Alix. His dynasty ruled uninterrupted until 1341, when Duke John III died childless, and the dispute over the title was carried on between the houses of Montfort and Penthièvre into the Hundred Year's War.* The Montfort side was supported by Edward III* of England; the Penthieve side by Philip VI* of France. This dispute lasted until 1365 when the two sides agreed that the duchy should be ruled by the house of Montfort continued to rule it until 1491. Brittany supplied France with knights and military leaders, the most famous of whom being Bertrand du Guesclin.* (Bibliog. 98, 100)

Britton, title of the earliest summary of the law of England written in the French tongue; it purports to have been written by command of King Edward I.* It had been attributed to John le Breton (fl. 1291), bishop of Hereford, but references to statutes enacted after his death in 1275 made his authorship questionable. It may well have been a royal abridgement of the work of Henry of Bracton,* but it makes the law appear in the king's name and in the form of royal precepts. (ed. S. E. Baldwin; tr. F. M. Nichols, *Britton: an English Translation*, Washington, 1901) (Bibliog. 68, 99)

Broceliande, massive forest in England containing a marvellous fountain around which both King Arthur* and Yvain* had some unique adventures; it was the location of Niniane's* beguiling Merlin* in the *Vulgate Merlin.* Here Merlin disguised of an ugly herdsman met Calogrenant.* Mentioned by Wace* in the *Roman de Rou,* it also was the location in *Claris et Laris*ined in which the two protagonists destroyed the enchantments of the chateau Perilleux, found themselves captives in Morgan la Fée's* sensual fairyland, and from which they escaped with the help of Madoine, Morgan's companion. Here also Joseph of Aremathia and Josephes met Argon, lord of the Castle of the Rock. (Bibliog. 10, 241)

Bron, guardian of the Holy Grail,* and father of Nascien. (Bibliog. 1)

Brough castle, fortress standing at a strategic point in Westmoreland* where roads crossed the Pennine Mountains. Adapting ruins from a ruined Roman fort, the Normans rebuilt it in the reign of William II.* William the Lion* of Scotland destroyed it in 1174, but English King Henry II* soon had it rebuilt. It passed into the hands of the Clifford family in 1204 who did little to maintain it. Only a half century later, it again had fallen into such disrepair that it required drastic restorations under the guidance of Edward I* and Edward II.* After the battle of Bannock Burn,* the town of Brough was burned, but the castle escaped damage. (Bibliog. 247)

Brubant. See Brabant.

Bruce, Scottish family founded between Cherbourg and Vallonges by a

Norman knight,+ Robert of Bruis, who followed William the Conqueror*
to England in 1066, and was granted estates in the northern portions
of the newly conquered kingdom, chiefly Yorkshire. His son, also named
Robert, settled in Scotland during the reign of King David I*
(1124-1153) and was granted huge estates in southwestern Scotland,
specifically the lordship of Annandale. His descendants increased
their power and influence to become one of the most important families
in Scotland by the end of the 13th century. Robert de Bruce,* was the
son and heir of Robert de Brus, lord of Annandale, by Isabel, second
daughter of David of Scotland,* earl of Huntingdon.* In 1267, he swore
fealty to King Henry III* and Prince Edward, the Lord Prince.* Being a
competitor for the crown of Scotland, claiming it as nearest in degree, he agreed to accept the decision about the Scottish throne made
by King Edward as his overlord, who however decided against him. He
married Isabel, daughter of Gilbert de Clare,* earl of Gloucester* and
Hertford. His grandson, Robert de Bruce, earl of Carrick,* became king
of Scotland in 1306. One of his descendants, Robert, defeated the
English under Edward II* at Bannock Burn* in 1314, and became a
national hero. See Barbour, John. (Bibliog. 47, 98)

Bruce, Edward (d. 1318), king of Ireland. Younger brother of Robert
Bruce, king of Scotland, he was a valiant and experienced soldier. He
led the right hand column of the Scottish army at the battle of
Bannock Burn* which was the result of his siege of Stirling castle.*
Bruce defeated the English 19 times in Ireland against the overwhelming odds of having five Engish oppose one of his men. He died at the
battle of Dundalk in 1318. (Bibliog. 47)

Brun. Names beginning with Brun were always borne by Saracens in the
chansons de geste*: Brun was a Saracen giant in *Aliscans**; Brun
d'Orcanie was a Saracen king in *Galien;* Brunamant was a Saracen king
of Esclaudie (a Saracen country in *Roland,** *Ogier,** *Girard de
Roussillon**), who was killed by Huon of Tabarie in *Bâtard de
Bouillon.** One exception occurred in Brunehaut, daughter of Judas
Maccabeus, wife of Caesarie and mother of Julius Caesar in *Auberon.**
(Bibliog. 128)

Brunamon de Misor, pagan king of Maiolgre (Majorca) who figured large
in the *chansons de geste** of *Enfances Ogier** and *Ogier le Danemarch*
where he was the Saracen champion who was fought, defeated, and killed
by Ogier* in Rome, thus freeing the city from Saracen control and re-
storing it to Christian hands. (Bibliog. 211)

Brunetto Latini (c. 1220-1295), Italian author and statesman. Born in Florence, Italy, about 1220, he became a notary by profession, and served his city well in many important matters. As a Guelph,* he was sent as envoy to Alfonso the Wise of Castile to seek his aid against Manfred and the Ghibellines.* As the outcome of the battle of Montaperti made it impossible for him to return to Florence, he went to France until the victory of the Guelphs in the battle of Benevento* in 1266 made it possible for him to return to Italy. For the remaining thirty years of his life, he was considered as an elder statesman in Florence. His main work, *Li Livres dou Tresor,* was a large encyclopedia written in French prose. The first of its three parts gave a history of the world and of Italy in particular, and of astronomy, geography, and natural history; the second part treated the virtues and vices; the third, rhetoric and politics. (ed. Charles Langlois, *La Connaissance de le Nature et du Monde,* Paris, 1927) (Bibliog. 126, 245)

Brunhild, one of the Valkyries whom King Gunther of Worms won as his wife with the supernatural help of Siegfried* in the German epic, *The Nibelungenlied.* * Her dispute with Kriemhild* in that epic caused the destruction and ultimate downfall of the German kingdom. (Bibliog. 161)

Brunswick, duchy in northern Saxony* created in 1180 when Frederick I,* Barbarossa accused and convicted Henry the Lion* of a felony, and forced him to cede Saxony, but allowed him to keep his family estates of Brunswick and Luneburg in northern Saxony as well as the ducal title. This title was changed to Brunswick in 1235 when Frederick II* bestowed it on Henry's grandson, Otto. Its dukes of importance included:

1139 - Henry the Lion, husband of Matilda of England
1195 - Henry the Long, and William, sons
1213 - Otto, son of William
1252 - Albert
1278 - Albert II
1318 - Otto, Magnus, and Ernest
1368 - Magnus II
(Bibliog. 100)

Brut, Middle English* poem composed by Layamon,* a parish priest at Arley Regis, Worcestershire, writing in the latter years of the 12th century. Supposedly the *Chronicle of Brutus,* the legendary founder of

Britain, this work was adapted by Layamon from the Anglo-Norman poem of the same name by Wace,* expanding Wace's original 14,800 lines to 32,200. To do so, he elaborated the details of events which Wace had recorded only briefly. For example, Wace reported that after King Arthur* had defeated the Roman emperor, Lucius, he had the body watched with great honor and sent home on a bier. Layamon enlarged that point to describe how Arthur ordered a tent pitched on a broad field, had the body of Luces (Lucius) borne there and covered with gold-colored palls, and guarded with honor for three days while a long gold-covered chest was made. Then the chest containing Luces' body was sent to Rome escorted by three kings. Layamon also added descriptions of behavior, which expressed feelings in speech, and which supplied dramatic incidents. A good example of such a series of speeches was the episode of the poisoning of Uther Pendragon* by Saxon spies. One of the best examples of his additions to Wace occurred in Arthur's dream which foretold Mordred's* treachery. (ed. and tr. Eugene Mason, *Arthurian Chronicles Represented by Wace and Layamon*, New York: E. P. Dutton, 1972) (Bibliog. 129)

Brut d'Angleterre (*Li roman de Brut*), free paraphrase of Geoffrey of Monmouth's *Historia Regum Britanniae* in 1155 by a Norman poet named Wace.* By incorporating into his work the French chivalric+ ideals then permeating the medieval court, Wace transformed it into a metrical romance.+ For example, he introduced a romance conception of Gawain*: he had the young knight praise peace even in a Council of War, and say that the pleasures of love were good, and that a young knight would perform feats of chivalry for the sake of his *amie*, his beloved. He depicted an Arthur* as the center of a court of knight-errantry,+ instead of as a world-conquering hero. He also was the first to mention Arthur's creation of the Round Table.* (ed. and tr. E. Mason, *Arthurian Chronicles represented by Wace and Layamon*, New York: E. P. Dutton, 1972) (Bibliog. 129)

Brutus, supposed first king of Britain which, with its people, was named after him. Geoffrey of Monmouth opened his *Historia Regum Britanniae** with an account of how Brutus was expelled by the Romans after he accidentally killed his father, Silvius. He travelled to Greece, again was expelled, went to France where he founded the city of Tours, and finally went to Britain which he named after himself. This account also was found in Malory's *Morte D'Arthur,** Layamon's *Brut,** *Arthour and Merlin,** and *Sir Gawain and the Green Knight.** (Bibliog. 139)

Buchan, earls of, united with, but later separated from, Mar. Among the early earls was Alexander Comyn, earl of Buchan(c. 1235-1290), one of the most powerful nobles of his time. He inherited large estates in Galloway, Fife and Lothians, and the office of constable in right of his wife. He was one of the nobles who in 1283 engaged to maintain the succession of the crown of Margaret of Scotland, and was one of the Six Guardians appointed after the death of Alexander III in 1285. His son, John Comyn (c. 1260-1308), was one of the nominees of Baliol in 1291. He fought against Robert Bruce* in December 1307 and again in May 1308 where he was totally defeated, after which he retired to England when his estates and honours+ in Scotland were forfeited. He married Isabel, daughter of Duncan, earl of Fife, and she took the oppositie side from her husband, placing, as her brother's representative, the crown on the head of Robert Bruce at Scone in 1306. For that act, the English imprisoned her in an iron cage at Berwich in 1306, and released her only in April 1313 in exchange for Humphrey de Bohun.* (Bibliog. 47)

Buckingham, English county that borders the Thames River. Once important for its castle+ as a defense against the Danes, it gave its name to titles of the highest honor for many brave and worthy knights, as well as those of royal blood. Earls of Buckingham included Walter Giffard, earl of Buckingham (1102); Richard Strongbow,* earl of Pembroke* (1164); Thomas of Woodstock, duke of Gloucester, lord constable+, created earl of Buckingham, in 1378 and then murdered in 1397; and Humphrey Plantagenet, created earl of Buckingham in 1397, but died a minor without issue in 1400. (Bibliog. 47, 101)

Bueves, Charlemagne's son in *Amis et Amiles.** (Bibliog. 128)

*Bueves d'Aigremont, chanson de geste** attached to *Renaut de Montauban* (see *Four Sons of Aymon)* with which it was published. Its hero was Bueve, lord of Aigremont, the son of Döon de Mayence,* and the father of Maugis* and of Vivien de Mombranc. (Bibliog. 128)

Bueves de Commarchis, son of Aimeri de Narbonne, and father of Girart and Gui in the *chansons de geste.** He was the hero of a work bearing his name written by Adenet le Roi.* (ed. A. Henry, *Les Oeuvres d'Adenet le roi,* II, Bruges, 1953) (Bibliog. 128)

Builth castle, castle+ in South Wales which came into the hands of King John* after the fall of William de Braose* in 1208. Early in the reign of Henry III,* it was recovered by William de Braose's son,

Reginald, who fortified it and held it against the crown's siege in 1223, until his death in 1230. Then it was handed to the Lord Edward,* heir apparent,* in 1254, but in 1260 was captured and destroyed by Llewelyn ap Gruffydd, and not rebuilt until 1277. (Bibliog. 104)

burg (Ger.), citadel of a town or castle,+ equivalent to the French "bourg." See also burh.

Burg Eltz, German castle+ built in the 12th century to protect an important bend in the River Eltz. By 1268, the family of the counts of Eltz had split into several branches which occupied the six *hauser* that surround the castle's courtyard. (Bibliog. 30)

de Burgh, Elizabeth (1292-1360), "Lady of Clare," sister and coheiress of Gilbert de Clare,* earl of Pembroke. At an earaly age she married John de Burgh, son and heir of Richard, earl of Ulster, who died in 1313. Then she married Theobald de Verdon who died in 1316, and finally she married Roger d'Amorie in Ireland who died in 1321. (Bibliog. 47)

de Burgh, Elizabeth (1332-1363), countess of Ulster, granddaughter and heiress of William de Burgh, earl of Ulster, who was son and heir of the Lady of Clare by her first husband. At age 10, she married Lionel,* second son of King Edward III,* and became earl of Ulster; he became duke of Clarence. Their only daughter was Philippa (1350-1381), countess of Ulster, who on her father's death inherited his dignities. In 1368, she married Edmund de Mortimer, earl of March, who also died in 1381. (Bibliog. 47)

de Burgh, Hubert (d. 1243), chief justiciar of England. Hired by King Richard I* and then by King John as the chief legal officer of England. King John sent him to ask for the king of Portugal's daughter in marriage for King John, even though John had married Isabelle of Angoulême* while Hubert was on that official errand. He was John's chamberlain and was sent with 100 knights to guard the Welsh march.* In 1204, when King Philip II,* Augustus, of France pronounced against John the second sentence of forfeiture of all English lands in France, Hubert was sent to Paris to declare John's readiness to answer all charges in his lord's court, and to demand a safe-conduct+ from Philip. He led the garrison on Chinon* in a year's defense against a stout siege, but was forced finally to leave the castle+ and fight the enemy on open battle where he was badly wounded, and captured. Later he stood beside King John at Runnymede for the signing of the *Magna*

*Carta Libertatum.** When Prince Louis* landed at Dover, Hubert was given the task of defending Dover* castle against the invaders. He withstood Louis' siege for four months, and then offered a truce to allow him to ask King Henry III for help. At that, Louis withdrew his siege. When in 1217, Louis' chances of success in England depended on receipt of reinforcements and supplies sent by his wife in a fleet led by Eustace, the Monk,* Hubert believed Dover castle was the "Key to England," and that if the troops and supplies landed, England would be lost. He begged William Marshal+ and other important barons to help. They refused. Hubert thereupon gathered every ship he could find in the Cinque Ports,* and staffing them with the stoutest men from Dover, set out with 16 large and 20 small ships to repulse the 80 large and numerous small ships of the French fleet. As the French headed for England, they saw Hubert sailing for what they assumed to be Calais* because his force was too small to cause the French any concern. However, as soon as he got his ships to windward of the French, Hubert changed course and bore down on the rear vessels. The remainder of the French invading fleet were helpless, for the wind was against them. Only 15 escaped; the rest were captured or sunk. As no quarter was asked or given, prisoners were beheaded or drowned, except for important and valuable knights and nobles who could be ransomed. He earned his high esteem with that battle.

After William Marshall's death in 1219 gave Hubert first place beside the young King Henry III,* his first step was to place the English government in English hands. His archfoe was Peter des Roches,* bishop of Winchester, whom the baronial leaders supported: William de Aumale* and Faulkes de Breauté.* Hubert had derived power and wealth by marring wisely first, Joan, daughter of William, earl of Devon* and lord of the Isle of Wight, and widow of William Brewer the younger; and second, Beatrice, daughter of William of Warenne* and widow of Lord Baldalf; and third, Isabelle, daughter of William, second earl of Gloucester,* and the repudiated wife of King John, who, at the time of her marriage to Hubert also was the widow of Geoffrey de Mandeville,* fifth earl of Essex.* In 1221, he married fourth, Margaret, sister of King Alexander II of Scotland, at the same time as Alexander II married Joan, King Henry III's sister. Frequently the barons would refuse to obey his directives, and not until the pope wrote in 1223 saying that Henry III was old enough to govern for himself did the barons obey Hubert unquestioningly as though the orders came from the King. But he had to fight the powerful barons all the rest of his life. Henry III's early invasions of France to reclaim some of the lands lost by King John were disastrous failures, and those failures were laid to Hubert and caused him to be removed from office in 1232. (Bibliog. 58)

Burghausen, Bavarian castle+ belonging to the counts of Burghausen. In 1164 it passed to the dukes of Bavaria* who maintained it for centuries as one of their most important castles. (Bibliog. 30)

Burghersh, Bartholomew (fl. 1340), English knight who fought in the Scottish wars of Edward II.* He joined with Thomas, earl of Lancaster* in his rebellion, was defeated with him at Boroughbridge,* and taken prisoner, but was restored to his lands and titles by Isabelle, the queen consort.* He was appointed constable of Dover castle* and warden of the Cinque Ports* in 1327, 1343 and from 1346 to 1350. During those years, he also served as chief justiciar in eyre South of Trent, became a banneret+ in 1341, was sent on an important embassy to the pope in 1343, fought at the battle of Crécy,* was chamberlain of the royal household, and constable of the Tower of London from 1355. He was nominated as one of the twenty-five original Knights of the Garter.* He accompanied Prince Edward* on almost all his expeditions, fought at Poitiers* in 1356, and was one of the most distinguished warriors of his day. (Bibliog. 47)

Burgundy (Fr. *Bourgogne),* geographical name whose location changed numerous times. In the older Burgundian kingdom, the northwest part formed a land known as the duchy of Burgundy* which in the 9th century was a fief of Karolingia, or the western kingdom. This territory known as the duchy of Burgundy in the east of France had been granted to a branch of the royal house in the early days of the Parisian kingdom under the Valois dukes. Despite its being a great power, its princes held no part of their dominions in wholly independent sovereignty. Rather, they were peers of their imperial and royal neighbors. Its capital was Dijon, and it always acknowledged the supremacy of the kings of Laon and Paris. By his marriage to Margaret of Flanders, Philip the Hardy, first duke of the house of Valois in Burgundy, obtained the counties of Flanders, Artois, Rhetel, Auxerre, and Nevers, all fiefs of the French crown, together with the county palatine* of Burgundy as a fief of the empire. The two Burgundies, duchy and county, and the county of Nevers, lay geographically together; Flanders and Artois lay together at a distance, with the small possession of Rhetel between them. This was the French duchy but was not the "royal" Burgundy, the middle kingdom. That kingdom, lying between the Alps, the Saône and the Rhône Rivers and the Mediterranean, was divided into two main parts: the northern part, the county palatine of Burgundy, and the southern, the Lesser Burgundy. Its main problem was that it had little real unity: the northern part, the county palatine of Burgundy, adhered to the empire, and frequently became totally independent of the other areas by reason of a strong leader. Situated at the center of the river system of France, it hence became a center of trade. When the Carolingian Empire disintegrated, Boron, the husband of Ermengarde, daughter of Louis II, founded the kingdom of Cisjuron, or Lower Burgundy, but in 882 he swore fealty to Charles the Stout. His territory included what later became Franche Comte, a part of the province of Burgundy, Dauphine, Provence, and part of Languedoc and Savoy. In 888, Rudolph, a Swiss count, established a kingdom known as Transjuran or Upper Burgundy. His son later traded his claim to the Italian crown for the Cisjuran kingdom, thus uniting both into what frequently was called the kingdom of Arles, which subsequently was united with the German Empire by Conrad II in 1033.

When Boron founded Cisjuran, his brother, Richard, remained faithful to Charles the Bald, and this loyalty was rewarded with the duchy of Burgundy which had been held by various members of the Carolingian family previously. King Robert II took it back and bestowed it upon his son, later Henry I, in 1015. It was held at one time by Emperor Frederick Barbarossa* in right of his wife; at another by King Philip V* of France through the marriage of one of his female descendants; then it was united with the French duchy of Burgundy under the dukes of the house of Valois.* (Bibliog. 79)

burh, fortification built by the Saxons as a communally owned walled enclosure, fortified and protecting a town, each encompassing a much larger area than that of a castle,+ and defended by a much larger garrison. (Bibliog. 90)

Burnell, Robert (d. 1292), chancellor+ of Edward I.* He was a bluff and not always scrupulous clerk who supported the king completely as the king's secretary since the battle of Evesham.* He was the younger son of Shropshire knight whom Edward appointed not only as chancellor to replace Henry III's* chancellor, William de Merto, but also as bishop of Bath and Wells, and would have appointed him as archbishop except for the pope's opposition. By the time of his death in 1292, Brunell held 82 manors in 19 counties as well as a large number of ecclesiastical preferments. At Wells, he built a large hall with battlemented+ wall, towers and gatehouse, and in Shropshire where he entertained both the king and the parliament, he built his home, Acton Burwell, with timber from the royal forests. (Bibliog. 34)

Byzantine romance, romance based on and shaped by the elements of plot and details of background which entered the literatures of Western Europe through the returning crusaders+ and the ever-broadening contacts with the Near East. The Middle English* romances, *Apollonius of Tyre,** and *Floris and Blauncheflur** revealed Byzantine atmospheres and scenes. (Bibliog. 202)

Byzantium, ancient Greek city on the shores of the Bosphorus. See Constantinople.

C

Caballero Cifar, el (Span.), first full-length chivalric novel in Spanish. Writing in the first half of the 14th century, its author, identified as Ferran Martinez, archdeacon of Madrid, drew on the *lais** of Marie de France* and the works of Chrétien de Troyes.* This story concerns the adventures of the knight Cifar, his wife, Grima, and his sons Garfain and Boboan; it resembles a Byzantine romance.* (ed. M. de Riquer, Barcelona, 1951) (Bibliog. 237)

Cador, earl of Cornwall, nephew of King Arthur* in Arthurian legend, and father of Constantine* who succeeded King Arthur. (Bibliog. 129, 145)

Caen, French castle+ built by Duke William I* on the Orne River, 9 miles from the seacoast of Normandy* soon after 1047. King Henry I* added a great keep. Later, Philip II,* Augustus, captured it from the English but twice during the Hundred Years War,* it returned to English control, in 1346 and again in 1417, before it finally returned to French hands in 1450. (Bibliog. 30)

Caer, Kaer, Celtic word for "fort" as in Caerleon, "fort [or city] of the Legion." An ancient fortress of the Britons on the River Clyde was called "Kaer Alclyde." (Bibliog. 96)

Caerlaverock, Scottish triangular castle+ which Edward I* besieged and captured in 1300. In 1313, Sir Eustace Maxwell, its castellan, declared for Robert Bruce* instead of Edward II,* and dismantled the castle in accordance with the Scottish policy of rendering useless any castle which might be of help to the English. (Bibliog. 30)

Caerlluel. See Carlisle.

Caerlon-on-Usk, location of Arthur's* second coronation, in Arthurian legend, which Wace* located in Glamorgan.* On the right bank of the

River Usk had been a colony and capital under Roman dominion; its name was a corruption of the Latin *Castrum Legionis,* which Nennius named Cair Leon. (Bibliog. 68)

Caernarvon, Welsh castle+ which King Edward I* intended to be the finest of all his castles, and the center of royal government in the north. He brought his wife, Eleanor, to Caernarvon to give birth to his son, Edward, to be known as Edward of Caernarvon, but also as the first English Prince of Wales who later became Edward II* of England. This castle had two flanking towers and two gateways: the Queen's Gate at the east, and the King's Gate at the North. (Bibliog. 30)

Caerphilly, Welsh concentric castle+ begun by Gilbert de Clare* in 1271. Later, Hugh le Despenser,* companion and favorite of King Edward II,* became lord of Caerphilly by marrying into the Clare family. Edward sought refuge here with his friend Hugh from his wife, Isabelle,* and other enemies. Even after the king had fled elsewhere, the queen persisted in its siege. When it finally surrendered some months later, Isabella was given its treasures and then, taking no chances on his returning to power, beheaded Despenser. (Bibliog. 30)

Cahn (Kahu, Quahn, Caii), Saracen god referred to in the *chansons de geste** of *Roland,** *Prise de Pamplune, Aquin,** *Aye d'Avignon,** and others. (Bibliog. 128)

Caithness, one of the seven transmarine provinces of Scotland in the 9th century, but not one of the seven earldoms (mormaerships; see Angus) of that kingdom. Until the 11th century, temporary possession of it was obtained by the Norsemen from Orkney,* which islands they had begun to colonize late in the 9th century when the title of jarl or earl of Orkney was bestowed on Sigurd, its leader. The earldom of Caithness was possessed for many generations by the Norwegian earls of Orkney who held the islands of Orkney under the king of Norway according to Norwegian custom by which the title of jarl was a personal one. They held Caithness under the king of Scotland and its tenure followed the laws of Scotland. Thorfinn, jarl of Orkney, was earl of Caithness; he was the son and heir of Sigurd II by the daughter of Malcolm II, king of Scotland.* On Malcolm's death in 1034, he disputed the right to the Scottish throne with Duncan, son of Malcolm's elder daughter. Joining with MacBeth, mormaer of Moray, he obtained dominion over the whole of the north of Scotland during MacBeth's usurpation of the crown of Scotland after Duncan's murder in 1040. (Bibliog. 176)

Calabria, province between Naples and Sicily in the southwestern part of the Italian peninsula. During the middle of the 11th century, it was conquered from the Byzantine Empire by the Normans, and by 1054 had become part of the state founded by Robert Guiscard* to serve as a base for the Norman conquest of Sicily. After the Sicilian Vespers* in 1282, and the establishment of separate kingdoms in Sicily and in Naples, it became a province in the Angevin kingdom of Naples, and by the 14th century had became a duchy+ under the control of one of the sons of the king of Naples. (Bibliog. 98)

Calais, minor fishing village on the French coast of the English Channel with a natural harbor at the mouth of a stream until 997 when Baldwin IV, count of Flanders, improved it. Philip II* of France, count of Boulogne, fortified it in 1224 to become one of the most strongly fortified localities in northern France. Edward III* of England besieged it in 1346 after defeating the French at Crécy* and captured it in 1347. Around its rectangular central market place were the walls and towers erected in the 13th century by Philip de Hurepel,* count of Boulogne; outside them were marshes and water courses. Where the road entered the town from the southwest, Count Philip had erected a castle+ surrounded by its own moat, and dominated by its own donjon which overlooked the countryside, the town,and the harbor. A mile from Calais, the main road bridged the River Hammes at a crossing called La Nieulay by the French but Newenham by the English. Because sluices there would permit the entire countryside to be flooded, that crossing was of great strategic importance, and therefore was heavily fortified in the later stages of the English occupation. By the Treaty of Bretigny,* the whole of the county of Guines was added to Calais so that the entire English possession was more than doubled. Thus, at no time were the English confined solely to the town of Calais, for "Calais" meant a wide protective zone between the port itself and the nearest French outposts. As such, it served as a bridgehead for any project of conquest for northern France, as a base for diplomacy and espionage, and as a haven for English shipping on the eastern side of the Channel.

To besiege and capture this important Channel port, Edward III raised an army unlike any army raised by his Plantagenet* predecessors. This 32,000-man army consisted of the Prince of Wales,* the earls of Lancaster,* Northampton,* Warwick,* Arundel,* Suffolk,* Huntingdon,* Oxford,* Pembroke,* Kildare,* and Hugh Despenser* as the earl of Gloucester*; the German count of Holstein and of Freiberg; the bishop of Durham; 78 barons and bannerets+; 1,066 knights; 4,182 squires, sergeants, and banner-bearers, thus totalling 5,340 mounted warriors. To these he added 26,963 footsoldiers: 52 centenars+; 794 vintenars (in charge of 20 foot soldiers); 528 hobilars+; 20,076 archers of whom 4,025 were mounted; 140 household yeomen of the king; 339 German panzenars (footsoldiers in mail); 111 crossbowmen; 6 standard bearers on foot; 6 armorers; 339 artificers (military repairmen); and 4,572 Welsh footsoldiers. Only 1,002 of the total were foreign auxiliaries: 107 barons and knights, 497 squires, 386 additional panzenars, 5 hobilars, and 7 infantry. Their rates of pay revealed the huge cost of such an undertaking for the king: the Prince of Wales received £1 per day; the earls and the bishop of Durham received 6 shillings 8 pence (half-mark) per day; barons and bannerets, 4 shillings; knights, 2 shillings; 4,182 squires and other mounted men-at-arms a shilling; the mounted archers and hobilars, 6 pence; the foot archers, 3 pence, the Welsh pikemen, only 2 pence. Estimating wages for others not listed brings the total daily cost for maintaining such an army to £710 17 shillings tuppence. Keeping it under arms for 41 days from midsummer (June 24, 1347) until its surrender on August 4 cost the king, the sum of £29,135, 3 shillings, 10 pence. If the knights' fee was based on a man's annual worth of £40 per fee, one can estimate the enormous impact of the king's enterprise on England's economy.

To counter this siege, King Philip VI* of France marched toward Calais to provide food for its starving inhabitants, but when Edward refused to emerge from his solid besieging positions and fight in the open, Philip departed and demobilized his army. At that news, the citizens of Calais surrendered. It had held out valiantly under the brave and resolute leadership of Jean de Vienne, its governor, until Edward starved it into submission. Its inhabitants were saved from the cruel fate which Edward had planned for them (see siege warfare+) by the devotion of Eustace de St. Pierre and six of the chief citizens who themselves were spared from execution by the intercession of Edward's queen, Philippa.* (Bibliog. 68, 104, 166)

Caledonia, ancient Latin name for Scotland. Nennius recounted that the seventh of Arthur's* twelve battles was fought in the Caledonian wood, that is, in Cat Coit Celidon. (Bibliog. 12, 169)

Calogrenant, knight of the Round Table* in Arthurian legend who was unsuccessful in attempting the adventure of the magic fountain during which he met Merlin* disguised as a huge ugly herdsman. *Le Morte D'Arthur** stated that he was slain by Lancelot* at Guenevere's* door. His name probably was formed from a combination of Kay le Grenant,* meaning Kay the "grumbler." (Bibliog. 1)

Calpe. See Gibraltar.

Calveley, Sir Hugh (d. 1393), distinguished English knight who became famous as a soldier of fortune. Thought to be a brother of Sir Robert Knollys,* Hugh participated in the Combat of the Thirty,* but was pardoned for it a year later. In 1364, he fought in the decisive battle of Auray* in which Charles of Blois* was killed, thus ending the struggle for the duchy of Brittany. When he was asked to command the rearguard, Hugh begged for a different assignment closer to the action. But his superior, Chandos,* refused, saying that no other man was equal to that important position. Hugh accepted the position, and by his steadfastness to discipline kept the army firm during the desperate charges of the enemy. Later, he joined Henry of Trastamare* in his struggle against Pedro the Cruel of Castile (see Peter IV). When Edward* the Black Prince joined Pedro, Calveley changed sides to fight under Chandos again, and then fought again under him at Navarette* in 1367. He next led 3,000 freebooters* warring in the territory of the earl of Armagnac. Appointed deputy of Calais in 1377, he led a small force to Bologne where he burnt ships in the harbor, destroyed part of the town, and returned with rich booty. In 1379, he and Sir Thomas Percy, as English admirals, conveyed the duke of Brittany to a haven near St. Malo with galleys laden with goods. The French fleet attacked them there, but were driven off by the ferocity of Calveley's bowmen. (Bibliog. 58)

Cambaluc, name by which the royal city of the Great Khan of the East was known in Europe. Later it became known as Peking. Jenghiz (Ghengis) Khan* captured the city in 1215; his grandson, Kublai, built a new city a few hundred yards from the old capital and called it Kaan-Baligh, Mongol for "City of the Khan." (Bibliog. 68)

Cambridge, county in England which has given its name to persons of distinction by the title of earl of Cambridge. This earldom was included with the earldom of Huntingdon which from 1115 to 1237 off and on was in the possession of the royal family of Scotland. In 1205, David* of Scotland, earl of Huntingdon, was in receipt of the third penny+ of the county of Cambridge, and so was recognized as earl of Cambridge and Huntingdon; he was the brother of William the Lion,* king of Scotland. Among its other earls were William de Meschines, son of Randolph, earl of Chester (see also Lincoln), 1139. Later, in 1330, it was bestowed upon William, marquis and duke of Juliers, who married Mary, sister and heir to Edward, duke of Geldres, nephew to King Edward III.* He was followed in 1340 by John de Hainault, uncle to

Queen Philippa, wife of Edward III, who lost it shortly thereafter by siding with the French king. Then, Edmund of Langley, duke of York, was created earl of Cambridge on November 13, 1362, and died forty years later in 1402. (Bibliog. 101, 164)

Cambridge castle, castle+ built on Castle Hill on the north bank of the River Cam by William I.* In 1173 Henry II* ordered the justiciar Richard de Lucy* to keep it in good condition. Later, when Richard I* went on his crusade in 1191, Cambridge was one of the castles he entrusted to his chancellor, William Longchamps.* Although on a potentially strategic location, it was not built up or strengthened by any English king until Edward I* began a series of major works on it destined to make it one of the strongest castles in England. He built a new gateway, new tower, and laid the new foundations for new walls. Even though his alterations were never finished, he did turn this decaying Norman bulwark into a major fortress. (Bibliog. 104, 247)

Camelot, King Arthur's* realm, his city, his castle+ in Arthurian legend; it was his chief residence, and was identified most convincingly with Cadbury in Somerset, but variously elsewhere as in Camelford in Cornwall, Camelon in Scotland, on the River Camlet near Montgomery, and Colchester in Essex. Camelot in Malory's *Morte D'Arthur** seemed often to mean King Arthur's castle at Carlisle,* and on other occasions to mean London, Arthur's capital, or as was often done by medieval monarchs, to mean the castle which flew his pennant or banner from a tower to show that he was in residence. (Bibliog. 12, 13, 96)

Campeador (Span.), surname given to Roderigo Diaz de Vivar, el Cid. He won this title, meaning "the champion," from the Arabs through successful single combat with the enemy's champion during the war between Sancho of Navarre and Sancho of Castile. See *Cid, Cantar de Mio.* (Bibliog. 65)

Candie, city of Gandia in Spain in the *chansons de geste.** (Bibliog. 128

cantare, Italian romance shorter than an epic and in a metrical form new to Italian poetry in the early 14th century. These were not recited but were sung by minstrels who accompanied themselves with simple stringed instruments. The two earliest such works were *Febusso e Breusso* and *Cantare di Florio e Biancifiore.* (Bibliog. 245) *cantastorie*   (It.),   Tuscan   "story-singers"   who   naturalized   the Carolingian epic in Tuscany. (Bibliog. 245)

Canterbury, Gervase of (d. c. 1210), a monk of Christ Church, Canterbury, in 1163, and its sacristan in 1193; author of *Chronica* covering the years 1135-1199 in which he showed a marked dislike for the Plantagenet* kings: Henry II* and Richard I.* (ed. W. Stubbs, London: *Rolls Series*, 1879-1880) (Bibliog. 99)

Canterbury, city in southeast England made famous by the murder in its cathedral in 1170 of Thomas à Becket.* Its royal castle has remained in the crown's control since 1086. On that site, William I* (1066-1087) erected a castle called Lodam's Castle containing the third largest keep+ in England; it was 80 by 88 feet, with walls 8 feet thick, and standing some 50 feet high. Henry II* (1154-1189) increased its defenses. Philip II* (1180-1223) of France controlled it for a brief time in the reign of King John (1199-1216), but after that its local importance declined, and it was used mainly as a county prison and headquarters for the sheriff of Kent. (Bibliog. 98, 247)

Canterbury, archbishop of. See archbishop of Canterbury.

cantred, English county containing a hundred townships. (Bibliog. 68)

Capellanus, Andreas. See Andreas Capellanus.

Capetian dynasty, rulers of France between 987 and 1314. Hugh Capet* (987-996) began the Capetian dynasty. Before he became king,+ he had been count+ of Paris, and abbot of St. Martin's of Tours, of Saint Denis, and of St. Germain-des-Pres. Supposedly from his abbot's hood he chose the name "capet." Though a brave man, he was personally retiring and really held little more power as king than some of his powerful nobles. He was succeeded by his son, Robert I the Pious, who reputedly was so pious that as thieves stole the fringe from his cloak while he walked through the city, he never lifted a finger to stop them. He repudiated his first wife, Susanna of Flanders, so he could marry his cousin, Bertha, but was excommunicated by the church for such a consanguineous marriage. This dynasty reached the peak of its power and prestige with the rule of Louis IX (St. Louis).* Finally, with the death in 1328 of Charles IV who had no sons, the Capetian line ended, and the throne went to collateral branch, the Valois, descendants of the younger son of Philip III, Charles of Valois. Capetian kings of France were:

987- 996 - Hugh (Hugues) Capet*
996-1031 - Robert II, the Pious*
1031-1060 - Henry I*
1060-1108 - Phillip I,* the Fat
1108-1137 - Louis VI*
1137-1180 - Louis VII*
1180-1223 - Philip II* Augustus
1223-1226 - Louis VII*
1226-1270 - Louis IX (St. Louis)*
1270-1285 - Philip III*
1285-1314 - Philip IV*
(Bibliog. 74, 124, 199)

Captal de Buch. See Grailly, Jean de.

Carados of the Dolorous Tower, Sir, huge knight in Arthurian legend who liked to capture and imprison other knights. Lancelot* arrived to see Carados carrying away Gawain* across his saddlebow.+ Lancelot killed Carados and freed Gawain and the other knights, but Carados' brother, Sir Turquine, died attempting to avenge Carados' death on Lancelot. (Bibliog. 145)

Carcassonne, city in the province of Languedoc+ in southern France on the main road between Toulouse and the shores of the Mediterranean. A part of the Visigoth kingdom until its collapse in 711, it was conquered by the Franks under Charles Martel in 735. By the 9th century, the city and its county were ruled by a local noble family under the suzerainty+ of the counts of Toulouse.* Through marriage, the title passed to the counts of Barcelona who, when unable to maintain control over the city, passed control to the Trencavel family of Beziers who assumed the title of viscounts+ of Carcassonne. The city and its area flourished under the Trencavels, but was conquered by the crusaders+ under Simon de Montfort* on the Albigensian crusade in 1210. In 1229 it was annexed to the French royal demesne becoming the seat of the royal seneschal.+ It was fortified in the 13th century, and its impressive walls still stand. (Bibliog. 98, 100)

Cardigan castle, once an outpost of Norman conquest, this decaying Welsh fortress during the reign of King Henry II* became a center of Welsh resistance when Rhys ap Gruffydd* rebuilt it in stone and mortar to make it the chief stronghold of his dominions. In 1199, however, his son, Maelgwn, was induced to sell both Cardigan and this castle+ to King John.* It was destroyed in 1231 by Llewellyn, but after his death in 1240, it was immediately rebuilt by Walter Marshal on behalf of his brother Gilbert, earl of Pembroke,* on whose death a few months later it reverted to the crown. In 1254 it was given to the Lord Edward,* heir apparent,* as part of his establishment in Wales, and ten years later, Edward transferred it to his younger brother Edmund.* In 1279, however, as king, Edward I resumed possession of the castle in order to make it the administrative center of the newly formed shire of Cardigan, and its maintenance became the responsibility of the justiciars and chamberlains of South Wales. (Bibliog. 104)

Carisbrooke castle, castle+ on the Isle of Wight. Built on an old Roman fort, this was given to William FitzOsbern* after the Conquest in 1066, but after he passed it to his son Roger, it reverted to the crown when Roger was stripped of his holdings for his role in the rebellion of 1078. It was granted by the crown to the family of Richard de Reviers* (Redvers) in whose family it remained until it was sold by the dying Isabelle de Forz, countess of Aumale,* to Edward I* in 1293. In 1308, Edward II* granted the castle to his favorite, Piers Gaveston,* who returned it to the crown a year later in return for the duchy of Cornwall.* Then in 1312, Edward II granted it to his son, the Lord Edward,* who in turn gave it to his daughter, Isabel, and her husband, Engurreand (Ingram) de Coucy,* earl of Bedford.* (Bibliog. 104, 247)

Carlisle (Caerlluel), principal city of Cumberland, England, located on the western marches* in the farthest part of the kingdom towards Scotland. It was fortified with a citadel and sundry bulwarks for a defense against the Scots to secure the border. Burnt to the ground by the Danes, it was rebuilt by William II* in 1092 to dominate and guard the north end of the city. During the reign of King Stephen* (1135-1154), King David* of Scotland supported Empress Matilda in her attempt to wrest the throne from Stephen. In gratitude, Cumberland and Westmoreland were ceded to Scotland, and Carlisle became a Scots city. There King David died. Four years later, in 1157, Henry II* received the castle back. In 1174, it was besieged by King Alexander* of Scotland, and after three months, its governor, Robert de Vaux, was about to surrender when he was saved by an English victory at the battle of Alnwick. An important bulwark, it was attacked frequently by William* the Lion of Scotland in his unsuccessful efforts to capture it. By 1256, the castle had fallen into disrepair through lack of interest and little was done to repair it until the emergency of the Barons' War* of 1264-1265 when a few repairs were effected. However, not until the Scottish wars of Edward I* was this castle maintained with basic repairs. Carlisle was made the center of military activity and its strength restored to its former position. It became the headquarters of the keeper of the West March, having finally been recognized as an important defense bastion and refuge of the lands adjacent to the Scots. In 1322, the earl of Carlisle, Andrew de Harcla,* fell from royal favor for treason. He was arrested, degraded (see degradation of a knight+), hanged, drawn and quartered. His head was spiked on London Bridge while his quarters were displayed at York, Carlisle, Shrewsbury and Newcastle. Carlisle itself had been made into a see by Henry I* which gave it wealth and credit. (Bibliog. 104, 247)

Carl of Carlisle, Arthurian poem from about 1400 detailing the adventures that took place in the hall of a terrible giant, the Carl (churl) of Carlisle where Gawain,* Kay* and Bishop Baldwin took refuge after a day of hunting. Undergoing successfully a series of tests for bravery, courtesy, and obedience imposed on him by his host, Gawain released the carl from his spell by cutting off his head. Once he was in normal human shape he promised to forsake his evil life and to build a chantry wherein priests would pray continually for the souls of all his previous victims. Gawain married the carl's daughter, and rich gifts were exchanged. Arthur* was summoned to a great feast at the castle+ after which he knighted the carl, conferred upon him the lordship of Carlisle, and made him a member of the Round Table.* (ed. A. Kurvinen, Helsinki, 1951) (Bibliog. 10)

Carmarthen castle, Welsh castle+ built by the Normans in the time of King Henry I* (1100-1135), but it was lost to the Welsh in 1137 and not recovered by the English crown until 1145 when Gilbert, earl of Pembroke,* rebuilt it. Even though it passed through the king's hands, it became part of the lands of South Wales under the control of the marcher lord, Hubert de Burgh* until it reverted to Gilbert Marshal, earl of Pembroke, after Hubert's fall from power in 1232. In 1254, as part of Lord Edward's* newly acquired Welsh estates, it was given to his brother Edmund. When he became king, however, Edward reclaimed it to make it the administrative center of the new shire of Carmarthen and the seat of the justiciar+ of Wales in 1279. (Bibliog. 104)

Carmen de proditione Guenonis, Latin work of the 12th century which described the combat of Roland (see *Song of Roland)* in an artificial style with a large number of puns and other strange literary devices; its author limited descriptions, and enumerations of names and similar things, and deleted passages such as Blancandrin's embassy,

Charlemagne's* vengeance, and the wager of battle concerning Ganelon's* crime. (tr. A. Livingston, *Romanic Review*, II, 1911, 61-79) (Bibliog. 231)

Carrick, earl of. Duncan, grandson of the Celtic Lord of Galloway (d. 1161), obtained from King William the Lion* of Scotland before 1161, Carrick, part of ancient Galloway, along with the title of earl of Carrick. When his granddaughter, Margaret, married Robert de Bruce* in 1271, he thus became earl of Carrick, but she had to pay a heavy fine because she had married without royal consent. Her husband was the son and heir of Robert de Bruce of Annandale, one of the competitors for the crown of Scotland. Their son, Robert de Bruce, earl of Carrick (1274-1329), obtained his father's lands in 1304 and then on March 27, 1304, was crowned king of Scotland as Robert I* when his Scottish dignities merged with the crown. His brother, Edward de Bruce, was made earl of Carrick by Robert I. He went to Ireland in 1315 and was crowned king of Ireland in 1316, but when he was killed at the battle of Dundalk in 1318, the earldom reverted to the crown. (Bibliog. 47)

Carrickfergus, one of Ireland's largest castles.+ Standing on a rocky peninsula in Belfast Lough, it consisted of a narrow enclosure covering the land of the peninsula and protected by a twin-towered gateway at the landward end. It was built between 1180 and 1205 either by John de Coucy or Hugh de Lacy. King John* stayed there on his visit to Ireland in 1210. (Bibliog. 30)

Castelfort. See Chastelfort.

Castile, kingdom located in the central part of Spain. Conquered first in the 5th century by the Visigoths who made Toledo their capital, it was conquered again in the 8th century by the Arabs who drove the survivors of the Christian population north, where at the end of that century, they founded the kingdom of Asturia. Then in the 10th century, the leaders of Asturia and Leon conquered the territory around Burgos from the Muslims, and built numerous castles+ there; hence the name: Castile. Throughout the next two hundred years it became the greatest monarchy in Spain. This was followed by intense civil eruptions, leading to its downfall late in the 14th century. (Bibliog. 98)

Castle Corbenic. See Corbenic, castle of.

Castle Rising, fortress built on the site of a Roman fort on the shore of Norfolk. William I* gave it to his half-brother Odo* of Bayeux, and then to William d'Aubigny* whose son started the castle.+ There, two centuries later, Isabelle, queen of Edward II,* was imprisoned. Its keep was 75 by 64 feet, and 50 feet high. (Bibliog. 247)

Castle Spofforth, castle+ in Yorkshire on land given by William I* to William de Percy, a Norman who arrived in England in 1067. There Percy set up his headquarters, and there the Percy family founded its fortunes. It basically was only a fortified manor house, and not a fortress. (Bibliog. 247)

Castle Sween, earliest stone castle built around 1220 in Scotland in the Norman style, it had a large rectangular keep with large pilaster and angle buttresses. (Bibliog. 30)

Cathars, religious sect which began in the southern French province of Languedoc. Even though they regarded themselves as Christians, the Cathars repudiated the authority of the Old Testament, but revered the Gospels which they interpreted in an allegorical way: they celebrated a form of communion in which a loaf was symbolically shared according to the Gospel description of the Lord's Supper. They denied Jesus corporeal sufferings and attacked the Catholic Church for its literal interpretation of the Bible, which they considered a corruption of the faith, "the work of the devil." For these reasons they rejected the sacraments and the liturgical role of the clergy, maintaining that the Church cannot mediate between God and the believer. They were opposed to the Church owning income-producing property; they forbade marriage and the consumption of animal products, but recognizing that such austerity could not be expected of everyone, they acknowledged two classes of the faithful: the "perfect" or pure, and the believers. They also were believers in Manicheeism, an ancient concept which founded its belief on the idea of two powers—one of good and one of evil. Their main aim was to follow the way of life set forth in the Gospels, and to do so they practiced fraternity, charity, poverty, renunciation, and tolerance. In Provence* they were known as the "good men"; one of their principal sects was in Albi in southern France, hence they were called the Albigenses. This belief spread rapidly and reached as far as Avignon and Lyon and on up to the Alps. Because he saw it as a threat, Pope Innocent III* in 1209 proclaimed a crusade against the movement. (Bibliog. 25)

ceiles. See Brehon law.

Cercle d'Or, crown of thorns adorned with precious gems in Arthurian legend. This holy relic was given to Perceval* for killing the Knight of the Dragon, Ardant.* It later was stolen and became the prize won by Gawain* at a three-day tournament+; he returned it to Perceval. (in *Perlesvaus*) (Bibliog. 241)

Chaitivel, lai* by Marie de France.* Its 240 verses told of a lady who loved four knights collectively but who could not bring herself to marry the one who survived a combat for her hand. Beyond the problem of the four lovers suing for the hand of the same lady, Marie was interested in who was to be the most pitied: the lovers who brought their suit in vain and died upon the field of combat, or he who survived that ordeal and still was not allowed to consummate his love. She seemed to be in favor of the latter. (tr. E. Mason, *Lays of Marie de France,* London and New York: E. P. Dutton, repr. 1966) (Bibliog. 147)

Champagne, province and county in northeastern France. After the county of Troyes was established in the 11th century, it was inherited by Count+ Eudes of Blois.* Subsequent counts of Troyes and Blois, even though vassals of the duke of Burgundy,* established a powerful rule at Troyes, and by the end of the century had become the most powerful of the Blois family and had imposed its rule on all of the family's holdings, and thereby became bitter enemies of the kings of France. With the marriage of William the Conqueror's daughter, Adele,* to Count Stephen of Blois,* they became relatives of the kings of England. While their younger son, Stephen,* became king of England (1135-1154), their elder son, Thibaut,* founded the county of Champagne. He allied himself with his uncle, Henry I* of England, against Louis VI* of France. He granted sanctuary to Peter Abelard and in 1122 set up a haven for him at Paraclete that became a famous intellectual center in France. He married Mary of Burgundy, and during the second crusade+ he preserved stability and order in France as one of the "wise old men". His son, Henry the Liberal, a colorful perfect knight, established at his court at Troyes a cultural center of Europe where the newest style of knightly life was presided over by his wife, Marie of France, daughter of Louis VII and Eleanor* of Aquitaine. There the greatest poets of the age gathered, among them Chrétien de Troyes.* (Bibliog. 68, 98)

Champart, Robert, abbot of Jumièges in Normandy,* who was protected and enriched by the dukes of Normandy, in order to become the archbishop of Canterbury. By this appointment Edward the Confessor

placed control of the Church of England in the hands of the Normans.
Robert and his men, however, were not strong enough to fight the control of Earl Godwine* and his underlings who had been allowed to return to England in 1053 from their year-long exile in France. On the
death of Godwin in 1053, Harold, his son, became the real master of
England and replaced Robert Champart at Canterbury with a man he could
trust and control, Bishop Stigand.* (Bibliog. 178)

Chandos, Sir John (d. 1370), English soldier. Descended from Robert de
Chandos, companion-in-arms of William I, John began his military career at the siege of Cambrai in 1337, and made a name for himself as the
military architect and tactician of the English victories at Crécy* in
1346 and at Poitiers* in 1357. After saving the life of Edward the
Black Prince,* he became his closest friend and advisor. In the Treaty
of Bretigny,* King Edward III* awarded him the lands in the Cotentin*
of Viscount Saint-Sauveur. About the same time, he was appointed
"regent and lieutenant" of the king of England in France, and
vice-chamberlain of the royal household. In 1364, he helped an English
ally, John de Montfort,* in his struggle for the duchy of Brittany,
and thereby prevented peace between Montfort and his rival, Charles*
of Blois. He was in command of Montfort's and the English forces at
the battle of Auray* in October 1364 at which Blois was killed and Du
Guesclin* was captured by Chandos; Du Guesclin was ransomed the
following year for 100,000 francs.

Two years later, Chandos tried unsuccessfully to dissuade the
Black Prince from going to Spain to help the unpopular Pedro the Cruel
(see Peter IV) reestablish himself on the throne of Castile from which
he had been driven by his natural brother, Henry de Trastamare, aided
by Du Guesclin and the free companies* of Gascony.* The English forces
met and defeated Trastamare's forces at the battle of Navarette*
(Najera). In command of the advance guard of the English army with
John of Gaunt,* Chandos displayed conspicuous bravery, and captured Du
Guesclin a second time. Chandos then was appointed seneschal+ of
Poitiers in 1369. In 1370, at Lussac between Poitiers and Limoges,
Chandos with a company of about 300 men clashed with a French force on
a hump-backed bridge over the River Vienne. Dismounting to fight on
foot, he slipped on the dew-moist grass, and fell. For some reason he
did not close his visor and when he failed to see and ward off the
blow of an enemy sword on the side of his blind eye, it penetrated
fatally between the nose and forehead. He was a chivalrous man whom
King Edward III characterized as the one man who alone could have made
peace between England and France, for his chivalric temper was recognized by friend and foe alike; even Du Guesclin strongly admired

Chandos as a man and fighter. His herald, the Chandos herald,* wrote a biography of the Black Prince which included many references to Chandos' actions, also. (Bibliog. 58, 223)

Chandos, the Herald of, author of a metrical biography of Edward,* the Black Prince of England* written in 1386 in continental French rather than in Anglo-Norman. Because the Herald probably was an eyewitness to the events he described, this work was especially valuable for the account of the Black Prince's Castilian expedition. He revealed that the Black Prince possessed and demonstrated the five major elements of chivalry:+ prowess, loyalty, courtesy, largesse, and prestige. The possession of prowess merited the term "chivalrous" or "bon chevalier," and such prowess was based on skill at arms which commonly was illustrated by good swordsmanship and was held to be governed by a code of fair fighting. Loyalty, more intricate and more significant, was a quality of the soul, and indicated a loyal heart. The Herald noted that the Black Prince undertook the Spanish campaign out of pity and concern, and found his pleasure there in giving aid to him who asked it on a plea of mercy. The Prince's largesse was illustrated amply by the rich gifts of gold, silver and jewels he gave away freely, and by the 400 men he entertained daily at his table at Bordeaux. His freedom and naturalness of manner and courtesy were illustrated by his actions on meeting his wife and son, Richard, during his triumphal entry into Bordeaux: he dismounted and walked into the city holding their hands. His courtesy was further shown by his conduct to the captured king of France to whom he tried to perform squires'+ duties, and by his humble manner of thanking his own knights. His prestige was obvious. (Bibliog. 148)

Channel Islands castles,+ fortresses controlled by England on the small islands of Guernsey and Jersey in the English Channel off the French coast. Only after the loss of Normandy to France in 1204 did these castles become essential for the protection of these small islands. Two castles, Gorey and Cornet, served as centers of royal administration for the next centuries. Gorey, also known as Mont Orgueil, stood on a hill on the east coast of Jersey, but Castle Cornet was built on an islet off St. Peter Post, Guernsey. Its principal function was to protect the roadstead which became an important shipping and base for operations against the neighboring coasts of Normandy and Brittany. (Bibliog. 62)

Chanson de Guillaume, Anglo-Norman *chanson de geste* * from the 13th century. Vivien, Guillaume's nephew, led Christians against the

Saracen forces of King Deramed of Cordova who had invaded France. Vivien swore never to retreat one step before the pagans, and as all his men were killed, he sent word to his uncle for help. He, too, lost all his men, and went back to Orange for thirty thousand more. These too were slain, but Guillaume found the dying Vivien, and administered the last communion to him. Deramed was killed, and Guillaume returned to Orange, and then left for Laon where he demanded feudal aid+ from King Louis I. At this point, Reneward*, or Rainouart, a huge giant, appeared, and took the field against the pagans with Guillaume's forces. Killing rank after rank of pagans with his huge club, he avenged the death of Vivien. On their return to Orange, Reneward inadvertently was not invited to the celebration dinner, and his wrath caused him to leave for Spain to gather a giant army to avenge the insult. However, he was appeased by Guillaume's wife, Guiborc,* who was his long lost sister. (ed. Jean Frappier, *Les Chansons de Geste du Cycle de Guillaume d'Orange,* Paris: SEDES, 1955, I) (Bibliog. 106)

Chanson de Roland. See *Song of Roland.*

chansons de geste, Old French epic poetry. These were narrative poems of moderate length, averaging 4,000 lines, usually in 10-syllable verse with assonanced and rhymed *laisses;* they were sung with an accompanying harp or viele. Basically these centered on the themes of the glory of the Franks, the Christian religion and the deeds of certain famous knights who owed allegiance to Charlemagne* or to his son, Louis the Pious.* Although most of the subject matter and characters were legendary, audiences believed them to be true history. None, except perhaps *Gormont et Isembart,* was older than 1100. Theories about their origin differed widely. One, the cantilena, held that after the battles of Charlemagne, lyric poems arose on the field of action and were chanted by soldiers and jongleurs+ to posterity; these lyric poems on the same or similar events were combined later into the epic form. A second held that these sprang from Germanic epics emerging from the time of the migrations of the people by the 5th century. Marked similarities existed between these Germanic epics and the *chansons de geste:* named swords and horses; status of the king among the nobles, and his constant search for advice; giants and other unusual characters; legal institutions; common occurrence of the number 12 as in the 12 peers; the quest for a bride. However, these motifs also occurred in popular literature of people who never had felt the Germanic influence; the German epic form differed greatly from the French in that the Germans never used *laisses,* and the German epic was pagan in spirit. A third theory held that soldiers and other eyewitnesses of the historic events narrated their experiences which thereby were transmitted through generations until eventually they were collected and put into epic form in the 9th and 10th centuries. A fourth held that they were extensions of saints' lives which were sung about the marketplace, church or shrine of the saint in question. Encouraged by the local clergy, their fame spread as did the fame of the tombs of their founders, many of whom had served under Charlemagne or his successors. As charters gave a fact or two about these local heroes, this fourth theory maintained that about the year 1000 some ingenious jongleur expanded the material into long narratives, well understanding that Charlemagne still was remembered fondly as the patron of Christianity and as the greatest French king. Added impact to such narratives was provided by the local popularity of the shrine. Roland,* for example, was celebrated at the church of Saint-Romain in Blaye; Ogier the Dane at the church of St. Burgundofaro at Meaux; William of Orange at Saint-Guilhelm-le-Desert. Bertrand de Bar-sur-Aube* in his *Girart de Vienne** (c. 1200-1220) categorized these *chansons de geste* into three *gestes* or cycles: the *gestes du roi,** those of a king, usually Charlemagne; the *gestes* of Doön de Mayence,* and the *gestes* of Garin de Monglane.* Of the eighty chansons which survived, thirty belong to the *geste du roi,** the cycle of the king. (Bibliog. 106, 231)

Charlemagne (Charles the Great) (742-814), great Frankish leader, and founder of a huge empire. Son of the first king of the Carolingian dynasty, Pepin the Short, and his wife, Berte,* Charles began to reign jointly with his brother, Carloman, in 768. Carloman was not loyal to Charles, but he caused little trouble, and died in 771. His widow and children, fearing Charles, fled under the care of a knight named Ogier to the court of Didier, king of Lombardy. To regain control over these fugitives, Charlemagne began his Lombardy wars. After capturing the fugitives between 772 and 773, he confined them in a cloister, and became the sole ruler of the country. He fought the Saxons* for thirty years (772-804) during which some 4,500 Saxons were slain, thousands baptized, and countless hundreds fled to other provinces. Between 778 and 812 his forces made seven expeditions into Spain but he led only the first one; his sons led the rest. Between 778 and 796, he fought against the Avars who occupied the vast region east of Bavaria* between the Danube and Illyria, and in 789, he fought against the Wiltzes between the Elbe and Oder Rivers. In 810, he gave orders that special boats be constructed for an attack against Barcelona, Spain. Recognizing that they needed to approach the enemy secretly, Charles ordered the boats built in sections so that each part could be transported overland by two horses or mules separately, and assembled at the point of embarkation across the Ebro River. With pitch, wax, and tow, the boats were reassembled and made waterproof for the crossing. By this means, they surprised and overcame the enemy.

On Christmas Day, 800, he was crowned emperor in the Church of St. Peter in Rome. He was a Frank, a German; he spoke Latin and his mother tongue, and understood Greek, but could neither read nor write any language. He was of medium height, thickset, and had a weak voice. He was famed for his generosity and was kind to strangers. For example, he was said to have decreed in 794 that he would hold court during the winter only in four places: at the palaces at Doue, Chaseneuil, Angeac, and Ebreuil so that after a lapse of three years, each place would support him during the winter in the fourth year. Those places then would have to offer sufficient provisions for the royal household when it came back in the fourth year only. He died on the Kalends of February, January 28, 814.

Einhard,* his biographer, wrote that Charlemagne had four wives: 1) the daughter of Desiderius, king of the Lombards, whom he married in 770, but repudiated a year later; 2) Hildigard, a noble Swabian who died in 783; 3) Fastrada, an East Frank who died in 794; 4) Luitgard, an Almannian who died around A.D. 800. He also was reputed to have had six concubines: Himiltrudis, Sigradane, Madelgard, Gersuind, Regina, and Adallindis. Children were born to all but his first and fourth wives. Charles (d. 811) and Pepin (d. 810) and Louis (the Pious) were the sons, and Hruotrud (d. 810), Bertha, and Gisla the daughters of Hildigard. Fastrada had two daughers: Theoderada and Hiltrud. Children of the concubines were Pepin (the Hunchback), Charles' firstborn (d. 811), son of Himiltrudis; Hruodhaidis, daughter of Sigridane; Tuothildis, daughter of Madelgard; Adalartrud, daughter of Gersuind; Drogo (d. 855) and Hugo (d. 844), sons of Regina; and Theodoric, son of Adallindis. Some said that Pepin, son of Hildigard, was originally named Carloman, perhaps after Charles' brother who died in 771. Note that Charles already had a son named Pepin.

In the *Chanson de Roland*,* Charlemagne appeared in his noblest and most authoritative manner: receiving with dignity the embassy from a rival monarch, behaving autocratically with his own barons, avenging ferociously the defeat of the rear guard, challenging to single combat the pagan leader Baligant;* he had to be revered, generous with gifts, and cautious in speech; when he acted impulsively, generally he was wrong. In the other *chansons* in which he appeared, he was a Christian Agamemnon whose breath was powerful, whose proportions were colossal, who represented, as Agamemnon represented, the ideal of royalty mod-

erated or tempered by wisdom. He appeared in the following
*chansons de geste** which gave him a poetic and legendary life (those
marked with an √ were part of the cycle known as the *gestes du roi**):

√ *Anseis de Carthage**
√ *Aquin**
√ *Aspremont**
  *Auberon**
√ *Basin** (or *Charles et Elegast*)
  Berte
√ *Berta au gran piés**
  Charlemagne (by Girard d'Amiens*)
√ *Chanson de Roland*
  *Couronnement de Louis**
  Desier
  *Destruction of Rome**
√ *Enfances Ogier**
√ *Enfances Roland*
√ *Entrée d' Espagne**
√ *Fierabras**
√ *Floovant**
  *Galien li restorés**
√ *Gaydon**
  *Girard de Viane**
√ *Gui de Bourgogne**
√ *Guiteclin de Sassoigne*
√ *Huon de Bordeaux**
√ *Jehan de Lanson**
  *Karleto**
√ *Macaire**
√ *Mainet**
  Ogier le Danois
√ *Otinel**
√ *Pèlerinage de Charlemagne**
√ *Prise de Pamplune*
  Renaut de Montauban (see *Four Sons of Aymon*)
√ *Chanson de Roland**
√ *Saisnes, Chanson de**
√ *Simon de Pouille**
  Voyage à Jerusalem (Bibliog. 88)

In England, Charlemagne appeared in the following Middle English*
romances*:

Duke Rowlande and Sir Ottuell
*Four Sons of Aymon**
*Huon de Bordeux**
Lyf of Charles the Grete
*Roland and Vernagu**
*Romance of Bevis of Hampton**
Romance of the Sowdon of Babylon
Sege of Melayne
*Sir Ferumbras**
Taill of Rauf Coilyear. (Bibliog. 202)

Charles IV, king of the Romans (1316-1378). Son of John of Luxemburg, king of Bohemia, Charles was made viceroy of Italy at the age of 16, but the job proved to be too great for him. Later he fought against the Emperor Louis* of Bavaria,* the great enemy of the pope. In 1346, on the death of his father at Crécy,* he became king of Bohemia, and later that same year he became emperor through the influence of Pope Clement VI, but he did so only by granting humiliating concessions to many by which he was made to appear as a tool of the papacy. He devoted all his efforts to aggrandizing his family to the almost total neglect of the empire. Crowned in 1354 in Milan, Rome and Ostia, he was forced to confirm the Visconti* in their usurpations, and then to leave for home with huge sums of money. He was remembered for being a lax emperor, and for the Golden Bull+ of 1356 which determined who should elect the king of the Romans. It decreed that the seven electors should make the choice: three ecclesiastical (bishops of Mayence, Cologne, and Treves), and four secular (king of Bohemia, count+ palatine,+ duke+ of Saxony, margrave+ of Brandenburg). Thus the king of the Romans, the future emperor, was to be elected by a majority of the electors at a meeting in Frankfurt. By this action, the pope lost all influence over this election. (Bibliog. 68)

Charles IV the Fair (1294-1328), last Capetian king of France. Third son of Philip IV, he succeeded his brother Philip V* who had no sons, and whose daughters were barred from inheriting the royal title. When Charles' officials tried to impose French royal authority in Gascony and Flanders, the native reactions led to the Hundred Years War.* He was survived only by a daughter. (Bibliog. 68, 98)

Charles V the Wise, king of France (1337-1380). He became regent when in 1356, his father, John II,* was taken prisoner at the battle of Poitiers.* With the able assistance of Bertrand du Guesclin* whom he appointed *connetable* (constable+) of France, he reorganized the army which subsequently defeated the English at Castile. This resulted in a return to order which helped him recover much of the territory lost to England, and a reorganization of the realm and the imposition of a new tax on salt, the *gabelle*,+ gave the treasury needed resources. (Bibliog. 98)

Charles the Bald (823-877), king of the Gallo-Franks. Son of King Louis I, the Pious, and grandson of Charlemagne, he was co-plotter with his brother Louis II, king of the Germans, to claim and divide the land of Lotharingia, the land of their brother, Lothaire.* Charles also was a co-swearer to the Strassburg Oaths. He was a forceful figure. He seized Aquitaine* from his nephew, Pepin II, in 848; in 869, he secured Lorraine (Lotharingia) but soon had to divide it with his brother, Louis II. He tried to seize Germany when Louis II died in 876, but was unsuccessful. He was crowned emperor of the West by Pope John VIII on Christmas Day, 875, seventy-five years to the day after his grandfather had been crowned Holy Roman Emperor. The various composers of the *chansons de geste** hopelessly confused this Charles with Charlemagne. On his death, the influence of the Carolingian kings had become minimal. (Bibliog. 106)

Charles le Chauve. See *Dieudonne de Hongrie.*

Charles of Anjou (1225-1285), king of Sicily and Naples (1266-1285). The tenth son of King Louis VIII* who left him the county of Anjou* as appanage,* Charles in 1266 was offered the throne of Sicily by Pope Clement IV, and with the consent of his brother King Louis IX,* he fought Manfred of Hohenstaufen* and conquered Sicily. His policies instigated open revolt against the Angevin magistrates on Sicily, and led to the bloody Sicilian Vespers* episode in 1282 which was the high point of the revolt that led to the loss of Sicily from Charles' control. (Bibliog. 68, 98)

Charles the Bad (1332-1388), king of Navarre who controlled much more than his small kingdom south of the Pyrenees Mountains; he also held several counties in Normandy and rich estates near Paris. He had a better claim to the French throne than Edward III* because his mother, Jeanne, was the daughter of Louis X (d. 1316), and therefore nearer to the succession than his aunt Isabelle (mother of Edward III). Jeanne's uncles had set aside her aunt's claims largely because of her reputation for promiscuity with Mortimer.* Had Charles the Bad been of age in 1328, he might well have been chosen as king of France instead of Philip of Valois. He was personable, smooth-talking and amoral and had

a sense of burning injustice. To add to his fury over losing the
French throne, he had been denied his wife's dowry of the counties of
Champagne* and Angoulême* due him when he married King John II's*
daughter; the dowry had never been paid. He chose to play the
Plantagenets* against the Valois* by offering to help Edward III and
then by persuading John II to buy a Navarese alliance. His first move
was far from subtle. He long had hated the constable of France, Don
Carlos de la Cerda, a man who had served as admiral at
Les-Espagnola-sur-Mer,* because King John had given Angoulême to him
instead of to Charles. Carlos was lured into Charles' Norman
possessions, was ambushed and then hacked to death. King John II was
infuriated by that murder, but was so afraid that Charles was plotting
with the English king that he pretended to forgive Charles and then
tried to buy him with a large slice of the Cotentin. John invited
Charles to a banquet at Rouen, and when he arrived had him thrown into
prison. He appealed to Edward for assistance, and all lower Normandy
revolted and declared for England. He died a horrible death. Tormented
by fever and chills, on doctor's orders he was wrapped each night in
cloths soaked in brandy to warm his body and cause him to sweat. Sewn
on him each night like a shroud to keep them in place, these wrappings
caught fire one night from a servant's candle as he leaned over to tie
a thread. (Bibliog. 203, 223, 228)

Charlot (Karlot), son of Charlemagne* in several *chansons de geste,**
such as *Enfances Ogier** and *Ogier.* In *Huon de Bordeaux,** the name
Charlemagne was used to represent Charles the Bald,* and Charlot,
killed by Huon, was Louis the Child, son of Charles the Bald.
(Bibliog. 128)

Charnay, Geoffrey de (d. 1356), "the perfect knight" of France, and
the author of *Book of Chivalry.* As lord of Pierre Perthuis, Montfort,
Savoisy and Licey, he first saw service in Gascony in 1337. In 1340 he
defended Tournai against the English, and in 1341 he served in
Brittany under the heir to the French throne, John, duke of Normandy.
Then in 1349, he led a band of Frenchmen who tried unsuccessfully to
recapture Calais by surprise. He rose to greater heights when his old
commander Duke John ascended the French throne as John II. He was
chosen to be a member of the Order of the Star,+ France's creation to
rival Edward III's Order of the Garter,* and in 1355 he was chosen to
bear the French royal standard, the Oriflamme+ of Saint Denis,* the
fork-tongued crimson banner of the king of France. In response to
King Edward III's invasion of France in 1355, King John II of France
issued an *arrière-ban+* to all men between 18 and 60 several times to

assemble a force to combat the English. One battalion led by Moreau de Fiennes, the future marshal of France, also contained Geoffrey de Charnay. Near Poitiers, Edward,* the Black Prince, drew up his forces, and was opposed by a larger force under King John. Confident of victory, the French king harkened to an appeal of Cardinal Talleyrand to delay the battle until the following day in order to observe the "Truce of God" and not fight on Sunday. Over strenuous objections, the king agreed. Geoffrey de Charnay proposed that the battle should be settled by 100 champions on each side, but his proposal was rejected by his companions because it would exclude too many from combat, glory and ransoms. Prince Edward, however, used the time to improve his position in the woods and hillside. At the battle the next morning, King John ordered his knights to dismount and fight on foot. They removed their spurs, cut off the long pointed toes from their poulaines,+ and shortened their lances to five feet. Geoffrey carried the Oriflamme. In the eighth hour of the battle, as the English forces of the prince attacked from the front, and the Captal de Buch's (see Jean de Grailly) forces from the rear, the French fought in ferocious despair. Bleeding from multiple wounds, de Charnay was cut down and killed, still holding the Oriflamme; the king's guard surrounding him in a mighty wedge tottered under the assault. And Denis de Morebecque* pressed forward to capture the French king. (*Le Livre de chevalerie,* ed. Arthur Piaget, *Romania*, vol. 26, 1897, pp. 394-411) (Bibliog. 119, 223)

Charroi de Nîmes (Carts to Nîmes), chanson de geste* belonging to the Garin de Monglane cycle written after 1140. Guillaume, returning from a chase, met Bertrand who informed him that King Louis I* had just distributed fiefs among his vassals, but had not awarded any to Guillaume. Furious, Guillaume rode into the palace and reproached the king for such obvious ingratitude, and then summarized all that he had done for him. (See *Couronnement de Louis.*) The king offered to make amends, even extending the offer of one-fourth of the lands of France, but the earlier insult was too great, and Guillaume refused to be appeased. Bertrand finally calmed Guillaume, and suggested that as fiefs he ask for the kingdom of Spain and the cities of Nîmes and Orange. Louis granted the request, but reminded Guillaume that those fiefs first had to be captured from the Saracens. Thirty thousand men flocked to Guillaume's standard to undertake that conquest. They began with Nîmes, a principal stop of the pilgrimage route, "via Tolosana."+ Guillaume hid the men in wine casks and had them taken into Nîmes in carts, and captured the city. (ed. Jean Frappier, Paris: *SEDES,* 1965) (Bibliog. 106)

Chartres, city in north-central France, famous for its 11th-13th century cathedral, noted for its sculptures and stained glass and as a center of learning. In the 9th century it became the seat of a county which the counts of Blois annexed to their estates in the following century. During the episcopate of Bishop Fulbert its cathedral school became a center for learning which was eclipsed by the University of Paris only in the second half of the 12th century. St. Bernard (see Bernard of Clairvaux) preached the fourth crusade+ in the cathedral in 1146. It was reunited with the French crown in 1346. (Bibliog. 98, 100)

Chastelaine de Vergi, French romance+ from the second half of the 13th century dealing with courtly love. The duchess of Burgundy* loved a knight, but was rebuffed by him. Seeking revenge for that insult, she told her husband that the knight had been a traitor because he pursued her and sought her love. When the angry duke+ confronted him with this accusation, the knight did not betray the duchess, but explained that he could not woo the duchess, for he loved another. The duke verified that the knight indeed loved the Lady of Vergy, the duke's niece. However, true to the courtly love tradition, the lady had told the knight that their happiness depended upon absolute secrecy so when vengefully the duchess made a public announcement of the affair, the lady died and the knight killed himself. The duke thereupon killed the vicious gossiping wife, and became a Templar. Historically, the Lady of Vergy was Laure de Lorraine who married Guillaume de Vergy between 1258 and 1267; her uncle, the duke of Burgundy, was Hugh IV and his duchess was Beatrice of Champagne; the endings in death were fictitious. As Guillaume de Vergy died in 1271, this tale probably was written after that date. A Middle English* version of this story, *The Knyght of Curtsey and the Fair Lady of Faguell,* was written in the late 14th century. (ed. R.E.V. Stuip, The Hague, 1971; tr. and ed. Alice Kemp-Welch, London, 1903; repr. 1909) (Bibliog. 47)

Chastelfort, Castelfort, castle+ home on the Rhone River of Ogier the Dane in the *chansons de geste*; he used its name for his battle cry. (Bibliog. 18)

Chateau de Louvre, small castle+ on the outwork of the system which French King Philip II,* Augustus, began in 1190 as a part of the general scheme of refortification of Paris. King Charles V* diminished the military significance of the castle by building an outer line of fortification beyond it and turning the buildings into more of a palatial residence than a fortress. The first building was square with towers at each corner; at the center of the south and east facades were towers guarding entrances. Siege towers marked the center of the other two facades, providing covering fire for the entire wall. Apartments were included in the south and east walls, but the north and west courtyards were bounded by a curtain wall. Inside the courtyard stood the Grosse Tour, a huge cylinder of stone some 18 1/2 meters in diameter, and standing in its own moat. This was the standard form of defense for a number of chateaux of which Coucy-la-Chateau in Picardy* in 1230 was considered the most important. Charles V enlarged the encircling wall, including a portion called the Bastille. That building relieved the Louvre of one of its chief functions—a prison for persons of distinction and a grim fortress. The remainder of the Louvre became a home for royal leisure. (Bibliog. 62)

Chateau du Milieu, one of the three castles+ which comprised Chinon.* (Bibliog. 30)

Chateau du Courdray, one of the three castles+ which comprised Chinon.* (Bibliog. 30)

Chateau Gailiard, King Richard I's "Saucy Castle," as he called it. Built in Normandy* by him in two years, 1196-1198, on a promontory 300 feet above the River Seine with a deep valley on either side, it was captured from King John in 1204 by King Philip II,* Augustus, of France. See Chateau Gailiard in volume I. (Bibliog. 92, 163)

Chateaudun, 12th century French castle+ overlooking the Loire 30 miles northwest of Orléans; it was dominated by the 148 foot high cylindrical keep dating from the time of Philip II,* Augustus (1180-1223). (Bibliog. 30)

Chatelain de Coucy, French romance* of adventure from the late 12th century, written either by Jakamon Sakesup or Jacques Bretiaus. It was the tale of the eaten-heart legend. Its protagonist was Gui, count de Couci (1186-1203). It related the story of the murder of a wife's lover by the jealous husband, and the serving of his heart as a supper dish for the wife. (See Konrad von Wurzburg, *Das Herzmaere,* ed. Crapelet, Paris, 1829) (Bibliog. 106, 127)

Chepstow, Welsh castle, also known as Striguil, built by an independent marcher* lord, William FitzOsbern.* After it was lost to the crown through the rebellion in 1075 of his son, Roger of Breteuil, it was granted to the family of Clare.* It remained in the Clare family after the marriage of the daughter of Richard, earl of Pembroke* into the Marshal+ family, and not until the death of Roger Bigod,* earl of Norfolk, did it revert to the king. (Bibliog. 30, 62)

Cheshire, custom of. Execution by beheading. William the Conqueror introduced this practice into England in 1066, and used it first to punish Waltheof, earl of Northumberland.* This ancient right was granted to the earls of Chester who allowed their sergeants or baliffs to behead any malefactor or thief. It was attached to the barony of Malpas. Later, in a roll of King Edward I* dated 1275, this method of execution was called the "custom of Cheshire." (Bibliog. 68)

Chester, principal city of Cheshire County, England, on the River Dee. There King Edgar once was rowed by seven petty kings of the Scots and Britons to the great joy of his people. Its first earl was said to have been Gherbod, a Fleming from the Abbey of St. Bertin who, early in 1070 in the dismemberment of Mercia soon after the Norman invasion in 1066, was granted a large portion of Mercia together with the city of Chester being formed into a county palatine+ under the name of Cheshire whereby he became the earl of Chester. William's object in creating that earldom was to create a powerful border stronghold in northwest England against the Welsh, and to some extent against the Scots. As a result, the earl of the area was granted palatine rights. He returned shortly afterwards to his native Flanders where he was captured and imprisoned after the battle of Cassel, 1071, and never returned to England. Shortly thereafter, within five years of the conquest, William the Conqueror bestowed this earldom on his nephew, one of his companions in arms on the invasion, Hugh d'Avranches, "le Gros" (or "Lupus" for his voracity), to be held "as securely by his sword as the king held England by his crown." Its castle was founded by William the Conqueror himself. This first earl died in 1101, and was succeeded by his son, Richard, age 7, who was brought up at the court of the king. Earl Richard married Maud, daughter of Stephen, count of Blois, by Adele, daughter of the Conqueror; he died in the White Ship* disaster in 1120. Richard's male heir was his cousin, Ranulph de Meschin, vicomte de Bayeux, son of Margaret, only sister of Hugh d'Avranches, the first earl. His son, Ranulph II, fought on both sides in the wars between King Stephen and the Empress Matilda with easy impartiality because of his own self-interest. Those fluid times afforded Ranulph excellent opportunity to consolidate his palatine holdings almost to the state of independence. During 1141, he married Maud, daughter of Robert, earl of Gloucester,* and died in 1153, supposedly poisoned by his wife, leaving an heir, Hugh, "of Kevelioc," aged 7, who became a ward of the crown. Later he joined young Henry* in his rebellion against his father, King Henry II,* was captured, but pardoned and released; later rebelled, but again was pardoned and had his lands restored to him. He died in 1181. His son, Ranulph de Blundeville, married while still under age in 1188, Constance, widow of Geoffrey,* earl of Richmond and duke of Brittany, and in her right occasionally styled himself with both of those titles, but divorced her in 1199. He bore the "Curtana,"+ one of the ceremonial swords at Richard I's* coronation, and continued his faithful allegiance to King John* by signing the *Magna Carta Libertatum+* as one of the few witnesses to in support of the king. John trusted him completely and made him sheriff of three counties—Lancaster, Stafford, and Shropshire—and steward of the house of Lancaster.   On John's death, the earl joined William Marshal in attacking the dauphin,* Prince Louis (VIII) of France, who had been persuaded by the rebellious barons to invade England to become its king. Leading the forces at Lincoln,* Ranulph was one of the main factors that secured the throne for the young King Henry III,* for which he was created earl of Lincoln in 1217. The earldom passed to his nephew, John le Scot, son of David, earl of Huntingdon,* and nephew of William the Lion,* king of Scotland. He died shortly after taking the cross in 1237, suspected of having been poisoned by his wife, the daughter of the Prince of North Wales. On his death, the earldom was annexed to the crown, and after the death of the last earl, the castle became a permanent royal castle.   In 1254, it was given to the Lord Edward* on the condition that it should never be alienated+ from the crown, but then after being captured at the battle of Lewes,* King Henry III bestowed it upon Simon de Montfort,* earl of Leicester, "having no other means to make his peace but by delivering the said earldom of Chester into Earl Simon's hands." Eight months after Earl Simon's death at the battle of Evesham* a year later, the earldom once again reverted to Prince Edward whose honours merged with the crown when he became king. As king, Edward bestowed it on his eldest son, Edward "of Carnarvon,"* at the same ceremony which designated him as Prince of Wales* in 1301. It remained as an honour of the later Princes of Wales: Edward,* the Black Prince, and Richard, "of Bordeaux," later Richard II.* (Bibliog. 47, 62, 66, 101)

Chetifs, Les (The Captives), crusader poem written by Graindor de Douai* between 1180 and 1200. It told how five knights, captured after the defeat of Peter the Hermit at Nicaea, were taken to the pagan city of Oliferne where they were put to work building. Corbarant of

Oliferne wanted to explain the fall of Antioch by showing that the Franks were superior to the Persians. One of the knights, Richard of Caumont, defeated the pagans Golias and Sorgales. As a result, the Christians were freed and made their way to Jerusalem. Another of the captives, Baldwin of Beauvais, fought and killed a giant serpent which had eaten Baldwin's brother. (ed. C. Hippeau, *Chanson du Chevalier au Cygne*, II, Appendix, Paris, 1877) (Bibliog. 106)

Chevalier à l'épée, composite Old French romance about Gawain.* Having lost his way through the forest, Gawain struck up an acquaintance with a mysterious knight who offered hospitality in his castle. There the host turned his daughter over to Gawain believing that as the two lay together at night, the sword which hitherto had protected her chastity would make an end to the hero. When Gawain was in her bed and was about to avail himself of her, she warned him about an enchanted sword suspended over the bed. He disregarded the warning, proceeded with his love-making, and was wounded twice slightly by the sword. At dawn, however, when her father saw that Gawain had passed the ordeal, he recognized him as the finest of all knights, and worthy of his daughter's hand. As Gawain and the girl set out for Arthur's court, the girl abandoned him for another knight, but he was killed by Gawain in a fight over the girl's dogs who were more steadfast that she in their attachment. Leaving the faithless wench to her fate, Gawain returned to his uncle Arthur's* court. (ed. E. C. Armstrong, Baltimore, 1900) (Bibliog. 113)

Chevalier Assigne, Middle English* metrical romance+ from the second half of the 14th century. In this English version of the French cycle of the *Chevalier au Cygne** (the Knight of the Swan, which was attached to Godfrey de Bouillon*), King Orviens of Lyon lamented that he had no children, but shortly thereafter his wife conceived and bore six sons and a daughter in a single birth, each child wearing a silver chain about its neck. Treachery by the king's mother brought hardships to the queen and the infants, for if the chain was removed from any child's neck, it would turn into a swan. Eventually all were restored to normal life except for one son who remained a swan for its entire lifetime. (ed. H. H. Gibbs, London: *EETS, OS* 1868; rep. 1973) (Bibliog. 202)

Chevalier au Cygne, cycle of French poetic romances+ developed in France in the latter half of the 12th century and attached to Godfrey de Bouillon,* hero of the first crusade.+ This cycle had five main parts: *Chanson d'Antioche,* *Chanson de Jerusalem,* *Les Chetifs,*

Helias, Les enfances Godefroi de Bouillon. (Bibliog. 202)

Chevalier au Cygne et Enfances Godefroi, 13th-century poem by a jongleur named Renaut; this story also went by the name *Beatrix.* In it, the swan knight was pulled in a boat by his swan brother. He arrived at Bouillon* in time to champion the duchess of Bouillon in a fight with Renier, the duke of Saxony. He won the fight and married Beatrice, the daughter of the duchess, but cautioned them never to question him about his origins. For seven years, they lived happily, but when the women succumbed to curiosity and asked, the swan knight climbed into his swan boat, and disappeared forever. Then seven years later, his daughter Ida, married Eustace of Boulogne by whom she had three sons: Godfrey, Eustace, and Baldwin. Historically, Godfrey was the second son of Eustace of Boulogne and of Ida, sister of Godfrey of Brabant. He was reared by his uncle and fell heir to his possessions, including the castle of Bouillon; his brothers, Eustace of Boulogne and Baudoiun, accompanied him on the first crusade+ in 1096. At the end of his *Parzival,** Wolfram von Eschenbach provided a short tale about Loherangrin (from the name Loherenc Garin) which connected the swan knight with the Grail* legend; the German epic *Lohengrin** (1276-1290) was based on Wolfram's story. (ed. C. Hippeau, Paris, 1874-1877 [contained both epics]; crit. ed. Gisela Pukatzki, DAI 32:2702A-03A, Alabama, 1971) (Bibliog. 106)

Chevalier au Dragon. See Ardant.

Chevalier aux Deux Epées (or ***Meriadeuc*)**, medieval French Arthurian verse romance+ from the first half of the 13th century. As the hero's name, Meriadeuc, was not revealed until the end of the romance, he was called the "Chevalier aux Deux Epées" (Knight with Two Swords) because he won a second sword at Arthur's* court by being the only one who could unfasten the sword worn by Lore, Lady of Garadigan, about her waist. After that, he disappeared, and Lore declared that she would have no other knight but him. Arthur sent Gawain* in search of this nameless knight, and he was attached treacherously by Brien des Illes, left for dead, recovered, survived other attempts on his life, championed a lovely damsel, fought incognito with Meriadeuc, and overcame Brien. After Gawain delivered Meriadeuc's mother from a siege, she pardoned him for killing her husband, and reconciled him with Meriadeuc. Earlier, Brien de la Gastine had obtained Gawain's services in his war with Bleheri, Meriadeuc's father, and Gawain unwittingly had slain him. Before he died, however, Bleheri explained that his son must avenge his death; and this Meriadeuc accomplished. After his reconciliation with Gawain, he returned to Arthur's court and married Lore. (ed. W. Foerster, Halle, 1877) (Bibliog. 10)

Chevalier de la Charette. See *Lancelot.*

Chevalier du Lion. See *Yvain.*

Chevalier du Papegau, French prose romance+ in which King Arthur* appeared as the hero. It was embellished with elements from the romances of Chrétien de Troyes,* and from the Middle High German* romance *Wigalois* by Wirnt von Grafenberg written about 1204, and the Italian *Carduino* (c. 1375). It also showed some connections with *Beaus Desconus,* the story of Gawain's son, Guinglain. (ed. F. Heuckenkamp, Halle, 1897) (Bibliog. 231)

Chevalerie Vivien, chanson de geste* of the Garin de Monglane* cycle composed between 1150 and 1170. It gave another version of the *Chanson de Guillaume.** This work began with Guillaume knighting his nephew Vivien, who left immediately with 10,000 men for Spain and spent the next four years capturing Barcelona, Balaguet, Tortosa, and other cities. At Portpaillart, he and his men horribly mutilated some Saracen* forces under King Deramed of Cordoba. Seeking revenge, the Saracens met Vivien at Aliscans. After a bloody battle, the wounded Vivien withdrew into a deserted castle from which he summoned the aid of his uncle, Guillaume, who raced to his side with all due speed. Before help could arrive, however, Vivien once more resumed the battle. Guillaume arrived to give him much needed support, but by then Vivien had been wounded again so severely that he did not recognize his uncle, and fought with him. When recognition finally occurred, Guillaume placed Vivien on his horse once again, and he rode back into battle to meet his death. See *Aliscans.* (ed. J. Frappier, *Le Chansons de Geste du Cycle de Guillaume d'Orange,* Paris: *SEDES,* 1955, I) (Bibliog. 106)

Chevalier Ogier de Danemarche, chanson de geste* of the Döon de Mayence* cycle. Although an epic dealing with Ogier the Dane already existed as early as 1160, the surviving *chanson de geste* detailing the rebellion of Ogier dated from 1190 to 1200, and incorporated the earlier epic, *Ogier,* and other stories. In this work, Ogier, a companion of Charlemagne,* frequently was mentioned as "li Danois" (the Dane), being a native of Denmark, but presumably his name was a corruption of "l'Ardenois" ("from the Ardennes"). In this story, Gaufrei, duke of Denmark, grossly insulted four of Charlemagne's messengers, and Charles swore vengeance which he easily could obtain because Gaufrei's son, Ogier, was hostage at Charles' court. Despite the pleas of his barons not to do so, Charles vowed to execute the young Dane, but before he could have his order carried out, he received word that Saracens had invaded southern Italy, and were about to attack Rome. Postponing his execution of Ogier, Charles hastened to Italy and took Ogier with him. Before he left, however, Ogier begot a son, Baudouinet. In Rome, Ogier distinguished himself by slaying the Saracen champion, Brunamor de Misor, freeing the city, and winning both his own knighthood and a pardon from Charles. By the time they returned to France, Ogier's son had grown to become a squire. One day, in a chess game Baudouinet was killed by Charlot, Charles' son, and Ogier demanded Charlot's life as atonement. When Charles refused that demand, Ogier left for the court of Desier, king of the Lombards, swearing unending war until he could capture and kill Charlot with his own hands. He finally found refuge at his own castle, Chastelfort,* where later he was captured by Archbishop Turpin* who found him asleep one day. Charles, refusing to pardon him a second time, ordered Turpin to jail and starve him. The Saracens, hearing false rumors about Ogier's death, invaded France as far as Laon. Ogier was released to drive them out, and despite being pardoned, refused to relent in his demand for Charlot's life. Charles sadly had to agree, and as Ogier was bringing down the sword blade in the death blow, an angel stayed his hand, and Charlot received only a slight nick to satisfy Ogier's sworn oath of vengeance. (ed. M. Eusebi, Milan, 1963) Historically, in 772, after the death of Carloman, joint ruler with Charlemagne, Carloman's widow and sons fled to Desier, king of Lombardy, under the protection of Count Ogier, but Charlemagne ultimately captured them. (Bibliog. 106)

Chevalier Vermeil, knight in red armor from the Forest of Quinqueroi, who, in Arthurian legend, insolently stole a cup from King Arthur,* and was killed with a javelin by Perceval who thereupon took his arms and armor for his own. (in *Perceval)* (Bibliog. 242)

chevauchée, raid technique by which Edward III devastated the French countryside in 1339. Its goal was to wreak as much devastation on both town and country as possible to weaken the enemy government by terrorizing the population. Its first stage consisted of obtaining food and drink for the army as it went on its way. Some food had been brought along, but most had to be obtained from the land if the army was to survive. Its second stage was the destructive process and plunder. On King Edward's march, his men looted and then put to the torch every town, every little hamlet, every house. Neither churches nor abbeys were spared, and hundreds of civilians — men, women, children, priests, bourgeois, peasants — were killed while thousands fled starving to the fortified towns. The English king saw these tactics as a way of making the French sick of war, and thus eager to capitulate. Although it may have terrified many, it did not bring the French to their knees. (Bibliog. 203, 224)

Chichester castle, built in the reign of William I* by Roger Montgomery (see Bellême-Montgomery), this castle+ in Sussex passed into the hands of the d'Aubigny* family in the 12th century and thence to the crown with the death of William d'Aubigny in 1176. Fearing it might fall into the hands of the French in 1216, King John ordered its destruction. This order was not carried out before John's death, and the castle fell into the hands of the French in 1217, and when it was recovered shortly thereafter, Philip d'Aubigny ordered it completely destroyed. (Bibliog. 62)

chief justiciar of England, duties of, most important lay position in the kingdom, the chief justiciar was the chief administrative and legal officer in the kingdom when the king was in England, and in the king's absence his representative who ruled in his name, subject always to the king's direction.   Hubert Walter* was one of the greatest justiciars. He governed England capably and efficiently, and contributed markedly to the governmental machinery which functioned smoothly and enabled administrative justice to succeed whether the king was there or not. He not only preserved the peace, and maintained law and order, but he also collected money and services from the king's subjects on an unprecedented scale without arousing the country to rebellion, for he was careful to adhere to customary and recognized forms of taxation, even though he pushed them to greater limits than hitherto seen. He realized the limitations of his power and his office. He differed markedly from the chancellor William Longchamps,* who sent out orders in his own name, under his own seal, and attempted to rule on his own authority. (Bibliog. 7)

Chievrefueil, La ("Honeysuckle"), *lai** by Marie de France* of 118 verses involving the Tristan* legend. When Tristan returned to Cornwall,* from exile in South Wales, he carved his name on a hazel rod to tell the queen of his presence, and left it in the road where she had to pass. She saw the rod, stopped her group on the pretext of resting, and left them to meet her lover. Though soon parted from the queen, Tristan composed a lay to remember the joy he had at the meeting, and to preserve the words she had him write. As he could not live without the queen, their affair was like the honeysuckle and the hazel tree: when the vine had encircled the tree, they endure together, but when separated they die. The queen's words provided the essence of the whole Tristan legend: *"Bel amie, si est de nus: ne vus sanz mei, ne mei sanz vus."** ("Dearest friend, this is how we must be: never you without me, never me without you.") (ed. E. Mason, *Lays of Marie de France*, New York: E. P. Dutton, 1966) (Bibliog. 147)

Chillon, castle+ on an island in Lake Geneva. Its earliest portions, the Tower of Alinge and the Duke's Tower, were built in the 10th and 11th centuries; they were modified and enlarged for Peter II of Savoy* by the architect Pierre Mainier who added mural towers+ on the vulnerable land side. (Bibliog. 30)

Chinon, huge mass of three stone castles+ in a row overlooking the town of Chinon and valley of the Vienne. Each of these three castles, Chateau du Courdray, Chateau du Milieu, and Fort St-Georges, was separated from its neighbor by a moat. Originally a Roman fortification, it was rebuilt by count Thibaud III de Blois* who ceded it to the count of Anjou,* Geoffrey Martel, in 1044. On the death of Geoffrey (Plantagenet)* of Anjou in 1151, Chinon was given to his second son, Geoffrey V of Anjou. His son, Henry II* of England, strengthened them and added Fort St-Georges; he died there in 1189, as did his son, Richard I,* ten years later. After Philip II,* Augustus, of France captured it in 1205, and reunited it with the French dominions, he strengthened it as did his grandson, Louis IX,* and his great-grandson, Philip III.* During the first half of the 15th century, it became the capital of France and the king, Charles VII, lived there. Its tower of Coudray contained a dungeon 25 meters high that held two vaulted rooms which served as a prison for the leaders of the Order of the Knights Templar,* who inscribed curious grafiti on the wall. One, signed by Jacques de Molay, grand master of the Order, showed a deer pursued by a hound. Their persecution and trial, convened on the orders of King Philip IV* and Pope Clement V, was conducted at Chinon under the direction of its governor Jean de Jeanvilles and three cardinal legates from the pope. The Templars were condemned to be burned alive as heretics, and were so executed at Paris in 1313. (Bibliog. 30, 196)

Chrétien de Troyes, 12th century French author who began to write when the literature of northern France had begun to correspond to the change in sentiment of the nobility,+ to exaltation of the lady, and to the refinement of manners known as "courtoisie," more commonly known as "Courtly Love." He was the author of the earliest extant and best Arthurian romances.* He listed his writings at the beginning of his *Cligés*.* His *Lancelot*,* or *Chevalier de la Charette*, was composed for the daughter of King Louis VII* and Eleanor of Aquitaine,* Marie,* who in 1164 married Henry, count of Champagne.* In the Prologue of his *Perceval** or *Conte du Graal*, Chrétien dedicated the work to Philippe of Alsace,* who became count of Flanders, and who embarked on the third crusade+ in 1190. Besides these three works, Chrétien wrote *Erec et Enide*,* *Yvain** or *Le Chevalier au Lion*, and he was reputed to have written *Guillaume d'Angleterre*.* (Bibliog. 44)

Christine de Pisan (1363-1431), poet and historian. Born of Italian stock in Venice, she was thought of mainly as French because of her work in French. Her father was astrologer at the court of Charles V* in Paris. She was educated at the king's court, and at the age of 15 married Charles' notary and secretary, Etienne du Castel. When both her father and her husband died shortly after the king's death, she found herself at age 25 without a protector and with three young children to provide for. She realized that she enjoyed writing, and thus she began to earn her livelihood with her pen. Between 1399 and 1405, she acknowledged that she wrote some fifteen major pieces, among them *Le Livre des faites et bonnes moeurs de roi Charles V*, which detailed the king's courage, chivalry,+ and wisdom. In addition, she was an accomplished poet, writing over 100 ballades dealing with her own early love, and a large number of religious poems. She was most famous for *Le Livre des Faits d'Armes et de Chevalerie* in which she gave, among other items, the five causes for war+: three were "lawful—for justice, against oppression, against usurpation; the other two were "unlawful—for revenge, and for aggression. (tr. and ed. William Caxton, London: *EETS OS* #189, 1932; repr. New York: Kraus Reprint, 1971) (Bibliog. 45)

Chronicon de Lanercost, work dealing with the general history of England and Scotland, 1201-1346, but generally favoring the English, (tr. Sir H. Maxwell, Glasgow, 1908-1913) (Bibliog. 99)

Chroniques de Saint-Denis. See *Grand Chroniques de France.*

Chronique de Turpin, work from the middle of the 12th century, supposedly written by Turpin,* the archbishop who took part in the battle at Rencesvcals.* Also known as the *Historia Caroli Magni et Rotholandi*, it related the entire story of Charlemagne's* Spanish expedition, but abridged and rearranged it. Over 300 different manuscripts survived to attest to its widespread popularity. (ed. André de Mandach, *Naissance et Développment de la Chanson de geste en Europe*, II, Geneva: Droz, 1963) (Bibliog. 231)

Chronique des quatre premiers Valois, chronicle written by a Norman clerk who supported the popular French side of the Hundred Years War,* this work was original only for the wars of Normandy* after 1350. (ed. S. Luce, *Société de l'histoire de France*, Paris, 1862, repr. 1965) (Bibliog. 99)

Chronique du religieux de S. Denys, written by a secretary to Charles VI, who was contemporary to the events he recounted, especially the revolt of 1381, this work was invaluable for the relations between England and France, 1380-1422. (ed. L. Bellaguet, *Documents inédits,* 6 vols., Paris, 1839-1852) (Bibliog. 99)

Chronique Normande du XIVe Siècle, written in French by a noble Norman after 1372, this chronicle provided valuable material for the history of the Anglo-French wars of the 14th century, especially between 1337 and 1372. (ed. A. and E. Molinier, *Sociéte de l'Histoire de France,* Paris, 1882) (Bibliog. 99)

Cid, Cantar de Mio, Spanish epic written about forty years after the death of the Campeador,* el Cid. It was written in 1140, the date of the betrothal of Dona Blanca of Navarre, the great-granddaughter of the Cid, to Sancho the Well-Beloved, which caused the minstrel to exclaim joyously in the poem that his hero had become related to royalty through this marriage: "today the kings of Spain are his relatives." It was a realistic work; almost everything in it was historically verifiable: characters, events, landscapes. It related how Roderigo (Ruy) Diaz de Vivar, a nobleman in the retinue of two brother kings, Sancho II of Castile and Alfonso VI of León, took part in the fratricidal wars of the ambitious Sancho. After Sancho's death at the hands of a traitor, however, Roderigo recognized Alfonso as rightful sovereign when he ascended the throne of Castile, but for reasons not clearly known, he was exiled by that king. He left Castile to enter the service of the king of Saragossa, and defeated this king's enemy, the king of Lerida, earning for himself the title of Cid [from the Arabic *sidi,* meaning lord]; he died in 1099. (tr. J. Gerald Markley, Indianapolis, IN: Bobbs-Merrill, 1961) (Bibliog. 65)

Cinque Ports, confederation of five seaports on the southeastern coast of England that had jurisdiction along the coast continuously from Seaford in Sussex to Birchington near Margate. Established in 1051, this was recognized as such by King Edward the Confessor* (1042-1066) when he granted to the men of these ports the profits of their courts of justice with the provision that in return they would supply the necessary ships and seamen for the royal fleet. William I* continued the confederation, as did all subsequent kings up to Henry II* who recognized their leader as a baron+ of the kingdom. Their barons were among those recognized by King John in the *Magna Carta Libertatum+;* during the Hundred Years War,* their fleet assured naval supremacy. In order of precedence, the five "ports" were Hastings, Sandwich, Dover, Romney, and Hithe, to which later were added the towns of Rye and Winchelsea. (Bibliog. 98)

Ciperis de Vigneaux, French epic about the Merovingian Era; Ciperis was Childeric II. (ed. William S. Woods, Chapel Hill, NC: Studies in Romance Languages and Literature, 7, 1949) (Bibliog. 106)

Cisjuran. See Burgundy.

Clare, Clarence, ancient English town on the border of Essex that gave its name to the noble family of Clare who in their times were earls of Hertford,* and Gloucester.* The ancestor of this historic English family was Count Godfrey, eldest of the illegitimate sons of Richard, duke of Normandy.* His son, Count Gilbert of Brionne, had two sons, Richard FitzGilbert, lord of Bienfaite and Orbec, and Baldwin, lord of Le Sap and Meulles, both of whom accompanied William I* to England in 1066. Baldwin received the shrievalty of Devon and great estates in the west country, and left three sons, William, Robert and Richard. This Richard, known as "de Bienfaite," or "of Tunbridge," or "of Clare," was the founder of the house of Clare (d. 1090). He derived his name from strongholds at Tunbridge and at Clare, on the border of Sussex and Essex. He served as joint justiciar+ in the absence abroad of King William, and took a leading role in suppressing the rebellion of 1075, for which he was rewarded by no fewer than 176 lordships of which 95 were in Suffolk attached to the honour+ of Clare. By his wife Rohese, he had five sons and two daughters. Roger was his heir in Normandy, Walter founded Tintern Abbey, Richard was a monk, and Robert, receiving the forfeited fiefs of the Baynards in the eastern counties of England, founded through his son, Walter, the house of FitzWalter, of whom the most famous was Robert FitzWalter, leader of the barons against King John.* Gilbert, the first earl, Richard de Bienfaite's heir in England, held his castle at Tunbridge against

William II* (1087-1100), but was wounded and captured. Under Henry I* (1100-1135), by whom he was favored, he obtained a grant in Cardigan. He died in 1115, leaving four sons. Gilbert II inherited Chepstow,* with Nether-Gwent* from his uncle Walter, the founder of Tintern Abbey, and was created earl of Pembroke by King Stephen* about 1138; he was the father of Richard Strongbow,* earl of Pembroke. The eldest son Richard was killed by the Welsh on his way to Cardigan in 1136, and left two sons, Gilbert and Roger. Gilbert was created earl of Hertford by King Stephen. Probably because they had no interest in Hertfordshire the family came to be styled as the earls of (de) Clare. Dying in 1152, Gilbert was succeeded by his brother, Roger, who constantly fought the Welsh for his possessions in Wales, and disputed his castle+ of Tunbridge with Thomas à Becket.*

He was succeeded by his son Richard as third earl, whose marriage to Amicia, daughter and co-heir of William, earl of Gloucester,+ brought him in 1218 the title of earl of Gloucester. He and his son Gilbert were among the signers of the *Magna Carta Libertatum*. His son, Gilbert, seventh earl of Clare, earl of Gloucester and Hertford, (d. 1230) married Isabel Marshal, the daughter of William Marshal,* earl of Pembroke.* Their son, Richard of Clare, earl of Gloucester and Hertford, (d. 1262) married 1) Margaret de Burgh, daughter of Hubert de Burgh*; 2) Maud de Lacy, daughter of John de Lacy, earl of Lincoln. Their son, Gilbert the Red, (1243-1295) ninth earl of Clare, eighth earl of Gloucester and seventh earl of Hertford, best known as the earl of Gloucester, married 1) Alice de Lusignan, daughter of Comte de La Marche; 2) in 1290, Joan of Acre (b. 1292), daughter of King Edward I. They had three children: the last earl, Gilbert de Clare, earl of Gloucester and Hertford, who died in 1314 without male issue at the battle of Bannock Burn,* when only twenty-three, rushing on the enemy "like a wild boar, making his sword drunk with their blood." They had a daughter, Eleanor, who married Hugh le Despenser the Younger* who was hanged in 1326; and a daughter, Margaret, who married Piers Gaveston* who also was hanged (1312). When these Clares bore no male children, Lionel, third son of King Edward III was made duke of Clarence, indicating the same place name. He had married the sole daughter and heir of William De Burg, earl of Ulster in Ireland whose mother was one of the sisters and co-heirs of Gilbert de Clare (d. 1295), the last earl of Clare and Gloucester of that name. (Bibliog. 47, 68, 79, 101)

Claris et Laris, long French verse Arthurian romance begun in 1268 by a minstrel of Lorraine. It concerned the fortunes of two friends and was divided into two parts. The first part centered on the love of

Claris for the wife of the aged king of Gascony, and led to their marriage after the king's death. In the course of the story, Claris confided his passion to his friend Laris who promised aid, but before he could do anything to help, Laris was carried off and imprisoned by a fée, Madoine. Claris and eleven other knights searched long before finding him. The second part of the story centered on the affair of Laris with Marine, sister of Yvain.* Her father, King Urien, was besieged by King Tallas of Denmark who wanted to carry off Marine by force. Urien sought Arthur's* help. Claris and Laris along with Gauvain and Yvain responded and defeated Tallas. Laris was taken prisoner and a large number of quests were undertaken to find him. Thirty knights divided into groups of ten set out, and with the help of Merlin,* Laris was located and rescued, and married Marine. The author used many "entrelacements"* in this story. (ed. J. Alton, Tubingen, 1884) (Bibliog. 10)

Claudas, king of "terre deserte" in Gaul, and enemy of Bors and Ban by whom, with King Arthur's* help, he was defeated in *Arthur and Merlin.** (Bibliog. 100, 202)

Clement's Inn. See Inns of Court.

Cleomadas, heathen knight in Arthurian* legend who had his hand severed in combat, but when it was restored miraculously by Joseph of Arimathia, he became a Christian. See *Joseph of Aramathia.* (Bibliog. 202)

Cléomadès, French romance of adventure written between 1274 and 1282 by Adenet-le-roi.* In it, suitors for the hand of the daughter of the king of Spain presented him with marvellous gifts. One of the suitors, the hateful magician Crompart, offered him a wooden horse that could fly. The king's son, Cléomadès, eagerly tried it out before learning all its secrets, so he was transported to Tuscany before he learned how to bring it to earth. There he saw and wooed the beautiful Clarmondine, and took her back to Spain. Crompart, however, stole her as revenge for his bad treatment. Cléomadès sought the world over before finding her, and returning to Spain where they married. (ed. A. Henry, *Oeuvres de Adenet le roi,* V, Bruxelles, rep. 1971) (Bibliog. 106)

Clifford, Robert de (1274-1314), English knight who served as hereditary sheriff of Westmoreland, as justice in eyre+ North of Trent from 1297-1307, and captain general of the Marches* of Scotland in

1299. He was made Lord Clifford after being summoned to Parliament in 1313. King Edward I* granted him manors in Yorkshire, and Edward II* made him marshal+ of England, and justice South of Trent in 1307, and warden of the Scottish Marches in 1308. He died at the battle of Bannock Burn* in 1314. His son and heir, Roger, Lord Clifford (1259-1322), sheriff of Westmoreland, joined with the rebellious barons led by Thomas of Lancaster.* He was defeated and captured with them at the battle of Boroughbridge* in 1322, and executed for his role in that rebellion. His grandson, Roger, (1333-1389), also sheriff of Westmoreland, served in the wars in Scotland and France with great distinction. By 1377 he had become the sheriff of Cumberland, the governor of Carlisle castle,* had been made a knight banneret,+ and appointed warden of the East and West Marches. He gave evidence in the famous Scrope-Grovesnor* controversy. His son, Thomas (1363-1391), tenth lord Clifford and sixth baron of Westmoreland, served as a knight in King Richard II's* chamber in June 1286. A man enamored of chivalry, Thomas issued a challenge in 1386 to Sir Bursigande, eldest son of the Sire de Bursigande in France, and crossed to France for this chivalrous combat in a tournament which he won in 1387. His license from the king allowed him, "our very dear and loyal knight...to perform all manner of feats of arms." After succeeding to his father's estate, he and 2 other English knights challenged 3 French knights to a tourney in the marches between Bologne and Calais. In 1390, he procured a safe conduct+ through England for William de Douglas who was journeying to the English court with 40 knights to a wager of battle+ with Clifford over certain disputed lands. His chivalric disposition endeared him to the youthful Richard II, but it provoked the baron's anger which resulted in his banishment from court in 1388. He died fighting "infidels" in Germany with Thomas of Gloucester in 1391. (Bibliog. 47, 58)

Clifford, Roger de (d. 1285), English soldier and judge. He accompanied King Henry III* to France in 1259 when the peace treaty was signed with French King Louis IX.* Three years later his loyalty was questioned by a letter to King Henry III which he sent as representative of the marcher barons, urging the king to observe the Provisions of Oxford.* As a result, he was forbidden to joust, to appear in arms, or to participate in any knightly activity without a royal license. In 1263, he joined Simon de Montfort,* ravaged the Welsh marches with Roger de Leyburne,* and took Hereford and Bristol, for which he was excommunicated. In the next year, however, he supported the king by capturing young Simon de Montfort, and was given the shrievalty of and the command of the castle of Gloucester.

Captured at the battle of Lewes,* he was released to appear at the Parliament controlled by Montfort when summoned. Once free, however, he allied himself with Roger de Mortimer,* and raised an army for the king in the west marches. In 1264, he and Leybourne saved Prince Edward* from capture at Hereford. Later after he distinguished himself at the battle at Evesham* in 1265, he was given estates as a reward, and then accompanied Prince Edward on his crusade. In 1282, he was surprised at Hawarden castle by David, brother of Llewelyn, and was wounded and taken prisoner after the garrison there was killed. He died in 1285. (Bibliog. 58)

Clifford's Inn. See Inns of Court.

Cligés, French Arthurian romance by Chrétien de Troyes* written in the middle of the 12th century. Alexander, a Byzantine prince who came to Arthur's* court seeking knighthood, married Gawain's sister, Soredamors, and they had a son, Cligés. Returning to Constantinople on the news of his father's death, Alexander found that his brother Alis, had usurped the throne. Then Alis married Fenice, daughter of the emperor of Germany with whom Cligés had fallen in love. She refused to emulate Isolde and be unfaithful to her lawful spouse, but through a magic potion, she was able to remain virginal because Alis embraced only air when he thought he was embracing her. Cligés went to Arthur's court to earn fame, took part in a four-day tournament in which he proved himself to be a better man than either Lancelot* or Perceval.* He returned to Greece, and professed his love for Fenice. She then was given a potion to simulate death so that they could live together, but their ruse was discovered, and they had to flee to Arthur's court. When the news arrived of Alis' death, they returned to Greece to be married and to rule. (ed. and tr. W. W.Comfort, *Arthurian Romances,* London and New York: E. P. Dutton, 1976) (Bibliog. 44)

Climborin, Saracen from Saragossa who gave his helmet to Ganelon*; he slew Engelier of Gascony at Rencesvals* and then was slain by Oliver* in the *Song of Roland.** (Bibliog. 210)

Clisson, Olivier de, (1336-1407) stalwart Breton knight in the battle of Auray* (Sept. 29, 1364) between mercenaries or "free companies" of Charles of Blois against those of John of Montfort. In this battle in which Sir John Chandos* captured Du Guesclin,* Olivier also displayed his abilities
bravely as he fought for the English. He had been only a boy in 1343

when his father, accused of treason, had been executed by the order of King Philip VI* of France. Suspected to have had dealings with King Edward III,* Clisson's father had been arrested in the middle of a tournament, thrown into prison, and conducted almost naked to his execution without trial. His wife carried his head from Paris to Brittany to display before her son and exact from the boy an oath of vengeance and eternal hatred for France. To avenge his father's "murder," de Clisson ordered in this battle that no prisoners should be taken, and as a result, the French lost about 1,000 dead and 1,500 prisoners. Although his savage conduct on the battlefield led to his being given the name of "the Butcher", he felt avenged. In this same battle, Charles de Blois also was killed, so John de Montfort* became indisputably Duke John IV of Brittany. Olivier had been brought up at the English court along with young John de Montfort, his duke, whose jealousy and dislike he reciprocated. Pursuing his vowed revenge against the French, Clisson fought against them with incredible ferocity at Reims, Cocherel and Najera* in Spain. He wielded a two-handed axe with such force that it was said that no one who ever received one of his blows ever got up again, though he failed to parry an enemy axe that cut through his helmet and cost him an eye. During the war in Brittany, Montfort enraged Clisson even further by favoring Chandos* and rewarding him with a castle and town. In a fury, Clisson assasulted and razed the castle intended for Chandos and used the material to build his own. By 1369, his anger had cooled, however, and then on learning that his squire, wounded and captured by the English, had been killed as a prisoner when he was discovered to belong to Clisson, he sided with the French against his formed friends, the English. Swearing never to give quarter to any Englishman, he attacked an English stronghold with such fury and took it with such slaughter that only fifteen defenders remained alive. Then, after locking them in a tower room, Clisson ordered them released one by one, and as each came through the door, he struck off each man's head with a single blow of his great axe, and thus with fifteen heads rolling at his feet, he avenged his squire. In 1370, he joined Bertrand Du Guesclin who had lately become constable of France, and followed him on his campaigns against the English. On the death of Du Guesclin, he received the constable's sword. In that capacity, he defeated the citizens of Ghent at Roosebek in 1382, he commanded the French army in Poitou and Flanders in 1389, and made an unsuccessful attempt to invade England in 1389. He died in 1407. (Bibliog. 223, 224)

Clisson castle,+ fortress situated near both Anjou and Poitou that maintained a totally Breton association. In the 12th and 13th centuries, its barons settled their claim to the area and built the castle consisting mainly of two strong paired towers. Its most famous baron was Olivier de Clisson.* (Bibliog. 196)

Cnut, Canute, Knut (995-1035), king of England (1016-1035); king of Denmark (1018-1035); king of Norway, (1030-1035). This Norseman completed the Danish conquest of England begun by his father, King Sweyn, and was proclaimed its king in 1016. Two years later he succeeded to the throne of Denmark, and built a powerful empire in the north. In 1028 he annexed Norway. He agreed to commercial treaties with Germany to facilitate English as well as Scandinavian trade with Europe; he became an ally of Normandy, and married Emma, widow of English King Ethelred and sister of Duke Richard of Normandy whose grandson became William the Conqueror. He appointed the Englishman, Godwine,* to be earl of Wessex, and made him his chief lieutenant in all matters pertaining to England. Godwine's son was Harold,* the successor to Edward the Confessor* on the English throne. Cnut began the special church tax called Peter's Pence.+ (Bibliog. 228)

Coarz Chevaliers. See Cowardly Knight.+

Cobham, Reynald, de (1295-1361), English knight who served with distinction in nearly all the battles in Flanders and France between 1327 and 1360. He was made a knight banneret+ in 1339, formed part of an important embassy to the pope in 1348, and served in the same contingent at Crécy in 1346 as the earl of Warwick,* Sir John Chandos,* and the Black Prince.* For his services he was granted an annuity of 500 pounds in 1347. His reputation led him to be selected as a Knight of the Garter* in 1353. He was marshal of the Prince's army at Poitiers* in 1356 where he led the captured French King John II* to the English quarters after the battle. Summoned to Parliament in 1341-2, in 1347, and again in 1360, he was created Lord Cobham, and died of the plague in 1361. (Bibliog. 47)

Cobbie Row's Castle,+ built on the Isle of Wyre in the Orkney Islands, this oldest Scottish stone castle+ was built by a Norse chief Kolbein Hruga about 1145; its name was a corrupted form of that Norse chieftain's name. (Bibliog. 30)

Cochem, German castle+ built on a hill above the Moselle River about 25 miles south-west of Koblenz around 1020. Three hundred years later, it was enlarged by Archbishop Baldwin of Trier, and it became a toll station on the Moselle by means of a chain drawn across to bar the river. (Bibliog. 30)

Cocherel, battle of (May 16, 1364), conflict in Normandy between Charles the Bad* of Navarre and John of Valois. His defeat in this battle eliminated Charles of Navarre as a chronic threat to Paris. It and Auray* (September 29, 1364) were the last battles in France before a period of peace began during the Hundred Years' War.* Cocherel was a battle fought out almost entirely by free companies.* Two-thirds of the French army and five-sixths of the Navarese army were veteran mercenaries. Professional soldiers on both sides remembered well the lessons of Crécy* and Poitiers.* At Cocherel, Du Guesclin* kept a small reserve of thirty horsemen who were ordered to wait until both sides were locked in combat and then dash at the leader, the Captal de Buch,* John de Grailly,* who had struck a decisive blow at Poitiers. As learned under the two Edwards, King Edward III* and Prince Edward,* the Captal took a defensive position on a slope, on which he awaited the attack of the superior numbers of his enemy. He was prevented from carrying out his plan, however, by the rashness of one of his wing-commanders, John Joel, a condotierri+ who was lured into the open plain by a feigned retreat by the clever du Guesclin. Captal had only 300 archers and 1,200 men-at-arms, not enough to have any real influence on the outcome of the battle. In it the Captal de Buch was captured, but was freed by King Charles V without ransom in the hope of winning him over to the French side. (Bibliog. 153, 166)

Coeur de Lion. See Richard I; *Richard Coeur de Lion.*

cog, English merchant ship designed for carrying cargoes which ranged from wool to wine and from livestock to passegers. It was small, ranging between 30 and 40 tons, though sometimes as large as 200 tons, but had a shallow draft which allowed it to use creeks and inlets inaccessible to larger ships. It had a broad beam and a rounded bow and stern, and was built to weather the storms of the North Sea. It had a square sail and a basic rudder which made it slow to maneuver. Edward's great cog, the Christopher, had been captured earlier by Hue Quéiret richly laden with wool and money. This ship was no match for the Mediterranean galley, the battle craft built by Philip. Armed with proper ram and a stone-throwing catapult, it had superior speed and maneuverability because of its oars. For forty years the French had maintained a dockyard producing these galleys. Their superior fighting ability did not give them the victory over the English in the Battle of Sluys,* however. They lost that battle through poor leadership. (Bibliog. 203)

Coggeshall, Ralph of (d. 1227), author of a work especially valuable for the reigns of King John and the early years of Henry III,* *Chronicon Anglicanum* (1066-1223), (ed. J. Stevenson, London: *Rolls Series* LXVI, 1875) (Bibliog. 99)

Colchester,+ largest and oldest tower keep in England. Its roots were laid before the Roman invasion of Britain. It had become the capital of King Cunobelin (whom Shakespeare named Cymbeline) in the first century A.D., and later a Roman fortress called Camulodunum. In 60, Queen Boudicca (Boadicea) attacked and destroyed Colchester and Verulamium (St. Albans). Following the withdrawal of the Romans, the Saxons and Vikings raided periodically, so these threats of Scandinavian invasions led to the building of this stronghold in Essex in the eleventh century, but as they were not repeated, the castle never was finished and in the fourtenth century its foundations were converted into a jail. (Bibliog. 30)

college of arms, office having authority over all heraldic matters in England. It was comprised of "kings of arms," "heralds,+" and "pursuivants of arms.+" Designations of most of the 13 members of the college of arms originated during the reign of King Edward III* (1327-1377). As for the 2 Provincial Kings of Arms, the one for the country north of the Trent River was called Nord Roy or Norroy, and the one south of the Trent was called Sud Roy or Surroy, which gave way in 1362 to Clarenceaux King of Arms in honor of Lionel duke of Clarence, second son of the king. Of the 6 heraldships, the first was the Windsor Herald founded by King Edward III, (Edward of Windsor) who had charge of the Order of the Garter* whose *caput** (headquarters) was at Windsor. The second herald was the Chester Herald which was instituted probably to honor Edward,* Prince of Wales, earl of Chester, the king's eldest son. Third was the Lancaster Herald, in honor of John of Gaunt,* duke of Lancaster, the king's third son. Fourth was the York Herald instituted in honor of Edmund,* duke of York, fourth surviving son of the king; and fifth was the Gloucester Herald, instituted in honor of Thomas, duke of Gloucester,* youngest son of the king, but this was abolished with the overthrow of Richard II* in 1399. (Bibliog. 47)

Combat of the Thirty, (March 27, 1351), chivalry's finest expression in contemporary eyes. At the center of Brittany lay two strong castles, Josselin commanded by Jean de Beaumanoir* on the side of Charles of Blois, and Ploermel commanded by an English knight, Richard Bramborough (Bembro) for the English side. For some time, these two garrisons had skirmished as they roamed the countryside in search of provisions. This famous fight began with a challenge to single combat issued by Jean de Beaumanoir to his opponent Bramborough. When their partisans clamored to join, a combat of thirty was agreed upon at a point midway between the two castles: thirty Breton knights under Beaumanoir against twenty English, six German and four Bretons under Bamborough. Terms were agreed, the site chosen, and after participants heard mass and exchanged courtesies, the fight began. With swords, boar spears, daggers and axes, they fought each other until four French and two English lay dead; then a recess was called. Bleeding and exhausted, Beaumanoir called for a drink, and received the era's most memorable reply, "Drink your blood, Beaumanoir, and your thirst will pass!" Resuming, the fight continued until every combatant on each side was wounded, and the French were considered to have won. Bramborough and eight of his side were killed, and the rest taken prisoner and held for ransom, including two English knights who later would become famous: Sir Hugh Calveley* and Sir Robert Knollys.* (Bibliog. 223, 224)

Committee of Twelve. See Oxford, Provisions of.

Committee of Twenty-four. See Oxford, Provisions of.

Compostella, city in the Galician province of Coruna, Spain, more frequently called Santiago in honor of its patron saint, St. James, whose shrine was considered one of the principal places of pilgrimage in Christendom. His tomb was believed to have been discovered there around 830, but not until the time of William,* count of Aquitaine (970-1029) was there evidence of a cult of followers so large that the pope authorized the bishop of Iria to build a new shrine to accommodate the large number of worshippers who made pilgrimages to the tomb. One of the locations along the main pilgrim route, the "via franca,+"through the Pyrenees Mountains between France and Spain was the pass at Rencesvals* where count Roland* and the other eleven of Charlemagne's douzepeers* were ambushed and slain, as recounted in the famous *chanson de geste,** the *Song of Roland.** (Bibliog. 79)

Comte de Poitiers, oldest French romance on the theme of wagering on the virtue of a woman. Here, Count Gerart de Poitiers boasts of his wife's virtue to the court, and challenges the duke of Normandy to bet against it. The duke won the bet by bribing the countess' attendant to get for him ten hairs from her head, her ring, and a piece of velvet from her skirt. Gerart believed the deception, and ordered his wife abandoned in a forest where she was found by his nephew, Harpin. By chance, Gerart learned about the deception from the duke himself, became reunited with his wife, and challenged and defeated the duke in single combat. (ed. Fr. Michel, Paris, 1831) (Bibliog. 231)

Comyn, Alexander. See Buchan, earl of.

Conisborough, castle+ in Yorkshire built of stone by Hamelin Plantagenet,* half-brother of Henry II,* to replace a wooden castle of his wife's ancestor, William de Warenne,* companion to William I,* and first earl of Surrey.* Its ashlar keep was a cylindrical tower with a splayed base and fitted with six large wedge-shaped buttresses. (Bibliog. 30)

Conquête de Constantinople, account of the capture and sack of Constantinople in 1204 written by one of the leaders of the fourth crusade,* Geoffroi de Villehardouin.* (ed. and tr. Sir Frank Marzials, New York: E. P. Dutton, 1958) (Bibliog. 230)

Conrad II (990-1039), Holy Roman Emperor (1024-1039). Son of the count of Spires, he was elected king after the Saxon dynasty became extinct. He pacified Germany and Lombardy and was crowned emperor the next year. He expanded German influence to the east beyond the Elbe River eventually extending it to Poland, Bohemia and Slavic tribes between the Oder and Elbe. To consolidate his authority, he promoted officials of low birth and granted his vassals full suzerainty+ over their subordinates, and thereby established feudalism in Germany. (Bibliog. 98)

Conrad III (1093-1152), Holy Roman Emperor, and founder of the Hohenstaufen* dynasty in Germany. He was made duke of Franconia* in 1117, and became the leader of the opposition to Lothaire III, but became reconciled with him in 1135, and was elected emperor on Lothaire's death in 1138. His elevation as emperor brought about the rebellion of Henry the Proud, duke of Bavaria* and head of the Welf family, which in turn became the root of the Hohenstaufen-Welf rivalry during the next two centuries. That conflict was transplanted to Italy where factions in the cities fought as Guelfs* (Welfs) or as Ghibellines* (from Weiblingen, the original Hohenstaufen castle in Swabia*). He took part in, and lost most of his army on, the disastrous second crusade.+ He joined with his ally Emperor Manuel Comnenos of Byzantium to attack Roger II* of Sicily whom Conrad blamed for the failure of the crusade, but withdrew to his homeland to suppress rebellions of Welfs there. (Bibliog. 68)

Conrad IV (1228-1254), Holy Roman Emperor (1250-1254), king of Jerusalem (1228-1245). Son of Frederick II* of Hohenstaufen* and Isabel of Brienne, queen of Jerusalem, he was proclaimed king of Jerusalem at his birth, but never reigned there. He was crowned king of the Romans (i.e., of Germany) in 1237 to ensure succession, but after his father died, he was unable to meet the demands of being king, and went instead to Apulia which he also had inherited, ruling it from 1252 until his death two years later. His death ended the Hohenstaufen dynasty. (Bibliog. 68)

Conrad of Montferrat (d. 1192), king of Jerusalem (1190-1192). He left Constantinople before the battle of Hattin,* and arrived in the Holy Land after that disaster. He organized the defense of Tyre, the last Christian stronghold in the kingdom, and was proclaimed its lord in 1187. By marrying Princess Isabel, heiress to the throne, he became king of Jerusalem. His death by an Assassin+ was laid to Richard I,* whose archenemy he had become, but that charge later was disproved. (Bibliog. 27, 99)

conservator of the peace, English royal official probably created in the reign of Richard I* by Hubert Walter,* the archbishop* of Canterbury to whom Richard entrusted the reins of government while he was on the third crusade.+ Chosen from among local knights, this forerunner of the justice of the peace was required to take an oath from all males over 15 years that they would keep the peace, and would pursue malefactors in full hue and cry,+ and having caught them, would thereupon turn them over to the conservators who then would deliver them to the sheriff to be guarded until they came up for trial. This curbed the sheriff's arbitrary power to make arrests, for conservators made the decision whether to hand over prisoners to the sheriff or not. (Bibliog. 94)

constable and marshal of England, chief military officers of the crown. They had cognizance of all military matters in England and overseas. Their office in time of war was to punish all who broke the statutes and ordinances made by the king to be obeyed by the army, and to punish offenders by the means cited in the statutes. Acting jointly on almost every occasion, with the marshal recognized as the lieutenant of the constable, these two officials were to investigate and punish all manner of crimes, contracts, pleas, quarrels, trespasses, injuries, and offenses committed beyond the sea in time of war between soldier and soldier, between merchants, victuallers, leeches, barbers, launderers, shoemakers, labourers and artificers necessary to the host. Their high court also had jurisdiction over disputes related to armorial bearings.   Later these officers came to be known as the lord high constable and earl marshal, and their court later as the Court of Chivalry.* (Bibliog. 212)

Constans, in Arthurian legend, king of Britain following his father King Constantine,* according to Layamon.* Sometimes he was called "moyne" meaning monk because he was said to have been removed from a monastery by Vortiger to be put on the throne. (Bibliog. 202)

Constantine, king of Britain in Arthurian legend, particularly in Layamon's *Brut.** He was father of Constans,* Aurelius Ambrosias,* and Uther.* (Bibliog. 129)

Constantinople, capital of the Byzantine Empire, with a circumference of 18 miles (c. 1170) located on the Aegean Sea at the entrance to the Bosphorus.   It was the location of the metropolitan seat of the pope of the Greeks in a place of worship called the St. Sophia. This holy place contained as many altars as there are days of the year, and possessed such untold riches which were augmented daily by contributions as to surpass all other places of worship in the whole world. It was ornamented with pillars and lamps of gold and silver. Near the wall of the palace was the Hippodrome, a public place set aside for the king's sports. Christmas was celebrated with public rejoicings at which representatives of all nations came with surprising feats of jugglery and other entertainments including fights between trained lions, bears, leopards, wild asses and birds. For his residence, King Manuel Comnenos* built on the seashore a large palace named Blachernes. Its walls and pillars were covered with pure gold, and decorated with pictures of wars of old as well as of his own wars. His gold throne was ornamented with precious gems over which, suspended by a golden chain, hung a jewel-encrusted golden crown whose diamonds were so lustrous that they illumined the room without any other light.   From all parts of the world came tributes every year: silks, purple cloths, and gold enough to fill many towers, riches unequalled anywhere in the world. The city of Constantinople alone paid a tribute to the emperor worth 20,000 florins gathered from the rents of hostelries and bazaars, and from the duties paid by merchants arriving by land and sea. Its inhabitants richly dressed in garments of silk and other valuable materials, and rode upon horses looking like princes. The country surrounding the city was rich, producing a variety of delicacies and an abundance of bread, meat, and wine. These Greeks hired soldiers of other nations, whom they called barbarians, to conduct their wars with the sultan of the Thogarmim, also called Turks, who possessed no martial spirit for themselves and were unfit for war. In 1203, the city was sacked by the crusaders on the fourth crusade,+ and the fabulous treasures of the city were destroyed or carried off to the west. Its capture and destruction were described by a member of the crusading forces, Geoffroi de Villehardouin,* who had become marshal of Champagne in 1185; his work, *Conquête de Constantinople,** was an unofficial history of the crusade compiled a few years after the events described by one who had access to letters, treatises, army lists and other similar documents to supplement his aged memory. (Bibliog. 50, 230)

Consuetudines et Justicie, document issued by William I* of England containing the clause concerning fortification: "No one was allowed to withhold the fortress of his castellany from the lord of Normandy should the latter desire to have it in his own hand." Such a statement was of importance for it allowed the duke to take control at his pleasure of fortresses in his duchy presumably just by placing his garrisons in them. If fully exploited this would extinguish the practical distinctions between fortresses of the ducal demesne owned and controlled solely by a duke, and those enfeoffed to a vassal over which presumably he had no such power. In return for the investment of his fief and the promise of the lord's protection which went with it, the vassal of whatever rank customarily undertook all the familiar service of court and host. He swore to attend his lord on judicial and military occasions, and made himself liable to certain other duties, but if the *caput* (headquarters or main residence) of his fief was fortified, that is, if his residence was fortified, then the lord required additional guarantees, and this document provided them. At least the king needed to be reassured that such a fortress would not be used in a manner prejudicial to his interests, and to safeguard himself completely he might insist on receiving control of the stronghold on his arbitrary pleasure to use so long as his need of it lasted. These were the vital matters in the custom of "jurability" whereby a fortress was liable to be sworn non-prejudicial to its tenant's immediate lord, and of "rendability" by which the lord could obtain possession of it any time so long as his need lasted. Thus, with these rights assured, the king saw no need to oppose any new fortresses being built, for they merely extended his power at no cost to himself. He just had to ensure those rights to control them. (Bibliog. 49)

Contrariants, name given to the English barons who sided with Thomas of Lancaster* against King Edward II* in 1321-1322. (Bibliog. 169)

Conway, battle of (January 22, 1295), English defeat of the Welsh near Conway castle. William, earl of Warwick,* was marching from Rhuddlan to rescue King Edward III* blockaded in Conway castle by a sudden Welsh uprising. The Welsh were camped on a hilltop between two woods into which they intended to retire if they were pressed too hard. Warwick marched his forces all night and not only surprised the Welsh at dawn so that they had no time to retire into the woods, but he also turned their flanks. Seeing themselves surrounded, the Welsh imbedded the butts of their spears into the earth with the heads pointing outwards to keep off the rush of the horsemen. Warwick responded to that tactic by placing an archer between each two knights, and when a large number of the spearmen had been picked off by volley after volley from these bowmen, he charged in with his horsemen and killed most of the rest, inflicting such a carnage as the Welsh had never seen before. (Bibliog. 166)

Corbenic (Carbonek) castle,+ magical castle where the maimed Fisher King* guarded the Holy Grail* until Galahad's* coming. (Bibliog. 117)

Corfe castle,+ one of the most famous of English castles which, though built in Dorset for strategic reasons by William I,* was valued more for its convenience as a stronghold for the safe custody of important hostages, political prisoners, and royal treasure. Henry I* replaced the wooden tower with a stone keep, and Henry II* had the entire area enclosed in stone walls and towers together with two gatehouses. It was one of King John's* favorite castles, and in the years of his reign he spent over £1,400 on it, including within its walls a 13th century ashlar+ house known as "la Gloriette," a great hall entered through a towered porch which also led to a vaulted apartment which contained a chapel. As the castle and its town were royal, every Saturday, the citizens of Corfe had to carry beer and bread from Wareham to Corfe for its constable's use. It remained in royal custody through the next two centuries until it was granted to John of Beaumont,* earl of Somerset, in 1407. (Bibliog. 62, 247)

Cornet castle. See Channel Islands castles.

Cornwall, earldom of, although Brient, younger son of a Breton count, Eudes, count of Penthièvre, and brother of Alan, earl of Richmond,* was said to have been given the earldom of Cornwall to reward him for

leading a band of Bretons for William I* at Hastings,* the first earl
of Cornwall of record was Reynold de Dunstanville, an illegitimate son
of Henry I* who was granted this earldom by the Empress Matilda* in
1141. He was sheriff of Devon in 1173-1175, and one of the king's commanders during the rebellion of young Henry* in 1173. Its title was
inherited by Henry FitzCount, Reynold's illegitimate son, and confirmed by King John* in 1215. After his death on a crusade+ in 1222,
the earldom then went next to Richard,* younger son of King John and
Isabelle of Angoulême,* born in 1209, and made earl in 1227. His
first wife was Isabel Marshal, widow of Gilbert, earl of Gloucester*;
she died in 1240. His second wife was Sanchia, daughter of Raymond,
count of Provence and sister of King Henry III's* queen; she died in
1261. Following this marriage, he renounced all rights to the property
of his father other than the county of Cornwall and a few minor
honours.+ His third wife was Beatrice of Falkenberg, who outlived him.
His great wealth from grants from the crown throughout his life encouraged an invitation for him to become titular king of the Romans,
and after a lengthy and scheming campaign, he succeeded in convincing
the electors* to choose him for that throne. Supporting his brother,
King Henry III,* on the throne of England, Richard fought beside him
and was captured at the battle of Lewes* in 1264, and kept prisoner
until the king's victory at the battle of Evesham,* the next year.
Richard was succeeded in the earldom by his son, Edmund of Almaine,
and when he died without issue in 1300, the earldom remained vacant
until Edward II* granted it in 1307 to his favorite, Piers Gaveston,*
who kept it until the barons captured and executed him in 1312. It
next was granted in 1331 to Edward II's second son, John of Eltham,
who died without male issue at age 20 in 1336. It never again was
granted, but instead was used by the king to found the dukedom of
Cornwall for his son, the Black Prince,* and has remained the title of
the heir apparent,* the Prince of Wales* ever since. (Bibliog. 66)

Cotentin, peninsula formed by the north end of Manche Department,
northwest France, between the Channel Islands and the Bay of the
Seine; it adjoined Brittany. Bayeux lay at its base. (Bibliog. 239)

Coucy-le-Chateau, castle+ associated with a family which long had been
allied with the royal house of France, England, and the Imperial house
of Austria: the house of Coucy. Enguerrand de Coucy* III (d. 1242) was
said to have chosen as his device the saying, "King I am not, nor
prince nor duke nor count also, I am just the sire de Coucy," when he
was supporting young Prince Louis* (IX) during the regency of Blanche
of Castile (1226-1234).* His castle reflected that pride. Nothing sym-

bolized it better than the circular dungeon extending 31 meters wide and rising 54 meters high, one of highest in the world. It sat on a promontory extending into the valley of Ailette in the Île de France.* (Bibliog. 196, 223)

Coudrey-Salbat, castle+ located near Niort in France. It played an important role in the history of Poitou. Its builder, William, the archbishop, lord of Parthenay, who was partisan toward the English, made this castle his base of operations around 1220. (Bibliog. 196)

Council of Fifteen. See Oxford, Provisions of.

Count of Eu. See Eu, Count of.

Count of Mortain. See Mortain, Count of.

Count of Poitiers. See *Comte de Poitiers.*

Count of Rouen, original title by which the dukes of Normandy were known. See Henry II.

counties, English, counties of England described in volume 1 of the *Domesday Book.**
Bedfordshire
Berkshire
Buckinghamshire
Cambridgeshire
Cheshire
Cornwall
Derbyshire
Devon
Dorset
Gloucestershire
Hampshire
Herefordshire
Huntingdonshire
Kent
Leicestershire
Lincolnshire
Middlesex
Northamptonshire
Nottinghamshire
Oxfordshire

Shropshire
Somersetshire
Staffordshire
Surrey
Sussex
Warwickshire
Wiltshire
Worcestershire
Yorkshire.

Volume II described Essex, Norfolk, and Suffolk. The counties of Northumberland, Durham, Westmoreland, Cumberland, and Lancashire were not reported in *Domesday*. (Bibliog. 144)

counties of Wales: Clwyd, Dyfed, Glamorgan, Gwent, Gwynedd, and Powys.

county, territorial division made of up hundreds+ in the same way that a hundred was made up of hides+: some of more, some of less than others, according as the land had been divided in the past. Thus the county was called after the count+ or earl,+ or alternatively, the count after the county name. He received the third penny+ of the profits from jurisdiction of the county. (Bibliog. 69)

Couronnement de Louis, one of the finest *chansons de geste** in the Garin de Monglane cycle.* It was written in a dialect occurring between Picardy* and the Île de France+ shortly after 1130, probably in commemoration of the coronation of Louis VII* in 1131 at the age of ll. Its story related how Charlemagne,* worn out by long years as emperor,+ crowned his 15-year-old son Louis at Aix la Chapelle.+ Louis hesitated timidly before lifting the crown from the altar, and this weakness infuriated the king. A traitor, Anseis of Orléans, offered to become regent for three years and thus strengthen the weak Louis, but was stopped when Guillaume, returning late from the hunt, recognized the traitor's real goal--the crown itself--and struck him dead with his fist. He thereupon crowned Louis, and was appointed protector of the young king. Five years later, Charlemagne gave Guillaume reluctant permission to make a pilgrimage to Rome. While there, Guillaume learned that the Saracens under Galafre had landed in Italy, and was put in charge of the pope's army. Single combat between Guillaume and the pagan giant, Corsolt, was to decide the war. Guillaume won the fight, but in it he lost the tip of his nose, so he was called "od le curt nes" ("with the short nose"). True to their pagan nature, the

Saracens did not keep the bargain, and renewed the war, but were thoroughly defeated, and Galafre, their leader, turned Christian. One of the Saracen captives freed by Guillaume, King Guaifer of Spoleto, was so grateful that he offered his daughter and half his kingdom to Guillaume. Their wedding was interrupted by messengers with news of a conspiracy against Louis in which rebellious barons wanted to crown as king the son of Richard of Normandy. Guillaume instantly abandoned his wedding and headed back to help Louis. In France he was joined by his nephews and 140 other knights who joined the thousand he already had. He rescued Louis from Tours where he was being besieged, slew the usurper, Acelin, trimmed Richard of Normandy's hair as a badge of servitude, and restored peace.

After several years, Louis and Guillaume were summoned to Rome because the pope and Guaifer both were dead, and Guy of Germany had seized the eternal city. Again, Louis showed his timidity, but Guillaume killed Guy in single combat and threw his body into the Tiber River. Louis was crowned king of Italy by Guillaume, who subdued new rebellions there, and then married his sister to Louis. Historically, Charlemagne crowned Louis in 813; Guaifer III of Salerno (871-873) was besieged by Saracens. (crit. ed. Yvan G. Lepage, Geneva: Droz, 1978) (Bibliog. 6)

Court of Chivalry,+ court held before the constable* and the marshal+ or their lieutenants by virtue of their respective offices, from which an appeal could be made to the crown in Chancery.+ Often referred to as proceedings "before the constable and the marshal," this was the same as the French "Court de Chevalerie," and Latin "curia militaris." But the Latin term was translated as "court military" by equating "miltarius" with "miles" or "soldier"; as "miles" meant "knight," so the "curia militarius" meant actually "court of knighthood." (Bibliog. 212)

courteous subsidies, voluntary contributions to King Edward I's* war funds for his fighting against the Welsh late in the 13th century. They were collected by John Kirkby,* archbishop of Ely. (Bibliog. 34)

courtesy titles, precedence+ by which the peers of England were ranked: duke,+ marquess,+ earl,+ viscount,+ baron.+ (Bibliog. 47)

Courtrai, battle of (July 1302), battle in which the French chivalric knights were badly defeated by Flemish footsoldiers in 1302. (See Battle of Courtrai in volume 1.) (Bibliog. 166)

cousin-german, first cousin; child of the brother or sister of one of a person's parents; "german" used in the sense of "germane." (Bibliog. 169)

Covenant Vivien. See *Chevalerie Vivien.*

Coventry, Walter of, English author of *Memoriale fratris Walteri de Coventria,* a chronicle whose entries from 1201 to 1225 were valuable for the reign of King John.* Nothing is known about the author. (ed. W. Stubbs, London: *Rolls Series,* 2 vols., 1872-1873) (Bibliog. 99)

Cowardly Knight (*li Coarz Chevaliers),* knight encountered by Gawain* in *Perlesvaus** in Arthurian legend riding facing backwards with the reins across his chest, his shield and lance reversed, and his hauberk and mail chausses hung about his neck. Although he ignored all taunts and refused to fight, later he fought, defeated and decapitated the Chevalier Roberes. As a result, Perceval renamed him the Brave Knight (*Hardi Chevalier).* (Bibliog. 241)

Crane, German chivalric story by Berthold von Holle; it was unusual, for it lacked the usual fantastic elements normally found in such tales, but included instead descriptions of the deeds of three knightly companions in the service of the emperor: Crane, Falcon, and Starling. Crane, the hero, after a variety of knightly adventures, gained the hand of the emperor's daughter. (ed. Karl Bartsch, Nurnberg, 1858) (Bibliog. 235)

Crécy, battle of (August 26, 1346), most humiliating defeat of the French chivalry by a smaller force of English knights and men-at-arms under the leadership of King Edward III* and the Prince of Wales, Edward, the Black Prince.* See Battle of Crécy in volume 1. (Bibliog. 166, 203)

crich. See Brehon law.

Crône, Diu (Die Krône), lengthy German courtly epic written by Heinrich von dem Türlin* about 1230. It was an Arthurian romance packed with fantastic adventures, in which, initially, Artus (King Arthur*) was the hero, but for the last two-thirds of the work Gawain* was the focus of the action. Heinrich used realistic details to describe his miraculous episodes and changed the locale from the usual spring to Carinthian winter. (ed G. H. F. Scholl, Stuttgart: *BLV,* XXVII, 1882) (Bibliog. 86)

Crooked Heir. See Desmond, earldom of.

Croquart, Breton captain in the Breton wars between John of Monfort*
and Charles of Blois. Beginning as a poor page, he rose by prowess to
become captain of a band of brigands worth 40,000 crowns whose military abilities and reputation caused him to be chosen as one of the
English side in the Combat of the Thirty.* Preferring to remain independent, he refused the offer of King John II of France of
knighthood, a rich wife, and annual salary of 2,000 livres to enter
his service. (Bibliog. 223)

crown,+ ancient worldwide symbol of monarchy.

cuaderna via (Span. "fourfold way"), Spanish type of verse form
written by clerics in the monasteries of Castile practicing the "mest-
er de clerecia"+ which was superseded early in the 15th century. In
the 13th and 14th century, the term denoted stanzaic structure of four
14 syllable lines divided by a caesura into equal hemistiches of 7
syllables each. One fully consonantal rhyme recurred throughout each
stanza. This was the "alexandrine"+ form derived from 12th century
French poetry. (Bibliog. 237)

El cuento de Tristan de Leonis, late 14th-century prose redaction in
the Aragonese dialect of the French prose *Roman de Tristan de Leonis.*
(ed. G. T. Northup, Chicago: University of Chicago, 1928) (Bibliog.
10)

Culhwch and Olwen, Welsh Arthurian story dating from about 1100; often
included as part of the *mabinogi,+* but not truly a *mabinogi* for it
showed no trace of continental influence. At Arthur's court, Culhwch
invokes the help of the king and all the warriors of his court before
he set out on a quest. The story lists an amazing miscellaneous items
from Irish and Welsh stories and history, including the Trojan War.
Two names in the story were well known Arthurian names: Cei and
Bedwyr, the Sir Kay* and Sir Bedevere* of later stories. (ed. Gwyn
Jones and Thomas Jones, *Mabinogion,* New York: E. P. Dutton, 1970).
(Bibliog. 10)

Cupientes, statute by which King Louis IX* regulated and reinforced
the organization of the Holy Office which was conducting the Inquisition* in southern France following the Albigensian crusade.+
(Bibliog. 25)

curia militarius. See Court of Chivalry.

curia regis,+ English court composed of the great officers+ of the state resident in the palace; it was called the King's Court. (Bibliog. 234)

"Curthose." See Robert II.

Cymaron, Welsh border castle+ built probably by the marcher* baron Hugh de Mortimer around 1140. In 1179, it was forfeited to the crown when Hugh's son, Roger, angered the King Henry II* by killing a Welsh prince who was travelling under a safe-conduct.+ After 1195, Roger Mortimer was allowed to refortify it, but subsequently it was deserted by the Mortimers in favor of the more favorably situated castle, Dinbaud. (Bibliog. 30)

D

Dacre, Sir Ranulph (1290-1339), English knight involved in the death of Piers Gaveston,* but pardoned by King Edward II to whom he renewed homage in 1318, and fealty in 1324. He performed military service frequently between 1318 and 1337, served in Parliament between 1321 and 1338 and became Lord Dacre. He went on the king's service to the Scottish marches* in 1322, in Gascony* in 1325, and in Scotland again in 1336. He was appointed constable of Carlisle castle in 1330, and granted the castle of Annandale in 1334. (Bibliog. 47)

Dagonet, Arthur's* fool in *Morte D'Arthur,* whom Arthur "loved passing well, and made him knight with his own hands." Once, donning the wounded Mordred's armor, he raced after King Mark so fiercely that Mark fled for his life until Palomides happened along to rescue him. (Bibliog. 100)

Dagworth, Sir Thomas (d. 1352), one of the most famous of English captains of his time. He accompanied his brother-in-law, the earl of Northampton,* on an expedition to Brittany* early in June 1345, and defeated the Franco-Breton forces at Cadoret near Josselin.* As King Edward III's* lieutenant in Brittany, he launched raid after raid in Brittany with his garrison captains, bringing more and more of the territory under English control. In 1346, after relieving the earl of Northampton in command of the English forces, he defeated Charles de Châtillon, called "de Blois" (who styled himself duke of Brittany), in June 1346. He defeated Charles again in 1347 and captured him at the battle of La Roche Derien.* For this victory, Dagworth was granted 25,000 florins *de scuto*. He received from the earl of Northampton all the castles and lands in Brittany forfeited by the lord of León, Hervé VIII, sire de Noylon. He was summoned to Parliament in 1347 by which he became Lord Dagworth. He married Ailanore, second daughter of Humphrey de Bohun,* earl of Hereford* and Essex,* by Elizabeth, daughter of King Edward I.* In 1352, he was ambushed and murdered by a Breton traitor, but his successor, Sir Walter Bentley, equally as vigorous, won an important victory at Mauron by using bowmen. (Bibliog. 47, 166, 203)

Dame Du Lac. See Lady of the Lake.

Dame Nicolaa (Nicolla) de la Haye. See Nicolaa de la Haye.

Dammartin, Renaud de (c. 1180-1220), count of Boulogne.* He was one of the greatest lords of his time and a special enemy of the king of France, and at the same time, also was a common brigand. He received money from the English and Germans to oppose King Philip II,* Augustus, and to raise money on all sides of that French monarch. He was reputed to have been good-looking, brave, strong, learned, and in-telligent, but in addition, he was a robber with an armed band, a vulgar pillager of peasants, merchants and citizens alike. He stole flocks of sheep from monks, sieze grain from their barns, and appropriated whatever suited him from his woodlands, lands and meadows. In 1190, he attacked the train of the exiled Bishop Longchamps,* when Longchamps arrived in Boulogne seeking refuge, and stole horses, baggage, the sacred vessels of his chapel; he even took the bishop's cope before allowing him to continue on his way. As punishment, he was excommunicated by the archbishop of Reims, but even that did not motivate him to return Longchamps' goods. All of the people under his control tried their best to escape him, and com-munities placed their accumulated wealth in areas which he could not touch to avoid being robbed. Citizens of Calais,* for example, en-trusted their wealth to the monks of Andres in 1191. Against his actions, the famous preacher Jacques de Vitry thundered,

> All that the peasant amasses in a year by stubborn work, the knight, the noble devours in an hour....As wolves and jackals de-vour a carrion, while the crows croak overhead awaiting their share in the feast, so...the barons and the knights pillage their subjects....Those lords who do not work and live off the work of the poor are like those unclean parasites which imbed themselves in the skin, prey upon it, and live off the substance which serves them as a home. (Bibliog. 143)

Damory, Sir Roger (d. 1322), English knight from Oxfordshire who in 1317 married King Edward II's* niece, Elizabeth, daughter of Joan of Acre (who was the daughter of King Edward I*). For his valor at Bannock Burn,* he was granted the manors of Sandal in Yorkshire, and Vauxhall in Surrey.* He was appointed keeper of several of the king's castles+ and honours.+ He took an active role in "pursuing" the Despensers* because the younger Despenser had taken lands from him, but was pardoned by the king in 1321. He was one of the principal Contrariants,* and engaged in the capture of Gloucester,* the burning of Bridgnorth,* and the siege of Tickhill.* His lands were taken into the king's hands and orders for his arrest were issued late in 1321. In retreat before the king's forces, either ill or wounded, he was left behind at Tutbury where he was captured in March 1322. Tried and condemned to death, he was respited, but died of his illness or wounds soon thereafter at Tutbury. (Bibliog. 47)

Dandolo, Enrico, doge of Venice (c. 1120-1205). His clever manipulations and shrewd financial dealings forced the crusaders+ on the fourth crusade+ to divert from their original goal of Alexandria, Egypt, and to capture Zara and then Constantinople.* See crusades.+ (Bibliog. 230)

Daniel von dem Blühenden Tal, Middle High German* courtly epic by der Stricker.* It described heroic Arthurian deeds of arms, and placed the love interest as secondary. In this, Daniel overcame many of Arthur's* chief knights. (ed. G. Rosenhagen, Breslau, 1894) (Bibliog. 235)

Danois, name meaning "the Dane" applied to the hero of a 12th century French *chanson de geste,* *Ogier le Danois.** This probably was a corruption of *l'Ardenois,* "from the Ardennes." In the *Chevalier Ogier de Danemarche,** the surviving version of the account of the rebellion of Ogier, however, he was referred to as being from Denmark. (Bibliog. 106)

Darcy, Sir John (1275-1347), English knight from Lincoln* who was outlawed for felony in 1306, and lost his inheritance in Nottinghamshire. He was pardoned in 1307 by King Edward II* at the insistence of Aymer of Valence,* earl of Pembroke,* who agreed to enfeoff+ him and the heirs of his body with 20 marks+ in land or rent. In return for the fief, Darcy was to take up knighthood within the quinzaine+ of Easter 1308, and during his life to serve the earl in peace and war at home and abroad, and to go to the Holy Land when the time should arrive. He served in the earl's retinue in 1313, 1320, 1321 and on an expedition to Scotland* in 1322. He was made banneret+ in 1323. He was appointed as justiciar of Ireland in 1323-1326 and again in 1328-1330, and was appointed special envoy to the king of France concerning the marriage of Prince Edward* in 1331. He was made Lord Darcy in 1334 by his summons to Parliament in that year. He led an army to Scotland in 1335 and wasted Arran and Bute, killing 700 Scots in the process. He was appointed to treat with the king of France, the emperor, and the count of Flanders,* and the king of Scotland in 1337 He was reappointed justiciar of Ireland* for life, but because the king needed his continued attendance, a deputy was appointed; he resigned in 1346. He fought at the battle of Crécy* and was the knight who was sent from Calais* in September 1346 to announce the victory to Parliament. At his death on May 30, 1347, he was pardoned for all homicides, felonies, robberies, etc., for all oppressions by color of any office he had held, for all trespasses of vert+ and venison, of any consequent outlawries, and for all arrears in debt. (Bibliog. 47)

Dares, supposed Phrygian who fought with the Trojans against the Greeks at Troy; he is the supposed author of *Historia de excidio Trojae.** He gave the Trojan side of the story, and prefaced his work by a letter purporting to be written by Cornelius Nepos to his uncle Sallust. In this letter, Cornelius wrote that he had come upon this book in Athens, and had translated it faithfully into Latin. He added that Dares had lived in Troy during the siege and wrote from first hand knowledge. In forty-four short chapters, the book described the events from Jason's expedition to the fall of Troy. (tr. Margaret Schlauch, *Medieval Narrative, A Book of Translations,* New York: Prentice-Hall, 1928, pp. 247-279) (Bibliog. 214)

Dauphin,+ designation of the sovereign counts of Vienne, rulers of a territorial principality east of the Rhône River, known in common usage as the Dauphine.* In time, it became the title bestowed on the eldest son of the king+ of France. (Bibliog. 225)

Dauphine, province in southeastern France bordering on Italy to the east and the Rhône River to the west and northwest. It became part of the Holy Roman Empire+ after 933. Its rulers assumed the title of dauphin*+ from dolphins on their arms.+ (Bibliog. 225)

David, St., uncle of King Arthur* in Arthurian legend. He was born about 496 to Prince Xantus of Cereticu (Cardiganshire) and a nun named Malearia. When the archbishop of Caerleon resigned his see to him, David moved his diocesan seat to Menevia which became the metropolis of Wales under the name of St. David's. He was said to have died in 642 at the age of 146. (Bibliog. 117)

David I (c. 1080-1153), king of Scotland (1124-1153). He spent many years at the court of Henry I* of England who was married to his sister. When his brother Edgar, king+ of the Scots, died in 1107, David was bequeathed the southern parts of the country, while his brother, Alexander, received the northern parts and the crown.+ David's possessions increased when he married Matilda, daughter and heir of Waltheof,* earl of Huntingdon,* in 1113 as she brought him the earldom of Huntingdon. In 1124 when his brother Alexander died, David inherited the crown of Scotland. Three years later, he swore a fealty oath to recognize Matilda* as heir of Henry I, so that when Stephen* usurped the crown of England in 1135, David invaded England on Matilda's behalf. He fought Stephen again in 1141 on behalf of Matilda and her son Henry (later Henry II*), but was captured, imprisoned for a while and then escaped. Thereafter, he stayed in Scotland and established a strong central administration becoming the first Scottish king to mint coins. (Bibliog. 176, 199)

David II, the Bruce,* (1323-1371), king of Scotland (1331-1371). As the son of Robert I,* the Bruce, at the age of 4 he married Joanna, the sister of the future Edward III* of England. He and his wife went to France in 1334 and remained for seven years. Captured in the battle of Durham in 1346, he spent eleven years in an English prison. Thus he spent most of his reign outside of Scotland either in exile or in prison. He died without issue and was succeeded by his nephew Robert,* high steward of Scotland.* (Bibliog. 176, 199)

Deganwy castle,+ fortress on the east side of the Welsh River Conway which long was one of the principal defenses of North Wales.* After the death of its builder, Robert of Rhuddlan, in 1088, it was long disputed between the princes of North Wales and the earls of Chester.* In 1241, the defeated prince of Gwynned yielded it to King Henry III* to indemnify the king for losses but destroyed it before surrendering it. Henry III ordered it rebuilt, and in 1254, he gave it to his son Edward,* the Lord Prince,* together with the earldom of Chester. In 1263, however, Llewelyn ap Gruffyd starved its garrison into submission, followed by orders for its complete destruction because it had represented the farthest extension of English authority in North Wales. (Bibliog. 104)

D'Eiville, John (1230-1291), English knight from Nottinghamshire, supporter of the barons in the Barons' War.* Although he did not participate in the battle of Evesham* in 1265, after the death of Simon de Montfort,* he became one of the most active leaders of the disinherited barons. With young Simon de Montfort, he occupied the

Isle of Axholme in the autumn of 1265, from which they were not dis-
lodged for months. Luckily escaping capture there, he became the leader of a group of discontented barons who took Lincoln and seized the
Isle of Ely in 1266 from which they plundered Norwich and Cambridge.
He joined the earl of Gloucester* at London in April 1267, and devised
a plan to seize the king in person, but the plot failed because the
duchess of Gloucester betrayed them. However, he was readmitted to the
king's peace in 1267, had his lands restored and the remission of his
first year's ransom, and following the accession of King Edward I,*
served the crown faithfully until his death in 1291. (Bibliog. 47)

de la Warre, Roger (1327-1370), English knight who served in the retinue of the Black Prince* at Crécy* and Calais.* He accompanied the
Black Prince to Gascony* and fought with him at Poitiers* in 1356.
Supposedly he and John Pelham were in the crowd which surrounded and
captured King John II* in that battle, Roger getting the king's sword
and John his belt. For their part in that action, Roger afterward
chose the crompet or chape+ of a sword and John a buckle as their
heraldic badges.+ He later accompanied the king on the invasion of
France in 1359. He was summoned to Parliament in 1363, and accompanied
the Black Prince again into Gascony on several occasions during the
next five years. He died in 1370, aged 43. (Bibliog. 47)

demesne, French royal, aggregate of territories over which the king of
France exercised the privileges of baron or independent lord on his
own behalf. Such territory had begun with the few palaces with which
Hugh Capet* had endowed himself in the regions of Paris, Poissy and
Senlis. When his uncle Henry, duke of Burgundy, died in 1002 without
heir, King Robert* gained them for his own inheritance, and by 1202,
this demesne had grown to include the duchy of Normandy* with its
forty "cities" (diocese centers) or chatellanies. To those were added
the demesne of the counts of Anjou* with Angers, Tours, and Le Mans;
the demense of the dukes of Aquitaine* in Poitou* and Saintonge with
Poitiers* and Saintes; and by fiefs that had been confiscated from
such rebellious vassals as the count of Boulogne.* Added to those were
the areas which Philip II,* (1080-1123) had wrested from the
Plantagenets*: Artois, Amiens, Montdidier, Roye and others. For more
than a century the royal demesne had been governed by provosts who
held their offices as a fief and tried to make them hereditary. These
royal officials farmed+ the king's lands, collected the revenues,
arrested and judged the lawbreakers, had charge of the royal tower in
town and summoned the host+ service. However, their brutal and
plundering methods proved far more of a liability than an asset as

they exhausted the resources of church, peasant and burgess alike. To stem such injustice, Philip II,* created a new official to handle those matters: the *baillus,* or bailiff.+ Then, before he departed for the Holy Land in 1190, Philip promulgated his Will* to handle these matters. By the time of King Louis IX* (1226-1270), the royal demesne had been reduced considerably by Louis VIII's (1223-1226) custom of establishing appanages+ for the younger sons of the king: he bequeathed Artois to his second son, Anjou and Maine to his third, Poitou and Auvergne to his fourth, but also stipulated that if the holder of an appanage died without heir, it was to revert to the crown. (Bibliog. 178)

de Monte, Robert. See Torigni, Robert of.

Denis, St., bishop of Paris and patron saint of France. Gregory of Tours wrote in the 6th century that Denis was one of the seven bishops sent to Christianize Gaul under the Emperor Decius, and after becoming the first bishop of Paris, he was martyred in 258. His relics were taken to the Benedictine abbey at St. Denis near Paris which Dagobert had founded. His cult spread rapidly, and the abbey became the burial place of the kings of France. As his grave became a revered shrine, his name was used as a battle cry+ for French knights and the oriflamme+ of the abbey was adopted by the kings of France as their banner.+ (Bibliog. 72)

Denis de Morbecque (fl. 1356), knight from Artois to whom King John II* of France surrendered at the battle of Poitiers* in 1356, but this claim was challenged by Bernard de Troie, a squire from Gascony.* Denis had been banished to England for manslaughter in 1353, and joined with forces of the Black Prince.* Supposedly Roger de la Warre* and John Pelham were in the crowd of English knights who surrounded and captured King John, Roger getting the king's sword and John his belt, but Denis was the man who grasped the French king by his hand and declared him prisoner. (Bibliog. 47, 223)

Derby, city in the English county of Derbyshire. Shortly after King Stephen's* victory at the battle of the Standard* (1138), one of his commanders, Robert de Ferrers,* was created earl of Derby. Third son of Henry de Ferrières, Sire de Ferrières and Chambrais in Normandy,* one of the *Domesday** commissioners for William I* who had granted him some 210 lordships and manors in England, Robert had succeeded to his father's estates in England. He was succeeded by his son, Robert II, by his grandson who died at the siege of Acre* in 1190, and by his great-grandson William II, who witnessed Richard I's coronation in 1189, and John's ten years later in 1199. William II's grandson, Robert, the sixth earl, seized three of Prince Edward's* castles at the outbreak of the Barons' War,* and at the head of large army, captured and destroyed Worcester. His actions caused the king to remove Derby from his control, and give it to Prince Edmund "Crouchback." All Robert's efforts to recover it failed. See Ferrers family. Edmund Crouchback also obtained the honour of Leicester* forfeited by Simon de Montfort,* and the honours of Lancaster* and Monmouth, but he never used any title but the earl of Lancaster. Edmund died in 1296 and his son and heir, Thomas* of Lancaster, fought against the king, was captured and executed in 1322. Thomas was succeeded by his brother, Henry, who died in 1345, leaving a son, Henry of Grosmont,* earl of Lancaster and Leicester and steward of England, and was, by the advice of Parliament+ in 1337, created earl of Derby "to him and his heirs" by girding on the sword and granting him £20 pounds per annum in lieu of the third penny.+ (Bibliog. 47, 66, 101)

de Reviers (Redvers). See Devon.

Desier de Pavie, in the *chansons de geste,** Didier of Pavia, king of the Lombards (Bibliog. 128, 173)

Desmond, earldom of. Thomas FitzAnthony, seneschal of Leinster, Ireland,* was granted by King John the custody of the counties of Waterford and Desmond in Ireland in 1215. His grandson and heir, Thomas FitzMorice, was called the "Crooked Heir" from a story that he had been left all alone by his nurses when the news of his father's death at Tralee had reached his castle. A pet monkey of the home, seeing him alone, took him out of the cradle, carried him to the top of the castle, unwrapped his swaddling clothes, licked and rocked the child, rewrapped him, returned him to his cradle safely, and then, finding the nurse beside the empty cradle, gave her a resounding blow to her ear as an admonition never to leave her charge alone again. (This event was said to have occurred to John FitzThomas, first earl of Kildare.) His son, Morice FitzThomas was made earl of Desmond by King Edward III* in 1329. Six years later, when the king cancelled all grants in Ireland made by his father or himself, Desmond and other Anglo-Irish lords refused to attend Parliament, but met to plan how to resolve their grievances; nothing came of their plans. Desmond even summoned a Parliament at Callan in 1344 to formulate actions, but no one attended. By 1349, however, he had obtained the king's pardon for all treasons, acts of war, and outlawries, and had been restored to his estates. He was made justiciar of Ireland in 1350. He died in 1356, and was succeeded by his son Morice FitzMorice. (Bibliog. 47)

Despensers, English family in the 13th and 14th century who became favorites of King Edward II* after the death of Piers Gaveston.* Hugh le Despenser (c. 1261-1326), a servant of the former earl of Chester,* had fought alongside Edward I* against France* and Scotland* and had served as the king's emissary. From 1312 he was Edward II's chief advisor and the object of the barons' jealousy and hate. The barons deposed him in 1315 when they had power, but after they had lost to the king's forces in the battle of Boroughbridge,* and their leaders, including Thomas, earl of Lancaster,* the king's cousin, had been executed, their opponents, including Hugh, regained power over the king. And the restored Despensers were granted enormous holdings in south Wales. Hugh the Younger (d. 1326), serving as chamberlain+ to the king from 1318 on, was an able administrator who tried to make the king's chamber an autonomous department, but in so doing made many enemies. During the revolt of Queen Isabelle* and Roger Mortimer, the Despensers remained loyal to the king. Both father and son were captured, tried and executed in 1326. In the sentence of execution, Hugh the younger heard the following words:

> [For your treacherous deeds]...the court awards that you be drawn for treason, hanged for robbery, beheaded for misdeeds against the Church: and that your head be sent to Winchester, of which place, against law and reason, you were made earl...and because your deeds have dishonored the order of chivalry, the court awards that you be hanged in a surcoat quartered with your arms and that your arms be destroyed forever. (Bibliog. 153)

Henry Despenser (1341-1406), grandson of Hugh the Younger, became bishop of Norwich after serving with his elder brother Edward in Italy. His career was more that of a soldier than of a churchman. Like his forebears, he was arrogant and headstrong. For example, in 1377, when he tried to have a mace carried before him at Lynn, usurping an honor reserved for the mayor of the town, he was warned about the possible town reaction in protest, but went ahead with his plan anyway. As soon as he and his mace-bearer set out, the people of Lynn closed the town gates, attacked him and wounded him with arrows and other missiles. Only a royal order aroused the sheriff of Norfolk to disperse the crowd. In the peasant's rebellion of 1381, Henry armed himself fully with sword, helmet and coat of mail, and in company of eight lancers and a few bowmen, set off to help suppress it. By the time he arrived at Walsham, his small force had grown considerably. He found the rebels entrenched, but he and his force charged and overran their position, defeated them in hand-to-hand combat, and captured and executed their leader. That display of violence at Walsham created hatred among the people, who began to conspire against him at Norfolk. One of the conspirators talked, however, and the others were apprehended and executed. Later, Despenser was chosen by Pope Urban VI to lead a crusade+ to Flanders against the supporters of "antipope" Clement VII. In his group he enlisted such stalwart knights as Hugh Calveley,* Sir William Elmham, Sir William Faringdon, and Sir Thomas Trivet, who crossed with him to Gravelines in Flanders.* After they won a battle near Dunkirk in 1382, and subdued the surrounding area, they besieged Ypres, but failed dismally because some of their troops were bribed into inactivity. This fiasco caused Despenser to return home to harsh criticism. Despite the accusations hurled against him, however, he still retained the loyalty of King Richard II* until that monarch was deposed in 1399. (Bibliog. 35, 58, 70)

despotate, Greek term for prince or ruler.

Destruction of Rome, fragmentary *chanson de geste** which served as a prefatory work to the *Fierabras***;* its subject was the war in Italy between the Saracens Balan and Fierabras, and a fight between Oliver* and Fierabras. The first part of the English poem *Sowdone of Babylone* was based on this *chanson.* (ed. G. Groeber, *Romania,* II, Paris, 1873) (Bibliog. 202)

Deus amanz, *lai** by Marie de France* in 254 verses, it told how a lover undertook to carry a maiden to the summit of a mountain in a contest for her hand in marriage. Although he had a specially prepared strength-giving potion, in his ecstasy he refused to drink it, and died of fatigue. The story took place at Pitre, a castle and town on the Seine located three miles above Rouen; the two lovers were buried at the foot of the Côte des Deux Amants upon which in the 12th century was built a Prieuré des Deux Amants. (Bibliog. 106)

Devereux, John, lord Devereux of Lyonshall in Hereford,* and soldier of fortune who joined the expedition of Bertrand du Guesclin* to assist Henry de Trastamare against Pedro the Cruel* (see Peter IV) of Castile. He was recalled with other English subjects by the Black Prince.* Later, after he distinguished himself at the battle of Najera* (Navarette) in 1367, he was appointed seneschal+ of the

Limousin between 1369 and 1371, and then, on the capture of Limoges by the Black Prince in 1370, he was appointed seneschal of Rochelle in 1372. Defeated and captured by du Guesclin at the battle of Chize in Poitou* in 1372, he assisted the duke of Brittany with his campaigns in that province in 1375, and then was awarded 200 marks a year for life by the Black Prince for his services during the Prince's journey into Spain; he was at the Prince's bedside at his death in 1376. On the accession of young King Richard II* in 1377, Devereux was appointed a member of the council constituted on July 20, 1377, to act during the king's minority. Shortly thereafter he was appointed constable+ of the castle of Leeds, Kent, during the king's pleasure in 1377, and for life in 1378 at a salary of 100 shillings+ per year charged to the manor of Leeds. He was appointed captain for the town of Calais in 1379-1380, as supervisor of the castles and fortalices (small forts) in the area of Calais, and a commissioner to deal with the king of France in 1381. He was summoned to Parliament in 1384 at which he became lord Devereux. Richard II made him a banneret,+ assigned him to guard the king's standard+ and chose him as a Knight of the Garter.* He served as steward of the king's household from 1378 until his death in 1392. (Bibliog. 47)

Devizes, Richard de (fl. temp. Richard I), monk of St. Swithins, Winchester,* who completed a chronicle about the reign of Richard I* around 1193. It began with Richard's coronation in 1189 and ended with his decision to leave the Holy Land in 1192. This work, *Chronicon Ricardi Divisensis de tempore regis Ricardi primi,* was one of the most valuable works on the early years of Richard's reign. In addition to the third crusade,+ it covered the political situation in England during the king's absence, and detailed Count John's* machinations in England, against the return of his unmarried older brother, and the efforts of the chancellor Longchamps* to preserve the kingdom until Richard returned. (ed. and tr. John Appleby, London, 1963). (Bibliog. 99, 174)

Devizes castle,+ founded by Bishop Osmund late in the reign of William II, this Wiltshire fortress became in the early 12th century one of the strongholds of Roger, bishop of Salisbury* (1107-1139), from whom it was captured by King Stephen* when he broke Roger's power in 1139. It remained in royal control thereafter, being used at first as a royal prison, and then more as an accommodation for the king and important visitors than as a jail. (Bibliog. 104)

Devon, county in western England, adjacent to Cornwall.* Its earls included:

c. 1080 - Richard de Reviers

1106 - Baldwin de Reviers*

1154 - Richard de Reviers; married Hawis, eldest daughter of Reginald, earl of Cornwall, natural son of Henry I

1162 - Baldwin de Reviers; married Alice, daughter of Ralph de Dol, in Berry

1184 - William de Reviers, surnamed de Veronna; married Mabel, daughter of Robert, earl of Mellent

1216 - Baldwin de Reviers; married Amicia, daughter of Gilbert, earl of Gloucester and Hertford

1235 - Baldwin de Reviers; married Avice of Savoy, related to Queen Eleanor of Provence

1262 - William de Fortibus, earl of Albemarle,* husband to Isabel, sister to the last Baldwin

1335 - Hugh Courtney, next heir of Isabel de Fortibus; married Agnes, daughter of John, Lord St. John

1340 - Hugh Courtney, his son and heir; married Margaret, daughter of Humphrey de Bohun,* earl of Hereford*

1377 - Edward Courtney, succeeded his grandfather; married Mary, daughter of Roger Mortimer, earl of March. (Bibliog. 101)

Dialogus de Scaccario (Dialogue of the Exchequer), written about 1179 by Richard FitzNeal,* bishop of London and treasurer for Henry II,* this document explained in dialogue format the methods and detailed procedures used in operating the king's treasury. (Bibliog. 69)

Diceto, Ralph de (d. c. 1201), priest who became dean of St. Paul's, London, in 1180, and remained there until his death. In his work, *Imagines historiarum,* 1148-1202, all the entries after 1172 were original, and after 1188, they were a valuable record of contemporary events, and contained letters, papal bulls, and other documents. (ed. W. Stubbs, London: *Rolls Series,* LXVIII, 1875) (Bibliog. 99)

Dictum of Kenilworth (October 31, 1266), statute worked out between King Henry III* of England and the rebellious barons of Simon de Montfort* by which the ways in which the accomplices of Simon might recover their lands seized by the crown in accordance with the Ordinance of Winchester* during and after the Barons' War.* Ten years later, King Edward I* reminded the justices in eyre+ that they had to distinguish between offenses committed in time of war and those committed in time of peace. Offenses committed in time of war were subject to the rules of the *Dictum* as interpreted by King Henry's judges in eyre, who were to have before them a transcript of that document and diligently observe its contents. These offenses did not involve the loss of limb or perpetual imprisonment because they came under the *Dictum*. Two qualifications, however, were attached to this declaration. Homicide, robbery and breaches of the peace committed during a period of war, but not under the guise of war were to be regarded as though they had occurred during a time of peace. Second, those persons who had been at the centers of rebellion at Axholme,* Kenilworth,* the Isle of Ely, Chesterfield or Southwark had to be dealt with according to the separate peace made with them, and not the terms of the *Dictum*. This agreement defined the way in which persons high and low who had been disinherited under the terms of the Ordinance of Winchester as accomplices of Earl Simon, could be restored to their places in society and recover their lands. Insofar as was possible it dissolved the effects of social revolution at that time. In 1266, the value of land in England was reckoned as ten times its annual value, to be used as the basis of the redemption plan: a man who had supported Earl Simon could be restored fully to the kings's peace+ and recover his lands if he paid half the price of their market value, that is, five years' purchase. A few persons were dealt with far more severely, however. For example, Robert Ferrers,* earl of Derby,* and Henry of Hastings, head of the garrison at Kenilworth among others, were forced to redeem their lands at seven, not five, times their annual value. At that time, the earl of Derby was held as a prisoner at Windsor, and may not have learned the terms of the *Dictum*. Nonetheless, he was forced to agree to those stark conditions as of his own free will, which made it impossible to redeem his lands, and prevented him from seeking legal redress after his release. His lands except Chartley were given to Edmund of Lancaster,* "Crouchback," whose grandson, Henry of Lancaster was created earl of Derby in 1337. (Bibliog. 70, 181)

Dictys, supposed Cretan author of *Ephemeris belli trojani,* an account of the Trojan War by a supposed eyewitness who gave the Greek side of the story. His work opened with a letter from Lucius Septimus to Quintus Aradius explaining that when Dictys died in Crete, his book written in Phoenician characters was placed in his casket and buried with him. In the reign of Nero, an earthquake broke open the tomb and exposed the casket. Found by some shepherds, this work was brought to Nero who ordered it translated into Greek letters and then placed in a library where its Greek was translated into Latin by Septimus. Dictys said that he had been with the Greeks at the siege, and that he supplemented what he saw firsthand by questioning Ulysses and others. He included accounts of the fortunes of the Greek leaders after the destruction of Troy. (Bibliog. 214)

Didot-Perceval. See Robert de Boron.

dienstmannen,+ German term for feudal vassal or liegeman in the 12th century. These were the dependents of nobles or princes, even of the emperor himself, who in return for military service received fiefs from their lords, and frequently attained considerable position and influence. (Bibliog. 186)

Dietrich und Wenezlan, anonymous Middle High German* poem written toward the end of the 13th century, of which only a brief fragment survived. Designed as a laudatory work for King Wenzel II of Bohemia (1285-1305), this work described a fight between Wenezlan (Wenzel) and Dietrich von Bern, but the fragment ended before the matter was settled. (Bibliog. 86)

Dietrich von Bern. See Theoderic the Great.

Dietrichsage, series of stories by which the adventures of Theoderic the Great,* the historic 5th-6th century figure, remained current in German lands. History became distorted as these legends became entwined with the story of the *Nibelungenlied.** Theoderic usually was called Dietrich von Bern (Verona). In legend, his father was Dietmar; his principal thane+ was Hildebrand; his principal opponent was Ermanrich who drove him from his realm and defeated him at the battle of Rabenslacht (Ravenna). Only after Ermanrich's death did Dietrich return to his country. The Norwegian *Thidreksaga* (c. 1250) contained a folk form of this series based on German oral tradition. Works in this series included
*Alpharts Tod**
Biterolf und Dietlieb
*Dietrich und Wenezlan**
*Dietrich's Flucht**
Eckenlied
Goldemar
*Hildebrandslied**
Hugdietrich
Jungeres Hildebrandslied
Laurin und Walberan
*Nibelungenlied**

*Ortnit**
Die Rabenslacht
*Rosengarten**
*Sigenot**
Virginal
Walther und Hildegund
Wolfdietrich
Die Wunderer.

(ed. O. Janicke, E. Martin et al. in K.   Mullenhoff, *Deutsches Heldenbuch*, 5 vols., Berlin: Weidmann, 1963-1973) (ed. and tr. H. Guerber, *Myths and Legends of the Middle Ages*, London and New York: George Harrap, 1924; repr. New York: Avenel, 1986) (Bibliog. 86, 197)

Dietrich's Flucht (Dietrich's flight), Middle High German* epic covering the ancestry of Dietrich von Bern and his expulsion from Italy. Dated about 1280, its author identifies himself as Heinrich der Vogler. This work described how Dietrich's wicked and cruel uncle, Ermanrich, urged on by his wicked counsellor Sibich, destroyed all his kin, and then forced Dietrich to flee. Taking refuge at the court of Etzel (Attila), Dietrich defeated Ermanrich several times with Hunnish assistance, but each time his own losses were so severe that he could not maintain his supremacy over his defeated foe, and thus he was forced back into exile. (ed. Ernest Martin, Dublin & Zurich: Weidmann, 1976) (Bibliog. 84, 235)

Dieudonne de Hongrie, late 14th century French epic, also known as *Charles le Chauve** (unedited). Because France was left without a king after Clotaire's death, an angel told the French to wait for Melisau of Hungary who had been appointed by God to become their new king. To Melisau's coronation, an angel descended from heaven to bring the Sainte Ampoule;+ at which miracle, Melisau instantly converted to Christianity, and was crowned as Charles le Chauve (Charles the Bald). His son, Philippe, exiled after being falsely accused by the Ganelon*-like traitor, Goubaut, of trying to poison his father, overcame a forty-foot giant named Merlangier, fell in love with and married Doriane, daughter of the king of Hungary, and eventually was crowned king of Hungary. In response to a dream vision, he left shortly thereafter to free Jerusalem. His son, born in his absence, was abandoned by traitorous servants, was rescued by a nobleman who, recognizing the kingmark+ on his shoulder, named him Dieudonne. See also Philip II,* Augustus. He became the focus of the remainder of the story.   He married Supplante, obtained magic gifts from a fairy, became the father of Dagobert, and finally retired to end his life as a hermit with his wife beside him. (Bibliog. 88, 121)

Dinadan, good-humored and practical knight of Arthur's* Round Table.* He never rushed headlong into battle for the sake of glory, but instead would find out if he had a chance of victory, and if he was fighting for the right side.   Best known as a scoffer, he was the brother of Breunor le Noir ("La Côte Male Taile"), and companion of Tristan.* (Bibliog. 145, 202)

Disinherited, The, disinherited nobles of the English party in Scotland* who had been supporters of the Plantagenets,* and backed by many English barons and knights who had lost estates in Scotland. The leaders of this group of Disinherited were Edward Baliol,* son of John Baliol,* king of Scotland (1292-1296); Gilbert Umphraville, earl of Angus*; David, earl of Athole; Henry de Beaumont who had married the heiress of Buchan*; Walter Comyn; and Walter de Mauny (see Walter de Manny), Dutch mercenary,+ among others. They had no more than 500 knights and men-at-arms, and between 1,000 and 2,000 archers. They defeated the Scottish host at the battle of Dupplin Moor* in 1332. (Bibliog. 166)

distraint of knighthood (1258), method used by King Edward I* to increase the number of knights in his realm. He was determined to turn country gentlemen who could afford the equipment into competent cavalry, serving under men on whose competence he could rely. His father, Henry III,* had used this tactic earlier in 1241-1242 and again in 1252-1254 as a financial measure: new knights meant more reliefs,+ wardships,+ and marriages.+ It also meant increasing the actual number of mounted armed men available in time of royal need. During Henry II's* reign (1154-1189), the total *servitium debitum*+ was about 5,000 knights, and the potential strength of the country in knights' fees+ was closer to 6,500. In only a century, by the time the first Welsh wars of Edward I began, the marshal's register of 1277 showed an official record of only 228 knights and 294 *servientes*+ or mounted men-at-arms (two of whom were rated as equivalent to one knight); that was a total of 375 knights. By the end of the 13th century, the number of fighting knights was about 500, and after the various distraints, probably there were about 700 more knights scattered throughout the shires. This marked decline was caused by the increase in costs of armor, equipment and horse. Sent to all sheriffs of England to enforce, Edward I's distraint read in part:

We order...you to distrain without delay all those of your baliwick who have lands worth twenty pounds a year, or one whole knight's fee worth twenty pounds a year, and hold of us in chief and ought to be knights but are not...to receive from us before Christmas or on that feast the arms of a knight.... (Bibliog. 70, 181, 185)

Dodinell, the savage, knight at King Arthur's* court, knighted by Arthur himself, but one whose character was elusive. He appeared in Chrétien's *Erec et Enide** and *Yvain** as one of the ten most important knights, and in *Sir Gawain and the Green Knight,* and *Morte D'Arthur,** yet he played no major role in any adventure, but merely accompanied Gawain* and Ywaine, and was in Guenevere's party when Meliagrance ambushed her. (Bibliog. 117)

Dolorous Garde, castle+ in Arthurian legend, located either in Northumberland near the Humber River, or in southern Cornwall* near the Devon* border and heavily guarded by enchantments. Lancelot* captured it, removed the enchantments, found his tomb there, and re-named it Joyous Garde. There Arthur* besieged him after he rescued Guenevere* from being burned at the stake. He changed the name of the castle to Dolorous Garde after he was forced to yield Guenevere to Arthur. There, Lancelot and Galehat, his friend, were buried in the same tomb. Both this tomb and the castle were destroyed by King Mark* of Cornwall because Tristan* and Isolde* had lived there for three years after leaving Cornwall. (Bibliog. 40, 117)

Dolorous Stroke, second blow with the Sword of the Strange Girdles by Balin, the Savage* against King Pellam*; the first blow had been the one with which Varlan had killed Lambors, the Grail* king, resulting in the kingdom of Logres becoming a waste land in *Morte D'Arthur,* and *Estoire del Saint Graal.** (Bibliog. 202)

Domesday Book,+ survey ordered in 1086 by King William I of "the whole country [of England], its woods, pastures and meadows, as well as its arable land, county by county." See *DomesdayBook* in volume 1. (Bibliog. 69, 144)

domestici, French king's court officials in the 10th and 11th centuries—ministers, secretaries, and counsellors—who travelled with the king were the nucleus to which were added the bishops and nobles who came to court and all later became the chief officers of the crown. Even though their positions were vague, their names appeared as signatories witnessing charters. (Bibliog. 178)

Don Juan, legendary figure based on a historical Spaniard at the time of Pedro the Cruel (1334-1369) or Charles V (1338-1380). Don Juan belonged to the illustrious Tenorio family, and lived a life of unrestricted licentiousness. In an attempt to abduct Giralda, the daughter of the governor of Seville, he fought and subsequently killed her father in a duel. When he mockingly defied the spirit world by visiting the tomb of the murdered man and challenging his statue to follow him to supper, it responded, and carried off the sceptical Don Juan to hell. (Bibliog. 68)

Doön, lai* written at the end of the 12th century. In it, the contestants for a girl's hand had to ride from Southampton to Daneborc, the girl's residence, in a single day. All but one of the suitors slept in beds provided for them, and were slain by the girl; Doön alone avoided her trap. He successfully passed a second test and won the girl's hand, and at the end, her father and Doön fought. (ed. Gaston Paris, *Romania,* XIV, 1885, 29ff.) (Bibliog. 106)

Doön de la Roche, chanson de geste* of the Doön de Mayence* cycle from the close of the 12th century, written in 4,638 verses in the Lorrain dialect. Its story related how Tomiles, Ganelon's* uncle, plotted the ruin of Olive, sister of Pepin, who had married Count Doön de la Roche. Tomiles persuaded a page to lie beside Olive without her knowledge, and then to convince her husband that she had been unfaithful. Doön cast her aside and married Tomiles' daughter, which broke Pepin's heart. Not content with breaking up the marriage, Tomiles continued his treachery by pursuing her relentlessly and forcing her and her son, Landri, into exile as both fled for their lives. In retaliation for his sister's disgrace and misfortunes, Pepin attacked Doön in La Roche, and forced him also into exile. Doön met his son years later in Constantinople where Landri had become one of the chief knights of the emperor of Constantinople. Olive, meanwhile, recaptured La Roche with the help of the bishop of Hungary. Doön and Landri arrived with a reinforcing army from Constantinople, captured Tomiles and his treacherous followers, and executed them with exquisite tortures. Landri scorned his uncle Pepin for not helping earlier in his life, but later saved his uncle's life. Finally all of them went back to Constantinople where Landri was given the throne by Emperor Alexander and married Salmandrin, the emperor's daughter. This story had no historical basis of fact. (ed. P. Meyer, G. Huet, Paris: SATF, 1921) (Bibliog. 106, 231)

*Doön de Mayence, chanson de geste** of late 13th century. This work linked all the heroes of the rebellious vassal* cycle of *chansons de geste*. Doön was brought up in a forest with his hermit father, a baron, Guy de Mayence, who was duty-bound to an oath that he prepare his son to avenge his mother's death. Doön eventually killed the traitors responsible. Later he fought with young Charlemagne, became his friend, and accompanied him to aid the Saracen Aubigant against the Danes. Doön eventually married Aubigant's daughter, Flandrine. Obvious similarities existed between this and *Huon de Bordeaux** and Chrétien's *Perceval*. (ed. A. Rey, Paris: APF 2, 1859) (Bibliog. 106, 231)

Doön de Mayence cycle. Of the three cycles of *chansons de geste** named by Bertrand de Bar-sur-Aube,* this one usually was known as the rebellious vassals cycle. In each poem of the cycle, Charlemagne* was forced to pursue some rebellious baron who had renounced allegiance to the emperor or had harmed some member of Charlemagne's immediate household. Unrelenting in his pursuit of enemies, Charlemagne often hounded them long after they had ceased to threaten him; many of the revolts, in fact, were caused by the emperor's own selfish actions or attitudes in the face of which the rebel tried to preserve his self-respect. In these works, however, Charlemagne became a matchless hero, and the rebels mere objects of pity. A king could function only because he was chosen by God, so God always was on the side of the emperor. If a divinely chosen king became a tyrant, however, God still was on his side, so therefore his tyranny was a punishment for the people who had to have been wicked. In this particular cycle of *gestes,* Charlemagne appeared tyrannical, but only because the family of the focus of his wrath had sinned and was accursed in the eyes of God. This cycle contained the following chansons: *Chevalier Ogier de Danemarch*; Doön de la Roche*; Girart de Roussillon*; Girard de Vienne*; Gormont et Isembart*; Raoul de Cambrai*; Renaut de Montauban,* otherwise known as *Four Sons of Aymon.** (Bibliog. 106, 231)

Doön de Nantueil, son of Doön de Mayence, and the father of Garnier de Nantueil in the *chansons de geste.** Only fragments of a *chanson de geste* by this name survived. (ed. Paul Meyer, *Romania*, XIII, 1884, 1-18) (Bibliog. 106, 231)

Dorset, county on the southern coast of England. It was famous primarily for the honorary titles bestowed on noble personages. Around 1099, Osmund de Sees, bishop of Salisbury* and chancellor to William I* was made earl of Dorset.* Three hundred years later, in 1398, John

Beaufort,* illegitimate son of John of Gaunt,* and earl of Somerset,* was made marquis of Dorset. His title of marquis was set aside in 1400 when the marquises of Albemarle,* Surrey* and Exeter* were deposed from their titles; however, because he was half-brother to King Henry IV,* he was appointed chamberlain of England for life. (Bibliog. 101)

Dorylaeum, battle of (July 1, 1097), first major battle between the crusading Franks on their way to the Holy Land and the Turkish native horsemen of eastern Turkey. These crusaders on this first crusade+ had crossed the Bosphorus at Constantinople* and had marched across Asia Minor towards the Holy Land in 1097, hoping to reach Jerusalem in five weeks. That journey took two years. One reason was the skirmish and battle near Dorylaeum on July 1, 1097. Marching in two divisions on separate roads seven miles apart, the crusaders were out of touch with each other. Turkish horsemen armed with bows attacked first the smaller group under Bohemund, Tancred,* and Robert of Normandy, but were driven off, and the crusaders' countercharge also was unsuccessful. A second Turkish charge was repulsed by the spears and bows of the crusader infantry. Then as the Turks encircled the crusaders and began their harassing tactics, the Christians fought back desperately. Word of these attacks finally reached Godfrey de Bouillon* in the other division, and he diverted the second column instantly to help the besieged crusaders. As the Turks retreated to the hillside above the Christian forces, the crusaders formed into a line of battle and charged the pagan marauders. Against such an irresistible force the Turks had no chance of success, and were scattered. Pursuing the enemy for several miles the crusaders obtained much booty. After the battle, the knightly author of the *Gesta Francorum* wrote,

> Who will ever describe the bravery, skill, and prowess of the Turks?....Please God, they will never be as strong as our forces...if they believed in Christ and the One God in Three...no one could have been able to find anyone stronger, braver, or more skillful in battle than they.

(Bibliog. 141, 166, 186, 201)

Douglas, Sir William (c. 1326-1384), Scottish knight who distinguished himself against the English in Scotland* in the decade between 1346 and 1356. Son of Sir Archibald Douglas, regent of Scotland in 1333, Willian slew his kinsman and namesake, William Douglas, the "Knight of Liddesdale," in August 1353. He was wounded at Poitiers* in 1356. Summoned to the Scottish Parliament in 1357, he was chosen as one of the eight nobles of whom three were to become English hostages for the release of King David II* in 1357. Shortly thereafter, he was made earl of Douglas. He attended the coronation of Robert II* at Scone* in 1371, and was appointed warden of the Marches, winning some battles against the English. He died in 1384. (Bibliog. 47

douzepeers,+ twelve peers of France, or paladins+ of Charlemagne,* in the *chansons de geste*.* Said to be attached to his personal retinue, these men were the bravest of his knights. Later, Philip II,* Augustus (1180-1223), using this idea straight from romances of Charlemagne, appointed twelve peers of France from among the important barons to serve the king as an advisory board. For the six lay peers, the king chose the dukes of Burgundy,* Normandy,* and Aquitaine,* the counts of Flanders,* Toulouse,* and Champagne* (the only one who was not a prince of his own domain, for his dominions were French). The six ecclesiastical peers were French bishops who were the subjects of their immediate sovereigns. These bishops were immediate vassals of the king in his position as king, a marked contrast to the electors of the German Empire who were bishops who became princes holding directly of the empire. Only one of those chosen was of the first rank: the archbishop and duke of Rheims; the other ecclesiastical peers of France chosen were the bishops and dukes of Langres and Laon, and the bishops and counts of Beauvais, Noyon and Chalons. (Bibliog. 79)

Dover castle,+ castle in Kent* which in the reign of Henry II* was considered to be "the key of England." Built first by the Romans, it was enlarged by William I* and entrusted to his half-brother, Bishop Odo* of Bayeux. Half a century later, Henry II recognized its important strategic value and completely transformed it. He built the tower keep,+ the inner curtain wall+ which formed its immediate protection, and the north east portion of the outer curtain wall which followed the line of the original earthworks and was designed to serve as the castle's first line of defense. Subsequent kings continued Henry's goals of strengthening the castle. Hubert de Burgh* led its successful defense against the siege of Prince Louis* of France in 1216-1217. After that siege, Hubert proposed and King Henry III* accepted and ordered into effect such changes in its structure as blocking up the old gateway on the north side because it favored an attacker, and extending the curtain walls to the edge of the cliff to fortify with the entire area with stone. By 1256, the work was complete, and the castle was in its final form. It remained one of the crown's most important castles. (Bibliog. 104)

dragon,+ beast of the Middle Ages which seemed as real an animal as an elephant and camel; people claimed to have seen a dragon even though they had not, for fighting and slaying dragons was a necessary accomplishment of many heroes, saints and gods. Among the many were Zeus, Hercules, Cadmus, Jason, Siegfried,* Beowulf, Frotho, Roland,* Lancelot,* Tristan,* Bevis,* and Guy of Hampton; St. George, St. Margaret, and St. Michael also killed dragons. Besides carrying off the dragon's hoard of gold as prizes, eating the dragon's heart gave the hero a knowledge of the beast's language, and painting himself with dragon's blood hardened the skin against all injuries. Some of the more famous dragon fights included Siegfried's fight with Fafnir and Tristan's fight with the Irish dragon. Two entries in an English chronicle, the *Annals of Winchester,* seemed to confirm that England was afflicted by dragons: "1177: In this year dragons were seen of many in England"; "1274: A fiery dragon frightened the English." Over 40 other sightings of dragons in Britain were recorded, and many dragon tales recounted both sightings and combats. At Linton, a dragon was killed by thrusting a fire-ball of peat attached to the end of a lance down the throat of the beast; at Nunnington near York, a poisonous self-healing dragon was killed by a knight in armor covered with razors and helped by a faithful dog. (Bibliog. 59)

Drayton, Lord Basset of. See Basset, Ralph.

Dreux, town and county northwest of Chartres in France which gave its name to the dynasty of counts related to the royal Capetian* line. Dreux was the major town of the county. Eudes II, comte de Chartres, received half of the county as part of the dowry he received when he married the daughter of Richard I, duke of Normandy.* Toward the end of the 11th century, he ceded Dreux to King Robert II of France. By 1135, it had been given to Count Robert I, son of Louis VI,* le Gros (1108-1137), who founded the dynasty of the counts of Dreux. Although the English King Henry II* captured it in 1188, Philip II,* Augustus, soon recaptured it and returned it to the Dreux dynasty until the end of the 14th century. (Bibliog. 98, 100)

Droit d'ainesse." See *"Jus Esneciae."*

Dublin, Marquess of, Robert de Vere,* ninth earl of Oxford.* At the request of King Richard II* (1377-1399), Parliament on December 1, 1385, created him marquess+ of Dublin with lordship and domain of Ireland* for the term of his life, and he was summoned by that title to Parliament on August 8, 1386. These letters patent,+ however, were surrendered and cancelled a few months later, and on October 13, 1386, he was created duke of Ireland with the lordship and domain of Ireland for the term of his life. His was the first dukedom conferred on a person not of the royal family, but in 1392, the same king created no less than five more dukedoms: Hereford,* Surrey,* Exeter,* Aumale,* and Norfolk,* of which only two were by male descent of the house of Geoffrey of Anjou.* De Vere was attainted and outlawed on February 3, 1388, when all his honours became forfeit. (Bibliog. 47)

Dudley castle,+ castle in Staffordshire built by William FitzAnsculf whose name appeared in the *Domesday Book.** By 1173, its owner was Gervase de Pagenel whose unsuccessful revolt against King Henry II* led to the demolition of the castle. A century later, Roger de Somery was given a license to crenellate.+ He fought on the king's side in the Barons' War,* and was captured at the battle of Lewes.* In 1300, it passed to his son, Sir John de Somery, who maintained himself as a "robber baron." (Bibliog. 247)

Du Guesclin, Bertrand (c. 1320-1380), one of the most famous of French knights of the 14th century who rose from lowly birth near Dinan in Brittany to the highest office France could bestow. Eldest son of ten children of poor French peasants, he spent his youth organising the local children into gangs to fight one another, with Bertrand always playing the commander. To a tournament in Rennes in honor of the marriage of Charles of Blois* to Jeanne de Penthièvre, Bertrand supposedly rode a carthorse and was met with the jeers of the well-to-do knights. In response, according to Cuvelier's apochryphal account, he borrowed the horse and armor from a cousin who was leaving, and with a closed visor to conceal his identity, he entered the lists and won every fight against him. In reality, however, in the service of Charles of Blois, this uncouth man, unspoiled by tournaments, learned to fight in the guerilla war of Brittany against the English troops of John de Montfort's+ forces from the safety of the forest of Paimpont. He pounced on isolated troop columns, he raided castles, he disrupted communications. His capture of the castle of Grand Fougeray revealed his ingenuity. He disguised his men as woodcutters bearing firewood to the castle. As the gates were opened to admit them, they threw down their wood to block the gates open and revealed their identities, as their companions raced in from nearby and joined them in the castle courtyard. He became skilled in the tactics of ambush and ruse, the use of spies, disguise, secret messengers, smoke screens to hide movements, bribes of money and wine, torture and killing of prisoners and surprise attacks launched during the supposed peace of the "Truce of God." He was intrepid, fierce, hard, tricky and ruthless, but had not received the recognition he deserved.

That changed when he rendered a simple but brilliant feat of arms to a senior French knight, the marshal d'Audrehem. After capturing the castle of Landal in northern Brittany, d'Audrehem turned his attention toward Becherel, a castle midway between Rennes and Dinan, and one of the major English strongholds in Brittany under the command of Sir Hugh Calveley.* Only six miles away lay Montmuran, a strong French-held castle whose owner was the widow of a French knight who had died in the battle of Mauron. When she invited d'Audrehem and his party (including du Guesclin) for Maunday Thursday celebrations in April 1354, du Guesclin warned his commander that Calveley was known for surprise and ambuscade, and might well attempt a raid on Montmuran to capture d'Audrehem. To guard against just such a surprise attack, du Guesclin concealed thirty archers along the road to Becherel with orders to prevent any approach of Calveley, and to warn the garrison at Montmuran. His assumption proved correct, and on hearing the skirmish, both du Guesclin and the Marshal raced to the scene. Calveley was flung from his horse by a French knight and captured. Immediately after this encounter, du Guesclin was taken aside by Eslatre des Maraes, a knight of Caux, and knighted on the field of battle as he girded him with his own sword. Once he was accepted by the other knights, du Guesclin's humble background was forgotten as his knightly virtues, especially his abilty to win battles, became obvious to all.

He distinguished himself during the Hundred Years War.* During the siege of Rennes he became noted for his bravery by entering the besieged city, stiffening its defense so it withstood the siege for a considerable time. Leading an expedition to Spain in 1365 to support Henry of Trastamere* against Pedro I, the Cruel,* he was captured by Edward the Black Prince,* and later released. In 1370, he was made constable+ of France by King Charles V,* and as such led many military operations against the English in Guienne (Aquitaine*) in 1374, Cherbourg in 1378, and others. He recognized the superiority of the English army, and urged his men to use such cautionary tactics as wearing out the enemy and attacking by surprise. He fell ill while besieging the castle of Chateauneuf de Randon, and was forced to lead the siege from his bed; he died on July 13, 1380. To honor him, King Charles V ordered his heart buried in his native Dinan in Brittany, his entrails at Puy, his flesh at Montferrand, and the remainder of his body beside the tomb which the king had prepared for himself at Saint Denis* near Paris. In his life, he was honored by many titles, among which were the count of Longueveille, duke of Molina, earl of

Trastamare, and constable of France. A French poet, Cuvelier, wrote his *Chronique de Bertrand du Guesclin,* a heroic poem, shortly after Bertrand's death in 1380. (ed. E. Charrière, *Collection de documents inédit sur l'histoire de France,* Paris, 1839) (Bibliog. 223, 224)

duke,+ next to the princes and princesses of the blood royal, and the archbishops+ of England, duke was the highest order and rank of the English peerage. (Bibliog. 47)

Duke Rowlande and Sir Ottuell, Middle English* verse romance from about 1400 that followed closely the story of Otuel but omitted many of the details from the original French version. Its best scene occurred when Charlemagne's daughter armed Otuel. (ed. S. Herrtage, London: EETS ES #35, 1880) (Bibliog. 202)

Dukus Horant, title given to a poem contained in a Hebrew manuscript of 1382 which was discovered in Cairo; its characters were Hebraic, but its language was German; it contained elements from stories of *Kudrun** and *Konig Rother.** (ed. P. F. Ganz, F. Norman, W. Schwarz, Tubingen, 1964) (Bibliog. 86)

Dunbar, Patrick (1152-1232), earl of Dunbar. A Scot who was the first to assume from his castle of Dunbar the territorial style of earl of Dunbar; he also was earl of Lothian.* He was a justiciar of Lothian and keeper of Berwick; he attended William the Lion* to Lincoln in 1200 to do homage to King John* for his lands in England, and also accompanied Alexander II* to York in 1221 on the occasion of that Scottish monarch's marriage to Joan, sister of King Henry III.* His great-great-grandson, Patrick Dunbar,* earl of March (from his father), was with his father at Caerlaverock* in 1300. Like his father, he favored the English faction, and after the defeat of Edward II* at Bannock Burn* in 1314, he welcomed the fleeing English king into his castle at Dunbar, and assisted his escape to England. After losing this unparalleled opportunity to serve his own Scottish people, he changed allegiance and served the Scottish Parliament at Ayr when the succession to the Scottish crown was settled in 1315. As sheriff of Lothian, he was at the capture of Berwick in 1318, signed the letter in 1320 to the pope asserting the independence of Scotland, and was at the defeat of the Scots at Dupplin Moor* in 1332 and Halidon Hill* in 1333. When the fort of Berwick surrendered to Edward III,* he changed allegiance for the second time, but as before, soon reverted to his Scottish support and fought against the English while his countess, "Black Agnes," survived and broke a nineteen-week siege by the English at Dunbar castle. Under the command of William de Montagu, earl of Salisbury,* the English advanced toward the castle under the cover of an enormous siege machine called a "sow," similar to a Roman *testudo*.+ The countess cried scornfully, "Beware, Montagu, for soon thy sow shall farrow!" and ordered a huge rock on the ramparts dropped onto the engine to crush it to pieces, as the men beneath fled from it like a litter of pigs. Dunbar was at the Scottish defeat at the battle of Durham in 1347, and was one of the sureties for the release of David II* from captivity in 1357, receiving various grants, among which was having the town of Dunbar become a free burgh, but by 1360, he was described as an enemy and a rebel whose lands were forfeit. (Bibliog. 47)

Dunstanburgh castle,+ fortress standing on the rocky coast of the North Sea, this, the largest castle in Northumberland,* was the northernmost possession of the house of Lancaster,* and became a royal castle with the accession to the throne of Henry IV of Lancaster in 1399. Built almost a century earlier in 1313 by Thomas,* earl of Lancaster, it was a large and strong castle of importance kept in good condition by the Lancastrians and then by the crown. (Bibliog. 104, 247)

Dupplin Moor, battle of (August 9, 1332), contest between the Disinherited* led by Edward Baliol,* son of King John of Scotland, and the Scottish forces under the earl of Mar near a bridge across the River Earn in Scotland. Facing a superior number of Scotsmen, Baliol and his followers realized that their only hope of success lay in a surprising and audacious move. They crossed the river at night and attacked the footsoldiers who lay on the outskirts. By then, however, the Scots had been aroused and had time to arm and form two massed columns on foot and advance on Baliol's group. Seeing the enemy approach in such force, the invading forces drew back from the Scottish camp and drew themselves up on the slope above it. The knights and men-at-arms dismounted and formed a solid mass at the center; their archers were drawn out in a thin line scattered among the heather on each flank; 40 continental mercenary men-at-arms were told to remain on horseback behind the group to serve as a reserve and to deliver a last desperate charge or to strike out as pursuers in case of victory. The Scots charged into the center of the mass with lances levelled, and the two forces were locked in a swirling mass of confused fighers. The archers on the wings showered the outer columns of Scots with a hail of arrows which had a devastating effect. Unable to break through at the front and stung severely by the archers on their flanks and rear, the Scottish host broke apart, and all who could escape from the massed confusion made their way toward the rear. Some of the Disinherited sprang to their horses and chased them for several miles. The Scots had been almost exterminated; only 14 knights escaped. Among the dead were the regent of Scotland, Donald earl of Mar; the earls of Mentieth and Moray; Robert Bruce, earl of Carrick; 18 bannerets, 58 knights, 800 squires, 1,200 men-at-arms, and an uncounted number of footsoldiers. Among the Disinherited, only 33 knights and men-at-arms, and not a single archer, fell. This battle taught the English a lesson: to dismount their heavily armed men to form the center of the formation around, and to place the archers forward on the flanks. (Bibliog. 166)

Durham, bishop of. As Durham was a strategic county and city in northern England close to the Scottish border, the bishops of Durham became great feudal lords. Because they often were entrusted with the defense of northern England, they became palatine counts,+ and commanded armies of their own. Two of the better known bishops were Hugh of Puiset* (1153-1195) and Anthony Bek* (1284-1311). (Bibliog. 98)

Durham, Simeon of (d. after 1129), author of a lengthy work which gave fundamental information about northern England for the 9th through the 11th centuries, *Symeonis monachi opera omnia.* (tr. J. Stevenson, *Church Historians of England,* London:Seeleys, IV, 1856) (Bibliog. 99)

Durmart le Gallois, medieval French Arthurian verse romance written between 1220 and 1250. In it Durmart, son of the king of Denmark, had an affair with the wife of his father's seneschal,+ but feeling remorseful, decided to change his profligate ways to make himself worthy of the queen of Ireland about whose beauty he had learned. Not long after, he met and won for her the sparrow hawk as a prize for beauty, not knowing who she was. He went on his way, and later, after learning her identity, he searched for her, but was diverted by other actions. He rescued Guenevere* from Brun de Morois, and won the tournament of the Blanches Mores. Arthur* and Guenevere welcomed him to Glastonbury,* but he refused to join the Round Table* until he had found his lady. He travelled to a land devastated by war, Ireland, and journeyed to a town being besieged by Nogant. Although Nogant called on Arthur for help against Durmart, he fled rather than face him in single combat. Durmart thus won the battle against Nogant and thereby won the hand of the queen, his lady, named Fenise. Afterward he founded abbeys, made a pilgrimage to Rome, and delivered it from a pagan army. (ed. E. Stengel, Tubingen, 1873) (Bibliog. 10)

Dymoke, Sir John (d. 1381), king's champion or the champion of England whose functions were confined to certain ceremonial duties at coronations. It was his duty as champion to ride his horse into Westminster Hall to begin the coronation banquet, and three times formally to challenge to combat any person who disputed the king's title. Then he flung down his gauntlet as soon as the herald announced the challenge. On no occasion was any opposition offered. When the champion took up the gauntlet for the third time, the sovereign drank to him from a gallon cup which afterwards was handed to the champion who drank to his sovereign, and then became owner of the cup. Dymoke's wife, Margaret de Ludlow, was the daughter and co-heiress of Philip Marmion, the last baron Marmion who claimed descent from the lords of Fontenay-le-Marmion. The Marmions were hereditary champions of the dukes of Normandy and supposedly had acted as the English king's champions at every coronation since the time of William I. Roger Marmion (d. 1129) was acknowledged king's champion in King Henry I's* reign; Philip Marmion may well have served as champion at the coronation of Edward I* in 1274. Dymoke was knighted in 1373 and represented Lincolnshire in Parliament in 1372, 1373, and 1377, and at the coronation of Richard II,* he claimed his right to serve as champion because he held the manor of Scrivelsby, previously owned by the Marmion family. (Bibliog. 58, 68)

Dynadan. See Dinadan.

Dynas, Sir, seneschal+ of King Mark,* and brother of Edward of Caernarvon in Arthurian legend; Lancelot* made him duke of Anjou.* (Bibliog. 100)

Dyserth castle,+ Welsh castle in Flintshire. Built by the king's orders after the defeat of David ap Llywelyn in 1241, it withstood a siege by David in 1254, and was handed over to the Lord Edward* by the king as part of his new possessions in North Wales. But in 1263, David's nephew, Llywelyn ap Gruffyd, captured it and demolished it completely. (Bibliog. 66)

E

Eadmer (d. c. 1130), monk at Christ Church, Canterbury, and the confidant of Anselm. His work *Historia novarum in Anglia* (c. 960-1122) gave a brief account of the 11th century, and detailed Anselm's pontificate as archbishop of Canterbury* from 1093 to 1109. (ed. G. Bosanquet, *Eadmer's History of Recent Events in England,* Philadelphia, 1965) (Bibliog. 99)

ealdorman. See earl.+

earldom and barony. An earldom was a title; an earl+ was a holder of office, ealdorman, under the early Anglo-Saxon crown, but under the Norman kings in England, it became a title, not an office. Except in the case of palatine+ earldoms (i.e., Lancaster, Chester, etc.), the earl had little to do with the government of the county which gave him his title. In fact, he had nothing to do with the county except to be girt with its sword, and to receive the third penny+ from its fines. But the dignity of an earl, both in origin and in nature, was entirely different than that of a baron. Taking shape after the reign of King Henry I,* this dignity was a personal grant to a tenant-in-chief already in possession of a substantial holding spread through many counties, yet not in itself emerging from the holding of that land, but rather from the standing and dignity of the recipient. An earl held the title of earl of a certain shire and was invested with that title by being girt with the sword later described as "the sword of the earldom." Like the greater barons, the earl had his personal summons to Parliament, to military service, and also to all the feudal obligations attached to the fief, but those obligations did not spring from his dignity as an earl. Originally, the earl held an office, but the baron did not; thus for the baron there was no ceremony of investiture. A barony was territorial, and with it went the right to be summoned to great councils such as Parliament simply as a part of the obligations of the baron; the descent to a barony continued to be governed by the law relating to the descent of land. When co-heirs appeared in the succession, the law maintained that each was entitled to an equal share in the whole of the territorial barony, and that the land continued to be held by baronial tenure as an essential part of the barony. The territorial right to summons thus became divided between all co-heirs and virtually fell into abeyance. Thus the logical development from this was that because all co-heirs had equal rights, no one could claim the dignity, yet the king could not deprive them of their joint right. The only solution was for the crown to choose one of them to inherit the dignity as the representative of the whole inheritance; yet this the heirs could not force, even if all agreed in naming their member. During his lifetime, a peer, on the other hand, could surrender his peerage to the sovereign, but if he died a peer,+ no statement in a will could prevent or change the succession of the dignity from the course detailed in the terms of the original grant; the same applied to real estate. A man holding such a title or estate could dispose of it during his lifetime, but if he died in possession of it, nothing could deprive his heir of the inheritance. When King Henry I* died in 1135, eight English earldoms were in existence:

Buckingham,* held by the Giffard family
Chester,* held by Ranulph de Meschin II
Gloucester,* held by Robert de Caen, illegitimate son of Henry I*
Huntingdon,* held by the royal house of Scotland
Leicester,* held by the de Beaumont family
Northampton,* held by the Senlis or St. Liz family
Surrey,* held by the Warenne family
Warwick,* held by the de Newburgh family.

Between 1135 and 1141 King Stephen* created nine new earls:

Arundel,* granted to William d'Aubigny late in 1141
Bedford,* granted to Hugh de Beaumont* in 1138, lost in 1141
Derby,* granted to Robert de Ferrers* in 1138
Essex,* granted to Geoffrey de Mandeville* in 1140
Hertford,* granted to Gilbert de Clare* late in 1141
Lincoln,* granted to William de Roumare* in 1139-1140, and Gilbert de
          Gant in 1147-1148; William d'Aubigny,* earl of Arundel
          appeared in two charters as earl of Lincoln
Norfolk,* granted to Hugh Bigod* before February 1141
Pembroke,* granted to Gilbert de Clare in 1138
Somerset,* granted to William de Mohun before 1141

After 1141, Empress Matilda created eight others:

Cornwall,* granted to Reginald FitzRoy in 1141
Devon,* granted to Baldwin de Reviers* before 1141
Hereford,* granted to Miles of Gloucester in July 1141
Oxford,* granted to Aubrey de Vere* in 1142
Salisbury* (or Wiltshire), granted to Patrick of Salisbury around 1149
York,* granted to William of Aumale.*

Over the next century, this number dwindled steadily from 23 in 1154 to less than a dozen in 1265 for several reasons. First, marriage and the failure of direct male heirs brought two earldoms into the hands of one man, as in the case of Lincoln which united with Chester in 1217; Gloucester with Hertford in 1225; Essex with Hereford in 1336. Second, some earldoms were withheld from lawful heirs or suppressed by royal acts which may have been lawful but which were inequitable as in the case of William de Fors* who in 1237 was denied the earldom of Chester to which he had unimpeachable hereditary claim so that King Henry III could annex it to the benefit of his eldest son, Edward.* These 23 earldoms were held to have been granted in fee, that is, of the grantee had no male heir, his earldom like his lands could be inherited by his collaterals and their descendants, and there were few if any limits to the remoteness of the common ancestor who established the kinship. A man could die without male issue, but rarely without blood relations, so it was by forfeiture and not the lack of heirs that Simon de Montfort's* earldom of Leicester passed through the king's hands to his son Edward after the battle of Evesham* (1265). Such extinction by forfeiture was rare, for Montfort was its only victim during the Barons' War* of Henry III's* reign. An earldom in fee could lapse through a plurality of co-heirs, because while the lands were divisible equally between co-heirs, the earldom was not, and if co-heirs were sufficiently numerous, no one might inherit enough land to support the rank of earl. For example, the earldom of Winchester disappeared for that reason in 1264; the earldom of Pembroke disappeared for half a century after the deaths of the great William Marshal's* five childless sons, and reappeared only through the daughter of one of Marshal's daughters. Robert de Ferrers lost his through force, the victim of Prince Edward's lawless greed. (See Derby.) (Bibliog. 47, 66)

earl marshal,+ originally, an officer subordinate to the constable, although they both acted and sat together on the military Court of Arms and Honors which came to be known as the Earl Marshal's Court.

The title of earl marshal was different from all the other titles of earl,* for while they denoted some particular place, this one was personal and official simultaneously. At first this position was designated only as the lord marshal, who carried only a wooden staff. Elevation by letters patent+ from King Richard II* (1377-1399) advanced him to the dignity of earl marshal, and gave him power to bear a staff of gold, enameled black at both ends, with the king's arms on the upper end and his own arms on the lower. Among the lords marshal and earls marshal were:

1135 - Gilbert de Clare,* lord marshal, created earl of Pembroke* by King Stephen* in 1139
1149 - Richard de Clare,* surnamed Strongbow, earl of Pembroke and lord marshal; died in 1176
1176 - John, surnamed Marshal from this office which King Henry II* conferred upon him on the death of Richard, earl of Pembroke*
1199 - William Marshal,* lord marshal, grandson of John; married Isabel, daughter and heir of Richard Strongbow, made earl of Pembroke by King John in 1201;
1219 - William Marshal, the younger, earl of Pembroke, son of William
1231 - Richard Marshal, earl of Pembroke, brother
1234 - Gilbert Marshal, earl of Pembroke, brother
1241 - Walter Marshal, earl of Pembroke, brother
1245 - Maud, countess of Norfolk,* eldest heir of Walter Marshal; allowed all rights thereto belonging;
1246 - Roger Bigod,* earl of Norfolk, as in right of Maud, his mother, one of the sisters and heirs of the five last marshals;
1307 - Robert de Clifford, made lord marshal by King Edward II*;
1315 - Thomas de Brotherton, earl of Norfolk, made lord marshal; followed by Margaret, his daughter and heir, honored with the title of lady marshal, afterward created duchess of Norfolk;
1343 - Thomas Beauchamp,* the elder, earl of Warwick*;
1373 - Edmund Mortimer,* earl of March,* served as deputy for the lady Margaret; resigned 1376;
1376 - Henry, Lord Percy, lord marshal at the coronation of King Richard II.* (Bibliog. 101, 212)

Earl of Pembroke. See Clare, Gilbert de.

Earl of Toulouse, Breton *lai*+ from the mid-14th century. In it, the earl fought on behalf of the innocent wife of the Emperor Diocletian whose life and honor were assailed. He finally became emperor himself. This story had a historical basis in the connection between Judith, wife of the Carolingian emperor, Louis the Pious,* and Count Bernard of Barcelona. The empress had to clear herself by oath before the assembly at Aix in 831. (ed T. C. Rumble, *Breton Lays in Middle English,* Detroit, 1965) (Bibliog. 63)

East Angles, fifth of the Heptarchy,* the seven kingdoms set up in England by Vortiger* around A.D. 449, and containing the counties of Norfolk, Suffolk, Cambridgeshire and the Isle of Ely; it was adjacent to the kingdom of the East Saxons*; among its kings were

575 - Uffa, the first king;
593 - Redwald, the first Christianized king;
870 - St. Edmund, who was murdered by the Danes and his kingdom was
        wasted by them; it was united with the West Saxons* by King
        Edward the Elder. (Bibliog. 101)

East Saxons, fourth of the Heptarchy,* the seven kingdoms set up in England. Begun in 527, some five years after the kingdom of the West Saxons, it comprised the counties of Essex,* Middlesex, and part of Hertfordshire. (Bibliog. 101)

ecclesiastical geographical divisions. As the Holy Roman Empire became Christian, it was mapped into patriarchates as well as prefectures. Under these lay the metropolitan and episcopal districts which later became known by their civil titles of provinces and dioceses. As the Church carried her spiritual conquests beyond the borders of the empire, new ecclesiastical districts were formed in the newly converted countries. As a rule every kingdom had at least one archbishop; the smaller principalities, provinces or divisions became the dioceses of bishops. Different social conditions in northern and southern Europe caused a marked difference in the ecclesiastical arrangements in the two regions. In the south and in the empire, each city had its bishop who always took his title from that city. In the north, and outside the empire, on the other hand, especially within the British Isles, both Celtic and Teutonic, a bishop of a tribe or principality bore a tribal or territorial title. Thus in Italy where there were more cities, bishops were more numerous and dioceses smaller than in the northern Gaul where cities were fewer, and dioceses larger. Outside of the empire, a diocese represented a tribe or principality larger than inside the empire. Within the empire, the territorial titles were used only in the case of metropolitans. A metropolitan was the chief ecclesiastical official belonging to an ecclesiastical metropolis, that is, the chief town or city of a country, especially one in which the government of a country was carried on, the capital. Prelates of that rank, besides their local title as archbishop of "X," often took a territorial title from the kingdom or principality within which they held metropolitan rank. These men bore such titles as Primate of all the Gauls, Primate of All England, Primate of Normandy, borne respectively by the archbishops of Lyons, Canterbury, and Rouen. (See also bishops, English; English ecclesiastical divisions.) (Bibliog. 79)

echevin, French municipal council and magistrate, corresponding to the English alderman. See Lord Mayor of London. (Bibliog. 169)

Eckenlied, Middle High German* romance about Dietrich von Bern (see Theoderic the Great) written in strophes of 12 lines which became known as the *eckestrophe** or *Berner Ton.* In this work, Ecke was transformed from an uncouth giant into a powerfully built knight who, seeking to prove himself, challenged Dietrich but was slain by him. Dietrich subsequently slew Ecke's brother, Fasolt. (ed. Mullenhoff, Janicke, et al., *Deutsche Heldenbuch,* Berlin: Weidmann, 1967) (Bibliog. 86)

eckestrophe, (Berner Ton), stanza form of 12 lines with a rhyme pattern *aabaab cdcd ee* used in the Middle High German* epic poems of *Eckenlied,* *Goldemar,* *Sigenot,* and *Virginal.* It may have been used first by Albrecht von Kemnaten, author of *Goldemar.* (Bibliog. 86)

Ector, Sir, father of Sir Kay,* and foster father of Arthur* in Arthurian legend. He participated in Arthur's early wars. He is not to be confused with Ector de Marys, natural son of Ban* by Agravadain's daughter, who, as half-brother of Lancelot,* later made him king of Guienne* and Benwick. (in *Merlin*, Le Morte Arthur*)* (Bibliog. 145, 202)

Edington, William, bishop of Winchester* who was appointed treasurer under Edward III* in 1345 and chancellor+ in 1356. He centralized the government finance under the Exchequer* because he recognized that only by pooling the entire revenue of the government could he hope to pay for the king's campaigns. By his efforts, Edward managed his continuing war against France without demanding too much more in taxes from his already heavily taxed population. (Bibliog. 203)

Edith Swannehals (Edith Swan's Neck), mistress of Harold Godwineson.* To win support of the house of Leofric* for his claim to the English throne, Harold put aside this woman who had borne him at least four illegitimate children in order to marry Edith, the sister of the earls Edwin of Mercia and Morcar of Northumbria. (Bibliog. 33)

Edmund Ironside, oldest surviving son of King Ethelred II,* the Unready (977-1016). He claimed the throne on his father's death, fighting the Danish Cnut* for it, but finally was defeated on October 18 at Ashington. Because Edmund was admired so highly by the common people, however, Cnut decided he should reach an agreement with him. On an island in the Severn River near Deerhurst, Gloucestershire, these two kings swore a solemn compact of mutual friendship, fixed a sum of money that should be given to Cnut's army, and agreed to a division of England which gave Wessex to Edmund and the remainder of the country beyond the Thames River to Cnut. This imposed a divided allegiance on every nobleman who held land in both Wessex and Mercia, but before that could cause trouble, Edmund died on November 30, 1016, and the West Saxons accepted Cnut as their king. (Bibliog. 213)

Ednyved, the Little (fl. 1230-1240). Welshman surnamed Vuchan (Vaughan), he was the most trusted counsellor of Llewelyn ap Iorwerth*; he also acted as seneschal+ and as negotiator for Llewelyn. Legendary history credited him with killing three English chiefs in a hard fight, and therefore he was allowed by Llewelyn to bear as his arms, "three Englishmen's heads couped." (See heraldry in Volume 1.) (Bibliog. 58)

Edward I, Plantagenet (1239-1307), king of England (1272-1307). Born in 1239 to Henry III* and Eleanor,* daughter of the count of Provence, Edward was named governor of Gascony* in 1256 to replace Simon de Montfort* with whom King Henry was dissatisfied. His marriage in 1254 to Eleanor of Castile* had secured for the English the undisputed possession of that province. Leading the government forces, he defeated the rebellious barons in the opening forays of the battle of Lewes* in 1264, but his later refusal to support the king's forces led quickly to the rout of the royal troops and his and his father's capture in that defeat. Five years later, he undertook a crusade+ to the Holy Land at the request of the Pope. After capturing Nazareth in 1271, he massacred all the Muslims found within its walls. In retaliation for this savagery, an Assassin* with a poisoned dagger stabbed him three times, but his life was saved by his wife's prompt action of sucking the poison from the wounds, and by his vigorous constitution which resisted whatever poison remained in his system. In that same year, his father died and so he was proclaimed king. However, instead of returning directly home to ascend the throne from Sicily where the news reached him, he crossed to Italy and thence to France to participate in a tournament in which he killed the count of Chalons in single combat. Thus he was not crowned until 1274. During the first year of his reign, he issued writs inquiring into the status of the realm. These resulted in the passage of the laws called the Statutes of Winchester+ which reformed many of the abuses of the feudal system. Although he conquered Wales in 1277, he had to fight against the rebellious Llewelyn until that stubborn Welshman died in 1282. His plan to raise money for the expenses of this Welsh war by summoning representatives of the shires, the boroughs, and the church for consultation in 1283 was the start of the English Parliament,+ although the first properly constituted Parliament did not meet until 1295. From 1295, the affairs of Scotland occupied his mind and attentions. He invaded Scotland several times, defeating them at Dunbar, losing to them at Stirling Bridge,* and defeating them at Falkirk.* Although he finally compelled submission of the Scots in 1304, he still had to invade a seventh time in 1307 to avenge the Bruce's* invasion and attacks on England. Edward determined to lead this army in person, but his health failed and he died on the fifth day of his march north from Carlisle. He had ordered that should that happen, his body was to be borne before the army until his enemies were vanquished, but his son, Edward II,* made no effort to abide by that wish, and buried the king at Westminster in October.

Called "Longshanks" because of his height, Edward was the product of his chivalric background. He loved and was famed for his abilities in the tournament,+ especially in the great tournament at Chalons on his way home from the crusade in 1272. He and his horse, Ferrant, were famous on the tournament fields. He loved hunting and hawking,+ feasting in castle or hunting lodge while being entertained by minstrels+ singing stories of battles and courtesy in action. He particularly enjoyed the tales of King Arthur.* Both he and Earl Gilbert of Gloucester* established Round Tables at which on occasion sat his battered and bruised knights fresh from the tournament field. His blond hair had darkened and his skin tanned by the Eastern sun, but he was in perfect health with vitality and good humor. From his Plantagenet+ ancestors he inherited a violent and overbearing temper, and from his father a drooping left eyelid and a slight stammer, but when he was excited, he spoke with intensity. His interests were broad: music, architecture, chess, books. He had married the ideal wife: Eleanor of Castile, the great-granddaughter of the Castilian king who had won northern Spain, the daughter of the king who had won Cordova, Seville and Cadis for Christianity, and the half-sister to

Alfonso the Learned who was one of the finest astronomers and mathematicians of the age. Even though they had married when he was 15 and she was a child, she assured as a grown woman that their court was an orderly and decorus place free from vice and grossness. Edward disliked every form of waste and extravagance, and by imposing a rigid economy he ensured that he could maintain everything he felt a king needed: castles, horses, armor, feasts and tournaments, tapestries and jewels, shrines, churches and monasteries.

His feudal nobles were for the most part men his own age. Four of his eleven earls were of royal blood: his brother, Edmund "Crouchback" of Lancaster, Derby, and Leicester; his cousin, Edmund of Cornwall,* son of the late King of the Romans (Richard of Cornwall) who ruled the southwest from Exeter to Land's End; his brother-in-law, John of Brittany, earl of Richmond; his uncle, William de Valence, earl of Pembroke.* Four other royal earls were: John de Warenne, earl of Surrey and Wessex; William de Beauchamp, earl of Warwick; Henry de Lacy, earl of Lincoln and Salisbury; Robert de Vere, earl of Oxford.* Only two earls stood out of the royal circle: Roger Bigod* of Norfolk, the hereditary marshal, and Humphrey de Bohun* of Hereford,* the constable. The final, and most powerful earl of all was Gilbert de Clare of Gloucester, great-grandson of William the Marshal,* a marcher+ lord who owed the crown the service of more than 450 knights because he was a landowner in twenty-two English counties and lord of the "land of Morgan" in south Wales. By his two wives, Edward sired sixteen children:

John, who died young
Henry, who died young
Alphonso, who died young
Edward,* prince of Wales, afterward Edward II
Eleanor, who married Alphonso of Aragon, and Henry, count of Bar
Joan, who married Gilbert de Clare, earl of Gloucester; and then Ralph
          de Monthermer
Margaret, who married John, duke of Brabant
Berengaria, who died in infancy
Alice,who died young
Mary, who became a nun at Fontevrault*
Elizabeth, who married John, earl of Holland; and then Humphrey, earl
          of Hereford* and Essex*
Beatrice,who died in infancy
Thomas, earl of Norfolk and marshal of England
Edmund of Woodstock, earl of Kent; who was beheaded in 1329
Eleanor, second of that name; she died young.

(Bibliog. 34, 47, 98, 124)

Edward II, Plantagenet (1284-1327), king of England, (1307-1327). The fourth son of King Edward I, he was a weak, indolent, faithless, and utterly incompetent king. He made no effort to pursue his father's war against the Scots for six years after his coronation. Immediately after his father's death, he recalled his favorite, the banished Piers Gaveston,* created him earl of Cornwall,* and appointed him to be guardian of the kingdom during his absence. Before being crowned, he went to France to marry Isabelle, daughter of King Philip IV* of France. His flagrant conduct with Gaveston so aroused the barons that they forced him to agree to banish Gaveston again before they would agree to his coronation in 1308. Edward agreed but went back on his word and recalled the exile within a year. At that, the barons, under the leadership of Thomas of Lancaster,* cousin of the king, banded together in 1310 and forced the king to appoint a committee known as the Lords Ordainers* to serve for a year as the royal executive in instituting reform. These men presented their program calling for annual Parliaments, responsibility of all royal ministers to Parliament, parliamentary control over war and the coinage, and the permanent expulsion of Gaveston and other royal favorites.

The king was inclined to accept this Ordinance, but refused to give up his favorite, Gaveston. At this, the earls took up arms, captured and beheaded Gaveston in 1312. Edward armed to avenge his friend, but the barons, believing their troubles were over, made their submission and agreed to a truce in 1313. Because the Scots under Robert Bruce* had united against the English again, Edward had to accept the barons' terms. Then after the English were badly beaten by the Scots at the battle of Bannock Burn* in 1314, the country was swept by discontent as famine, bad crops, the plague, and rebellion in the Marches* and in Wales made life intolerable. Meanwhile, Edward had replaced Gaveston by the Despensers,* father and son, as his favorites, and secretly plotted to avenge himself on his cousin Thomas of Lancaster, who had led the opposition. In 1322 after the king defeated the rebellious barons at Boroughbridge,* and beheaded Lancaster and three other earls as their leaders, he issued the Statute of York which restored conditions to the way they were before the ordinance, and returned to his old habits of being dominated by his favorites. For the next four years, the king and Despensers tyrannized England, taxing heavily and ruling badly. The Scots continued to defeat the English forces in almost every battle of their continuing war; the French pushed hard against the English forces in Gascony; the barons smouldered in resentment.

In 1325, Queen Isabelle* went to France to arrange a treaty with her brother, the king, and there met Roger Mortimer,* a Marcher lord who had fled to France after escaping from the Tower of London where he had been imprisoned after the battle of Boroughbridge. Becoming intimate, these two soon conspired to rid England and themselves of her incompetent husband-king. When they landed in England in 1326 with an armed force, and declared open war against Edward II, they were supported by London and most of the country; Edward fled to Wales, but was captured and brought back to prison; both the Despensers were executed. In January 1327, the Parliament asked the young Edward III* to replace his father on the throne. The king was given the opportunity to abdicate rather than face deposition, and agreed to do so on promises of personal safety and honorable treatment. Those promises were broken before the year was out and Edward was murdered horribly at Berkeley* by having a red hot poker jammed up his rectum. By his wife, Isabelle of France, he sired four children:

Edward, afterwards Edward III*
John of Eltham, earl of Cornwall
Joan, who married David, prince of Scotland, son of Robert Bruce*
Eleanor, who married Reginald, earl of Gueldres.
(Bibliog. 47, 124, 203)

Edward III, Plantagenet (1312-1377), king of England (1327-1377). One of England's most formidable monarchs, he had unbelievable energy for three decades after his coronation. After dispossessing Mortimer, who with his mother, Isabelle, had usurped the throne, he quickly established his authority over the barons, and by the time he was mid-twenty, he had achieved his full power. He was unusually tall, and strikingly handsome with a pointed yellow beard and long drooping mustaches. He could speak English as well as French, could write Latin and understand German and Flemish. His actions revealed him to have been extravagantly elegant, warm in friendship but mercilessly cruel and hardhearted in enmity. He was a self-indulgent womanizer whose motto conveyed a realistic appraisal of himself: "It is as it is." Born in 1312 at Windsor* castle, he had been appointed guardian of the kingdom on October 26, 1326, and he became king on the death of his father, Edward II, in 1327, but did not ascend the throne until he was crowned in February of the next year, 1328. However, following the death of Edward II, and the young age of Edward III, England was ruled by Queen Isabelle* and her lover, Roger Mortimer, who had assumed the title of earl of March. Their greed and their ineptitude in foreign policy made their rule even worse than that of their predecessor. To complicate matters, Bruce* was recognized as king of Scotland; and Mortimer had concluded a treaty which called for the Scots to pay the English £20,000 in return for which England would recognize the independence of the Scottish crown. Such a treaty was unpopular in England. Further, an indemnity was paid and land ceded to France to settle the problem on the Gascony border, while homage was paid to Charles IV* and then later to Philip VI* for the English possessions in France. Henry of Lancaster had become leader of the barons as his executed father had been, and tried to consolidate their power against Mortimer and the queen. But when Mortimer thwarted their plans by maneuvering Edmund of Kent, the dead king's younger brother, into open treason, and then having him executed, young King Edward III asserted himself and overthrew the regent, Mortimer. In 1330, Mortimer was arrested by the king's men, charged with treason, tried before Parliament and executed; the queen, Isabelle, was given an allowance of £3,000 per year, and was permitted to live at her favorite residence, Castle Rising.* Later she voluntarily entered a convent of the sisters of Santa Clara for the remainder of her life, and died there in 1358. Edward III became king at age 18 in 1330.

Subsequently, when Edward Baliol's* attempt to mount the Scottish throne was overturned in 1333, the English decided to invade Scotland once again. On July 19, King Edward led the English forces to victory at the battle of Halidon Hill,* and forced the Scottish nobles to submit to the English crown, following which Edward annexed the whole of Scotland south of the Firth of Forth; Edward Baliol was allowed to remain titular king over the rest, but not for long. By 1336, he again was a fugitive seeking the help of the English king to the south. Edward again invaded and ravaged the countryside as far as Aberdeen, but was forced to break off the actions to turn his attention to the worsening conditions with France in which through his mother he claimed to have a titular right to the throne. To further that claim, on February 6, 1340, in Ghent, Edward publicly assumed the arms of France, quartering+ the golden lilies on their blue background with his own golden leopards+ on red, and styled himself king of France. In addition, he issued a cleverly worded proclamation, addressed both the French lords and the common people of France, in which he promised to "revive the good laws and customs which were in force at the time of St. Louis our ancestor," to reduce taxation and to stop debasing the coinage (which Philip had been forced to do earlier), and to be guided by the counsel and advice of the peers, prelates magnates+ and faithful vassals of the kingdom. By that move, he posed as a champion of local independence against Valois* centralization, offering an alternate monarchy. He capped off this maneuver by challenging Philip to trial by battle,+ "as we do purpose to recover the right we have to the inheritance which you so violently withhold from us." Such a fight was to be held between the two kings or between a hundred of Philip's best knights and a hundred of Edward's. This certainly was a chivalrous offer by Edward, but it was hardly fair, for he was only 28 and Philip was 47. The challenge was never withdrawn.

In 1338, he created six new earls, but he appointed as his commanders men like Sir John Chandos,* a poor knight from Derbyshire; Sir Thomas Dagworth* a bold professional soldier from a family of Norfolk squires; and Sir Walter Manny,* who had come from Hainaut with Queen Philippa.* In 1339 Edward sailed for France, and although he was unable to lure King Philip* into open battle, he defeated the French fleet off Sluys* in the following year, and concluded a peace treaty with them shortly thereafter. His interest in King Arthur* led him to order a tournament held at Windsor in honor of his great English predecessor, and a few years later in 1348, to found the Order of the Garter.* In 1346, he again went to France on an expedition which before it concluded saw the English victory at Crécy* and the capture at Calais.* After this Edward retired into the background to let his son, Edward,* the Black Prince, assume military control of the French expeditions. About this time, too, the black death* swept across Europe and ravaged the countryside. By 1360, the Treaty of Bretigny* resolved many of the difficulties between England and France; its provisions set a ransom on the French king, John,* and although Edward renounced his claim to the French throne, he kept sovereignty over the duchy of Aquitaine, the counties of Ponthieu and Guignes, and the town of Calais. Between 1369 and 1375, King Charles IV of France succeeded in recovering from the English all but Bayonne and Bordeaux in the south and Calais in the north. By 1376, the "Good Parliament" had virtually seized control of the government from the hands of the king and his ministers, and had forced Alice Perrers, the king's powerful mistress, out of his life, never to see the king again. He died in 1377, one year and two weeks after the death of his oldest son, the Black Prince. The crown then passed to his grandson, the 11-year-old Richard,* son of Edward the Black Prince. By his wife, Edward sired 12 children:

Edward, prince of Wales, the Black Prince, who married Joan, the Fair
     Maid of Kent
William of Hatfield, who died early
Lionel,* duke of Clarence,who married Elizabeth de Burgh,* and then

Violante, daughter of the duke of Milan

John, of Gaunt,* duke of Lancaster, who married Blanche of Lancaster, and then Constance of Castile, and late in life, Catherine Swynford

Edmund of Langley, earl of Cambridge and duke of York; who married Isabelle, daughter of Peter, king of Castile and Leon; and then Joan, daughter of Thomas, earl of Kent

William of Windsor, who died young

Thomas of Woodstock, duke of Gloucester; who married Eleanor, daughter of Humphrey de Bohun,* earl of Hereford, Essex, and Northumberland

Isabel, who married Engurrand* de Coucy VII, who was created earl of Bedford

Joan, who contracted to marry Alphonso, king of Castile, but who died before the ceremony

Blanch de la Tour, who died in infancy

Mary, who married John de Montfort, duke of Brittany

Margaret, who married John Hastings, earl of Pembroke.

(Bibliog. 34, 47, 68, 184, 203)

Edward, the Black Prince (1330-1376), eldest son of King Edward III* and Philippa of Hainault, he was born in 1330 and created duke of Cornwall* in 1337, the first English duke.+ He was appointed guardian of the realm during his father's absences in France in 1338, 1340, and 1342, and on his father's return in 1343, was created the Prince of Wales.* In 1346, at age 16, he accompanied his father's fourth expedition against France and won honor and fame by the leadership he showed when the division he led took the brunt of the French and Genoese attack at the battle of Crécy.* In 1355 he commanded the main of three armies raised by the English for the invasion of France, and landing at Bordeaux, captured and plundered its main fortresses and towns. In the following year, he gained a great victory at Poitiers* and took the French king, John II, prisoner. During the peace which followed the 1357 Treaty of Bretigny,* he married his cousin Joan,* more familiarly known as the Fair Maid of Kent, as third husband. In response to urgent pleas in 1363, the Black Prince agreed to help Pedro, the deposed monarch of Castile, regain the Spanish throne in return for Pedro's assuming the cost of maintaining Edward's army in Spain. The English forces marched across the Pyrenees, defeated Henry de Trastamare in the savage battle of Najera,* and two days later, accompanied Don Pedro in triumph into Burgos. Don Pedro, however, promptly forgot his promises, and after months of waiting vainly for the money, Edward returned to his duchy with only one-fifth of his army;

the remainder had died in Spain of sickness. To recoup some of the money, he imposed a hearth tax in Aquitaine, against which the Gascon lords complained to the king of France. When summoned to Paris to explain this tax, Edward replied that he would enter with helm+ on his head and with 60,000 men. Thus between these two countries, warfare resumed. Two simultaneous invasions of English territory were planned by the French—one led by the duke of Anjou and the other by the duke of Berry. The siege of Limoges by the duke of Berry was successful through the treachery of its bishop, who for money persuaded the inhabitants to surrender. But the prince fell ill to degenerative dysentery which gave way to dropsy, and almost completely incapacitated him. As his degenerative illness began to affect his mind, it intensified his anger, and verging on madness, Edward swore to recover Limoges, and after only a month's siege, succeeded. He swore to make an example of it for surrendering to the duke of Berry which would prevent further defections. Late in 1370, commanding from a litter, he watched his forces attack and overcome the meager defense of the city easily by mining the outer wall, and entering the city. He was so enraged by their earlier surrender to the duke of Berry that he ordered the city destroyed. Its gates were sealed, it was sacked and burned, and the entire population was put to the sword: men, women, and children alike. This brutal stain on the prince's record never could be removed. His illness worsened, making him too ill to govern so that he turned the government over to his brother, John of Gaunt.* His desperate condition then was further shattered by the news of the death of his eldest son, Edward, age six. When he left for England from Bordeaux in January 1371, his constitution and spirit were broken. He died in 1376 and was buried in Canterbury Cathedral. His second son, Richard of Bordeaux, became Richard II* at age 10 in 1377 on the death of his grandfather, King Edward III. (Bibliog. 68, 153, 203, 223)

Edward, The Confessor (1004-1066), king of the Anglo-Saxons (1042-1066). Surnamed the Confessor because of his piety, he was the son of Ethelred II* and Emma,* daughter of Richard I* of Normandy. He and his family fled to the Norman court when Swein* took over the throne of England in 1016, and in 1017, even after his mother married Cnut,* Edward remained in Normandy until he was recalled by Harthacanute* in 1041. He was elected king on the death of Hardicanute in 1042. Under his rule, Godwine,* the West Saxon earl, grew to have enormous power and influence over the throne. Godwine's reluctance to punish the town of Dover for the deaths of several Norman soldiers caused him to flee the wrath of Edward. During Godwine's absence from the country, William,* duke+ of Normandy, visited Edward, and presumably received from him the promise of the English crown. On Godwine's death in 1053, his son Harold* became the most powerful earl, and virtually ruled all of the country in the king's name. Toward the end of 1065, Edward's strength began to fail, and his one wish was to preside at the consecration of the newly rebuilt abbey of Westminster on December 28. His strength gave out, and his role in that ceremony had to be taken by a deputy; he died on January 5, 1066. (Bibliog. 124)

Edwin of Warwick, grandson of Leofric,* earl of Mercia and husband of Godiva.* He declined in 1066 to send men to aid King Harold* at Hastings,* but had to forfeit his lands to William I* because of his feeble resistance to the Normans in 1068. In reaction, William built a castle at Warwick and entrusted it to Henry de Newburgh, son of Roger de Beaumont, who was created the first earl of Warwick* shortly after the date of *Domesday.** (Bibliog. 238)

Egbert, first absolute monarch of the entire Heptarchy,* that is, of England. In 800, Egbert, son of Alemond, king of West Saxons, having vanquished all or most of the Saxon kings, and added their estates to his own, commanded that the entire country be called by the name of England. (Bibliog. 101)

Eginhard. See Einhard.

Egypt, huge ancient country on the northern coast of Africa. Orosius, a Spanish priest of the 5th century, who compiled an encyclopedia, *Historia adversum paganos,* to show that greater calamities had befallen the world in pagan times than those since Christianity began, described Egypt as being of two parts: Lower Egypt and Upper Egypt. Lower Egypt was bounded by Syria and Palestine on the east, by Libya on the west, by the Mare Nostrum (Mediterranean) on the north, and on the south by the mountain which was called *Climax,* together with Upper Egypt and the Nile. This river issued from a spring near the mouth of the Red Sea at a place called Mossylon, flowed westward for a great distance, forming in its midst the island called Meroe, finally bending to the north, and when swollen by seasonal floods, watered the plains of Egypt. Upper Egypt stretched eastward a long way: to the north was the Arabian Gulf, to the south, the Ocean (Indian), in the west, Lower Egypt, in the east, the Red Sea; all told, Egypt contained twenty-four tribes.

        Isidore of Seville's description differed somewhat from

Orosius. He stated that Lower Egypt was comprised of 5,000 country estates, and was surrounded by the course of the Nile which watered the
estates, for the Egyptian skies were never obscured by rain clouds.
Egypt's capital was Babylon (Cairo), built by Cambyses. The island of
Meroe lay in Upper Egypt. Drawing both on Isidore and Orosius,
Honorius of Autun stated in his *De imagine mundi*, written in 1100,
that to the west of Egypt lay the provinces of Libya, named for a
queen of that name; Cyrenaica, called that from the city of Cyrene;
Pentapolis, from the five cities of Berenice, Arsinoe, Ptolemais,
Apollonia, and Cyrene; Tripolis, from the three cities of Occasa,
Berete, and Leptis Magna; Heusis, containing the site of Carthage;
Getulia; Numidia in which lay Hippo, the home of St. Augustine, and
finally Mauretania.

    Later writers were more exact in their descriptions, having
visited the place as merchants. Benjamin of Tudela, a Spanish rabbi
who travelled throughout southern Europe and the Near East beginning
about 1160, testified to the enormous trade carried on there with the
West. Alexandria was the principal port through which spices and
luxuries of the Far East were transshipped to Europe. He spoke
glowingly about the wide straight streets of the city, of the
architectural beauty of its buildings, and of the swarms of merchants
from all over the world who congregated in its streets and markets.
William of Tyre* enlarged by detailing the items which found their way
through that great port: peppers, spices, ointments, drugs, elec-
tuaries, precious stones and silks from the Orient. The Church tried
to impose severe restrictions on commerce with the pagans, in
particular by prohibiting the importation into Egypt of wood and iron
because those two items were of vital importance to the Saracens and
therefore much in demand. Such restrictions, however, were ignored,
and trade flourished between southern Europe and Egypt through
practically the entire period, especially during the crusades.+
William of Tyre reported that Alexandria in 1215-1216 contained more
than 3,000 Frankish merchants. Furthermore, he gave a vivid picture
of the fertile strip of the country, bordered by two deserts, "in
which the land was so burned and sterile that it supported no herb and
no manner of tree, except where the River Nile watered the ground when
it was in flood; in these parts alone a great abundance of wheat
grew." He described the flood of the Nile between the months of June
and September leaving a rich deposit of silt, and the palm gardens
like forests along the banks of the river. He described the caliph's
palace at Cairo and the Mameluke's or sultan's bodyguard recruited
from the children of captured enemies. Legend recorded that among the
diverse deserts lived such wonderful beasts and monsters as pards,

tigers, satyrs, cockatrices, adders, serpents, the cacothephas,+ and monsters. (Bibliog. 122, 126, 160)

Eilhart von Oberg, author of *Tristant*, the first German version of the famous love story, and the oldest German version of a Celtic fable. Based presumably on the same French source used by Béroul for his *Tristan,* this work displayed courtly refinement and a lively dialogue. But it lacked psychological insight into the characters and sped over some events so quickly that the action was confusing. (ed. Hadumod Bussmann, Tubingen, 1969) (Bibliog. 235)

Einhard, Eginhard, author of *Vita Karoli,* a life of Charles the Great (Charlemagne*) that was modelled in form and content on the lives of the Caesars by Suetonius. Einhard was born in the valley of the Maine River about 775, was educated at the monastery of Fulda and later at the court of the emperor. Louis the Pious,* Charles' son, who had been his schoolmate, appointed Einhard as his secretary, and later placed his son Lothair under Einhard's tutelage. He withdrew from public life in 828 and died in 840. His work described Charlemagne after being crowned emperor in 800, and not the actions of a young king in his early years. (ed. and tr. Lewis Thorpe, Penguin, 1969) (Bibliog. 106)

ekupedes, (equibedes), race of devils who dwelt in the air, one of whom was Merlin's* father. See incubus. (Bibliog. 241)

Elayne, Elaine, various characters in Arthurian legend, including: 1) wife of King Ban of Benwick, and mother of Lancelot du Lac*; as a result of her husband's defeat by Claudas she was forced to become a nun (in *Merlin*); 2) daughter of Howel, the Hende,* she was ravished and killed by the giant of Mont St. Michel in Layamon; 3) daughter of Sir Bernard of Astolat whose token Lancelot wore into the lists, and who died for love of Lancelot; 4) sister of Morgause and Morgan la Fée and wife of Nentres of Gorlot; and 5) the Fair Maid of Astolat who became enamored of Lancelot; 6) the Fair, Sans Peur, daughter of Pelles, mother of Galahad* by Lancelot. (Bibliog. 117, 129, 145)

Eleanor, "La Brette," sister of Arthur* of Brittany, and daughter and heiress of Geoffrey,* duke of Brittany and earl of Richmond, by Constance. On Geoffrey's death, she was his heir presumptive* to the duchy. King Philip II,* Augustus of France claimed her wardship because King Henry II* of England would not agree and procrastinated. Her claim ended with the birth of Prince Arthur. In 1193, a clause in the treaty by which King Richard I* was released from his German prison stipulated that Eleanor should marry Leopold, son of the duke of Austria. She was sent to that wedding in 1194 in the care of Baldwin de Bethune, but returned to Brittany when she learned that Leopold had died. When Richard made peace with Philip in 1195, the two agreed that Eleanor should marry Philip's son and heir, but this project also failed. Later King John* imprisoned her in Burgh castle in Westmoreland, one of the strongest castles in England, and then in Bowes in Yorkshire, and finally in Corfe* castle in Dorset to prevent her from marrying and having a child who would be the true heir to the crown. She died unmarried in 1241. (Bibliog. 47)

Eleanor of Aquitaine (1122-1204), wife of two kings, and mother of two kings, Eleanor was the daughter of William IX,* the last duke of Aquitaine, and Aenor, viscountess of Châtellerault. At her birth, she was named Alia-Aenor, "the other Aenor," a new name which in time was shortened to Eleanor. She succeeded her father to the dukedom in 1138, and shortly thereafter in the same year, she was married to Prince Louis of France, who became Louis VII.* Because she was a lively, frivolous, and pleasure-filled woman, and her husband was somber and pious, their marriage was strained from the start. She accompanied him on the ill-fated second crusade+ to the Holy Land in 1147, but they became estranged, and agreed to a divorce on their return to France. On their way through Italy, they were guests of the Pope who cleverly sought to prevent the breakup of their marriage by having them sleep in the same bed; he hoped that Eleanor would become pregnant. She did, but despite the birth of a daughter nine months later, Eleanor still wanted a divorce. That child, Marie,* later became the wife of Henry of Champagne.* Eleanor's divorce from Louis became final on March 18, 1152, on the grounds of consanguinity.+ Six months later, she married Henry of Anjou,* who, in 1154 ascended the throne of England as Henry II Plantagenet.* Because she brought the duchy of Aquitaine with her in marriage, Louis VII was reluctant to lose control of such a vast portion of his country, but Eleanor took it with her in her marriage to Henry, nonetheless.   She bore Henry eight children, despite his numerous infidelities:

William (1153-1156)
Henry* (1155-1183)
Matilda (1156-1189)
Richard* (1157-1199)
Geoffrey* (1158-1186)
Eleanor (1161-1214)
Joanna (1165-1199)

John* (1166-1216)

When she intervened in her husband's affairs, and encouraged her sons to rebel against him, he captured her and imprisoned her for ten years in England. After Henry's death in 1189, she helped her son Richard* with the government of England, and on his death in 1199, tried to save the empire from collapse because of the actions of her son John.* The last few years of her life were spent in the convent at Fontevrault* where she was buried beside her son and husband in the church at the convent. Her interest in the fine arts and in a courtly life filled with light and beauty and music and liveliness led her at her court in Poitiers* in 1173 to hold entertainments which resulted in the formation of courtly love and in the composition by Andreas Capellanus* of the *Art of Courtly Love*.* (Bibliog. 154, 162, 163)

elector, one of the princes in the Holy Roman Empire entitled to take part in choosing the emperor. In the Golden Bull+(1356) of Charles IV,* seven electors were recognized: archbishop of Mainz (Mayence), archbishop of Trier (Treves), archbishop of Cologne, king of Bohemia,* count palatine+ of the Rhine, duke of Saxony, and margrave+ of Brandenburg.* See also titles of dignity.+ (Bibliog. 169)

*Eliduc, lai** by Marie de France* which presented the problem of a married knight who gradually fell in love with another woman. His problem was resolved by the first wife who withdrew to a nunnery. It resembled the romance of *Ille et Galeron** by Gautier d'Arras.* (tr. Eugene Mason, *Lays of Marie de France,* London and New York: E. P. Dutton, 1966) (Bibliog. 147)

Elie de Saint Gille, one of the two *chansons de geste** in the cycle of St. Gilles, which narrated the adventures of the father of Elie. His birth was referred to in the *chanson de geste, Raoul de Cambrai*;* his father was Julien, son of Bernier and Beatrice of Saint Gille. When Julien rebuked Elie for not proving his prowess, Elie left in anger. He tried unsuccessfully to save Guillaume d'Orange from his pagan captors, but was himself captured. Subsequently, he escaped, and with his companion, Galopin, entered the town of Sorbrie. The pagan princess Rosemond saw him, fell in love with him, and when the town was besieged by Macabre, she aided Julien, Elie, and Guillaume to end the siege. She was converted because she wanted to marry Elie. Unfortunately, she was found to be consanguinous with him, and therefore could not marry him, but was forced to marry Galopin instead. Elie married Avisse, sister of Louis of France.   (ed. W.

Foerster, Heilbronn, 1876-1882) (Bibliog. 106, 231)

Elioxe. See *Naissance du Chevalier au Cygne.*

Ellesmere castle,+ Shropshire fortress given by Henry I* to William Peverel, but in 1154 it was returned to Henry II* who kept it until he gave it to David ap Owen on his marriage to his sister Emma in 1177. King John* insisted that it be returned to the crown, yet gave it away himself as part of the marriage portion to Llewelyn on his marriage to John's illegitimate daughter, Joan. Henry III* awarded it to Hamon Le Strange for his services to the throne during the Barons' War.* (Bibliog. 104)

emir, emeer, amir, Saracen* military commander or independent chieftain. The term originally was an honorary one given to the descendants of Mohammed through his daughter Fatima. (Bibliog. 169)

Emma of Normandy (d. 1044), daughter of Duke Richard I of Normandy, sister of Duke Richard II* of Normandy, and wife of Ethelred II* of England. From this marriage came the kinship of William the Conqueror,* grandson of Richard II, with Edward the Confessor,* which was a vital element in his claim to the English succession. Ethelred and his family had found asylum at the Norman court after Swein's* conquest of England in 1013. This was followed by Edward's long exile in Normandy, the Norman claim upon his gratitude for help in time of need, and by his own Norman sympathies as King of England between 1042 and 1066. Emma was a remarkable woman, dominating English politics for 40 years, and losing her influence only shortly before her death when Edward confiscated her lands and property in 1043. After the death of her first husband, Ethelred, in 1015, she married Cnut in 1017, and became known as Aelgifu-Emma. By these two marriages, she became queen to two English kings, and mother of two more: Edward the Confessor, son of Ethelred II, and Harthacanute, son of Cnut. She had married Cnut to prevent any intervention by Normandy on behalf of Edward and Alfred, her exiled sons by Ethelred; this second marriage achieved its goal because relations between the two countries remained friendly during the reign of Duke Richard II (996-1026), even though the aethlings+ were being sheltered at the Norman court. See William I. (Bibliog. 33)

emperor,+ *imperator,* title formerly borne by the sovereigns of the Roman Empire, and since then by a variety of other potentates.

emperors of the Eastern Roman Empire. Rulers of the Eastern Empire between 969 and 1425 and Latin emperors of Constantinople between 1204 and 1372 were as follows:

John Tzmisces, 969-976, co-emperor, husband of Theodora
Zoe, 1028-1050, and Theodora, 1028-1056, daughters of Constantine VIII
Romanus III Argyrus, 1028-1034, husband of Zoe
Michael IV, 1034-1041, husband of Zoe
Michael V, 1041-1042, nephew of Michael IV
Constantine IX, 1042-1054, husband of Zoe
Michael VI, 1056-1057, adopted by Theodora
Isaac I Comnenos, 1057-1059
Constantine X Ducas, 1059-1067
Romanus IV Diogenes, 1067-1071, husband of Eudocia, widow of
        Constantine X
Michael VII, 1071-1078, son of Constantine X and Eudocia
Nicephorus III Botoniates, 1078-1081, husband of Marie, widow of
        Michael VII
Alexius I Comnenos, 1081-1118, nephew of Isaac Comnenos
John II Comnenos, 1118-1143, son of Alexius
Manuel I, 1143-1180, son of John
Alexius II, 1180-1183, son of Manuel
Andronicus I, 1183-1185, cousin of Manuel
Isaac II Angelus, 1185-1195
Alexius III Angelus, 1195-1203, brother of Isaac II
Isaac II restored, 1203-1204, and Alexius IV, his son
Alexius V Ducas Murtzuphles, 1204, son-in-law of Alexius III
Theodore I Lascarius, 1204-1222, son-in-law of Alexius III at Nicaea
John III Vatatses, 1222-1254, son-in-law of Theodore I
Theodore II, 1254-1258, son of John III
John IV, 1258-1261, son of Theodore II
Michael VIII Paleologus, 1259-1282, restored empire to Constantinople
Andronicus II, 1283-1328, son of Michael VIII
Michael IX, 1295-1320, co-emperor, son of Andronicus II
Andronicus III, 1328-1341, son of Michael IX
John V, 1341-1376, son of Andronicus III
John VI Cantacuzenos, 1347-1354, co-emperor, father-in-law of John V
Andronicus IV, 1376-1379, son of John V
John V, restored, 1379-1391
John VII, 1390, son of Andronicus IV, grandson of John V
Manuel II, 1391-1425, younger son of John V, uncle of John VII

Latin emperors of Constantinople:

Baldwin I (IX of Flanders), 1204-1206
Henry I, 1206-1216, brother of Baldwin I
Peter I de Courtenay, brother-in-law of Baldwin I and Henry I
Robert I, 1219-1228, son of Peter I
Baldwin II, 1228-1273, son of Peter I
John de Brienne, 1231-1237, co-emperor, father-in-law of Baldwin II
Philip I, 1273-1285, son of Baldwin II
Catherine de Courtenay, 1285-1302, daughter of Philip I
Catherine of Valois, 1313-1346, daughter of Catherine de Courtenay
Philip II of Taranto, husband of Catherine de Valois
Robert II, 1346-1364, son of Philip II and Catherine de Valois
Philip III, 1364-1376, son of Philip II and Catherine de Valois
(Bibliog. 124)

empire,+ term used to denote either the territories governed by a person bearing the title of emperor,* or, more generally, any extensive dominion. (Bibliog. 169)

emprise,+ using the same word as the word for device, "emprise," this referred to the adventures, undertakings, and enterprises of a knight-errant.+ (Bibliog. 169)

d'Enéas, Roman, 12th-century French romance adaptation of Virgil's *Æneid.* Its 10,156 verses in octosyllabic rhymed couplets recounted the ancient story of Aeneas and Lavinia but changed it into a love story of great passion. It included long monologues of self-analysis by Lavinia, extended descriptions of Aeneas groaning in misery, bestiaries, the seven wonders of the ancient world, and distortions of classical mythology. (tr. John Yunck, New York and London, 1974) (Bibliog. 106)

Eneit, German adaptation of the French *Roman d'Enéas,** by Heinrich von Veldeke. In this version of Virgil's *Aeneid,* the Roman epic became a love romance. All the characters of Virgil's work were transformed into knights and ladies of 12th-century France, and the main emphasis was shifted to deeds of chivalry and courtly love. Although it was begun before 1174, it was not completed until after 1190. (ed. T. Frings and G. Schieb, *Enide,* in *Deutsche Texte des Mittelalters,* #58, 1964;, #59, 1965) (Bibliog. 86)

enfance (Fr.), story of a hero's youth from his conception to his early manhood. It detailed his training for knighthood. (Bibliog. 106)

*Enfances Garin de Monglane, chanson de geste** in 5,000 verses of twelve-syllable lines from the 13th century. This work detailed the youthful experiences of Garin, son of Savari d'Aquitaine and Floure. (crit. ed. Jack D. Brown, DAI 32:2676A, University of North Carolina at Chapel Hill, 1971) (Bibliog. 106, 121)

Enfances Gauvain, fragmentary French verse romance from the early 13th century. This 712-line work related how Arthur's sister, Morcades, bore a love-child by Lot, her page. These two lovers gave the infant to a knight named Gauvain le Brun, who, after baptizing it with his own name, placed it in a cask and set it adrift in the sea. A fisherman rescued him, learned his secret from a letter tucked beneath the child in the cask, reared him and finally took him to Rome where he was educated and knighted by the Pope, and then made a name for himself in tournaments. (ed. P. Meyer, *Romania*, XXXIX, 1910, 1-32) (Bibliog. 10)

*Enfances Guillaume d'Orange, chanson de geste** from the 13th century in 3,400 lines of ten-syllable assonance, this work told how Guillaume first heard about the Saracen princess Orable, and how he contended for her with Tibaut of Orange. Tibaut was unable to consummate his marriage with Orable because of magic used against him; and when he attacked Narbonne, he was driven off by Guillaume and his brothers. This work related basically the same story as *Prise d'Orange.** (ed. J. L. Perrier, New York: University of Columbia, Institute of French Studies, 1934) (Bibliog. 106)

Enfances Hector, poem written in French by an Italian during the 14th century which served as an introduction to Benoît de Saint-Maure's* *Roman de Troie.** (Bibliog. 231)

Enfances Ogier, 13th-century enlargement into a separate poem by Adenet le Roi* of the first part of the 12th-century work, *Chevalerie Ogier le Danois,* by a poet named Raimbert de Paris. (ed. Albert Henry, *Oeuvres d'Adenet le Roi*, Bruges, III, 1956) (Bibliog. 106, 231)

*Enfances Vivien, chanson de geste** of the *Garin de Monglane** cycle, this work was written between 1165 and 1170 in 3,200 ten-syllable assonanced lines.   It described some of the events between the *Prise d'Orange** in which Guillaume was just beginning his career, and *Aliscans** in which he was a mature man. Its story related how the Saracens* had captured Garin d'Anseune and were torturing him at Luiseme-sur-Mer in Spain. They offered to free him if his wife,

Wistace, would offer their son, Vivien, in exchange. In Paris where she went to seek the advice of her kinfolk she was told by Guillaume d'Orange, her brother-in-law, that the exchange had to be made, but that he, Guillaume, would avenge the boy's death many times over. The exchange was made, but Vivien was rescued miraculously just before the pagans were about to torture him. The remainder of the poem described his early days of training and knighthood until the day he almost was killed in capturing Luiserne. This is the first *enfances* epic in the *chansons de geste*. The remainder of his life is recounted in *Covenant Vivien,* sometimes called *Chevalerie Vivien.** (ed. C. Wahlund and H. von Feilitzen, Upsala and Paris, 1895) (Bibliog. 106, 231)

Engelhard, 13th-century Middle High German* courtly epic of 6,000 lines written by Konrad von Wurzburg*; it combined the themes of friendship and the healing of leprosy by innocent blood. Here, Engelhard and his friend Dietrich, as alike as identical twins, visited the court of Denmark. Engelhard fell in love with the king's daughter, Engletrude, and the two were discovered in an innocent nocturnal embrace by Prince Ritchier of England, who denounced them. To prove his innocence in a trial by battle, Engelhard summoned his double Dietrich, who impersonated him and was victorious. Engelhard and Engletrude were married and she bore him children. Dietrich, meanwhile, was afflicted by leprosy which he told Englehard could be cured only by the blood of innocent children. Against Dietrich's wishes, Engelhard sacrificed his children for the friendship he bore Dietrich, and Dietrich recovered. God, however, intervened, and re-stored the children to life. See also *Amis and Amiloun; Der Arme Heinrich*; *Athis und Prophilias.* (ed. P. Gereke, 2nd ed., rev. I. Reiffenstein, *Altdeutsche textbibliothek*, XVII, 1963) (Bibliog. 86)

Engelier de Gascoigne, one of the *douzepeers** killed at Rencesvals* by Climborin, the pagan, who earlier had given his helmet as a present to Ganelon* in the *Song of Roland.** Engelier was avenged when Oliver* killed Climborin in the battle. (Bibliog. 210)

England, during the Anglo-Saxon and Norman periods, the kingdom of England did not include Ireland, which remained independent until the reign of Henry II,* nor Wales which was not conquered until the reign of Edward I*; nor Scotland which was not united with England until the reign of James I in the early 17th century. Having patrolled Britain for over 400 years, the Roman legions finally departed in the 5th century, leaving a free entry for the German invaders to establish petty little kingdoms with little permanent remains. Early in the 8th century the Danish and Norse invaders colonized great areas of the north and east of England which King Alfred the Great* abandoned to them by the Treaty of Wedmore in the same way that they colonized Normandy when it was given to them by Charles the Simple. During the first part of the 11th century, the Danes conquered all of England. Finally it was invaded in 1066 by Duke William the Conqueror* of Normandy with recruits from Flanders, Picardy, and the Armorican peninsula of Brittany. From the time in A. D. 800 when it was called England by King Egbert (see English Saxons), who ruled for 37 years as the 18th king of the West Saxons, 19th king of the English, and the first king of England, the following were its kings:

837 - St. Ethelwolf, 20 years
857 - Ethelbald, eldest son of Ethelwolf
858 - Ethelbert, second son of Ethelwolf, 5 years
863 - St. Etheldred, third son of Ethelwolf; martyr; 9 years
873 - Alfred; totally reduced the Saxons to one monarchy; 23 years
900 - Edward the Elder, son of Alfred, 24 years
925 - Athelstan, son of Edward, 16 years
940 - Edmund, brother to Athelstan, 6 years
946 - Eldred, brother to Edmund; he called himself king of Great
        Britain, 9 years
955 - Edwin, eldest son of Edmund; 4 years
959 - St. Edgar, 16 years
975 - St. Edward the Martyr; son of Edgar, 3 years
978 - Ethelred, 14 years
1016 - Edmund Ironside,* son of Ethelred
1017 - Cnut,* king of Denmark, 30 years
1037 - Harold Harefoot, fourth son of Cnut, 4 years
1041 - Harthacanute,* elder brother of Harold, 4 years
1045 - St. Edward the Confessor,* youngest son of King Ethelred, 21
        years
1066 - Harold Godwineson, son of Godwine; usurped the throne; lost it
        to William of Normandy
1066 - William I,* 7th duke of Normandy, 21 years
1087 - William II,* Rufus, 13 years
1100 - Henry I,* Beauclerc, 35 years
1135 - Stephen,* earl of Blois, 19 years
1154 - Henry II,* Plantagenet, 35 years
1189 - Richard I,* Coeur de Lion, 9 years
1199 - John Lackland,* 17 years
1216 - Henry III,* 56 years
1272 - Edward I,* 34 years

1307 - Edward II,* 20 years
1327 - Edward III,* 50 years
1377 - Richard II,* 22 years
1399 - Henry IV of Lancaster, 13 years
(Bibliog. 101, 124, 178)

English counties (in *Domesday Book*). See counties, English.

English ecclesiastical divisions. Pope Gregory I, the Great (540-604), divided Great Britain into two provinces nearly equal in size: the metropolital chairs going to the two greatest Roman cities of London and York; Wales was to be part of the south, and Scotland part of the north. Circumstances of conversion caused the metropolital see to be centered at Canterbury, and the original division did not work, for although Wales came under Canterbury, Scotland never fell under York. Accordingly, under Canterbury fell the following bishoprics: Rochester; London; Dorchester; Winchester from which Sherbourne (later Salisbury), Ramsbury, and Wells then separated; Worcester; Hereford; Litchfield; Selsey; Crediton and Bodmin which united to form Exeter; Ely and Dorchester to Lincoln; Somerset to Bath; Lichfield to Chester then Coventry; and Thetford to Norwich. The four Welsh dioceses were St. David's, Llandaff, Bangor, and St. Asaph. York had only three: Lindesfarn, Durham, and Carlisle. Ireland had Armagh (for Ulster), Dublin (for Leinster), Cashel (for Munster), and Tuam (for Connaught). (Bibliog. 79)

English Saxons, though divided into seven kingdoms, the Heptarchy,* the Saxons in Britain for the most part were subject to one king, *"Rex gentis Anglorum"*—King of the English People. This king was stronger than the rest, giving unto them the law until they in turn became incorporated into the empire of the West Saxons. Those monarchs were

455 - Hengest,* king of Kent
481 - Ella, king of the South Saxons
495 - Cerdic, king of the West Saxons
535 - Kenrich, king of the West Saxons
561 - Cheuline, king of the West Saxons
562 - St. Ethelbert, king of Kent
616 - Redwald, king of the East Angles
617 - Edwin, king of Northumbria
634 - Oswald, king of Northumbria
643 - Oswy, king of Northumbria
659 - Wolfhere, king of Mercia

675 - Ethelred, king of Mercia
704 - Kenred, king of Mercia
709 - Chelred, king of Mercia
716 - Ethelbald, king of Mercia
758 - Offa, king of Mercia
794 - Egfride, king of Mercia
796 - Kenwolf, king of Mercia
800 - Egbert,* son of Alemond, king of West Saxons.
(Bibliog. 101)

Enguerrand I, de Coucy, count of a domain in the center of Picardy.* A man of scandal, obsessed by inordinate desire for women, he lusted after Sybil, wife of a lord in Lorraine, and persuaded the bishop of Laon, his first cousin, to help him divorce his first wife on the grounds of adultery. Afterward he married Sybil with the sanction of the church while her husband was away at war, and while she herself was pregnant with a child from a third liaison. His first wife, Adele de Marle, bore Thomas de Marle* who swore to avenge his mother by continuing the ceaseless war against Enguerrand which was begun by the discarded husband of Sybil. Using incredible gusto, both Thomas and Enguerrand tried to ruin each other by killing or maiming as many of the other's peasants, by destroying as many crops, vineyards, tools, buildings and other possessions as possible, thereby reducing his sources of revenue. Men were blinded and maimed in this senseless private war. Both men participated in the first crusade,+ and returned with their mutual hatred undiminished to the death of Enguerrand. Thomas succeeded to the Coucy domain as well as his mother's property on Marle and La Fere in 1116. (Bibliog. 223)

Enguerrand III, de Coucy (d. 1242), grandson of Thomas de Marle,* he was called "the Great" because he built or rebuilt castles+ and ramparts on six of his fiefs+ in addition to Coucy; he took part in the slaughter of the Albigensian crusade,+ and fought in every available war he could find. He even fought against the diocese of Reims over feudal rights. He was accused of having pillaged its lands, cut down its trees, seized its villages, forced the doors of the cathedral, imprisoned the dean in chains and reduced the canons to misery. His excommunication in 1216 for those acts forced him to yield in 1219 after he performed penance. He continued his extravagances until his accidental death at the age of 60 when in 1242 he fell from a horse onto the point of his sword. He was succeeded by his second son, Enguerrand IV. (Bibliog. 223)

Enguerrand IV, de Coucy (d. 1311), violent follower of his father's practices, he became the center of a controversy between the peers and the French King Louis IX.* Enguerrand had apprehended in his forest three young squires armed only with bows and arrows but no hunting dogs.+ Even though they obviously were not out for important game (see hunting+), Enguerrand hanged them without any trial or legal process of any sort. That action no longer was considered as a right of the landowner; he could not execute such people with impunity, and so the king ordered him arrested, not by his peers, but by sergeants+ of the court like any criminal, and imprisoned in the Louvre. Brought to trial in 1256, he was accompanied by the greatest peers of the realm including the king of Navarre,* the duke of Burgundy,* the counts of Bar and Soissons who foresaw this trial as a test of their prerogatives. Enguerrand refused to submit to investigation of the case as touching his person, honor, rank and noble heritage, and demanded judgment by his peers and trial by combat.+ King Louis IX, however, firmly refused because he saw such a fight as unjust and obsolete. After a long and heated debate, the king ordered de Coucy to stand trial, and he was convicted. Although the king wished to impose the death sentence, he was persuaded by the peers to forgo it, imposing on Enguerrand instead a fine of 12,000 livres+ to be used partly to pay for masses in perpetuity for the souls of the men he hanged, and partly to be sent to Acre+ to aid in the defense of the Holy Land. Even though Coucy was restored to royal favor by loaning Louis 15,000 livres in 1265 to buy what the king thought was the True Cross, he continued his outrages and died in 1311 at the age of 75 without issue. (Bibliog. 223)

Enguerrand VII, de Coucy (1340-1397), sire de Coucy, count of Soissons and Marle, chief butler of France. One of forty hostages sent to England in compliance with the Treaty of Bretigny* in 1360, Coucy and the other hostages had to live at their own expense, but were received favorably by the English court. During his five years in England, he met Chaucer (they were approximately the same age), and Chaucer's description of the squire in the *Canterbury Tales* may well have described Enguerrand aptly. These Frenchmen brought splendor to the English court as they moved about freely joining the English in hunting,+ hawking,+ dancing and flirting. Sharing a common language and a common culture, both French and English chivalric knights took pride in treating one another courteously as prisoners, regardless of the size of the ransom involved, and Coucy certainly was no exception. He felt right at home in England, for his family owned land there inherited from his great-grandmother, Catharine de Baliol. At Windsor

Castle on July 27, 1365, he married Isabella, second child but oldest daughter of King Edward III.* Four months later, they returned to France with Edward III's permission, but returned frequently to visit Isabella's parents. In 1366, Edward bestowed upon him the vacant earldom of Bedford with a revenue of 300 marks a year; he appeared in English records thereafter as Ingelram of Bedford. Shortly thereafter the king made him a Knight of the Garter.* In 1371, he accompanied his cousin Amadeus VI* of Savoy, the Green Count, on an invasion of Piedmont, Italy, and was made Lieutenant-General for Piedmont. Later he was captured at the battle of Nicopolis in 1386, he was held prisoner in Brusa, Ottoman capital in Asia. Despite frantic efforts by his wife and many other notables to ransom him from the Ottoman prison, he died on February 18, 1397 in Brusa and was buried there. (Bibliog. 223)

ensign, correct term for the armorial bearings of a kingdom, of an office, or a community. (Bibliog. 26)

Entrée d'Espagne, epic written in a hybrid Franco-Venetian language by an unknown writer of Padua early in the 14th century, and dealing with traditional French themes. In it, Charlemagne* undertook to conquer Spain and in the resulting fight, eleven of the twelve peers of France were defeated by a giant named Ferragu whom Roland finally slew after a fierce three-day duel. Later, after he and Charlemagne had a serious disagreement, Roland left for the Orient where he saved a charming princess, Diones, from a brutal marriage, became the bailiff of Persia, and following other exotic adventures, returned to the court of Charlemagne and his wife, Aude, bringing with him the young Persian prince, Sanson. (ed. Antoine Thomas, Paris, *SATF*, 1913, 2 vols.) (Bibliog. 106, 231)

Enzio, king of Sardinia (1225-1272), who played a large role in the conflict between the empire and the papacy in the first half of the 13th century. As one of the natural sons of the Emperor Frederick II* by his mistress Bianca Lancia, he was born in the same year that his father married his second wife, Iolanthe of Jerusalem. His name is thought to have been a corruption of the Germanic name, Hans. When he was only 13, he fought beside his father against the Lombards in the battle of Courtenuova, and in the following year (1238), he was married to the widowed heiress of Sardinia and Corsica, and received the title of king of Sardinia. He also was knighted by his father in the same year. He then was appointed in charge of the German and Saracen troops in the imperial army, and from then on, he was his father's right hand in war. He and his father were so successful, and the papacy so fearful of them, that Pope Gregory IX excommunicated them both, and preached a crusade against them. This opposition did not deter them. In 1241, Enzio, already famous for a victory over the Genoese, was entrusted with the command of the fleet, and on May 3 near Meloria, he led his vessels against a fleet of Genoese ships carrying numerous prelates to Rome in response to the pope's summons for a council to depose Frederick II. Three vessels were sunk and nineteen were captured; the prisoners included three cardinal-legates, and numerous archbishops and bishops; the booty was enormous. All the prisoners were taken to Naples and kept in close confinement, bound mockingly with silver chains. After the death of the pope, Enzio joined his brother Conrad,* king of the Romans, with a large army to battle the invading Tatars; these two defeated the invaders decisively to end their threat to Western Christendom forever. Then he went to Lombardy for several years. He and the emperor were excommunicated again by Pope Innocent IV, but that did not stop him. He captured the castle of Arola, but he stained his reputation by executing more than one hundred Guelphs* who were taken prisoner there. On May 29, 1249, at the age of 24, he was wounded and captured at Fossalta by Bolognese troops. He was so hated and feared by his captors that they kept him in perpetual imprisonment for the remaining 23 years of his life, and nothing the emperor could do nor ransom promised could obtain the freedom for Enzio, his favorite son. After his death, he was embalmed, robed in scarlet, and then lay in state for several days wearing a golden crown and a sceptre before he was buried in the church of St. Dominic. (Bibliog. 68)

Ephemeris belli Trojani, history of the Trojan War written by the supposed Cretan, Dictys* Cretensis. (ed. Meister, Leipzig, 1872) (Bibliog. 202)

Epirus, division of Greece. Following the conquest of Constantinople* in 1204 by the crusaders,+ an independent despotate* (lord or prince) of Epirus was set up by Michael Angelus until 1318, when, after a brief domination by the Serbs, it passed to Turkish control. Despots who ruled it were

1205 - Michael I Angelus Comnenus
1214 - Theodorus Angelus Comnenus
1230 - Manuel
1237 - Michael II
1271 - Nicephorus I

1296 - Thomas
1318 - Nicolo Orsini
1323 - Giovanni Orsini
1335 - Nicephorus II
(Bibliog. 100)

equibedes (ekupedes), race of evil spirits to which Merlin's* father belonged; the name perhaps was a corruption of *incubi demones*. (Bibliog. 202)

*Equitan, lai** of 320 verses by Marie de France* that told the story of a lover killed in a trap prepared for the husband. In it, the lover was a king and the mistress was the wife of his vassal. (tr. E. Mason, *Lays of Marie de France,* London and New York: E. P. Dutton, 1966) (Bibliog. 147)

Eracle, French romance by Gautier d'Arras* which has three main episodes. In the first one, reminiscent of the life of Saint Alexis, Eracle, the only son of an aged nobleman, was endowed with three gifts from birth: the abilities to judge precious stones, women, and horses. After his father died, he was sold by his mother to the seneschal+ of Rome for 1,000 bezants* so she could get the money to pray for her husband's soul. At the emperor's* court, Eracle displayed his talents, and selected a wife for the emperor. In the second episode, war broke out and the emperor departed to fight. Against Eracle's advice, the emperor's young wife was locked in a tower for safety. There she verified the emperor's concern by having an affair with Paradis. When the emperor returned from the war, he renounced his wife who thereupon married her paramour. In the third episode, a Persian named Cosdres invaded Jerusalem and carried away the True Cross to Persia. Because of his services to the emperor in Rome, Eracle was chosen emperor of Constantinople to replace the old emperor, Foucar, who had been slain treacherously; Eracle thereupon set everything right. (ed. E. Löseth, Paris, 1890) (Bibliog. 106, 231)

erbarmde (Ger.), Germanic chivalric-courtly virtue of mercy drawn from Christian teaching. (Bibliog. 235)

ere (Ger.), chivalric word for honor. (Bibliog. 86)

Erec, poem by Hartmann von Aue*; the first Arthurian romance in German. It was a *roman à thèse:* its 10,000 lines treated the problem of how to maintain a just balance between knighthood+ and the demands of love. Its main point verified that a perfect knight+ should not devote himself too much to the one at the expense of the other. Although this work used Chrétien de Troyes'* basic plot, it was not a simple German adaptation of either Chrétien's *Erec et Enide,** nor his *Yvain,** for those two works dealt with opposite cases of immoderate devotion to the fundamental demands of ideal chivalry. In this work, because of his immoderate love for his wife, Erec neglected his obligations so that he became slack he had to take part in the vigorous activities of the tournaments and chivalry to re-establish his knightly honor. (ed. A. Leitzmann, 3rd ed. rev. L. Wolff, *Altdeutsch Textbibliothek,* 39, 1963) (Bibliog. 86, 235)

Erec et Enide, oldest of Chrétien de Troyes'* Arthurian romances. It detailed how Erec, son of King Lac of Nantes, was a knight at King Arthur's* court. While pursuing a dwarf who had struck one of the queen's maidens, he met Enide, brought her to court where they were wed, and then took her to his father's kingdom. There he spent so much time with his wife that he ignored his knightly duties, and people's gossip began to blame her. Overhearing his wife's bitter lament at his fallen esteem, he angrily ordered her to follow him from the castle on his search for knight-errantry, but not to speak to him. Every time she disobeyed his command and warned him of a danger, he chided her for breaking the silence he commanded her to keep. When he was badly wounded, she nursed him back to health, faithful all the while. He forgave her and they returned to Arthur's court where he learned of his father's death. They returned to Nantes where he was crowned. This story ended with an episode called "Joie de la Cort."* Erec was the guest of a King Evrain at a castle named Brandigan. Going to a garden surrounded by a wall of air, Erec saw a row of heads impaled on stakes, and one stake from which hung a horn. Then he came upon a beautiful damsel reclining on a couch under a tree. He was attacked by a tall knight named Mabonagrain who fought lustily until his strength began to wane after noontime, and he yielded to Erec. He told Erec to blow the horn which would release him from his captivity in the garden. At his release, he and the court of Evrain rejoiced merrily—the "Joy of the Court"—and the lady alone grieved in her garden. (tr. and ed. W. W. Comfort, *Arthurian Romances,* London and New York: E. P. Dutton, 1976) (Bibliog. 44)

Ermonrich, traditional enemy of Dietrich von Bern (Theodoric the Great* of Verona) in legend; historically, he was Odoacer, king of Italy. (Bibliog. 86) *ernaans.* See Brehon law.

Escalidars, in the *chanson de geste* Enfances Ogier,* sword of Richard of Normandy.* (Bibliog. 128)

Escanor, medieval French Arthurian romance written about 1280 by Girard d'Amiens. This work intertwined two stories. One centered on Keu (Kay)* who distinguished himself in the eyes of the young Andrivete at the tourney of Banborc organized by her father, Canor of Northumberland, to find a valiant husband for her. Keu fell in love with her, and left for Caerlon before he revealed his feelings for her. However, after her father's death, her uncle tried to marry her to a man of low degree so he could claim the kingdom, but Andrivete avoided his scheme, and his plot was foiled. The other story centered on the enmity between Gauvain (Gawain)* and Escanor le Beau who unjustly accused him of the murder of his cousin. When Gauvain hesitated to defend his honor, young Galantivet, brother of Gifflet, stepped in and fought the false accuser, Escanor, on the road, leaving him half-dead. The accuser's uncle, Escanor le Grand, tried to capture Gauvain, but caught only Gifflet instead, and sent him as a prisoner to the queen at Traverses. Arthur* besieged the town to rescue Gifflet, and Gauvain defeated young Escanor in a duel and they became reconciled. (ed. F. Michelant, Tubingen, 1886) (Bibliog. 10)

Esclabarie, city in Spain destroyed by Charlemagne* during the siege of Narbonne, and rebuilt by the Sagettaries, centaurs who inhabited the city, in the *chanson de geste,* Mort Aymeri de Narbonne.** (Bibliog. 128)

Esclavon, Escler, Escles, generic name given to Slavs from Esclavonie, and frequently confused with and used to mean Saracens.* It is found in the *chansons de geste* Aliscans,* Anseis de Carthage,* Antioche,* Aquin,* Bueves de Commarchis, Fierabras,* Fouque de Candie,* Galien, Ogier,* and others. (Bibliog. 128)

L'Escopart, Saracen* giant in *Bueves de Hamptone;* he also appeared as Escofaut, a Persian giant, whom Maugis killed in the *chanson de geste,* Maugis d'Aigremont.* (Bibliog. 128)

Escosse, name for the kingdom in Scotland* containing the territory northeast of the Firth of Forth in Arthurian romances where its most famous ruler was Anguisel. (Bibliog. 242)

Escoufle, French romance written by Jehan Renart (see Jean Renaut) between 1195 and 1202, and dedicated to Count Baldwin,* later Baldwin VI of Constantinople.* Count Richard de Montevilliers journeyed to the Holy Land, and on his return was urged by the emperor of Rome to pause for a visit. While there, his wife and the empress of Rome bore children on the same day: the empress, a daughter named Aelis, and the countess, a son named Guillaume. These two later were betrothed. When the count died, the emperor dissolved the betrothal, but the two eloped. A buzzard (*escoufle*) carried off Aelis' purse, and when Guillaume rode in pursuit, the two became separated. After many wanderings and much disappointment, they were reunited at Saint Gilles, and married. They lived at Montevilliers for three years, but when the emperor died, they returned to Rome and ruled the empire. (ed. Charles Langlois, *La Vie en France au Moyen Âge,* Paris, 1926, pp. 36-71) (Bibliog. 127)

escuyer. See esquire.+

Les-Espagnols-sur-Mer, sometimes called the battle of Winchelsea,* this sea battle was fought between Edward III* and Philip IV* of France in 1350. In response to the plunder of English merchant ships by a Castillian fleet, a squadron of fifty small English vessels and pinnaces* assembled at Sandwich. Manned by the flower of English chivalry including nearly all the original Knights of the Garter,* the group also included John of Gaunt,* the king's seven-year-old son. Sighting the Spanish fleet late in the afternoon, the English king ordered the attack from his flagship *Thomas.* Just as at Sluys,* so here also, the English triumphed by the use of archers who outshot the Spanish giant crossbows, stone-throwing catapults and cannon. Their marksmanship was followed by English knights and men-at-arms swarming over the Spanish ships to complete the slaughter. Both the king and Black Prince* had their ships sunk beneath them and only survived by boarding enemy vessels. After a ferocious combat lasting till nightfall, the English ended the day in complete victory by capturing fourteen galleons, throwing their crews overboard, and driving off the rest of the enemy vessels in panicked flight. Crowds of English cheered from the cliffs at Winchelsea. (Bibliog. 35, 203)

Esperveris, Saracen,* son of Borel; slain by Engelier de Gascony in the *Song of Roland.** (Bibliog. 210)

Espiet, dwarf, spy, the nephew of the fairy, Orianda, the Lady of Rocheflour. He played a large role in the *chanson de geste,** *Maugis* *d'Aigremont.* (Bibliog. 128)

esquire+ (L. *armiger;* Fr. *escuyer),* knight's attendant or shield bearer; frequently a candidate for knighthood. See esquire in volume 1.

Essex, portion of England which early on belonged to the East Saxons before being made a part of England. The kingdom of the East-Saxons was the fourth part of the Heptarchy,* begun in A. D. 527 some five years after the West Saxons. It included the counties of Essex, Middlesex, and part of Hertfordshire. Its kings were:

527 - Erchenyn
587 - Sledda
595 - S. Sebert, the first Christian king of the East Saxons
617 - Seward and Sigebert
623 - Sigebert the Little
648 - Sigebert III
661 - Swithelme
664 - Sighere
664 - S. Sebba, who entered the monastery of St. Paul's in London
         after 30 year's reign
694 - Sigherd
694 - Seofride (Senfredus)
701 - Offa
709 - Selred
747 - Suthred, who was subdued by Egbert king of the West Saxons, and
         his kingdom made a part of that area.
(Bibliog. 101)

Essex, earls of. After the Norman conquest, Geoffrey de Mandeville, one of the Conqueror's prominent companions, was granted a fief extending through eleven counties. He chose every means to increase his holdings and advance his personal standing during the struggles of King Stephen* and Matilda FitzEmpress* for mastery. He was a famous turncoat and blackmailer. He convinced King Stephen to appoint him constable of the Tower of London, and to make him earl of Essex in for reasons which were obscure. He deserted the king shortly thereafter, and was recognized by Matilda FitzEmpress as earl of Essex and hereditary constable of the Tower of London, and was granted by her 100 librates+ of land, the services of 20 knights, and the offices of hereditary sheriff and chief justice of Essex. He soon changed allegiances again, and obtained from King Stephen 400 librates of land, custody of the Tower, the offices of sheriff and justice of

London, Middlesex, Essex, and Hertfordshire, and 60 knights. After driving the rebels from the Isle of Ely in 1142, he changed his allegiance once again to Matilda when he learned that the king was desperately ill. From her he obtained a charter confirming all the grants both she and the king had made to him. Then he tried to return to King Stephen's good graces but the king had had enough. In 1143, Geoffrey was accused of treason, but he ridiculed the charge. Nonetheless, he was arrested and imprisoned until he surrrendered all his castles to avoid being hanged. On his release, he broke into open revolt, making Ely his headquarters, and sacking and ravaging Cambridgeshire with ferocious cruelty. He raided monasteries, villages, anywhere he could find any wealth; those unfortunate enough to be captured by him were tortured until they paid exorbitant ransoms.+ For this, he was declared outlaw,+ but he continued his rapacious activities until his death. In August 1144, when besieging Acton Burnell* castle, he removed his helmet in the heat of the day, and was struck by an arrow shot by a guard posted on the castle wall, and he died of this wound a month later. Because he had been excommunicated with his son for his gross sins, no one would bury him; it took the monks of Waltham Abbey twenty years before they could finally bury his embalmed and coffined remains.

Geoffrey II, his son and heir, succeeded to the inheritance of his father and grandfather, eleven years after his father's death, and died without issue in 1166. He was succeeded by his brother, William, the third earl of Essex, a faithful supporter of King Henry II.* A vigorous soldier, he commanded a campaign in northern France in 1173, joined with the count of Flanders on a crusade+ to the Holy Land in 1177, and was with that count and the count of Tripoli in an ineffectual siege of Harenc in November 1178, and thereby missed the great battle of Ramleh* where King Baldwin scattered the forces of Saladin.* Returning to England later that year, he assisted the count of Flanders against the count of Hainault, and was one of four generals who were appointed in May 1187 to conduct the war with France. He retaliated for the bishop of Beauvais burning of his castle at Aumale* with the burning of Saint Clair-sur-Epte. He carried the crown at Richard I's* coronation, and was appointed justiciar+ of England jointly with the bishop of Durham during King Richard's absence on the crusade. He died in 1189 on a mission to the king of France, and was succeeded by his aunt, Beatrice de Say (or de Mandeville), sister to the first earl.

Because she was of great age, her son, Geoffrey de Say, was allowed to occupy her place. Her older son, William, died in 1177 leaving two daughters as co-heirs, so on the death of Geoffrey, the title went to the husband of Beatrice's eldest daughter, Geoffrey FitzPiers, who was girded with the sword in 1199. He was succeeded by his son, Geoffrey, the fifth earl, who seems to have been forced into a second marriage to Isabel, countess of Gloucester, divorced wife of King John. By this marriage he became earl of Gloucester for which he agreed to pay the ruinous fine of 20,000 marks.+ When the first installment of 5,000 marks was not paid, the king ordered the sheriffs to reclaim any lands belonging to the countess, but that sum seems to have been paid soon thereafter, for Geoffrey became earl. Siding with the barons against the king in 1215, Geoffrey and his brother, William, were excommunicated by the king in December 1215. Two months later, he was killed at a tournament in London, dying without issue. His younger brother, William, was his heir, but because he was excommunicant, his lands had been forfeit to the king. He did homage to Prince Louis* of France at Rochester in 1216, and saved himself at the battle of Lincoln in the following year by fleeing. A year later, having returned his allegiance to the English crown, he was restored to his lands, except for the money still owing from his brother for the earldom of Gloucester. He died without issue in 1226, leaving only his sister, Maud as heiress. Her first husband had been Henry de Bohun,* fifth earl of Hereford,* who had died in 1220. Her son, Humphrey, earl of Hereford,* succeeded her as the seventh earl. In the Baron's War* he and his son took opposite sides, the father siding with the king and being one of the twelve arbitrators who drew up the *Dictum of Kenilworth*.* Because his son, Humphrey, predeceased him, the title fell to his grandson, Humphrey de Bohun, in 1277. He, the eighth earl, sided with the barons, and became one of the leaders against King Edward I.* Even though he and his co-conspirator, Roger Bigod,* earl of Norfolk, were deprived of their offices of constable+ and marshal,+ in the end they proved too strong for the king to oppose and still conduct his wars against the Scottish, the French and the Welsh. Humphrey died in 1298 leaving as his heir a son, Humphrey, who married Elizabeth, daughter of King Edward I, and was killed at Boroughbridge* in 1322. (Bibliog. 47, 66, 101, 180)

Estanhangues, Stonehenge, where Wace* claimed the remains of Uther Pendragon* reputedly were interred. (Bibliog. 232)

Este, aristocratic family of Ferrara, Italy. In 1296, Azzo VI became *podesta** of Ferrara, and established his rule over a group of towns in the Po River valley. By 1208, he had eliminated rival familes and had become *signore* (lord) of Ferrara. In the 13th century, the Este family had become one of the leading Guelph* dynasties in northern Italy, and in that role, continuously fought the Emperor Frederick II* in Germany. (Bibliog. 98)

Estoire de la Guerre Saint. See Ambroise.

L'Estoire del Saint Graal, prose French Arthurian romance written between 1215 and 1230, and included as part of the Vulgate* cycle. Its story related that on Good Friday, A. D. 750 its author had a vision in which Christ gave him a book of which this *Estoire* was a faithful copy. This romance described how Joseph of Arimathia collected the blood of Jesus in a dish used at the Last Supper. Imprisoned by the Jews, and kept alive for 43 years by this vessel, Joseph was finally freed by Vespasian. He was baptized, and on divine orders, left with his wife and son, Josephes, to preach the Gospel. He converted Evelake, the king of Sarras who took the name of Mordrain, and his brother-in-law who took the name of Nascien on their baptisms. These men worked to convert the people in the east. Joseph, in the meanwhile, had taken his family and the Grail on a ship to Britain where in due time they were joined by Mordrain, Nascien and his son, Celidoine. The Grail continued to work its miracles; it multiplied the bread and fish which Alein, nephew of Joseph, and the twelfth son of his brother-in-law, Bron, had caught. In their old age, Joseph and his wife had a second son, Galahad de Galafort. On his death, Joseph committed the vessel to Alein, first of the Fisher Kings,* who took it to the Terre Foraine, built Castle Corbenic,* and there successive guardians of the Grail awaited the coming of the Good Knight. (ed. H. O. Sommer, *Vulgate Version of the Arthurian Romances,* Washington: Carnegie Institute, 1909, I) (Bibliog. 10)

Estoire des rois d'Angleterre et de Normandie, account of the wars between England and France at the beginning of the 12th century, compiled by an anonymous writer of Bethune in Picardy.* (ed. Delisle, *Recueil des historiens des Gaulois,* Paris, 1905, XXIV) (Bibliog.106)

Estoire des rois de France, French translation of the Latin work, *Historia regum Francorum,* 1185-1204, by monks of St. Denis.* (ed. Delisle, *Recueil des historiens des Gaulois,* Paris, 1905, XXIV) (Bibliog. 106)

Estorgant, one of the Saracen* twelve opposing Charlemagne's* *douzepeers** at Rencesvals;* he was slain by Aton in the *Song of Roland.** (Bibliog. 210)

Estout de Lengres (Langres), French baron, son of Odon, but not the Odon who was the uncle of Aubri le Bourgoing, the traitor in the *chanson de geste,* * *Aubri.* He became a heroic-comic figure; he was petulant when Roland* ordered him to stay to guard the camp, but replied that he would guard it by becoming a leopard. He appeared in the *chansons de geste, Rolandslied,* * *Gaufrey,* * and *Ogier.* * (Bibliog. 128)

Estramariz, one of the Saracen* twelve sent to oppose Charlemagne's* *douzepeers* * at Rencesvals*; he was slain by Berengier in the *Song of Roland.* * (Bibliog. 210)

Ethelred II (Aethelred) the Unready, king of England (979-1016). As his name literally meant "noble counsel," the epithet "Unready" must have been given to him as a play on words. During his reign, when a crisis demanded a concentration of the national energy, this king could neither give direction to his people nor hold his greater subjects to their allegiance. When he needed money on short notice, he would write to the shire courts to have them raise the needed funds. These informal communications, called King's Writ,+ were written in English and were authenticated by the impression of his seal hanging from one corner. (Bibliog. 213)

Ethiopia, huge country in Africa stretching from the Atlas Mountains in the west to the ends of Egypt in the east, and by the ocean on the south and the Nile River on the north. It was first called "blue men's land" for it was believed to be inhabited by men of that color; it also was inhabited by black men who gave the country its name. Many nations and many men with diverse faces were located therein. Other residents included Trogodites who lived in caves and dens instead of houses, and ate serpents and had a terrible voice; Garamantes who lived like beasts with women without marrying them; Graphasantes who went around naked and did no work; Benii who had no heads, but their eyes were fixed in their breasts; and men who lived only on honeysuckle dried in smoke, but they didn't live past the age of 40. It also contained many marvels including such beasts as rhinoceros, chameleon, cockatrice,+ dragons* with precious stones in their heads, and such precious gems as jacinth,+ chrysophrase, and topaz among many others. (Bibliog. 18)

Eu, count of, Guillaume (William), illegitimate son of Richard I,* duke of Normandy, received from his father the *comte* of the Exmesin or Hiemaes. He rebelled against his half-brother, Duke Richard II,* and was imprisoned at Rouen. Escaping, he surrendered to the duke, was pardoned, and was given the *comte* of Eu, of which his nephew, Gilbert, ancestor of the family of Clare,* recently had been deprived. Guillaume's son and heir, Robert, count of Eu, together with Roger de Mortemer, commanded the Norman army at the battle of Mortemer in 1053. After the invasion in 1066, Duke William I gave him the honour of Hastings. In 1069, he and Robert, count of Mortain,* were left in charge of Lincolnshire, and defeated an invading band of Danish at Lindsey. Later, like the count of Aumale* and other Normans, he deserted Duke Robert II,* Curthose, and placed his castles at the disposal of William II.* His son and heir, William, count of Eu and lord of Hastings, possessed in 1086 an extensive honour which included holdings throughout England and the lands of Striguil (see Chepstow), but he took part in the rebellion against William II in favor of Robert of Normandy, invaded Gloucestershire, and destroyed Berkeley town. By 1093, William II had won him over by bribes and promises, but in 1095 he participated in Mowbray's plot to kill William II and place the count of Aumale* on the throne. At the council of 1096, he was charged with treason as one of the conspirators of 1095, was vanquished in single combat+ by his accuser, was condemned to be blinded, and at the insistence of his brother-in-law, Hugh, earl of Chester,* also was emasculated.

This William's grandson, John, as count of Eu and lord of Hastings, was given the custody of Tickhill* by King Stephen* but lost it when captured at the battle of Lincoln* in 1141, and did not recover it when his other lands were restored; he died after 1189. When his sister and heir, Alice, countess of Eu, married Raoul de Lusignan of Exoudoun, Raoul became count of Eu. King Richard I gave him Driencourt. In 1200, Raoul and his brother, the count of La Marche, swore fealty to King John* who gave him a castle in Poitou* for which he did liege homage.+ In 1201, John quarreled with the Lusignans because he had married Isabel of Angoulême,* even though she was engaged to the count of Lusignan. At the time, he confiscated the English possessions of the count of Eu, including Driencourt and all his other possessions in Normandy, because the count had defied him. When Raoul and his brother appealed to King Philip II,* Augustus, of France, the king besieged Driencourt, but lifted the siege when he learned of John's success at Mirabeau.* Count Raoul's granddaughter, Marie, married Jehan de Brienne, called "d'Acre," son of Jehan de Brienne, king of Jerusalem, and so he became count of Eu in 1249. Then in 1251, he obtained a safe-conduct+ to go to Canterbury on a pilgrimage. Shortly after King Louis IX* of France knighted him at Jaffa* in 1253, he became champion of France until his death in 1270. Louis requested Henry III* to restore to Jehan the castles of Hastings and Tickhill, but Henry refused. Jehan accompanied Louis on his crusade, died in 1270 and was buried beside King Louis IX in the chapel of Saint-Martin at the abbey of St. Denis.* Jehan's great-great-grandson, Raoul de Brienne, count of Eu and Guines, and constable of France, was captured at Caen in 1346 by Sir Thomas Holand,* and did not regain his liberty for four years. So important a prisoner was he that King Edward III* paid 80,000 florins+ to Holand for him. On his return to Paris in 1350, he was accused of treason, and condemned to be beheaded. He was executed "à l'heure de matines" (midnight) on November 19, 1350. This honour died with his sister and heir in 1389. (Bibliog. 47)

Eudes II (995-1037), count of Blois, and one of the most undisciplined of the great French vassals of the 11th century. Although he had been a faithful vassal of Hugh Capet,* he constantly warred against King Robert II* the Pious and Henry I,* and particularly against the counts of Anjou* over control of the Loire valley. After Fulk III Nerra* defeated him in 1017, he turned eastward and his claims to Troyes brought him into direct conflict with King Robert II. In 1023, he disobeyed a summons to appear at the royal court, and hence went to war with King Robert, but defended successfully his actions in a remarkable document which explained the principle of the obligation* between king and vassal. His document to King Robert II read, in part,

> I am astounded that without having heard me in my own defense, you should hasten to pronounce me unworthy of the fief I hold of you. Consider my ancestry: by dint of it I am entitled to succeed to the counties of Meaux and Troyes. Consider the fief you have bestowed on me: it was not granted out of your royal fisc, but is part of the lands which have come down to me by hereditary right and of your royal grace. And consider the feudal services I have done you: you are well aware that for the favors I have had from you I have served in your household, on your travels and in your wars. And now you have deprived me of your favor, and seek to take away from me the things you have given to me. It may be that in defending myself and my fief, I have committed certain offenses against you. I was driven thereto by necessity and the wrongs I have suffered. By God and my immortal soul, I had rather die defending it than live deprived of it....Wherefore I implore you to show me that clemency which is as a well-spring within you, and which only evil counsel can cause to dry up. And I pray you to cease persecuting me, and let me be reconciled with you. (Bibliog. 74)

In 1032, Eudes claimed, as nephew of Rudolph III, the inheritance of the kingdom of Burgundy* against the claims of the Emperor Conrad II, and he siezed power in Arles, but held it for only two years before being forced to yield it to the forces of the Imperial army in 1034. (Bibliog. 74, 98)

Eustace, the monk, ("le moine"), French monk who left the monastery at Samer, France, to demand justice from the count of Bologne against Hainfrois de Hersinghen, the murderer of his father. When the appeal+ of battle went against his champion he went into the service of Count Renaut of Bologne and by 1203 had become his seneschal.+ His old enemy, Hainfrois, however, convinced Count Renaut that Eustace should be delivered to him. Eustace fled, swearing vengeance. Living as an outlaw near Bologne, he warred against Hainfrois so intensely that when the count sought assistance from the king of France, Eustace took service with King John* in England as a sea captain. John rewarded that service by granting him lands in Norfolk. In 1212, however, when the count of Bologne and King John entered into an alliance, Eustace turned to serve the king of France, and was promoted rapidly to the rank of admiral. When Prince Louis* invaded England in 1215, Eustace's ships transported the prince to England from Calais and landed the French siege machines at Folkestone. He was killed in a great English naval victory off Sandwich in 1217.

His reputation as an unscrupulous sea fighter led him eventually to become known as the archpirate, one who from a black monk became a demoniac. His fame had grown so legendary that in the early years of the 14th century, 100 years after his death, he was described as a tyrant of Spain named Monachus who had wasted many lands until at last, hearing that England was ruled by a child, the infant Henry III,* he aspired to conquer that country also. (Bibliog. 39, 120)

Evelake, king of Sarras, an eastern kingdom thought to lie near Jerusalem, but probably a corruption by abbreviation of the word Sarrasin or Saracen* in Arthurian legend. Upon his baptism, he changed his name to Mordrains. He played an important role in the mission of Joseph of Arimathea. When he foolishly approached the Grail too closely, he was blinded, but was allowed to live until the arrival of Galahad. He appeared in *Estoire del Saint Graal* and *Joseph d'Arimathie*. (Bibliog. 145, 202)

Everingham, Adam de (b. 1307), English soldier who fought at the siege of Berwick* in 1333, at Halidon Hill* in 1333, and then beside King Edward III* at Antwerp in 1338 and at Sluys* in 1340. When later he was captured in France in 1342, the king paid 200 marks in gold for his ransom. He went on to serve with the earl of Derby* in Gascony* in 1346, with the earl of Lancaster* at Calais* in 1347, and with the king on the Franch invasion in 1359-1360. (Bibliog. 47)

Evesham, battle of (August 14, 1265), final conflict of the Barons' War* between the forces of King Henry III* of England and Earl Simon de Montfort.* Montfort's forces were resting at Evesham, a small town in western England situated on a spit of land in a deep loop of the river Avon; the town was at the base of the slope. Thus the location was a good place to defend but almost impossible to escape from if attacked from both land and river sides. Prince Edward* discovered the location of the barons' forces and marched to challenge them. Displaying banners captured in recent encounters with some of Simon's supporters to deceive Earl Simon's lookouts, Edward's forces approached in three armies which blocked the avenues of escape. When he learned of the identity of the forces approaching his position, the earl knew instantly that he had to fight or flee, but the only path out led through the prince's forces. His Welsh footsoldiers were no match for the mounted men in armor, and were slaughtered like sheep. The barons formed a circle with Montfort in their midst, but their cause was futile. In the battle, Earl Simon, his son Henry, Peter de Montfort, and Ralph Basset* were killed. Guy de Montfort and Humphrey de Bohun* the younger were wounded and captured. King Henry was wounded and would have been slain had he not been saved by Roger Leybourne*—the man who almost single-handedly had fomented the revolution that led to the Barons' War, but who turned away from the barons after their severe disagreement had split their forces. In the ensuing fight, the barons lost 180 knights, 200 squires and 7,000 footsoldiers; the prince lost only 2,000 footsoldiers and reportedly only 2 knights. De Montfort's body was dismembered by William Mautravers,* one of his knights at Lewes. His head was sent to Roger Mortimer's* wife at Wigmore; his body was buried at Evesham where he fell. (Bibliog. 166, 184)

Excaliber,+ King Arthur's* sword. Called Caliburn by Geoffrey of Monmouth, and Caledfwlch in the *Mabinogion*, this was the sword which Arthur drew from the stone to establish his claim to the throne; the name was reputed to mean "cut steel." It supposedly was unearthed at Glastonbury* when Henry II* ordered Arthur's tomb exhumed in 1181, and later given by Richard I* to Tancred* in Sicily on his way to the Holy Land on the third crusade.+ (Bibliog. 27, 202, 241)

Exchequer,+ administration of finances in Anglo-Norman England and Norman Sicily. Its origins lay in the practice of using a chequered table or board on which money due the ruler would be placed by peasants, barons, sheriffs alike, and counted. Such a board was called an "exchequer" so that the term came to be applied to the court which sat with the Exchequer. (Bibliog. 69)

Exeter, chief city of Devonshire, England. Its first duke was John Holand, earl of Huntingdon, and son of Thomas Holand*; his mother was Joan,* the Fair Maid of Kent, widow to Edward, the Black Prince.* He married Elizabeth, eldest daughter of John of Gaunt.* John was made duke and lord chamberlain for life by King Richard II,* but was deposed from this title in 1400, and later that same year was beheaded by King Henry IV* at Pleshy in Essex. (Bibliog. 101)

Exeter castle,+ fortress built in Exeter by William I* in 1068, but not kept in good repair over the next few centuries so that much of it collapsed in the reign of King Edward I.* Edward ordered it repaired and granted it to his son, the Prince of Wales (later Edward II*), for life. (Bibliog. 104)

Eye castle,+ fortress in Suffolk* founded shortly after the Norman Conquest by William Malet as the *caput* of the extensive honour+ of Eye. In 1157, it was one of the castles which Henry II* took from William, count of Boulogne,* Stephen's surviving son and heir, and granted it to the custody of Thomas à Becket.* It was damaged in the fighting surrounding Hugh Bigod's* rebellion in 1173-1175. Richard I* granted it to Henry, duke of Lorraine,* whose wife had a hereditary claim to the honour. (Bibliog. 104)

Eynesford castle, castle+ on land in Kent* held by the archbishop of Canterbury.* Originally intended to be a defensive fortification, this castle consisted basically of a watch tower surrounded by a wooden wall which, in 1100, William de Eynesford I replaced with a stone wall 30 feet high and 6 feet wide at its base, and built of flint rubble laid in a herringbone pattern. His son, William II, known as Gurham, built the stone hall and raised the curtain wall. When William III (all lords of Eynesford were christened William) disputed Thomas à Becket* about a priest for Eynesford, King Henry II* intervened. William V opposed King John* and was captured at Rochester castle. Although the king threatened to hang those captured, he relented and held them for ransom instead. Following King John's death, William V became an important official for King Henry III.* (Bibliog. 247)

F

Fair Unknown. See *Libeaus Desconus*.

Falaise, Treaty of, also known as the Treaty of Montlouis, this was the +surrender signed in 1174 by the rebelling sons of King Henry II of England. When Henry had tried to give some of young Henry's* castles in Anjou as a marriage portion for his youngest son, John, in 1173, his sons Henry, Richard and Geoffrey rebelled. They fled to Paris where they were to be joined by their mother, Eleanor of Aquitaine,* but she was captured by Henry II's forces and kept in prison for fifteen years. The rebelling princes were joined and supported by the kings of France* and Scotland* and a few Anglo-Norman barons. By 1174, Henry had defeated the Scots and the rebels, had driven the French from Normandy and had forced his sons into complete submission. The rebellion ended with the princes signing this treaty which restored them to their titles and granted them pensions; John, however, was given the castles which had started the war, and the king of Scotland was forced to pay homage to Henry for his entire kingdom. (Bibliog. 92, 124, 162)

Falkirk, battle of (July 22, 1298), conflict between the English King Edward I* and Scots under William Wallace* in which the Scots used footmen grouped in a rectangular formation called shiltron.+ (See Bannock Burn.) At the approach of Edward's forces, Wallace took a position on a hillside two miles south of Falkirk, not far from the edge of a thick forest. With his front protected by a broad morass, he arrayed his pikemen in four great shiltrons behind which were two to three hundred mounted men-at-arms. On each flank and between the shiltrons were a few thousand archers. Edward formed his army into three battles.+ Roger Bigod,* earl of Norfolk, the marshal, and Humphrey de Bohun,* earl of Hereford,* led the right or vaward battle; Edward led the main battle in the center; and Anthony Bek,* bishop of Durham, led the one on the left. Each battle contained thirty to thirty-five banners of barons and bannerets.+ Starting the charge, the vaward was turned back by the morass and began to circle around it. Seeing that movement, the third battle led by Bek also wheeled around to flank the morass to await the arrival of the king's forces. Impatient at this delay, some English knights dashed foolheartedly into the impenetrable mass of spears held by the Scottish shiltron on two levels, and were killed. Then, even though Bigod's forces charged the left flank and scattered its archers, the English were unable to penetrate the shiltron. Edward's arrival changed the plan of attack. He had his knights pause while his bowmen concentrated their fire at point-blank range against the shiltron, causing devastation. The Scots could not retaliate for their own bowmen had been scattered. After a few moments, the shiltrons had been so weakened in places that Edward commanded his knights to charge a second time at the weakened points of the Scots' line. This time the English horsemen burst through the lines where the dead and wounded were the most numerous, and the result was little more than a massacre. One third of the Scottish host of an estimated 10,000 footmen and 200 horsemen lay dead on the field; the survivors, including Wallace, fled to the forest to save themselves. As a result, the English losses were light, and the Scottish heavy. From this attack, military men learned a lesson similar to that from Hastings*: even the best of infantry, if not supported by cavalry and situated where their flanks could be turned, could not hope to withstand a forceful combination of archers and cavalrymen. (Bibliog. 166)

familia regis, king's personal retinue; a standing nucleus of armed men—knights and bannerets—around which a king mobilized his army. In normal times, this consisted of thirty to forty knights and from sixty to ninety sergeants. (Bibliog. 166)

Fantôsme, Jordan, chancellor+ in the diocese of Winchester, and author of a rhymed chronicle, *La Guerre d'Ecosse* (1173-1174), written before 1183, detailing Henry II's* war against his eldest son, young Henry,* the king of Scotland, and King Louis VII* of France in 1173-1174. He had been an eyewitness to part of this conflict. (tr. Joseph Stevenson, *Church Historians,* London: Seeleys, 1856, IV, 1, pp. 245-288; ed. Philipp Becker, *ZrP,* lxviv 1944, 478-535.) (Bibliog. 99, 231)

Fatamid, dynasty which challenged the power of the Abbasids* in Egypt.* Said ibn Husayn, claiming descent from Fatimah, set himself up in Tunis as the Mahdi of the Ismailian sects of North Africa in 909. Expanding both east and west, by 973 the Fatamids had set up a powerful center in a new city, Cairo, which they had built. Their armies overran Africa and raided Sicily, Corsica, Malta, and the coasts of Italy and southern France; they pushed into Arabia, captured Mecca, Medina and Hedjaz, and even controlled Damascus for a while.

Under the caliph+ Al Azziz (975-996), they controlled an empire that stretched from Morocco to Mosul. Azziz was followed by one of the most bizarre of all the caliphs, Al Hakim* (996-1021). His insanity was interpreted as godliness, so his sect believed him to be God. His religious persecution was extraordinary: he destroyed the Church of the Holy Sepulchre in Jerusalem, closed all churches, destroying many; Christians and Jews were forced to wear distinctive dress; Muslims were forbidden to make their pilgrimage to Mecca; all dogs were exterminated; all chess boards burned, and women were forbidden to appear on the streets or at windows. To ensure women's place inside buildings, he forbade them to possess shoes; and once he decreed that all shops and places of public business should be closed during the day, and all business conducted at night. He ruled for twenty-five years before being assassinated. One of the most interesting sects of the Ismailites were the Assassins+ with headquarters at Alamut in northern Persia and with a branch in Lebanon. By the end of the 11th century, the Fatamid's control over Egypt, western Arabia, and southern Palestine* had become so feeble that it was easily overthrown by the crusaders+ and in 1171 finally by Saladin.* (Bibliog. 205)

Fata Morgana. See Morgan la Fée.

Faulkes de Breauté. See Breauté, Faulkes de.

fée, fay, fairy or demi-goddess from Celtic and Teutonic tradition that abounded in medieval stories. These creatures affected the fortunes of adults. Nigellus Wirkere, contemporary of Thomas à Becket,* described in his work, *Speculum Stultorum,* how three fays, or Fates as he called them, relieved misfortune. One of them, *domina,* restrained the malevolent zeal of the other two when she showed the difference between two young ladies. One used the riches given her to the disadvantage of other people; the second, a young and lame peasant girl, became a fine lady with her riches despite her physical handicap. In his *Roman de Rou,* * Wace* related that he had been assured that he would see fays in the forest of Broceliande* but did not find any there. Perhaps the most famous one was Morgan le Fée* in Arthurian legend. (Bibliog. 150)

Felton, Sir John (d. after 1334), English knight from Norfolk who served in the army in Scotland in 1310, and was knighted later that same year. He served as keeper of the castle+ and manor of Alnwick,* constable+ of the castle of Newcastle upon Tyne. In 1317, he was ordered to deliver to Henry Percy* the castle and honour of Alnwick in 1318, and to pay £100 to Percy due from Felton as keeper of that castle. Then he was ordered to join King Edward II* at Coventry and set out against the Scots and the Contrariants* in 1322. In 1326, the king ordered him to remain at the march* of Wales for its defense against the rebels. He demonstrated his fidelity to the king shortly thereafter, when he was appointed constable of Caerphilly* castle where he resisted a siege by Queen Isabelle's party directed by Sir Roger Chandos.* On December 26, 1326, and again on February 15, 1327, he received letters supposedly from the king at Kenilworth ordering him to deliver the castle and the king's goods to Roger de Chandos and William la Zouche of Ashby, and then discharged Felton from his office and from his oaths to keep the castle. Because the countersignature of the king was missing from them, these orders were ignored. Even though agreements including pardons were offered to him and his garrisons at repeated intervals in January and February 1327, he held out against Zouche until these agreements included Hugh, son of Hugh Despenser* the Younger, who was in the castle, and who had been specially excepted from the earlier pardons to Felton. (Bibliog. 47)

Felton, Sir William (d. 1367), seneschal+ of Poitou.* Son of Sir William Felton of Northumberland,* he held important commands during the wars with Scotland.* He fought at Halidon Hill* in 1333, was summoned to Parliament, accompanied the Black Prince* to Poitiers* in 1359, and fought at the siege of Reims which the English were forced to raise and retreat to Brittany. While there, Felton participated in the siege of the castle of Pontorson defended by du Guesclin.* He was defeated and captured, but shortly thereafter, du Guesclin became a hostage for John de Montfort,* and was entrusted to Felton. One day du Guesclin went riding in the charge of Felton's young son, and escaped to Guincamp. From there, du Guesclin sent a message to Montfort exonerating Felton from any complicity in his escape, and challenged anyone who might assert that Felton had broken his word of honor. Felton wanted to accept the challenge but was forbidden to do so. (Bibliog. 58)

Ferdinand III, king of Castile (d. 1252). One of the two leaders (the other was James I* of Aragon) who carried through their decisive efforts to reconquer from the Muslims* most of eastern and southern Spain between the early 11th century and 1250. (Bibliog. 118)

Fergus, medieval French Arthurian verse romance written by Guillaume le Clerc about 1225. Fergus, son of a peasant, saw Arthur* and a hunting party ride by the field he was plowing, and decided to become a knight. He eventually was knighted at Carduel and set out on knight-errantry.+ He met the beautiful Galiene, +Lady of Lothian, and rejected her favors because he felt unworthy until he could prove his worth by the perilous adventure of Nouquetran. He removed the wimple and horn from an ivory lion by killing the black knight defending it. When he returned to Galiene's castle, she had disappeared but he set out to find her. He defeated the king who was besieging the castle where she was staying, and then left to participate in the tourney held by King Arthur at Gedeorde. There he was recognized by Galiene and they married. (ed. E. Martin, Halle, 1872) (Bibliog. 10)

Ferguut, middle Dutch Arthurian verse romance which was a redaction of the French *Fergus** of Guillaume le Clerc. (ed. J. Verdam, Leiden, 1908) (Bibliog. 10)

Fernan Gonzalez, Poema de, anonymous Spanish narrative poem (c. 1260) in the *cuaderna via** meter detailing the exploits of Count Fernan Gonzalez (c. 915-970). Based on a lost epic, *Cantar de Fernan Gonzalez,* this poem centered on the hero's struggle during the fights of Arlanza, Gonzalez, and Castile for independence from the province of León. (ed. modern Spanish, A. Alarcos Llorach, Valencia, 1955) (Bibliog. 237)

Ferrara, province in north central Italy. It became a powerful principality and flourished as a seat of the Este* family whose court was famous throughout Europe for their patronage of arts and letters. (Bibliog. 200)

Ferrers family (De Ferraris), descendants of Henry de Ferrers, a *Domesday+* commissioner in Worcestershire, and the son of Walkelin, lord of Ferrières St. Hilaire in Normandy* who had been killed in Normandy during the early years of the dukedom of William I.* Henry had fought at Hastings* and was rewarded for his efforts by being granted 114 manors in Derbyshire. His principal seat was Tutbury castle in Staffordshire which previously had been held by Hugh d'Avranches, earl of Chester.* His son, Robert de Ferrers (d. 1139), was one of the leaders of the English in the battle of the Standard.* He was created the first earl of Derby in 1138, and died a year later (see Derby). His great-great-grandson, Robert de Ferrers, sixth earl of Derby (d. 1279), was chosen by King Henry III* to marry Isabella, one of the daughters of the king's eldest half-brother, Hugh XI of Lusignan, count of La Marche. On her early death, her sister, Mary, aged 7, married the bridegroom Robert, aged 9. On the death of his father, Robert became a ward of the king, and custody of him fell to the Lord Prince.* In 1257, the queen and Peter of Savoy* gave the king 6,000 marks to obtain the custody of the Ferrers estates. Three years later, however, Robert came of age, did homage for his estates and recovered them. He soon sided with the barons against King Henry III, much to the displeasure of the king who felt his niece's husband should have supported the crown. In 1263, Robert captured three castles from Prince Edward, and then captured Worcester* after a lengthy siege and several attacks. Because of its resistance, Robert wasted much of the city, destroying the ghetto, ravaging religious and secular palaces alike, and devastating the king's parks. From there he marched to Gloucester, saved the earl of Leicester's (Montfort) sons from being attacked by Prince Edward, captured Edward and kept him prisoner for a while. Robert was one of the five barons summoned by the king to answer for their conduct, and he was attacked so violently by the king that Simon de Montfort* had to put him in the Tower of London for safekeeping. His lands were seized and he was brought to trial. He avoided condemnation only by submitting completely to the king's mercy.+ Because Robert had supported him, Montfort's fall delayed his release from imprisonment until 1266. He was so angry at the king's action when he was released that he gathered the Disinherited* whom the king's harsh treatment had forced to revolt, and formed an army in Derbyshire. His army was surprised and defeated by Henry of Almayne, and he was captured while he lay helpless with gout. He again was imprisoned at Windsor* for three years. At the *Dictum of Kenilworth,** he and de Montfort were singled out, and were required to redeem their lands at the huge fine of seven years' rent. King Henry III then granted Robert's lands to his own son, Edmund "Crouchback" of Lancaster.* In May 1269, Robert promised to pay Edmund the enormous sum of £50,000 in one payment on July 8, 1270, for his interest in the estates. Such an arrangement was impossible to fulfill, so most of the Derby lands stayed permanently in the hands of the earldom of Lancaster, despite many lawsuits to recover them. He died in 1279, ten years after being released from prison. His son, John de Ferrers (d. 1312) like his father petitioned in vain for redress and for recovery of the family estates. He sided with Bohun* and Bigod* in 1297 and with them was pardoned by name in pardons of October 10 and November 5, 1297. (Bibliog. 47, 58, 71)

Ferte Milon. French castle+ which the count of Valois* gave to Charles, the young son of Philip III,* the Bold. It was fortified by his brother, Philip IV,* the Fair. In 1371, the Valois family gave it to Louis d'Orléans, second son of King Charles V.* (Bibliog. 196)

Fierabras, name borne by William II, count of Poitiers* (963-990), and not invented by the poet of the *chanson de geste** of the same name. William was surnamed Fierabras or *Fera brachia* ("strong arm") because of his great strength, just as Baldwin, count of Flanders, was named *Bras-de-fer* ("iron-armed"). Subsequently, William Ferrabras, son of Tancred the Norman, acquired the signories of Apulia* and Calabria* about 1230. (Bibliog. 205)

Fierabras, geste du roi* written in the Picard dialect about 1170, describing events which supposedly happened three years before the *Song of Roland*.* The work opened with a fight between Oliver* and Fierabras of Alexandria. Fierabras' father, Balant, the *emir*+ of Spain, had captured Rome, destroyed the Church of St. Peter, killed the pope, and had carried away such important holy relics as the crown of thorns and the ointment with which Jesus had been anointed. That ointment was so powerful that it could heal any wound no matter how serious. When Charlemagne* attacked the camp of the pagans, the giant Fierabras, 15 feet tall, emerged from his tent and demanded to be allowed to fight a Christian champion. Oliver alone accepted the challenge even though he himself already was badly wounded; he defeated Fierabras who subsequently was baptized. Oliver and four other *douzepeers** were captured. Seven other peers, including Roland and Ogier the Dane, sent by Charlemagne to rescue the five captured knights also were captured. Fierabras' sister, Floripas, fell in love with Guy of Burgogne, and with her aid and weapons, the *douzepeers* defended themselves until they were rescued by Charlemagne. Floripas was baptized and married Guy; and the *emir* was killed rather than forfeit his religion, so Spain was divided between Guy and Fierabras. (ed. M. A. Kroeber and G. Servois, Paris, 1860) This story was so popular outside of France that it was recited in four versions in English: *The Sowdon* (sultan) *of Babylon*; *Sir Ferumbras**; *Firumbras*, and a prose story, *Charles the Great*; and *Destruction of Rome*.* (Bibliog. 106, 231)

Fisher King, guardian of the Grail* at the Grail castle (see Corbenic). Wounded by the Dolorous Stroke* in the thighs by a javelin, he was unable to ride a horse so that his only recreation was fishing—hence the name. The title Fisher King came from the history of the Grail. When Joseph of Arimathea and his followers came to Britain with the Grail, they gave it into the care of Nascien's great-great-grandson Alain (Helias) le Gros. Alain had, at Joseph's bidding, caught a fish in a British pond to feed the sinners of the company. Miraculously, it had grown large enough to feed all. As a result, Alain and his followers became known as the Rich Fisher or the Fisher Kings. Although Alain's descendants ended in France, one of them being Lancelot du Lak,* the Grail-keeping responsibilities passed to Alain's brother, Josue, from whom Pellam,* the last Fisher King, descended. (Bibliog. 117, 242)

FitzAlan, Brian (d. 1306), English knight from Richmondshire who served in Wales* for King Edward I* in 1277 and 1287. He was granted letters of protection for a pilgrimage overseas before he was made guardian of Scotland* in 1291. He was summoned to Berwick in October and November 1292 to discuss the various claims to the crown of

Scotland, and as a guardian of Scotland, was one of the men appointed to give seizin+ of that kingdom to John de Balliol* in November 1292. He was appointed a keeper of the march of Scotland in Northumberland* in 1293, and was paid £2,000 salary, the same amount paid to his predecessor, John, earl of Warenne.* He fought at Falkirk* in 1298 and at Caerlaverock* in 1300. Summoned to Parliament in 1304, he became Lord FitzAlan. (Bibliog. 47)

FitzGerald, Sir John FitzThomas (d. 1316), earl of Kildare, and fifth lord of the barony of Offaly, Ireland.* Appointed as guardian of part of the marches of the English Pale,* he built a castle in Sligo to protect his lands in Connaught from an assault by Richard de Burgh, earl of Ulster. He was appointed keeper of the castles of Roscommon and Randown in the same year. In 1294, he captured the earl of Ulster, and disputed with another noble, William de Vesci, lord of Kildare and justiciar+ of Ireland, and challenged him to a wager of battle.+ When King Edward I* ordered the duel stopped, and them to appear before him to explain, Vesci fled to France. Then FitzGerald was forced to free the earl of Ulster because Ireland was upset by his imprisonment; as a result, for a time he lost his land in Connaught, but a year later had been reappointed keeper of the two castles. When he was summoned to Parliament in 1298, he signed a truce with the earl of Ulster, and this became a peace pact by which Sir John paid the earl 3,000 marks and the earl gave him his daughter to marry John's son. King Edward I summoned him for military service in Scotland* and Flanders* for which he was pardoned his offenses and rewarded with gifts of land. In 1309, King Edward II called upon him to cooperate with the earl of Ulster in assembling an Irish force to fight in Scotland in 1310. In 1314, when Edward Bruce,* brother of King Robert* of Scotland, came to Ireland and was crowned king of Ireland, FitzGerald and others who were strong enough to resist him, met and only squabbled about what should be done; they took no action. In 1316, for services to the late and present king, FitzGerald was granted the castle and town of Kildare, and was created earl of Kildare with it passing to his lawful male heirs, to he held by service of two knights' fees.+ His son, Thomas FitzThomas FitzGerald, was his survivor as earl of Kildare. (Bibliog. 47)

FitzHugh, Sir Henry (d. 1356), English knight from Richmondshire who supported Thomas* of Lancaster against Piers Gaveston,* but was pardoned in 1313 for any part he had in the actions against and subsequent death of that favorite of King Edward II.* Appointed constable of Barnard* castle between 1315 and 1319, later as a follower of John Mowbray he was pardoned for all felonies committed in pursuit of the Despensers.* He was summoned to Parliament in 1321 and again in 1315, and thus became Lord FitzHugh. In February 1323, he was ordered to arrest Sir Andrew Harcla,* earl of Carlisle, on the charge of having deserted the king's forces and siding with the Scots. (Bibliog. 47)

FitzJohn, Sir John (c. 1240-1275), English knight from Surrey* whose father was a sometime justiciar+ of Ireland.* On the death of his father, the lands reverted to King Henry III,* and Sir John had to purchase them back from the king. He became one of the most conspicuous members of the barons' party, strongly supporting Simon de Montfort,* and agreed on St. Lucy's Day (December 13, 1263) to submit to and to abide by the arbitration of King Louis IX* of France in the barons' dispute with King Henry III. He broke his agreement when Louis decided against them, and he joined with William de Munchanesey and the earl of Gloucester* as commanders of the second division of the army of the barons at Lewes* in 1264. After Montfort's victory at Lewes, Sir John was appointed sheriff of Westmoreland in June 1264, and constable of the castle of Windsor* in July 1265. He was wounded and captured at the battle of Evesham,* and his lands given to the earl of Gloucester and Roger de Clifford.* In 1266, the countess of Aumale* agreed to take him before the king if called upon to do so, and so the king committed him to her charge. He was pardoned in 1266, and recovered his lands by the *Dictum of Kenilworth,** but lost them to the king again in 1268 for contempt by failing to appear before the king on a given day to do homage.+ He was restored to the king's good graces after Edward I* came to the throne, and served as one of the king's proxies at Lyons in May-July 1274. (Bibliog. 47)

FitzNeal, Richard (d. 1196), treasurer of England, great-nephew of Roger of Salisbury,* and the reputed author of the *Dialogus de Scaccario** (*Dialogue on the Exchequer*). See Exchequer.+ (Bibliog. 99)

FitzOsbern, William, close friend and counsellor of William the Conqueror.* Son of Osbern, seneschal+ of Duke Robert I* of Normandy* and one of the guardians of young Duke William after Robert's death, he married a daughter of Rudolf, count of Ivry, half-brother of Duke Richard I, and established the honour+ of Breteuil on the Eure River. Osbern had died defending the young duke. Of his two sons, one, Osbern, became a chaplain to King Edward the Confessor* in England; the other, William, grew up in the household of young Duke William, and played a major role in the young duke's capture of Domfront and Alençon. He inherited Breteuil from his father, and strengthened his position by marrying a daughter of Roger of Tosny. Confidant to the Conqueror, he became his seneschal, and quite probably advised him to invade England, basing his advice on good intelligence from his brother the monk in King Edward's household. That advice was well followed, and after William's success at Hastings,* he placed FitzOsbern in command of the western part of the country already conquered, with possession of the Isle of Wight* and his capital at Winchester,* and gave him the earldom of Hereford, already a march* against the Welsh. Building on that authority, FitzOsbern organized Gloucestershire, Herefordshire, and some of Worcestershire as a military region, establishing castles at Monmouth and Chepstow* to control the whole region of Gwent. In 1069, he was in Normandy helping Queen Matilda* in the government and defense of Normandy. While there, he received an appeal from the widow of count Baldwin VI of Flanders, King William's sister-in-law, to help her protect her two young sons from the designs of their uncle, Robert le Frison. To do that, she offered to marry FitzOsbern. That marriage would have given him, a man with vast estates in England, Normandy, and Wales, the chance to make himself the count of Flanders, the richest principality in France. Hurrying to that expedition, he was killed at the battle of Cassel in February 1071. He was succeeded in his Norman lands by his elder son, William of Breteuil, and in his England and Welsh lands by his younger son, Roger of Breteuil. This William, with some lapses, was a faithful vassal of Duke Robert Curthose (see Robert II). In 1100, for example, he was in the hunting party in the New Forest when King William II,* Rufus, was killed, and rode to Winchester to urge the claims of his absent lord, Duke Robert, against those of Henry I.* He died in 1102, leaving only an illegitimate son, Eustace. (Bibliog. 130)

FitzWarin, Fulk I (fl. 1156), second son of Warin de Metz, he was head of the family in 1156 when King Henry II* gave him the manor of Alveston in Gloucestershire. His grandson, Fulk III, claimed Witinton (Whittington) castle as his right as adjudged to him by the *curia regis*.* He was knighted with his brothers, and with them journeyed overseas to the continent to enter every tourney and joust that they could find. On the death of his father, he was called home by King Richard I,* and with his inheritance, was given the job of keeping the march* of Wales for the king. In 1201, Meuric de Powys bribed King John* to oust Fulk and his brothers and to confirm him in the possession of Witinton. At this Fulk became an outlaw, but his outlawry was revoked in 1203, and his castle was restored by the king in 1204. Ten years later, he lost his fiefs, and became one of the discontented barons who were excommunicated by Pope Innocent III* in 1215. Fulk III made his peace with King Henry III* in 1218, and died around 1256. His son, Fulk IV, drowned at the battle of Lewes,* 1265. In the traditional story of FitzWarin, outlaw, Fulk I was omitted and Fulk III and Fulk IV were combined into the figure of Foulke le Brun. This folk hero roamed throughout the countryside with his four brothers, his cousins, and the nimble-witted John de Rampayne, seeking adventures of the Robin Hood+ type, helping the poor, and defying the king because the king (John) had denied him justice. His outlawry was told in the *Romance of Fulk Fitzwarin* (ed. Joseph Stevenson, in R. Coggeshall, *Chronicon Anglicanum,* London: *Rolls Series,* 1875) (Bibliog. 58, 120, 171)

Flambard, Ranulph (d. 1126), Norman ecclesiastic who became chaplain to King William I,* clerk to the chancellor+ of England, and was given custody of the royal seal under William I. After William II* appointed him justiciar+ in 1087, he imposed the royal will on the realm with such unscrupulous methods that he made many enemies. On the complaint of barons in 1100, King Henry I* imprisoned Flambard in the Tower of London, but he escaped in 1101 and regaining royal favor, served as bishop of Durham* for the remainder of his life. (Bibliog. 98)

Flanders, part of the kingdom of France in the Low Countries along the shores of the North Sea. At the division of the Carolingian Empire, it became a fief dependent on the French crown, but its powerful counts extended their power to the east. Their additions, held as a fief of the Holy Roman Emperor, became known as Imperial Flanders in contrast to Crown Flanders held of the French crown. Struggle for succession in Flanders during the 12th century resulted in the loss of Artois* and other of its western and southern districts to the French crown. At the same time, Flemish cities were given vast privileges because of their prosperity from the cloth industry: Ghent, Ypres, Courtrai, Bruges. Flanders thus became a feudal principality which French King Philip II,* Augustus, brought under control of the crown. In 1180, King Philip had married Isabella, the daughter of Count Baldwin V of Hainault and niece of Philip of Alsace, count of Flanders. Philip of Flanders held as his domain not only Flanders proper, but Artois which encompassed Arras, Bapaume, Ruhout, Saint-Omer, Saint-Pol, Lilliers and Hesdin. Philip of Alsace had married in 1159, Elizabeth of Vermandois, daughter of Raoul of Vermandois (brother of King Philip I) and Petronilla (sister of Eleanor of Aquitaine*). On the death of her brother, Countess Elizabeth of Flanders had inherited Vermandois, Amienois and Valois. Her husband, Philip of Alsace, forced her to give these areas to him, and then had King Louis VII* and then later Philip II confirm these gifts. Thus the French largely dominated the region, but were defeated at the battle of the Golden Spurs in 1302. This was followed two decades later by the accession in 1322 of the pro-French Louis de Nevers as count of Flanders which threw the country into civil war, Bruges and Ypres fighting against the count, and Ghent for him. The pro-French side won. Then, when King Edward III* of England began the Hundred Years War,* and stopped the wool trade to Flanders because of its sympathies with France, Flanders faced economic disaster until it switched its allegiance under the leadership of Ghent, sided with England and took part in the battle of Sluys* in 1340. (Bibliog. 74, 79, 100)

flaths. See Brehon law.

Fleck, Konrad, author of *Floire und Blanscheflur,* a Middle High German* poem written about 1220, and a lost poem, *Clies,* based on *Cligés* of Chrétien de Troyes.* Little else is known about him. (ed. W. Golther, *Deutsche National-Litteratur,* IV, No. 3, 1885) (Bibliog. 86)

Fleta, Latin treatise (c. 1290) which was an abridgement of Bracton.* It commented on the English legislation of King Edward I,* it described the royal law courts and royal household, and it contained a Latin version of a tract on estate management which in its French version was ascribed to Walter of Henley. (ed. and tr. H. G. Richardson and G. O. Sayles, London: Selden Society, LXXII, 1953; LXXIX, 1972) (Bibliog. 99)

Floire et Blancheflor, one of the oldest 12th-century adventure stories. Its popularity was widespread. Konrad Fleck* translated it into Middle High German* in the first half of the 13th century. Its story detailed the adventures of Floire, son of the pagan king of Spain, who was born on the same day as Blancheflor, a Christian maiden born to a woman held in captivity by Felis, the pagan king. When the young Floire and Blancheflor fell in love, the angry Felis sent Floire away and sold Blancheflor to a merchant ship. When Floire returned, he was told that Blancheflor had died, but believing Blancheflor to be alive, he threatened suicide unless his parents told him the truth. They relented and revealed their actions, and then allowed him to leave to search for her. Meanwhile, she had been sold to the emir* of Babylon for seven times her weight in gold, and was being kept in a harem for maidens. Eventually, Floire located her, and, concealed in a huge flower basket, gained entrance to her rooms. He was discovered, and was sentenced to death for his presence in that chamber, but the love shown by the two so softened the emir's heart that he relented and let them marry. Shortly thereafter, they learned that Felis had died and they returned to govern his kingdom. (ed. Merton Hubert, Chapel Hill, NC: University of North Carolina Press, 1967). The English version, *Floris and Blancheflur,** a free rendering of the French original, appeared in England about the middle of the 13th century. (ed. and tr. Bradford B. Broughton, *Richard the Lion Heart and Other Medieval English Romances,* New York: E. P. Dutton, 1966) (Bibliog. 28)

*Floovant, chanson de geste** based on a legend of Dagobert, son of Clotar II in the 7th century. One of the *gestes du roi** cycle composed at St. Denis, France, it made no reference to the relics at that chapel, and was the only *chanson de geste* to center on Clovis. Floovant was the eldest of Clovis' four sons. As a prank one day, he cut off the beard of his teacher and master-at-arms, a baron of high rank. That was an indignity which only criminals endured. Clovis was so angry at his son's impudence that he would have slain him with his own hands had not the queen and clergy intervened. Floovant, however, was banished from France for seven years during which time he experienced many knightly adventures and searched for a wife. His shield-bearer, Richier, shared his exile and adventures. They arrived back at Clovis' court in time to free him from a siege in Laon, and father and son were reconciled. (ed. F. H. Bateson, Loughborough, 1938) (Bibliog. 106, 231)

Florence de Rome, 13th-century *chanson d'adventure* that was divided into two main parts: the war against Gausire of Constantinople and the adventures of Florence after she was abducted by Milon. In the first portion, she was the daughter of the emperor of Rome who refused to allow her to marry the aged emperor of Constantinople, Gausire, who tried to win her by force. Two sons of the king of Hungary, Esmere and Milon, went to Rome to join in the ensuing battle. Esmere won the hand of Florence and became emperor of Constantinople in Gausire's place, but before he could make his triumphal entry, Milon stole Florence for himself. As her chastity was protected by a magic brooch, Milon was thwarted in his seduction attempts, and hanging her up by her hair, he left to join Guillaume de Dôle. After many harrowing adventures, she finally was reunited with her husband, Esmere, and returned with him to rule Constantinople. (ed. S. Wallenskold, Paris: *SATF,* 1907-1909, 2 vols.) (Bibliog. 106, 231)

Florent de Varenne, appointed in 1270, he was thought to have been the first French admiral.* (Bibliog. 68)

*Florent et Octavian, chanson de geste** based on the earlier *Octavian.** The story centered around Florent and Octavian, twin sons of the Emperor Octavian who exiled his wife, Florimonde, the sons' mother, because he thought that the birth of her twins had proved that she had been unfaithful. Separated, the twins grew to manhood, and with their mother became reconciled with their father. Then the story proceeded with accounts of the loves of young Octavian. (no edition) (Bibliog. 106, 121)

Flores historiarum, chronicle from the Creation to 1326, this work long was attributed to a Matthew of Westminster who later was identified as an "entirely imaginary writer." Matthew Paris was the presumed author, with additions by various monks of Westminster.* The section between 1259 and 1265 was important for its favorable views of the barons' side of the conflict between king and nobility. (tr. C. D. Yonge, *The Flowers of History to 1307*, London: Bohn's Antiquary Library, 1853, 2 vols.) (Bibliog. 99)

Floriant et Florete, French Arthurian verse romance written in the middle of the 13th century. After his father, the king of Sicily, was murdered by his seneschal,+ Floriant was taken by Morgan la Fée* to Morigibel where she trained him in the arts and chivalry before sending him to Arthur's court. Hardly had he taken up his life at Arthur's court when he was summoned back to Sicily by the news that the seneschal was besieging his mother at Monreal. Arthur* joined him in his fight against the seneschal and his overlord, the emperor of Constantinople. Floriant fought valiantly, defeated the seneschal in trial by combat,+ fell in love with the emperor's daughter, Florete, and married her. He journeyed to England a second time, killing a dragon* and a sultan in Calabria* on his trip. After his return to Palermo with Florete, his calm life was disrupted one day by chasing a white stag until it led him to a pleasant region on Mount Etna where Morgan la Fée held court in her castle. Florete also was led there. [The ending was lost.] (ed. H. F. Williams, Ann Arbor, MI: University of Michigan Publications in Language and Literature, XXIII, 1947) (Bibliog. 97, 209)

Florimont, French love romance written by Aimon de Varenne around 1188 in a dialect of the Île de France.* Florimont, the grandfather of Alexander the Great,* assisted King Philippe Macemus in his war against the Bulgarians, killed a monster (as Siegfried* did) and extracted from its dead body an ointment that made him invulnerable, and endured similar events in his *enfances,** including falling in love with a *fée.** (ed. A. Hilka, A. Risop, Gottingen: Gesellschaft für romanische Literatur, 1933) (Bibliog. 231)

Floris and Blancheflur, Middle English* metrical romance written about 1250 in the southeast Midlands and relating the basic French story of *Floire et Blancheflor.** Floris and Blancheflur have loved each other since childhood. They were separated, and Floris searched until he found her in a seraglio. He was reunited with her by secretly hiding in a huge basket of roses. When the sultan heard of Floris' impudent behavior, he ordered the two to be burned alive. At the last moment, Floris urged Blancheflur to wear the talismanic ring he gave her to protect her from the flames. She refused, preferring to die with him.

When the sultan was informed of this steadfast devotion, he forgave them and they were united. Boccaccio included a version of this in his *Filocolo*. (ed. and tr. Bradford B. Broughton, *Richard the Lion Heart and other English Metrical Romances*, New York: E. P. Dutton, 1966) (Bibliog. 28)

Foix, county in southern France founded by the lords of the castle+ of Foix who were vassals of the counts of Toulouse.* By the 12th century it had grown into an important commercial town, and then by the 13th century, its counts wielded great power. They supported the count of Toulouse in his opposition to the Albigensian crusade.+ In 1290, when Count Roger-Bernard III married Margaret of Bearn, he inherited the principality of Bearn and thus established one of the most important noble houses of southern France. Through marriages and inheritance, this family established one of the most prestigious courts in France. They remained faithful to the French crown during the Hundred Years War.* (Bibliog. 98)

Folko. See *Fouque de Candie.*

Fontevrault, town in France located 10 miles southeast of Saumur, and 2 miles from the junction of the Loire and Vienne Rivers. Its abbey was founded in 1099 by a Breton hermit, Robert d'Arbrissel, and because of the liberality of the local nobility and especially counts of Anjou,* Robert soon built several large self-contained monasteries: St. Mary's for nuns, St. John's for monks, St. Mary Magdelene's for unfortunates, and an infirmary, St. Lazarus, for the sick. Both monks and nuns went by the name of Benedictines of Fontevrault; all were under the unusual control of a woman, the abbess. The first famous abbess was Matilda of Anjou, daughter of Fulk, fourth king of Jerusalem; wife of William, grandson of William the Conqueror*; and aunt of Henry II* Plantagenet of England. Later, Adele of Champagne, widow of King Louis VII* and mother of Philip II,* Augustus, was abbess, as was Alice, sister of Philip Augustus. Its chapel of the south transept became the final resting place of King Henry II,* Eleanor of Aquitaine,* Richard I,* and Isabelle of Angoulême,* wife of King John Lackland.* (Bibliog. 179)

Foraine, Terre, name given in Arthurian legend to Logres* after the Dolorous Stroke.* (Bibliog. 53, 145, 202)

Fordun, John (d. 1384), chantry priest in the cathedral at Aberdeen; the author of the first attempt to chronicle a complete history of Scotland.* Sometimes known as the *Scotichronicon*, this work was highly valuable for its discussion and details of relations between England

and Scotland. (ed. W.   F.   Skene, *Historians of Scotland*, I, IV, Edinburgh, 1871-1872) (Bibliog. 99)

Fornham, battle of (October 17, 1173), decisive encounter which crushed some of King Henry II's* enemies in the rebellion of the king's sons in 1173. Marching across Sussex* toward his own county with 80 knights and a large body of Flemish mercenaries+ whom he had imported to strengthen his rebellion, the rebel earl of Leicester* was intercepted by the constable+ of England, Humphrey de Bohun,* and the justiciar,+ William de Lucy at the head of a force of a few loyal knights and 300 of King Henry's horsemen. Leicester's Flemish mercenaries had made themselves so hated by their cruel ravages in Norfolk that many local peasants came out readily to join the constable's forces. Even though de Bohun's forces outnumbered Leicester's forces four to one, the earl had a more formidable following of trained men, while the constable led a rabble. Falling upon the earl suddenly as he was passing a marsh, de Bohun's forces overpowered the earl's men, and destroyed the Flemish infantry by cavalry charges. Then the infuriated peasants took over and gave no quarter with their forks and flails, thrusting the foreigners down into the bog and ditches until more were drowned than slain by swordstroke. Leicester fled but was captured nearby with his wife, Petronilla, who had accompanied him. She was reported to have thrown away an easily identifiable ring and then tried to drown herself in a ditch to avoid being captured. Such a rout of trained soldiers by a few hundred horsemen backed by the shire levy+ demonstrated that even mercenary infantry were helpless if deprived of cavalry, and attacked by horse and footmen in combination, even though the footmen were raw and untrained. (Bibliog. 166)

fortalice, a small fort, or the small outer fortifications of a large fortress. (Bibliog. 169)

Fougères, castle+ which legend and Einhard* credited as having belonged to Roland, Charlemagne's* nephew, and prefect of the marche of Brittany.* It was in a military zone defended constantly. It was besieged in 1166 by Henry II* of England who razed it. Raoul II de Fougères and his successors rebuilt it, and made it one of the main fortifications of the duchy. In the 13th century it passed by marriage to Jeanne de Fougères of the Lusignans who built the tower named Melusine, and christened it in the name of that fairy fée* from whom they claimed their descent. On 1350, in the Hundred Years War,* the new French king, John II,* the Good, sent an army to besiege it because he recognized that it held the key to the Breton/Norman border. That attack was beaten off by the defenders under the able leadership of Sir William Bentley. Later, du Guesclin* took possession of it in 1372 for the French count of Brittany. (Bibliog. 196, 224)

Fouque de Candie, *chanson de geste** by Herbert le Duc de Dammartin* that continued the story begun in *Aliscans.** Folko, as the hero was named, was the grandnephew of Guillaume Fierabras*; he went with Vivien and Guy to rescue Guillaume who was besieged by Tibaut d'Orange (see *Enfances Guillaume d'Orange)*. There he won the love of Anfelise, a beautiful Saracen* princess, and with her love, he won the possession and rule of Candie (Gandia) in Spain. Most of the poem was occupied by an account of the siege of Candie by the Saracens, and after Guillaume and King Louis I* had raised that siege, the poem described the siege and capture of Arrabloi by the Christians. (ed. O. Schultz-Gova, *GrL*, Dresden, XXI, 1909 and XXXVIII, 1915 and Halle, XLIX, 1936) (Bibliog. 231)

Four Sons of Aymon, *(Quatre Fils Aymon)*. One of the most popular French epics; also known as *Renaud de Montauban*, it was translated into English, Italian, German, and Scandinavian. The oldest surviving version dated from the end of the 12th century. In the opening Prologue, Bueves d'Aigremont refused to pay homage+ to Charlemagne,* and among Charlemagne's messengers whom he killed was Lohier, Charlemagne's son. Bueves' two brothers, Doön de Mayence and Girart de Roussillon, joined him in his fight against the emperor, but eventually they submitted to him. On his way to Aix to pay homage, Bueves was slain by treachery. Then Aymon de Dordonne, Bueves' third brother, took to Charlemagne's court his four sons Renaud, Aalars, Guichers and Richart who were well received and immediately knighted. Tragedy soon struck, however, when Renaud accidentally killed Bertolai, Charlemagne's cousin in a quarrel over a chess game. At this, the four brothers were instantly exiled, outlawed+ and hounded by Charlemagne. They built a castle Montessor in the Ardennes, but after five years, the emperor learned their whereabouts, besieged their castle, and drove them forth again penniless. After three years of wandering in the Ardennes, they were found by their father, but because he was honor bound by his oath of homage to the emperor, he had to fight them as rebels. When at last they managed to return to his castle to beg for help, their mother gave them gold and silver, and they left for Bordeaux where they joined the service of King Yon of Gascony. While there, they built Castle Montauban ("Alien's mount"), and Renaud married Yon's daughter who bore him two sons. This peaceful life once more was interrupted when Charlemagne, returning to Aix from Galicia, discovered them, and besieged them again with his huge army. These four sons enlisted the aid of Maugis, son of Bueves of Aigremont.

Because Charles feared and detested Maugis the most, he offered to reconcile with the four sons if they would yield Maugis to him. Refusing to turn over their sworn ally, the brothers continued to withstand the siege until they found a subterranean passageway out of the castle, and fled to Tremoigne (Dortmund in Westphalia). Once more the emperor tracked them down and besieged them. This time, however, because the emperor's barons were tired of sieges and battles, and wanted to return home, they insisted the emperor make terms with the rebels. He agreed only if Renaud would make a pilgrimage to the Holy Land. Renaud agreed, and on his return retired to Cologne where he wished to expiate his sins by serving as a humble porter. He was murdered by jealous comrades, and was buried at Tremoigne where he was worshipped as a saint. In history, Charles the Bald* warred in the Ardennes, and then against King Yon of Gascony. (ed. and tr. William Caxton, London: Oxford, *EETS ES* #44, #45, 1884-1885; tr. Robert Steele, *Renaud of Montauban*, London: G. Allen, 1897) (Bibliog. 73, 106)

France, huge territory in Europe between the Low Countries at the mouth of the Rhine River and the Pyrenees Mountains, and roughly lying west of the Rhône and Rhine Rivers. Between 888 and 920, principalities on its periphery were formed through the efforts of Charles the Bald* entrusting command to certain powerful underlings. Flanders,* Burgundy,* Aquitaine,* Normandy* (under Rollo), and Brittany,* each of these principalities was governed hereditarily, and each formed a valuable state in which the prince exercised authority which previously had devolved upon a king. Each brought together several districts (*pagi*) which were held directly by a territorial prince, with other districts subjected to less rigorous control. In the half-century between 920 and 970, *comtes* (counts), holders of a single *pagus*, profiting from battles between Carolingians and Robertians (the ancestors of Capetians*) made themselves politically autonomous, as in Anjou,* the Maconnais, Auxerres, Nivernais, and in the Midi when around 900 the entire area south of the Loire was dominated by a dozen families, but by 975, had been divided among some 150 lineages of independent counts and viscounts. From then on, even the *pagi*, as small as they were, could not remain independent, so new political formations appeared: castellanies whose holders possessed the *ban*, that is, its military command. To maintain these, castles+ played an essential role. During this early period, France was a country of castles. Even the *curtes*, or social and administrative centers of aristocratic or royal estates, had to have some defensive elements. Buildings began to be arranged within the area of a hectare or one and one-half hectares, surrounded by an earthen bank and sometimes with a ditch on the outer side, and reinforced with a palisade of logs, stakes, and interwoven branches. This was surrounded by a second wall which enclosed the gardens and plots of cultivated land. By the 10th and 11th centuries, these new fortifications had mottes+ topped with palisades, and ditched around the base. These castles were divided into three categories: 1) those which the holder of public activities (such as a duke, or count or lord having command) kept in his own hands; 2) those he entrusted as a fief+ to officers, relatives, faithful lieges and vassals; and 3) adulterine+ castles, private castles erected illegally by adventurers or powerful nobles without the knowledge of the territorial prince.

The Frankish territory tended to divide itself early: the eastern or Teutonic land, Austria* or Austrasia; and Neustria,* or the western or romance land. These grew into the kingdoms of Germany* and France. The name Francia shifted its geographical use according to the geographical wanderings of the people from whom it was taken, and gradually settled down as the name of Germania and Gaul where it still applies. Still, Teutonic Francia kept the name of Franken or Franconia. Originally called Karolingia, Neustrian Francia or the kingdom of the West-Franks gradually came to be known as France after the accession of the Capetian dynasty in 987. Karolingia meant all France west of the Rhône and Saône Rivers, and nothing east of them. It also included the march* of Flanders, the Spanish march to the south, the Norman islands (in the English Channel), and fiefs south of the Loire River. The chief of these fiefs were the duchy of Aquitaine which meant the land between the Loire and Garonne, the duchy of Gascony* between the Garonne and the Pyrenees Mountains, the march of Septimania and the march of Barcelona. North of the Loire were Brittany, the march of Flanders, the duchy of Burgundy, and the rest, the duchy of France, called variously western France, or *Francia Occidentalis,* or *Latina.* The kings of Karolingia or the western kingdom and the dukes of western Francia were the same persons. France then, the western or the Latin Francia, as distinguished from the German Francia or Franken, properly meant only the king's immediate dominions. Although Normandy, Aquitaine, and Burgundy owed homage to the French king, they were not part of France. Thus the name *France* supplanted the name *Karolingia.* Kings of the western kingdom kept the title *Rex Francorum* after it had been dropped by the eastern kingdom, and thus the title came to mean *not* the king of the Franks, but the king of the French. The name *France,* however, at this stage in its development meant only the immediate territory of the king, and the name spread to cover every increase of that territory whether by incorporation of a fief or by annexation of a territory wholly foreign: every land permanently annexed to the crown sooner or later became French. (For eastern kingdom, see Germany.) This original duchy of western Francia had been reduced considerably by the great grant of Normandy and by the practical independence of the counts of Anjou, Maine, and Chartres. The dukes of France claimed that small territory which had been in the immediate possession of the West-Frankish kings at Laon. Along with the crown and the immediate territory of those kings, the French kings at Paris also inherited their claim to superiority over all states which had risen within the bounds of the western kingdom.

The French king's court officials, called *domestici** in the 10th and 11th centuries, were ministers, secretaries, and counsellors who travelled with the king and became the nucleus to which were added the bishops and nobles who came to court, and all later became the chief officers of the crown. Even though their positions were vague, their names appeared as signatories witnessing charters. However, a compete lack of unity among these signatories revealed the disintegration of the Carolingian Empire, and the insecurity of the newly formed Capetian dynasty. The king of France did not summon his court to legislate, for the kingdom had no common laws, nor did he call it to raise money, for there was no taxation as yet, and he had to rely on his own demesnes* to supply his money. Furthermore, any questions of justice to be resolved in his court were understood only insofar as the fact that the king could do little to punish anyone found guilty of a crime. Even if the summons to court was obeyed and the individual was indicted for an action, he still could withdraw from court and defend his rights by arms. Only when the strength of his army or the powers of his baronage gave him the power to execute the sentences of his court was the king considered the fount of justice. Because he was forced to depend on the feudal host+ to conduct a campaign or to carry out a simple civil matter, he also was forced to bargain for that service with his vassals, and their regular service was by no means guaranteed. The power of the early French monarch was best expressed in a letter from Count Eudo II, count of Chartres,* to King Robert. In reaction to the king's attempts to take some of Eudo's territories into his own hands, Eudo responded with a letter of protest. Why, he wrote, without giving him a chance to explain his case, was the king seeking to deprive him of a hereditary fief which the king himself earlier had recognized as belonging to him. Eudo went on to state that he had served him "in his palace, in his wars and on his journeys," and even though he might have committed some imprudent acts, those were to be expected and certainly were not grounds for so serious an action by the king. Punning on the term "honor (honour),"+ Eudo claimed that he could not live "dis-honored," and sought reconciliation with the king:

> This discord, my lord, will destroy your office root and branch,
> justice and peace alike, and therefore I beg amd implore that the
> clemency which is natural to you...permission to become reconciled

with you either by the mediation of your ministers or of the princes. (Bibliog. 178)

Among the fiefs annexed, a distinction must be made between the great princes who really were national chiefs owing external homage to the French crown, and the lesser counts whose dominions had been cut off from the original duchy of France. And a distinction must be made between this last group and the immediate tenants of the crown within its own domains, vassals of the duke of France as well as king. To the first class (national chiefs) belonged the dukes and counts of Burgundy, Aquitaine, Toulouse* and Flanders. To the second (lesser counts) belong the counts of Anjou, Chartres, and Champagne.* Historically Normandy belongs to this second class as the grant to Rollo originally was cut off the French duchy. But the circumstances of that duchy made it a national state owing only the merest homage to the French crown. Brittany was held to owe its homage to the duke of the Normans. These areas were controlled by the so-called *douzepeers** of France. At their accession, the royal house took over the greater part of the Île de France,* a small territory surrounding Paris. The rest of the country was held by dukes and counts. The Channel coast was held by princes of Brittany, Normandy and Flanders; the ocean coast was held by rulers of Brittany, of Poitou* and Aquitaine under a single ruler, and Gascony to the south of them. Along the Mediterranean coast, the counts of Toulouse and Barcelona held sway. Of these great feudatories, the princes of Flanders, Burgundy, Normandy and Champagne were all immediate neighbors of the king. To his west lay domains of several states of second rank. Chartres and Blois* for some time were united with Champagne. Beyond these, besides some smaller counties, were Anjou, Tourraine, and Maine, the borderland between Normandy and Anjou. Thus, the kings of Paris were surrounded by their own vassals, and held territory smaller than a duchy. By the end of the eleventh century, however, the Île de France had begun to grow by the acquisition of the Gatinois and the viscounty of Bourges, a small part of the later province of Berry, but an addition which made France and Aquitaine more clearly neighbors than before. Towards the end of the twelfth century, France made a more important advance toward the northeast at the expense of Flanders. Philip II,* Augustus, added the counties of Amiens, Vermandois and Artois* to the crown.

Later in his reign came an acquisition of a far greater scale which was the result of causes begun in the 11th century. Aquitaine and Normandy had been united under the hands of a single king of a powerful foreign kingdom: Henry II* of England. Besides the county of Poitou, the Aquitaine duchy contained a number of fiefs of which the most important were those of Perigueux, Limoges, the dauphine* of

Auvergne,* and the county of Marche which gave kings to Jerusalem and Cyprus. To these, the duchy of Gascony with its subordinate fiefs was added, and the dominions of the lords of Poitiers stretched to the Pyrenees Mountains. Meanwhile, Duke William* of Normandy, before his conquest of England, had inceased his continental holdings by adding Ponthieu, the small district of Domfront, and the whole of Maine. Aquitaine was added to the French crown with the marriage of Eleanor* of Aquitaine to Louis VII,* but lost to him with her divorce and subsequent remarriage to Henry, duke of Normandy and count of Anjou, later king of England. Later, by a marriage of his son, Geoffrey, to the heiress of Brittany, Henry also gained control of that territory, also. The house of Anjou, then, had territory greater than the French kingdom and its vassals, and controlled the mouths of the three great Rivers: Seine, Loire and Garonne, and was further strengthened by the possession of the kingdom of England. On the death of Richard I* of England and Normandy, the crown went to his brother John,* but Richard's nephew Arthur* pressed his claims as heir to Brittany; had he been successful, the Angevin possessions on the continent would have been possessed by the duke of Brittany and not the king of England. On Arthur's disappearance and presumed death in 1203, King Philip II, by the clever help of jurisprudence devised for that particular purpose, declared that all the fiefs held of the French crown by King John were forfeited to that crown; this did not apply to the fiefs held of his mother, Eleanor of Aquitaine.* In the next two years, Philip executed that ruling, and thereby joining the continental Normandy, Maine, Anjou, and Touraine to the dominions of the French crown; by a later Treaty of Paris in 1258 these formally were surrendered to the French King Louis IX* by the English King Henry III,* John's son. Poitou went with those lands. English kings still kept Aquitaine with Gascony and the Norman islands of Guernsey, and Jersey in the Channel. Thus France had obtained a large seaboard on the Channel, and a small seaboard on the Atlantic Ocean.

Another chain of events incorporated a large territory with the crown which heretofore had had little relationship to it, and gave France a third seaboard on the Mediterranean. To the south, the greatest princes had been the counts of Toulouse. During the later part of the 11th century, the counts of Barcelona and the kings of Aragon who succeeded them acquired by various means a number of Tolosan fiefs, both French and Imperial. Carcassonne, Albi, and Nîmes were all under the crown of Aragon. Then the Albigensian+ crusade seemed likely to lead to the formation of the house of Montfort* as the chief power in southern Gaul, but the struggle ended in the increase in power of the French royal house at the expense of the houses of Toulouse and Aragon.* The dominions of the house of Toulouse were divided; a number of fiefs such as Béziers, Narbonne, Nîmes, and Albi were annexed to the crown; the capital and the county itself passed to the crown fifty years later, and the name of Toulouse, except for the name of the city itself, passed away. This new territory came to be known by the name of the language which was common to them as to Aquitaine and Imperial Burgundy: Languedoc.+ Louis IX also enlarged the royal holdings by purchasing the areas of Blois and Chartres to which Perche afterwards was added. Later in the 13th century, the marriage of Philip IV,* the Fair, with the heiress of Champagne extinguished another peerage and briefly made the French kings also the kings of Spain. Champagne had for two generations been united with the kingdom of Navarre. These dominions were held by three kings of France in right of their wives. Then Navarre, though it passed to a French prince, was completely separated from France, while Champagne was incorporated within the kingdom. In the 14th century, the Hundred Years War* with England resulted in the acquisition for the French crown of Aquitaine.

Paris was the capital of this area called by its princes *Duces Francorum* (meaning French rather than Frankish). From it gradually several great fiefs were cut away: Anjou, Champagne, and between the Seine and Epte Rivers, land was granted to a Norseman, a Scandinavian named Rolf or Rollo, whose territory grew into Normandy with its capital at Rouen. After the reign of Charles the Fat (839-888), the crown of the western kingdom passed to and fro between the dukes of the French at Paris and the princes of the house of Charlemagne whose immediate dominion was the city and district of Laon near the Lotharingian border. Thus for 100 years, the royal city of the western kingdom sometimes was Laon and sometimes Paris, and the king of the western Franks was sometimes the same person as the duke of the French and sometimes not. After Hugh Capet,* though, the kingdom and duchy never separated. Sovereigns of France after Charlemagne were

768 - Charles the Great, Charlemagne, king of the Franks (768); emperor (800-814)
814 - Louis I, the Pious (*"le Debonnaire"*)
840 - Lothaire, (emperor)
843 - Charles, the Bald (king of the Franks, 840-877), (emperor, 875-877)
877 - Louis II, the Stammerer, king of the Franks, 877-879
879 - Louis III, king of the Franks, 879-882
879 - Carloman, king of the Franks, 879-884
884 - Charles, the Fat (*"le Gros"*), 884-887
877 - Eudes or Hugh, count of Paris, 887-893
893 - Charles, the Simple, 893-922
922 - Robert, brother of Eudes
923 - Rodolf, duke of Burgundy, 923-936

936 - Louis IV, d'Outremer ("from overseas"), 936-954
954 - Lothaire, 954-986
986 - Louis V, the Indolent, 986-987
987 - Hugues Capet, 987-996
996 - Robert II, the Sage, 996-1031
1031 - Henry I, 1031-1060
1060 - Philip I ("*l'Amoureux*"), 1060-1108
1108 - Louis VI, the Fat ("*le Gros*"), 1108-1137
1137 - Louis VII, the Young, 1137-1180
1180 - Philip II, Augustus, 1180-1223
1223 - Louis VIII, the Lionheart, 1223-1226
1226 - Louis IX (Saint Louis), 1126-1270
1270 - Philip III, the Bold ("*le Hardi*"), 1270-1285
1285 - Philip IV, the Fair ("*le Bel*"), 1285-1314
1314 - Louis X, the Headstrong ("*le Hutin*"), 1314-1316
1316 - Philip V, the Long, 1316-1322
1322 - Charles IV, the Fair ("*le Bel*"), 1322-1328
1328 - Philip VI, of Valois, 1328-1350
1350 - John II, the Good, 1350-1364
1364 - Charles V, the Wise, 1364-1380
1380 - Charles VI, the Beloved, 1380-1422

The 14 provinces of France, long constituted virtually sovereign states in themselves, were

Alsace (or Elsas)
Anjou
Aquitaine
Brittany
Burgundy
Champagne
Dauphine
Gascony
Le Marche
Lorraine
Navarre
Normandy
Poitou
Provence.

Of secondary rank to the provinces, but still basically self-governing and autocratic in all executive details were the baronial houses of Angoulême, Armagnac, Artois, Auvergne, Bayonne, Blois, Bologne, Bourbon, Chalons, Chartres, Dombes, Dreux, Franche-Comte, Ligny, Limoges, Maine, Narbonne, Nevers, Orange, Penthièvre, Perigord,

Perpignan, Ponthieu, Roussilon, Saintonge, Soissons, Thouars, Toulouse, Turenne, Valentois, Valois, Vendôme, Vermandois, and Vienne. (Bibliog. 79, 100, 178)

Franche-Comte, region of east central France bounded by Lorraine,* the Swiss Confederation, Burgundy,* and Savoy.* It originally was part of Burgundy, but became a fief of the king of Arles* in the 10th century, and under the control of the Holy Roman Empire after 1034. (Bibliog. 241)

Francia Media, area extending from the North Sea through parts of Germany* and France* to Switzerland and Italy* which was given to Lothaire I, son of Louis the Pious,* by the terms of the Treaty of Verdun* in 843. (Bibliog. 124)

Franconia, country in central Germany.* Located between the Neckar and Fulda rivers, it was annexed to the royal demesne of Austria in 720, and was used by the Carolingians as a base for their advances into Germany. In 840, Louis the German made it one of the duchies when he established the kingdom of Germany. When Conrad I,* count of Worms, became king of Germany in 906, he granted Franconia to his brother Eberhard, who, a few years later, revolted against the emperor, Otto I,* and was killed. Otto divided some of the duchy among some bishops and abbots, and granted the rest to members of the Conradin family. Conrad II,* duke of Franconia, was elected emperor in 1027, and until 1125, the Conrads continued to use Franconia as a seat of imperial power as they retained the ducal title, but gave away the major portion of its lands to the church and vassals.+ In 1168, Frederick I,* Barbarossa, gave the title to the bishop of Wurzburg whose successors held it for centuries. (Bibliog. 98)

Franks, group of Germanic tribes from east of the Rhine River who gave their name, France,* to the Roman province of Gaul in the 5th century after they conquered it. Good footsoldiers, they were adept in making and using arms, and had been trusted soldiers for many Roman emperors. (Bibliog. 233)

Frazer (Frezel), Simon (d. 1306), king's banneret+ of Edward I* at the battles of Falkirk* and Caerlaverock.* As the eldest son of Simon Frazer, ancestor of the houses of Saltoun and Lovat, he had been captured at Dunbar in 1296 and gained liberty only by swearing to serve the English king; this he did well at Falkirk, but he was captured by the Scots in September 1299. After being held prisoner by them until late June 1300, he deserted to the Scots side in 1300. After he was captured by the English and executed in 1306, his head was displayed on London Bridge with a fanfare of trumpets. (Bibliog. 56)

Frouendienst, courtly Middle High German* poem written in 1225 by *minnesinger** Ulrich von Liechtenstein (ca. 1200-1275). This work, a unique autobiography, detailed his career in the service of his lady as he attempted to live the life of the conventional lover. Critics believed that he actually did most of what he related. For example, he boasted that he drank the water in which his lady had bathed, cut off his little finger and sent it to her as a token of his love, and dressed as Venus to challenge all comers in jousts as he travelled from Venice to the Bohemian frontier. (ed. R. Bechstein, Leipzig, 1888, 2 vols.) (Bibliog. 235)

Frederick I, Barbarossa (Redbeard) (1123-1190), emperor of Germany (1155-1190), called *Rotbart* in Germany* and *Barbarossa* in Italy.* Becoming king of Germany in 1152 and emperor in 1155, Frederick was determined to extend German dominion over Italy, and to stop the expansion of papal power into Germany. He appointed his own bishops in Germany in defiance of the pope's opposition; he invaded Italy four times between 1158 and 1176, and established partial control over it until he suffered a catastrophic defeat at the battle of Legano* in 1176. By subtle negotiation with the Lombard League* in 1183, and by the marriage of his son Henry to Princess Constance, heiress of Sicily, he succeeded in obtaining the power in Italy which force of arms had denied him.   In his youth he had participated in the second crusade,+ but then in 1187, Frederick again sewed the cross on his tunic and embarked on the third crusade.+ Like a true chivalric knight, he sent a challenge to his enemy, the Saracen* leader, Saladin.* However, he drowned in the Kalycadnus River in Armenia in 1190 en route to meet his enemy.

A few years before his death, however, he became an ideal and legendary hero of chivalry. When he held the *swertleite* for his two sons, Henry and Frederick, at Whitsuntide in 1184, his attitude toward chivalry and knighthood were made obvious to the world. Over 70,000 knights from all over Western Europe, especially from France and Germany, assembled for the three days of ceremonies as the guests of the emperor. He had a city of tents erected on a plain near the Rhine to accommodate them. Chivalry manifested itself there in all its panoplied glory, splendid raiment, dignified ceremony, and knightly skill and valor. Even though he was 60, he broke lances with the best of the knights there assembled. Heinrich von Veldeke,* major poet of the new courtly epic, called this ceremony a greater festival than that which he had described for the marriage of Aeneas to Lavinia in his *Eneit*. (Bibliog. 68, 99, 186)

Frederick II (1194-1250), Holy Roman Emperor (1212-1250), king of Sicily (1197-1250), and of Jerusalem (1226-1250). Nicknamed *stupor mundi** ("amazement of the world"), this son of Henry VI and grandson of Frederick Barbarossa* was one of the most intelligent men of his generation. He was proclaimed king of Sicily at three years of age on his father's death, and when his mother died the following year, he reigned under the guardianship of Pope Innocent III* and the regency of his father's German and Sicilian advisors. In 1212, when Innocent III excommunicated Otto IV,* he sent Frederick north to claim the throne of Germany. After his election, he defeated Otto at the battle of Bouvines* as an ally of Philip II,* Augustus, of France. As one of the conditions of his election as emperor, Frederick was forced to make concessions both to the Church and the German princes. One such concession was the Golden Bull of Eger which recognized the privileges of the German nobility, and led to the feudalization of Germany. He was crowned in Rome in 1220, and then left to crush a rebellion in Sicily and established a centralistic government based on bureaucratic service of royal officials. When actions like these proved to Innocent III that Frederick was not a man to be controlled by anyone, the pope encouraged the Guelph* (Welf) constituents in Italian cities to revolt, and continued his own pressure on Frederick to embark on the crusade+ he had promised to undertake earlier.

To stimulate that interest, the new pope, Honorius III, arranged a second marriage for Frederick to Isabelle of Brienne, heiress to the throne of Jerusalem. Once he had married her, Frederick ordered her father, John of Brienne, to remain in Italy and to leave the government of Jerusalem to Frederick. Pope Gregory IX brought matters to a head in 1228 by excommunicating Frederick; this action encouraged revolts against the emperor in Italy by making them legitimate rebellions against an excommunicate. It also encouraged Frederick to embark on his crusade, and he left for Acre* in 1229 but not before concluding secret negotiations with the Ayyubid sultan of Egypt,* Al-Malik Al-Kamel, which allowed Christians to run the civil governments of Jerusalem and Nazareth. However, because he was an excommunicate, the French-speaking nobility in Jerusalem refused to have any contact with him, the Templars+ and Hospitallers+ ignored him, and the officials of the church openly condemned him. Nevertheless, he reached Jerusalem and in the Church of the Holy Sepulchre, he crowned himself king of Jerusalem. His crusade achieved more than any other in the entire 13th century, but was not recognized because he had been excommunicated by a jealous pope. He returned to Germany to suppress a rebellion by his son Henry whom he dethroned and imprisoned for the remainder of his life for that action. He appointed his illegitimate son Enzio* as king of Sardinia, and by his strong positions had become sovereign of almost all of Italy. Pope Innocent IV deposed him in 1245 and once again thus made legitimate all revolts against him. Frederick died in 1250 at his palace near Luccera, Italy. His courts had become brilliant centers of learning at his encouragement. He even wrote a treatise on falconry, *De arte venandi cum avibus,* about 1248 after thirty years of observation, research and study. It was more than a manual for training birds; it was a zoological study written from a scientific point of view. (ed. and tr. Casey A. Wood and F. Marjorie Fyfe, *The Art of Falconry,* Stanford, CA: Stanford University Press, 1943) (Bibliog. 68, 99)

free booter, one who took booty+ by force, usually considered the same as a man in a free company.* (Bibliog. 169)

free companies, bands of mercenaries of many nationalities swarming into France* and Italy* between 1340 and 1380 by their desire for profit in the wars of Charles V.* The people of France called these bands of ruthless adventurers "The English" because they frequently were led by English knights, and their operations resembled the actions these men had carried out on behalf of the king of England. They were different from the English mercenaries, however, by their international composition, their utter ruthlessness, and the sheer unpredictability of their movements. Each company of no more than a hundred men operated independently. All they had to do was capture a castle and hold the local populace for ransom. France under Charles V and northern Italy under the Visconti* both proved ideal pickings for these men. Beginning in 1334 with the "Knights of the Dove," a band of Germans who terrorized central Italy, this idea next emerged as the "Company of St. George," a band of Germans under the orders of Ludovico Visconti, the head of a Milanese family controlling much of northern Italy. Three years later, a former Provençal Hospitaller, Montreal d'Albarno, formed the "Great Company," a collection of ruffians from France, Hungary and especially Germany who, after their leader was decapitated in Rome by Cola de Rienzo, were led by Count Conrad von Landau. This band was defeated badly by the Tuscans at Biforco in 1358. With this defeat, the goups changed. The companies no longer were just temporary associations whose primary aim was to exploit the native population who had been reduced to mere victims; they became permanent military units entering into, or trying to enter into, the service and pay of one or another of the Italian states. Sir John Hawkwood,* son of an English tanner and minor landowner near Colchester,* had campaigned in France, and found himself in 1360 at the head of a composite group of mercenaries, made up mostly of Englishmen. For a while he served in a great company under the marquis of Montferrat* in the service of the counts of Savoy* against the Visconti of Milan. For nine years, he was the most redoubtable captain in Italy at the head of the White Company.* The last great foreign company on Italian soil was that of the Bretons under Sylvestre Budes whose deeds ended with their defeat at the battle of Marino in 1380 by Alberigo da Barbiano at the head of a third company of St. George. (Bibliog. 48, 224)

free-lances. See White Companies.

La Fresne, lai* by Marie de France* based on the superstition that the birth of twins pointed to the mother's conjugal infidelity. In this story, a mother abandoned one of her twin daughters in the fork of an ash tree in a nunnery garden because she knew that accusations of adultery would follow the birth of her twins. The child was reared by the abbess and was christened La Fraisne ("fraisne" = ash), but ran away to become the mistress of a knight, Sir Garoun. His men persuaded him to marry her sister, but at the last moment her mother identified her lost child, and he married La Fraisne instead. (ed. and tr. Eugene Mason, *Lais of Marie de France*, New York: E. P. Dutton, 1966) (Bibliog. 147)

Frisia, country located between the mouths of the Rhine and Weser along the coast of the North Sea. This area was settled by a western group of the Germanic tribes, the Frisians, who gave it their name. (Bibliog. 98)

Frithiof, hero of Icelandic myth, *Frithiof's Saga*, who married Ingeborg, daughter of a minor king of Norway, and a widow of Sigurd Ring, to whose dominions he succeeded. His name meant "peacemaker," and his adventures were recorded in a saga which bore his name. Scholars believe that it was based on the Floris and Blaunchflore* story. (ed. Ludvig Larsson, *Altnordische Saga-Bibliothek*, 1901; tr. Margaret Schlauch, *Medieval Narrative*, New York: Prentice-Hall, 1928) (Bibliog. 134)

Friuli, country in northeastern Italy* between Venice and Istria used in the early Middle Ages as an entryway to Italy by invading Visigoths and Lombards. During the Carolingian Empire, it was considered to be an important march,+ but after the establishment of the Holy Roman Empire, it lost its importance. (Bibliog. 98)

Froissart, Jean (d. c. 1410), celebrated chronicler of France. His *Chroniques* provided a principal source for the Hundred Years War* between 1361 and 1400. He was in England from 1361 to 1366 as secretary to Philippa* of Hainault, queen to King Edward III.* His work concentrated on knightly exploits and chivalric details. (tr. G.

Brereton, Baltimore: Penguin Books, 1978) (Bibliog. 99)

Fromont de Lens, one of the traitors in the *chansons de geste*.* He was the son of Hardré,* brother of Guillaume de Monclin, and father of Fromondin in *Garin le Loherenc*,* and *Girbert de Metz*. He was the villain in *Jourdain de Blaives*.* (Bibliog. 128)

Froncin, dwarf of King Mark* of Cornwall* in the *Tristan* story of Béroul.* Skilled in sorcery and astrology, he was hostile to both Tristan and Isolt. However, when he revealed the secret that King Mark had horse's ears, Mark killed him. (Bibliog. 97)

fuidhirs. See Brehon law.

Fulcher of Chartres (1058-1127), chronicler who accompanied Baldwin of Boulogne* on the first crusade+ as chaplain, and later became canon of the Holy Sepulchre in Jerusalem after Baldwin had become king of Jerusalem in 1100. His chronicle of the first crusade and the kingdom of Jerusalem was a highly important source because he had been an eye-witness to the events he narrated. (Bibliog. 98)

Fulk I (Fulque) the Good, early count of Anjou*; author of the comment that "an unlettered king is a crowned ass." (Bibliog. 68)

Fulk III (Fulque) Nerra (987-1040), founder of the feudal state of Anjou.* When his overlord Hugh Capet* ascended the French throne, Fulk annexed a number of seignories in western France, and then swung south to include portions of Aquitaine* under his control. In his later years, he began a continuous dispute with the counts of Blois,* and became an ally of King Henry I* of England. (Bibliog. 98)

Fulk IV (Fulque) le Rechin ("the Grumbler") (1068-1109), count of Anjou,* and father of Fulk V.* (Bibliog. 98)

Fulk V (Fulque) (1095-1143), count of Anjou* (1109-1128), king of Jerusalem (1131-1143). Entrusted with the government of Anjou by his father, Fulk IV, he became vitally interested in the structure of its administration and its defenses. He built many fortresses and castles to maintain the peace. Fearful of the claims against Anjou of King Henry I* of England, who also was duke of Normandy, Fulk supported the claims of William Clito,* Henry's nephew, but reversed himself after 1125, and negotiated with Henry himself. These two agreed to the marriage of Matilda, Henry's daughter recently widowed by the death of her husband, the Holy Roman Emperor, Charles V,* to Fulk's son, Geoffrey Plantagenet.* Part of the agreement called for them to be given the county of Anjou immediately, and to be declared heirs of England* and Normandy.* This laid the groundwork for the Angevin Empire built by his grandson, Henry II* of England. In 1128, he turned Anjou over to his son, spent the rest of his life in the Holy Land, ascending the throne of the kingdom of Jerusalem in 1131. His strong hand there maintained peace, ensured good diplomatic relations with Damascus, and established a strong realm. (Bibliog. 98)

Fulk Fitzwarin. See FitzWarin, Fulk I.

Furnival's Inn. See Inns of Court.

G

Gaheret, third son of Lot,* king of Lothian* and Orkney*; he was the brother of Gawain,* Agravaine* and Gareth* (Gaheris), and fought against the heathen invaders of Britain. He rescued Lyones from Ironsyde, and then married her. He killed his mother when he found her in bed with Lamorak,* but was himself killed accidentally by Lancelot* in the abduction of Guenevere.* For that death, Gawain swore eternal hatred for Lancelot. (Bibliog. 117, 145, 202)

Gaimar, Geoffrey, French poet who between 1135 and 1140 adapted Geoffrey of Monmouth's *Historia Rerum Brittaniae** for Anglo-Norman and French readers at the request of Constance, wife of Robert FitzGilbert of Scrampton. To it, he added a rhymed chronicle of England, *L'Estoire des Angles* up to the reign of William II* (1087-1100). (tr. Joseph Stevenson, *Church Historians of England,* London: Seeley, 1854, II, part 2) (Bibliog. 10)

Galafers, king of Foraigne, the Waste Land in Arthurian and Grail* legends. He was cured of leprosy after his baptism under the name of Alphasan; he then ordered Castle Corbenic* to be built. (Bibliog. 202)

Galahad, son of Lancelot* and Elayne the Fair* in Arthurian legend. Because Lancelot's name had been Galahad before it had been changed by Viviane, Elaine used the same name for their son. He achieved the Siege* Perilous and the Grail.* (Bibliog. 1, 117, 145)

Galeholt, duke of the Long Isles and Surluse in Arthurian legend; close friend and confidant of Lancelot* in his affair with Guenevere.* (Bibliog. 117)

Galeron le Bretayne, short French romance by Jehan Renaut* about 1225; it closely resembled Marie de France's *lai* la Fresne.** A good knight, Brundore, lived with his good wife, Gente, near Rouen. When Marsile, wife of one of his vassals, bore twins, the childless Gente jealously announced to her husband at the Ascension Day+ celebration the old folk belief that only by sleeping with two men could a woman conceive twins. Shortly thereafter, Gente was repaid for her slander by giving birth to twins. Desperate, she abandoned one in a tree in a nunnery garden where the nuns found and reared it. When grown, the young woman fled from the nunnery and lived with a handsome knight, Sir Galeron, without marrying him. Galeron, however, married her sister. After the wedding, the unfortunate girl was recognized by her mother, and the wedding was annulled, after which the girl, La Fresne, was married by Galeron. (ed. L. Foulet, Paris: *CFMA*, 1925) (Bibliog. 106)

Gales, 1) Wales; 2) country renamed from Hoselice in honor of Galahad*; it was Perceval's* native land, and the kingdom of Varlan whose Dolorous Stroke* in killing Lambar caused it to become the Waste Land. More broadly, it was the land occupied by Britons from the English Channel to the Firth of Clyde, in Arthurian legend; 3) according to Gottfried von Strassburg,* it was the land of the Saxons before they drove the Britons from Great Britain. He believed that the name England (Engelant) was derived from the name of Gales. (Bibliog. 97, 241)

Galicia, province in the northwestern part of the Iberian peninsula which became a part of Asturia in the 9th century. In the 11th century when the bones of St. James supposedly were found in Compostella,* so many pilgrims began flocking to worship at the shrine erected to house the remains of the saint that the city's name was changed to Santiago. Struggling constantly for freedom from the domination of its neighbor, León, it finally was integrated into the kingdom of Castile in the 13th century. (Bibliog. 98)

Galien le restorés, 13th century *chanson de geste** which united the *Pèlerinage de Charlemagne** with the *Song of Roland.** In fulfilling his boastful "gab"+ about his sexual prowess with Jaqueline, the daughter of Hugh of Constantinople, Oliver sired a son, Galien, during the fateful night-long encounter with her. When he was grown, Galien sought his father, and eventually found him on the battlefield of Rencesvals* where he and five other peers had survived the attack described in the *Song of Roland.* This work later was incorporated into the cycle of the *gestes* of *Garin de Monglane.** (ed. Edmund Stengel, Marburg: *AA*, 84, 1890) (Bibliog. 231)

Galloway, lords of, ancient rulers of a section of southwestern

Scotland.* The last ruler was Alan, lord of Galloway, constable of Scotland, who died in 1233 with no male heir, leaving three daughters of whom one, Devorgild, daughter of his second wife, Margaret of Scotland, was the mother of John Baliol,* king of Scotland 1292-1296. (Bibliog. 47)

Galvoie, Gavoie, locality confusingly identified either as Galloway in Scotland* or Galway in Ireland.* (Bibliog. 242)

"Gambaron," nickname of Robert II* of Normandy because of his short fat figure and fat face. (Bibliog. 68)

Gamelyn, Middle English* romance. The son of an English knight of the shire, Gamelyn was deprived of his rightful inheritance and turned outlaw. His fight with the sheriff, his flight to the forest and subsequent fellowship of a band of outlaws, his animosity to the greedy clergy, his constant feud with the unjust sheriff, yet beneath all, his loyalty to the king—all echoed the story of Robin Hood.+ Although not written by Geoffrey Chaucer (1344?-1400), this poem frequently was included in complete editions of the his works. (ed. Neil Daniel, DA 28 (1967): 2241A-2242A Indiana) (Bibliog. 102)

Gand. See Ghent.

Ganelon, archtraitor of the *chansons de geste.** He was Roland's step-father, and hated his stepson. Possibly that hatred emerged from Roland's besting him in a financial deal, or from Roland's greater wealth achieved by actions during Charlemagne's* seven year crusade in Spain. In the *chanson de geste, Song of Roland,** Ganelon plotted with Marsile,* king of Saragossa, to betray Roland and the *douzepeers** at the battle of Rencesvals* in which Roland and the *douzepeers* died. Ganelon was tried by Charlemagne at Aix la Chapelle. His defense against the charge of treason lay in his public proclamation against Roland just before he left as the ambassador to Marsile's court to deliver Charlemagne's ultimatum to the pagan king. By that public announcement, Ganelon maintained that he had done nothing behind the king's back, so he was not guilty of treason against Charlemagne. Charlemagne countered by reminding Ganelon that Roland had been Charlemagne's official representative as guardian of the baggage train, and thus actions against the king's representative amounted to treason against the king himself. Found guilty by the trial by combat+ between Pinabel, Ganelon's champion, and Thierry,* Charlemagne's champion, Ganelon was sentenced to death, and was executed by being drawn and quartered, and the thirty members of his family who served as hostages were hanged. (Bibliog. 112, 210)

Gannes, Arthurian locale thought to mean Gaul. King Bors of Gannes was the father of Bors of Ganis. (Bibliog. 117)

garde de mer, home guard raised between 1338 and 1340 along the southern coasts in every southern English county. People residing in those costal villages had cause for alarm, for French privateers under such notable French brigands as Nicholas Béhuchet and Hue Quiéret had made sporadic attacks on the English coast, burning Portsmouth and later Southampton to the ground in 1338; they raided from Cornwall* to Kent,* attacking Folkestone and Dover,* and burned the Isle of Wight.* (Bibliog. 203)

Garel von dem Blühenden Tal, Middle High German* courtly epic by der Pleier.* Modelled on the tale of *Daniel von dem Blühenden Tal* by der Stricker,* this work seemed to answer Stricker's poem, for it re-affirmed the chivalric qualities of Arthurian poetry in contrast to the unchivalric aspects of *Daniel.* In this work, Garel was successful in his various adventures because of his valor and not his cunning, and ended his adventures at a great feast and celebration at King Arthur's* court. (ed. M. Walz, 1892) (Bibliog. 86)

Gareth(Gaheris)ofOrkney,"Beaumains,"youngestsonofMorgawse*and King Lot.* His accidental death at the hands of Lancelot* in the abduction of Guenevere* caused an unending hatred of Lancelot by Gawain* and eventually brought down Arthur's Round Table.* (Bibliog. 117, 145)

Garin d'Anseune, son of Aimeri de Narbonne and father of Vivien in the *chansons de geste.** (Bibliog. 128)

*Garin de Monglane, chanson de geste** cycle containing twenty-four poems in three groups: the group around Garin de Monglane himself; the group around Aimeri (father of William); and the group around William of Orange (Guillaume d'Orange) himself. Even though Bertrand de Bar-Sur-Aube* identified the cycle with the name of the family ancestor, Garin de Monglane, most people consider this cycle to be the cycle of William of Orange. Garin was the great-grandfather of the historical Count William of Toulouse* whose exploits against the Saracens* in the later years of the 8th century were added to adventures of his brothers, father and great-grandfather to form a whole family history, largely imaginary. *Chansons de gestes* comprising this cycle included from the 12th century:

Chanson de Guillaume*
Couronnement de Louis*
Charroi de Nîmes*
Prise d'Orange*
Aliscans*
Chevalier Vivien* (or *Covenant Vivien*)
Moniage Guillaume*
Enfances Vivien*
Guibert d'Andrenas*
Siege de Barbastre*
Prise de Cordres et de Sebille*
Mort d'Aimeri de Narbonne.*

From later centuries, it grew to include

Enfances Garin*
Garin de Monglane*
Girart de Vienne*
Narbonnais*
Bueves de Commarchis*
Enfances Guillaume*
Bataille Loquifer*
Moniage Rainouart.* (Bibliog. 106, 231)

Garin de Monglane, French *roman* composed in the second half of the 13th century. In it, Garin was told by an angel to abandon his heritage in Aquitaine* to his brothers and to win Monglane from an Albigensian+ heretic named Gaufroi. After defeating Charlemagne* in a game of chess, Garin obtained Charlemagne's permission to acquire that fief. In that game also, Garin won as his bride the woman already engaged to Hugo of Auvergne. His adventures from that point on deteriorated into the actions of a romance hero. (ed. Hermann Menn, Book III, Griefswald: dissertation, 1913; Max Müller, Book II, Griefswald: dissertation, 1913) (Bibliog. 106)

Garin le Loherenc (Lorrain), *chanson de geste** written by Jean de Flagy in the 13th century. Garin, the center of a cycle of poems, supposedly lived during the reign of Pepin the Short. Like Beguè, this son of Hervis de Metz was famous for his fights against the Saracens.* Beguè's investiture with the duchy of Gascony and his upcoming marriage to the daughter of the king of Moriane (Arles) aroused the envy and hatred of the Bordelese family. This family included the count palatine,+ Hardré, his brother Lancelin de Verdun, Lancelin's son Fromont, and sons-in-law, Hamion de Bordeaux and William de Blancafort. Their first hostile encounter, in which Hardré was killed, began a long series of wars in the neighboring regions of Cambrai, Saint-Quentin, Soissons, and Bar-le-Duc. Slanderous remarks by the Bordelese against the Lorrains led to a single combat in which Beguè overcame and killed Fromont's son, Isoré. After only a short truce, the warfare broke out again, and shifted to southern France where it was finally settled. Then a Bordelese hunter accidentally killed Beguè and war resumed. In it Garin cruelly avenged his brother's death, but was himself killed at the end. (ed. and tr. into modern French, Gaston Paris, Paris, 1862) (Bibliog. 106)

Garnier de Nanteuil, son of Doön de Nanteuil, husband of Aye d'Avignon, and father of Parise la Duchesse, lord of Nanteuil in the *chansons de geste.** (Bibliog. 128)

Garter, Order of, the most famous English order of knighthood, founded in 1348 by King Edward III.* Stirred by the formation at Lincoln* of a voluntary association of knights in 1344, Edward determined to found such an order himself. At the close of a great tournament at Windsor,* and after a stately service in Windsor Chapel, the king swore a solemn oath to found a Round Table like King Arthur's* Table of 300 knights. The outbreak of the war with France* prevented Edward from carrying out that purpose immediately, but in October 1347, the king returned to England and set about fulfilling his oath. He may well have been prompted by an additional desire to commemorate his extraordinary victory at the battle of Crécy.* For the Order's badge and name, the king gallantly chose the garter dropped accidentally at a ball in Calais* by the loveliest woman in England, the princess Joan of Kent,* wife of the earl of Salisbury.* As he bound the garter around his knee, the king was said to have spoken the words which became its motto, *"Honi soit qui mal y pense,"* ("Evil to him who thinks it evil"). Two months after his return from Calais, he ordered for himself and the knights of his Order twelve garters of royal blue embroidered with the words of the motto and the cross of St. George. Members of the Order, the "valyantest men of the realm," were directed to tie the garter about their leg for their renown, and to wear it "as the symbol of the most illustrious Order, never to be forgotten or laid aside, that thereby thou mayst be admonished to be courageous, and having undertaken a just war,...that thou mayst stand firm and valiantly and successfully conquer." In the jousts which took place in January 1348 at Eltham, twelve of the most renowned knights were chosen on the king's side and received garters and robes from his wardrobe to wear there. Twelve other knights received similar gifts from Edward,* the Black Prince, and were chosen for his side of the tournament. These twenty-five knights and the king—twelve knights-companions for the king, and twelve for the Prince of Wales—made a total of twenty-six members in the Order, dedicated to St. George, the patron saint of all Christian warriors, and henceforth of England. These twenty-five were be linked by vows of eternal friendship for the "advancement of piety, nobility and chivalry." These knights wore their badges for the first time at a tournament at Eltham in January 1348. At one of the nineteen tournaments held that winter and spring, Edward wore the wardrobe fashioned for his Order, a mantle, surcoat, tunic and hood of long blue cloth powdered with garters and furnished with buckles and pendants of silver gilt. Edward took pains that membership in this order should not be confined to the high and mighty. He directed that if membership fell vacant, the names of three dukes or earls, of three barons and of three knights were to be offered for consideration, and the worthiest should be chosen to fill the single vacancy. The original twenty-five members were:

1. Edward (Plantagenet*), prince of Wales (d. 1376)
2. Henry (Plantagenet*), earl of Derby, afterwards duke of Lancaster (d. 1361)
3. Thomas (Beauchamp*), 11th earl of Warwick (d. 1369)
4. John de Grailly, vicomte de Benanges et Castillon, Captal de Buch* (d. before April 4, 1377)
5. Ralph (Stafford), lord Stafford (d. 1372)
6. William (de Montagu), 5th earl of Salisbury* (d. 1397)
7. Sir Roger (Mortimer), 4th lord Mortimer* of Wigmore, afterwards 2nd earl of March (d. 1360)
8. John (de Lisle), 2nd lord Lisle de Rougemont (d. 1356)
9. Sir Bartholomew de Burghersh,* afterwards 3rd lord Burghersh (d. 1369)
10. Sir John Beauchamp, afterwards lord Beauchamp de Warwick (d. 1360)
11. John (Mohun), 2nd lord Mohun de Dunster (d. 1376)
12. Sir Hugh Courtenay, son and heir apparent* of Hugh, earl of Devon (d. before September 2, 1349)
13. Sir Thomas Holand,* afterwards 7th earl of Kent (d. 1360)
14. John (Grey), 1st lord Grey of Rotherfield (d. 1359)
15. Sir Richard FitzSimon of Simons Hide, Hertfordshire (d. after 1349)

16. Sir Miles Stapleton of Bedale, Yorkshire (d. 1364)
17. Sir Thomas Wale of Wedon, Pinckney, Northamptonshire (d. 1352)
18. Sir Hugh Wrottesley of Wrottesley, Staffordshire (d. 1381)
19. Sir Nele Loring of Chalgrave, Bedfordshire (d. 1386)
20. Sir John Chandos* (d. December 31, 1369)
21. Sir James Audley of Stratton Audley, Oxfordshire (d. 1369)
22. Sir Otho Holand, brother of Thomas (d. 1359)
23. Sir Henry Eam (d. before 1360)
24. Sir Sanchet D'Abrichecourt (d. after 1349)
25. Sir Walter Pavely of Boughton Aluph, Kent (d. 1375)

The following replacements were appointed by the king before he died
in 1377:

26. Sir William Fitzwaryne (d. 1361); replaced #24
27. Robert (de Ufford), 1st earl of Suffolk (d. 1369); replaced #15
28. William (de Bohun)*, 5th earl of Northampton (d. 1360); replaced
        #12
29. Reginald (de Cobham), 1st lord Cobham of Sterborough (d. 1361);
        replaced #7
30. Sir Richard de la Vache (d. 1366); replaced #8
31. Thomas, (Ughtred), lord Ughtred (d. 1365); replaced #23
32. Sir Walter Manny, 1st lord Manny (d. 1371); replaced #14
33. Sir Frank van Hale (d. 1376); replaced #22
34. Sir Thomas Ufford (d. 1368); replaced #7
35. Lionel (Plantagenet) of Antwerp,* earl of Ulster, afterward duke
        of Clarence; 3rd son of Edward III (d. 1368); replaced #10
36. John (Plantagenet) of Gaunt*; 4th son of Edward III (d. 1399); re-
        placed #13
37. Edmund (Plantagenet) of Langley*; 5th son of Edward III (d. 1402);
        replaced #28
38. Edward (Despenser), 5th lord Despenser (d. 1375); replaced #2
39. Sir John Sully (d. 1388); replaced #29
40. William (Latimer), 4th lord Latimer (d. 1381); replaced #26
41. Humphrey (de Bohun), 12th earl of Hereford (d. 1372); replaced #16
42. Enguerrand VII de Coucy,* sire de Coucy, afterwards 2nd earl of
        Bedford, husband of Isabella, daughter of Edward III (d.
        1397); replaced #31
43. Sir Henry Percy, afterwards 1st earl of Northumberland (d. 1407);
        replaced #30
44. Ralph (Basset),* 4th lord Basset of Drayton (d. 1390); replaced
        #35
45. Sir Richard Pembrugge (d. 1375); replaced #34

46. John (de Nevill), 3rd lord Nevill de Raby (d. 1388); replaced #9
47. Sir Robert de Namur (d. 1392); replaced #27
48. John (Hastings), 12th earl of Pembroke (d. 1375); replaced #3
49. Sir Thomas de Granson (d. 1376); replaced #21
50. Guy (Bryan), lord Bryan (d. 1390); replaced #20
51. Sir Guichard D'Angle, afterwards 12th earl of Huntingdon (d. 1380); replaced #32
52. Sir Alan Buxhull (d. 1381); replaced #5
53. Thomas (Beauchamp) (d. 1401); replaced #41
54. John (de Montfort or of Brittany), duke of Brittany and count of Montfort and earl of Richamond; husband of Mary, 4th daughter of Edward III (d. 1399); replaced #48
55. Sir Thomas Banastre (d. 1379); replaced #25
56. William (de Ufford), 2nd earl of Suffolk (d. 1382) replaced #45
57. Hugh (Stafford), 2nd earl of Stafford (d. 1386); replaced #38
58. Thomas (de Holand), 8th earl of Kent (d. 1397); replaced #11
59. Sir Thomas Percy, afterwards 2nd earl of Worcester (beheaded 1403); replaced #49
60. Sir William Beauchamp, afterwards 18th lord of Abergavenny (d. 1411); replaced #33
61. Richard (Plantagenet),* prince of Wales,* afterwards King Richard II (d. 1400); replaced #1
62. Henry (Plantagenet), 9th earl of Derby, afterwards duke of Lancaster and King Henry IV (d. 1413); replaced #4

(Bibliog. 14, 35, 204)

Gascony, duchy of southwestern France bounded by the Bay of Biscay, the Pyrenees Mountains, and the Garonne River. In 1058, the duke of Aquitaine* absorbed it from Basque-speaking people who had been fighting for centuries with the Visigoths, Franks, and Arabs. It passed to English control in 1154 under Henry II.* (Bibliog. 98)

Gaufrey, *chanson de geste** of the 13th century. It related the story of the adventures of Gaufrey, eldest son of Doön de Mayence,* and father of Ogier; it included the adventures of Bernart de Mondesier (Montdidier), son of Thierri d'Adrenne, and of Robastre, son of a mortal woman and an impish elf. It also features incidents involving Malabron, a counterpart of Oberon. (ed. M. F. Guessard, Paris: *APF,* 2 & 3, 1859) (Bibliog. 106)

Gaunt, John of. See John of Gaunt.

Gaurel von Muntabel, Middle High German* epic from the late 13th century by Konrad von Stoffeln.* Gaurel loved a fairy, but lost her and his own good looks when he told her so. He regained both by defeating three Arthurian knights in a series of combats. He was accompanied on his adventures by a male goat so naturally he was known as the Knight of the Goat, "der Ritter mit dem Bock." This and other features were derived from Hartmann von Aue's* *Iwein** ("der Ritter mit dem Lowen") which in turn was indebted to Chrétien de Troyes'* *Yvain,** the Knight of the Lion. (ed. F. Khull, Graz, 1885) (Bibliog. 86, 235)

Gautier d'Arras (c. 1160-1202), powerful noble in Arras who belonged to the Notre Dame des Ardents, an association of minstrels at Arras. He served under Philippe d'Alsace, count of Flanders* and Baudouin V of Hainaut.* He wrote *Eracle** after 1164 and dedicated it to Baudouin V and to Thibaut V, count of Blois* in 1152-1191, husband of Alice, daughter of Louis VII* and sister of Marie of Champagne. Between 1167 and 1170, he wrote a romance, *Ille et Galeron,** and dedicated it to Baudouin V and to Beatrice, second wife of Frederick I,* Barbarossa. (Bibliog. 106, 231)

Gautier d'Aupais, French romance of the 13th century. After the hero, Gautier, gambled away his horse and his clothing, his father mistreated him so badly that he left home and wandered about France. Taking a job as a watchman, he fell in love with his employer's daughter, and declared his love. Only after his identity was verified was he accepted. Then he became reconciled with his family. (ed. E. Faral, Paris: *CFMA,* 1919) (Bibliog. 106)

Gaveston, Piers (d. 1312), earl of Cornwall*; favorite and foster brother of King Edward II* of England. He was banished by King Edward I,* but after the accession of Edward II in 1307, Piers was recalled to the English court and created earl. He was betrothed to Margaret, the sister of Gilbert de Clare,* seventh earl of Gloucester.* At the coronation+ of Edward II, he walked immediately ahead of the king bearing the sword of St. Edward, angering both the clergy and the laity. He also bore the left spur, and had the honor of redeeming the sword Curtana+ from the altar after the oblation. This conduct so offended the barons that they forced the king to banish him again, but once again he was favored by his friend the king, and was made lieutenant of Ireland in 1308. He was recalled in 1309, made earl of Cornwall, and gave fresh offense by his insolence and outrageous extravagance. He accompanied the king to Scotland in 1310-1311, but again his banishment was demanded by the Ordainers* in 1311. Returning

secretly from Bruges, he joined the king at York. He surrendered con-
ditionally to the earl of Pembroke* and other Ordainers at
Scarborough, but was kidnapped by the earl of Warwick* and executed at
Blacklow Hill in the presence of Thomas of Lancaster* and other
barons. (Bibliog. 58, 182)

Gawain, one of the most famous knights of Arthur's Round Table*;
eldest son of Lot,* king of Lothian* and Orkney* and Anna (Enna) also
called Morcades; grandson of Uther Pendragon* and Ygerne, and nephew
of King Arthur,* Anguisel and Urien. He was the brother of Agravaine,*
Gaheris,* Gareth* and Mordred,* and of the damsels Clarissant and
Soredamor. His prowess in combat and his courtly manners were matched
by his great attractiveness to women. Conceived out of wedlock, he
was educated by the pope. He sired two sons by the sister of Brandle,
and his wife, Ragnell, bore him Guinglain. See *Libeaus Desconus.* He
played a principal role in practically all English Arthurian works,
and met his death in the final battle between Arthur and Mordred after
Mordred usurped the English throne. His unrelenting hatred and pursuit
of Lancelot* to avenge the deaths of his two brothers by Lancelot in
the abduction of Guenevere* eventually brought about the downfall of
Arthur's Round Table. His favorite horse was Gringalet and his sword
was Galatyn. (Bibliog. 10, 29, 202, 242)

Gaydon, chanson de geste written between 1218 and 1240 which related
the story of Thierri d'Anjou, also called Gaydon, who defeated Pinabel
in Ganelon's* trial by combat at Aix la Chapelle* in the *Song of
Roland.* The traitors accuse him of treason against the emperor, and
Charlemagne,* aged and weak-minded, believed the accusations. Gaydon
then fled for his life and had many adventures in which he was
victorious, returning just in time to save the emperor whom the
traitors were about to execute. (ed. M. F. Guessard and S. Luce,
Paris: *APF,* 1862) (Bibliog. 106)

Geoffrey I, Grisgonelle ("Greygown") (960-987), count of Anjou.* Son
and heir of Fulk I,* the Good,* count of Anjou, Geoffrey was a
faithful vassal of Hugh Capet.* He spent much of his rule in organizing the county, basing his power on the great abbeys which supplied
him military materiel and supplies in return for protection. His name
came from his custom of wearing a coarse grey woolen tunic of the
Angevin peasantry. He was popular with the bards and storytellers who
made him the hero of marvellous combats and of implausible deeds of
knightly prowess. (Bibliog. 162)

Geoffrey II, Martel ("the Hammer") (1006-1060), count of Anjou*
(1040-1060). Son of Fulk III,* Nerra, he became part of his father's
government in 1030 when he was granted the county of Vendome. As
count, Geoffrey became one of the most important feudal lords in
France by marrying his stepdaughter to the Emperor Henry III.* He
sided with King Henry I* of France against his most bitter enemy,
Count Thibaut of Blois.* By capturing Tours in 1044, Geoffrey removed
the influence of the family of Blois from the county of Touraine, and
gave him control over the roads of France from north to south and east
to west. His control of Tours also gave him control of its mint, one
of the most important in France. Being childless, he named his
sister's sons, Geoffrey and Fulk, as his heirs. (Bibliog. 98, 162)

Geoffrey III, the Bearded (d. 1096), count of Anjou* (1060-1080).
Eldest son of Ermengarde, sister of Geoffrey II,* Martel, Geoffrey had
inherited the roughly united dominion of his uncle. Consisting of
Anjou, Touraine, Maine and Saintonge, this dominion began to dissolve
immediately after Martel's death. Only Touraine and Anjou were loyal;
the other two had been held in the count's control only by the terror
he instilled in them. Not the man his uncle was, he lost control of
his dominions, was defeated by the dukes of Normandy* and Aquitaine,*
and was excommunicated by the papacy for his attempts to control the
churches in his territory. He was deposed by his brother Fulk in 1080,
and died as his brother's prisoner at Chinon* castle+ in 1096.
(Bibliog. 98, 162, 180)

Geoffrey (1154-1198), illegitimate son of English King Henry II*
(1133-1189), by a whore named Ykenai, he was brought up with Henry's
legal children, educated at Northampton* schools, among the nation's
finest. In 1172, he was elected bishop of Lincoln and sent by Henry II
to Tours to complete his studies. He proved to be a great fighter
against Henry's sons (Richard,* Geoffrey* and John*) in the rebellion
of 1173-1174. Henry was so pleased that he wanted to make him a
bishop, and exerted such influence on the pope that Geoffrey's im-
pediments of illegitimacy and age were waived. Geoffrey, however, had
ambitions of a great secular career and refused the appointment. In
response, the pope told Geoffrey to accept the see or resign from the
church; Geoffrey resigned. Henry II then appointed him as his
chancellor,+ and Geoffrey served him well and faithfully to the end of
the king's life. Henry II's successor, Richard I* (1157-1199), knew
that his half-brother was ambitious, and fearful of that ambition, ordered the canons of York to elect Geoffrey as archbishop* of York,* a
post vacant since 1181. At this, Hugh le Puiset,* bishop of Durham,*

and Hubert Walter,* dean of York, protested because Hubert wanted the position for himself and Hugh wanted it for his son Bouchard. Ranulph de Glanville,* chief justiciar and uncle of Hubert, also protested the appointment. In response, Richard appointed Walter as bishop of Salisbury, and Bouchard as treasurer of York, and the objections disappeared. Geoffrey, however, still was unhappy at this church position. His stubbornness angered the king who promptly stripped him of his land and possessions on both sides of the sea to verify to him that his future depended on the king's good will. Despite his high secular ambitions, Geoffrey accepted Richard's next move to ordain him (by force), and thereby remove him from any possible claim on the throne. Richard later restored Geoffrey's lands. While Richard was preparing for and leaving for the crusade,+ he once more appointed Geoffrey as archbishop of York to serve as a counterbalance for the actions of William Longchamps,* the chancellor, while the king was out of the country on the crusade. Geoffrey was highly regarded and highly respected for his unswerving loyalty to Henry II, Richard's father. Alone of Henry's sons, he stood beside the king to the end, comforting him in his last moments. He spent most of his life in England, and had shown courage and loyalty by his actions; he was liked and admired by the English populace. His troubles arose because of his temperament and his character. He was impatient and hot-tempered, and having lived and worked for many years with his father, he was unable to work in another sphere in which he was not backed by royal authority. Furthermore, he was unsuited for episcopal office. He had declined to be consecrated bishop; he had neither the character nor the training that would fit him for such an office, and he accepted it only as a last resort, when Richard's accession to the throne forced him to find another niche for himself. His selection also revealed the problems that arose in the entire selection process of English church officials of that high position. Bishops were almost always nominated by the king, and the priests in the chapters they were to control were practically never allowed to choose their own candidates. See bishops, English. (Bibliog. 7)

Geoffrey, Gefreit, Geifreit of Anjou, one of Charlemagne's* *douzepeers** who carried the Oriflamme+ into battle, and who overthrew Amborre, Baligant's* standard-carrier at a critical moment in the battle; his brother was Thierry,* Charlemagne's champion in the duel over Ganelon's guilt or innocence in the *Song of Roland.** (Bibliog. 210)

Geoffrey de Clinton, one of the chamberlains+ of the English treasury, who also was prominent in Henry I's* judicial and financial administration in England where he acquired great wealth, and also in Normandy* where he was treasurer and a justice, and perhaps a baron of the Exchequer.* Though his family name was taken from Glympton in Oxfordshire, his hereditary estates were in Normandy, a castle in Semilly (Saint-Pierre-de-Semilly and Le-Bar-de-Semilly, 7 miles east of St. Lô), and other lands in the Cotentin.* (Bibliog. 130)

Geoffrey de Mandeville, earl of Essex. See Essex.

Geoffrey de Preuilli, the reputed inventor of tournaments; he was said to have died in a tournament in 1062. (Bibliog. 46)

Geoffrey of Anjou. See Anjou.

Geoffrey of Monmouth, author and creator of Arthurian legends. As a clerk and teacher at Oxford after 1129, he wrote *Libellus Merlini (The Prophecies of Merlin*)* between 1134 and 1135 at the request of his superior, Alexander, bishop of Lincoln.* His greatest work was his *Historia Regum Britanniae* (History of the kings of Britain)* begun seemingly by 1130 and not finished until after the death of King Henry I* in 1135. (Bibliog. 10)

Geoffrey Plantagenet (1158-1186), duke of Brittany* (1166-1186). The fourth son of Henry I,* king of England, and Eleanor of Aquitaine,* he married Constance, daughter of Conan IV,* duke of Brittany, and ruled the duchy only nominally; his father ruled it in actuality. He rebelled frequently against his father, joining his older brothers in their unsuccessful attempts to oust their father from his control of his French dominions in 1173. He developed a close relationship with Philip II,* Augustus, of France. He died in a tournament in Paris in 1186, shortly before the birth of his son, Arthur.* (Bibliog. 98, 162, 180)

Geoffrey Ridel, baron of the Exchequer,* and a prominent minister in England during the earlier part of King Henry I's* reign. He married a daughter of Earl Hugh of Chester* (who also was hereditary *vicomte* of Avranches). Even though to his grandson the Empress Matilda* and Duke Henry of Anjou* restored all his inheritance "both in England and Normandy," there is no evidence that he acted in any official capacity in the duchy. The only occasion he was known to have been there with the king was just before the wreck of the White Ship* in which he sailed and was drowned. (Bibliog. 130)

Geoffroi de Villehardouin. See Villehardouin, Geoffroi de.

Gerald de Barri. See Giraldus Cambrensis.

Gerald of Wales. See Giraldus Cambrensis.

Gerard de Camville, constable+ of Lincoln* and sheriff+ of Lincolnshire, husband of Dame Nicolaa de la Haye,* daughter and heiress of the hereditary constable of Lincoln castle.+ Gerard was appointed by King Richard I* as castellan of Lincoln castle for a fee of £700. When the justiciar+ Longchamps* demanded in 1191 the surrender of the castle, Gerard fled to Count John (Prince John*), leaving the castle in the hands of his wife, Dame Nicolaa who defended it stoutly like a man. Gerard was one of the four justiciars+ who were excommunicated by the pope in 1192 for their seemingly treasonous actions against King Richard in support of John. On Richard's return to England in 1194, the charges laid against him were more severe. At the instigation of William Longchamps, Gerard was accused of harboring robbers and thieves who sallied forth from Lincoln castle to rob merchants on their way to the great fair at Stamford. Further, he was assumed guilty of contempt for the king's majesty since he refused to appear before his majesty's justiciars when summoned by them, or to turn over to them the alleged robbers. To these summons, Gerard replied that he was Count John's man and would stand trial in John's court. Finally, he was accused of being a close supporter of John and others of the king's enemies and of having helped them seize the castles of Nottingham* and Tickhill.* He denied all the charges. He ended up having to pay 2,000 marks "for the lord king's goodwill," and his wife Nicolaa to pay 300 marks "to marry her daughter where she will, except to his enemies." He paid off this debt by 1197, and settled the last £8 of it by giving the king two fine horses. No sooner had that been paid than he was levied another fine of £100 because the knight service+ he owed to the king's forces in Normandy had not been served as required. (Bibliog. 7)

Gerart of Roussillon. See Girard de Roussillon.

Gerbert de Metz. See *Girbert de Mez.*

German chivalry. No German could be knighted unless he had four knightly ancestors, according to the *Constitutio de pace tuenda* of the Emperor Frederick I,* Barbarossa, in 1152, Only after Frederick I's sons were knighted at Mainz in 1184 was chivalry recognized as a socially acceptable institution. (Bibliog. 235)

German duchies. See Germany.

Germany, country in central Europe populated by Germanic tribes. Its areas ranged from the Alps to the North and Baltic Seas and from the Meuse (Maas) River in the west to Poland in the east. Although this area was called by the Romans *limes Germaniae* (*limes* meant a fortified frontier), and was perpetuated by Tacitus in his book, *Germania* it was called *Deutschland* by its inhabitants after the Thioi tribes, called *Tedeschi* by the Italians, and *Alamanni* by the French. With the decline by 843 of the system of *missi dominici* established by Charlemagne,* the defense of the eastern areas was left to the counts of duchies, powerful political units within Germany. As royal prestige and power declined, their status and power increased. Under Charlemagne, these counts had been royal officials who were replaceable at least in theory by the emperor. But by the 10th century, these counts were ruling Germany often as dukes. Within each territory each duke had far more power than the king; his office had become hereditary and only an extraordinarily strong king was powerful enough to replace him. Different tribal customs and traditions further strengthened the independence of these duchies. By 911, it contained four hereditary tribal dukedoms: Saxony, consisting of northwestern Germany between the lower Rhine and Weser rivers, the area conquered by Charlemagne, protected the eastern frontier on the north; Franconia* with its focus in the Main River valley and the closely grouped towns of Mainz, Worms, Speyer, and Frankfort, lay in the center; Swabia,* formerly called Alemannia, in southwest Germany from which Alsace tended to separate itself owing to its natural barrier of the Rhone River above Strassburg, protected the Alpine passes; Bavaria centering on the upper Danube and Inn river valleys, protected the eastern frontier against the Magyars and Slavs. A fifth, the western duchy of Lorraine* (Lotharingia), was poised uncomfortably between France* and Germany. Basically it was the Holy Roman Empire, an assemblage of Christian states ruled by the twin heads, temporal and spiritual: the emperor and the pope.

German heroic epics drew their material from native Germanic history and legend, such as Theoderic the Great* (known as Dietrich von Bern in German epic poetry), whereas its courtly epics were French in origin and its stories centered around the court of King Arthur.* Towards the end of the 12th century, however, the heroic epics became obsolete and were superseded by the court epic when the French courtly influence began to change the outlook of society.

Kings and emperors of Germany from the time of Charlemagne:

800 - Charlemagne
814 - Louis* the Debonnaire
840 - Lothair I, Louis the German
876 - Carloman, Louis the Young
881 - Charles* le Gros
887 - Arnould, natural son of Carloman
899 - Louis, Arnould's son
912 - Conrad I, king of Germany; Charles the Simple, king of France
919 - Henry the Fowler
936 - Otto I, king of Germany; king of Italy, 961; emperor, 962
961 - Otto II, king of Germany; emperor, 973
983 - Otto III, king of Germany; emperor, 996
991 - Otto III and Adelaide, his grandmother
1002 - St. Henry II of Bavaria, king of Germany and of Italy;
           emperor, 1014
1024 - Conrad II, the Salic
1039 - Henry III, king of Burgundy in 1038,
           emperor 1045
1056 - Henry IV, king of Germany, emperor in 1084;
           Rudolph, duke of Swabia, pretender;
           Herman of Luxemburgh, pretender;
           Egbert, margraf of Thuringia, pretender
1106 - Henry V, emperor in 1111
1125 - Lothair, duke of Saxony, emperor in 1133
1138 - Conrad III of Hohenstaufen
1169 - Henry VI, king of the Romans, emperor and king of Italy, and
           the Two Sicilies
1198 - Philip, a Tuscan nobleman, king of Germany Otto IV, king of
           Germany and Italy, and emperor
1212 - 1250 - Frederick II, son of Henry VI
1246 - 1248 - Henry Raspe of Thuringia; anti-king
1250 - 1254 - Conrad IV
1257 - The Great Interregnum:
           Richard, earl of Cornwall
           Alfonso V, king of Castile
1273 - Rudolph of Hapsburg
1292 - Adolphus of Nassau
1298 - Albert I of Hapsburg, duke of Austria
1308 - Henry VII of Luxemburgh, king of Romans and of Italy; emperor
1314 - 1322 - Frederick of Austria, son of Albert I
1314 - Louis IV of Bavaria

and emperor
1349 - Gunther of Schwarzburgh, king of the Romans
1378 - Wenceslas of Luxemburgh
1400 - Robert, count Palatine+ of the Rhine
(Bibliog. 24, 68, 199)

Gervase, chronicler who became a monk at Canterbury in 1163; his *Chronica*, 1135-1199, described the burning and restoration of the cathedral in detail. Up to 1135, he used Geoffrey of Monmouth's* work, but the coverage of the reigns of Henry II* and Richard I* provided some useful insights. Gervase did not like the Plantagenet* kings, and was severely critical of them in his writings. (tr. Joseph Stevenson, *Church Historians of England,* London: Seeley, 1858, V, pt. 1) (Bibliog. 63, 99)

Gervase of Tilbury, marshal of the kingdom of Arles* around 1200, who travelled widely from England to Sicily in his official capacity. Dedicated to his patron, Otto IV* of Germany, his *Otia imperialia* contained legends, history, descriptions of natural phenomena, artificial and natural wonders, and an interesting account of the kings of England from 1066 to 1199. Presumably this was written for the amusement of his patron, the emperor. (ed. G. G. Leibnitz, *Scriptores Rerum Brunsvicensium,* I, 881-1004; II, 751-784, Hanover, 1707-1710) (Bibliog. 63)

Gesta Edwardi de Carnarvan, valuable contemporary chronicle of the reign of King Edward II* of England written by a canon of the priory of Bridlington; it was continued through the reign of Edward III.* (ed. William Stubbs, *Chronicle of the Reigns of Edward I and Edward II,* ii, 25-151, London: *Rolls Series,* 1883) (Bibliog. 99)

Gesta Herwardi incliti exulis et militis, life of the outlaw Hereward* the Wake, supposedly compiled from a life of Hereward by his priest, Leofric,* although it probably was written about 1150 by Richard, a monk of Ely who died before 1189. (ed. and trans. S. H. Miller, *De gestis Herwardi Saxonis,* in *Fenland Notes and Queries,* III, Peterborough, 1895) (Bibliog. 99)

Gesta Regis Henrici secundi Benedicti abbatis, chronicle of the reigns of Henry II* and Richard I,* 1169-1192, known commonly under the name of Benedict* of Peterborough. It contained valuable information on the reigns of those two monarchs. (ed. William Stubbs, London: *Rolls Series,* 1867) (Bibliog. 99)

Gesta Stephani, chronicle describing the deeds of King Stephen,* 1135-1154. It was one of the most detailed sources for Stephen's reign, written by a contemporary, thought to have been Robert of Lewes, bishop of Bath and Wells, 1136-1166. Its author supported Stephen's side against Matilda, but chose no sides between Stephen and Henry II.* (ed. and trans. K. R. Potter, *The Deeds of Stephen,* London: Medieval Texts, 1955) (Bibliog. 99)

geste, French word meaning history or recording of deeds and events, and gradually incorporating with it the entire lineage of a family involved, that is, those who accomplished the deeds. As most of these accounts were related in verse and generally sung to the accompaniment of lute, rebec or viol, the entire unit came to be known as a song of deeds, or *chanson de geste.** (Bibliog. 106, 231)

La Geste francor, anonymous Italian cycle of poems that freely modified and enlarged the French *chansons de gestes.** It added to the Italian epic certain features which later Italian epic writers kept. Roland was said to be an Italian by birth; all traitors were grouped as members of the single house of Maganza; and the main narrative of the story frequently was interrupted by adventures of love. (Bibliog. 245)

gestes du roi, cycle of *chansons de gestes** which centered on Charlemagne and his immediate family. He was the embodiment of Christianity successful before the Saracen* infidels; he was the great emperor of the west. Usually the king or emperor of France formed only the background of the stories involving his faithful and immediate vassals, because these vassals were more active in the poems than the king who served as a court of appeal or as their accepted leader in peace and battle. Most of the action lay in his court or his camp. For a list of these *chansons,* see Charlemagne. See also *Girart de Vienne.* (Bibliog. 106, 231)

Ghent, Gand, city in Flanders* which grew to become one of the most important centers of wool and cloth industry in Europe. (Bibliog. 98)

Ghibelline, Italian political party from the 12th to the 14th centuries in northern and central Italy, which strongly supported the Hohenstaufen* dynasty on the throne of the Holy Roman Empire, especially Frederick I,* Barbarossa (1123-1190) and Frederick II* (1194-1250). They were vigorously opposed by the Guelphs.* (Bibliog. 98)

Gibraltar, peninsula in southern Spain which commanded the strait between the Mediterranean Sea and the open Atlantic Ocean. Known to Greek and Roman geographers as Calpe or Alybe, and coupled with an eminence on the northern African coast called Abyla (Ape's Hill), these two formed the Pillars of Hercules, the limits of enterprise to the seagoing people of the Mediterranean Sea for centuries. Moors who crossed from Africa in the 8th century chose this place as the site for a fortress which they called "gebel Tarik" (Tarik's Hill) from the name of their leader, Tarik ibn Zeyad. It was considered so impregnable that no siege was laid against it until 1309 when Alonzo Perez de Guzman captured it for Ferdinand IV of Spain. To attract inhabitants to it, Ferdinand offered asylum to swindlers, thieves, and murderers and promised to levy no taxes on the export or import of goods. (Bibliog. 68)

Giffard, Sir John (c. 1232-1299), English knight from Brimsfield, Gloucestershire, who was a supporter of the baronial party opposing King Henry III.* He was among those who made a treaty with Prince Edward* in 1263, and was pardoned later that year for not observing the Provisions of Oxford.* In April of 1264, he was in command of Kenilworth* castle+ from which he surprised and destroyed Warwick* castle, capturing the earl and his countess. Taking an active role at the battle of Lewes* in 1264, he was captured, but only after he had captured William la Zouche. His strong opposition to the tactics of Montfort* caused him to change his allegiance, and by the battle of Evesham* in 1265, he, along with the earl of Gloucester and others, was in the king's army. For his services in that battle, he was pardoned for his support of Montfort at Lewes, and for all other trespasses up to October 1265. He was appointed as one of the commissioners to draw up a truce at Montgomery in 1274 between Llewelyn ap Gruffyd, the Prince of Wales,* and Humphrey de Bohun.* He was summoned to Parliament in 1295 and again in 1299 by which he became Lord Giffard. He had been engaged at age 4 to Aubrey de Camville, also age 4, but he never married her. His son and heir was John, Lord Giffard (1287-1322), who took livery of his father's land in 1308 although he still was a minor. A hot-headed young man, John was forbidden under pain of forfeiture from participating in the tournament at Newmarket in 1313, and again that same year was enjoined to abstain from tourneying, bourding,+ jousting,+ or seeking adventures or performing any other feats of arms without the king's license. He fought at the battle of Bannock Burn,* and was captured. After his release, he was appointed keeper of the castles, manors, towns and lands of Glamorgan, lately belonging to Gilbert de Clare,* earl of Gloucester* and Hertford, recently deceased. By 1316, he had become a banneret+ of the king's household, and was granted 200 marks per year for life, and to serve the king in peace and war with 30 men-at-arms; this grant was revoked two years later. He was one of the barons who ravaged the lands of the Despensers* in 1321, but was pardoned for that action by act of Parliament two months later. At the outbreak of hostilities, he held Gloucester against the king, and then opposed the king's forces at Bridgnorth* the following January, burning the town and destroying the bridge to prevent the king's forces from crossing the Severn River. Soon after, Giffard joined Thomas* of Lancaster at the siege of Tickhill* castle and at the fight at Burton-on-Trent. His lands had been taken into the king's hands by writs of 1321 and 1322, and orders were issued for his arrest. He was captured at the battle of Boroughbridge* on March 17, 1322, and hanged as a traitor at Gloucester a month later. (Bibliog. 47)

Gilbert de Clare (d. 1314), ninth earl of Clare,* known as "the Red", Gilbert was knighted at the age of 16 by Simon de Montfort* along with his brother Thomas de Clare, and Robert de Vere,* earl of Oxford,* before the battle of Lewes* in 1264. He led the center of the baronial army, and it was to him that King Henry III* surrendered his sword when the battle was over. Later, after violent quarrels with Simon and his sons, he joined Prince Edward whose victory he shared at Kenilworth.* He was at Evesham* in 1265 when Montfort was killed. On the death of the King Henry III in 1272, Gilbert took the lead in swearing fealty to the new king, Edward I,* and was joint guardian of the kingdom in the king's absence on the crusade. He married as his second wife Joan, second daughter of Edward I. His earldom died with him in 1314. (Bibliog. 56)

Gilbert of the Haye, author of a 15th century translation into Middle Scots, *Boke of the Law of Armys,* of Lull's+ handbook for knights, *Libre del Orde de Cauayleria.* (ed. J. J. Stevenson, London, 1901) (Bibliog. 16, 119)

Gille, daughter of Pepin, sister of Charlemagne,* and mother of Roland, she became wife of Milon d'Aiglent, who died; then she married Ganelon* in the *chanson de geste,* Berta aus grans Piés.* (Bibliog. 128)

Gilles de Chin, romance by Gautier le Cordier of Tours, based on the life of a real person, Gilles de Chin, who died on August 12, 1137. Giselbert de Mons, the chronicler, reported that Gilles was one of the most valiant knights of the 12th century. This work was regarded as the first historic-biographic *roman*. In it, with his friend Gerart de Saint-Aubert on the tourney circuit, Gilles saw and fell in love with the countess of Duras, 18 years old. Promising to be faithful to her, he departed for a crusade where in her honor he performed marvellous deeds. While he was there, the queen of Jerusalem fell in love with him, but he remained constant to his countess. Regrettably, she died while he was away, so on his return he married Domisin de Chievres (historical fact), and once more began following tourneys. Tiring of that, he enlisted to aid the count of Hainault against the duke of Brabant.* He died of a lance thrust in a battle of Rollecourt in a war between the count of Namur and the duke of Louvain. (ed. Baron de Reiffenberg, *Mon. pour servir à l'histoire des prov. de Namur,* VII (1847), pp. 1 ff.) (Bibliog. 106, 231)

Ginglain, son of Gawain* and his wife Ragnell.* He was raised in seclusion by his mother and was known by the epithet *Libeaus Desconus.** (Bibliog. 145)

Giraldus Cambrensis, Gerald of Wales, Welsh historian also known as Giraldus de Barri. Born in Pembrokeshire in 1146 or 1147, he was descended on his mother's side from Nesta,* the famous mistress of King Henry I* and daughter of Rhys ap Tudor, Prince of South Wales. He studied in Paris and England, and returned to become the archdeacon of Brecon. Nominated twice to become bishop of St. David's in Wales, he was never elected to that post because the archbishop of Canterbury feared elevating a Welshman to such a high position. He was a voluminous writer, and an important one for the period. Among his works are the following:

Topographica Hibernica, a description of Ireland and its inhabitants based on his visits to that country in 1183 and again in 1185-1186 as secretary to Prince John, later King John. (trans. John J. O'Meara, *The Topography of Ireland,* Dundalk, 1951; trans Sir. Richard C. Hoare, rev. Thomas Wright, London, 1863, repr. 1867)

Itinerarium Cambriae, a account of Archbishop Baldwin's tour of Wales in 1188 to preach the third crusade.+ He also included descriptions of topography and natural history. (tr. T. Jones, *Gerald the Welshman's Itinerary through Wales and Description of Wales,* Aberystwyth: National Library of Wales, 1950)

De principis instructione, a work which purported to instruct princes

in proper conduct. In it, Giraldus included a description of the exhumation of King Arthur's body between two stone pyramids and buried
deep in a hollow oak at Glastonbury* "in our days." On the casket was
a cross of lead inscribed "here lies buried the renowned king Arthur
with Wenneveria his second wife in the isle of Avalonnia." He continued by recounting that the body of a woman lay in the same tomb
with a lock of yellow hair still well preserved, which crumbled when a
clumsy monk tried to handle it. (tr. Joseph Stevenson, *Church
Historians of England,* London: Seeley, 1858, V, i, 131-241)

Expugnatio hibernica, describing the English conquest of Ireland,
1166-1185. (ed. Frederick J. Furnivall, London: Kegan Paul, Trench,
Trubner, 1986: *EETS OS,* 107) (Bibliog. 73)

*Girard de Roussillon, chanson de geste** written between 1155 and
1170. In this story, Girart was the brother of Doön de Mayence.* Here
Charles Martel took away from Girart his bride, Ellisent, younger
daughter of the emperor of Constantinople, in order to marry her
himself instead of the older and less beautiful daughter, Bertha, who
had been promised to him. He also intended to deprive Girart of his
castle+ of Roussillon in Burgundy, but to obtain Ellisent, he reluctantly had to grant Girart his feudal independence. Charles then
married Ellisent, and Girart married Bertha. Later Charles was determined to have Girart become his vassal again, thus breaking his
faith. He encamped before Roussillon and demanded Girart's
allegiance. These two marshalled their forces and began a huge battle
south of Vezelay, but the fight was stopped by divine intervention,
only to resume again after a short period. Finally, Girart was forced
to flee to the Ardennes forest where he led the life of a charcoal
burner for twenty-two years while his wife supported them as a
seamstress with her high-quality needlework. They finally returned to
France and were restored to their estates through the efforts of
Ellisent, but war between Charles and Girart broke out once again and
raged for seven more years before Girart finally yielded. Converted as
a result of a miracle, Girart consecrated the remainder of his life to
pious works, including bringing the body of Mary Magdelene to Vezelay
where he founded a monastery to honor that precious relic.+ He and his
wife were buried beside their son in the valley of Roussillon at the
abbey of Pothieres. Historically, Rossilho was a castle at Isère near
Vienne that belonged to a nobleman named Girard de Fraite who once revolted against Charles the Bald. Since 1040, the Abbey of Vezelay
claimed to possess the body of Mary Magdelene, and three times a year
pilgrims flocked by the thousands to worship at her shrine: Easter,

Pentecost, and on Mary Magdelene's Day (July 22). (ed. Mary Hackett, Paris: *SATF*, 1953-1955, 3 vols.) (Bibliog. 106, 231)

Girart de Roussillon, one of the *douzepeers** slain by Marsile* at Rencesvals* in the *Song of Roland.** He was surnamed *le Vieil* ("the elder"). (Bibliog. 210)

*Girart de Vienne, chanson de geste** by Bertrand de Bar-Sur-Aube* written between 1190 and 1217. In its opening lines, Bertrand divided the French *chansons de geste** into three common cycles: the gestes of the king (*gestes du roi)* (Charlemagne and his successors); of Doön de Mayence (ancestor of Ganelon and many other traitors); and of Garin de Monglane whose family distinguished itself by its service to the kings of France and Christianity. This *chanson* belongs to the third cycle. Girart was the son of Garin de Monglane, and had three brothers: Hernaut de Beaulande, Milon de Pouille, and Renier de Gennes. Its story centered around a dispute between Girart and the duchess of Burgundy. The duchess had been promised to Girart but Charlemagne took her instead, rewarding Girart with the fief of Vienne. Angry with the lady for rejecting him, Girart scorned her so that she determined to get revenge. On her wedding night, she tricked him into kissing her toe instead of Charlemagne's, and then boasted about it to Girart's sons years later. War followed that insult. Charlemagne besieged Vienne where Girart was aided by his brother, Renier, and by Renier's son, Oliver.* Hostilities ceased when single combat was arranged between Oliver and Roland to settle the matter. Their fierce combat on an island in the Rhone River was stopped by the intervention of an angel who demanded that these two paragons of knighthood should love one another, and should fight pagans instead of each other. Charlemagne accepted Girart's homage, the beautiful Aude, Oliver's sister, was affianced to Roland; and new wars against the pagans were announced to arouse all warriors in France. This work served as an introduction to the *Chanson de Roland.** (ed. W. Van Emden, Paris: *SATF*, 1976). (Bibliog. 231)

*Girbert de Mes, chanson de geste** of the 12th century which forms a continuation of *Garin le Loherenc,** containing the same general style and motifs of its predecessor, and introducing the second generation of Lotharingians and Bordelais. Here, Girbert, out to avenge the death of his father, Garin, sought Fromont of Lens, nephew of the traitor Hardré* and leader of the Bordelais, who had fled to Spain, and had concluded an alliance with King Marsile and his Saracen followers. Girbert killed Fromont, made a drinking cup of the dead man's skull, and then offered Fromontin, Fromont's son, a drink from that grisly cup. Fromontin took a bloody revenge, but fell victim to Girbert in the end. (ed. Pauline Taylor, Namur: Bib. de la Fac. de Phil. et Letters de Namur, XLIX, 1952). (Bibliog. 106, 231)

Gisors, castle+ of Robert de Bellême (see Bellême-Montgomery), famed military engineer who owed much to King Henry II* of England. It owed its strength to the continuing rivalry between Henry II and King Louis VII* of France, both husbands of Eleanor of Aquitaine.* Called the "outpost of France" against Normandy, it was located on the right bank of the Seine River in prime position for the king of England to defend his possessions in Normandy in face of the Île de France* and served as the capital of the Vexin.* Built on an artificial mound, it had an octagonal donjon surrounded by a polygonal wall encompassing seven acres. Its buttresses supported bretesche+ and hoarding.+ Inside the donjon was a chapel which Henry II had dedicated to the memory of Thomas à Becket.* (Bibliog. 196)

Glamorgan and Gwent, castles+ of. When William, earl of Gloucester* and lord of Glamorgan died in 1183, the custody of his lands passed to the crown. Thus the English king had the task of defending his Welsh castles of Cardiff, Kenfig, Neath, Newcastle, Newport and Rhymny against the Welsh population which rose after William's death. As the lordship of Striguil* (the whole of Nether Gwent) also was held by the king at this time, its main castles at Chepstow* and Usk also were his responsibility. In 1189, the royal custody of the lordship of Striguil was given to William Marshal, and the lordship of Glamorgan to Henry's youngest son, John,* who married its heiress. Though John divorced his wife soon after he ascended the throne in 1199, he kept her estates and entrusted them to William de Braose,* lord of Gower. In 1207, the king was forced to yield them to Faulkes de Breauté,* and then in 1214 to Geoffrey de Mandeville (see Essex) on his marriage to Isabelle of Gloucester in whose family hands they remained. (Bibliog. 104)

Glanville,+ Ranulph de (d. 1190), chief justiciar+ of England under Henry II* (1154-1189). He had a long and distinguished career. He had been sheriff of Yorkshire between 1163 and 1170 until he lost it at the Inquest of Sheriffs+ in 1170, and had participated in the revolt of King Henry II's sons in 1173-1174. After he distinguished himself at the battle of Alnwick* where he had captured the king of the Scots, Henry rewarded him by reappointing him sheriff of Yorkshire and itinerant justice. Later, as chief justiciar, he was the king's most trusted servant, serving as vice-regent when the king was out of the country. When he and King Richard I* had serious differences of opinion, Richard imprisoned him, and for his release forced him to pay £15,000 of the money he had amassed as sheriff. Despite these differences, however, Richard used Glanville to ensure the continuity of the government in his absence. He died in 1190 en route to the Holy Land with Richard I. In the last few years of Henry II's reign, Glanville wrote a *Treatise on the Laws and Customs of England,* which was the most important legal treatise in English before Bracton.* Written as a practical manual for judges and other royal officials, this work was based on his own experiences and discussed royal statutes and the distinction between civil and criminal cases. He presented writs+ from Henry II's reign described the procedure for handling each one, and then added his own commentary. His main theme was the role of the royal court as administrator of justice.   (ed. and trans. John Beames, London: W. Reed, 1812; repr. J. H. Beale, Washington, D.C., 1900) (Bibliog. 7, 98, 99)

Glastonbury, abbey in Somersetshire where supposedly Joseph of Arimathia* was buried; a tomb there also was identified as the burial place of King Arthur.* This locale often was identified as Avalon.* See also Giraldus Cambrensis. (Bibliog. 1, 12, 96)

gleeman, poetical musician in Anglo-Saxon Britain; he was a court favorite, and was offered asylum by the courts of kings and by residences of the rich. Basically, a gleeman was a merrymaker, and did mimicry, dancing, tumbling, sleight of hand, as well as singing and storytelling. (Bibliog. 215)

Gliglois, French Arthurian verse romance written in the first half of the 13th century. Gliglois, son of a German noble, was sent to Arthur's* court by his father, and became Gawain's* squire. Both men fell in love with Guenevere's* handmaid, Beaute, but she rejected both, secretly preferring Gliglois. When he was left behind by Gawain going to a tourney,+ Beaute secretly armed him and he won the prize. By so doing, he demonstrated his devotion and valor, and was rewarded by her hand in marriage. (ed. C. H. Livingston, Cambridge, MA: Harvard Studies in Romance Languages, VIII, 1932) (Bibliog. 10)

Gloucester, Robert of, chronicler of the Barons' War* against English King Henry III* in the 13th century. His work spanned English history from Brutus to 1270. (tr. Joseph Stevenson, *Church Historians,* London: Seeley, 1885, V, i) (Bibliog. 99)

Gloucester, city in the county of Gloucestershire in western England which borders on Oxfordshire. Bictric, son of Algar, a great thane+ in the time of Edward the Confessor,* held various lordships in Gloucester. In her youth, Matilda, afterwards wife of William I,* sought to marry Bictric, but he refused her. When she became queen, she imprisoned him, and on his death, the honour of Gloucester was given to her. On her death in 1083, the king took possession of it, and gave it to Robert FitzHamon for services to the king and his father. He married Sibyl, daughter of Roger de Montgomery,* earl of Shrewsbury,* who bore him a daughter, Mabel, who later was married to Robert de Caen (or de Mehlent), illegitimate son of King Henry I. Sometime between 1121 and 1123, the king bestowed the earldom of Gloucester on Robert, who, by 1130, had a grant of £20 a year in lieu of the third penny+ of the county pleas. When Stephen* seized the throne in 1135, Robert was in Normandy, but the following year he crossed the Channel and did conditional homage for his lands. In 1137, he quarreled with the king, and lost his lands. In 1139, he brought Matilda FitzEmpress* to England and acted as her commander-in-chief in the civil war that resulted. Even though Robert was captured in the battle of Lincoln,* he soon was exchanged for King Stephen who also had been captured in that battle. He died in 1147 leaving a son and heir, William, called FitzRobert, who died in 1183, leaving three daughters, the youngest of whom, Isabelle, married Prince John,* youngest son of King Henry II.*

When her marriage to John was dissolved in 1199, Isabelle retained the earldom because John had obtained it only through marriage. Isabelle, who had been kept in prison since her divorce from John, was sold in marriage to Geoffrey de Mandeville, earl of Essex.* On his death without issue, the honour of Gloucester again reverted to the king's hands. On King John's death in 1216, the Countess Isabelle once more was restored to her lands, and married as her third husband, Hubert de Burgh,* the justiciar, but she died shortly after their marriage. Following the death of Isabelle, the sole remaining heiress of William, earl of Gloucester, was his third daughter, Amice; she was styled countess of Gloucester until her death in 1225. By her husband, Richard de Clare, earl of Hertford,* Amice had a son and heir, Gilbert I, who had fought on the side of the French at the battle of Lincoln and had been captured by William Marshal, earl of Pembroke,* and regent. Gilbert was allowed to make his peace with the regency, and to be recognized as earl of Gloucester on the death of his aunt. He married Isabelle, daughter of William Marshal, and died in 1230 leaving a son and heir, Richard de Clare II. This Richard, who had become earl of Gloucester through his grandmother's inheritance and earl of Hertford through his father's inheritance, did homage to

King Henry III* in 1243 for all his lands. He had been ward of Hubert de Burgh and had secretly married Hugh's daughter, Megotta. The king was outraged, but soon forgave him the action when Megotta died. Shortly thereafter, he married Maud, daughter of John de Lacy, earl of Lincoln. He died in 1262, and was succeeded by his son, Gilbert II,* known as the Red Earl. He was the most powerful English noble of his day. Besides owning immense estates in Wales and Ireland, he also possessed land in twenty-two English counties. The earldom died with him in 1314. It was not again granted in fee, but was granted to favorites of the king later in the 14th century. Included among its later earls and dukes were the following:

1324 - Hugh Despenser* the younger; married Eleanor, daughter of
         Gilbert de Clare; hanged and quartered in Hereford in 1326
1337 - Hugh, lord Audley
1386 - Thomas of Woodstock,* duke of Gloucester and lord constable;
         married Eleanor, eldest daughter and co-heiress of Humphrey de
         Bohun,* earl of Hereford, Essex, and Northampton; murdered by
         Thomas Mowbray, earl marshal, 1397
1398 - Thomas Lord Spencer, grandson of Eleanor, co-heiress of Gilbert
         de Clare, earl; married Constance, daughter of Edmund Langley,
         duke of York; beheaded at Bristol, 1400
(Bibliog. 47, 66, 101)

Gloucester castle,+ fortress in Gloucester built early in the reign of Henry I,* and given to Walter of Gloucester. Henry II* continued the association by granting its custody in fee to Roger, earl of Hereford,* son and grandson of its previous castellans, Miles and Walter of Gloucester, but Roger's rebellion in 1155 ended his family's connection with the castle, and Henry kept it as a royal possession. At the outbreak of the barons' rebellion in support of young Henry and the king's other sons in 1173, Gloucester castle was readied for defense, but the baronial army besieged it, and gained access to it with the help of some prisoners who unwisely had been released to help with its defense. Over half a century later, Lord Edward* recovered it for the crown, and entrusted it to Roger de Clifford.* Following the battle of Lewes,* in 1264, it once again fell into the hands of the barons, but yet again was retaken by Lord Edward after a three-week siege. From 1273 until her death in 1291, it was held by Eleanor of Provence as part of her dowry. (Bibliog. 104)

Godfrey de Bouillon (c. 1061-1100), duke of Lower Lorraine and one of the leaders of the first crusade+ who appeared in legend as the perfect Christian knight, a peerless hero of the whole crusading era. He was hardly that. His resources resembled those of Count Robert of Normandy, but Godfrey had the capacity to lead. Actually, his dukedom was a barren title given to him by the Holy Roman Emperor, Henry IV,* and he sold his two small estates, extorted money from the Jews in his territory, and pledged his castle of Bouillon to raise a considerable army and to finance his crusade. However, on the crusade itself, accompanied by his brothers Baldwin and Eustace, he distinguished himself as a brave soldier. Physically, he was tall, well-built, fair with blond hair and beard, appearing every inch the ideal northern knight.   As a soldier, however, he was indifferent, and was over-shadowed by the abilities of his brother Baldwin. (Bibliog. 195, 201)

Godfrey of Louvain, duke of Lower Lorraine. When he married his daughter Adeliza to King Henry I* of England as his second wife, he established relations of importance with Brabant. Among those who accompanied her to England were her chancellor Godfrey who became bishop of Bath in 1123, and her half-brother, Jocelin of Louvain, or as he preferred to be called, Jocelin the Castellan, who was granted the honour+ of Petworth. (Bibliog. 180)

Godfrey of Luci (Lucy), son of one of King Richard I's* most trusted servants, Richard of Luci. For money, he persuaded Richard to appoint him bishop of Winchester.* He went on to purchase the manors of Meon and Wargrave for his church for £3,000, was granted his inheritance for 1,000 marks, became sheriff of Hampshire and obtained custody of Winchester castle. (Bibliog. 7)

Godiva, Godgifu, wife of Leofric,* earl of Mercia, mother of Aelfgar, earl of East Anglia, and grandmother of Edwin* and Morcar,* and of Aldgyth, who became the wife of Gruffyd, Prince of Wales,* and after his death, the wife of King Harold.* Legend reported that Countess Godiva, wishing to free the town of Coventry from a heavy tax, asked her husband the earl to lift it. He scolded her for wishing to harm him by that suggestion, and forbade her from mentioning it to him again. She persisted until in exasperation he told her to mount her horse and ride naked through the market place of the town from one side to the other wherever people were congregated, and when she re-turned from that ride he would grant her whatever she wished. She made him confirm that promise, and then accompanied by two soldiers, she mounted her horse naked, loosed the bands of her hair and let it veil her whole body except her legs. Passing through the town she was seen by no body except for her white legs. When she returned she demanded of him what he had promised, and Earl Leofric freed the town of Coventry and its inhabitants from the servitude, confirming that he had done so by a charter. (Bibliog. 238)

Godwine, Godewine, Godwin, Anglo-Saxon baron who was appointed earl of Wessex by King Cnut* (1016-1035). He had married the king's niece, and had been made the king's chief lieutenant in all matters pertaining to England which gave him incredible power, and when Edward the Confessor* ascended the throne in 1042, Godwine had his daughter Edith marry the new king, and secured earldoms for his sons Swein* and Harold.* Both Saxon and Norman nobles were so angered by his power that they convinced the king to exile him and his five sons. At this time, 1051, King Edward promised the throne to William,* duke of Normandy. Godwine, however, was too strong and too powerful to remain in exile for long, and he returned in 1052 and ejected the Norman counsellors of the king. He replaced Robert of Jumièges* as archbishop with his man, Stigand, but he did so without the consent of the pope who thereupon became an enemy of the house of Godwine. Godwine really ruled both England and its king, however, and after his death by choking on a piece of bread while dining with the king in 1053, his son Harold stepped into his place and virtually ruled England until the king's death in January 1066.   (See Ordeal by bread and cheese in Volume 1.) (Bibliog. 228)

Golagrus and Gawain, Middle English* romance which centered on King Arthur's* journey to and from the Holy Land. Its chief incident was a battle between Gawain* and Golagrus, the lord of the castle which Arthur was besieging. Although Gawain was the winner, he allowed himself to be treated as the loser and follow Golagrus humbly as if a prisoner in order to save Golagrus' life. By such courteous and chivalric behavior, Gawain convinced Golagrus to become his friend and a subject of Arthur. (in F. J. Amours, *Scottish Alliterative Poems,* Edinburgh, PSTS, 27, 1918) (Bibliog. 202)

Goldemar, Middle High German* poem by Albrecht von Kemnaten in the late 13th century; only the first nine stanzas survived.   With the help of giants, Dietrich von Bern (see Theoderic the Great) liberated a beautiful maiden held captive in a mountain by the dwarf king, Goldemar. This work adapted the heroic Dietrich legends to courtly presentation. Albrecht may have been the originator of the twelve-line German stanza known as *eckestrophe.* (Bibliog. 86)

Gore, kingdom of, small kingdom, strongest for its size in all of

Arthurian Britain. Presumably it lay on a peninsula in southwest Wales, the one which included the city of Pembroke,* but more probably on one of the western isles which may have been Avalon* or have contained Avalon. In the Vulgate,* Uther Pendragon* warred against King Urien of Gore, captured him and threatened to hang him. Urien's nephew, Baudemagus,* surrendered the land to Uther to save Urien's life. Urien later reconquered it, and gave it to Baudemagus as reward for his earlier noble gesture. (Bibliog. 96, 117)

Gorey castle.+ See Channel Islands castles.

Gorlois, earl of Cornwall* and lord of Tintagel,* he was Uther Pendragon's* vassal, and husband of Igerne.* He was slain during Uther's siege of the castle. (Bibliog. 129, 145)

Gormont et Isembart, oldest *chanson de geste*ation* in the cycle of *gestes** concerning the rebellious vassals *Doön de Mayence.** Also known as *Le Roi Louis,* only a fragment of the original late 11th-century or early 12th-century version survived, and its plot was reconstructed because it was included in several later works: Philippe Mousket's *Chronique rimée,* and the German romance *Loher und Maller.* Isembart, a rich young vassal of King Louis, Charlemagne's* son and successor, was opposed at court by his enemies. Louis, a weakling, sided with the opposition, and forced Isembart into exile in England. There he was well received by Gormont, a Saracen* king, who converted him to the Saracen faith. Raising an army, Isembart and Gormont returned to France to retake his confiscated fiefs in Ponthieu and Vimeu, and to confront King Louis in a final battle. Louis killed Gormont, but was mortally wounded himself, and died a month later. Isembart took over command of the Saracen army, but he, too, was wounded fatally, and reconverted to Christianity just before his death. Historically, the Norseman Godrun invaded Vimeu and Ponthieu from England in 880-882, and burned the abbey of St. Riquier before being defeated at St. Valery by King Louis III shortly before Louis died of pneumonia. (ed. Alphonse Bayot, Paris: *CFMA* 14, 3rd ed., 1931) (Bibliog. 106)

Gottfried von Strassburg (d. 1210), German author of the Middle High German* courtly poem *Tristan.* He seemingly wrote the work for a person named Dietrich, for that name is spelled out acrostically in the poem's opening verses. Gottfried was one of the three great names of the *Blutezeit** in the field of narrative poetry, the other two being Hartmann von Aue* and Wolfram von Eschenbach. (Bibliog. 86)

Gowther, Sir, Middle English* romance from about 1400 that was a redaction of the 12th century French romance, *Robert le diable.** When
the wife of the duke of Estryke prayed for a child by any means
because of her ten years of childlessness, a stranger visited her in
her garden, and impregnated her. Only on his departure did he reveal
himself as a devil. She told her husband that an angel had visited her
and had told her that she would have a child. The child, Gowther, was
born and, true to his demonic background, grew to have enormous
strength. By the age of 15, he was so terrorizing the whole area that
his supposed father died of grief when his mother tearfully revealed
his true parentage. Gowther fled to Rome and confessed his sins to the
pope who told him as penance to eat only what he could snatch from
dogs, and not to speak again until he received a sign from heaven. As
Hob the Fool he visited the court of Almayne where three times he
routed the Saracens,* who were seeking the emperor's daughter, before
being wounded. The daughter, previously mute, fell from a tower when
she recognized Hob as the unknown knight who had saved the court, and
recovered her speech by the fall. The pope absolved Gowther of his
past, married him to the daughter, after which Gowther and his wife
ruled Almayne. (ed. K. Bruel, Oppeln, 1886) (Bibliog. 202)

Graeco-Byzantine romances, 12th-century French romances whose main
settings were in southern Italy, Constantinople or Rome, and whose
characters often had names distorted from the Greek. Romances so considered were *Eracle** (*Heraclius*) by Gautier d'Arras*; *Florimont** by
Aimon de Varenne; *Ipomedon** by Hue de Roteland; *Athis und Prophilias**;
*Floire et Blancheflor**; *Cligés* by Chrétien de Troyes.* (Bibliog. 106)

*Graelent, lai** by Marie de France* which used the same plot as her
*Lanval.** Its title came from a legendary historical figure, Gradlon,
king of Cornouaille in the 6th century. (ed. E. M. Grimes, *Lays of
Desire, Graelent, and Melion,* New York, 1929) (Bibliog. 147)

graf, German count. See titles of dignity, German.+

Graf Rudolf, Middle High German* poem from the 12th century of which
only 900 lines survived. Its story recounted how Rudolf, on a crusade+
in response to a summons by the pope, quarreled with the king of
Jerusalem, and threw in his lot with the Saracen* sultan. The sultan
refused to send him back to the king of Jerusalem because Rudolf was
in love with the sultan's daughter. They were separated...[*gap in the
manuscript*]...she was found, and baptized in Constantinople; he was
found, wounded and captured, but he escaped and joined his beloved,

and they departed secretly from Constantinople.* Dual emphasis in this work was placed on military and moral virtues of the knight and on love (*minne+*). It also recognized knightly virtues in Saracens—a remarkably tolerant view for the time of its composition. (ed. P. F. Ganz, *PsQ*, XIX, 1964) (Bibliog. 197)

Grail, Graal, Holy, cup of the Last Supper in which Joseph of Arimathea caught the blood of the crucified Christ. Later he carried it to Britain where in Castle Corbenic* it was entrusted to Joseph's descendants, ending with Galahad.* It was endowed with supernatural properties of Christianity; it was a source of healing and inspiration and visions, and its finding or its "achievement" was a transcendent mystical experience. But its details varied widely. Another name for a grail, tailleor, meaning a serving or carving platter became associated with the Holy Grail legends. In Chrétien de Troyes'* account of *Conte del Graal,* it was a vessel of different dimensions and shape than a goblet and it represented a conflation of two accounts in one of which the damsel bore a grail and in the other a tailleor. Chrétien stated that the Grail did not contain a pike or a lamprey or a salmon, but merely a single wafer, a sight curious enough to cause attention. Wolfram von Eschenbach, the German poet, presented a different Grail in *Parzival*; he made it wonder-working stone with heavenly origins. See Grail, Holy in Volume 1. (Bibliog. 10, 96, 138)

Grail keepers, when Joseph of Arimathia took the Grail to Britain, Josephes, his son, accompanied him as the Grail keeper. On his death, the keeper became Alein*; then Josue, son of Bron, became keeper; his father-in-law, Galafers,* built Corbenic* as the Grail castle. The Grail kings followed in succession, father to son from Galafers: Galafers to his son Alphanye, to his son Amynadape, to his son Carcelois, to his son Mangel, to his son Lambor, to his son Pellam, to his son Pelles. The *Grand Saint Graal* named the kings in succession differently: Joseph of Arimathia; Josephes, his son; Alein; Josue; Aminadappe; Catheloys; Mangel or Manaal; Lanbar; Pellean; Pelles, whose daughter bore Lancelot's son Galahad. (Bibliog. 1, 96)

Grailly, Jean de, Captal de Buch (d. 1369), one of the most famous of the feudal family from Gascony, who entered the service of the kings of England. His title, *Captal,* derived from the Latin *Capitalis,* meaning chieftain. Grailly was the closest Gascon ally of the Edward,* the Black Prince, and the first foreign knight to be chosen for the Order of the Garter.* Toward the end of the battle of Poitiers* in 1356, the

Prince ordered the Captal to lead a small mounted force in an attack upon the French rear while he led his forces in a frontal assault. That assault led to the defeat of the French and the capture of the French King John II.* Two years later, Grailly and the count of Foix, Gaston Phoebus, returning from a "crusade" in Prussia, rode to the relief of the nobility at Meaux from an attack by the peasantry. With a company of 40 lances (120 men), and leading 25 knights in bright armor with pennons flying, the Captal and Gaston charged into the city across a narrow bridge filled with angry peasants who had unwisely chosen that place to fight. Wielding weapons from horseback, the knights cut down their opponents, trampled them, threw their bodies into the water, forced the rest back across the bridge, and inflicted general carnage. Poorly armed and led, the peasants gave way before the lances and battle axes of the footmen, and the slashing blades of the mounted knights. Several thousand were slain, and the fleeing rest were pursued and butchered across the countryside; the village was destroyed and its inhabitants slaughtered. As a supporter of King Edward III,* Grailly joined an extraordinary group of able soldiers. Besides Phoebus and the Black Prince, Grailly fought beside Chandos,* Knollys,* Sir Walter Manny,* and Sir Hugh Calveley.* (Bibliog. 223)

Graindor (Graind'or) de Douai, 12th century poet who redacted a 1130 *chanson de geste** by Richard le Pèlerin (the Pilgrim) on the capture of Antioch, *Chanson de Antioche.* This work by Graindor constituted the starting point of the entire epic poetry of the crusades, for he revised also a continuing epic, the *Chanson de Jerusalem,* dealing with the conquest of Jerusalem. This dual work began with the crucifixion of Christ who prophesied to the thief also being crucified that the crusaders would come. This was followed by the description of the misfortunate crusade of Peter the Hermit,+ the preparations for a new crusade, the descriptions of the crusaders' trip to the Holy Land including their stay in Constantinople, the capture of Nicaea, a detailed description of the siege and fall of Antioch,+ and the siege by the Turks and the raising of that siege. Godfrey de Bouillon* was highlighted as the crusaders' leader, and Adhemar* de Puy was described as going to war carrying the holy lance. See *Antioche, Chanson de;* Peter Bartholomew.+ (Bibliog. 111)

Gran conquista de Ultramar, anonymous Spanish *libro de Caballeria* written early in the 14th century, detailing the story of the crusades up to 1271. For its 1,100 chapters, it drew on old French epics including *Helias, Les Chetifs*,* and the *Chanson d'Antioche** for its intermingling of fact, fancy and fantasy. (ed. P. de Gayangos,

Biblioteca de Autores Espanoles, 44, 1858) (Bibliog. 237)

Grandasso, king of Sericana in *Orlando furioso,* who invaded France to win Orlando's sword, Durindana, and Rinaldo's steed, Bayard. Eventually Orlando killed him. (Bibliog. 8)

Grandes Chroniques de France, also known as the *Chroniques de Saint-Denis,* this huge ten-volume work was regarded as historical historiography inspired by Louis IX* and compiled from time to time by the monks of St. Denis. Much of it deals with relations with England. (ed. Jules Viard, Paris: Société de l'histoire de France, 1920-1953) (Bibliog. 99)

Grandison, Sir Otes de (c. 1250-1328), English knight who served in the household of Prince Edward* around 1265. He accompanied the prince on his crusade until the death of King Henry III* brought the prince back to become King Edward I in 1272. He received a grant at the king's pleasure of the islands of Guernsey and Jersey at a rent of £500 a year in 1275, and was reconfirmed in that grant for life the following year for his long and faithful service to the king from an early age. He particularly was commended for his wise care and solicitude of the king's affairs at the court of France. In 1278 he married the daughter of the count of Burgundy, was appointed to the king's household and served as the king's secretary in 1280. In 1281, he was nominated to serve as the peace negotiator between the king of the Romans and the count of Savoy.* On his return to England, he continued to serve the king, being sent on frequent trips to the king of France and the Roman emperor. Summoned to Parliament in 1299, he became Lord Grandison. On the accession of Edward II,* he was opposed to Piers Gaveston,* and with the count of Savoy he left England permanently, and died in 1328. (Bibliog. 47)

Grandison, Sir Piers de (c. 1290-1358), English knight from Herefordshire who accompanied the earl of Richmond* to Gascony* in 1310. He joined with Thomas* of Lancaster in 1322, was captured at the battle of Boroughbridge* by Sir Hugh Despenser* and held in prison until the manor of Liddiard in Wiltshire, an inheritance of his mother's, was given to Sir Hugh as a fine. In 1322, his brother, Otes de Grandison,* was security for his good behavior under penalty of 600 marks. By 1323, he had been restored to his lands in Kent* and County Hereford.* He took livery of his father's lands, did homage to the king in 1335, and was summoned to Parliament in 1337. In 1355 he vowed to visit the shrine at Santiago de Compostella, but was allowed for illness and weakness to commute that vow into other works of piety. (Bibliog. 47)

Graphasantes. See Ethiopia.

Gray, Thomas (d. 1369), English knight and lord of Heaton manor in Northumberland,* and the author of *Scalacronica,** a chronicle of England and Scotland between 1066 and 1362. In 1355, he was constable of Norham* castle, and while attempting to intercept a Scots foray, he was ambushed and captured. During his captivity in Edinburgh he wrote his "Ladder Chronicle" in French, beginning in 1355. He apparently was the first English layman to write a chronicle. (Bibliog. 99)

great barons' meeting, meeting called at Poitiers* in 1159 by King Henry II* of England to undertake the recovery of Toulouse* from Count Raymond V who refused to return it to its heiress. Among those present at that muster were the king's chancellor, Becket,* with 700 knights of his own personal following, and the first vassal of the English crown, King Malcolm III of Scotland, who came to win his spurs which Henry had refused to grant him a year before. Others who appeared were Raymond de Trencavel, viscount of Béziers and Carcassonne; William of Montpellier; and the count of Barcelona. (Bibliog. 162)

Great Company. See free companies.

Great Interregnum (1254-1273), period of German history during which two emperors vied for the imperial throne, and neither exerted any real power. On the death of Conrad IV* (Hohenstaufen*) in 1254 after only a four-year reign filled with prolonged civil war for control of the empire, William of Holland was chosen by the electors.* He reigned for only two years. On his death in 1256, the electors were divided; one party chose Richard of Cornwall,* the brother of King Henry III* of England, and the other party chose Alfonso V, king of Castile. Neither exerted any real authority in Germany,* and as a result the country was plunged into anarchy as each prince went his own way unlimited by any superior authority. This Interregnum was brought to a close in 1274 by the election of Rudolph of Hapsburg. (Bibliog. 124)

Great Painted Chamber, large room in Westminster,* about 80 feet long by 26 feet wide by 30 feet high, originally chosen by King Henry III* as his bedchamber, and decorated on his orders with biblical and other murals which gave it its name. It was in the small private chapel in the northeast corner of this room that Simon de Montfort* married the king's sister in 1238. Used for royal audiences, this room probably had long been used as the "place customary for our parliament" when its members were summoned to Westminster prior to the various elements withdrawing to their separate deliberations. King Edward II* used it on March 16, 1310, for the meeting of the lay and clerical magnates for the election of the Ordainers.* (Bibliog. 182)

Green Knight, epithet of Sir Bercilak* in the Middle English* metrical romance, *Sir Gawain and the Green Knight.** (Bibliog. 206)

gregois, grigois, gregeois, grezois, grecois, name or term used with incredible variety in the *chansons de geste.** For example, in *Girard de Roussillon,** it was used for a bishop's name; in *Ogier le Danois,* to refer to a spy, a helmet+ and a hauberk.+ In others, it referred to a destrier, a palace, gold, and a mantlet. Most frequently, it referred to Greek fire,+ a weapon of awesome aspects. (Bibliog. 128)

Gregorius, Middle High German* poem by Hartmann von Aue* written around 1190. With this work, Hartmann created a new type of German literature, the so-called courtly legend in which an edifying story was told with all the refinements of the courtly style of writing which Hartmann had helped to create in such of his earlier works as *Erec.** In this work, Hartmann told of a child born of an incestuous union of a brother and sister who, once he was born, was set adrift, and drifted to a foreign shore where he was reared by an abbot. The young man, Gregorius, desired to be a knight and not a monk, so he set out after being knighted to be a knight-errant.+ One of his adventures took him to the castle+ of a lady being besieged by an unwelcome suitor. Gregorius saved her and then married her, only to discover shortly thereafter that his wife was in fact his mother. He fled into the wilderness in despair, and had himself chained to a rock in the middle of a lake by a fisherman. He lived there in penance for seventeen years, subsisting only on rain and dew. When the pope died, two cardinals learned by a dream that Gregorius was destined to be the next pope, so they set out to find him. After a lengthy journey, they found him still chained to his rock. He was escorted to Rome, and crowned pope. At the end, he was happily reunited with his mother who came to Rome seeking absolution from the pope, unaware that he was her son. (ed. and tr. E. H. Zeydel, and B. Q. Morgan, Chapel Hill, NC: University of North Carolina Press, 1955) (Bibliog. 235)

Gregory VII (Hildebrand) (1021-1085), pope from 1073 to 1085. A Cluniac monk, after he was elected pope in 1073, he continued the work he already had begun, especially the moral and political elements of the reform movement. He worked to purge the church of corrupt clergy, to maintain priestly chastity by opposing marriage for priests, to prevent buying and selling church offices (simony), to restore unity in the orthodox church, and to continue the holy war against Muslims* to free Spain and Palestine* from Muslim rule. In 1075, he proclaimed his *Dictatus Papae (The Pope's Dictate)* which revealed his political appraisal of the papacy. Among other items, it stated that the Roman pontiff was the sole and universal pope; that he alone was entitled to depose bishops or to forgive their sins; that he had the power to depose an unworthy emperor; that no one could judge the pope; and those who did not obey the Roman Church were not Catholics. To implement these claims, he appointed legates who would represent him in various countries, and who were granted imperial power to intervene in local affairs and to depose unworthy bishops and abbots. These dictates were in open and direct opposition to the current practices in Germany,* rooted in the Constitution of the Holy Roman Empire. Therefore, Henry VI* denounced them in 1076, and confrontation between the two men became imminent. In 1076, Henry deposed Gregory as being a rebel against imperial authority; Gregory responded by excommunicating Henry, and cancelling the oath of fidelity owed to him by his subjects. At this, his vassals rebelled against him. Henry then took advantage of the ecclesiastical procedure of penance, journeyed to the pope, made penance and requested absolution in accordance with ecclesiastical practice. By that tactic, the emperor beat the pope with his own weapons, for the rebels in Germany no longer had a legal basis to oppose the emperor and were left to his mercy. Thus the pope lost the upper hand in Germany; Henry was able to defeat the rebels and reaffirm his authority in 1080. Gregory tried to save face by excommunicating him again, but was ineffective. Henry thereupon invaded Italy, appointed an antipope, Clement III, and in 1081, besieged Rome. Gregory was forced to flee, and died at Salerno in 1085. (Bibliog. 98)

Gret Gest off Arthure. See *Morte Arthure.*

Gromer Somer Joure, one of the knights who surprised Guenevere* and Lancelot* in their assignation, as described in *Morte D'Arthur.** He also was the brother of Dame Ragnell,* the ugly crone whom Gawain* agreed to marry to save King Arthur's* life if she would answer Gromer's question, what women love best, in the mid-15th century English romance, *Wedding of Sir Gawain and Dame Ragnell.* (Bibliog. 202)

Grosmont castle,+ one of three fortresses in South Wales—Grosmont, Skenfrith and White Castle—which formed a unit for the defense of Upper Gwent. Early in his reign, King Stephen* (1135-1154) had acquired them from the marcher* baron, Pain FitzJohn (d. 1137), in exchange for lands elsewhere. Half a century later, King John* (1199-1216) granted these three castles to Hubert de Burgh* who held them until his fall in 1239. They then remained in King Henry III's* hands until 1245 when, with the extensive possessions in Wales* and elsewhere, he bestowed them on his younger son Edmund, earl of Lancaster,* in whose hands they remained. Edmund's son, Henry,* became the second English duke+ when Edward III created him Henry of Grosmont, duke of Lancaster, on March 6, 1250. (Bibliog. 104)

Guarin de Glapion, seneschal+ of Normandy under King John.* He besieged and captured the castle+ of Driencourt belonging to the count of Eu* in 1201 for that nobleman's opposition to King John's marriage to Isabelle of Angoulême. (Bibliog. 47)

Guelders, Guelderland, province of east and central Netherlands.

Guelphs, Italian political party of the 12th-14th centuries which opposed the Hohenstaufen* (Ghibelline) emperors, especially Frederick I,* Barbarossa (1123-1190), and Frederick II* (1194-1250). (Bibliog. 124)

Guenevere, Guenever, Guinevere, daughter of King Leodegrance of Cameliard whom Arthur* rescued from King Ryons and married; besides being the wife of King Arthur, she was loved by Meliagrance and became the lover of Lancelot.* Her treatment of Lancelot as a courtly lover was the core of the story, *Knight of the Cart** (see *Lancelot)* by Chrétien de Troyes*; Malory's treatment of her was extensive in *Morte D'Arthur.** She married Mordred* illegally after he usurped Arthur's kingdom while Arthur was pursuing Lancelot in France. She ended her days as a nun after the deaths of Arthur and Mordred. (Bibliog. 49, 145)

Guerrino il Meschino, fantastic Italian adventure story written by Andrea da Barberino* late in the 14th century. The hero moved through childhood slavery to the discovery and release from imprisonment of his royal parents, his marriage to a Persian princess, happy years of kingship and a saintly death at the age of 56. Throughout this work, Guerrino fought monsters, duels and battles, thwarted treacheries, and lived a good kingly life. (Bibliog. 245)

Guesclin, Bertrand du. See du Guesclin, Bertrand.

Gui de Bourgogne, French *chanson de geste** detailing the adventures of one of Charlemagne's* barons, the son of Sanson de Bourgogne. Written late in the 13th century, this work assumed that Charles had been in Spain for twenty-seven years instead of seven, and that he was exhausted and needed men and supplies desperately. Gui responded to the emperor's plaintive plea and brought to Spain a company of young men, the sons of the warriors accompanying Charlemagne. This energetic group succeeded in doing what Charlemagne had been unable to accomplish--they conquered Spain. Out of gratitude, Charlemagne rewarded Gui with Spain as his fief.+ (ed. Guessard and Michelant, Paris: *APF* 1, 1859) (Bibliog. 106, 231)

Gui de Nanteuil, sequel to *Aye d'Avignon,** this *chanson de geste** from the last years of the 12th century summarized the *Aye d'Avignon* before recounting the adventures of Gui, lord of Avignon as well as of his father's fief of Nanteuil (of unknown location). Arriving in Paris, Gui was made standard-bearer by Charlemagne.* Defamed at court by Hervieu of Lyons, grandson of Doön de Mayence, one of Ganelon's* relatives, Gui vanquished his slanderer in single combat. Charlemagne, however, supported Hervieu in their dispute for the hand of Ayglentine, daughter of Yon of Gascony, because Hervieu had bribed the king to find in his favor. Gui fled to Nanteuil where he was pursued by both Charlemagne and Hervieu. Receiving unexpected help from Ganor, Gui killed Hervieu and forced Charlemagne to agree to and witness his marriage to Ayglentine. Charlemagne returned to Paris angry and humiliated by the traitors who surrounded him. During the 13th and 14th centuries, this *geste* was enlarged by the addition of poems on Garin's father, Doön; on Gui's sister, Parise; and on his son, Tristan. (ed. James R. McCormack, Genève: Droz, 1970) (Bibliog. 53, 106, 231)

Gui de Warewic, French romance of adventure written between 1232 and 1242. Its author may well have been a monk of Osney in Warwickshire who wrote to glorify the families of Warwick and Wallingford. Gui was supposed to be an ancestor of Wigod of Wallingford, cup-bearer for King Edward the Confessor.* While in love with his lord's daughter, Felice, Gui fought in tournaments+ at the German emperor's court, at Constantinople, and at Alexandria. He returned to England, slew a dragon,* and won the hand of his beloved Felice. On his wedding night, however, he left for a pilgrimage to the Holy Land, and was gone so long that when he returned, he lived in his own house as a beggar unknown to his wife. He fought and defeated the evil knight, Colebrant, and then retired to a monastery. The remainder of the poem as devoted to his son. See *Guy of Warwick*. (ed. A. Ewert, Paris: CFMA, 1933) (Bibliog. 106)

Guibert d'Andrenas, chanson de geste* of the *Garin de Monglane* cycle*, this work belonged to the Aimeri de Narbonne group. Written about 1185, it described how Aymeri, seeing his four oldest sons well endowed with fiefs, determined to leave Narbonne to his godson, Aymeri. For his remaining and youngest son, Guibert, he determined to obtain the Saracen city of Andrenas and the daughter of its king for Guibert's wife. The aged man assembled an army to help Guibert with its capture. Despite encountering stiff resistance, they captured Andrenas, and Guibert married Augaiete, the daughter of King Judas who had been killed in the battle. Guibert assumed the throne, and his father returned to Narbonne to confirm his godson in his succession. (ed. Jesse Crosland, London: Longmans, Green and Allen, 1923) (Bibliog. 106)

Guiborc, Guibor, Guibour, Guibort, baptismal name assumed by Orable before she married Guillaume d'Orange (Count William of Toulouse).* She was the Saracen daughter of Emir Desrame of Cordoba in Spain, and had been the wife of King Thiebaut whom she betrayed and abandoned to marry Guillaume. She appeared in *Aliscans,* Chevalerie Vivien,** and *Fouque de Candie.** (Bibliog. 128)

Guienne, Guyenne, duchy in southwestern France. Its name was a popular contraction of Aquitaine,* and both names were used interchangeably for the territory of Aquitaine until 1258 when Aquitaine was divided by the Peace of Paris, agreed to by Henry III* and Louis IX.* That division called for Guienne, the southern part of the duchy including Gascony,* to remain under the control of the kings of England as vassals of the king of France. It played an important role in the Hundred Years War.* It was an important source of income for the English king, Edward III,* because its bridge-tolls along the Garonne River and its wine exports fattened the English treasury. It also served as an important English base for the operations of Edward,* the Black Prince, in his battles against the French. (Bibliog. 98, 203)

Guigemar, lai* by Marie de France* telling the story of a knight who wounded a doe that was a fée* in reality. His arrow bounded back to wound him in the thigh. That wound would not heal until the knight had undergone the pangs of love. He left his country in a ship which landed him at a seaside castle+ in which a beautiful young wife was being confined by her elderly husband. These two young people fell in love, but eventually were found out. They pledged mutual constancy on the oaths that she would marry no man who could not undo a certain belt of hers, and he would marry no woman who could not untie a knot in his shirt. He left on the same ship that brought him. They subsequently met and after the knight killed her husband in a fight, they were united. (Bibliog. 147)

Guilford castle,+ though this bulwark in Surrey was one of the many castles readied for defense against the rebellion of Henry II's* eldest son, young Henry, in 1173, its primary role afterwards was as part of the dowry of successive queens. After the death of Henry III* in 1272, his widow, Queen Eleanor, held it until her death in 1291, then Queen Margaret until 1317, and Queen Isabella from 1327 to 1330, though they undoubtedly stayed at the adjoining palace rather than in the castle itself. It was so weak a fortress that in 1391 fourteen prisoners escaped from its dungeon as a consquence of its "want of repair." (Bibliog. 104)

Guillaume. See also under William.

Guillaume, Chanson de, also known as *L'Archanz,* this was the oldest *chanson de geste** of the *Garin de Monglane* cycle.* Composed in the Anglo-Norman dialect, this work perhaps was written about the same time as the *Song of Roland.** Landing at Archamps with a huge force of Saracens, King Deramed of Cordova was met by Vivien, nephew of Count Guillaume, who assumed command of the situation after the previous Christian leader, Count Tedbalt of Bourges, had fled shamefully in terror. Count Guillaume of Barcelona was Guillaume "al curb nez" ("with the aquiline nose"). Vivien swore never to retreat one step before the Saracens. His men were slain and he was seriously wounded, but he sent a message begging help from his uncle. Guillaume's forces arrived to assist Vivien, but they, too, were killed by the huge numbers of Saracens. Going to obtain more men whom his wife Guiborc* had gathered for him, Guillaume returned to the fight, but those men, too, were killed. Guillaume then found the dying Vivien on the battlefield, and administered the last rites before returning to his wife in Barcelona. He set out on the next day with 30,000 more men, but unknown to him, Vivien's 15-year old brother, Gui, secretly followed them. This third army also succumbed to the numerical superiority of the Saracen forces, and when Guillaume's life itself was threatened, it was saved by Gui who, through intervention of God, routed 20,000 pagans. Then Guillaume found Deramed, cut off one of his legs to prevent him from fleeing, and Gui decapitated him to prevent him from begetting an heir who someday might come back to avenge his father.

At this point, the second episode, the Rainouart (Renewart) episode, began. In this, Guillaume no longer was "le curb nez," but now was called "le court nez," so his identity had shifted to Guillaume of Orange, Count William of Toulouse,* or William Shortnose. In this new episode, William found Vivien on the battlefield, administered the last rites, and then, disguised as a Saracen, fled to Orange on a Saracen horse. His wife, however, refused to believe it was he, for her husband would never retreat before pagans, she declared. He finally convinced her of his identity by freeing 100 Christian prisoners from 7,000 Saracens marching past. Later he travelled to the court of King Louis the Pious,* Charlemagne's son, and his brother-in-law, in Laon to demand the aid due him in their feudal contract. After he witnessed Guillaume's legendary wrath—throwing his gloves at the king's feet in anger—Louis finally agreed to send the 20,000 men he demanded, and off he went. Accompanying him was an uncouth scullion from the kitchen, Rainouart, carrying only his tinel, his club. Guiborc soon discovered that Rainouart was her brother, son of Deramed and Oriobel, but did not tell him so. His hot temper got him in trouble with the Franks who hurled insults at him, but on the battlefield, he was a powerful force, slashing horse and warrior to pieces, and freeing captured Christians. Even after his sword broke, he fought on fiercely using just his bare fists. After the battle, he inadvertently was not invited to the victory celebration. Furious at this oversight, he returned to Spain to gather a huge army to bring on the Christians the same ruin he had brought on the pagans. Guiborc succeeded in reconciling him with William, and he was baptized and reconciled with his sister. (ed. E. S. Taylor, New York: Oxford Press, 1919) (Bibliog. 106, 231)

Guillaume d'Angleterre, poem commonly attributed to Chrétien de Troyes,* and written about 1170. Concerning an imaginary King William of England, this work centered on a King William of England and his wife, Queen Graciene, living in Bristol. After seven years of marriage, she became pregnant, but a voice kept sounding in the evening for the king to flee. As they did so, she bore twins, and somehow the four got separated. Twenty-one years passed as William worked as a steward in the household of a burgher of Galveide, Graciene ruled a fief of Sorlinc, and the twin boys, Lovel and Marin, ended up in the service of the king of Quatnasse. William arrived in Sorlinc by accident and was recognized by Graciene, and on a hunting trip, he met two knights who turn out to be his long lost sons. The reunited family returned to Bristol where the throne was returned to them. (ed. Maurice Willmotte, Paris: *CFMA*, 1927) (Bibliog. 106)

Guillaume de Dôle, French romance by Jehan Renaut* written between 1210 and 1214. Sometimes known as *Roman de la Rose* (but not the famous allegorical poem with the same name), this work was a variation of the theme of virtue tested. The heroine here was Lienor, the maiden sister of the hero, Guillaume de Dôle. Her honor was slandered by the emperor's seneschal+ who boasted that because he knew she had a birthmark like a rose on her thigh, he therefore proved that she had lain with him. Lienor undertook her own defense and proved to the court that she had been slandered. She then married the German emperor who had fallen in love with her upon hearing praise of her virtue. (ed. Rita Lejeune, Paris, 1925) (Bibliog. 106, 127)

Guillaume de Palerne, French romance written for Yolande of HainaulT,* countess of St. Pol. Events in this story paralleled events in the history of Sicily. The siege of Palermo (Palerne) in the story echoed the deposition in 1194 of King William III of Sicily when Emperor Henry VI* surrounded the forces of the Queen Regent in Palermo Palace and slaughtered the game in the Royal Park to feed his troops. Ebron, king of Apulia, married Felise, daughter of the emperor of Constantinople, and their son, Guillaume, was to inherit the kingdom, but was prevented from doing so by the actions of his uncle who tried to kill him. Guillaume was saved by a werewolf, the enchanted son of the king of Spain, who carried him away to the woods. After many adventures, Guillaume arrived at Constantinople where the young Princess Melior fell in love with him. To prevent her scheduled marriage with the son of the emperor of Greece, they fled with the help of the werewolf, and took refuge at the palace of the widowed Felise. Guillaume helped his mother in her battles against the king of Spain whom Guillaume captured. After becoming reconciled with his family, the king of Spain disenchanted his son, and Melior and Guillaume were married. (ed. H. Michelant, Paris: *SATF,* 1876) (Bibliog. 106, 202)

Guillaume le Breton, chaplain of King Philip II,* Augustus, of France. Also known as William of Armorica, this poetic biographer was the continuator until 1223 of Rigord's "Vie de Philippe-Auguste" in his *Gesta Philippi Augusti,* and his long poem, *Philippide.* Both works were valuable for his descriptions of the relations between France and England in the reigns of Henry II,* Richard I* and John.* (tr. into French in

Guizot, *Collection des Mémoires*, Paris, 1825, IX, pp. 183-351)
(Bibliog. 99)

Guineman, French baron whom Charlemagne* chose to bear Roland's horn,
Olifant, after the death of the *douzepeers** at Rencesvals* in *Song of
Roland.** He and Rabel were the two barons who replaced the fallen
Roland and Oliver,* and who opened the battle against Baligant* who
subsequently killed him. Der Stricker,* in *Karl,** called him and Rabel
two "princes of France." (Bibliog. 173, 210)

Guinemer, Ganelon's* uncle who held his nephew's stirrup as Ganelon
said farewell to his men just before departing on his mission to
Marsile's* camp for Charlemagne* in the *Song of Roland.** That act was
considered an act of homage, of humility. (Bibliog. 210)

Guingamor, lai* by Marie de France.* After being rejected by him, a
proud fairy queen provoked Guingamor to slay a boar. Then he followed
her into fairyland where he lived with her for 300 years, but which
seemed like only three days to him. She permitted him to return to
normal life for a visit, but warned him not to eat. Forgetting her
admonition, Guingamor ate some wild apples, and instantly was
shrivelled to extreme age. The fairy recalled him to her fairyand and
he was never seen again. (Bibliog. 147)

Guinglain. See *Le Bel Inconnu.*

Guiscard, Robert. See Robert Guiscard of Hauteville.

Gundulf (b. 1024), bishop of Rochester, and celebrated castle-builder
in 11th century England. As a son of Norman peasants born in the
Vexin* about 1024, he vowed to make a pilgrimage to the Holy Land
before entering the monastery at Bec where Lanfranc* was prior.
Associating himself with Lanfranc, he went to Duke William's new abbey
of St. Stephen at Caen with Lanfranc, and thence to England when
Lanfranc became archbishop* of Canterbury in 1070 under William I.* In
1077, Gundulf became bishop of Rochester. He erected at his own expense, but at the urging of Henry, earl of Warwick,* a stone castle
which showed his unusual knowledge of masonry construction. He was the
logical choice for William I to select to supervise the replacement in
London of William I's hasty defenses with a massive stone tower to
overtop the other complex of buildings on the shores of the Thames
River. For this Tower of London, Gundulf built a remarkable structure
three stories high. Within its massive fifteen-feet-thick walls (at

their base), he built all the essential accommodations of the royal residence, including a great hall and an aisled chapel. Entrance was gained by means of a doorway at the first-floor level, well out of reach of hostile fire or battering ram, and accessible only by means of wooden stairs which could be withdrawn in case of danger. Such a tower was capable of withstanding any assault by any siege engine known in the time of William I. (Bibliog. 104)

Gunther, king of Worms. Through Siegfried's* supernatural help, he won the hand of Brunhild, took her to Worms as his queen, where her dispute with his sister, Kriemhild,* wife of Siegfried, led to the destruction of the Nibelungs at Etzel's court in Hungary. Their dispute was the focus of the action of the German epic *Nibelungenlied.** (Bibliog. 161)

Die Gute Frau, anonymous Middle High German* romance written before 1242 for the duke of Zahringen. Its stated source was a French poem told to its author by the French chaplain of Margrave+ Heinrich V of Baden who died in 1242. Its heroine, "die gute frau" or "la bone dame," was the daughter of a count who married a knight of low degree. After they had a religious experience, they decided to renounce wealth and possessions and live their lives as beggars. In time, they became separated from each other and from their children. Later the wife married first the count of Blois, and then the king of France, but neither marriage was ever consummated because God protected her from infidelity. At the end, the family was reunited in health and prosperity. (ed. E. Sommer, *ZfdP*, II, 1848) (Bibliog. 235)

Der Gute Gerhard, Middle High German* poem written around 1220 by Rudolph von Ems.* It told the story of the German Emperor Otto who was proud of his piety but was warned by a voice from heaven that he lacked true humility, and that he should take a lesson in true humility from a rich merchant of Cologne known as the "good." He had earned his reputation by the goodness of his heart and the charitable use he made of his great wealth by journeying to redeem Christian captives from infidels. Among his captives had been a princess of Norway betrothed to the missing King William of England. When after two years there still was no sign of the missing king, the princess was betrothed to Gerhard's son. On the eve of the wedding, the missing king appeared, and Gerhard respectfully waived his son's claim to the bride. Thus the emperor learned true humility from the lips of the merchant himself. (ed. J. A. Asher, *ATB*, LVI, 1962) (Bibliog. 86)

Guy of Lusignan (1129-1194), King of Jerusalem (1186-1192) and of Cyprus (1192-1194). Coming from the family of Lusignan in Poitou,* he journeyed to the Holy Land as an adventurer, and in 1179, he married Sybil, sister of King Baldwin IV. He was endowed with the county of Jaffa* and Ascalon, and then in 1186, after the death of the child king Baldwin V, was crowned king with the support of some of the barons. He was not a leader, either in military or political matters. That ineptitude led him into direct conflict with Saladin* and to his defeat by Saladin at the battle of Hattin* in 1187 where he was captured. On his release, he tried to recover his title but was unsuccessful because his rival, Conrad* of Montferrat, blocked his admission to Tyre. In 1192, King Richard I* of England forced him to renounce his claim to the throne of Jerusalem and gave him instead the crown of Cyprus. (Bibliog. 195, 201)

Guy of Warwick, huge Middle English* version of the Anglo-Norman *Gui de Warewic** was composed about 1240. Its 11,000 lines divided the story of Guy into three parts: Guy before marriage, Guy after marriage, Guy's son Reinbrun. Basically it was a story of a dragon-slaying, giant-killing knight who followed in the footsteps of the crusaders, and ignored the advances of infidel maidens. He was the grand exemplum of chivalric conduct: a defender of the faith against every infidel, a ready rescuer of damsels in distress, and a very proper knight of unswerving loyalty to kin, kith and king. (ed. William B. Todd, Austin, TX: University of Texas, 1968) (Bibliog. 202)

Gwent castle. See Glamorgan and Gwent, castles of.

Gymnosophists, people in a Far Eastern land filled with marvels. See Prester John; *Alexander and Dindimus.*

Gyrth, Anglo-Saxon earl; son of earl Godwine* of England. When he was exiled with his family by King Edward the Confessor* in 1051, he lived with Baldwin in Buges for a year, returning to England in 1052. He fought beside his older brother, Harold,* and fell at the battle of Hastings* in 1066. (Bibliog. 228)

H

Hab, battle of (August 14, 1119), indecisive conflict between King Baldwin II* of Jerusalem and the Turks under Il-Ghazi, emir of Mardin. Baldwin sought to rescue Antioch from the Muslims* with the help of his vassal Pons, count of Tripoli, and an army of 700 knights and several thousand footsoldiers. Against them, the enemy sent an army of some 20,000 horse archers. Baldwin used a formation more complicated than that used normally by crusaders against the Turks. His front line was formed by three corps, each consisting of a body of cavalry supported by a body of infantry so that each could protect the other. Behind the center of this line Baldwin placed himself and the knights of his household in three corps; on the right and slightly to the rear was the count of Tripoli with his vassals, and on his left and also slightly to his rear was Robert Fulcoy, lord of Zerdana, with the barons and knights of Antioch. This formation was used to prevent the Muslims from turning the crusaders' flanks, and to allow Baldwin to strengthen the center of the front line if the main attack was thrown at it. As the battle was joined, fighting became confused and neither side was able to use its main weapons to its advantage. Fighting all day, neither side won a decisive victory. Thus Il-Ghazi left at night believing he had won; Baldwin retired to Hab at sunset, returning to the battlefield the next day to recover his dead and strip the fallen Turkish warriors. (Bibliog. 166)

Hadleigh castle,+ built in Essex* by Hubert de Burgh* in 1230, this fortress surrendered to King Henry III* in 1239, but nothing was done by the king to maintain it. In 1292, despite its being assigned to Queen Margaret, and then to Queen Isabella as part of their dowries, little money was spent on its upkeep. Only when Edward III* began extensive repair in the 1360's did it become a fitting royal residence and a substantial military fortress which Richard II* granted to Aubrey de Vere, earl of Oxford,* for life. Its bailey extended some 350 feet from east to west and 200 feet from north to south, and was surrounded on three sides by a ditch. (Bibliog. 104, 247)

Hagen, vassal and kinsman to King Gunther* of Worms, lord of Troneck and brother of Dancwart; murderer of Siegfried* because Siegfried's wife, Kriemhild, insulted Brunhild, wife of his overlord, Gunther. Kriemhild violated the code of chivalry by killing him as a captive in bonds at Etzel's capital, Gran, and was herself slain for that reprehensible action in the German epic, *Nibelungenlied.** (Bibliog. 161)

Hainault, Hainaut, Flemish province bordered by Brabant,* Flanders,* France,* and the province of Namur. Established in the 10th century, it owed its allegiance to the duchy+ of Lotharingia, a part of the German Empire, but as its counts intermarried with the counts of Flanders, their histories became closely intermingled. To avoid the difficulties of plural homage, a separate junior branch of the counts of Flanders was given the title of counts of Hainaut. This province finally was united with the Low Countries by a marriage in the early 15th century. (Bibliog. 79, 100)

Halidon Hill, battle of (July 19, 1333), conflict between King Edward III* and the Scots in which Edward tasted victory for the first time by combining archers and dismounted cavalry to defend a strong position and thereby defeating the Scots' light horse and spearmen. After the Scots' advance had been repulsed by volley after volley of arrows from his archers, King Edward had his knights mount their horses and charge the retreating Scots. The Scots lost many earls and knights in this fight. To the English this battle made up for their defeat at Bannock Burn.* When he returned to England after this victory, the king received a triumphant reception, "universally loved and honored by high and low....so much so that one and all said that he was King Arthur* come again." (Bibliog. 166, 203)

Hamelin Plantagenet, earl of Warenne, illegitimate half-brother of English King Henry II,* who became a staunch supporter of Richard I's* chancellor,+ William Longchamps,* during the early years of the king's absence from England on the third crusade.+ Hamelin frequently went on official duties for the chancellor, such as journeying to Dover in September 1191 to secure the release of the imprisoned archbishop* of York, Geoffrey,* who had returned to England against the express wishes of the chancellor. He accompanied Longchamps to the meeting with Count John at Lodden Bridge. He later was one of the custodians of the ransom being raised for Richard I's release from German prison. (Bibliog. 7)

Hanley castle,+ castle begun in Worcestershire at the order of King John* in 1206-1207, presumably for its strategic value in commanding the high road from Worcester* to Upton. Henry III* granted it to Gilbert de Clare* and it remained in his family's hands until 1314 when the last of the Clares fell at the battle of Bannock Burn.* Then it passed in dower to the earl's widow, Matilda, but soon thereafter passed to Hugh Despenser* the Younger as part of his share of the Clare inheritance, obtaining it in right of his wife Eleanor, the earl's eldest sister and co-heiress. In May 1321, however, when his baronial opponents were plotting his fall, Despenser surrendered Hanley to the crown, after which it was attacked and burned by the in- surgents in the following winter. After the king's victory at Boroughbridge* in 1322, the Despensers were reinstated, and Hanley was restored to Hugh, along with considerable financial assistance from the crown to restore it. In 1328, it was granted to Eleanor, the widow of Hugh Despenser the Younger, and remained with her descendants. (Bibliog. 104)

Harbottle, motte and bailey+ castle+ built in Northumberland* by the Umphraville family around 1157 as a center for their operations, and captured by King William the Lion* of Scotland on his invasion of northern England during the rebellion of young Henry,* and the other of King Henry II's* sons in 1173. (Bibliog. 79)

Harcla (Harclay), Sir Andrew, degraded knight. Because knighthood was such a sacred honor, betrayal of it became an unforgivable and irremediable horror. The culprit was regarded as a traitor not only to his honor but also to his God. He was exposed on a scaffold in nothing but his shirt, after being stripped of his armor which was broken before his eyes, and thrown at his feet; his spurs were thrown on a dunghill, his shield was fastened to the croup of a cart horse and dragged through the dirt; his charger's tail was cut off. Three times a herald-at-arms asked "Who is there?", three times the name of the knight being degraded was given, and three times the herald answered, "No, it is not so, for I see no knight here, but only a coward who has been false to his plighted oath." Then carried to a church on a litter like a corpse, he was forced to lie and listen to a burial service being read over him, for he had lost his honor without which a knight could not live, and he was looked on as dead.

Sir Andrew Harclay was degraded on February 27, 1322. He had served his king and country well for years. He had been sheriff of Cumberland from 1285 to 1298, from 1312 to 1315, and again from 1319 to 1322. He was warden of Carlisle in 1296, served in the Scottish wars between 1304 and 1311, and was member of Parliament for Cumberland in 1312. He was made earl of Carlisle in 1321 by the first patent of creation into honor using a preamble imparting the merits of the person so designated:

> to him and the heirs of his body, with a grant of land to the value of 1500 marks a year because he routed the insurgents at Boroughbridge* on 16 March 1322, and captured their leader, the earl of Lancaster. (Bibliog. 246)

However, because he was jealous of the favoritism shown by the king for the Despenser family, he conspired with the Scots, and their king, Robert the Bruce,* and sought to marry Robert's sister. After his treason was discovered, he was led to the bar as an earl, fully attired with his sword belted on, wearing boot and spurs. There he was accused of taking money from James Douglas, a Scot, for not coming to the assistance of the king at the battle of Highland. For this the king ordered him to be degraded so that lower knights might learn from this lesson. His judge, Sir Anthony de Lucy,* then said to him:

> Sir Andrew, the king...did unto you much honor, and made you earl of Carlisle, and thou, as a traitor to thy lord the king, led his people of this country, that should have helped him at the battle of Highland,...away by the country of Copeland, and through the earldom of Lancaster, wherefore our lord the king was discomfited...by the Scots through thy treason and falseness; and if thou had come in time, he [would have] had the mastery. And all that treason thou did for the great sum of gold and silver that thou took from James Douglas, a Scot, the king's enemy. And our lord the king's will is that the order of knighthood by which thou undertook all thy worship and honor upon thy body, be all brought unto nought, and thy state undone so that other knights of lower degree may after thee beware. (Bibliog. 246)

Then his spurs were removed, his sword broken over his head, the same sword which had been given to him by the king when he created him earl, and he was stripped of his fur-edged tabard, his hood, his coat of arms, and his girdle. When thus shorn of all symbols of knighthood, Sir Anthony said to him, "Andrew, now thou art no knight, but a knave, and for thy treason the king's will is that thou be hanged." Then he was hanged, beheaded, drawn, and quartered, his head mounted on London bridge, and his four quarters sent to four towns of England as lessons to others. (Bibliog. 212, 246)

Hardicanute. See Harthacanute.

Hardré, member of the family of Ganelon* whose name became traditional as a traitor. His characteristic role in the *chansons de geste** can be understood by his role in *Garin le Loherenc** where he belonged to a small group of conspirators who gave the king dishonorable advice to further their own greedy ends, and to harm the king's loyal barons. Because Hardré chose the moment when the king had his head bowed in the symbolic posture of deep thought to make a treacherous proposal, the king was deeply moved by it, and accepted it. His whole lineage was tainted. His son Fromont* carried on the tradition by secretly marrying without the king's permission, and then quickly consummating a marriage to a woman who would secure his position among the barons. Thus the king was unable to stop the marriage. Their son, Fromondin, carried on the tradition: he denied Jesus, deserted the king's cause and joined the Saracen* army. Hardré appeared in *Gaydon,** *Gui de Bourgogne,** *Amis et Amiles,** *Parise le Duchesse,** *Gaufrey,** *Renaut de Montauban,* (see *Four Sons of Aymon),* and *Jourdain de Blaives** among others. (Bibliog. 52)

Harlech castle,+ concentric fortification standing on the estuary of the River Dwyryd in Wales* begun in the spring of 1283 and finished in 1290 during the second Welsh war of King Edward I.* It was one of the superb accomplishments of Master James of St. George, castle builder for the English king (see castle+). The Welsh besieged it in 1294, but were forced to cease their operations when a relieving force arrived from Conway and Caernarvon.* (Bibliog. 30)

Harold I, Harefoot, king of England (1035-1040), illegitimate son of King Cnut whom he succeeded. He ruled ferociously, and on his death, the English people willingly sent for his stepbrother, Harthacanute.* (See the genealogical chart 1 in the Appendix.) (Bibliog. 213)

Harold II, Godwineson (c. 1022-1066), king of England, 1066; ablest of all Earl Godwine's* sons. As hard as his father and his brother Swein,* he was a good military man, and made himself so indispensable to King Edward the Confessor* (1042-1066) of England that he was made earl of East Anglia in 1046. Between 1046 and 1051, Godwine and his sons fought the king in a power struggle but in 1051, they were exiled by the king. They were so powerful, however, that after only one year they were invited back to England in 1052. Harold had joined the Vikings in Ireland for his exile. He became earl of Wessex upon the death of his father in 1053, leaving vacant the earldom of East

Anglia. After several years of careful manipulation, Harold obtained that earldom for his younger brother Gyrth,* and a new earldom comprising Hertfordshire, Essex, Surrey, Kent and Buckinghamshire for his youngest brother, Leofwine.* By 1063, he had stopped the uprisings in Wales and had made himself the top soldier in England. In the next year, King Edward sent him to Normandy with a formal promise that the English throne would go to Duke William* when Edward died; Harold was to act as regent until William could claim the throne.

While in Normandy, he did homage+ to the duke by the *immixtio manuum*,+ and then took an oath of fealty+ to William "by the sacred right of Christian men." In the last article of the established form for that oath, Harold distinctly stated that he would be the representative (*vicarius*) of Duke William at the court of his (Harold's) lord, King Edward, as long as he [Edward] should live. He promised also that he would employ all his influences and resources to assure William the possession of the English kingdom after the death of King Edward; that he would turn over the castle+ of Dover to the custody of William's knights fortified with his [Harold's] own effort and cost, and that he would similarly supply and hand over other castles in various ports of the land where the duke should order them fortified. By these acts, Harold became William's man, his vassal, and bound to support William's accession. However, Harold cared only about his own career and not about oaths.

By Christmas 1065, King Edward was dying. Having William declared the next king, he felt that he had done everything he could to keep the throne out of the hands of the sons of Godwine. Westminster cathedral had just been completed and only eight days after it had been consecrated on December 28, 1065, the king was dead. His funeral ceremonies were followed in the cathedral by Harold's coronation. To heal internal breaches, Harold put aside his mistress, Edith Swannehals,* who had borne him four illegitimate children, and married Edith, sister of Morcar and Edwin,* earls of Northumberland and Mercia. Then the invading force of Harold "Hardrata,"* king of Norway, sent Harold and his forces north to defeat the invaders at Stamford Bridge+ on September 25. No sooner had he won that fight than he heard of William's invasion at Pevensey* on the southern coast. In 13 days he marched his army the 190 miles south to London where he collected whatever men he could find, and by forced march covered the 50 to 60 miles to the battlefield where he arrived on Friday, October 13, 1066. Meeting the forces of William on the field of battle at Hastings* on the next day, Harold, his brothers Gyrth and Leofwine and the greater part of the English barony were killed. Harold had miscalculated by forcing the attack against William so quickly. He had

had time on his side, time to prepare, to group his forces, to gather an army of superior size, but he sought to strike an unexpected blow against the duke by a night attack, and he failed.

Above his perjury and dishonest practices to get and keep the throne, the weakest point of his claim was his lack of "kin-right." He had not one single drop of royal blood. Without even a right of conquest behind him, a right which could be regarded as God's judgment, such a peaceful ascension to the throne by a non-royal noble was unprecedented, revolutionary, and politically dangerous. (Bibliog. 33, 110)

Harold "Hardrata" ("Hard Ruler") (c. 1015-1066), king of Norway, brother of King Olaf II of Norway, and the last and probably the greatest of the warrior-Vikings. He claimed the English throne through King Cnut.* After the battle of Stiklestad in 1030 in which Olaf died, Harold made his way east to the eastern Baltic Sea and on through Novgorod and down the great Russian rivers to the Black Sea where he joined the Varangian Guard+ at Constantinople. He returned to Norway as a hero, and became its king in 1047. Because he was a harsh but effective ruler, he became known as Hardrata or "Hard Ruler." The events in England in 1066 gave him the opportunity to prove to the world that he indeed was the greatest Norse conqueror of all time. Gathering a huge fleet of some 300-500 ships, he sailed to Scotland to rendezvous with Tostig,* and then sailed down the east coast of England to the Humber River, and up the River Ouse to anchor 10 miles from York at Riccall. He fell in defeat when his and Tostig's forces were met and defeated by Harold Godwineson's* forces on September 25, 1066, at the battle of Stamford Bridge.+ (Bibliog. 110)

Harthacanute, Hardicanute, king of England (1040-1042). He was Cnut's son by Emma of Normandy.* He invited his half-brother, Edward,* son of Emma and King Ethelred* the Unready, to come to England from Normandy and to hold the kingdom together with himself, and to ensure that Edward would succeed him. He was the only legitimate son of King Cnut. (Bibliog. 110)

Hartmann von Aue, first German poet to introduce Arthurian epic into Germany; he lived around 1160-1210, probably in the Swiss Thurgau. He was one of the three great names in the *Blütezeit*+ in the field of narrative poetry; Wolfram von Eschenbach* and Gottfried von Strassburg* were the other two poets. He was an educated man well acquainted with the classics, and could read French fluently. He endowed his works with more humane values than had his predecessors.

When he returned from a crusade,+ he wrote his greatest narrative poem, *Der arme Heinrich*.* He followed this with his *Gregorius*,* and two Arthurian romances adapted from Chrétien de Troyes'* works, *Erec** and *Iwein*.* (Bibliog. 86, 97)

Harun al-Rashid (766-809), sixth Abbasid* caliph.+ His reign was considered to be the most brilliant period in the Abbasid caliphate because it was marked by a long period of peace and economic prosperity and the development of international trade all through the Mediterranean Sea and Europe, as far north as the Baltic Sea. The wealth brought to Baghdad by those traders allowed him to establish a magnificent court, best described in the stories of *A Thousand and One Nights*. (Bibliog. 98)

Hastings, battle of (October 14, 1066), decisive battle between the forces of Harold Godwineson,* usurper king of England, and Duke William* of Normandy in the fall of 1066. To assert his claim to this throne which had been promised him earlier by King Edward* the Confessor, and agreed to by Harold, William assembled a force of about 3-4,000 knights, and sergeants, and 7-8,000 men-at-arms, and on September 28, 1066, sailed for England. His ships for the invasion fleet had the lines of the Norseman's drakkar, a long lean serpentine look with a head rearing in the prow and a tail curving upward to form the stern. Two-masted with square sails, the largest could carry 200-300 men and horses; the smaller ones were not decked over, and were oar-powered, and could carry only 40 men and a few horses. Landing unopposed at Pevensey, he grouped his forces and moved eastward to the larger borough of Hastings where he immediately erected a motte and bailey+ castle.+ Harold Godwineson still recovering from his bloody victory over Harold Hardrata* at the battle of Stamford Bridge+ seven days earlier, hurried south from York to rebuild his army to meet the invading forces. Without pausing long enough to await the arrival of his infantry from the north or fresh troops summoned from distant shires, he set out from London on October 11 in a forced march to meet the invaders. He hoped to surprise the invading William by a night attack, but his approach was reported by William's scouts. Harold arrived on the evening of October 13, 1066.

Fearing a night attack, William kept his troops in arms all night. Harold's army took a position on a long narrow spur of land some 600 yards long where the ground fell sharply away at either end to protect the flanks of the army. His 7,000 men, including half-armed peasants, all were dismounted and prepared to fight on foot, forming a tightly compacted line atop the hill. His army's primary strength lay in the heavily armed men, mostly his housecarls+ and those of his brothers who had been transformed into infantry for this battle. In William's forces, Normans formed the center with William himself; Bretons and other auxiliaries were on the left; Robert de Beaumont led the forces on the right. The invaders advanced in three lines: first the light infantry armed with bows and slings; then the heavy infantry; and in the rear were the horse troops. William was in the center with the strongest squadron so he could control every section with his voice and hand. William's men tried to provoke the Anglo-Saxons into breaking their line by shooting stones and arrows, but Harold's men held firm, retaliating with javelins, axes and stones. As the Norman infantry failed to break the Anglo-Saxon line, his cavalry rode up between the retreating footsoldiers, and attacked Harold's men, but were repulsed by fierce fighting. Dismayed by the fierceness of this defense, the Breton horsemen and footsoldiers fell back, and almost the entire line of the invaders gave way in a general panic. As they fled, they were chased by light infantry which had come through Harold's main line as the housecarls opened their ranks. Duke William stemmed the panic by lifting his helmet to show that he still was alive. Rallying, his Normans turned on the English and slew all who had advanced so rashly. William had his men attack the line again, and again they were unsuccessful, but feigned a panicked retreat to draw more English out of the line in pursuit as before. All the while, the English line began to weaken from the arrows, and other missiles were being volleyed at it. King Harold also fell, mortally wounded by an arrow seemingly striking him in his eye. When they saw their leader was dead and that night was approaching rapidly, the English forces broke and fled. The battle was over. William's forces included the following companions:

Aimeri, viscount of Thouars
Engenulf de Laigle, seigneur of Laigle
Eustace,* count of Bologne
Geoffrey de Mowbray, bishop of Coutances
Geoffrey of Mortagne, afterwards count of Perche
Goubert d'Auffay, seigneur of Auffay
Hugh de Grandmesnil,* seigneur of Grandmesnil
Hugh de Montfort, seigneur of Montfort-sur-Risle
Odo* (Eudes), bishop of Bayeux, afterwards earl of Kent*
Ralph de Toeni,* seigneur of Conches
Robert de Beaumont,* afterwards count of Meulan and first earl of
         Leicester
Robert, count of Mortain,* afterwards first earl of Cornwall

Turstin FitzRou
Walter Giffard,* seigneur of Longueville
William de Warenne,* afterwards first earl of Surrey*
William FitzOsbern,* afterwards first earl of Hereford*
William Malet, seigneur of Graville
(Bibliog. 47, 166, 244)

Hastings castle,+ fortress erected in September 1066, on or near the site of the battle in Sussex* during which William I* won England. Within a few years of the battle, he entrusted it to Robert, count of Eu,* whose descendants were so constantly rebelling against their king, that in the 11th and 12th centuries, the castle rarely was out of the crown's control. Henry II* held it, and made some repairs and modifications; Richard I* kept it in repair. Barons on their way to oppose King John* were welcomed by the knights who garrisoned it in 1216. In 1225, however, the crown resumed possession from the countess of Eu, on the understanding that it would be restored to her in the event of peace with the French king. It was never restored to her, and in 1249, the king granted it to Peter of Savoy,* but took it again into royal custody on Peter's death in 1268. Then in 1331, Edward III* granted it to the dean and chapter of the chapel within the castle, and it deteriorated steadily from that time on. (Bibliog. 104)

Hastings, Henry (d. 1268), English knight from Norfolk who was knighted by Simon de Montfort* just before and became one of the baronial leaders opposed to King Henry III* immediately after the battle of Lewes* in 1264. He became constable+ of the castle+ of Winchester* in 1265, succeeding Humphrey de Bohun,* and shorly thereafter was wounded and captured at Evesham.* Later, because he, along with John de la Warre, had defended Kenilworth* castle against the king's siege in 1266, his lands were subject to seven years' purchase price by the *Dictum of Kenilworth,* in order for them to be redeemed. He died in 1268, and was succeeded by his son, Sir John of Abergavenny* (1262-1313), who claimed one-third of the kingdom of Scotland* by reason of his being grandson and heir of Ada, fourth daughter and co-heiress of David, earl of Huntingdon,* but that claim was rejected at Berwick castle in 1296. (Bibliog. 47)

Hattin, battle of (July 4, 1187), conflict in eastern Galilee also known as the battle of Tiberias in which Muslims* led by Saladin* defeated crusaders led by Guy of Lusignan,* king of Jerusalem. When Saladin had attacked Tiberias several days earlier, he found it inhabited only by the wife of Count Raymond III of Tripoli who was without the knights she needed to defend the place. Fleeing into the citadel, she called on Guy of Lusignan for assistance. Turning to Raymond for support, Guy was informed that such an attack was ill-conceived and probably would result in the loss of the kingdom because the march to assist the besieged forces in Tiberias could be made successfully only if the Muslim resistance to it was overcome, and that was unlikely. Defeat in the battle would result in the loss of the army needed to support the kingdom. As Raymond had been Guy's enemy until recently, his advice was considered suspect, and Guy decided to march the five leagues to relieve the citadel, not to do battle. As predicted, their march was subjected to the usual Muslim attacks of harassment all day long, especially the rear of the column. Guy ordered the column to halt to rest. That turned out to be a fatal mistake. For the remainder of the day and through the night of July 3-4, the crusading forces lay encamped without water for men or horses exposed to brutal heat, dust and thirst; their wounds and weariness went unrelieved in the constant presence of a harassing enemy. On the next day, their army weas annihilated as a fighting force. Their will to resist had been destroyed by the desertion of Count Raymond, the treason of six knights, and the mutiny of some footsoldiers all the while the forces were suffering an ordeal of heat, thirst and dust which Saladin had intensified by fire and smoke blowing over the exhausted Franks constantly. This battle led subsequently to the fall of the kingdom of Jerusalem which led, in turn, to the third crusade.+ (Bibliog. 98, 166, 209)

Haut Koenigsberg, castle+ on the lower Rhine River which dominated the Rhine plateau in the 12th century, and was the property of the dukes of Lorraine,* dukes of Alsace,* and the bishop of Strassbourg. (Bibliog. 196)

Haute Prince, epithet given to Galahad* in *Morte D'Arthur.** (Bibliog. 145)

Havelock, Middle English* metrical romance written in the last quarter of the 13th century. This was based on a story in Geoffrey Gaimar's* *Estoire des Engles* about Havelock the Dane, written as though the events had taken place between A.D. 495 and 556. Havelock's father, the king of Denmark, died, leaving his son as the ward of Duke Godard who sought to seize the throne of Denmark for himself. Havelock was given to a fisherman named Grim to be killed. However, when Grim saw the miraculous light issuing from Havelock's mouth as he slept, and the royal kingmark+ on his shoulder, he realized that this lad was destined to be a king, and so he fled with him and his family to England where he reared the boy as one of his own sons. At Grimsby, Havelock became scullion to Godrich of Lincoln, earl of Cornwall. Because Godrich had promised King Ethelwold on his deathbed that he would give in marriage his daughter, Goldborough, to the strongest man in the kingdom, Godrich married her to the strong scullion Havelock, and thus removed her claim to the throne. But when Goldborough saw Havelock's light and kingmark, she knew that her husband would be king. The couple went back to Denmark where Havelock was knighted, defeated Godard to become king of Denmark, and then returned to England where he defeated Godrich and became king of England. (ed. W. H. French and C. B. Hale, *Middle English Metrical Romances,* New York: Russell and Russell, 1964, I, 71-176) (Bibliog. 156, 202)

Haverford castle,+ originally the property of the marcher* lords of Braose* and Bohun,* this South Wales castle was acquired by Queen Eleanor* in 1289 in an exchange of property with Humphrey de Bohun. She enlarged it considerably although her reasons for doing so remained obscure. On her death in 1290, the castle was held by Edward,* the Prince of Wales, until he ascended the throne in 1307, then by Aymer de Valence, earl of Pembroke,* until 1324, and then by Queen Isabelle from 1331 until 1358. (Bibliog. 104)

Havering, John de (c. 1240-1309), English knight from Dorset who served as yeoman for Eleanor, countess of Leicester, wife of Simon de Montfort* and sister of King Henry III.* After the battle of Evesham,* he was granted lands by Prince Edward* when John's father, Richard, gave up the castle of Berkhamstead* to the Prince. John later became constable+ of Marlborough* castle around 1270 when he and his wife Joan acquired for 500 marks the manor of Grafton in Wiltshire for the service of a pair of gilt spurs. He was granted a license to hunt hare, fox, badger and cat in the forest of Huntingdon and Wiltshire with his own dogs. He was appointed keeper of the castle of Devizes* from 1272 to 1278, and deputy under Otes de Grandison* in Snowdon, Wales, in 1284. While he was steward+ of Gascony* in 1291, he was imprisoned by the king of France, and later petitioned King Edward I* and was granted relief of £297, 13 shillings 4 pence as relief from debts incurred for his maintenance and ransom from that French prison. He was summoned to Parliament in 1299, by which he became Lord Havering. (Bibliog. 47)

Hawkwood, John (d. 1394), English adventurer and general. Son of an English tanner, he was impressed for the French wars and served first as an archer for King Edward III.* By 1359, he was in Gascony* in charge of a troop of free-lances (see White Company) who survived by pillage. To avoid the plague in France, he led his troop to Italy where he joined with another band of free booters* under Bernard de la Salle. Then taking a village near Avignon where Pope Innocent VI was in residence, they exacted a substantial sum of protection money from him. Then they were hired by the marquis of Montferrat* for his war with the Visconti* family of Milan. Defeating a band of Hungarians under Count Conrad Landau of Swabia,* Hawkwood's band forced the Visconti to sue for peace. They moved next to fight in Pisa's war with Florence, receiving 10,000 gold florins per month as their fixed wages. After several assaults, Hawkwood found himself deserted by all but 800 of his White Company, the rest having been bought off by Florentine gold. Hawkwood retreated to Pisa, and found that the Florentines were marching to besiege Pisa. Seeking to destroy this invading force, Hawkwood with a small force attacked the Florentine He entered the stronghold but was overpowered by the size of the enemy force, and was forced to retreat to Pisa. With this reversal of fortunes, the Pisan doge was overthrown, and with the help of Hawkwood, a new doge was chosen in 1364. His first act was to sue for peace, and to pay a tribute to Florence of 10,000 gold florins a year for ten years. Hawkwood then resumed his free-lance ways until he entered the service of Bernabo Visconti after the marriage in 1368 of Lionel,* duke of Clarence, second son of Edward III, to Violante, daughter of Galeazzo Visconti in Milan. Over the years in the Visconti service, he fought against Florence, against the pope, and against Emperor Charles IV, but in 1372 he went over to the pope's side against Galeazzo Visconti whom he defeated at the battle of Chiese in 1373. Once Milan and the papacy were reconciled, Hawkwood was left without employment, so he turned against France whose territory he menaced and pillaged. By 1375, however, he once more was in the service of the papacy in Tuscany. Florence bought him off with payments of 130,000 florins, which, with added money from Pisa, Lucca, Arezzo and Siena, totalled 225,000 florins. When Florence tried to protect itself further by offering him an annual salary for life, he rejected their offer, and remained in the employ of the papacy. He was responsible for the massacre of Cesena in 1377 in which 5,000 people died. A few weeks later he reentered the service of Florence for a salary of 225,000 florins per year. Then he married Dinnina, illegitimate daughter of Bernabo Visconti, became the owner of a castle and lands, and remained faithful to Florence for the rest of his life. He was considered to be the first modern general. His genius for organization which enabled him to transform a rude bunch of free booters into a disciplined army, his effective strategy, his energy and his resourcefulness all distinguish him from his predecessors. He was an effective and prudent tactician, always on the move. He was appreciated by his men whom he paid regularly, and who never mutinied against him. He had known defeat, but afterwards would regroup. Despite large payments, he never amassed a fortune. Shortly before his death in 1392, he sold his villa near Florence and castle near Arezzo, and went back to England to die. Where, when, and by whom he was knighted was not known. (Bibliog. 48, 58)

Hedingham castle,+ fortress in Essex which had a superb example of the solid square Norman type of keep.+ Its keep rose to the height of 110 feet to the battlements+ with 20-foot towers rising above them. It had a basement and three stories. At the base, the walls were 12 feet thick, and the only openings on the ground floor were small loopholes, making a direct attack against that floor difficult. On the west, the entrance was approached by an outside staircase which prevented attackers from gathering momentum to attack the door with a battering ram, and was further protected by a portcullis+ and a barbican.+ It was the seat of the de Vere family, the earls of Oxford.* (Bibliog. 247)

Hegira, Arabic word *Hajira* meant "the emigration," given to the flight of Mohammed and his followers of Mecca to Medina in 622. Islam dates its beginnings from this event. (Bibliog. 98)

Schloss Heidelberg, massive fortress in Germany with round towers which from 1225 served as the seat of the counts palatine+ of the Rhine. (Bibliog. 30)

Heinrich, Die arme, Middle High German* poem of some 1,500 lines by Hartmann von Aue* written after 1195. Heinrich, a prosperous nobleman of humane temperament and courtly demeanor, was afflicted with leprosy. He was told by a doctor in Salerno that the only cure was to be washed in the heart's blood of a marriageable virgin, willingly given. The daughter of a tenant farmer with whom Heinrich had chosen to live offered herself as a sacrifice, despite her parents' and Heinrich's protestations to the contrary. At Salerno, she was bound naked to the operating table, and Heinrich, hearing the surgeon sharpening his blade, and seeing her innocent beauty, ordered the surgeon to stop, much to the distress of the girl. However, because Heinrich had been moved by the grace of God to halt the operation, he was cured of the leprosy and he and the girl were married. That story also occurred in *Amys and Amiloun,** *Athis und Porphilias,** and *Engelhard.** (ed. Hermann Paul, Tubingen, 1966) (Bibliog. 86)

Heinrich der Löwe. See Henry the Lion.

Heinrich von dem Türlin (fl. 1225), Middle High German* author of a huge Arthurian romance, *Diu Crône** which he intended to be the crowning achievement of all Arthurian works. Its 30,000 lines reveal that he was highly educated, understanding not only French and Latin, but also Italian. He was extremely well read in French literature and in the literature of his native Germany, studying the works of Hartmann von Aue,* Wolfram von Eschenbach,* and Wirnt von Gravenberg. But because he was not from the knightly class, he did not understand knightly ideals, and paid them only lip service in his poetry. (Bibliog. 235)

Heinrich von Kempten, short Middle High German* verse narrative written for Berthold von Tiersburg in Strassbourg around 1270 by Konrad von Wurzburg.* It related the story of Heinrich von Kempten who angered the Emperor Otto. When the emperor swore by his beard to be avenged on him, Heinrich seized him by his beard and with the point of a sword, made him swear not to harm him. Some years later, he saved the emperor's life by rescuing him from robbers, and in return received forgiveness for his earlier offense and a rich reward. (ed. E. Schroder, *Kleinere Dichtungen Konrad von Wurzburg,* Halle: Altdeutsche Textbibliothek, 3 vols., 1924-1926) (Bibliog. 235)

Heinrich von Veldeke (c. 1140-c. 1210), German poet who introduced the epic of chivalry+ into Germany. Born near Maastricht, on the lower Rhine River, he was in a good geographical position to come into contact with and pass along to German courts the new literary and cultural influences from France. He also was influenced deeply by the proximity of French and Flemish knights who took a prominent part in the first crusade.+ He received a classical education and wrote some attractive love lyrics, a legend of St. Servatius in verse, and his *Eneit,* a celebrated adaptation of the *Roman d'Enéas,** which transformed the Latin work into a work of chivalry. His fellow poets praised the work, calling him "master" and "the wise man von Veldecke." In his description of the marriage of Aeneas and Lavinia, he said he could go no further in his elaborations of the splendors of the wedding than to compare it with the great Whitsun Festival of 1184 at which Frederick I,* Barbarossa, had knighted his two sons. (Bibliog. 97, 186)

heir apparent, an heir whose right to inheritance was indefeasible by law, provided he survived the ancestor. The eldest surviving son of an English king was the heir apparent to the throne. (Bibliog. 169)

heir presumptive, an heir whose claim could be defeated by the birth of a closer relative before the death of an ancestor. The second son of a king could be considered the heir presumptive, behind the eldest son who was the heir apparent, until the eldest son sired a son of his own. Roger Mortimer (1374-1398) was declared heir presumptive to the English throne in 1385 by King Richard II.* Roger was the eldest surviving heir (grandson) of Lionel* of Clarence, second son of King Edward III.* Richard II was son of the Prince of Wales, Edward the Black Prince,* but if he died without issue, the throne would go to the eldest surviving son of the next surviving son of King Edward III, in this case, Lionel. His claim as heir presumptive would have been voided had Richard II had any children; his legitimate claim to the throne in 1399, however, was ignored by Henry of Lancaster who usurped the throne as Henry IV. (See genealogical chart 5 in Appendix.) (Bibliog. 169)

Hengest, mythical king of Denmark and Sessoine (Saxony); brother of Horsa and father of Octa and Rowene, he invaded Britain with his Saxon forces and occupied large portions of the realm until he was defeated and slain. (Bibliog. 129, 202)

Henri le Waleys, Guyennois native who was elected mayor of both Bordeaux and London. That role was typical of the interdependence of the two countries of England and Aquitaine* (Guyenne). The Plantagenets seemed to regard Guyenne (Aquitaine) as far more an integral part of their domains than Wales or Scotland, for many Guyennois served in Edward's armies for the wars in Scotland, and a decision from a Guyennois court could be appealed in England. (Bibliog. 203)

Henry I, Beauclerc (1068-1135), king of England (1100-1135). Third son of William I* and Matilda, he was the first Anglo-Norman monarch born to the purple—that is, the first child born to a crowned king and queen on English soil, and thus by birth, though not by descent, entitled to rank as an English aethling.+ With a legacy of £10,000 given him by his father, he shrewdly manipulated his elder brothers, William* (later II) and Robert II,* Curthose whose empty treasuries forced them to come to him for loans. For £3,000, Henry obtained the whole western end of the Norman duchy consisting of the Cotentin,*

Avranchin, and Mont-St-Michel. Later, he bargained with Fulk V of Anjou* for the marriage of his heir. Those two actions revealed his two strongest qualities which his brothers lacked: self-control and the ability to endure troubles. Simply, he was a man of business. Immediately after the death of his brother, William II, in the New Forest in 1100, Henry first took possession of the treasury at Winchester, and then sought to obtain the support of his barons. In his coronation oath, he swore to abolish his brother's evil customs, and to return to just government according to the law of the land. See coronation oath.+ To solidify his claims to the throne, he married a maiden of old English royal blood, Eadgyth (Edith) of Scotland, great-granddaughter of Edmund Ironside,* and had her name changed to Matilda. Later, when the armies of his brother, Robert Curthose and his own almost came to confrontation near Alton, Henry convinced his brother to settle their differences peacefully: Robert renounced his claim to the throne for a yearly pension, and Henry gave up his Norman possessions except for Domfront.

In Normandy during 1117 and 1118, he suppressed a rebellion of some of his barons. His wife Matilda had died that year, as had his faithful counsellor Robert de Meulan, first earl of Leicester.* In December 1118, the town of Alençon rebelled against his nephews and was occupied by Fulk of Anjou. To ensure the peace, Henry ordered Eustace de Pacy, husband of his illegitimate daughter Juliana (see below), and lord of Breteuil to send him his two little daughters as hostages for his good faith, and put a castellan, Ralph Harenc, in charge of his tower at Ivry, making him send his son as a hostage to Eustace. On the advice of Amaury of Montfort, Eustace, who was on the rebel's side, blinded the boy. Livid with rage at this insolence,King Henry sent his two granddaughters, Juliana's daughters, to Harenc that he might respond by treating them in the same way. Harenc tore out their eyes, and cut off the tips of their noses. Juliana and Eustace then fortified all their castles against her father, and Juliana gathered a force and shut herself in the castle of Breteuil. The townspeople were loyal to Henry, however, and did not oppose him when he appeared before the castle demanding surrender. Juliana tried to kill her father by a shot from a siege engine but failed, and was forced to surrender. Henry refused to let her leave the castle except by letting herself down into the icy moat and wading through the icy water. Later that year, Henry's son William joined him in Normandy, and an agreement was struck between Henry and Fulk of Anjou. William was to marry Fulk's daughter Matilda, ending the ancient dispute between Anjou and Normandy. It also allowed Henry to concentrate on ejecting King Louis VI's* men from Normandy, and punishing his rebellious vassals.

In August Henry with 500 of his best knights, was riding toward Andelys to make war when his scouts reported that the French king, who had ridden out from Andelys with 400 of his best knights was close at hand. The two forces met on the plain of Bremûle (Brenneville). Henry's force included his son William, and two illegitimate sons, Richard and Robert; Richard with 100 knights stayed mounted, and the rest dismounted to fight on foot. Among Louis' forces was William Clito,* son of Robert Curthose and Henry's nephew. Louis neglected to marshall his forces, so they were scattered. William Crispin, a rebel Norman, charged Henry's men with 80 horses. He and his men were surrounded, but he fought his way to Henry and struck him a deadly blow on the head. Henry's headpiece saved him, though it was shattered by the blow and wounded him so that blood streamed down his face. All 80 knights were captured. When Louis saw that Crispin and his men had not returned, he fled back to Andelys. Henry had captured 140 men and the French king's banner.+ He returned the banner to the French king with his charger, and young William returned the charger of William Clito. Henry also sent back some knights who owed allegiance to Louis as well as to himself. Only three knights were slain of the 900 engaged in the fight, for all were clad in armor and seemed to share a feeling of knightly comradeship, and a desire to take prisoners rather than to kill the enemy. This fight resembled a tournament more than a battlefield. On the return trip to England of Henry and his entourage later that year of 1120, his son was drowned in the White Ship disaster.* When his son-in-law, the Emperor Henry V,* died in 1125, Matilda was summoned home.

Then, in 1126 Henry had the prelates and barons swear that if he died without male heir they would accept Matilda as Lady both of England and Normandy. Among those who swore were David I,* king of Scots, and Stephen, count of Bologne, the king's nephew. No woman had ever reigned in her own right over England or Normandy, but Henry ordered the oath to put an end to the hopes of supporters of William Clito. To further solidify matters, Henry had his daughter Matilda marry Geoffrey, son of Fulk, count of Anjou, in 1128, after knighting him with much ceremony at Rouen. However, it was reputed that Henry said on his deathbed that he wished the crown to go to his nephew Stephen rather than to his daughter Matilda. Henry died in 1135 after eating a "surfeit of lamprey." He had been a builder and repairer of castles on a large scale. At Rouen, Normandy, he built a great wall around the keep+; at Caen, he built the keep itself; at Arques, the tower and other defenses. At Gisors,* Falaise, Argentan, Exmes, Domfront, Ambières, Vire, Gavrai, and Vernon, he executed similar works; he had works erected in Sussex to oppose the landing of Robert Curthose, and in Wales after the campaign in 1114 against Gruffyd, king of Powys.

Besides the two legitimate offspring his wife bore him: Prince William who drowned in the White Ship disaster* and Matilda FitzEmpress, Henry sired at least twenty illegitimate offspring: nine sons and eleven daughters. No one knew the order of their birth, or their dates of birth, nor even their mothers' names. Eight of his sons and their subsequent titles were, first, Robert the king's son, (born c. 1190) called de Caen who was created earl of Gloucester in 1122. Then Richard, born around 1101, who fought the French in 1119, was captured at Les Andelys, was set free by the French king, and then fought beside his father at Bremûle in 1119; he died in the wreck of the White Ship+ in 1120. The next son was Rainald de Dunstanville who was created earl of Cornwall by his half-sister, the empress Matilda; when he died in 1175, his earldom reverted to the crown. Then there was Gilbert about whom nothing is known. Next was William de Tracy, who died soon after his father in 1135, leaving a wife and son. He was followed by Henry the king's son, whose mother was daughter of the prince of South Wales; he was killed in Henry II's* invasion of Anglesey in 1157. Then came Fulk the king's son who became a monk at Abingdon and died young. Finally there was William, called brother of the queen (Sibyl; she was one of Henry's illegitimate daughters, and married Scottish king Alexander I; see below).

The daughters were: Maud, married to Routrou, count of Perche, who went on the first crusade,+ fought against the Moors in Spain for his cousin King Alfonso I, king of Navarre and Aragon, and beside Henry I at the siege of Bellême in 1114; she died in the White Ship disaster in 1120. Then Maud, who married Conan III, duke of Brittany. Then Juliana married to Eustace de Pacy, lord of Breteuil and Pacy, who subsequently rebelled against Henry I, but was forgiven (see above.) Then Eustacie married to William Gouet, lord of Montmirail. Constance married Roscelin de Beaumont, vicomte of Maine to whom King Henry gave South Taunton in Devon when he married Constance. Alice (or Aline) married Matthew de Montmorenci who later became constable of France, and after Alice's death, married Adelaide, widow of Louis VI, king of France. Isabel, whose mother was Isabel, daughter of Robert de Beaumont, count of Meulan and first earl of Leicester. Sibyl, married Alexander I, king of Scotland, with whom she was said to have been a founder of Scone Priory. Maud, abbess of Montivilliers, called the Sister of the Empress Matilda. Then Gundred, of whom nothing was known but her name. Rohese married Henry de la Pomerai, a great Devonshire baron who fought for Henry in the rebellion of 1123, and later became an assistant constable in the king's household. And finally an unnamed daughter whom Henry agreed to marry to William de Warenne,* the second earl of Surrey. Of the six women bearing him children whose names were known, two were English, two were Norman, one was Welsh, and one was half Norman and half French. (Bibliog. 47, 58, 104, 162, 166)

Henry II, FitzEmpress (1133-1189), king of England (1154-1189). Eldest child of Matilda,* daughter of Henry I,* and Geoffrey Plantagenet,* count of Anjou* (1113-1150). At his birth, he was declared heir to his grandfather, King Henry I, but on whose death two years later, the barons repudiated that allegiance and turned to Stephen* for their king. By 1147, he had been given the lands which his mother and father had been holding in trust for him. In 1149, he ventured to England, and was knighted at Carlisle* on Whitsunday by his great-uncle, King David I* of Scotland. Two years later, he was invested with Normandy and his father's dominions in Anjou on his father's death. To these he added in 1152 the great duchy of Aquitaine* by his marriage to its heiress, Eleanor,* recently divorced wife of King Louis VII* of France. By this, he found himself strong enough to stand up to both Kings Stephen and Louis VII,* and at the treaty of Wallingford in November 1153, Henry and King Stephen adopted each other as father and son, Henry leaving the crown to Stephen for his life on a promise of its reversion to Henry on Stephen's death, and Stephen undertaking to govern according to Henry's advice. On Stephen's death in October 1154, Henry became king of England. With that crown he assumed a unique king-duke responsibility for his domains, for as king of England, he acquired another feudal empire, the empire of the dukes of Normandy.* By the usual methods of marriage, aggression and exploiting feudal suzerainty, the counts of Rouen, as the dukes of Normandy originally were styled, had acquired not only the historic duchy of Aquitaine,* but were prepared to take possession of or to acquire considerable interest in Brittany,* Maine, the Vexin,* Ponthieu, Flanders,* and England.*

He first reaffirmed the oath declaring restitution of liberties which his grandfather, Henry I, had promised at his coronation in 1100. See coronation oath.+ Then he demolished all the private adulterine+ castles erected over the previous two decades by individual barons without royal licenses, and restored to royal control many castles appropriated by private barons during the anarchy of Stephen's reign. William of Aumale* in Yorkshire, and Hugh of Mortimer* and Roger of Hereford* in the west all resisted that decree, but all submitted before another year passed. Then Henry turned his attention to building an empire on the foundations laid by his grandfather. At that time, his empire spread from Flanders* to the Pyrenees and covered the whole of western France. It was made up of five distinct fiefs and claims of suzerainty over some half a dozen others, all held on different tenure, and all jealous of one another. In 1156, he went to France, renewed his homage to Louis VII, bought off his brother, Geoffrey, in Anjou for a money payment, and secured his claims over Aquitaine. Then on returning to England, he forced the surrender of a few royal castles still held by the earls of Warenne* and Norfolk,* and demanded and obtained from King Malcolm* of Scotland the homage due from a Scot to an English king, and the return of three northern English counties to English control: Northumberland, Westmoreland, and Cumberland, and at sword's point he obtained the homage of the Prince of Wales.* In 1158, he returned to France to claim the county of Nantes on the death of his brother Geoffrey, and successfully to assert his rights over Brittany, and to obtain the blessing of the French king through the betrothal of his daughter Margaret to Henry's eldest son, young Henry. In the next year, 1159, he exerted his wife's claim to the overlordship of Toulouse, and when that claim was denied he was prepared to enforce it with an army consisting of the great barons* of his realm with the Scottish king at their head, and the help of a crown of mercenaries hired with the proceeds of scutage.+ Only when King Louis himself entered Toulouse did Henry withdraw the siege out of obedience to the feudal etiquette which forbade a vassal to fight against his overlord in person. In 1160, a truce was made and young Henry married Margaret, thus gaining possession of her dowry, the Vexin.

In between his trips to the continent, Henry revised the royal administration. In 1158, he replaced all the debased currency of his predecessor with a new and uniform currency (see coinage+); he instituted the "great assize"+; he removed the crown's reliance on military tenants for military assistance by instituting the practice of scutage. By the Constitutions of Clarendon+ he broke down the barriers which kept clerical people free from any restraints except church law and he applied the principle of jury inquest to criminal cases by his Assize of Clarendon.+ In sum, he sought to put forth a code of law based on custom and precedent, and on the right and duty of a people to govern itself in its own courts. He strengthened alliances of Germany and Castile by the marriages of his two elder daughters, Matilda and Eleanor in 1168-1169; he betrothed his youngest daughter to William, king of Sicily, in 1169. He broke the opposition of the Bretons in three direct military campaigns in 1166-1169, and had obtained the French king's approval of his plans for his three sons by the Treaty of Montmirail in January 1169. He ordered a thorough investigation of the sheriffs of the country by the Inquest of Sheriffs+ in 1170 which suspended all sheriffs from their counties and all bailiffs from their demesnes,+ and appointed a special commission to investigate every detail of every administration over the previous four years. At the end of two months, only seven of the original twenty-seven sheriffs were reinstated; the other offices were filled with officers of the Exchequer* whom Henry knew and trusted.

He made one bad mistake: he had his successor, young Henry, crowned as king in 1170. This innovative step had no precedent, and led to considerable trouble for him. Later that year, also, by wrongfully interpreting one of his angry comments, four knights "avenged" the king on the troublesome archbishop* of Canterbury, Thomas à Becket, by murdering him in the cathedral on December 29, 1170. With that action, the world seemed to turn against him, but instead of succumbing to pressure, Henry turned his attention to Ireland to help Diarmait MacMurchadha recover the throne of Leinster. Henry sent troops there under the command of Richard de Clare,* who later married MacMurchadha's daughter and was named heir to the Irish throne. Meanwhile the young King Henry demanded to be recognized as the actual ruler of England or at least of Normandy and Anjou. When Henry refused, young Henry fled to the court of the king of France and began an complicated conspiracy involving the French king, the counts of Blois, Flanders, and Boulogne, the king of the Scots, a crowd of barons in England, Normandy, Anjou and Aquitaine, his brothers Richard and Geoffrey, and his mother, Queen Eleanor. Henry gathered every supporter he could find and began resisting their moves. Over the next few weeks, the count of Boulogne died, the king of Scots was captured at Alnwick,* a rapid assault by Henry saved Brittany, and he suppressed the rebellion of his sons Richard and Geoffrey. The king of Scots was released after doing homage to the English king for his crown, and surrendering five of his strongest fortresses. Queen Eleanor had been captured in men's attire trying to reach her sons at the French court. Henry kept her in prison for the remainder of his life. With that, the rebellion collapsed, and Henry returned to his pursuit of administrative reforms. In his Assize of Arms on 1181, he imposed on every free man the obligation of bearing arms for the defense of his country, and each man's liability for that defense should be determined not by the amount of land he owned but by his annual revenue. Meanwhile, Louis VII had died in 1180 and his son Philip II* ascended the throne. And young Henry had died in 1183 and his third son Geoffrey in 1186. Then in response to an impassioned plea from the patriarch of Jerusalem, Henry decided to go on a crusade+ to help free the Holy Land from pagan hands. That decision was intensified with the news of the fall of Jerusalem.* At that, both Kings Henry and Philip decided to take the cross.+ Richard also wanted to go, but first demanded that Henry recognize him as the heir apparent.* Henry demurred, hoping to name his youngest son, John, as his successor. Henry's continued refusal drove Richard into the camp of Philip in 1188 to force Henry to recognize him. Tired, ill, and fever-stricken, Henry met Richard and Philip and agreed to their demands, and then died on July 6, 1189.

Henry was a reddish-headed man of medium height with a square leonine face and goggle eyes which were soft and gentle when he was in a good humor, but flashed when he was angry. He had horseman's legs, a broad chest, and athletic arms. He took no care of his hands except when hawking. He was restlessly involved in all the affairs of state. He fought off obesity by sobriety and the constant exercise of walking and horsemanship. He sat only to eat or to ride a horse, and often rode in one day the distance four or five times the normal days's length. His followers were subjected to severe tests by being forced to wander through unknown forests for three or four miles after dark before they found lodging in hovels. By this restlessness, he was able to catch enemies off guard, and his underlings by surprise for an inspection. He was quick-witted and eloquent, and regarded peace as the greatest good a king could bestow on his people. He undertook enormous tasks to maintain peace and spent large income to obtain it by financial rather than by military measures.

His children by Eleanor of Aquitaine were:

William, who died in childhood in 1156
Henry,* who died in 1183
Matilda, who married to Henry the Lion, duke of Brunswick, died in
        1189
Richard* who reigned afterwards Richard I, and died in 1199
Geoffrey,* earl of Brittany and Richmond, who died in 1186
Eleanor, who married Alphonse, king of Castile, died in 1214
Joan, who married first, William II, count of Sicily, and second,
        Raymond, count of Toulouse; she died in 1199
John,* who afterwards reigned as King John, died in 1216

His two illegitimate children by his mistress, Rosamund Clifford, were William Longespee,* and Geoffrey,* afterward archbishop of York. (Bibliog. 42, 52, 146, 161)

Henry III, of Winchester (1207-1272), king of England (1216-1272).

Eldest son of King John* by Isabelle of Angoulême,* he was born at Winchester and named after his grandfather, Henry II.* Despite their oath to the dying King John to support the young Henry on the throne, the barons were opposed to being ruled by an intolerable tyrant any more, and were committed to deprive an innocent child of his rightful inheritance, and to place a foreign prince, Louis* of France, on the English throne. However, with the support of Pope Honorius III, Henry was crowned at age 9 in Gloucester on October 28, 1216, but reigned until 1226 under the regency of William Marshal, and the justiciar, Hubert de Burgh,* whom he dismissed in 1232 in order to begin his own personal reign. In 1236 he married Eleanor of Provence* and peopled his court with her relatives and other nobles from Provence. His defeat in France in 1241 in which he lost Poitou and Angoulême, his support of the pope against the Hohenstaufen* dynasty, his attempts to place his brother Edmund on the throne of Sicily, and his urging his brother Richard, earl of Cornwall,* to try for the imperial throne in Germany—all these angered his nobles into a revolt in 1258. In that year, fully armed, they strode into Parliament and demanded reforms. Henry agreed to their demands, known as the Provisions of Oxford* which reaffirmed the *Magna Carta Libertatum*+ and imposed on him a government controlled by the nobility. A few years later, after he refused to abide by the Oxford Provisions, the barons revolted in 1264 in the Barons' War* defeating the royal forces in the battle of Lewes* in 1264 and capturing Henry and his son, Prince Edward.* On his release he and Edward reversed their fortunes and defeated the rebels under Simon de Montfort* at Evesham* in 1265, and imposed upon the defeated rebels the *Dictum of Kenilworth.* He died in 1272, and was succeeded by his son, Edward I. His children by Eleanor of Provence were:

Edward, who afterward reigned as Edward I*
Edmund Plantagenet, surnamed Crouchback, earl of Lancaster
Richard, earl of Cornwall, afterwards elected as Holy Roman Emperor
John, who died young
William, who died young
Margaret, who married Alexander III, king of Scotland
Beatrice, who married John, first duke of Brittany
Catherine, who died in infancy.
(Bibliog. 47, 58, 184)

Henry I, the Fowler (c. 876-936), king of Germany (919-936). He reformed the Saxon army, training small groups of the basic infantry to become mounted fighters able to beat back the attacking Magyars who were accustomed to live and fight on horseback. Further, he strengthened the eastern frontier by building a number of castles+ along and behind it, for against a well-stocked and defended castle, the Magyar cavalry was able only to ravage the countryside, but could not mount a successful invasion of the Saxon territories. Henry thus shaped the pattern of war that followed his lifetime by demonstrating the value of castles in defense and of trained mounted cavalrymen, the knights, in attack. Wars thereby became the affairs of knights, and became less destructive and costly in human life. (Bibliog. 199)

Henry III, the Salian (1017-1056), German emperor (1039-1056) who took the German Empire to its height. A devout man, he was dedicated to ecclesiastical reform, and by so doing, won back the support of the clergy who had been alienated by his father, Conrad II.* He maintained relative peace in both Germany* and Italy,* suppressed revolts and secured full submission and vassalage of the rulers of Bohemia,* Poland, and Hungary.* His greatest accomplishment, however, was his intervention in papal affairs, and his re-establishment of imperial control over the church. He conquered Rome in 1046, deposed rival popes, and successively appointed German bishops in their place. During his reign, no papal election was considered valid unless he approved the candidates. By the middle of the 11th century, he had become the leader of Western society. He died suddenly at age 39. (Bibliog. 228)

Henry IV (1050-1106), German emperor (1056-1106). Son of Emperor Henry III,* he was seven when he ascended the throne. After eight years of having his mother, Agnes of Poitou, serve as regent for him, he assumed the throne in 1065 and began his attempts to regain power to the imperial throne. In 1058, Pope Nicholas II did not wait for imperial approval of his candidature, and immediately issued a decree that proclaimed the exclusive right of the College of Cardinals in papal elections. When Pope Gregory VII* (Hildebrand) issued in 1075 his *Dictatus Papae,* he did so in open opposition to Henry, thus beginning the Investiture contest between them. Henry was excommunicated. However, when his barons were revolting against him shortly thereafter, Henry decided on a cunning plan of action. He rushed to Canossa in 1078 to meet with the pope, begged forgiveness, made his penance, and was absolved. By that move, the German barons' rebellion became illegitimate, so the emperor could call on the bishops to help him crush it. Once that had been taken care of, Henry turned his attention once again to the pope. He conquered Rome once again in 1083, appointed an antipope to replace Gregory VII who had fled to Salerno where he died the following year. The new pope, Urban II, helped raise German public opinion against Henry at time when Henry's own sons were revolting against him. He died in 1106 in the middle of a war against his second son. (Bibliog. 98, 228)

Henry V (1081-1125), German emperor (1106-1125). He was the son of and successor to Henry IV. After finally pacifying Germany* from the revolts in which he himself had participated against his father, he journeyed to Rome in 1110 to discuss the Investiture question with Pope Pascal II. Refusing to budge on this issue, he imprisoned the pope, aroused new opposition to the empire, and renewed the contest between them. In 1121, German princes organized the Concordat of Worms (1122) to force a compromise between the emperor and the papacy which ended the investiture conflict. Henry tried unsuccessfully to restore imperial authority over the papacy, and died childless in 1125. His widow was Matilda,* daughter of King Henry I* of England, whom he had married in 1114 when she was 12. At age 26, she subsequently married the 15-year-old Geoffrey of Anjou* in 1128, and bore him the future Henry II* of England. (Bibliog. 98)

Henry VI (1165-1197), German emperor (1190-1197). Son of Frederick I,* Barbarossa, he was elected king of Germany* in 1169. He assumed the imperial crown on the death of his father in 1189, and by marriage he obtained the right of succession in Sicily. Before he could claim the Sicilian throne, however, it was usurped by Tancred.* Henry hurried to Rome, was crowned emperor in 1191, but did not try to obtain the Sicilian crown while there. Unrest at home called him urgently back to Germany. He was helped by the ransom paid to him by King Richard I* of England who had been captured on his return from the third crusade.+ His imprisonment of Richard I provided him with a prize of inestimable value. First, Richard was the brother-in-law of Henry the Lion,* duke of Saxony and leader of the Welf (Guelph*) faction against which the emperor was fighting bitterly. Second, Richard was an ally of Tancred, king of Sicily, whose kingdom the emperor planned to take; and third, he was hated by King Philip II* of France whom he planned to bring under his control. Henry ignored the fact that as a crusader, Richard was under the protection of the church, and hence should not have been captured or held. He skillfully played Philip against Richard, knowing that Philip would give almost anything to prevent Richard's release so that he might continue his intended subjection of Normandy and eventually all English lands on that side of the Channel. Only in 1194 could Henry turn his attention to the Sicilian crown, and subdue Naples and Sicily. He planned to extend his power over all of Europe, and to make the imperial crown hereditary in his own house, but he died in 1196 from a chill contracted while hunting. Henry's life was a conflict between the real and the ideal. As a minnesinger,+ he wrote tender and passionate lyrics, and was listed on the rolls of the minnesingers, and one of his poems stands at the head of a collection of their works. In his youthful exuberance, he stated that he would rather lose his crown than his beloved. Yet, despite those seemingly tender mercies, he was cruel and merciless. He rarely showed any chivalric qualities or virtues. In 1194, for example, he ordered suspects in a plot in Palermo to be executed by incredibly cruel means. Count Jordan was executed by being placed on a red-hot throne with a red-hot crown nailed to his head. Others were buried alive or burned or hanged or dragged through the streets at the tails of horses. He was succeeded by his son Frederick II.* (Bibliog. 7, 186)

Henry, archdeacon of Huntingdon (c. 1084-1155), author of a work of dubious value, *Historia Anglorum* (55 B.C.- A.D. 1154), because some of its details were pure figments of his imagination. A chronicler for the troublesome reign of King Stephen,* Henry demonstrated sympathy for neither figure, but tried to remain neutral. He justified his work in the prologue to the seventh edition, "For nothing is more distinguished in life than to trace and frequent the tracks left by outstanding lives." (tr. Thomas Forester, *The Chronicle of Henry of Huntingdon,* London: Bohn's Antiquarian Library, 1853) (Bibliog. 99, 174)

Henry, "of Grosmont" (c. 1300-1360), earl of Lancaster* and Leicester,* and steward+ of England was born probably at Grosmont castle, Monmouth. He became active in public affairs early in life and devoted his life to service of his king and country. He was summoned to a council at Nottingham as Henry of Lancaster in 1335, and then two years later he was made earl of Derby* on advice of Parliament, invested by the girding on of a sword, and the granting of £20 per annum in lieu of the third penny+ of the county pleas. He served as steward of England at the famous tournament held by King Edward I* at Windsor* in 1344, and was made Knight of the Round Table* at that time. On his father's death in 1345, he became earl of Lancaster and earl of Leicester and steward of England. In 1347 he became lord of Bergerac with the king's grant of the castle of Bergerac. He became a founder knight of the Order of the Garter,+ his name being second on the list following that of the Prince of Wales,* Edward,* the Black Prince. Two years later, he was created the earl of Lincoln,* and in the following year, 1350, was created duke+ of Lancaster by Parliament and invested with the girding on of the sword along with the chancery in the county for life and other liberties. By David II* of Scotland, he was made earl of Moray in 1359. He was a military man from his youth until a few months before his death. On those occasions when he was not bearing arms, he was serving as a plenipotentiary to arrange a truce or as an ambassador to negotiate a peace. In that busy career, he raised men and served in Derbyshire for the invasion of Scotland; while there he was then sent by the king to London to consider measures for defense of the realm. Shortly thereafter he accompanied the king to Flanders, and then as one of the sureties of the Treaty of Bretigny* was left on the continent with the duke of Brabant.*

In 1339, he accompanied King Edward III back to Flanders leading to the great naval victory of the battle of Sluys.* These activities were typical of his life-long activity on the service of his king. By 1345, he was so highly regarded by the king that he was appointed commissioner to govern Aquitaine* with full military and judicial powers. He was relieved of that command to aid the king at Calais* in 1347. By 1350, he was appointed as admiral* of the fleet from the Thames mouth south and west. In the following year, after a truce had been made with the French, he went to Prussia with a view to fighting the Turks, but before he arrived peace had been made with them. On his journey to and fro he was treated so insultingly by Otto, duke of Brunswick, that he insisted on fighting a duel with him. This matter was referred to the king of France. In Paris, Otto attempted to withdraw, but Henry insisted on the duel not only for his own but for his king's and the English nation's honor against the charge of cowardice. Otto finally refused to fight, and the king of France made a great feast offering Henry many great gifts. Of these, he accepted only one—a spike from the Crown of Thorns which he gave to his church at Newark in Leicester. He married Isabel, daughter of Sir Alexander Comyn, lord Beaumont.* He died of the plague in 1360, and as he was survived only by two daughters, the dukedom of Lancaster became extinct. His second daughter, Blanche, married John of Gaunt,* the fourth but third surviving son of King Edward III by Philippa* of Hainaut; through Blanche, John became duke of Lancaster. (Bibliog. 47)

Henry Jasomirgot (1156-1177), first duke of Austria*; appointed by Emperor Frederick I* in 1156, he participated in the second crusade.+ After his death, Austria and Styria were declared as part of the Holy Roman Empire and placed under the control of the Hapsburgs. (Bibliog. 68)

Henry Lovelich. See Lovelich, Henry.

Henry Plantagenet (1235-1271), second but first surviving son of Richard of Cornwall,* king of the Romans, and nephew of King Henry III* of England. Knighted on the day of his father's coronation as king of the Romans, he fought beside and was captured with his father at the battle of Lewes* in 1264 where he commanded the left wing of King Henry III's army. He married the widow of the Infant Alfonso, son and heir of Jayme I, king of Arragon, and then journeyed to the Holy Land. On his return from that crusade,+ he was murdered while at mass in a chapel of the cathedral of San Nicolo, Viterbo, Italy, by Simon and Guy, sons of Simon de Montfort,* in revenge for the indignities inflicted upon their fathers's dead body after his defeat at Evesham* in 1265. (Bibliog. 47)

Henry the Lion, (Heinrich der Löwe) (1129-1195), duke of Saxony (1142-1180) whose symbol was a bronze lion, he reconquered Bavaria* which his father, Heinrich der Stolze (Henry the Proud), had lost, and held as its duke from 1156 to 1180. Because he quarreled with the Emperor Frederick I,* Barbarossa, he was outlawed and deprived of his possessions in 1180. He lived in exile at the court of Henry II* of England in Normandy from 1182 to 1185, and in 1190, he regained some of his possessions. He was patron of Pfaffe Konrad* who wrote the *Rolandslied* * for him and his consort in 1170. (Bibliog. 86)

Heptarchy, seven states established by the Angles, Saxons and Jutes of Anglo-Saxon England in the 6th century. These seven kingdoms were Kent, East Anglia, East Saxons (Essex), Wessex, Sussex, Mercia, and Northumbria. They completed the conquest of the Celtic Britons while they struggled for power among themselves, finally coming under the vague but general leadership of King Ethelbert (560-616) of Kent. During his rule Roman Christianity was brought to the British Isles by St. Augustine in 597, establishing the first English bishopric of Canterbury. With the coming of the Danes, England united for the first time under the house of Wessex, and Alfred the Great* (871-899) became the first important English king. (Bibliog. 124)

herald, trusted servant of a king or a lord who, by being sent on private diplomatic or military missions, learned to identify important men by their heraldic devices or insignia. Frequently, these heralds wandered from lordship to lordship, from county to county wherever they heard rumors of tournaments at which their services as criers or masters of ceremonies might be needed. A luckier few were retained as household officers by knights, lords or princes, and hence had authority over their fellow heralds; such were called Kings of Heralds. The first recorded private English herald appeared to be the Lancaster* herald who at Calais* in 1347 proclaimed judgment in a plea of arms of Burwell versus Morley. The earls and dukes of Lancaster kept a Lancaster herald until Henry of Lancaster ascended the throne as King Henry IV when the Lancaster herald passed into the king's establishment and became the king's herald. Among the officers of the Scottish crown, Carrick* possibly was the herald of the Bruces* as the earls of Carrick before they attained the throne in 1306; and Rothesay was herald and Bute was pursuivant+ of the high stewards of Scotland before their accession to the throne in 1371. Some heralds were hired by private knights between 1360 and 1383: Chandos herald was hired in 1360 by Sir John Chandos,* a Knight of the Garter,* and he kept the title even after Sir John's death when King Richard II* appointed him as "roy d'armes d'Angleterre" (king of arms of England); in 1381, he was on the staff of the earl of Buckingham and in 1382 he was named the Ireland king of arms. Derval, the herald of Sir Robert Knollys,* brought dispatches from Normandy to King Edward III* in 1361-1362; he was called Derval because John de Montfort* gave Knollys lands of Derval and Rouge with 2,000 livres per year as a reward for his help in Montfort's struggles against Charles of Blois* in Brittany, and sometimes he was called Sire de Derval. Other English heralds were the Aquitaine herald who probably was king of arms between 1366 and 1367 as an officer of Edward,* the Black Prince; the Bordeaux herald, William Moulton by name, performed between 1390 and 1398. Henry Grene was the Leicester herald in 1386 and 1390, and he specifically was the officer of John of Gaunt,* duke of Guienne, duke of Lancaster, and earl of Leicester, and transferred to royal service a few years later. John Lake was the March herald to Edmund Mortimer,* earl of March,* who granted him an annuity in 1377, and after the earl's death, when he transferred to royal service but retained the title of March herald, the king continued his annuity. Mowbray, herald for the dukes of Norfolk, first appeared in 1392 when the Lancaster and Mowbray heralds attended Henry Bolingbroke (later King Henry IV) on his journey to the Holy Sepulchre. The Gryphon pursuivant held in 1385 by Thomas Turville was Salisbury herald in 1388, evidently as an officer of William Montagu, earl of Salisbury. In 1369, Richard was Hereford herald to Humphrey de Bohun,* earl of Hereford, Essex and Northampton, on whose death in 1373, Richard entered royal service but kept the name of Hereford. (Bibliog. 47)

Herbert le Duc de Dammartin, French author of a long and tedious *chanson de geste,* *Fouque de Candie,** written around 1170. (Bibliog. 231)

Herbort von Fritzlar, author of Middle High German* poem for the Thuringian court of Landgraf+ Herman about 1190-1210. This work, *Das Lied von Troja,* was a coarse adaptation, abridgement and translation of Benoît de Sainte-Maure's immense *Roman de Troie,** reduced from the original 30,000 lines to 18,000, and filled with gory battle scenes and vulgar utterances by lords and ladies. (ed. G. K. Frommann, Quedlinburg, 1837) (Bibliog. 235)

Hereford, city in Herefordshire, England, which was made an earldom two years after the Norman invasion in 1066. To William FitzOsbern, siegneur de Breteuil, one of the major planners for and the king's companions at Hastings,* William* the Conqueror granted the Isle of Wight* and the county of Hereford. FitzOsbern held it practically as a palatinate,+ dividing it into a number of "casteleries" (a moated and palisaded mound which formed the fortress of the time). In Hereford, he rebuilt the castle+ erected by a nephew of King Edward the Confessor* around 1048 which had been badly damaged by the Welsh in 1055. After many months of vigorous fighting to subdue his territory, FitzOsbern crossed the Channel to help Queen Matilda with the administration of the duchy of Normandy,* and while there, went to fight in Flanders and was killed in 1071. He was succeeded in his English lands by his second son, Roger de Breteuil; his elder son had received the Norman fiefs. Earl Roger kept the March against the Welsh until 1075 when in the king's absence in Normandy, he conspired against him with his sister's husband, Ralph, earl of Norfolk,* and Waltheof (see Huntingdon), earl of Northumbria. Archbishop Lanfranc,* acting as Regent, moved swiftly and prevented Roger from joining his two co-conspirators, so the revolt came to a speedy end. Ralph fled to Brittany,* his father's home, never to return; Waltheof was accused of treason, and executed; Roger, tried under Norman law, was imprisoned for life. In accordance with feudal law, for those crimes, these men lost their titles as earl and their lands in England; the Hereford fief was broken up. Later, Miles of Gloucester,* son of Walter of Gloucester, hereditary sheriff of Gloucester and one of the royal constables, was confirmed by King Stephen* in the honour+ of Gloucester, and later was confirmed again when he switched sides to support Queen Matilda* who bestowed upon him the title of earl of Hereford in 1141. He was known by that title during the remainder of his life. He was succeeded by his son, Roger FitzMiles, who opposed King Henry over the castle of Gloucester, and not only was excommunicated by the bishop of

Hereford, but was forced to surrender his castles, fees and the earldom itself, until he entered a monastery just before his death when the title reverted to the crown. Henry de Bohun,* grandson of Humphrey I de Bohun, by Margaret, the eldest daughter, and eventually a co-heir of Miles de Gloucester, who not only was earl of Gloucester and earl of Hereford but also was hereditary constable of England, inherited through his grandmother Margaret the Gloucester portion of the inheritance. Siding with the barons, Henry was chosen as one of the twenty-four* appointed to secure the observance of the *Magna Carta Libertatum*+ in 1215, and was among those excommunicated by the pope. After the death of King John,* he sided with Prince Louis* of France, and was captured at the battle of Lincoln* in 1217, and died shortly thereafter. His son, Humphrey de Bohun, was one of the twenty-four counsellors who draw up the Provisions of Oxford* in 1258, being chosen among the barons' twelve, and being chosen to be one of the fifteen chosen to advise the king on all points. Its first earls and dukes were:

1066 - William FitzOsbern, earl of Hereford and lord of Wight; married
          Adeliza, daughter of Roger de Tony, standard-bearer of
          Normandy; d. 1071
1071 - Roger de Bretville, second son of William; died without issue
1141 - Miles de Gloucester, lord constable; married Sybil, daughter
          and heiress of Bernard de Newmarch, lord of Brecknock
1143 - Roger, lord constable, son of Miles
1154 - Walter, lord constable, his brother Henry, lord constable, his
          brother Mahel, lord constable, his brother; all died without
          issue.
(For later earls, see Bohun.) (Bibliog. 47, 66, 101)

Hereward the Wake, notorious legendary English outlaw. As the leader of the English forces at Peterborough against the Normans, he became the subject of a series of poems about his activities fighting for freedom. In 1070, King Swein* of Denmark crossed the North Sea to lead a Danish fleet awaiting him in the Humber River estuary. Sailing down the coast to the Wash,+ he planned to meet one of the last groups of English resistance fighters led by Hereward of Bourne, a Lincolnshire thane,+ who had based themselves in the fen country around Peterborough and the Isle of Ely. Earl Morcar had fled from the court, pursued by King William I* and his forces. Hereward rallied his forces to mount a strong defense of the Isle of Ely, and thwarted all the king's attacks until the Isle fell by the treachery of the monks who believed the false promises of the king and surrendered. Hereward and his close companions escaped to the fens where they continued to harass the Norman forces with a group of about 100 mounted and 200 footmen and a few men armed with crossbows.

Physically he was reputed to be a short, stocky, but quite agile man with long golden hair, an oval face and pale flashing eyes. His Flemish wife, Torfrida, was skillful in magic and the study of the liberal arts, and when she was apart from her husband, all sorts of evils befell him because of the lack of her advice. One of the poems about him described how he was outlawed at his father's request, roamed through Bernicia, Ireland* and Cornwall,* and finally took service under the count of Flanders.* He returned to England after the Norman invasion to avenge the murder of his brother by the Normans and to help purge his homeland of the invaders. (Bibliog. 55, 213)

Hermitage castle,+ Scottish fortress built in the 13th century on a bluff on the Liddesdale, England's "western way into Scotland." One of its earliest owners was the de Soulis family, hereditary king's butlers of Scotland, but it changed hands frequently between the English and Scots. In 1335, Edward Baliol* granted it to an English supporter, Ralph Neville, but in 1338 it was captured by the famous knight of Liddesdale, Sir William Douglas.* In 1342, he seized his enemy Sir Alexander Ramsay, imprisoned him at Hermitage and starved him to death. Douglas subsequently joined the English at which King David II granted Hermitage to William, afterwards first earl of Douglas, who ensured he had no opposition by murdering his predecessor in nearby Ettrick Forest. Nevertheless, after the knight of Liddesdale's widow had married an Englishman named Dacre,+ the castle changed hands once more and with the backing of Edward III,* remained in the Dacre family until after 1365. (Bibliog. 192)

Hernaut de Beaulande, son of Garin de Monglane and father of Aimeri de Narbonne in the *chansons de geste.** (Bibliog. 128)

Hertford, county and town in England. Its castle+ originally had been built by a son of King Alfred the Great* when he erected a mound on each bank of the River Lea. On the south mound, William I* erected a Norman castle which a century and a half later was under siege by Prince Louis* of France in 1216, but later was returned to crown control. This locality also had the longest title of honour remaining in the same family of any in England; it began with the family of Clare.* In 1138 Gilbert de Clare,* lord of Clare, son and heir of Richard FitzGilbert, lord of Clare, succeeded his father to the great family estates, the honour+ of Clare and Tonbridge castle, and was created the first earl of Hertford by King Stephen.* His uncle Richard was the earl of Pembroke,* after which the Clares were known as earls of Hertford or of Clare, just as the younger line were known as earls of Pembroke or Striguil. He appeared to have sided with Matilda,* for when in 1145 the king captured the earl of Chester,* Gilbert gave his nephew as hostage for his liberation. He died between 1151 and 1153 without issue. His brother and heir, Roger de Clare (d. 1173), second earl of Hertford, but generally styled earl of Clare, was allowed this earldom by Henry II.* In 1163, he disputed with the archbishop of Canterbury over the latter's claim to fealty with respect to Tonbridge castle, and in the following year, he took part in the Constitutions of Clarendon,+ and in 1170 in King Henry's Inquest of Sheriffs.+ His son and heir, Richard de Clare, third earl of Hertford, received a grant of half of the Giffard* estates from King Richard I*: de Clare received all Giffard's English holdings, and William Marshal and his wife, Isabelle, received the holdings in Normandy. Clare attended Richard I's coronation, and was one of the eleven knights chosen by Longchamps* to settle with the eleven chosen by Prince John the questions between them. In 1193, he accompanied Longchamps to Richard I's prison in Germany. On the accession of King John* in 1199, Clare was one of the knights about whom the archbishop, Hubert, and the king's other supporters had the most doubt. He was summoned to Northampton where an oath was taken that King John would restore to every man his right if they would keep the peace with him; they swore accordingly. He attended John's coronation in 1199, and did homage to William, king of Scotland, at Lincoln. He sided with the barons against John, and he played a leading role in the negotiations for the *Magna Carta Libertatum,*+ being chosen as one of the twenty-four barons* who were guardians of the Charter. He lost his land and was excommunicated by the pope in 1216 and died in 1217. By marrying Amice, daughter and heir of William FitzRobert, earl of Gloucester,* he brought the earldom of Gloucester to his family; it was inherited by his son and heir, Gilbert de Clare who became the fourth earl of Gloucester and the fourth earl of Hertford. (See Gloucester for remaining earls.) (Bibliog. 47, 101)

Herupe, Hurepe, part of Neustria* whose barons—Normans, Angevins, Bretons, and knights of Maine and Tours—refused to pay tribute, a head tax of four deniers+ imposed on them as on everyone else by Charlemagne;* however, they agreed to serve him in his battle against Guiteclin, the Saxon, as detailed in in the *chanson de geste,* *Chanson de Saisnes** (Saxons). (Bibliog. 106, 128)

*Hervis de Mes (Metz), chansons de geste** in the Lotharingian* or Lorraine cycle. Thierri, Hervis' bourgeois father, was provost of Metz. Angry that his son showed little financial acumen because of his continuous largesse,+ Thierri forced his son and his wife, Beatrice of Hungary, to undergo severe privations because he felt Hervis had wasted the 15,000 marks he paid as her dowry. Only after her royal background was revealed to him did Thierri become reconciled with his son. An aged king of Spain coveted Beatrice, meanwhile, and threatened war unless she was yielded to him. Beatrice's brother, Floire, took her away secretly, but Hervis found and rescued her, but refused to give her to the aged king. Finally, all worked out happily after the Spanish king agreed to become a monk. (ed. Edmund Stengel, Dresden: *GrL* 1, 1903) (Bibliog. 106)

Der Herzemaere, short Middle High German* verse romance by Konrad von Wurzburg* which told the story of a married woman who deeply loved a knight. To allay her husband's suspicions, she sent her lover on a crusade,+ but he died of heartbreak after giving instructions for his heart to be sent to her. The husband intercepted it, learned the truth about his wife's affair, had the heart cooked and set before his wife. After she had eaten it, he revealed the truth. The horrified wife declared that after that meal she would eat no more food, and like her lover, she died of a broken heart. (ed. E. Schroder, *Kleinere Dichtungen Konrad von Wurzburg,* Halle: Altdeutsche Bibliothek, 3 vols., 1924-1926) (Bibliog. 86)

Herzog Ernst, Middle High German* epic poem by Ulrich von Etzenbach around 1280. It told of a quarrel between the emperor and his stepson which ended in a reconciliation. In the first part of the poem, Duke Ernest's mother married Emperor Otto and they lived happily together until an intriguer, Pfalzgraf Heinrich, poisoned the emperor's mind against his stepson. Ernest avenged himself for this vile deed by assassinating Heinrich with the help of his faithful follower, Wetzel. As a result, he was outlawed, and shortly thereafter left on a crusade.+ The second part of the poem described his adventures in the Orient, including his meeting some marvellous creatures (e.g., people with cranes' bills for mouths), and rescuing an Indian princess. His ships were shipwrecked on a magnetic cliff; he secured a magic stone which he took home with him to become a part of the imperial crown when he finally returned to become reconciled with his stepfather. Interestingly, the first part of the poem fused two historical events as its base: the quarrel of Duke Liudolf with his father Otto I in 953-954, and the revolts of Duke Ernest I of Swabia against his stepfather, King Conrad I, in 1026-1027. (ed. F. H. von der Hagen, *Deutsche geschichte des Mittelalters* I, Berlin, 1808) (Bibliog. 86)

Hesse-Cassel, landgraviate+ in western Germany. Enfeoffed+ first to the dukes of Franconia* and later to the counts of Thuringia,* Hesse emerged in 1247 as a landgraviate under a branch of the house of Brabant.* (Bibliog. 100, 200)

"l'heure de matins," midnight; the hour when Roual de Brienne, count of Eu* and constable of France, was executed for treason at the Hôtel de Ville+ in Paris in 1350. (Bibliog. 47)

Hexham, Richard of, prior of Hexham who compiled a valuable detailed contemporary narrative of the period 1135-1139, written before 1154. Much of it was concerned with the invasion of King David I* of Scotland.* It covered the battle of the Standard.* Richard was elected prior in 1141 and seems to have died between 1162 and 1174. (tr. Joseph Stevenson, *Church Historians,* London: Seeleys, 1876, IV, pt. i, 35-58) (Bibliog. 99)

Hiaumont, son of Agolant,* defeated at Aspremont by Roland; he became the symbol of the valiant Saracen in the *chanson de geste,* *Fouque de Candie.** (Bibliog. 128)

Higden, Ranulph (d. 1363-1364), monk of St. Wereburgh's Abbey, Chester,* he was the author of *Polychronicon* that covered events from the creation of the world to 1352. This was the most popular work on universal history during the 14th and 15th centuries. Using classical and medieval sources, Higden arranged his work in seven books. Book I described the geography of the countries of the earth; the remaining six books comprised a universal history from Adam and Eve to the 14th century. In 1385, John Trevisa translated Higden's chronicle into English and carried it down to 1360; Caxton continued it up to 1460 in English and printed Trevisa and his continuation in 1482. (ed. David Fowler, *Traditio,* XVII, 1962, 289-317) (Bibliog. 99)

Hildebrandslied, fragment of Old High German alliterative heroic poem which narrated the encounter between Hildebrand and his son Hadubrand. Hildebrand was a voluntary exile with his king, Dietrich von Bern (Theoderic the Great,* the last East Gothic ruler of Italy, 493-526). As the king's chosen champion he confronted a young man who was ready for combat. It was his son, Hadubrand, but as so much time had passed since last they had met, neither recognized the other. In the custom for such a fight, Hildebrand first asked the name and kin of the challenger, and was overjoyed to recognize his own son whom he hadn't seen for over thirty years. But Hadubrand was suspicious, for he had been told by sailors that his father had been killed in battle. In vain, Hildebrand tried to convince him, offering him gold rings which his son scornfully refused, saying that the old man was a coward who had survived only because he always practiced treachery. After such an insult, there was no possibility of reconciliation. The evil fate must be fulfilled: either father would kill the son or the son would kill the father. Unfortunately, the poem broke off before the conclusion was revealed, but there can be no doubt about the outcome—one of them had to die. (tr. Bruce Dickins, *Runic and Heroic Poems of the Old Teutonic Peoples,* Cambridge, England: University Press, 1915) (Bibliog. 24, 235)

Hincmar, Bishop, archbishop of Reims (845-882). He was one of the first and strongest supporters of the ordeal of cold water+ to test the innocence or guilt of someone. He said,

> He who seeks to conceal the truth by a lie will not sink in the waters over which the voice of God has thundered; for the pure nature of water recognizes as impure and rejects as incompatible human nature which, released from falsehood by the waters of baptism, becomes again injected with untruth. (Bibliog. 132)

He cited baptism in the River Jordan, passage of the Red Sea and the crowning judgment of the Deluge as strong evidence to support his belief. He was a loyal supporter of Charles the Bald,* and he helped to secure the succession to the throne of Louis II,* becoming one of his chief counsellors and regent for his son. (Bibliog. 98)

Historia de excidio Trojae, history of the Trojan War by the supposed Phrygian, Dares (Dares Phrygius). This gave the Trojan side of the war; Dictys Cretensis' work, *Ephemeris belli trojani,* spoke for the Greeks. See Dares; Dictys. (Bibliog. 214)

Historia Meriadoci, Arthurian romance written in Latin no later than 1277. It contained the usual stock motifs of romance such as the faithless guardian ordering the murder of his royal wards, but their successfully talking their way out of the plight; fights against a Red Knight, a Black Knight, and a White Knight; Arthur's* refusal to begin a banquet until some adventures was announced; a marvellous place which no one had ever seen before, and so on. This was an important document for Arthurian legend of the 12th century. (ed. J. D. Bruce, *Hesperia,* Baltimore: 1913) (Bibliog. 106, 231)

Histoire van den Grale, remarkably free poetic version of Robert de Boron's* *Joseph* by the Dutch poet Jacob van Maerlant written about 1261. Not only did van Maerlant omit material from his original source, but frequently he attacked that source. When Boron differed from Scripture, Maerlant called him a liar; when Boron recounted how Judas retained a tithe of the money received by Jesus, Maerlant declared him a thief. He ended Boron's work at verse 1926, and then continued uninterrupted with a translation of the French prose version of Boron's *Merlin* to verse 10,398. Lodewijk van Velthem then continued it for nearly 26,000 more lines which corresponded to the *Livre d'Artus.** (ed. J. van Vloten, *Jacob van Maerlants Merlijn,* Leiden, 1880) (Bibliog. 10)

Historia Regum Brittaniae, Geoffrey of Monmouth's* spectacular Latin history of the kings of Britain, completed shortly after the death of Henry I* in 1135. Because he was a strong advocate of Matilda* in the controversy over the English throne, he dedicated this work to her brother and chief supporter, Robert, earl of Gloucester, whom he called "another Henry." When the crown went to Stephen,* Geoffrey rewrote his dedication to the earl of Worcester* and count of Meulan (see Beaumont, Robert de), who enjoyed the new king's special favor. This proved to be a wise political move for Geoffrey because he obtained preferment from King Stephen. Much of this work may have been Geoffrey's own creation despite his avowed source of an old book which he claimed had contained stories of all the previous kings of Britain from Brutus to Cadwalader. A recent work disputed that position, and accepted Monmouth's assertions as correct. (See Bibliog. 96.) Even though he drew material from numerous sources, especially Nennius, Monmouth's own two main creations seem to have been the stories of Merlin* and Arthur.* From Nennius he borrowed the accounts of Vortigern and his tower, the dragons* in the underground pool, and the clever young boy without a father, Ambrosius, whom Monmouth transformed into Merlin by the simple tactic of saying that Merlin also was called Ambrosius.

His treatment of Arthur was the most notable portion of the book. Here, Uther Pendragon* was credited with begetting Arthur, and Arthur fought the battles named by Nennius. By surrounding Arthur with nobles and barons from all over western Europe, Geoffrey made Arthur's court into a glorification of the courts he actually had seen. He had Arthur defeat the emperor of Rome and Gaul, and thus reign over a huge empire that surpassed even that of Charlemagne.* To show that the French kings were subject to the English kings, Geoffrey recounted that as Brutus had ravaged Aquitaine,* and Belinus had conquered France, so Arthur, too, defeated the French before the time of Charlemagne. Arthur also had to be defeated by treachery, so Geoffrey introduced the figure of Mordred. (ed. and tr. Lewis Thorpe, Baltimore: Penguin Books, 1977) (Bibliog. 10, 89, 96)

höfische dichtung (Ger. "courtly poetry"), Middle High German* courtly literature, both lyric and epic, of the *Blütezeit* period, 1150-1250, in which the poetry written by knights or their more literate retainers was composed not to be read, but to be performed especially during long winter evenings. It was to be sung, chanted or declaimed in the courts of princes to whom the knights paid homage+ or from whom they sought favor. Although its primary goal was to entertain, it also expressed the high ideals of knightly life. (Bibliog. 86)

höfische epos (Ger. "courtly epic"), type of Middle High German* poem read or recited at the courts of German nobles during the 12th and 13th centuries. Often of considerable length, these works sought not only to entertain, but also to stress the chivalric virtues of *maze+* (harmonious self-control), *milte+* (chivalric generosity), and *minne+* (respectful love) which the society of the time respected highly. The poems, generally on Arthurian subjects, were freely translated or adapted from French sources, especially Chrétien de Troyes* and Thomas of Britain.* These began with Eilhart von Oberg's *Tristant und Isolde* and Heinrich von Veldeke's* *Eneit,* and reached their zenith with the works of the three great poets, Hartmann von Aue's* *Erec** and *Iwein*;* Wolfram von Eschenbach's* *Parzival;* and Gottfried von Strassburg's* *Tristan,* all of which were written about 1200. Other lesser and later writers of this type of poetry included Ulrich von Zatzikhoven (*Lanzelet**), Heinrich von dem Türlin* (*Diu Crône,** *Der Mantel**), Wirnt von Grafenberg (*Wigalois),* der Striker* (*Daniel von dem Blühenden Tal**), K. Fleck* (*Floire und Blancheflur**), Rudolf von Ems* (*Alexander**), Konrad von Wurzburg* (*Engelhard*; Partenopier und Meliur*; Der Trojan Krieg*).* (Bibliog. 86)

Hohenstaufen, German dynasty which ruled the Holy Roman Empire in the 12th and 13th centuries; they chose the name from their castle Staufen in Swabia.* Originally, they were counts of Weiblingen which was corrupted in Italy* to Ghibelline.* In 1079 the head of the family, Frederick I,* married Agnes, daughter of Emperor Henry IV,* and was appointed duke of Swabia after crushing a revolt there led by Duke

Rudolf of Swabia. The family controlled the Holy Roman Empire for the next century until 1202 when Pope Innocent III,* fearing the great power of the family, called for the election of Otto, duke of Brunswick, the heir to the Welfs (Guelph in Italy). Civil war broke out in Germany which led subsequently in 1266 and 1268 to the deaths of Manfred and Conradin, illegitimate sons of Frederick, when the dynasty became extinct. (Bibliog. 98)

Holand, Robert (1270-1328), English knight from Lancashire who grew up to become a favorite of Thomas,* earl of Lancaster, and hence matured surrounded by wealth and importance. Knighted in 1307, he participated in tournaments before being employed by Thomas of Lancaster at Beeston* castle in Chester.* He was summoned for military service against the Scots at Newcastle in 1314 and 1316, and served as commissioner of array+ in Lancashire. He was summoned to Parliament in 1314 and 1321 by which he became Lord Holand. Siding with his patron, Earl Lancaster, he was pardoned for any complicity in the death of Piers Gaveston* in 1314. He helped suppress the rising of Adam Banastre* in 1315, and again in 1318 was pardoned for his adherence to the earl. Because of the earl's affinity for him, he and his family in 1321 procured a curious variation in the tenure of Upholland and the remainder of his hereditary holdings: he and his successors for the earl's soul each December 29 (feast day of St. Thomas the Martyr) were to distribute certain specific charities. On that day, they were to distribute meal and meat in the value of £10 to poor people coming to the hall at Upholland by serving to 240 poor men on that day a meal of two courses, and on the morning next, a meal of one course, and giving to each guest either 4 pence or a pair of shoes. He was said to have played a treacherous and cowardly part in the earl's final uprising in 1322. Although he collected 500 men in Lancashire to support the earl, he took them to support the king instead. On the earl's flight northward, before the fight at Boroughbridge,* Holand surrendered to the king at Derby, and was sent to Dover* castle, but he was released in time to join the earl at Boroughbridge, and he surrendered after the battle. Treated as a rebel, he was stripped of all his lands, and imprisoned at various places. On the accession of King Edward III,* he petitioned for the return of his holdings, and the king agreed. In 1328, he was captured at Boreham Wood in Hertfordshire by some adherents of his former patron, the Earl Thomas, and was decapitated for his treachery. His head was sent to Henry, the new earl of Lancaster at Waltham Cross. His son and heir, Robert (1312-1373), was 16 at his father's death. After proving himself and being knighted in the war with Scotland, he continued to prove his valor on the battlefield by participating in the wars in France in the retinue of the earl of Warwick* at Crécy* and with the king in 1347 at other battles. (Bibliog. 47, 84)

Holand, Thomas (c. 1320-1360), brother of Sir John and one of the founding Knights of the Garter* in 1348. He was summoned to a council and then to Parliament in 1354 by which he became Lord Holand. He was one of the young bachelors+ who had taken the Vow of the Heron+ instigated by Robert of Artois* to incite Edward III* to invade France for vengeance against King Philip VI.* This action started the Hundred Years War.* Thomas played a leading part in the capture of Caen in 1346 with one of his eyes still covered in compliance with the bravado of the oath he took in the Vow of the Heron, "that they would see with but one eye until they had done some knightly deeds in France." He married Joan,* daughter of Edmund of Kent, third son of King Edward I,* and sister of John, earl of Kent,* on whose death Thomas assumed the earldom. He later was summoned to Parliament as the earl of Kent. His younger son, John Holand, by Joan of Kent, was created earl of Huntingdon* with the title to continue to the heirs male of his body, when he married Elizabeth, daughter of John of Gaunt*; he was created duke of Exeter by King Richard II,* but was degraded from his dukedom in November 1399, and beheaded in 1400. Parliament that same year attainted him as earl of Huntingdon by which the earldom was forfeited. (Bibliog. 47, 84)

Holland, county belonging to the duchy of Lotharingia, which covered part of the territory of western Frisia between the Amstel and Rhine rivers. This county was organized in the 10th century by Dirk who reconquered it from the Normans and was made count of Holland by Charles the Simple, king of France. Under Count William II (1234-1256) Holland gained powerful such influence in the Germany that he was elected anti-king in 1247 by the German princes who rebelled against Frederick II.* In 1296 the Frisian dynasty died out, and Holland was ruled by John of Avesnes, count of Hainaut.* (Bibliog. 98)

Holy Land. See Palestine.

Holy Office. See Inquisition.

Horn, 12th century Anglo-Norman poem written in the form of a *chanson de geste,* but was basically a romance of adventure. This was the basis for the English *King Horn* story. (ed. R. Brede and Edmund Stengel, Marburg: *AA* VIII, 1883) (Bibliog. 21)

Horn Child, revision of the *King Horn** English romance written about 1320. Son of King Hatheof who ruled all of England north of the Humber River, Horn Child was taken to the protection of King Houlac in the south of England after King Malkan of Ireland invaded his father's land and slew him. Horn fell in love with Rimnild, the king's daughter, but was accused of seducing her, and was forced to flee. Rimnild promised to wait seven years for him, and gave him a ring to serve as a token of her fidelity. Horn then changed his name to Godebounde, and served the king of Snowdon in Wales, and then King Finlak of Youghal in Ireland in whose service he killed King Malkan, and thus avenged his father. He returned to England, recalled by Rimnild's ring, just as she was about to be married to an unwanted suitor named Moging. Putting the ring in the goblet he served her disguised as a beggar, Horn revealed himself to her. One of his boyhood friends there revealed for him the heraldic devices of Horn's enemies in the tournament to celebrate Rimnild's wedding. Thus he identified and overcame his enemies and rivals, married Rimnild, and returned north to reconquer his own land. (ed. J. Hall, London: Oxford University, 1901) (Bibliog. 202)

Horn et Rimenild, romance by the Anglo-Norman poet Mestre Thomas in the last years of the 12th century. It was the source for the English *King Horn.** In this poem, Horn's father, a foundling, overcame many difficulties to win the throne at the court of King Silaf, but then was killed in a fight against invaders. His son, Horn, was set adrift in a rudderless boat, and eventually landed on the shores of King Hunlaf in Brittany. He was educated there, fell in love with the king's daughter, Rimnild, was falsely accused, and again was forced into exile. He returned in disguise, saved Rimel from an unwanted marriage on two occasions, and finally won his lady and his heritage in the end. (ed. Brede and Stengel, Marburg: *AA* 8, 1883) (Bibliog. 202)

Horsa, legendary Saxon invader of Britain, brother of Hengest.* (Bibliog. 129, 202)

Hoveden (Howden), Roger of (d. 1201), author of the most valuable narrative for the reigns of Henry II* and Richard I* of England, *Chronica Rogeri de Hovedene* (A.D. 732-1201). Roger was a royal clerk who accompanied Henry to France in 1174 and was an itinerant justice+ of the forest on several occasions between 1185 and 1190. He accompanied Richard on the third crusade,+ but had returned to England by Christmas of 1191. (ed. and tr. H. T. Riley, *Annals of Roger de*

Hoveden, London: Bohn's Antiquarian Library, 2 vols., 1853; repr. New York: AMS Press, 1968) (Bibliog. 99)

Howel, the Hende, father of the maiden Elayne,* who was murdered by the giant of Mont St. Michel in Arthurian legend; perhaps he was the same as Howell, king of Brittany, father of Isolde* le Blanche Mains who married Tristan. (Bibliog. 1, 129, 145)

Hubert Walter. See Walter, Hubert.

Hue de Roteland, author of *Ipomedon,** an English love romance possibly Byzantine,+ and *Prothesilaus.** Written between 1174 and 1191, both of these works revealed that he was well versed in French literature of his time. A native of Hereford,* whose patron was Gilbert FitzBaderon, he was a skillful writer, well versed in the tastes of a chivalric audience, and clever in adapting material of proved quality. (Bibliog. 106)

Hugh, bishop of Lincoln* under Richard I* who performed the burial rites over that king's tomb at Fontevrault* in 1199. He was a saintly man who shortly after his death was canonized, not for the way he died, as Thomas à Becket* was, but for the way he lived. (Bibliog. 92)

Hugh (Hugues) Capet (941-996), founder of the Capetian* dynasty of French kings. Son of Hugh the Great, duke of the Franks, Hugh became duke on his father's death in 956, and thus became the most powerful feudal lord in the country. In 978, he joined with his cousin, Emperor Otto II,* and Adalberon, archbishop of Reims, against King Lothaire; subsequently, after the death of Louis V in 987, the nobles of the kingdom elected Hugh king against the candidacy of the last Carolingian, Charles of Lorraine. He withstood a revolt of Charles' supporters within the church and the nobility to keep the throne and to begin the Capetian dynasty. (Bibliog. 98)

Hugh of Puiset (d. 1195), bishop of Durham.* Great-grandson of William* the Conqueror, and distant cousin of Richard I* and Philip II* of France, he was appointed bishop of Durham in 1153 after being treasurer of York.* At the time he was elevated to become chief justiciar,+ Hugh was made earl of Northumberland* for £10,000, and given complete jurisdiction over that county which was jointly administered with Durham as a county palatine.+ Not only was he earl palatine+ of his shire, but his diocese extended over the whole of

Northumberland as well. King Henry II* also sold him the manor of Sadberge for 600 marks more. He had been bishop of Durham since 1153, and did not actively help Henry II win the throne even though he was one of the richest and most powerful men in the north of England. Staying neutral in Henry's quarrel with Thomas à Becket* in 1173, Hugh schemed against his king by doing nothing in his northernmost area to prevent the invasion of England by William the Lion,* King of Scotland. He was dismissed from office and left England for several years. When Richard ascended the throne, Hugh hoped to become archbishop of York, and so as a move to achieve that goal, he bought the position of sheriff+ of Northumberland on his return. However, when he did not pay on the specified day the 2,000 marks he had promised for that sheriffship, he was dismissed by Chancellor William Longchamps,* and the sheriffship sold to William de Stuteville. Longchamps' brother, the sheriff of Yorkshire, kept Hugh restrained under close house arrest after seizing his person, castles, manors, and all other possessions, until he died in 1195. To pay his debts to King Richard, he used the money he had collected for the third crusade,+ and then sent messages to the pope begging to be released from his crusader's vow on the excuse of old age. He was grave, courteous, stately; a gentleman, a patron of the arts, a builder, and a lover of the good life. (Bibliog. 7, 94)

Hugues Capet, French romance from the middle of the 14th century which recounted how the hero, descended from a butcher's family, went to Paris, squandered his father's wealth in a knightly manner, and who, after saving the widowed queen, and marrying her daughter, Marie, was made king of France. (ed. André Ferrière, *Positions des thèses de l'Ecole des chartes,* Paris, 1950) (Bibliog. 23, 106)

Hulagu, Mongol khan* of Persia and Mesopotamia, grandson of Jenghiz (Genghis) Khan. In 1256, he crossed the Oxus River, subjugated Persia, Mesopotamia, and the sultanate of Rum in Asia Minor and brushed aside the remnants of a dozen dynasties between the Caucasus and the Indian Ocean. His first major setback occurred in 1260; after he had annexed all Syria and Palestine not in Christian hands, his Syrian governor had been defeated by the Mameluks in the great battle of Ain Jalud or Goliath's Spring near Mount Tabor. The Mongols were forced back across the Euphrates and the Mameluks had a free hand in Syria. He was succeeded by his son, Abagha,* in 1265. (Bibliog. 184)

Humbaut (Hunbaut), incomplete French Arthurian romance written by a poet from Hainaut* between 1250 and 1275. Despite its title, the chief

character was Gawain* whom King Arthur* sent to the king of the Isles
to demand submission. Humbaut accompanied him. On their way, they
stopped at a castle+ where an imperious host told Gawain to kiss his
daughter. He did so four times and was nearly blinded as punishment,
but Humbaut with his glib tongue talked them out of further trouble.
Their final destination was guarded by a hideous peasant who proposed
the mutual beheading game. (See *Sir Gawain and the Green Knight.*)
Gawain won by holding back the peasant's body from its head, so that
it died. Their message was delivered and they returned to rescue
Gawain's sister who had been stolen by the knight errant to whom
Gawain had entrusted her. (ed. J. Sturzinger and H. Bruer, Dresden:
GrL, 1914) (Bibliog. 10, 219)

Hundred Years War, name given to a series of conflicts between
England* and France* between 1337 and 1453. It was fought as a result
of the claim of Edward III* to the crown of France because he was the
grandson of Philip IV* of France. It began on May 24, 1337, when King
Philip VI* of France commanded his seneschal+ of Perigord to take the
duchy of Aquitaine* and the county of Ponthieu into his hands. That
action was necessary because Edward III, who was the king of England,
a peer of France, the count of Ponthieu, the duke of Aquitaine, and
liegeman of the king of France by reason of the duchy, peerage and
county, had given aid to Robert of Artois,* a capital enemy of the
king of France who had banished him from the kingdom for many crimes.
To harbor such a man was contrary to Edward's obligations as a liege+
vassal+ by universal feudal custom, and it entailed the confiscation
of fiefs. It also meant taking possession of such territories, and
because any such action would be resisted, it also meant war. And as
French troops immediately overran Ponthieu and invaded Edward's lands
in Aquitaine, it started the war which was to run for over a hundred
years. Such a feudal relationship between the two countries had been
established by the Treaty of Paris in 1259 between Henry III* and
Louis IX.* That treaty was intended to bring to an end the war between
the two countries which had existed more or less since the accession
to the throne in 1180 of Philip II.* By that treaty, Louis IX gave to
Henry III the rights he had as king of France in the dioceses of
Limoges, Cahors and Perigeux, and part of Saintonge. He also recognized Henry's rights to those parts of France of which he at that
moment was in effective possession—fragments of the duchy of Aquitaine
and the Channel Islands. In return, Henry abandoned his rights in
Normandy, in Anjou, Maine and Touraine, and in Poitou, and agreed to
hold by liege homage and as a peer of France not only what he acquired
by the treaty, but what he had possessed in the kingdom of France at

the time when the treaty was being negotiated. That treaty lasted roughly for fifty years, and the tension between the two countries was intensified by the death of the last two Capetian kings, Philip V* in 1322 and Charles IV* in 1328, without male heir.   Edward II* had married Isabelle, sister of these two kings of France, so their son, Edward, felt he had a more logical and legal claim to the throne than Philip VI, son of Charles of Valois and cousin to the previous two kings. Thus claims to the throne and insults to a king's honor lay behind the opening of this extended conflict. (Bibliog. 130)

Hungary, country in central Europe in the plains of the Danube River, bounded by the Alps, the Carpathian Mountains, and the Balkans. Its people, the Hungarians or Magyars, related to the Huns, Avars and Bulgars, settled during the last years of the 8th century in the lower Danube regions which later became the provinces of Bessarabia, Moldavia, and Walachia. In 895, they were forced by pressure from the Bulgarians to move westward again across the Carpathian Mountains and on to the Pannonian Plain, from where they began to raid the west. From 899 to 955, they raided Italy and France at least 33 times, but Germany suffered the most. These Magyars formed a kind of military re-public, linking several tribes. Only men fit for war exercised political rights. Each tribe elected its chief (Hungarian, *hadnagy*, Latin, *dux*) from the same family. These chieftains in turn selected a *princeps,* who at the time of the invasion, belonged to the Arpad tri-be. These warriors were formidable, not so much by their numbers, but by their strategy, their swift movements and surprises, their wariness on the march, and their greed and cruelty. As warriors on horseback armed with sword, spear and bow, these fighters were protected only by a light felt headpiece. They were so ferocious, however, that their war cry of "Hui! Hui!" created panic. They were suspected of drinking their enemies' blood. They were incapable of besieging a walled town or of standing firm against the shock of hand-to-hand fighting. Instead, their tactics were adopted from the steppes in western Asia, an attack accompanied by a rain of arrows followed by a simulated re-treat to encourage pursuit. Then, when the integrity of the enemy's line was broken, they would wheel about, attack and overwhelm their opponents. Lacking siege engines, they were highly mobile. They tried to recover and burn their war dead to carry home their ashes. (Bibliog. 48, 166)

Huntingdon, town on the River Ouse in Huntingdonshire, England, which was situated in a heavily forested area until King Henry II's* reign when it was deforested to the delight of hunters; hence it was called

"Hunters-down" at first. It became an earldom at the time of the
Norman Conquest when Tostig,* brother King Harold,* was banished in
1065, and replaced as earl of Huntingdon by Waltheof, son of Siward,
earl of Northumberland.* He did not oppose William, and was taken to
Normandy* in 1067. He joined the Danes in their attack on Yorkshire in
1069, distinguishing himself in their attack on the city of York, but
surrendered to William when the Danes left England early in 1070, and
was restored to his earldom as well as that of his father in 1072.
Three years later, he conspired with the earls of Norfolk* and
Hereford* to seize England for themselves. He quickly repented and
begged the king's pardon. Seemingly forgiven because he had married
the Conqueror's niece, Judith, he was suddenly brought to trial at
Westminster, condemned and executed, in 1076. Simon de St. Liz
(Senlyze), a Norman, then assumed both titles on his marriage to Maud,
daughter of Waltheof, around 1090. He died on his second journey to
the Holy Land, and his widow married David I* of Scotland, youngest
son of Malcolm III of Scotland. His marriage also brought to him the
titles of Earl of Huntingdon and Northhampton. He succeeded his brother, Alexander I,* to the Scottish throne in 1124, but he also had retained his English earldoms. He sided in 1127 with the Empress
Matilda's* right to ascend the throne on the death of her father, Henry I.* Thus, when Stephen* seized the throne in 1135, David warred
against him, but made peace soon thereafter, and resigned his earldom
to his son Henry, who did homage to Stephen for it. Despite the re-
sumption of the war soon thereafter, in which David was defeated at
the battle of the Standard,* Henry remained a favorite of King
Stephen.

On his death in 1152, the title was assumed by Simon de St.
Liz, son of Simon, the second earl of Huntingdon, who had been a minor
on the death of his father, and had become a ward of his stepfather,
David I, until he became king of Scotland, and then a ward of his
great-uncle, Stephen, count of Aumale.* He became as staunch a
supporter of King Stephen as King David and Earl Henry had been
supporters of Matilda, fighting beside him at Lincoln. He died in
1153. Malcolm, king of Scotland, son of Henry, earl of Huntingdon,
succeeded his grandfather, David I, as king of Scotland, and resigned
his right to Cumberland and Northumberland to King Henry II. He was
confirmed by that English monarch in his right as Earl of Huntingdon.
He accompanied Henry II on one of his tours of Toulouse* and was
knighted by him on their return in 1159 at age 18. Dying six years
later, he was succeeded by his brother, William the Lion* as king of
Scotland, born in 1143. After Henry II recognized him as earl of
Huntingdon, but refused his right to Northumberland, William became an

enemy of the English. He joined with young Henry* in the rebellion of 1173, invaded England, was defeated and captured, and deprived of his earldom. In 1189, he purchased from Richard I* a release of all claim of allegiance from Scotland for the sum of 10,000 marks. The title was assumed by Simon de St. Liz, son and heir of Simon de St. Liz II but he died in 1184 without male issue. David of Scotland, younger brother of Malcolm and William, kings of Scotland and earls of Huntingdon, became earl of Huntingdon on the resignation of the earldom by his brother William of Scotland, and was held in high esteem by the English crown. He carried one of the three swords at Richard's coronation, and with his brother-in-law, the earl of Chester,* besieged Nottingham* castle+ in 1194 when it was held by followers of Prince John* in Richard I's absence. He was succeeded by his son, John the Scot, who was created earl of Chester in 1232 in succession of Ranulph de Blundeville, his mother's brother. When he died in 1237 without male issue, the earldom became extinct. King Edward III* bestowed the earldom on William de Clinton in 1336 for his services in conducting William, count of Hainaut and his daughter, Philippa,* to the English court, and for his large role in seizing Roger de Mortimer at Nottingham castle in 1330; he even was pardoned for slaying two knights who resisted him at that time. He became an admiral* for Edward III, fighting in the Scottish wars, at Sluys,* and in the Crécy* campaign. Robin Hood,+ or Robin of Lockesley or Robert Fitzooth, the legendary outlaw whom folk legends ennobled as earl of Huntingdon, never possessed that earldom nor any other. (Bibliog. 47)

Huntingdon, Henry of (1084-1155), author of *Historia Anglorum* (55 B.C.- A.D. 1154). Drawing much of his early information, particularly for his Arthurian material, from Nennius, Bede and the *Anglo-Saxon Chronicle* up to the year 1126, he then provided statements from oral reports but provided little new material. He referred to Arthur* as *dux milittum et regum Brittaniae*. When he discovered new material in Geoffrey of Monmouth's* work, he included it in his own as an appendix rather than incorporate it into his own writing. His famous letter to Warinus written some time after January 1139, after Henry had found a copy of Geoffrey of Monmouth's *Historia Rerum Brittaniae* at the monastery of Bec in Normandy,* summarized Geoffrey's work for his friend, but changed some of Geoffrey's ideas. For example, he said that Uther was Aurelius' son instead of his brother, and he omitted the story of Vortigern's tower. He gave an interesting account of the final confrontation between Arthur and Mordred.* He wrote,

When Arthur saw that he could not retreat [from the superior forces of Mordred], he said, "Friends, let us now avenge our dead. I will now smite off the head of that traitor my nephew; after which death will be welcome." So saying, he hewed a way through the host, seized Mordred in the midst of his men by the helmet, and severed his armored neck as if it had been a straw. In the act he himself received so many wounds that he fell, although his kinsmen the Britons deny that he was mortally wounded, and seriously expect that he will yet come. He was a hero surpassing all the men of his time in valor, generosity, and *facetia*. (Bibliog. 77)

In the controversy for the throne, he supported neither Stephen* nor Matilda.* In his letter to his friend Walter, called *de Contemptu Mundi*, he gave some neatly executed sketches of great and small men of his time. (ed. and tr. Thomas Forster, London: Bohn's Antiquarian Library, 1853) (Bibliog. 77, 99, 174)

Huntley castle.+ Sometimes called Strathbogie, this Scottish fortress was erected at the confluence of the rivers Bogie and Deveron in the 11th century when the Scottish kings were imposing Norman civilization and institutions on their mainly Celtic subjects. Scottish kings invited Norman barons from England to settle north of the Tweed River by giving them lands to be held in feudal tenure from the crown. Because the Celts opposed the "Normanizing," the Scottish kings had to face continuing revolts among their subjects. Strathbogie was situated on one of the routes northward which the king had to keep open to make sure that his royal garrisons could be reached. Duncan, earl of Fife, was the first Norman to settle there sometime late in the 12th century. He built a conical flat-topped motte which was called de Strathbolgyn. Surrounded by a deep wide ditch and a palisade, its interior buildings were of earthwork and timber, for stonework was too costly. In 1307, to recover from illness, King Robert the Bruce* came to the Peel of Strathbogie, as it had come to be called. Pursued there by his enemies, he left his sickbed on Christmas Eve 1307 to defeat them at the battle of Barra. David de Strathbolgyn turned against the Scottish king shortly before the battle of Bannock Burn,* and as a punishment had his lands taken from him and granted to Sir Adam Gordon of Huntley in Berwickshire. (Bibliog. 192)

*Huon d'Auvergne, chanson de geste** relating events in the time of Charlemagne.* Surviving only in a Franco-Italian verison from the 14th century, it described that Huon even had a meeting with the Devil in Hades, showing a marked influence of Dante's *Inferno*. (ed. Arturo

Graf, *Giorn. de fil. roman.*, I, #2, 1877, 92-110) (Bibliog. 21, 231)

Huon de Bordeaux, late 12th-century *chanson de geste** which showed considerable influence of the romances.+ It was considered a part of the *gestes du roi** cycle, but it also could be considered a part of the Doön de Mayence* cycle (rebellious barons cycle). After the death of Seguin, duke of Bordeaux, his two sons, Huon and Girard, neglected to go to Paris to do homage+ for their fiefs+ as his heirs. Aumeri de Tour de Rivier, an evil schemer, coveted their land, and proposed to the king that these two be dispossessed as rebels. Instead, Naimes, their uncle, proposed that they be summoned to court to explain their actions. Charlot, Charlemagne's* eldest son, followed the evil suggestion of Aumeri that he lay an ambush for these rebels, and was killed by Huon in the ensuing fight. Charlemagne's fury was almost uncontrollable, but he relented in his demand for the life of Huon only after his peers refused to countenance that action. He insisted, though, that as penance Huon make a long and perilous trip into the land of the Saracens*; Girard was to remain home and take care of the fief. Throughout his fanciful adventures, many echoing episodes in romance, Huon was aided by Auberon, the fairy king who was the second son of Julius Caesar and the fairy Morgain.* Huon returned safely to find that his brother Girard had usurped the entire fief. With Auberon's assistance, he recovered the fief, hanged Girard for his treachery, and reconciled himself with Charlemagne. Then he married the beautiful Saracen princess, Eslarmonde. Auberon departed but promised to yield the crown of fairyland to Huon in three years. (ed. Pierre Ruelle, Bruxelles: Presses Universitaires de Bruxelles, 1960) (Bibliog. 99)

Huon of Bordeaux, Middle English* romance translated from the French *Huon de Bordeaux* by Sir John Bourchier, Lord Berners, around 1530 and published probably by Wynken de Worde about 1534. It was an extremely close and faithful translation of a French prose version. By order of Charlemagne,* Huon had to get the beard and four teeth from the admiral of Babylon. On his way he met and obtained the favors of Oberon, king of the fairies, who helped him obtain the needed trophies, and had the admiral's daughter fall in love with him. He returned home, set things right with his emperor, and recovered his lands from his brother. This work contained episodes involving magic and splendid jewels, rings, armor, supernatural swords, apples of youth, and other marvels. (ed. H. Guerber, *Myths and Legends of the Middle Ages*, London and New York: George Harrap, 1924; repr. New York: Avenel, 1986) (Bibliog. 202)

Hurepel, Philip de (fl. 1225), count of Boulogne. Son of Philip II,*
Augustus, of France by his third wife, Agnes de Meran, he joined in an
alliance with King Henry III* of England, Pierre Mauclerc, count of
Dreux, the duke of Burgundy* and others against young Louis IX* during
the regency of Blanche of Castile.* (Bibliog. 124)

Huth Merlin. See *Suite de Merlin.*

I

I Reali di Francia. See *Reali di Francia.*

Ibn al-Athir (c. 1160-1233), Mesopotamian author whose most famous work, *Kamil at-Twarikh* (*The Perfect History* or *The Collection of Histories*), was a history of the Muslim world based on Arabic and Hebrew legends up to the year A.D. 1231. He witnessed Saladin's* role in the crusades+ and used Ibn al-Qalanisi*; Baha ad-Din* and 'Imad ad-Din* as sources. His goal of presenting the essential facts of the events he recorded made him one of the chief historians of the crusades. (ed. Tornberg, Leiden, 1853-1864) (Bibliog. 83)

Ibn al-Qalanisi, Arab historian writing in Damascus A.H. 465-555 (A.D. 1073-1160). He was the earliest Arab historian to write about the crusades.+ His chronicle, *Dhail ta'rikh Dimashq* (*Appendix to the History of Damascus*), covering the period from A.D. 974 to 1160, the year of its author's death, was written from firsthand experience in the first and second crusades up to the time of Nur ed-Din's entry into Damascus. (ed. Amedroz', Leiden, 1908) (Bibliog. 83)

Ibn Shaddad. See Baha ad-Din.

Ibn Wasil, Arab government official under the last Ayyubid and early Mameluk dynasties. His work, *The Dissipator of Anxieties Concerning the History of the Ayyubids,* focussed chiefly on Saladin's* career, and then described the Mameluks up to 1282. It was one of the best sources for the fifth crusade,+ Emperor's Frederick II's* journey, and Saint Louis'* crusade.   Unfortunately, it has not been published. (Bibliog. 83)

Iceland, last region in Europe in the north beyond Norway.* Stretching on the cliff of ocean toward the north where the sea was frozen by great and strong cold, it, too, always was ice-covered and frozen. Emperor Frederick II* in his treatise on falconry stated that gerfalcons+ came from a certain land between Norway and Gallandia (Greenland) called in Teutonic "Islandia" which was translated as "region of ice." Its capital, Isenstein, was the home of Brunhild* in the *Nibelungenlied.** (Bibliog. 18, 161, 248)

Ich Dien (Ger. "I serve"), motto and crest of the blind King John* of Bohemia. At the battle of Crécy,* he rode to the English lines, and after he reached them, he ordered his attendant knights to lead him forward so that "I may strike one stroke with my sword." Somehow this small party, tied to each other by their reins, managed to ride unharmed through the archers to charge the men-at-arms. There, however, all of the Bohemians fell with their king, except for two who fled back to the French lines with the news. Their bodies were found at dawn still tied together. The Prince of Wales was so moved that he adopted the old king's crest and motto—three ostrich feathers with the legend, *Ich Dien.* (Bibliog. 203)

Idain, (Yde), (Ydain), 1) daughter of Florent and Clarisse who was changed into a man in the *chanson de geste,** *Yde et Olive;* 2) daughter of the Knight of the Swan and of Beatrix, wife of Wistace de Boulogne; she also was the mother of Godefrey of Boulogne, Wistace, and Baudouin in *Beatrix* (see *Chevalier au Cygne);* and in *Baudouin de Sebourc.* (Bibliog. 128)

Igerne, Ygerne, wife successively of Hoel, duke of Cornwall; Gorlois,* earl of Cornwall (Tintagel*); and Uther,* king of England. She was the mother of Arthur,* Anna, Morgawse,* Belisent,* Hermesent, and Morgan la Fée.* (Bibliog. 145, 202)

*Ignaures, Lai d', lai** written at the end of the 12th century by an unidentified poet known only as Renaut. In this poem, Ignaures, a Breton knight, regularly visited the castle of Wrial where twelve knights lay beside their twelve beautiful wives. He became the secret lover of all twelve. Eventually, in gossiping about their preferred lover, these twelve found that they all loved the same man. In anger, they arranged a collective rendezvous to kill him. Cleverly talking his way out of that predicament, he agreed to choose only one, and did so. Unbeknown to the wives, however, this secret arrangement was revealed to the husbands who secretly killed Ignaures and served up his heart and his genitals to their wives. When the truth about the meal was revealed, the wives refused to eat any inferior dish, and starved to death. (ed. K. Bartsch, *Langue et Littérature française,* Paris, 1887, 553ff.) (Bibliog. 106)

Ile de France, domain claimed by the Parisian dynasty of Hugh Capet* in 987. It included the greater part of Orléans, the counties of Clermont, Dreux, Moulins, Valois,* and the Gatinois. Even though two of the great rivers, the Seine and the Loire, flowed through royal dominions, the king was cut off from the English Channel by the great feudatories held by the princes of Brittany,* Normandy* and Flanders,* and the smaller county of Ponthieu which lay between Normandy and Flanders. (Bibliog. 79)

Ille et Galeron, Breton romance begun between 1167 and 1170 by Gautier d'Arras,* a contemporary of Chrétien de Troyes.* Ille was the son of a knight, Eliduc of Brittany. After many experiences common to heroes of *chansons de geste,** Ille fled into exile following his father's death, returned to recover his hereditary estate, and married Galeron, sister to Duke Conan from Brittany. Disfigured by the loss of his left eye in a tournament, he felt unworthy of his wife and secretly left for Rome without her. There, after freeing the city and its people from besieging enemies, he was forced to accept the hand of Ganor, the emperor's daughter. Before he and Ganor could be married, however, Galeron found him, convinced him that she still loved him, and returned with him to Brittany. There he learned that Galeron had vowed to take the veil, so Ille left her and returned to Rome where he rescued Ganor from evil men, and married her. (ed. Wendlin Foerster, Halle: *RB* 7, 1891) (Bibliog. 106)

'Imad ad-Din (1125-1201), Arab scholar, rhetorician and historian who was secretary to Nur ed-Din and then to Saladin.* His *Lightning of Syria* chronicled Saladin's life and deeds from 1175. (ed. Landberg, Leiden, 1888) (Bibliog. 83)

L'Image du Monde, poetic description of the world written about 1245 in Lorraine. The first of three parts centered on science, including God, human intelligence and nature; the second on each of the four elements: earth, air, fire and water; the third on astronomy—the phenomena which occur in air. The section covering geography was further subdivided into three parts: the first described Asia, or the ancient realm of a queen called Madame Asia, hence the name; the second described Europe, called after King Eutrope; the third described Africa the name of which came from Affer. (ed. Charles Langlois, *La Connaissance de la Nature et du Monde,* Paris, 1927) (Bibliog. 126)

indenture (lettres de retenue), method of raising military leaders frequently used by Edward III.* It called for a carefully drawn-up contract for the man to raise a given number of troops of a specific type to serve for a fixed period and for a fixed scale of pay. (Bibliog. 203)

India, country in the Far East abounding in wonders. Huge beasts were bred there, and hounds greater than in any other lands. Trees grew so high that no man could shoot an arrow over them; fig trees grew so broad that many companies of knights could sit at meat under the shade of one tree. Some men there grew to be over five cubits+ tall; others never spit, nor had a headache nor toothache nor sore eyes bothered by the sun. Gymnosophists* there stood in boiling hot gravel from morning till evening and stared at the sun without hurting their eyes. Other inhabitants had their feet turned backwards and grew eight toes on each foot, while others had hounds' heads and spoke only like hounds barking; still others had no mouths and subsisted only on the odor of such things as flowers and woodapples. See Prester John. (Bibliog. 18)

Ingham, Oliver (1287-1343), English knight from Norfolk* who at age 33 in 1320 was appointed to assemble the horse and footsoldiers in Wiltshire and Berkshire against the forces of Thomas,* earl of Lancaster. Actively supporting King Edward II* against this rebel again in 1322, he was appointed as keeper of the county of Chester and the lands of Flint with the power of imprisonment accompanying that appointment; he also was ordered to accept delivery of all the castles+ and fortalices* in those counties. A few days later, he was ordered to raise forces in County Lancaster to go against the rebels, but not to interfere with the powers granted to Sir Andrew Harcla.* On March 3, 1322, he was appointed to take into the king's hands all the castles, lands, and goods of the earl Thomas of Lancaster in County Lancaster, the Marches of Wales,* and then on March 12, to take also the lands of Robert Holand* in County Chester.* He was one of the 12 counsellors for the young Prince Edward* in 1326, and yet three years later he was one of the principals in the last plot of Roger Mortimer, earl of March. On October 18, 1330, young King Edward III* entered Nottingham castle at night, and captured Mortimer, Oliver Ingham and other prisoners and sent them to London. Even though Oliver's lands and goods were forfeit for that action, in consideration for his service to King Edward II, he was pardoned and restored to his property in 1330, and served as seneschal+ of Aquitaine* for ten years with distinction, and died in 1343. (Bibliog. 47)

Innocent II, pope (1130-1143). As cardinal on diplomatic missions to England and France, he became acquainted with the leaders of the monastic movements of the Cluniacs and the Cistercians. In 1130, he was elected to the papacy by a minority of the cardinals, but because he failed to be accepted by Rome, he returned to France where he sought and received the support of Peter the Venerable, abbot of Cluny, Bernard of Clairvaux,* and King Louis VI.* With Bernard's support, he gained the endorsement of King Henry I* of England and Lothaire* of Germany so that he was able to ascend the throne in 1134. (Bibliog. 68)

Innocent III, pope (1198-1216). A member of one of the highest ranking Italian noble families, the Segni, he studied theology and law and became a cardinal at age 30, and pope at age 38. As a supporter of the theory of papal supremacy at a time when the imperial throne of the Holy Roman Empire was being disputed, he involved himself in the politics of Sicily because he was the suzerain+ of the kingdom of Sicily and thereby tutor of its infant king, Frederick II. He also intervened in the imperial elections, opposing Philip of Swabia,* head of the Hohenstaufen* dynasty, in favor of Otto of Brunswick, the Welf (Guelph*) leader, on his belief that, although the princes of Germany had the right to elect the emperor, the pope had the right to determine the worthiness of the candidate because the coronation and investiture of the emperor lay in the hands of the pope. He also had had an interest in the crusades,+ proclaiming a crusade (the fourth) in the first year of his pontificate and finally organizing it in 1204. Further, in his fervent efforts to combat heresies of all kinds, he called for a crusade against the heretics in southern France that resulted in the Albigensian+ crusade. In 1215, he summoned the Fourth Lateran Council which brought him the support of the laity and clergy of the world, and revealed the broad sphere of his concerns. (Bibliog. 68, 98)

inquest, method of governmental investigation in Europe by which royal officials conducted inquiries into the revenues owed to the king. Although the system was begun in Normandy* in the 11th century, its most famous example occurred in England when William I* ordered the inquest that led to the writing of the *Domesday Book** (1081-1087). Later English King Henry II* legalized that procedure as part of the judicial administration carried out by a sheriff+ in the presence of a jury. One of his most famous inquests, the Inquest of Sheriffs+ (1170), called on the counties+ to provide evidence about how the sheriffs had been performing their duties, and then using that evidence to rectify their abuses and to bring the powerful sheriffs into line. (Bibliog. 98, 228)

Inquisition, "Holy Office" of the church which enforced the old belief that the church was bound to correct all immorality or misbelief. Basically, it created a system of spying, denunciation and terror that extinguished the culture and wealth of the lands in the south of France after the Albigensian crusade+ had almost destroyed the physical area in 1209-1213. Instigated at the urging of St. Dominic and Blanche of Castile,* the Holy Office of the Inquisition was based on the theory that a suspected man was to be hunted down and trapped like a wild beast because his guilt was to be assumed. Then his judges were directed to obtain enough evidence to warrant the extortion of a confession from him but without allowing him any means of defense. Because these were done in secret, they deprived the accused of one of the great safeguards accorded him under Roman law: that any accuser who failed to prove his accusation was to be subjected to the same punishment as the accused was forced to endure. Staffed by high ecclesiastical officers who tried to curb the excesses of their representatives, this high office authorized atrocities in the name of righteousness. Young King Louis IX* (St. Louis) of France supported and regulated the Holy Office by means of the statute *Cupientes*, and supplied it with funds out of the royal treasury. He was fond of ordering the lips and noses burned off people who were guilty of blasphemous language. Further, he felt that only clerics should dispute with heretics; others should treat them with a sword, which they "should plunge well into the belly as far as it will go." (Bibliog. 25, 133)

Inverness castle,+ fortress erected on a hilltop in this Pictish capital of Scotland.* By the 11th century, a royal castle had been erected there. To avenge his father King Duncan, murdered by MacBeth in his castle of Inverness in 1039, Malcolm III of Canmore razed the castle of MacBeth and erected another nearby in 1057 on a location known as Castle Hill. This stronghold was captured by troops of Edward I* in 1303, but was recaptured by Robert the Bruce* in 1310. (Bibliog. 192)

Ipomedon, Ipomadon, French romance written between 1174 and 1191 by Hue de Roteland. Ipomedon, a prince of Apulia, wooed the princess Fiere of Calabria by showing his prowess in numerous ways, and finally won her after his performance in a three-day tournament.+ Hue included in this work elements from *lais** of Marie de France*; a version of the

Tristan* theme; *Le Bel Inconnu* (*Guinglain**) of Renaut de Beaujeu, and its Middle English* version, *Libeaus Desconus*.* Other versions of the story appeared in *Carduino*, an Italian poem ascribed to Antonio Pucci (c. 1375); in Book 7 of Malory's *Morte D'Arthur**; in the romances of Thebes, Troy, and Eneas, and Chrétien de Troyes' *Cligés*.* Similar elements were found in the Middle High German* *Wigalois* by Wirnt von Gravenburg. (ed. Kolbing-Koschwitz, Breslau, 1889; English version: ed. Henry Weber, *Metrical Romances of the 13th, 14th, and 15th Centuries*, Edinburgh: A. Constable, 1810, II, 281 ff.; ed. David Anderson, DIA 29:3968A-3969A, Davis, CA: U. C. Davis, 1969) (Bibliog. 106, 202)

Ireland, island lying west of Britain and separated from it by the Irish Sea. Populated by Celtic or Gaelic tribes, it was organized by clans who established five kingdoms in the country: Ulster, Northern Leinster, Southern Leinster, Munster, and Connaught. In 432, St. Patrick, a student from Gaul, was sent to Ireland to preach Christianity. He won the support of the royal families, converted the country, and founded many monasteries organized on tribal and regional lines. Constant warfare between chieftains led some Irish to emigrate to Scotland and imposed their rule over the Picts. However, Norsemen began to attack Ireland and gain important victories. The Danes conquered the south and the Norsemen the rest, establishing Dublin as their capital. Defeating the Norse at Clontarf in 1014, the Celts freed Ireland from Norse domination with the exception of the Norse enclave at Dublin. The ancient kingdoms were restored and their centers moved to new cities established by the Norse: Cork, Limerick, and Waterford. Constant warfare and feuds between the princes of the various royal families led Henry II* of England to intervene. In 1170 he obtained papal benediction for his Irish expedition. Irish opposition united under the kings of Connaught, but Henry prevailed and established a feudal regime by creating royal demesnes+ in and around Dublin, and granting the rest of the country to English barons. (See Clare; Pembroke.) Under Prince John,* English dominion increased and a new nobility was formed under the leadership of Anglo-Irish families who imposed a severely repressive policy. Even though Edward I* created a central government controlled by a viceroy sitting in Dublin, the English could not destroy the Irish social structure of clans and tribes. These continually erupted into revolt, particularly during the reign of Edward II.* England's attempts to suppress such revolts led to the establishment of three distinct societies in Ireland: the English high nobility who ruled vast estates and were supported by an English urban middle class, the Anglo-Irish emerging from the integration of the lesser nobility with the Irish privileged class, and the Irish serfs or peasantry. Robert de Vere,* close friend of King Richard II,* was created marquess+ of Dublin in 1385, and a year later was appointed duke of Ireland, the first such titles bestowed by the English monarchy for its appointed rulers of Ireland. (Bibliog. 47, 68, 98)

Iron Arm. See William of Hauteville.

Ironsyde, Red Knight of the Red Lands, and Gareth's* chief adversary in the rescue of Lyones in Malory's *Morte D'Arthur*.* He became a knight of the Round Table* after Gareth defeated him. (Bibliog. 145)

Isaac II, Angelus, emperor of Byzantium (1185-1195 and 1203-1204). When Frederick I,* Barbarossa sought and obtained permission to lead his troops through Byzantium on the third crusade,+ Isaac, secretly seeking an alliance with Saladin,* tried every trick he could to block their way. Only Frederick's force of arms cleared their passage and forced Isaac to abide by his agreements. Deposed and blinded in 1195, he was imprisoned by his brother Alexius* for eight years. Because his mind and body had been so enfeebled by the imprisonment, he survived for only six months when he was restored to the throne in 1204. He was one of the weakest and most vicious princes ever to rule Byzantium. He was vain, superstitious, and sensual, surrounding himself with all the pleasures the great wealth of the throne could provide. (Bibliog. 68, 172)

Isabelle of Hainaut (1170-1190), queen of Philip II,* Augustus, of France (1180-1190). As the daughter of Baldwin V of Hainaut, she was married to Philip II in 1180, and brought the province of Artois* to him as her dowry. She failed to win the affection of her husband, and in his war against Flanders* in 1184, he became so angered at Baldwin for supporting his enemies that he called a council to repudiate her, but was dissuaded from so severe an action. She died in 1190 giving birth to Louis, later Louis VIII.* (Bibliog. 68)

Isidore Hispalensis. See Isidore of Seville.

Isidore of Seville, one of the most influential writers of the early portion of the Middle Ages, flourishing in the latter part of the 6th and early part of the 7th century. He was the son of a wealthy and distinguished native of Cartagena named Severianus, and his elder brother, Leander, was bishop of Seville. He succeeded his brother to the bishopric early in the 7th century and became highly known and respected both for his government of his see and for his voluminous writings on theological, historic and scientific matters. His most elaborate writing, *Etymologiarum Libri*, sometimes called *Origines*, was an encyclopedic presentation of the sum of knowledge of the age on all branches of scientific research. Book 5 contained a sketch of universal history; book 9 of language. (portions tr. Ernest Brehaut, *Encyclopedist of the Dark Ages*, New York, 1912) (Bibliog. 68)

Islam, name given to the religion founded by Mohammed, counting its beginning from the Hegira* in A. D. 622. Its basic foundation was the revelation of the Word of God to the Prophet, as expressed in the Koran. Such revelation implied the transmission of the divine will which was sovereign and must be executed by the faithful, who were called Muslims* (Moslems). Its central doctrine was the absolute unity of God (Allah) who had predestined all things. Several times Allah had sent prophets such as Moses, Jesus Christ, and Mohammed to reveal His word. Mohammed was the most important prophet. Every Muslim recited the profession of his faith in God and Mohammed, His prophet; recited ritual prayers five times daily; fasted during the month of Ramadan, and undertook a pilgrimage to Mecca at least once during his lifetime. (Bibliog. 98)

Isle Saint Sanson, island in the Scilly group off the southwest coast of England on which the combat between Tristan and Morholt* took place in *Tristan*. (Bibliog. 241)

Isles, Lord of the, designation from the 12th century of the lordship of the islands off the coast of Scotland.* The first lord was Somerled I (d. 1164), thane of Argyll, a Celtic chief who was said to have acquired the western islands,and assumed the designation of king of the Isles. His son, Reynold (Reginald) (d. 1207), the second lord, was called king of the Isles, and lord of Argyll and Kintyre. In a charter to the monastery at Paisley, which gave eight cows and two pennies for one year, and one penny in perpetuity from every house in his territories from which smoke issued, he was called lord of the Isles. His son, Donald, after whom the clan Donald was named, the third lord of the Isles, was a turbulent ruler; he continued the grant to Paisley and died around 1250. He was succeeded by his son, Angus Mor (d. 1296), fourth lord of the Isles, and the first to acknowledge the subjection of the Isles to the king of Scotland. His son and heir, Alexander, the fifth lord of the Isles, fought against Robert Bruce,* and was appointed admiral* of the Isles under the English crown.

Alexander's brother and heir, Angus Og, the sixth lord of the Isles, fought for Robert Bruce at Bannock Burn* in 1314, and died at Finlaggan castle in Isla in 1330. His son and heir, John, seventh lord of the Isles, supported Baliol,* but subsequently submitted to King David II.* He fought beside the French at Poitiers* in 1356 where he was captured. He married Margaret Stewart, daughter of King Robert II* of Scotland, and became the father of Donald, eighth lord of the Isles, who married Mary, countess of Ross, the daughter of Sir Walter Leslie and Eupheme, countess of Ross. In right of this marriage, Donald claimed the earldom of Ross, and the battle of Harlaw was fought in 1411 as a consequence of that claim. (Bibliog. 47)

Isolde, la Belle, daughter of Anguysh, king of Ireland in legend. She married King Mark* and became the beloved paramour of Tristan* in *Tristan.* (Bibliog. 97)

Isolde Le Blanche Mains, Isolde with the White Hands, daughter of King Howel of Brittany, married Tristan after he was expelled from King Mark's* court in Cornwall, and falsely reported to him as he lay dying that the color of Isolde la Belle's* ship's sails was black. (Bibliog. 97)

Istria, margraviate+ of Austria* in the peninsula bounded by Trieste and stretching between the Gulf of Trieste and the Gulf of Quarnaro in the Adriatic Sea. It was pillaged by the Longobardi and the Goths, and later was annexed to the Frankish kingdom by Pepin in 789. About the middle of the 10th century it fell into the hands of the dukes of Carinthia. From there, it fell successively into the hands of the dukes of Meron, the duke of Bavaria,* and the patriarch of Aquilea, ending finally under the control of the republic of Venice. (Bibliog. 68)

Italy, kingdom on the Italian peninsula which did not include the entire peninsula. Below its southern border reaching a little below Rome lay the separate principalities of Benevento and Salerno, and the lands belonging to the eastern empire. The Italian kingdom itself included Lombardy, Liguria, Friuli (including Trent and Istria), Tuscany, Romagna (or the Exarchate of Ravenna), Spoleto and Rome itself. Its capital moved from the old Lombard capital of Pavia to Milan which became the crowning place for kings of Italy. Desiderius (or Didier), the last king of the Lombards, was captured by Charlemagne* in 774 and the kingdom of Italy was united, first to France, and afterwards to the empire, until 888, when it separated on the death of Charles the Simple, and was ruled by Berenger,* duke of Friuli. He was deposed in 900 by Louis III,* the Blind, but restored in 905. In 962, the Emperor Otto reduced Italy and reunited it with the German Empire. Under the Saxon and Frankish emperors, the old Lombard names of Austria and Neustria disappeared. Several marches lay along the Burgundian frontier: Savona on the coast; Ivrea among the mountains to the northwest; and between them Montferrat, Vasto, and Susa whose princes, as special guardians of the passage between the two kingdoms, bore the title of marquess of Italy. During the centuries, the marquesses of Montferrat* played important roles as feudal princes quite apart from the lords of the cities growing in importance in the area. In the northeast corner of the territory were the great marches of Verona, Friuli, Trent, the marchland between Verona and Bavaria, and the peninsula of Istria on the Slavonic side of the Adriatic Sea. Between the border districts lay the central land of Lombardy. There, by the middle of the 12th century, every city had become a separate commonwealth, owing only nominal allegiance to the German emperor. The Guelph* cities opposed him; the Ghibelline* cities welcomed him, but both were practically independent. This attitude led to the long wars between the Swabian emperors and the Italian cities of the 12th and 13th centuries. Around the Guelphic Milan and the Ghibelline Pavia gathered such cities as Como, Bergamo, Brescia, Lodi, Cremona, Piacenza and Parma. Verona and Padua became the seats of commonwealths and then of tyrants. Trent to the north split off and became an ecclesiastical principality under the German suzerainty. The patriarchs of Aquileia grew into powerful princes at the northeast corner of the Adriatic, while within the marches of Verona the lords of Romano and the more important marquesses of Este* grew strong. Romano produced its famous tyrant Eccelino during the reign of Frederick II,* and the marquesses of Este, kinsmen of the great Saxon dukes, came to rank among the chief Italian princes.

Further to the south, Pisa, one of the commonwealths of Tuscany, stood apart from the rest as one of the great commercial and maritime states of Europe. In the 11th century, it won back the island of Sardinia from the Saracens,* and became a power which colonized and conquered beyond the seas. Three additional great commonwealths grew so powerful that eventually they divided the land between them: Lucca, Siena, and Florence. Genoa, beyond the borders of Tuscany, after long disputes with Pisa, won possession of Corsica. Perugia, as a commonwealth and tyranny in the center of Italy, grew to eminence among Italian cities. And of course, there was Rome itself, whose bishops claimed much temporal power, and the disputes between the church and the emperor occupied much of the next few centuries. When Rudolf of

Hapsburg granted power to the popes in 1278, a distinction was drawn between imperial and papal territory in Italy. While certain princes and commonwealths still acknowledged at least the nominal superiority of the emperor, others felt that they stood in the same relationship with the pope. By this time, the marquesses of Montferrat had claimed the crown of Jerusalem and had worn the crown of Thessalonica. On each side of this principality developed two great powers, the duchy of Milan and the principality of Venice. Milan, like most other Italian cities, came under the influence of party leaders who grew first into tyrants and then into acknowledged sovereigns. After the short domination of the Della Torre, Milan came under the influence of the Visconti* whose rule finally was solidly established when the coming of the Emperor Henry VII* strengthened the rule of the lords of cities throughout Italy. At the end of the 14th century, their informal lordship was changed by royal grant from the emperor Wenceslaus into an acknowledged duchy of the empire. Their dominion included all the great cities of Lombardy, especially those of the Lombard League* who had united against the Swabian emperors. Pavia, ancient rival of Milan, formed into a county, but the duchy granted by the emperor to Gian-Galeazzo stretched far on both sides of the lake of Garda. It took in the mountain lands which later became the two Alpine confederations; it included Parma, Piacenza and Reggio south of the Po River, and Verona and all the old Austrian Venetian land. Besides all of this, Padua, Bologna, and even Genoa and Pisa passed under the control of the Visconti. On the death of Gian-Galleazzo in 1402, the duchy of Milan and county of Pavia separated, and the restored duchy never again rose to its eminence.

To the west, in Tuscany, political circumstances differed. There smaller cities grouped under the power of the larger ones. Lucca had a great power in the 14th century under the tyrant Castruccio, but after his fall, it declined in importance. Meanwhile, Pisa kept her former maritime greatness, and her continuing rivalry with Genoa spurred that city to even greater political ambitions so that finally, she established dominion over the coast on both sides of her. Pisa fell from strength and her control over Sardinia passed to become a kingdom of the house of Aragon, and she herself passed into the dominion of Florence, just then rising to prominence. (Bibliog. 79, 164)

Itinerarium Peregrinorum et Gesta Regis Ricardi (1187-1199), history of the third crusade+ under Richard I,* long thought to have been written by Geoffrey de Vinsauf. It closely resembled the work of Ambroise.* (tr. "Itinerary of Richard I," *Chronicles of the Crusades,*

London: Bohn's Antiquarian Library, 1848; K. Fenwick, *The Third Crusade,* London: Folio Society, 1958) (Bibliog. 98)

Ivry-la-Bataille,   Norman   border   fortress   situated   in   the *arrondissement* (district) of Evreux on the River Eure. Ancelin Goel, son and heir of Robert d'Ivry, took part in William I's* invasion of the French Vexin* in July 1087, and destroyed the vineyards around Mantes. He built a strongly fortified castle+ at Breval. In 1089, he took the castle of Ivry by strategy from William de Breteuil, and delivered it to Duke Robert II,* Curthose. De Breteuil redeemed it from the duke, and deprived Ancelin of the provostship of Ivry.   Ancelin then captured de Breteuil and imprisoned him at Breval until be bought his freedom for money, cession of the castle to Ivry and marriage of his daughter Isabel to Ancelin. After William de Breteuil tried unsuccessfully   to   recapture   the   castle   in   the   following   year,   he appealed first to the king of France and then to the duke of Normandy for assistance. The duke came to his aid by summoning the *levée en masse+* on the surrounding population, and besieging Ancelin at Breval. Ancelin surrendered and returned the castle to William before he died in 1117. (Bibliog. 47)

Iwein, model Arthurian romance in Middle High German* literature; this was Hartmann von Aue's* adaptation of Chrétien de Troyes'* *Ywain* or *Chevalier au Lion.** It was Hartmann's major achievement. Here, *Iwein* was the reverse of *Erec**: instead of neglecting his knightly duty, Iwein neglected his wife. (ed. G. F. Benecke and K. Lachmann, 6th ed.; rev. L. Wolff, 1959) See also *Yvain.* (Bibliog. 235)

J

Jaffa (Joppa), battle of (August 5, 1192), confrontation between Saladin's* forces and the crusaders led by Richard I.* The Muslims* were on the verge of capturing the newly fortified town of Jaffa when Richard arrived by sea with eight vessels but only a few men. Learning that these reinforcements were sparse, the Muslims rushed the crusaders' camp at daybreak to surprise them. Warned in time, Richard composed his small force of 55 knights and 2,000 men-at-arms into a front line of infantry armed with spears backed up by the crossbowmen from the Genoese and Pisan vessels which had brought Richard's forces. Kneeling with one knee in the sand, the infantrymen levelled their spears at the height of a horse's breast. Behind them stood the crossbowmen, one in each interval between two spearmen, backed up by another man whose duty was to load and hand him a crossbow. This way there was no intermission in the discharge of missiles. The Saracens never dared cross the spears. They did some damage with their own arrows but suffered far more from the constant barrage from the crusaders. When they were in disorder, Richard and five mounted knights charged them, and cut right through them. He wheeled and charged back toward his camp, saving by his own valor the earl of Leicester and Ralph de Mauleon who had been surrounded and nearly captured. When Richard brought up reserves from the galleys, the enemy fled, leaving 700 men and 1,500 horses dead on the field. Of the crusaders, many had been wounded but only two had been killed. (Bibliog. 166, 195, 201)

Jakemon Sakesap, French writer of the late 13th century who treated the theme of the *herzmaere* in his romance *Le Châtelain de Coucy* in which his hero was the *châtelain* Renaut de Coucy, hence his title. (ed. Craplet, Paris, 1829) (Bibliog. 231)

James I of Aragon, one of the two men who carried through the decisive efforts to reconquer from the Muslims* the greater part of southern and eastern Spain between the early part of the 11th century and the middle of the 13th century. The other leader was Ferdinand III of Castile.* (Bibliog. 118)

Jarl. See Caithness.

Jaufre, Arthurian romance written at the end of the 12th century in the *langue d'oc*+ by a poet who lived near Catalonia or just north of the Pyrenees Mountains. It described how the hero, Jaufre, son of Dovon, set out from Arthur's* court for the court of Monbrun where he became involved in two series of events. First he responded to lamentations from Melion de Monmelior for injuries inflicted on him by Taulat de Rogimon, a knight who had previously insulted Arthur in this romance. This second injury gave Jaufre a double debt to settle with Taulat. While there, Jaufre also met the mistress of the castle of Monbrun, and their mutual attraction led to a union. (ed. C. Brunel, Paris: *SATF*, 1943) (Bibliog. 10)

Jedburgh castle,+ bulwark in Roxburghshire, Scotland, which was occupied many times by the English. It was one of the five fortresses ceded to the English under the Treaty of Falaise,* in 1174 to provide security for the ransom of King William the Lion.* Eventually, it became a royal Scottish residence. King Malcolm IV died there in 1195, and Alexander III* was married to Jolande, daughter of the count of Dreux, in Jedburgh abbey in 1285. It finally was demolished by the Scots early in the 15th century because they had found the frequent English occupations to be embarrassing. (Bibliog. 223)

Jehan de Lanson, chanson de geste* from the 13th century. Its protagonist was Ganelon's* nephew who harassed the *douzepeers** in Italy. Material in this work was similar to episodes in *Renaut de Montauban* (see *Four Sons of Aymon).* (ed. John V. Myers, Chapel Hill, NC: *UNCSRLL* #53, 1965) (Bibliog. 106)

Jehan et Blonde, French romance written between 1270 and 1280 by Philippe de Remi,* Sire de Beaumanoir. This story described the adventures of young Jehan de Dammartin, oldest son of an elderly knight who went to England to seek his fortune, and entered the service of the count of Oxford. There he fell in love with Blonde, the count's daughter. On his father's death he returned to France, and went to Paris to pay homage to the French king, and to enroll his three brothers in the king's service. He returned to Oxford to find that Blonde had been promised to the count of Gloucester. Jehan eloped with her, and eventually was knighted by the king of France. (ed. H.

Suchier, *Philippe de Beaumanoir, Oeuvres poètique,* Paris: *SATF,* 1884-1885) (Bibliog. 106, 127)

Jenghiz (Genghis) Khan (1162-1227), Mongol emperor. Born while his father was absent on a successful campaign against a Tatar chieftain, Temuchin, he held in his newborn fist a clot of coagulated blood like a red stone when his father finally saw him. His superstitious father believed that the clot referred to his victory over the Tatar chieftain, so he named his son Temuchin. He was only 13 when his father died, leaving him the difficult task of keeping the allegiance of tribes which only his father's iron rule had held. He held some of the tribes under him, and warred with his neighbors until 1206 when he felt strong enough to proclaim himself ruler of an empire. At that time, he summoned the notables of his kingdom to a meeting and at their unanimous request adopted the name of Jenghiz Khan or "perfect warrior." Defeating one enemy on the Mongolian steppes, he began to expand his territory by adding city after city and province after province in China. He was merciless and ruthless, not hesitating to destroy captured cities completely. He sent a message to Mahommed, the shah of Khwarizm, to whose border in the west his control now reached, that he had conquered all of China and the Turkish nations north of it, and that now he needed no other lands. This peaceful message was received by the shah, but a governor under him seized and put to death traders sent by Jenghiz to open up trade routes. When Jenghiz demanded the extradition of the offending governor, the shah beheaded the Mongol ambassador and sent the others back without their beards. Such an insult made war inevitable, and in 1219, Jenghiz set out on an four-pronged invasion that reached as far west as Samarkand. He continued his merciless ways. Once, when the citizens of Herat deposed the governor set over them by Jenghiz's youngest son, Tule, and set up their own governor, Jenghiz punished their rebellious act by a six-month siege which captured the city, followed by a week of rape, pillage, and the massacre of one million six hundred thousand people. He fell ill and died in 1227 on a campaign in western China. By the terms of his will, his son Ogotai was appointed his successor, but so essential was it that Ogotai be proclaimed before Jenghiz's death become known that as the funeral procession moved to his burial place, they killed everyone they met. Jenghiz was one of the greatest conquerors the world ever knew, establishing his empire from the China Sea to the Dnieper River and the western shore of the Caspian Sea. (Bibliog. 68)

Jerusalem, Chanson de, *chanson de geste** written by Richard le

Pèlerin* about the first crusade.+ This original version was lost, but the work survived in a version by Graindor de Douai* between 1180 and 1200. It related the story of the capture of Jerusalem and the election of Godfrey de Bouillon* as king of Jerusalem. (ed. C. Hippeau, Paris, 1868) (Bibliog. 106)

Joan, name given to a female pope who, under the title of John VII or John VIII, was said to have occupied the papal throne between Leo IV (847-855) and Benedict III (855-858). As a young woman, she supposedly fell in love with a young Benedictine monk, and to be near him, assumed male monastic attire and lived for some time with him at the monastery of Fulda. Her lover died while they were pursing their studies together at Athens. After his death, she continued her studies in Rome in male guise, and became so successful a professor there that the cardinals on one vote elected her as pope. She performed her duties as pope admirably until she suddenly gave birth to a male child during a procession to the Lateran palace. She was said to have died either in this childbirth or was stoned to death. Her story was first mentioned by Stephen de Bourbon who died in 1261, and who said he took the information from the lost chronicle of the Dominican, Jean de Mailly. (Bibliog. 68)

Joan of Kent (1328-1385), "The Fair Maid of Kent"; wife of Edward the Black Prince* and mother of King Richard II.* She was declared by Jean Froissart* to be "the most beautiful woman in the whole realm of England, and the most attractive." Her father was half-brother of Edward II,* so that when in Joan's infancy, Roger Mortimer and Queen Isabelle* persuaded her father, Edmund,* earl of Kent that his half-brother was still alive, Edmund mistakenly allied himself with a non-existent rescue operation. As a result, in March 1330, he was arrested on a charge of conspiracy against his young nephew, King Edward III,* and was summarily beheaded. Joan and her brother, Edmund, and their mother were arrested and imprisoned at Salisbury Castle. Nine months after her father's execution, the verdict against him was reversed and Joan was adopted by the sympathetic Queen Philippa,* and spent her childhood at the royal manor of Woodstock under the tutelage of Sir William and Catherine Montague, soon to become the earl and countess of Salisbury.* Among her playmates were two of her future husbands: Edward, Prince of Wales, her third, and William Montague, her second. Her first husband, Thomas Holand,* was eight years older than she. She was fascinated by Thomas and he made a contract of marriage with her, but left for continental military service before the marriage could be solemnized. While Thomas was gone, William

Montague entered into a marriage contract with her in 1340. When Holand returned, he challenged that marriage, and petitioned Pope Clement VI to restore his marriage rights. In 1349, the pope ruled in his favor—an action which the chroniclers of the time mistakenly viewed as a divorce from Salisbury based on Joan's infidelity with Holand. She remained with Holand until his death in 1360, bearing him three sons and two daughters. Within three months of being widowed, she again was engaged, this time to her second cousin, Edward, the Black Prince. That marriage took place on October 6, 1361, after Edward had received a papal dispensation to marry her. They moved to France where Edward was the governor of Aquitaine until his death in 1376. There Joan presented him with two sons, Edward who died at age 6, and Richard of Bordeaux who, in 1377, became king of England on the death of his grandfather, Edward III. Her garter became the symbol for the most famous order of chivalry.+ See Order of the Garter. (Bibliog. 84)

Joceran, Jozeran de Provence, one of Charlemagne's* chief barons in the *Song of Roland,** who shared, with Duke Naimes, the duty of forming the Frankish army into ten divisions; he shared with Godselm the command of the Poitevins and Auvergnais. (Bibliog. 210)

John II, the Good (1319-1364), king of France (1350-1364). As son of Philip VI* of Valois, he was educated in the spirit of knighthood and chivalry rather than as a king. He ascended the throne with the intention of erasing the defeats suffered by his father over the past decade, but because he inherited an empty treasury, he had no money with which to pay an army. But he was impetuous and impolitic, never choosing the wiser of alternatives. His first act as king was to execute the constable of France, the comte d'Eu,* and sixteenth *comte* de Guines, a man well loved by high and low alike. He had been captured by the English at Caen in 1345, but had been unable to raise the ransom+ demanded by Edward III,* for that king ignored the chivalric principle about ransoms that set the figure at an amount which would not ruin the captive nor be in excess of one year's income. Guines finally gained his liberty by ceding to the English king his strategic castle and county of Guines which adjoined Calais. For that action, John II considered him a traitor and ordered his instant execution with no trial or public procedure of any kind. This alienated the French nobility. He angered them even further when he immediately appointed his relative and favorite, Charles d'Espagne, to be the constable. That position had considerable importance as being the military command second only to the king, and on its holder bestowed many lucrative perquisites attached to building up the armed forces; Charles abused the privileges. John was brave in battle but not a good captain. His subjects called him "the Good" seemingly because of his sense of chivalric honor. To rebuild his army, John published the Royal Ordinance of 1351 to introduce the principles of dependability and command. This document raised the pay of soldiers to 40 sous+ (2 livres) a day for a banneret, 20 sous for a knight, 10 for a squire, 5 for a valet, 3 for a footsoldier, and 2 1/2 for an armor-bearer or other attendant. (See knight+; sergeant+; soldier+) Of more significance was the provision in this ordinance which prevented independent withdrawal from the battlefield. This new provision required every man in the army to be subordinate to some captain, and to take an oath not to leave the company of their captain without an order. That reversed the old feudal concept of departure from the battlefield at will when military wisdom seemed to dictate, or when one's leader had fallen. Defeated and captured by Edward the Black Prince* at the battle of Poitiers* in 1356, he was taken back to England and imprisoned in the Tower of London until his ransom of 4 million gold ecus could be paid. His son, Louis, duke of Anjou,* was one of the hostages+ sent to England as guarantee for the payment of the full ransom. See spoils of war.+ When Louis broke his parole and fled to France, John considered his son's act as a felony upon the crown, and he insisted on returning to prison in England until the full ransom was paid. He fell ill in London two months after returning, and died in April at age 45. King Edward III gave him a huge funeral service at St. Paul's during which 4,000 torches each 12 feet high, and 3,000 candles each weighing 10 pounds were consumed. (Bibliog. 124, 199, 223)

John II Comnenos (1088-1143), Byzantine emperor. He was the eldest son of the Emperor Alexius whom he succeeded to the throne in 1118. A mild ruler, he did little to rid his government of the excesses and abuses he inherited. His subsequent successes against the Hungarians, Serbs, and Turks won for him the admiration of his soldiers, but did not stabilize his kingdom. He spent much of his reign fighting Roger II of Sicily who was trying to establish his dominance over Albania, Epirus and the islands in the Ionian Sea. He was killed accidentally during a boar hunt on Mount Taurus on April 8, 1143. (Bibliog. 68)

John, bishop of Lisieux, advisor to English King Henry I.* Son of Norman the Dean, he was already known to the king when he came to England as a refuge in 1103, and may have made Henry's acquaintance possibly while he was lord of Domfront. Between 1103 and 1107, he was one of Henry's principal advisors, and after that was in touch with Roger of Salisbury, for some of the ideas from which the exchequer evolved seemed to have been worked out between them. In 1107, when he became archbishop of Liseux, he seemed to have a position in the administration of Normandy similar to that held by Roger of Salisbury in England. He accepted King Stephen's* rule, and died shortly after being forced to give up his cathedral city to Geoffrey Plantagenet* in 1141. (Bibliog. 130)

John de Beauchamp. Baron of Kidderminster. See Beauchamp, John. (Bibliog. 105)

John Lackland (1167-1216), king of England (1199-1216). Youngest son of Henry II* and Eleanor of Aquiatine,* he was nicknamed Lackland by his father who had divided his kingdom among his elder sons. Although he was his father's favorite, and was educated by Ranulph de Granville,* he developed none of the chivalric virtues which feudal monarchs were expected to possess. True, he was imaginative and ingenious, but he loved to dissemble, and to create complicated and twisted maneuvers; he was coarse and vulgar; he seduced ladies of his court with no poetry or charm, and considered tournaments a waste of manpower and a dangerous potential source of trouble. And finally, he had a complete lack of military ability or interest in military affairs; he led troops only once in his entire reign—to relieve Mirabeau* castle in 1202, and even then others were the real leaders in that battle. During his reign, he spent his energies and intelligence in developing his royal authority in England. His characteristics began to be formed early. When he was five years old, he was contracted to marry Alice, daughter and heir of Humbert III, count of Maurienne with the provision that if Humbert had no sons, John would inherit the kingdom, but if Humbert did have sons, John was to inherit money. That marriage never took place. His father promised him castles+ and the districts of Chinon, Loudon, and Mirebeau which already were the possessions of Henry's eldest son, young Henry,* who refused to give any of them up, and a war between the king and his sons ensued. In the end, Henry gave John instead certain castles in Normandy,* Anjou,* Touraine, and Maine.* When he was nine, Isabelle of Gloucester,* more commonly called Hawise or Avice, was given to him in marriage by her father William of Gloucester, and he became the heir to lands in western England and Glamorgan in Wales. Only a year later, when John was ten, Henry declared him king of Ireland, and appointed Hugh de Lacy as his viceroy. On the death in 1183 of young Henry, the king tried to persuade his oldest surviving son and heir to the

throne, Richard,* to surrender Aquitaine to John. When Richard re-
fused, Henry urged John and his other brother Geoffrey* to war on
Richard, but the king stopped the conflict and summoned them all to
England for a reconciliation.

Henry II knighted John when he was 18, and sent him to govern
Ireland. John immediately alienated the Irish people, and within a
year was in such a weak position that the king recalled him to
England. In 1187, he accompanied Henry II to France; his brother
Richard, thinking Henry still sought the Aquitaine, allied himself
with the French king, Philip II.* John plotted behind his father's
back, and the realization of that treachery hastened Henry II's death
in 1189. With his brother Richard I* on the throne, John married
Isabelle of Gloucester in 1189 and received the counties of Mortain*
in Normandy and Derby, Somerset, Devon and Cornwall and several
castles in England. He returned to England in 1191 and during the
king's absence on the crusade,+ John led the opposition to the lord
chancellor William Longchamps,* and had himself declared heir
apparent* to the throne. Then, on the news of Richard's captivity by
the German emperor, John rendered homage to the French king for his
continental dominions in 1193, and tried to have Richard's captivity
prolonged. For that treasonous act, Richard, on his release, deprived
John of his English holdings, but through the efforts of his mother,
Eleanor, restored them to him.

On Richard's death in 1199, John declared himself the king,
but was resisted by the people of Brittany who were adherents to the
claim of Arthur,* son of John's deceased older brother, Geoffrey* of
Brittany. Because Henry II had been unsuccessful in establishing the
rule of primogeniture+ in England as it was in France, on Richard's
death three considerations instead of just one and the right of the
eldest son entered the decision about the succession: the law of inheritance, the wishes of the barons and great officers of the realm,
and the desires of the late king. Because the Angevin empire was merely a collection of feudal principalities, each with its own law of
succession, the question of Richard's successor was complex. The
English barons knew John who was still in his early thirties; Arthur
was an unknown boy of twelve who had been reared by the nobles of
France. Richard may or may not have declared for John in his last dying moments, but chroniclers recounting his death maintain that he
did. In any event, John was crowned in 1199, and made a treaty with
the king of France whereby Philip II acknowledged him as king of
England and duke of Normandy. After John captured Arthur in 1203,
young Arthur disappeared, presumably killed by his ambitious uncle,
John. He had divorced his wife in 1200, but kept her inheritance, and

then married Isabelle of Angoulême* who already was betrothed to Hugh le Brun. Her relatives proceeded against him, and as a result he was forced to forfeit all his French fiefs for refusing to submit to his suzerain Philip II about this claim of Hugh's against him. He then lost to the king of France all of Normandy and most of Poitou in 1204-1205. When he refused to accept Stephen Langton as archbishop* of Canterbury, all of England was laid under an interdict in 1208. In retaliation, John seized the property of the bishops who had published the interdict. In the following year, he went to Ireland to establish English supremacy, and overthrew the power of the de Lacys in 1210. John continued to oppress and anger the English barons by such actions as allying himself with the counts of Flanders* and Boulogne* against Philip of France. They were displeased even further when John appointed Peter des Roches* as justiciar. He then invaded Poitou* and had some successes in recovering lost domains, but he fled before the dauphin+ of France. This was followed in 1214 by his and his allies' defeat by Philip of France at the battle of Bouvines.* That was the final action that caused the barons to force his submission to their demands at Runnymede on June 15, 1215, in the *Magna Carta Libertatum.*+ In retaliation, John had the pope excommunicate the barons who had participated in the Runnymede affair, and this caused division among the barons. He was deserted by many of the barons who then encouraged the invasion in 1216 of Prince Louis (later Louis VIII) of France who claimed the throne. Even though Louis' claim was invalid, most of England but the western counties refused to support John. He was pursued from Windsor castle, and ravaged the country mercilessly north through Lincolnshire in retaliation for its lack of support. He fell ill and died, possibly of poison on October 19, 1216. He was succeeded by his infant son and heir, Henry III, for whom William Marshal served as regent until his death in 1219. (Bibliog. 58, 162, 171)

John of Gaunt (1340-1399), third son of King Edward III* of England. He became duke of Lancaster in 1362 on his marriage to Blanche of Lancaster. In time, he became one of the wealthiest men in England. He fought in the Hundred Years War* beside his father and his brother, Edward,* the Black Prince,* and led some brutal campaigns in France. He became one of the most powerful men in England during the early years of the reign of the child king, Richard II* (1377-1399). He led the crown's forces to suppress the peasant's revolt of 1381, but later he broke with Richard and left the court. His second marriage to Costance of Castile,* daughter of Pedro the Cruel,* led him to claim the crown of Castile, but he never obtained it. In 1389, he mediated between Richard and his brother, Thomas of Gloucester. By his mistress, and later third wife, Catherine de Swynford, he sired four children whom Parliament legitimized under the name of Beaufort,* but excluded from any claim to the throne of England. These four were John Beaufort, who became earl of Somerset; Henry Beaufort, bishop of Winchester and cardinal priest of St. Eusebius; Thomas Beaufort, created earl of Dorset in 1412, and duke of Exeter for life in 1416; and Joan Beaufort, who married Sir Robert Ferrers.* Their family name of Beaufort came from their father's castle in Champagne which devolved to him through his first wife, Blanche of Lancaster, who herself was descended from Blanche of Artois, the second wife of Edmund "Crouchback," earl of Lancaster. This Blanche of Artois had married as her first husband Henry, count of Champagne and king of Navarre, and had bought the lordship of Beaumont in 1270. (Bibliog. 9, 47)

John of Salisbury (d. 1180), bishop of Chartres.* As a student of Peter Abelard, he learned humanism at the famous school at Chartres, and became a prolific writer. His classical education and his familiarity with classical authors went beyond the ability to quote them; he understood and appreciated them. His most famous work, *Polycraticus (Statesman's Book),* contained eight books on government, philosophy, learning, and so on, and disclosed many of the vices of the court and the corruption of the church. In it, he maintained that a tyrant could properly be slain by his subjects. He went on to distinguish carefully between a good king and a tyrant, and was careful to point out that a tyrant could not be slain for a private cause, but only in the public good. He was a firm supporter of Thomas à Becket* against King Henry II*; he dedicated his work to Becket because he was in the cathedral at Becket's death. (tr. into English by John Dickinson, New York: Knopf, 1927) (Bibliog. 87, 124)

John the Blind (d. 1346), king of Bohemia. As a knight who loved fighting for its own sake, not caring whether the conflict was important, he fought in every European quarrel he could find, and in tournaments when wars were unavailable. In one he received the wound that blinded him, although legends credit that affliction to divine punishment for his digging up a synagogue in Prague for money beneath the pavement, and then for greed, digging up the tomb of St. Adelbert in the Prague cathedral for which the desecrated saint was said to have struck him blind. As an ally of French King Philip VI,* he led 500 knights in the *avant garde* against the English through Picardy.* At Crécy,* he rashly demanded to be led into the enemy lines to strike a blow against the English, a foolish act which caused his death. His crest of three ostrich feathers and his motto, *"Ich Dien,"** was taken by the Prince of Wales* and attached to his title thereafter. (Bibliog. 203, 223)

"Joie de la cort," ("joy of the court"), 1,592-line final episode in the Arthurian romance of *Erec et Enide** by Chrétien de Troyes*; it concerned the release from an enchanted garden by a knight who was held captive by a lady. (tr. W. W. Comfort, New York: Dutton, 1976) (Bibliog. 44)

Joinville, Jehan de (1224-1315), seneschal+ and close friend of King Louis IX* of France, as well as second great writer of early French history, following Geoffroi de Villehardouin* and succeeded by Jean Froissart.* He is best remembered for being the author of *Livre des saintes paroles et des bonne actions de Saint Louis.* Born to a noble family in Champagne,* he was connected by marriage to Frederick II.* He first appeared in court as the carver for his feudal lord at the knighting ceremony of Louis IX's younger brother, Alphonse. Seven years later at the age of 24, he took the cross to follow his monarch on the seventh crusade+ (1248-1254), but refused to accompany him on the eighth (1268-1270). He returned with the king in 1254. His reverence for his king knew no bounds, for he certainly had the chance to see firsthand the king's strategic faculties. He spent as much time as he could on his own domains, while making frequent visits to the royal court. His close association with Louis made him a chief witness at Louis' canonization hearing in Rome in 1272. Seventeen years later at the age of 74, he was present at the exhumation of the saint's body. Later even than that he began his literary work at the request of Joan of Navarre, wife of Philip IV,* the Fair, and mother of Louis X.* He did not finish the work until 1309. As the queen had died before the completion of the work, six years before he died at the age of 95 in 1315, Joinville dedicated it to her son, the future Louis X.

Writing as a very old man, he described circumstances which occurred in his youth. His work was divided into three parts: the first dealt with the character and conduct of its hero, King Louis; the second with his acts and deeds in Egypt,* and in the Holy Land as Joinville knew them; and the third with his subsequent life and death, including some anecdotes on the king's "justice," his favorite and distinguishing attribute during the sixteen years between crusades. (tr. M. R. B. Shaw, London: Penguin, 1976) (Bibliog. 230)

Joppa. See Jaffa, battle of.

Jordan Fantôsme. See Fantôsme, Jordan.

Joseph d'Arimathie, French poem by Robert de Boron* which related the story of the Holy Grail.* This vessel, supposedly the Grail which Christ used at the Last Supper, was given by a Jew to Pilate who gave it to Joseph of Arimathia who used it to catch the last drops of Jesus' blood as Joseph washed his corpse. This poem recounted Joseph's adventures after that. His sister, Enygeus, and her husband, Bron, joined Joseph's wanderings with the Grail. At the table around which members of a Grail community gathered to show reverence for the Grail, one seat always was left vacant for its future guardian. Bron's nephew supposedly was to be its last guardian. This romance was translated into English around 1350, and was elaborated to include the history of Joseph's actions between his release from prison to the conversion of the heathen King Evelake's subjects, including Joseph's arrival in Britain, his establishing the succession of Grail kings at castle Corbenic,* and his burial at Glastonbury. (French version: ed. P. Nitze, *Roman de l'Estoire dou Graal,* Paris: *CFMA,* 1927; English version, ed. W. W. Skeat, Oxford: *EETS OS* #44, 1871; repr. New York: Kraus, 1973) (Bibliog. 10, 231)

Josephes, son of Joseph of Arimathia* who went with his father and the Grail* company to Britain, and helped with the conversion of pagans there. He became the Grail keeper there and died shortly after his father. See Grail; Grail Keepers. (Bibliog. 202)

Josselin, 11th century French castle+ dominating the valley of Oust at Josselin. Dismantled by Henry II* of England, it was rebuilt sufficiently by the 14th century to be commanded by Jean de Beaumanoir* (d. 1366), one of the knights who took part in the Combat of the Thirty.* In 1370, it passed to the constable Olivier de Clisson,* who had married the widow of Beaumanoir. Clisson rebuilt the castle and added nine towers. (Bibliog. 196)

Joufrois, anonymous French adventure romance from the mid-13th century containing characters based on real people: King Henry I* and his Queen Aelis of England; Alienor of Poitou (see Eleanor of Aquitaine), who was the mother of the hero, Joufrois; and Alphonse of Saint-Gilles (Toulouse). Joufrois, the son of the count of Poitiers and his wife, Alienor, was handsome, wise and brave. He asked his father to send him to the court of King Henry of England to become a knight. There, he dispensed largesse+ liberally. When the king's treacherous steward+ accused the queen of having an affair with a kitchen knave, Joufrois rose to her defense on the field of battle+ after being knighted by the king. There he defeated the traitorous steward to prove the queen's innocence. Then he had to return to Poitou because his father had died. After receiving homage as count of Poitou, he embarked on the tournament+ circuit with 25 of his knights as his mesnie.+ When one of his minstrels told him that the most beautiful woman in the world was Madame Agnes de Tonnere whose husband kept her locked in the tower of his chateau, Joufrois decided to enter incognito the tournament which the count of Tonnere declared. Calling himself Cocayne, he won the tournament, overcoming such notable opponents as the king of France, and then helped the imprisoned Agnes to escape. He went on to other similar adventures in the remainder of this story. (ed. Percival Fay and John Grigsby, Geneva: Droz, 1972) (Bibliog. 106, 127)

Jourdain, Alphonse (1103-1148), count of Toulouse.* His father died when he was two years old, and he remained under the guardianship of the count of Cerdagne until he was five. When ten, he succeeded to the government of Narbonne, Toulouse, and Provence, but Toulouse was taken from him by the duke of Aquitaine,* still in his minority. After the duke died, the people of Toulouse revolted and recalled Jourdain, and he returned in triumph in 1123. His retaliatory treatment of the people of St. Gilles who had sided with the duke brought about his excommunication. He warred with Raymond Berenger for the sovereignty of Provence* until 1125 when he won absolute mastery of the regions lying between the Pyrenees and the Alps, and Auvergne* and the sea. His firm rule for the next fourteen years brought culture and prosperity to the region. Further disputes with the church, including a second excommunication, led him to take the cross for the second crusade+ in 1144. He arrived in Acre* in 1148, but was poisoned and died there before hostilities began. (Bibliog. 68)

*Jourdain de Blaives, chanson de geste** from the early 13th century which continued the story of *Amis et Amiles.** Here, the protagonist was a grandson of Amis. Fromont, the traitor, killed Jourdain's parents, and seized his land, forcing Jourdain to flee with his godparents. They were captured by Saracens* and separated. Jourdain married the princess Oriabel who bore him a daughter, Gaudice. They, too, became separated, but eventually the entire family was reunited and Jourdain succeeded to his father's kingdom and Gaudice became empress of Constantinople. Fromont was defeated and Blaye (Blaives) was given to Jourdain's godfather, Renier de Vautamise. (ed. Peter Dembowski, Chicago: University of Chicago, 1969) (Bibliog. 106)

Jouvent, mountain in the *chanson de geste,** *Esclarmonde,* where the fountain and fruit of youth were found. (Bibliog. 128)

Jufaret. See Jurfaleu.

Jumièges, Guillaume de (fl. c. 1070), author of a history of the dukes of Normandy,* *Gesta Normannorum ducum.* Using a contemporary source for the description of the years 1028-1070, it was especially valuable for its account of Norman invasion of England. (tr. French: F. P. G. Guizot, *Collection des Mémoires,* xxix, 1-316: "Histoire des Normands," Paris, 1826; into English (Book VIII), Joseph Stevenson, *Church Historians,* London: Seeleys, 1876, V, pt.1) (Bibliog. 99)

Jungere Hildebrandslied, Middle High German* poem from the 13th century giving a version of the Hildebrand* and Haudabrand story. Here Hildebrand rode home after 32 years service with Dietrich von Bern (see Theoderic the Great). On the way, he did battle unwittingly with his son, Alebrant, whom he overcame. Following a recognition scene, Alebrant escorted his father home for a reunion with his wife, Ute. (Bibliog. 86)

Jurfaleu, Jurfale le Blont, Jufaret, son and heir of King Marsile*; he was decapitated by Roland at Rencesvals* in the *Song of Roland.** (Bibliog. 210)

"Jus Esneciae," ("Droit d'ainesse"), English principle of succession which expressed the exclusive right, in the event of co-heirship, of the senior co-heir in line to succeed to certain impartible inheritances. It was based on the idea of preventing partition in order to leave rights and services in a single hand and so preserve the individual identity of a fief and office. This principle also applied to some of the offices of an honour,* the *caput** of baronies, honours and earldoms, palatinate+ regalia, some sergeanties, and in a measure to certain conquered Welsh marcher* fiefs nominally held of the crown. To continental military tenants, the unity of the fief and the possession of a fortified *caput* were essential. It was equally essential for the overlord that the control of the military forces should be in unified leadership. (Bibliog. 66)

K

Kamal ad-Din (1192-1262), Arab historian* born in Aleppo and died in Cairo. His work, *The Cream of the Milk in the History of Aleppo*, gave a history of that city in the 12th and 13th centuries, and provided an Arabic account of the crusade+ events in northern Syria. (ed. Sami Dahhan, Damascus, 1954) (Bibliog. 83)

Karaheut, Caraheu, Saracen* king, son of Gloriant; defeated by Ogier in the *chansons de geste*.* (Bibliog. 211)

Karl, retelling of the *Song of Roland** by the German poet, der Stricker* about 1170. (ed. Karl Bartsch, *Karl dem Grosse von dem Strickere,* Quedlinburg, 1857; repr. Berlin, 1965) (Bibliog. 235)

Karlamagnus Saga, Carolingian epic from the Scandinavian countries containing all ten sagas relating to Charlemagne.* Not a single composition, this work was created in two stages: one in two manuscripts from Iceland containing eight branches of epic material, and the second also represented by two manuscripts but including two new branches and with significant additions to the other eight. Taken as one work with ten parts, this Saga recounted the history of Charlemagne from Pepin's death when Charles was 32 years of age, until his own burial. These ten parts were:

I. *Karlamagnus Saga ok Kappa Hans (The Saga of Charlemagne and His Knights).* Giving a detailed account of the early years of the emperor, it served as an introduction to the other nine branches. Here among other events, Karl (Charles) was warned by an angel to associate with a thief, Basin, and to earn his living by stealing. Doing so, he learned of a plot against his own life which he thwarted. In this also, he appointed twelve knights to go against the heathens: Rollant, Oliver, Archbishop Turpin, Gerer, Gerin, Baeringur, Hatun, Samson, Engeler, Ivi, Ivori, and Valter.

II. *Af Fru Olif of Landres Syni Hennar* (*Lady Olive and Landres Her Son*). This was found only in the Iceland collection based on an original written in English and not in a Romance nor Latin language. It centered on the folktale of the calumniated wife and the persecuting mother-in-law, and was attached to Charlemagne's sister.

III. *Af Oddgeri Danska* (*Ogier the Dane*). This corresponded with the first part of the Ogier epic, the *Enfances Ogier*.* Here Ogier's father, the king of Denmark, executed Karl's son, and the emperor ordered Ogier executed in retaliation, but before the sentence could be carried out, Ogier performed such valuable services for the king that he was made royal standard-bearer, and saved Karl's son, Karlot, who had rushed into battle impetuously. His other adventures resembled those of other romance heroes.

IV. *Af Agulando Konungi* (*King Agulandus*). This contained the first thirty-two chapters of an almost literal translation of the *Historia Karoli Magni*, commonly known as the *Pseudo-Turpin*, (see *Chronique de Turpin*), the fictitious chronicle written in Latin about 1130. The rest of the story here came from the *Chanson d'Aspremont*,* a 12th century *chanson de geste** recounting Charlemagne's wars in southern Italy.

V. *Af Guitalin Saxa* (*Guitalin the Saxon*). Derived from a source earlier than that used by Jean Bodel* in his *Chanson des Saisnes** at the end of the 12th century.

VI. *Af Otuel* (*Otuel*). This followed the Anglo-Norman *Otinel*,* which was the same as the French *Otuel*. It was a favorite story in England where at least five English romances of *Otuel* were known. Otuel was a valiant heathen warrior who went to Charlemagne's Christmas court at Paris to announce that his master King Garsis of Syrland had captured Rome. He was so impudent that one of Charlemagne's knights attacked him, but Roland* protected him, and agreed to meet him in single combat. During that fierce encounter, the holy spirit descended in the shape of a white dove and landed on Otuel's shoulder, and he became a Christian, and went on to fight for Charlemagne and rescue Roland, Oliver and Ogier.

VII. *Af Jorsalaferth* (*Journey to Jerusalem*). This was the amusing account of Charlemagne's trip to Constantinople and Jerusalem in which the *douzepeers** "gabbed"+ (bragged) about their abilities, and were called upon to live up to their boasts, and set about to do so. (See *Pèlerinage*.)

VIII. *Af Runzivals Bardaga (The Battle at Rencesvals)* This version closely resembled the English manuscript of the *Chanson de Roland.**

IX. *Af Vilhjalmi Korneis (William of Orange)* This gave an account of how Charlemagne's veteran supporter, Guillaume d'Orange or Guillaume au Court Nez retired to a monastery, but returned to help his aged lord in an hour of need. It was based on the French *Moniage Guillaume.**

X. *Um Kraptaverk ok Jartegnir (Miracles and Signs).* This material from the *Pseudo-Turpin* (see *Chronique de Turpin)** recounted Charlemagne's last days, but also included some from Vincent of Beauvais' *Speculum Historiale* which appeared in 1250. (ed. and tr. Constance B. Hieatt, Toronto: Pontifical Institute of Medieval Studies, I, 1975; II, 1975; III, 1980) (Bibliog. 116, 134)

Karleto, anonymous Italian version of the French *Mainet** which described the deeds of Charlemagne's* youth, his *enfances,** written at the end of the 12th or beginning of the 13th century. This was included by Andrea de' Magnabotti in his prose compilations of French epic poetry, *I Reali di Francia** and *Storie Nerbonesi.* (ed. Pio Rajna, Bologna, 1872) (Bibliog. 231)

Kartagene, Carthage in Africa, one of the four regions under the rule of the Algalife* in the *Song of Roland.** (Bibliog. 210)

Karthen, Carinthia, German march* alongside the Croatian border. (Bibliog. 79)

Kay (Cei, Kai, Keu), Sir, son of Ector* and King Arthur's* foster brother. He became a knight of the Round Table* and seneschal+ at Arthur's court, and figured in many of Arthur's adventures, especially those involving Gawain.* He often was portrayed as a braggart, an indifferent fighter, a dangerous enemy, disliked by other knights for his venomous tongue, boorishness and jealous disposition. His churlishness was explained by the fact that he was supplanted at his mother's breast by his foster brother Arthur, and was raised instead by a rough-speaking and boorish wet nurse. (Bibliog. 117, 145)

Kenilworth castle,+ stronghold in Warwickshire, England, built by Godfrey de Clinton. This was one of the four castles put at the disposal of the barons as security for King John's* observance of the provisions of the *Magna Carta Libertatum,+* although it probably never was surrendered to them from the king's control. It certainly was in John's possession in 1216 when he sent Ralph de Normanville with two other knights to help garrison the castle under William de Cantilupe. Originally part of the royal manor of Stoneleigh given by Henry I* to Geoffrey de Clinton, his chamberlain, this structure had a great keep+ 80 by 60 feet with projecting square towers at each angle. Its walls were 20 feet thick at the base and 14 feet thick at a height of 10 feet. In the rebellion of young Henry* in 1173-1174, King Henry II* assumed control of it when he stationed 20 hired troops and 120 footsoldiers in the castle. Richard I* had it repaired and set in order. John then spent £2,000 to have the old castle surrounded by an outer curtain wall+ with towers. Despite these efforts of maintenance, Henry III* let it fall into disrepair. Then in 1244 he appointed his brother-in-law, Simon de Montfort,* earl of Leicester, as warden of the castle, and in 1253 granted Simon and the countess Eleanor custody of the castle for life. After Simon's death at Evesham* in the rebellion in 1265, its defenders against the king's siege were allowed to recover and keep it by the *Dictum of Kenilworth.** Then Henry III gave it to his son, Edmund, "Crouchback," whom he created earl of Lancaster. In 1279, Edmund held there his famous concourse called the "Round Table" consisting of 100 knights engaged in tilting and in martial exercises under the presidency of Roger Mortimer and 100 ladies. On Edmund's death, Kenilworth went to his son, Thomas,* earl of Lancaster, who later on led the opposition to King Edward II* resulting in his conviction and beheading for open rebellion in 1322. The king, Edward II, then held Christmas court there in 1323, and there he was taken prisoner three years later by Henry, the Earl Thomas' brother, and forced to abdicate the throne. Then the king was taken to Berkeley* castle where he was murdered. Subsequently, Kenilworth passed to Blanche of Lancaster, daughter of Henry of Grosmont,* duke of Lancaster, and then to her husband, John of Gaunt,* who converted it from a stronghold into a palace. (Bibliog. 238)

Kent, county of southeastern England. After Vortiger (A.D. 449) called in the Saxons to resist and repel the Scots and other people from the northern part of Britain, he created seven kingdoms, the heptarchy,* Kent being the oldest. Among its kings were: Hengest* (457); Octa or Otha (512); Ethelbert I
(561), first Christianized king who founded St. Paul's, in London; Baldred (805-827), who lost the kingdom to Egbert, king of West Saxons. William* the Conqueror made it an earldom, and bestowed it on his half-brother, Odo,* bishop of Bayeux, who had fought at Hastings* beside him. For that support, Odo was granted several hundred manors,

the most profitable of which were in Kent, and he was made earl of that county. His principal feudal obligation was the defense against invasion of the southeast portion of England. Although he had been a loyal supporter of the Conqueror, by 1082, however, he was arrested on a charge of subversion and deported to Normandy,* and his English estates were seized. Odo accused Archbishop Lanfranc* of being behind those charges, but remained in custody in Caen for the rest of William I's life. When his nephew, William II,* ascended the throne, Odo was restored to lands and titles, but because he had joined Duke Robert* in Normandy and raised rebellion in England, his property was confiscated. After he died in 1097, the earldom reverted to the crown for over a century until King John* rewarded Hubert de Burgh* by bestowing upon him the custody of the county of Kent in 1215. As justiciar* Hubert held Kent and the castles of Canterbury and Dover at royal pleasure. He was one of the regency chosen by the barons on King John's* death. A strong supporter of William Marshal as regent, after Marshal's death, Hubert became supreme in the regency government, and was created earl of Kent in 1227, receiving £50 per annum in lieu of the third penny.+ He fell out of favor with the young King Henry III* through the conniving of Peter des Roches* and lost his holdings, but had them returned to him two years later when he had restored the king's confidence in his advice. Rather than risk his territory any more, he retired from active life in the government and died in 1243. His daughter and heiress died without issue so the earldom became extinct until Edward II* girded his youngest brother Edmund* of Woodstock with the sword of the earldom in 1321. Some of its other earls were:

1057 - Tostig,* brother of King Harold*
1330 - Edmund Plantagenet, the fourth earl who was the son of Edmund, and who died unmarried
1333 - John Plantagenet, the fifth earl, and brother of the fourth earl; he married Elizabeth, daughter of the duke of Juliers
1352 - Joan of Kent,* the sixth earl, and daughter of Edmund of Woodstock; she married Thomas Holand*
1360 - Thomas Holand, the seventh earl, and son of Thomas Holand; he married Alice, daughter of Richard FitzAlan, earl of Arundel
1397 - Thomas Holand, the eighth earl, and the duke of Surrey; son of Thomas Holand, he married Joan, daughter of Hugh, earl of Stafford
1401 - Edmund Holand, ninth earl, brother of Thomas; he was lord admiral and married Lucy, surnamed Le Viscount, daughter of Barnabas, viscount of Milan.

(Bibliog. 66, 101)

Kerak-in-Moab, castle+ in "Outre Jourdain" in the Near East, built in 1142 to launch raids on Muslim* caravan and pilgrim routes. Rainald de Chatillon's ruthless exploitation of this potential led to its being besieged in 1183 and 1184, and finally to his death at Saladin's* hands after the battle of Hattin* in 1187. It finally fell after an eight-month siege in 1188, and though it was regarded by the crusaders+ as essential to the security of Jerusalem, it never again was in their hands. (Bibliog. 30)

kern, 14th century Irish scouts and skirmishers armed with dirks and javelins whose speciality was creeping beneath men-at-arms' horses and stabbing them in the belly, and cutting the throats of the enemy wounded. (Bibliog. 203)

"Key to England," Dover. See de Burgh, Hubert.

khan, lord, or prince, used as the title of sovereigns of territory conquered by Jenghiz (Genghis) Khan* and ruled by his successors. (Bibliog. 169)

khanate, dominion or jurisdiction of a khan.* (Bibliog. 169)

Kidderminster, baron of. See Beauchamp, John.

Kildare, earl of. See FitzGerald, John FitzThomas.

Kildrummy castle,+ fortress in Aberdeenshire, Scotland, built by the last Scottish saint, St. Gilbert, along the design of the massive Chateau de Coucy* near Laon, France. Its enormous semicircular curtain wall+ was protected by five projecting round towers, the largest of which was called the Snow Tower. It was completed near the end of the 13th century at a time when Scotland was under the control of the English King Edward I,* and Kildrummy under the earl of Mar became involved deeply in the attempts to place Robert the Bruce* on the throne. After his defeat at Methven in 1305, Bruce sent his queen to Kildrummy for safety while he fled to the Western Highlands. In 1306, Prince Edward* besieged it, and Sir Nigel Bruce, the Scottish king's youngest brother, was forced to surrender it, but not before the queen had escaped northward. From then on, the castle led a peaceful existence. (Bibliog. 192)

King Arthur and King Cornwall, badly damaged English ballad that re-counted a story similar to *Pèlerinage de Charlemagne** with the boast-ing of the *douzepeers.** Here Arthur,* Tristan, Gawain* and two other of Arthur's knights travelled to the land of King Cornwall whose court was said by Arthur's queen to be richer and more splendid than Arthur's. Cornwall boasted of having a miraculous sword, horn, and horse, and a seven-headed, fire-breathing fiend who served him. Arthur and his knights succeeded in overcoming King Cornwall. (ed. Helen Sargent and George L. Kittredge, *English and Scottish Popular Ballads,* Cambridge, MA: Houghton Mifflin, 1932; repr. Kennebunkport, ME: Longwood, 1978) (Bibliog. 177)

King Horn, Middle English* romance written around 1225; it retold the story of Mestre Thomas' Anglo-Norman *Horn et Rimenild* (c. 1170).* (ed. George McKnight, London: Oxford *EETS OS* #14, 1901; repr. 1962) (Bibliog. 202)

King Mark. See Mark, King.

"king of all earthly kings," Matthew Paris' term for the king of France in the 14th century, referring to the French monarch as the first ruler in western Europe. He was far more powerful than the Holy Roman Emperor, and he had basically controlled the papacy by serving as both protector and quasi-jailer since 1309 when the papacy had been established at Avignon. Further, these French kings had controlled the counts and barons, instead of being controlled by them as in other lands. (Bibliog. 203)

King of Heralds. See herald.

King's Inn, Dublin, legal school in Ireland corresponding closely to the English Inns* of Court. (Bibliog. 68)

Kirkby, John, archdeacon of Coventry and indispensable Chancery+ official and Exchequer* baron for King Edward I.* He later was elevated by the king to become treasurer of England and subsequently rewarded by being appointed bishop of Ely. During the fighting against the Welsh, when King Edward needed cash to pay his army, he sent Kirkby, as vice-chancellor, around England to beg individual magnates for contributions, called "courteous subsidies," to his war chest. Kirkby asked for these contributions with the utmost politeness, because the king felt he should remain on good terms with and cooperate with his subjects. This fund enabled the king to raise a disciplined military force. (Bibliog. 35)

Die Klage, Middle High German* poem in couplets appended to the *Nibelungenlied.** Written in Bavaria about 1220, this diffuse and sentimental work continued the epic after the debacle at Etzel's court, describing in detail how the dead were buried, how Etzel's messengers brought the news of the tragedy to Bechlaren, Passau and Worms, and how Bishop Pilgrim of Passau ordered Meister Kuonrat to record the story in Latin. (ed. F. Lachmann, *Die Nibelung Nôt mit der Klage,* 6th ed., Berlin, 1961) (Bibliog. 235)

Knaresborough castle,+ fortress in Yorkshire built by Serlo de Burg who received the land from Sir Hugh de Morville, one of the four knights who murdered Thomas à Becket.* King Richard II* also was imprisoned there shortly before his death. On the banks of the River Nidd, this castle had two baileys enclosed by a curtain wall+ 40 feet high; its keep measured 64 by 52 feet. (Bibliog. 247)

Knight of Courtesy and the Fair Lady of Faguell. See *Chastelaine de Vergi.*

Knight of the Cart. See *Lancelot.*

Knight of the Lion. See *Yvain.*

Knight of the Parrot. See *Chevalier du Papegau.*

Knight with the Goat. See *Gaurel von Muntabel.*

Knighton, Henry (d. 1396), canon regular in St. Mary's in the Meadows in Leicester,* he began his *Chronicon* with the genealogy of William* the Conqueror, and extended it from 1066 to 1395, with a gap from 1366 to 1377. It was a principal source for the reign of Richard II,* and was partial toward John of Gaunt,* duke of Lancaster. (ed. J. R. Lumby, London: *Rolls Series,* 1889-1895) (Bibliog. 99)

Knollys, Robert (d. 1407), English military commander. Possibly a brother to Hugh Calveley,* Knollys was a native of Cheshire.* Early in his military career, he served in Brittany* at the siege of La Roche d'Orient in July 1346 with Calveley and Walter Hewett under Sir Thomas Dagworth.* Knighted by 1351, Knollys took part in the famous Combat of the Thirty* where he was one of the survivors taken prisoner. On his subsequent release, he remained in Brittany where he made a name for himself as a soldier. He became leader of a company of free-lances (see White Company) and free booters.* He bought custody of Fougeray and other castles in Brittany for 2,000 florins. In 1356 when Henry of Grosmont* raided Normandy in support of Philip of Navarre and Geoffrey de Harcourt, Knollys came to his assistance with 300 men-at-arms and 500 archers. This expedition ravaged Normandy up to the walls of Rouen. He besieged Domfront, and tried to join Edward,* the Black Prince in Poitou* but he was unable to cross the heavily guarded Loire River. He served under du Guesclin* at Rennes before leaving on his own with a large body of mercenaries called the Great Company (see free companies) to plunder Normandy, and to amass for himself 100,000 crowns as his share of the booty. By his military ability, he controlled the Loire valley by becoming master of 40 castles. He claimed that he fought neither for the king of England nor for the king of France, but for himself alone. He continued to ravage the French countryside up to a distance of 10 leagues from Pope Benedict XII at Avignon. His ravages were so destructive that the charred gables which marked his route were called "Knollys' mitres."

By 1358, he declared in support of the English, and sent word to King Edward III* that all the towns and castles he had captured were at the king's disposal. Pleased, the king pardoned all Knollys' informal tactics. In 1359, he battled and captured his former teacher and friend, du Guesclin, and then in 1364 at the siege of Auray,* he captured him again and the count of Auxerre and killed Charles of Blois.* John de Montfort,* contender for the county of Brittany, rewarded him for killing his competition by granting him with lands in Derval and Rouge in 1365 so that sometimes he styled himself Sire de Derval. He went south with a select group of the Great Company to join the Black Prince. At the battle of Najera,* he supported and then rescued Sir John Chandos,* and then returned to Brittany. Summoned to England by the king in 1370, he was ordered to return with the king to Calais* as commander of 1,500 men-at-arms and 4,000 archers to plunder Artois, Picardy and Vermandois, inflicting as much damage as possible on a *chevauchée,* and exacting as heavy ransoms as he could. On the news that du Guesclin had been recalled from Aquitaine to counter this proposed invasion, the king cancelled it. He rode beside young King Richard II* to meet the rebels outside the walls of London in 1381. In his later years, he became a great benefactor to London giving freely of his money. He and Calveley and John Hawkwood* even founded a hospital in Rome. (Bibliog. 58)

König Rother, Middle High German* epic recounting a repeated wooing urged on King Rother of Apulia, by advisors who urged him to marry to ensure an heir to his kingdom. He was advised to woo the daughter of the Emperor Konstantin of Constantinople who opposed any marriage of his daughter, and executed all suitors. Rother was well received by the princess, outwitted Konstantin, and took the girl home to his capital at Bari with him. Konstantin sent an emissary who enticed her aboard his ship, and then carried her back to Constantinople with him. Rother undertook a second wooing in disguise, was captured, identified, and condemned to death. He was rescued in the nick of time, and sailed home with his bride. This work was thought to have been written by a Bavarian priest for the entertainment of a noble public around 1150. (tr. English, R. Lichtenstein, 1962) (Bibliog. 237)

Konrad von Stoffeln, Middle High German* poet from Hohenstoffeln in Hegau, northwest of Lake Constance, in the mid-13th century. His verse romance, *Gaurel von Muntabel,** described Gaurel's love for a fairy. As he was accompanied by a goat, he was known as the "*Ritter mit dem Bock,*" the Knight with the Goat. (Bibliog. 86)

Konrad von Wurzburg (c. 1225-1287), Middle High German* poet who was born a commoner and spent his life as a professional poet writing for wealthy patrons in Strassburg and later in Basel. He wrote 23 *minnelieder+* in which nature played a considerable role, but his best known works were his short verse romances ranging between 300 and 1,300 lines: *Der Herzmaere,** *Heinrich von Kempten,** and *Der Schwanritter.** Similar in style to those romances was his *Das Turnei von Nantiez,* a verse account of an imaginary tournament which included a great deal of heraldic description. He also wrote three legends of saints in verse: *Silvester* about Pope Sylvester, *Heilige Alexius,* and *Pantaleon,* the story of a Roman physician and a Christian martyr and three long verse romances: *Engelhard,** *Partenopier und Meliur,** and the unfinished *Der Trojan Krieg.** (Bibliog. 86)

Krain, Carniola, German march* alongside the Hungarian border. (Bibliog. 79)

Krak des Chevaliers, huge concentric fortress on the west bank of the Orontes River in the county of Tripoli in the Near East. Originally an 11th-century Arab fort called the castle of the Kurds, it was acquired by the Hospitallers+ in 1142 who strengthened it. Earthquakes in 1157, 1170, and 1201 forced massive reconstruction, but it remained an impregnable bulwark. A small rectangular castle with square towers was incorporated into a concentric fortification. First the outer curtain with evenly spaced towers and box machicolation,+ then an inner bailey with tall towers rising out of sloping walls. Unsuccessfully besieged on many occasions, this fortress finally fell to the Mameluke sultan of Egypt,* Baibars, in 1271 when there was no hope for its being relieved. (Bibliog. 30)

Kriemhild, sister of King Gunther of Worms, wife of Siegfried* and his avenger against Hagen. See *Nibelungenlied.** (Bibliog. 161)

Kudrun, Middle High German* epic ranking second in importance only to the *Nibelungenlied.** Written by an Austrian poet between 1230 and 1240 in stanzas resembling the *Nibelungenlied,* its 32 *aventiuren+* related the story of three generations: 1-4 told of the birth to Siegebant and Uote of Hagen who was carried off by a griffin+ which he later killed, of his finding three ladies also carried off by the creature and of his returning home with them, and eventually marrying one, Hilde; 5-8 related how Hagen and Hilde, reigning in Ireland, had a daughter, also named Hilde, whose suitors Hagen slew. King Hetel, wishing to woo Hilde, sent a party led by Wate, the warrior, and Horant, the minstrel. Horant's music won Hilde and she fled with Hetel's men pursued by her father who became reconciled to the marriage. The remaining 24 *aventiuren* related the main story of Kudrun, the daughter of Hetel and Hilde, who was wooed by Hartmunt and Herwig, refused both at first, but later accepted Herwig. Hartmunt kidnapped her and took her to Ormanie (Normandy), but her relatives who pursued them were defeated. Kudrun, however, refused for years to marry Hartmunt and as a result was treated badly by Hartmunt's mother, Gerlint. Finally after 13 years, she was rescued by Kerwig who slew Gerlint and captured Hartmunt. The happy couple returned home and were married; Hartmunt was pardoned and later married Hildeburg, Kudrun's companion in captivity. (ed. B. Sijmons, Tubingen: *ATB* #5, 4th ed. rev. B. Boesch, 1964; English tr. M. Armour, London: Everyman, n.d.) (Bibliog. 197)

Kyng Alisaunder, also known as *Lyfe of Alisaunder*, this 14th-century English romance was a free adaptation of the *Roman de toute Chevalerie.** The first of its two main parts related Alexander's mysterious conception, his birth and youth, his coming to the throne, and his conquest of Darius; the second told of his conquests eastward, the marvels he encountered, his seduction by Candace, and his death by poisoning. (ed. G. V. Smithers, *EETS* #227, London, 1952; repr. 1961) (Bibliog. 202)

L

Lacy, Richard de, castellan+ of Falaise Castle in Normandy,* who was in such favor with the English king, Stephen,* that in time he became justiciar of England, castellan of the Tower of London and Windsor* castle, and sheriff of Essex and Hertfordshire. (Bibliog. 94)

Lacy, Roger de, honorary constable+ of Chester* to whom Longchamps* gave the castles of Nottingham* and Tickhill* after recovering them in 1191 from their constables, Robert of Crockston and Eudes of DeVille who had turned them over to Prince John.* Lacy sought to punish them for that act, but forewarned, they fled, and refused to stand trial. He then arrested Alan of Leek and Peter of Bovencourt, two associates of the constables. Peter swore before Prince John, Longchamps, and the entire king's court that the castles had been turned over to the prince against his will. Longchamps refused to believe him and sent him to Lacy to be purged of his crime. Lacy also refused to listen to the two men and hanged both on a gallows with iron chains. On the third day after the hanging, when a squire was found driving away birds feasting on the corpses, he too was hanged. For that, Prince John took away Lacy's lands as punishment. Later, after John had become king, he turned over the defense of Chateau Gailiard* to Lacy whom he considered to be a man of dauntless courage and high military capacity. When the French forces of Philip II* began to pressure the village of Les Andelys at the foot of the castle, Lacy made the fatal blunder of admitting its 2,200 terrified citizens into the fortress. When he found that they were useless mouths he had to feed, consuming precious stores that would have furnished a year's food for the small garrison within the castle, he tried to turn them out. However, when the French king realized what he was doing, he ordered that every person emerging from the castle should be driven back inside. These poor unfortunates endured existence for three months without shelter and with barely enough food. King John did nothing to relieve this blockade so within a few months, Richard's "Saucy Castle"+ fell to the French. (Bibliog. 7, 101, 180)

Lady of Clare. See de Burgh, Elizabeth.

Lady of the Lake, three distinct Ladies of the Lake appeared in Arthurian material: one raised Lancelot* in France, one gave Arthur* his sword, and the other was Niniane.* Viviane generally was the name of the lady who raised Lancelot; the other two were called by either Niniane or Viviane, and also known as Ninene, Nynyue and Nimue (thought to be a clerical error for Ninene). First cousin of Lunete (Linet) the Damsel Savage (in *Morte D'Arthur*), this Niniane learned how to practice sorcery from Merlin* who was infatuated by her, and then she laid a spell on him, trapping him in his tomb. Occasionally she helped Arthur, but primarily she was protectress of Lancelot, Lionel* and Bohort. (Bibliog. 44, 241)

lai,   lay, short form of French romance in octosyllabic couplets. Also called *conte, contoise,* or *dit,* this story differed from the romance in that it was much shorter, usually under 1,000 lines; its details converged on one main scene or climax; and its poetic style was subordinate to the action which sped towards the climax. The term *lai* came from the Celtic word *laed,* song. (Bibliog. 106)

Lai de Courant, also known as the *Lai d'Haveloc,* this French *lai,* written between 1130 and 1140, detailed the Danish-Saxon racial saga associated with the fate of the Viking Reginwald, ruler of Northumbria and his nephew, Anlaf Cuaran. Haveloc was forced to flee from his enemies and leave his native country, the Danish kingdom. Under the name of Courant, he went to England, served as a scullion at the court of King Alsi, and finally won the hand of the king's daughter together with several kingdoms. (ed. Alexander Bell, Manchester, 1925) (Bibliog. 231)

Lai de Lanval, French *lai* by Marie de France* relating a fairy story based upon the Arthurian legend which concerned the love of a hero for a fairy who enjoined him not to reveal their love. Although the hero broke his promise, the fairy came to his rescue in his time of need, and led him away to safety in Avalon.* (tr. E. Mason, *Lais,* New York: E. P. Dutton, 1966) (Bibliog. 147)

Lai de l'espine, French *lai* which described the love of a young prince and princess. His father married her mother in a second marriage, and when the young children were seen embracing in all innocence, they were separated, and she was confined. Years passed, and the prince finally sought to prove his valor by waiting and watching beside a ford (*l'espine*) for some difficult adventures eight days before the feast+ of St. John (June 24). The young princess learned of his plan, and slept at the ford so he would find her. He defeated a series of knights, and won a noble steed. On their triumphant return to court, they were married. (ed. Rud. Zenker, *ZrP* 17, 1893, 223ff.) (Bibliog. 231)

Lai de l'ombre, French *lai** written between 1217 and 1221 by Jehan Renaut.* It was a story of perfection in a lover which was mainly courtesy. In it, the most courteous of knights visited the most courteous of ladies. As the two of them sat by a well, he tried to convince her to grant him her glove as a love token, and to wear his ring by slipping it on her finger by a trick. She insisted that he remove the ring. He gallantly thereupon bestowed it upon her shadow (*l'ombre*) in the well. This so impressed her that she yielded and gave him her glove. (ed. Joseph Bedier, Paris: *SATF,* 1913) (Bibliog. 106)

Lai de Tyolet, French *lai** which rendered the well-known theme of a simpleton recounting a dangerous adventure that a hero underwent to win his bride. (ed. Gaston Paris, *Romania,* VIII, 1879, 40-50) (Bibliog. 106)

Lai du Cor, Breton *lai** by Robert Bicket written in the third quarter of the 12th century. Its hero was a figure known to Chrétien de Troyes* as Karadues Briebraz (Shortarm), to the Bretons as Karadoc Brech Bras (Armstrong), and to the Welsh as Caradawc Vreichvras. In it, the ivory drinking horn (*cor*) sent to King Arthur's* court at Caerleon* by King Mangoun of Moraine had the property of exposing the slightest infidelity of a wife. Arthur insisted on trying it, and when he did, he was drenched in wine. He would have killed his queen had not his knights intervened. He recovered his good humor, however, when he found that all the knights who tried it were similarly disillusioned by being drenched, and he pardoned his wife with a kiss. Then Caradoc took the full cup, and after he drained it without a drop being spilled, Arthur bestowed upon him Cirencester in perpetuity. (ed. and tr. Isabel Butler, *Tales from the Old French,* New York: Houghton Mifflin, 1910; in Richard Brengle, *Arthur King of Britain,* New York: Appleton Century Crofts, 1964) (Bibliog. 10)

Lai la Freine, incomplete English imitation of a French *lai** from the beginning of the 14th century. It recounted the tale of a young girl, one of a set of twins, who, with a gold ring identifying her as well-born, was exposed as an infant in a hollow ash tree (hence the title: *freine* = "ash"). She was reared by an abbess as her niece, fell in love with a knight, Sir Guroun, who took her away as his mistress. He later was persuaded to marry, and chose her twin. Their relationship was discovered, and Freine was married to her true knight after all. This was not a close imitation of Marie de France's* version of the same story (see *La Fresne).* (ed. D. B. Sands, *Middle English Verse Romances*, New York: Holt, Rinehart, and Winston, 1966) (Bibliog. 202)

Lake, Lady of the. See Lady of the Lake.

Lambors, Grail* king, son of Mangel and father of Pellam;* he was slain by the first Dolorous Stroke* delivered by Varlans with the Sword of the Strange Girdles. (Bibliog. 202)

Lamorak of Wales, son of Pellinore* and brother of Perceval* in Arthurian legend. When Gaheris* found him lying with his mother, Morgawse,* he killed his mother; Lamorak later was slain by Gawain* for that infidelity. (Bibliog. 202)

Lampete, Amazon queen. See Amazonia.

Lamprecht, *pfaffe,* German priest who translated Aubry de Pisançon's* *Alexanderlied** into Middle High German* by 1130; Lamprecht called the author, *Alberich von Bisinzo.* This was the first extant translation of a French literary work into German. Included in it were such elements from fable as a letter from Alexander* to Aristotle describing the wonders of India, and Alexander's experiences at the gates of Paradise. For Lamprecht, the whole Alexander story was only a symbol of the transience and worthlessness of worldly fame; for he found the deeds of the conqueror damnable and he could not bring himself to praise them. A continuator of his work from Strassburg, however, saw Alexander as a knightly ruler possessing all the virtues of a model 12th-century king. (ed. F. Knorr, *Das Alexanderlied des Pfaffen Lamprecht, ZfdG,* 1942) (Bibliog. 235)

Lancarote de Lago, early 14th-century Spanish romance which contained part II and II of the French *Lancelot,** beginning with the departure of Galeheut for Sorelis, and ending with the tales which Gawain,* Bors,* and Gaheret* told of their adventures. (portions in *ZRP,* XXVI, 1902, 202-205) (Bibliog. 10)

Lancaster, town on the Irish sea above Cheshire* in the county palatine+ of Lancashire in the northwestern part of England. It became an earldom when King Henry III* conferred that title upon his second son, Edmund, "Crouchback." In addition to the county of that title, the king conferred on him the confiscated estates of the earls of Montfort* and Ferrers,* and the barony of Monmouth. It was made a county palatine by King Edward II.* It passed to Thomas Plantagenet* who was beheaded for treason in 1322. Its fourth earl and first duke was Henry, "of Grosmont,"* earl of Lancaster, earl of Leicester* and steward of England. In 1350, he was made duke of Lancaster by Parliament, and served his king well as a renowned military man. On his death the dukedom of Lancaster became extinct. Its next duke was John of Gaunt,* earl of Richmond,* third surviving son of King Edward III* through his marriage to Blanche, second but only surviving daughter of Henry of Grosmont. His son, Henry, "of Bolingbroke," afterwards ascended the throne as Henry IV. Into this earldom by marriages accrued in time the great estates of William de Fortibus, earl of Aumerle* and lord of Holderness, Beaufort, and other lands in France; the earldom of Lincoln* and a large part of Salisbury; and the lordships of Ogmore and Kidwelly in Wales* which once had been held by the Chaworths. To these vast holdings John of Gaunt added the castles and honours+ of Tickhill,* and his son, Bolingbroke, added one-half of the lands of Bohun,* the earl of Hereford,* Essex,* and Northampton.* After Henry Bolingbroke ascended the throne of England as Henry IV, all the lands and honours+ belonging to and incorporated into the duchy of Lancaster were brought to the crown of England. (Bibliog. 47, 101)

Lancaster, Thomas, earl of. See Thomas, earl of Lancaster.

lance, unit of cavalry. See White Company.

Lancelot, major Arthurian character who was the son of Ban* of Benwick, father of Galahad* by Elayne* daughter of Pelles,* and lover of Guenevere.* He was the hero of the Round Table* and as such was considered the paragon of chivalric virtues; he fell in love with Guenevere, committed adultery with her, and after rescuing her from being burned at the stake, was the sworn enemy of both Arthur* and Gawain.* That enmity basically destroyed the Round Table. He ended his days as a hermit and priest at Glastonbury.* He appeared in three of Chrétien de Troyes'* Arthurian romances: *Lancelot** or the *Chevalier de la Charette*, *Erec et Enide*,* and *Cligés*;* in the *Vulgate** cycle: *Lancelot* proper,* *Quest del Saint Graal*,* and *Mort Artu**; in Ulrich Von Zatzikhoven's *Lanzelet**; in *Lancarote de Lago**; and in a

15th-century Scots poem, *Lancelot of the Laik;** he also was mentioned in the *chanson de geste,** *Girard de Roussillon** when Girard cited him as a model of "*preux.*"+ (Bibliog. 10, 202)

Lancelot, also known as *La Chevalier de la Charette* (Knight of the Cart), this was one of the most famous Arthurian romances written by Chrétien de Troyes'* for Marie de Champagne in the late 12th century. As Lancelot was riding to rescue Queen Guenevere,* his horse died and he was ordered by a dwarf to mount a cart, but hesitated for two steps before entering. He was chided for that hesitation, because love should have made him do instantly anything asked of him. He underwent a series of adventures to rescue the queen, including crossing a bridge made of razor-sharp sword blades arching across a stream, and fighting in a tournament so poorly as to play the coward, even though on the third day of the tournament he distinguished himself. Finally he vanquished and slew the villain Meleagant* at Arthur's court for kidnapping the queen. (ed. and tr. W. W. Comfort, London and New York: Everyman and E. P. Dutton, 1955) (Bibliog. 44)

Lancelot-Grail. See *Vulgate* version of Arthurian romance.

Lancelot of the Laik, late 15th-century Scots poem in heroic couplets which made reference to contemporary political events in Scotland of the time of composition. It was a poorly written rehandling of the first portion of the French prose *Lancelot proper.** (ed. Margaret Gray, *PSTS*, II, 1912) (Bibliog. 10)

Lancelot proper, long French prose romance in two parts written between 1215 and 1230 as part of the Vulgate* cycle: from Lancelot's birth to the preparation for the quest, and the preparation itself for the quest. In the first part, even though he was descended from King David, Lancelot appeared a child of calamity. King Claudas of Terre Desert (Berry) defeated Lancelot's father, King Ban of Benoic, while Lancelot was still in his cradle. The infant was snatched from the cradle in front of his mother by the Dame du Lac (see Lady of the Lake) and brought up with his cousins, Lionel and Bohort, who already had avenged their own father's death by killing Claudas' son. At 18, Lancelot was taken by the Dame du Lac to Arthur's court and knighted with arms presented by the Dame du Lac, and not from Arthur.* Thus when Arthur forgot to gird on the sword, Queen Guenevere* did, thereby providing the impetus for Lancelot's loyalty to her rather than to Arthur. To become a *preudhomme,** Lancelot engaged in a series of strenuous adventures: incredible vows, combats, enchantments, all leading to the conquest of Dolorous Garde* castle and the discovery there of his name on the lid of a tomb where his body ultimately was to lie. After he removed the enchantment from the castle, he changed its name to Joyeuse Garde.

The second part, the preparations for the quest for the Holy Grail,* contained events crucial to the story: the begetting of Galaad (Galahad*). Lancelot, under the influence of a potion given him by the duenna Brisane with the connivance of the Grail king, Pelles,* lay with the king's daughter under the impression that he was with Guenevere. That union begot Galahad. Veiled references were made throughout this second part to the final catastrophe of the treachery of Mordred,* the conflict between Lancelot and Arthur, and the ultimate collapse of the empire. (ed. H. O. Sommer, *Vulgate Version of the Arthurian Romances*, Washington: Carnegie Institute, III, 1910; IV, 1911; V, 1912; repr. New York: AMS, 1979) (Bibliog. 10)

Landgraf Herman of Thuringia (d. 1217), ruler from 1190, he was involved in the conflict for the imperial crown of Germany between Philip of Swabia* and Otto IV.* His court at Thuringia was a haven for *minnesingers+* and the poets of the time, including Wolfram von Eschenbach and Walter von der Vogelweide. He commissioned the "learned scholar," Herbort von Fritzlar, to produce in German a version of the French *Roman de Troie** using Latin sources. (Bibliog. 86)

Lanfranc (1005-1089), abbot of Bec in Normandy* whom William I* made archbishop* of Canterbury. Born in Italy, he studied in France and began a school at Avranches, and then in 1045, began and headed at Bec one of the most famous schools in Europe. Chosen by William to be one of his closest advisors, he was given the task of oganizing the church in England after the Conquest, and of maintaining close and harmonious relations between the English crown and the papacy. (Bibliog. 98)

Langtoft, Peter of (d. after 1307), canon of the priory of Bridlington in Yorkshire, he wrote his *Chronicle* of English history from Brutus to 1307 in French verse with a translation. Up to the end of Henry II's* reign, he used Geoffrey of Monmouth,* Huntingdon,* and Malmesbury,* and other well-known writers, but for the years 1272-1307, it was a contemporary record, much of which was devoted to the Scottish wars of Edward I;* he was hostile to the Scots. (ed. Thomas Wright, London: *Rolls Series,* 1866-1868, 2 vols. Extracts 1190-1307) (Bibliog. 99)

Lanval, Lai de. See *Lai de Lanval.*

Lanzelet, Middle High German* courtly epic by Ulrich von Zatzikhoven. It recounted the hero's life story from birth to death. On the death of his royal parents, Lanzelet was reared by a sea fairy, and was destined to war against King Iwert. In due course, he set out on his adventures, defeated various adversaries, and finally met and defeated Iwert himself whose daughter Iblis he married. The second part of the poem focussed on his quest for Arthur's queen, Ginover, who had been abducted. He liberated her and eventually settled happily with Iblis until death claimed them on the same day. (ed. and tr. K. G. T. Webster; rev. R. S. Loomis, New York: Columbia University, 1951) (Bibliog. 227)

Laostic, French *lai** by Marie de France* telling how a jealous husband slew a nightingale (*eostic* in Breton) because unknowingly and innocently it furnished entertainment to his wife and her lover. (tr. E. Mason, New York: E. P. Dutton, 1966) (Bibliog. 147)

Lastours (or Cabaret), four castles+ in the Black Mountains of Languedoc which played a large role in the Albigensian+ war, serving as important refuges for the Cathars.* Simon de Montfort* besieged them futilely in 1209. In 1210, he renewed his assault at the head of an army of crusaders led by his wife, Alix de Montmorency. This time he was successful, and to punish the defenders, he cut off their ears and blinded them. One was left with one eye to lead Montfort to the final castle called Cabaret. (Bibliog. 196)

Latimer, William (1330-1381), knight who fought at Crécy,* beside Edward,* the Black Prince and was chosen for the Order of the Garter* in 1362. He served the crown in various military and administrative roles, among them being in charge of making the king's dies at the mint in the Tower of London, and witnessing Baliol's* surrender of his claim to the Scottish crown in 1356. He was lieutenant and captain-general in Brittany,* and fought beside John de Montfort* at the battle of Auray* in which Charles of Blois,* Montfort's rival for the duchy of Brittany, was killed. Latimer served as ambassador to Portugal, became warden of the Cinque Ports* and constable of Dover in 1372 and shared in the *chevauchée** of 1373. He was impeached by the Good Parliament of 1376, and for his trial the commons set the procedure for impeachment; to Latimer's demand for an accuser, he was told by Sir Peter de la Mare, one of the knights representing Hereford, that he and his fellows in Parliament would maintain all their charges in common. Every time Latimer would make a point in his own defense, they would produce an answer, maintaining their role as prosecutors.   After paying a fine of 20,000 marks, he was released, but soon sought and was granted a pardon for all debts, actions, treasons and felonies by the king. He died in 1381 from a stroke of paralysis suffered while dismounting his horse. (Bibliog. 47, 153)

Launcelot, son of Jonas and the sixth in the line of holy men; he was the father of Ban and Bors of Gaul, and the grandfather of Lancelot of the Lake. (Bibliog. 145)

Launceston castle,+ stronghold built originally by Richard,* earl of Cornwall,* brother of King Henry III,* in the middle of the 13th century.   On the death of Richard's son, Edmund, in 1300, the castle reverted to the crown, and Edward II* gave it to Piers Gaveston* a few years later. In 1337, it was granted to Edward* the Black Prince as duke of Cornwall. It had a strong central tower rising from the circular keep. (Bibliog. 247)

Launfal Miles. See *Sir Launfal.*

Laurin, anonymous Middle High German* heroic epic from the second half of the 13th century. Its setting was Tyrol. From his henchman Witege, Dietrich von Bern (see Theoderic the Great) learned of the physical prowess of the dwarf Laurin ("laur" = cunning) who fiercely defended his rose garden against all intruders. It was surrounded by a silken thread, and whoever broke that thread had to forfeit a hand or a foot. Dietrich, accompanied by Witege and Dietlieb, set out to prove his own superiority. Witege was defeated by Laurin whose superior strength came from a magic girdle. After Dietrich cut that girdle, Laurin easily was defeated, and then revealed that he had abducted Dietlieb's sister, Kunolt, to marry her. He invited all to a banquet in his palace where he drugged the wine, and imprisoned his guests after they became unconscious.   Kunolt rescued them with the aid of the weapons she brought them and a magic ring which allowed Dietlieb to see in the dark. Laurin was carried off to Bern (Verona) where he was baptized and became a thane+ of Dietrich. (ed. G. Holtz, Halle, 1897) (Bibliog. 235)

Layamon, early 13th-century translator into English and enlarger of Wace's* *Brut,** a history of the kings of England. He increased Wace's 14,800 lines of Anglo-Norman verse to 32,200 lines. He added to the story to make it more specific and dramatic. For example, Wace said that after Arthur killed Lucius he ordered the body of the emperor to be taken, watched with great honor and then sent it to Rome on a bier for burial. Layamon related that Arthur ordered a tent pitched in a broad field, had the body of Lucius carried there and covered with gold-colored palls, and watched for three days while he had a long gold-covered chest made. Then with the emperor's body inside he had it sent to Rome under escort of three kings. Even more important were his additions which described behavior, expressed feelings in speech and supplied dramatic incidents. It is a highly important work in the Arthurian corpus. (ed. and trans. Eugene Mason, *Arthurian Chronicles*, New York: E. P. Dutton, 1928; repr. 1972, pp. 116-264) (Bibliog. 129)

Le Bel, Jean (d. 1370), canon from Liège, who took part in the English King Edward III's* campaign against the Scots in 1327. Covering 1272-1361 and written in French, his *Chronique de Jean le Bel* dealt mainly with the wars of England and France for which it was one of the most important historical sources; Le Bel was an admirer of Edward III. (ed. Jules Viard and Eugene Deprez, Paris: *ShF*, 2 vols., 1904-1905) (Bibliog. 99)

Legend of King Arthur, ballad of 100 verses in which Arthur* recounted his own history from his begetting to his last battle after Mordred's* treason. (in Bishop Thomas Percy, *Reliques of Ancient English Poetry*, ed. Henry Wheatley, Gloucester, MA: Peter Smith, 1966) (Bibliog. 177)

De Legibus et consuetudinibus Angliae libre quinque. See Bracton, Henry of.

Legnano, battle of (May 28, 1176), decisive battle fought north of Milan in 1176 between Frederick I,* Barbarossa, and the cities of the Lombard League.* At first, the heavy German cavalry broke through the ranks of the Lombards, and threw them into confusion, but around Carroccio, the German forces were checked by the desperate resistance of a handful of heroes defending a central point. By such stiff resistance the League's forces routed the imperial army. Frederick lost his shield,+ banner,+ cross, lance,+ and his war chests of gold and silver. His defeat in this battle not only destroyed his hopes for an Italian empire but also forced him to negotiate a humiliating peace with Pope Alexander III* and to focus his efforts on his German rival, Henry the Lion,* whom he held responsible for the battle's outcome by not participating. (Bibliog. 166, 228)

Leicester, town in Leicestershire, England, honored with the reputation of an earldom even before the Norman Conquest. Leofric,* husband of Lady Godiva,* was one of its earliest earls. Then, with the Norman invasion, the earldom changed. Roger de Beaumont, seigneur de Beaumont and Pont-Audemer, was a faithful supporter of the young Duke William,* even supplying 60 ships for William's invasion of England. He chose not to accompany that expedition, but remained in Normandy as a principal advisor of the Duchess Maud to whom William had entrusted the government, and as a custodian to whom William had sent Anglo-Saxon Earl Morcar as a prisoner. His son and heir, Robert de Beaumont, served with the Conqueror at Hastings* and received large grants of lands in Warwickshire and smaller ones in Leicester and elsewhere. In 1181, he inherited from his mother the *comté* of Meulan (Mellent) and was generally known as the count of Meulan. After he succeeded to his fathers's inheritance in Normandy, he became one of the wealthiest men in both Normandy and England. He sided with William II* and then with Henry I,* Beauclerc, so that he became one of the most highly trusted men in the country. Ivo de Grandmesnil, one of Robert II,* Curthose's strongest supporters when that claimant had invaded England at the instigation of his partisans in the baronage, had held large estates in Leicester which were confiscated. After peace had been restored between Henry I and Duke Robert, Ivo's confiscated estates were given to Beaumont for custody, and the king was adroitly persuaded not only to grant them as permanent holdings, but also to grant Beaumont interest in the remainder of the Leicester farm.+ With this, Robert Beaumont became earl of Leicester. He died in 1118 leaving three sons: Waleran and Robert (twins), and Hugh.

Waleran was granted the Norman and French fiefs, and was styled count of Meulan; Robert II, the English fief, with which as early as 1119 he styled himself earl of Leicester. When Henry II* ascended the throne in 1154, Robert II sided with him and made available to him thirty "fortresses." That support earned Robert the stewardships of England and Normandy, and the position of justiciar which he shared with Richard de Lucy.* He was the first baron to attest to the Constitutions of Clarendon,+ and side with King Henry against Thomas à Becket.* He died in 1168, and was succeeded by his only son and heir, Robert III. Unlike his father, though, Robert III, styled "Blanchemains" ("White hands"), was disloyal to Henry II: after siding with the young Henry* in his rebellion in 1173, he was deprived of his fief, and fled to France. He returned to England, landing in Suffolk, to join his fellow conspirator, Hugh Bigod,* the earl of Norfolk,* but was defeated and recaptured by Henry II's forces. After peace had been restored between Henry and his sons, one of the conditions was that the earl of Leicester be forgiven and released. By 1177 he was freed after Henry levied sufficiently large fines to defray his expenses. At Richard I's* coronation in 1189, Leicester carried one of the swords of state. He died in 1190 on his way home from the crusade,+ leaving as his successor his eldest son, Robert IV, who also had accompanied Richard I on his crusade and who was knighted at Messina on the outward trip to the Holy Land.

Robert IV defended the duchy of Normandy for Richard against the incursions of Philip II* during Richard's captivity, but was captured and held by the French monarch. After Richard's death, he supported King John,* acting as steward for the coronation in 1199, after a tight contest for the position with Roger Bigod, earl of Norfolk. He died in 1204 without male issue, leaving his two sisters Amice and Margaret, as co-heiresses. His English inheritance was extensive; King Philip II,* Augustus, of France appropriated his Norman estates when King John lost the duchy of Normandy. His sister Amice married Simon de Montfort,* siegneur de Montfort and Rochfort, and their son, Simon II, born in 1170, claimed the earlship of Leicester. Making the mistake of declaring his loyalty to Philip II, Augustus, Simon II lost his English lands when King John declared that double loyalty was incompatible. He became one of the most violent of the leaders of the Albigensian crusade+ in 1209, and died in 1218 while besieging Toulouse* when he was hit in the head by a rock thrown by a woman from the ramparts of the city. He left four sons. Aumary, the eldest, succeeded as heir of his father to his French holdings and to whatever English lands the English king could be persuaded to restore. As constable of France, he strongly supported the French crown. Because he hardly would jeopardize his strong French position by supporting the English crown, he tried to transfer his English holdings to his brother, Simon III, and wrote to Henry III* about it. Surprisingly, Henry accepted the offer, and in 1231, Simon III had his sword and homage accepted by the English king. By 1239, Simon III had been invested with the earldom of Leicester, and confirmed as steward of England. In 1259, he led the baronial opposition to the king which resulted in the Barons' War.* At Lewes,* Simon's forces routed the king's troops and captured the king and Prince Edward. For more than a year, Simon ruled England as a dictator in the king's name, and summoned to Parliament only supporters of his cause. During this period he gave himself the earldom of Chester.* A little more than a year later, however, he was killed at the battle of Evesham,* his forces were scattered, and all his lands and honours forfeit to the crown. Within a few months of Evesham, Edmund "Crouchback," second surviving son of Henry III, was given possession of the lands of Leicester and made its earl. He died in 1296 and was succeeded by his son, Thomas* of Lancaster, who was tried and beheaded for treason in 1322. Eventually, the earldom merged with the crown when Henry IV* ascended the throne in 1399. (Bibliog. 66, 101)

Leodegran (Leodegrance), king of Carmelide, father of both Gueneveres.* He was besieged by Rion and his pagan hosts, and ultimately was rescued by King Arthur's* forces. (Bibliog. 145)

Leofric, earl of Mercia in England; he married Lady Godiva.* See also Leicester. (Bibliog. 238)

Leofwine, Godwine's* next to youngest son. He followed the lead of his bother Harold* and became an English earl. He was exiled with the family by King Edward the Confessor* in 1051, joined Harold in Ireland, returned to England in 1052, and was killed in the battle of Hastings* in 1066. (Bibliog. 228)

Leopold V, duke of Austria* and Styria (1177-1194) who became the leader of the German crusading forces on the death of Frederick I,* Barbarossa. His conflict with Richard I* of England at Acre* led to Richard's being captured and imprisoned on his way back to England from the Holy Land in 1192. In 1192, he annexed Styria to the duchy of Austria and developed Vienna as his capital. (Bibliog. 199)

Lewes castle,+ originally granted to William de Warenne* when King William I* appointed him as justiciar in 1074, this fortress on the River Ouse in Sussex differed from the usual Norman castle by having two mottes of quaried chalk, one overlooking the town and containing the keep,+ the other overlooking the river. By the end of the 11th century, its wooden palisades had been replaced by stone walls built of flint rubble in the common Norman herringbone pattern. For that construction, the first course was of flat stones, and then the next course was placed sloping to the right, and the next sloping to the left, and then the pattern repeated. Despite its important geographic location, Lewes saw little fighting after the battle between Simon de Montfort* and the king's forces in 1264. (Bibliog. 247)

Lewes, battle of (May 14, 1264), battle in which tactics decided the battle between the forces of English King Henry III* and those of Earl Simon de Montfort* in the Barons' War.* To oppose the forces with which the rebellious Montfort had secured London, Henry III raised a large army in the Midlands which easily captured the towns of Nottingham,* Northampton* and Leicester.* He should have marched on London immediately, for the fall of the capital would have ended the war immediately, but he was delayed. When Montfort saw that the king was not going to attack London, he counterattacked and besieged the royalist stronghold of Rochester to the southeast of London. Hearing that Rochester was under siege, the king sent his son, Prince Edward* (later Edward I), with his forces in a huge sweep around London toward the coastal towns, and then along the south coast. His relentless drive crippled many horses and left thousands of foot-soldiers straggling along the 150-mile line of march. In reaction, Montfort amassed as large an army as he could and marched to attack Henry's main forces near Lewes. By approaching from the west, Montfort forced Henry and his troops either to fight in town, or to cross the River Ouse and fight at the foot of hills commanded by Montfort's men. Catching the king by surprise, the earl's smaller force had been divided into four battles+ of men, three to oppose the king's three battles, and the fourth kept in reserve. Accompanied by his French half-uncles, William de Valence and Guy de Lusignan,* Prince Edward commanded the right division. The center was commanded by the king's brother, Richard of Cornwall, king of the Romans, accompanied by his son Edmund, and three Scottish barons, Robert de Bruce,* John Baliol,* and John Comyn; the left division was under the command of the king himself. When the battle was joined, Montfort's men fought so ferociously that the king and Prince Edward realized that they had been beaten and surrendered. By the "Mise of Lewes," the king lay down his arms, gave up his son as hostage, and agreed to the terms to be settled by arbitration. Simon had won because his surprise attack had forced his opponent to fight in disorder before being able to array his host, and because he had kept a fourth battle in reserve to be used at the proper moment and place; that proper moment and place never materialized and the king lost. Tactics were all-important. (Bibliog. 166)

Leybourne, Roger de (d. 1271), English knight who slew Arnold de Montigny at a joust at Walden, Essex,* in 1252. He professed sorrow for the accident but because his lance was found to have been unbated+ he was suspected of murderous intent, for it was remembered that Arnold had unhorsed Roger and broken his leg in an earlier tournament. When he assumed the cross+ for a crusade, he was pardoned by the king. He became an intimate of Prince Edward,* and accompanied him to tournaments throughout England and France as steward and keeper of the prince's purse. In 1258, he sided with the baronial party and swore to the Provisions of Oxford.* Later, acting as the prince's steward in the Welsh marches* in 1260, he hanged some servants of Richard de Clare, the fifth earl of Gloucester.* When he was accused of hanging them unjustly and without trial, he and the prince quarreled. Queen

Eleanor, angered by Leybourne's association with the barons, persuaded Prince Edward to demand an accounting of Leybourne's stewardship of the prince's money. After an audit by the Exchequer determined that Leybourne was £1,000 short, probably a false accusation, he was stripped of his holdings. To survive, he turned to marauding, allying himself first with Roger de Clifford* and then with Simon de Montfort.* By August, he had become reconciled with Prince Edward, and had become his steward once again. He was captured at Lewes* and he fought beside the prince at Evesham* and saved the wounded king's life. For that and his help with the pacification of the country after that battle, he was granted estates confiscated from the rebelling barons. He promised to accompany Prince Edward on the crusade, but his health prevented him from going, and he died in 1271. (Bibliog. 58)

Leybourne, William de, first English admiral*, appointed in 1286 by King Edward I* under the title of "Admiral de la mer du Roy d'Angleterre." (Bibliog. 68)

Libeaus Desconus, also known as the "Fair Unknown," this Middle English* romance was written in the second quarter of the 14th century by a Kentish poet who may have been Thomas Chestre, author of *Sir Launfal,* and *Octavian.* It paralleled three other works: Renaud de Beaujeu's *Le Bel Inconnu* (c. 1190), the Middle High German* *Wigalois* (c. 1210),* and the Italian *Carduino* (c. 1375). Guinglain, the hero, was the bastard son of Gawain* and Ragnell.* Raised in seclusion by his mother, he was knighted by King Arthur* as Libeaus Desconus (Le Bel Inconnu the Handsome Unknown) because he did not know his own name, and was trained by Gawain. He won the Lady of Sinadoune despite her mockery of his actions; he defeated the steward of the castle+ of Sinadoune, and slew the evil necromancer, Maboun, who had put an evil magical spell on the lady. In this story, he became famous for his chivalrous deeds for the maiden Elene. This story was reminiscent of the *enfances** of other heroes, including Perceval.* (ed. M. Mills, London: *EETS OS* #261, 1969; modern version tr. by Jessie Weston, London, 1902) (Bibliog. 10, 202)

Limoges, city in west central France which in the 10th century became a viscountship. Near it at Chaluz in 1199, Richard I* of England was killed while besieging a castle.+ Its worst memory concerned Edward,* the Black Prince, heir to the throne of England. In August 1370, the French King Charles persuaded the bishop of Limoges to renounce his oath of fealty to the Black Prince, and to bestow his allegiance to the French king. With only a small garrison to defend it, Limoges found itself the focus of the Black Prince's wrath. He was determined to make an example of it for its defection. So ill that he had to command from a litter, the Black Prince ordered an assault of the town. He had miners tunnel under the walls, propping them with wooden posts. When these were set afire, the tunnels collapsed, causing great sections of the wall to collapse. The English forces raced into the city, blocked the gates, and massacred the inhabitants. Despite their pleas to the prince for mercy, he ordered no one spared, although he made some exceptions for a few important dignitaries who were valuable for ransom.+ See spoils of war.+ After the massacre, it was sacked and burned and its fortifications were razed. Although this horror slowed resistance to the English forces for a brief period, it led to such hatred of the English that fifty years later it brought Joan of Arc to Orléans. (Bibliog. 223)

Limousin, city in western France which became part of the duchy and kingdom of Aquitaine* in the 8th century. In the 10th century, the title passed to the dukes of Aquitaine while the land was subdivided into a large number of feudal seignories. By the 12th century, it was called the "land of the troubadours," and was a hotbed of revolutionaries. Henry II* of England, who became its suzerain* on his marriage to Eleanor of Aquitaine,* had to use hired English troops to maintain his control of the territory, and in 1173 entrusted that duty to his second son, Richard Coeur de Lion,* who was crowned duke of Aquitaine at Limoges. Dispute over the territory continued until 1386 when it finally fell to French control. (Bibliog. 98)

Limousin astronomer, anonymous writer from Limousin, known as the astronomer because of his interest in heavenly bodies, who wrote a life of Charlemagne's* son, Louis I,* the Pious, after 840. Entitled *Vita Hludovici Pii,* it depicted Louis in admirable terms, for the writer was an admirer of his subject. He presented Charlemagne's expedition into Spain as a veritable crusade+ destined to lead the Moors to the true faith. (in *Monumenta Germaniae historica,* II, 604-648) (Bibliog. 106, 231)

Lincoln, town in Lincolnshire, England. It was a town of great renown and strength from the time of the Britons; in Norman times, it was one of the largest and most vigorous cities in England. William d'Aubigny, earl of Aumale,* who married Queen Adeliz, widow of King Henry I* (died 1135), was created the first earl of Lincoln shortly after the accession of Stephen of Blois* to the throne. With that creation, the king granted to him lands recently forfeited by the late bishop of

Lincoln. Other than those lands, William owned no land in the county, and being created an earl of a locale in which he owned no land was an exception to the usual rule of the time. Stephen, however, may well have bestowed that earldom to enlist the support of a man who had extensive fiefs elsewhere, including the useful castle-port of Arundel. Stephen also recognized the claim to this earldom of William de Roumare who owned large tracts of Lincolnshire land from his mother. He had supported Henry I, and was supposed to have sailed to England on the White Ship* with Prince William in 1120, but did not embark and so was saved. After a violent quarrel with Henry I about his land, Roumare fled to his native France until he and the king resolved their dispute; thereafter he became a favorite companion of Henry I. When Henry died in 1135, Roumare was one of those placed in charge of the defense of the frontier of Normandy. He was made earl of Cambridge* first because William d'Aubigny, earl of Aumale, was at first the earl of Lincoln, and thus kept him out of the title. After being captured at Lincoln, Stephen purchased de Roumare's support by granting him the earldom of Lincoln about 1141; d'Aubigny was created earl of Sussex.* Roumare spent most of his time strengthening his positions in Lincolnshire, building among others the castle of Bolingbroke. His son, William II, predeceased him in 1151, so the land and title passed to his grandson, William III, a man who made no mark on history, and when he died without issue in 1198, the earldom became extinct.

The next creation occurred in 1217 when the 60-year-old Earl Ranulph of Chester* became the earl of Lincoln. He was one of the two leading barons supporting the regency of the infant King Henry III,* the other being William Marshal, earl of Pembroke.* When Ranulph died without issue, the earldom passed to his sister, Hawise, in 1232, and thence to her son-in-law, John de Lacy. His grandson, Henry de Lacy (1251-1311), was girded with the sword of the earldom in 1271. He became a noted military leader and devoted servant of the king. For example, he was sent overseas to arrange the marriage of the king's daughter to the son of the duke of Brabant,* and then to Scotland* to escort Alexander III* on a visit to England. Because both of his sons died in accidents, the earldom passed to his daughter, Alice, who married Thomas* of Lancaster, son of Edmund Lancaster, the king's son. Thomas was a continual thorn in the king's side, and ended by opposing him in open revolt at the battle of Boroughbridge* during the reign of Edward II,* and was disinherited, had his lands and honours forfeited to the crown, and then executed in 1322. His wife was left a life tenant of the property she had inherited, but on her death in 1348, the title of earl of Lincoln reverted to the crown. King Edward III* bestowed it upon Henry of Grosmont,* earl of Lancaster, in 1349. Among its later earls were John of Gaunt,* third son of Edward III, and his son, Henry Bolingbroke, who became King Henry IV* in 1399. (Bibliog. 47, 66, 101)

Lincoln, battle of (February 2, 1141), fight between the forces of King Stephen* and those of Ranulph of Chester,* Robert of Gloucester* and other supporters of Matilda FitzEmpress.* With his characteristic fatal view of chivalry, before the battle began Stephen threw away the advantage of his position on the easily defendable heights by descending to the plains for a "fair fight." Five of his earls (Richmond, Norfolk, Northampton, Surrey and Worcester) even suggested starting the battle with a formal joust. When the actual confrontation occurred, however, Stephen's cavalry were unable to withstand the ferocity of Ranulph's charge. At that, the same five earls fled in disorder, and his forces on the left flank deserted him. Those retreats left him and his reserves of dismounted knights to face the combined attack of enemy horse and footsoldiers. Stephen personally put up a staunch fight, slashing with his sword+ until it snapped in his hand, and then with his Danish axe+ until it, too, broke. He was felled with a stone. William de Kahains sprang forward and seized him by the nasal of his helmet and forced him to yield himself prisoner to Gloucester. (Bibliog. 11, 180)

Lincoln Fair, battle of. See Dame Nicolaa de la Haye.

Lincoln's Inn. See Inns of Court.

Lion de Bourges, chanson de geste from the 14th century glorifying the viscount of Bourges. Its hero, Lion de Bourges, followed the adventures of *Huon de Bordeaux,* including the Grateful Dead motif. (ed. William Kibler, J. L. Richerit, and T. S. Fenster, Geneva: Droz, 1980) (Bibliog. 135)

Lionel of Antwerp (1338-1368), duke of Clarence; second surviving son of King Edward III* of England. At age 4 he married Elizabeth, aged 10, daughter of William de Burgh, third earl of Ulster, but did not consummate the marriage until he was 14. By this marriage, he became the earl of Ulster, and acquired the right to vast estates in Ireland, and a large part of the estates of the de Clare family by right of his wife's paternal grandmother, Elizabeth, "Lady of Clare."* He was created duke of Clarence in 1362. At age 7, he had been made "Guardian of England," and as earl of Ulster, had been made a Knight of the Garter,* and chief governor of Ireland in 1365. As Duke of Clarence, he took an active role in court affairs, and actively participated in the Hundred Years War* under his father's command. His wife died in 1363. When he died without male issue in 1368, the dukedom of Clarence became extinct and the Irish earldom of Ulster and the honour of Clare* devolved on his daughter Philippa, who, in 1368, married Edmund Mortimer, earl of March.* Their son, Roger Mortimer, was proclaimed by Richard II to be the heir presumptive* to the throne which Henry IV usurped on the death of King Richard in 1399. When their great-great-grandson and heir ascended the throne in her right as Edward IV in 1461, the honour of Clare became vested in the crown. (Bibliog. 47)

"Little Charlemagne." See Peter of Savoy.

Livre d'Artus, continuation of Robert de Boron's* *Merlin** in late 13th century French. Its principal hero was Gauvain (Gawain*) who went through a series of battles, duels, spells, imprisonments, and amours until the story ended abruptly as he came to the aid of a lady being dragged by her hair. (ed. H. O. Sommer, *Vulgate Version of Arthurian Romances*, Washington: Carnegie Institute, VIII, 1913) (Bibliog. 10)

Llewelyn ap Iorwerth, the Great (d. 1240), prince of North Wales, afterwards called Prince of Wales (but not the heir apparent* to the English crown). About 1176, he was expelled from his country by his half-brother, Davydd ap Owein. In 1194, with the help of an uncle and some cousins, he drove Davydd from Wales. After Davydd died in England in 1203, Llewelyn laid the foundations for his forty-year reign. King John's* troubles with his barons, followed by King Henry III's* problems with civil wars early in his youthful reign, gave Llewelyn ample opportunity to consolidate his hold on Wales. He extended his power into South Wales in 1207, opposed King John with some success between 1208 and 1211, regained possessions and finally conquered all of South Wales from 1212 to 1215 so that by 1216, he had become prince of all Wales not ruled by the Normans from the English throne. He did homage to King Henry III in 1218, fought against the English in 1228, and finally submitted again to Henry in 1237. (Bibliog. 58)

Llwyd, Gruffyd (fl. 1321), Welsh hero called the "lion of Trevgarnedd." Son of Ednyved Vychan, he was knighted by King Edward I* for bringing him at Rhudddlan the news (rumors+) of the birth of his son Edward at Caernarvon.* After a long period of good relationship with the English, Llwyd grew disgusted with their oppressions and negotiated with Edward Bruce,* brother of Robert

Bruce, in Ireland. Failing in his negotiations with the Irish, Llwyd rose in revolt and was defeated by the English, captured, and imprisoned in Rhuddlan castle. (Bibliog. 58)

Loenais, Lothian, territory in Arthurian romance between the Firth of Forth and the River Tweed in Scotland,* including part of Northumbria in England. (Bibliog. 242)

Logres, kingdom located in Britain south of the Humber and east of the Severn River in Arthurian romance. Its name supposedly was derived from Locryn, Brutus' successor. The name later was given to the capital city and subsequently called London. (Bibliog. 202)

Lohengrin, Middle High German* epic poem of unknown authorship written around 1280. At one point in the work an acrostic spelled out the name NOUHUSIUS which has been interpreted as Neuhaus or Neuhausa, but no such poet has been recorded. This story centered on the hard-pressed fortunes of the duchess of Brabant* whose rights were maintained by the Knight of the Swan whom she then married. When later she transgressed his injunction not to ask his name, he departed. The story was filled with descriptions of chivalric and courtly life, battles, banquets, tourneys, and hunts, and included a history of the reigns of German kings Henry I* and Henry II.* (ed. H. Ruckert, 1858; trans. H. A. Junghaus, Reclams *Universal-Bibliothek* 1199-1200) (Bibliog. 235)

Lohot, King Arthur's* son by Guenevere,* according to Geoffrey of Monmouth.* Malory's *Morte D'Arthur,*, however, named him the illegitimate offspring of Arthur and Lysanor who was slain by Sir Kay. He also was called Borre le Cure (Coeur) Hardy by Malory. (Bibliog. 89, 145)

Lombard League, association of cities and communes in northern Italy* which organized in 1164 to oppose the imperial policies of the Emperor Frederick I,* Barbarossa. Actively supported by Pope Alexander III,* thisz league mobilized against the emperor. It continued to oppose him until 1177 when he and the pope came to an agreement. His subsequent attempt to destroy the league backfired, however, and two years later his humiliating defeat at Legnano* at the hands of the pope forced him to give up his dream of including Italy in the empire. The league continued as a powerful force in Italian politics until the death of Frederick II* in 1250 caused its dissolution. (Bibliog. 98)

Lombardy, province in northern Italy named for the Lombards who in the 6th century conquered most of Italy and divided it into duchies. In the 7th and 8th centuries, the name became restricted to the northern and central parts of Italy ruled directly by the king from the capital at Pavia. Charlemagne* annexed it to his empire in 774. (Bibliog. 98)

London, Treaty of (January 1358). Treaty negotiated between the French and the English for the release of French King John II* who had been captured at the battle of Poitiers* (1365). It it, the Dauphin* agreed to surrender the sovereignty of Guienne,* and other territories comprising at least one-third of France. (See Treaty of Bretigny.) In addition, John's ransom was set at 4 million gold ecus,+ payable at fixed installments, to be guaranteed by the delivery of forty hostages. King Edward III* was to renounce his claim to the French throne. Edward was so encouraged by the Dauphin's difficulties with this, that he decided he wanted more, and proposed a second treaty. He added the demand for Anjou,* Maine, Normandy,* and the Pas-de-Calais, together with the overlordship of Brittany. Because of those excessive demands, the Estates of France found this second treaty to be unacceptable, and so they rejected it, and the Hundred Years War* continued. (Bibliog. 203, 223)

Longchamps, William (d. 1197), grandson of a Norman serf who rose to become bishop of Ely and justiciar+ of England under King Richard I.* A greedy and rapacious man not of noble descent, he was driven by ambition. He bought the chancellorship+ from Richard I in 1189 for £3,000, even though Reginald, bishop of Bath and Wells offered £4,000. Giraldus Cambrensis* gave a powerful portrait of this man whom he hated:

> He was short and contemptible in stature and crippled in both haunches, with a big head and with the hair on his forehead coming down almost to his eyebrows like an ape. He was very dark, with little sunken black eyes, a flat nose, a snarling face. His beard below his eyes and his hair above them were all shaggy; his chin was receding, and his lips were spread apart in an affected, false and almost continual grin which he very suitably used as a disguise. His neck was short, his back was humped, his belly stuck out in front and his buttocks at the rear. His legs were crooked and although his body was small, his feet were huge. (Bibliog. 7)

He was elevated to justiciar after the death of the earl of Essex,* whom Richard had chosen to be joint justiciar with the bishop of Durham* in the north of England. Simultaneously, in the absence of Baldwin, archbishop* of Canterbury, Longchamps was appointed papal legate by Pope Clement III, thus controlling both the secular administration and the powerful episcopate in England. In Richard I's absence in 1190, he was papal legate, chancellor, and the king's representative in England besides being bishop of Ely. He arranged a treaty with King William* of Scotland whereby the king of the Scots agreed to recognize Prince Arthur,* son of Geoffrey* of Brittany, who was his nephew also, as heir to the throne in opposition to Richard's announced preference for John. His triple position of legate, chancellor, and justiciar was more than he could handle. Despite his unquestioned loyalty to the absent Richard I, he was overbearing, flamboyant, and extravagant, and his insatiable lust for power brought about his downfall in October 1191. On the death of Baldwin, archbishop of Canterbury, Longchamps hoped to be elected to that position, and seized its temporal possessions which reverted to the throne so long as the seat remained vacant; he already controlled the assets of the see at York.   Richard I reversed his opposition to his half-brother Geoffrey* and asked the pope to consecrate him as archbishop* of York, and thus to provide some control over Longchamps as bishop of Ely at least in church matters. Longchamps realized that he was losing power and faced problems accounting for the revenues from York which he had wasted. He tried unsuccessfully to prevent Geoffrey's return, and then had him arrested. News of this outrage so inflamed England that Longchamps realized he had made a fatal blunder. He sent Hamelin,* earl of Warenne, to release Geoffrey from Dover castle. Count John* ordered a meeting to discuss Longchamps, but Longchamps chose not to attend. After hearing from Archbishop Geoffrey and Walter of Coutances, bishop of Rouen, with his letters from King Richard, the barons+ of the *curia regis** forcibly removed Longchamps from office and appointed Walter; at the same time, they gave Prince John the title of regent and heir apparent.*

This action was the precursor of the baronial revolt which led to the *Magna Carta Libertatum+* in 1215. Longchamps was deprived of his offices of chancellor and chief justiciar, and surrendered his castles seized after Richard had left the country, but he was allowed to keep Dover,* Cambridge* and Hereford castles because they were too far apart to cause any threat. Taken to his castle at Dover, and despite the dangers to his brothers who were hostages for his word, he tried to flee the country against his oath not to do so, and became a laughing stock for his efforts. Disguising himself as a woman in a long green gown with a hood pulled over his face, he stood on the shore of Dover with a length of cloth draped over his arm as though for sale and a staff in his hand while his servants sought a ship for him to cross the Channel. As he waited, a fisherman, wet and cold from the sea, attempted to warm himself by embracing the chancellor. With his left hand around Longchamps' neck, the fisherman attempted certain familiarities with his right hand that revealed the chancellor's sex. When the fisherman tried to summon his mates to admire this marvellous masquerade, Longchamps' servants drove them away. Next came a woman who fingered the cloth and asked the price. Since he knew no English, he couldn't answer her. The woman called a friend, and together they pulled away the hood to reveal the dark close-shaven man's face. Their shrieks drew a crowd to help stone this monster. His servants were helpless, and could only watch as he was dragged through the streets of Dover being stoned, spit upon, and jailed for a week. King John ordered his release, and he went to Flanders.* He returned to England with Richard's return, but he never again had the power he once enjoyed. (Bibliog. 7, 38, 228)

Longespee, William (d.1226), illegitimate son of King Henry II,* perhaps by Rosamund Clifford, William was made third earl of Salisbury* when in 1198 he married Ela, daughter and heiress of William, second earl of Salisbury. He held the castle of Pontorson in Normandy* which he exchanged early in King John's* reign for land in England, but surrendered them to the king in 1203. He was appointed sheriff of Wiltshire, a post he held for most of his life. Other appointments included being made lieutenant in Gascony* in 1202, constable+ of Dover castle and warden of the Cinque Ports* until 1206, warden of the Welsh marches* in 1208, and ambassador to the prelates and princes of Germany on behalf of his nephew Otto,* who later that year was crowned emperor. During King John's excommunication, he was thought to have been one of his evil counsellors who were ready to do anything the king wished. His name was also associated with one of the king's most tyrannical deeds. On orders from the king, William seized Geoffrey of Norwich at Dunstable. Geoffrey was one of John's ablest clerks, but he withdrew from the Exchequer,* for he said it did not believe it fitting for a clerk to keep company with an excommunicate. On orders from the furious King John, Geoffrey was imprisoned at Bristol castle and had a heavy leaden cope placed on him so that it crushed him to death. Later, in 1213, along with the count of Holland and the count of Boulogne,* Longespee led a fleet of 500 ships and 700 knights across the English Channel to destroy the French invasion fleet amassed by King Philip II* at Damme, near Bruges in Flanders.* So large that the harbor couldn't hold them all, this French fleet was attacked by Longespee. He sent to England the 300 ships laden with provisions and arms he captured outside the harbor, burned 100 that were beached, and then attacked the remainder within the harbor the next day. His force was driven off by King Philip, but the severe loss of ships and materiel caused the French to abandon the invasion. Next, Salisbury was made marshal of John's army in Flanders, and joined with the Emperor Otto IV* and other allies of the English king to move against Philip. Captured at the battle of Bouvines,* he was exchanged for Robert, son of the count of Dreux, who had been captured a few days previously. Then, after he stood beside King John at Runnymede in 1215, he was made captain of the army in the south so that he and Faulkes de Breauté* could watch London and sever the supply lines to the barons; then the two men ravaged Ely. When Prince Louis* landed in 1216, Salisbury believed that John's cause was lost, so he switched allegiance, and gave his castle at Salisbury to the French prince, but reversed his allegiance after John's death in 1216, and supported the new King Henry III* by helping William the Marshal against the Welsh in 1223. He died in 1226. (Bibliog. 58, 98, 107)

"Longshanks," nickname given to King Edward I* of England because his unusual height (6 feet 2 inches) when he stood in his stirrups made him appear extraordinarily tall. He was at least eight to ten inches taller than the average man of his day. (Bibliog. 35)

Longsword, William. See Longespee, William.

lord, from the Anglo-Saxon *hlaford* meaning *dominus* or senior, this word in the medieval sense denoted the head of a household in his relationship to his servants and dependents who "eat his bread"; it came to be used for anyone who had vassals and held lands, cultivated by dependent peasants. This lord could be a vassal of a higher lord, and so on up a feudal pyramid to the king who was the chief lord of the kingdom. (Bibliog. 98, 169)

Lords mayor of London. In 1190, London acquired from William Longchamps,* lord chancellor+ of England, the right to elect its own sheriffs. Previous attempts to organize a communal type of government similar to that of French towns had been suppressed sternly by King Henry II* but by 1193, like the communes of northern France, it had a mayor and echevins.* By 1206, this governing group had won the confidence of the citizens of London, and became the accepted govening body of London; its mayor at first held his office for life. King John* in 1215 granted the citizens of London a charter which allowed them the right to elect their mayor annually. The inclusion of the mayor of London among twenty-four barons elected to carry out the terms of the *Magna Carta Libertatum*+ showed the importance of the position. The lord mayor signed himself with his surname only, in the manner of a peer, and added the title of Mayor, his original title. The first allusion to lord mayor occurred in 1283. By the 14th century, the lord mayor was the head of the city corporation, its chief magistrate and the chairman of its two governing bodies: the Court of Aldermen and the Court of the Common Council. Its first lord mayor was Henry FitzAlwyn who served from 1191 until his death in 1212. (Bibliog. 101, 180)

Lord Prince, name for the heir apparent* to the English throne. Before he became king, Edward I* was known as Edward the Lord Prince; while he was king, Edward I created the title of Prince of Wales* for his son, the English heir apparent who became King Edward II.* See Edward I. (Bibliog. 183)

Lords Appellant, group of English earls who were opposed to the concessions which King Richard II* and his supporters were offering to the rebels in the Great Revolt (Peasant's Revolt) of 1381. One of the king's closest advisors and supporters was the earl of Suffolk.* The earl of Gloucester* allied with parliament to oppose the king; this group soon was joined by the earls of Warwick* and Arundel,* and called itself the Lords Appellant. They impeached and imprisoned the earl of Suffolk, but he was promptly released by the king. Then they marched on London and seized control of the government. Under their control and guidance, the Merciless Parliament of 1388 impeached and executed two of the king's ministers, and issued a general proscription to the royalists. By 1389, the king felt he could resume control alone, and demanded the resignation of several ministers appointed by the Lords before he took the government into his own hands. (Bibliog. 124)

Lords Ordainers, group of nobles assembled to control the actions and government of King Edward II.* Basing their idea on the committee formed by the Provisions of Oxford* fifty years before, the barons, after Piers Gaveston,* the king's favorite, had been exiled a second time in 1310, forced the king to issue letters patent+ permitting "the prelates, earl, barons and others, whomever they may choose,...to ordain and establish the state of our realm and household according to right and reason" before Michaelmas,+ 1311. The king bound himself to accept the resultant ordinances and in return, the archbishop* of Canterbury and ten bishops, eight earls, and thirteen barons issued a declaration that the king's concession should not form a precedent. Elected on March 20 in the Great Painted Chamber* at Westminster,* the Lords Ordainers were to be chosen in the following manner. The prelates were to elect two earls, these two earls to elect two bishops, and then those four were to elect two barons; those six were then to choose fifteen others. The final composition was comprised of the archbishop of Canterbury, six bishops: London, Salisbury, Chichester (who was the Chancellor of England), Norwich, St. David's, and Llandaff; eight earls: Gloucester,* Lancaster,* Hereford,* Lincoln,* Pembroke,* Richmond,* Warwick,* and Arundel*; and six barons: Hugh de Vere,* William Marshal, Robert FitzRoger, Hugh Courtenay, William Martin, and John Grey of Wilton. All these men swore to make ordinances to the honor and profit of the church, king and people according to right reason and the king's coronation oath.+ (Bibliog. 182)

Lorraine, province in eastern France which originally was part of the Frankish kingdom, but by the Treaty of Verdun* (843) was given to the Emperor Lothaire,* eldest son of King Louis the Pious,* and was known as Francia Media.* It passed to Lothaire's son, Lothaire II, and was renamed Lotharingia.   From 869, it was contested by the kings of Germany and France. In 925 it became a duchy under the Holy Roman Empire. During the 13th century, several fiefs escaped ducal control: the bishoprics of Metz, Toul, and Verdun were three of them.   The dukes of Lorraine supported the empire and derived support from it. (Bibliog. 98, 100)

Lot, Loth, Lott, king of Lothian* and Orkney* in Arthurian legend. Brother of Urien* and Augwys, he married Arthur's* half-sister Anna (in Layamon*) or Morgawse (in Malory*) or Belisent* (in *Merlin*) and became the father of Gawain,* Agravaine,* Gaheret,* Gareth* (Gaheris). He was a rebellious vassal in the early years of Arthur's reign, but later became reconciled with Arthur through his son's efforts on Arthur's behalf in battles. Arthur unknowingly begot Mordred* on his own sister, Lot's wife. (Bibliog. 202)

Lothaire (795-855), as eldest son of Louis I,* the Pious, he was destined to inherit the imperial title of the Carolingian Empire (840-855). From 811 he assisted his father, but in 828 he revolted against him, and defeated him in 831. His first years as emperor were marked by constant struggles with his two brothers, Charles the Bald* and Louis the German.* An agreement, signed at Verdun* in 843, divided the empire: Lothaire was to receive the imperial title and the Francia

Media*: the middle kingdom, Italy, Burgundy, the land along the Rhine, Rhône, Meuse and Scheldt rivers, including the two capitals of Rome and Aix la Chapelle.* Shortly before his death, he divided his lands among his three sons: Louis II, Charles, and Lothaire. (Bibliog. 98, 124)

Lothian, kingdom in Arthurian legend located in southern Scotland between the Firth of Forth and the River Tweed, and including a portion of Northumbria; its king was Lot,* father of Gawain.* (Bibliog. 202, 242)

Lotharingian cycle, five *chansons de geste** dealing with figures from Lorraine: *Mort Garin le Loherenc** and *Girbert de Mes** from the 12th century, and *Hervis de Mes,** *Anseis, fils de Gerbert,** and *Yon* from the 13th century. It centered on the bitter strife between the Lotharingians* and the Bordelais.* (Bibliog. 106, 231)

Loudon Hill, battle of (1307), conflict between Robert Bruce* and Aymer of Valence,* earl of Pembroke* which forecast Bannock Burn.* Bruce with 600 followers was on Loudon Hill where de Valence came to hunt him down. Bruce took a position about two bow-shots wide through which a road ran. He narrowed the position by digging ditches on the banks to leave an opening of only about 50 yards on each side of the road. On this position he drew up all his men dismounted with pikes levelled. De Valence could have destroyed Bruce had he sent his archers first, but instead chose to charge with his cavalry, expecting to ride over the Scots easily. Twice his charges were repulsed, leaving over a hundred men-at-arms dead. Seeing those dead lying in front of the Scots line, de Valence immediately withdrew before his infantry and rear-battle could strike a blow. (Bibliog. 166)

Louis I, the Pious (778-840), Carolingian emperor also called *der Fromme* (Ger. "Pious"), and *le Debonnaire* (Fr. "Easy"), who succeeded his father Charlemagne* in 814 and ruled until 840. Youngest son of Charlemagne, he was destined to inherit Aquitaine,* but as the sole survivor of his father, he inherited the whole empire. Even though he clamped down on all opposition, his empire was turbulent and difficult to govern. He sought support from the high clergy in return for which he granted them extensive privileges. In 795, fearful that the attractions of the flesh might lure him into wrong alliances, Louis married Irmingard, daughter of Count Ingramnus who held castles along the borders of Aquitaine. Following the precedent set by his father in 806, he divided his empire among his three sons, Pepin,*

Lothaire,* and Louis,* but in 823, after a fourth son, Charles (afterwards Charles the Bald), was born by his second wife, Judith of Bavaria, Louis cancelled the division of the empire and gave Alemannia to Charles when he was only 9; this was followed by granting him Aquitaine a year later in 833, and Burgundy,* Provence,* and Septimania in 837. In 838, after Pepin died, he reassigned the whole empire and in 839 gave all the provinces in the Jura and the valley of the Rhône, east of Muen, to Lothaire; Bavaria* to Louis; the romance-speaking territory of the west to Charles, his favorite. Aquitaine continued in the hands of Pepin's son, Pepin II, until 848. Louis was a weak ruler who served as a model of an ungrateful or pusillanimous king for writers of later *chansons de geste** who needed a model around whom to center the action. (Bibliog. 6, 98, 117)

Louis II, *le Bègue*, the "Stammerer" (846-879), king of France and son of Charles the Bald,* and grandson of Louis I,* the Pious. On the death of his elder brother Charles, second son of Charles the Bald, he was consecrated king of Aquitaine* in 867, and ten years later succeeded his father on the imperial throne, being crowned by Hincmar,* bishop of Reims, under the title of "king of the French by the mercy of God and the election of the people." He died after a feeble and ineffectual reign of only eighteen months. (Bibliog. 69)

Louis III, the "Blind" (880-928), son of Boso, and great-grandson of Lothaire, he became king of Provence* in 888. He was crowned Roman emperor after defeating his rival, Berenger I, in 901. In 905, while residing at Verona, he was surprised by his rival, blinded, and ultimately sent back to live a life of inactivity in Provence until his death. (Bibliog. 68)

Louis the Child (893-911), known as Louis III (and sometimes as IV), he was the son of the emperor Arnulf, and succeeded to the throne of East Francia or Germany* in 900 when he was six years old. During his brief reign, Germany, weakened by internal factions and strife, was desolated by continuing raids by invading Hungarians who defeated every force sent against them. As a result of the ensuing anarchy, the country was divided into several great duchies, the rulers of which, while acknowledging the supremacy of the king, became virtually independent themselves. (Bibliog. 68)

Louis IV, *"d'Outremer"* (921-954), son of Charles III, the "Simple," and grandson of Louis II.* As a result of disasters which befell his father in 922, he was taken by his mother Odgiva, sister of

Athelstan,* to England where he spent his boyhood. On the death of
Rodolf of Burgundy,* who had been elected king in place of Charles,
the choice of Hugh the Great, count of Paris, and other nobles fell
upon Louis who was brought to Germany and consecrated king in 936.
Count Hugh expected to dominate the young king, but found that Louis
was not easily maneuvered. He was captured and released only after
surrendering Laon to Hugh, but once released, he was able to reconquer
his kingdom with the help of the Germans and English. He died in 954.
(Bibliog. 68)

Louis IV (or V), the "Bavarian" (1286-1347), German king and Roman
emperor. The son of the duke of Bavaria,* after the death of the
Emperor Henry VII,* he was elected to the throne by five of the electors,* the others giving their votes to Frederick, duke of Austria.*
This split election led to civil war between Frederick, supported by
the church and many nobles, and Louis supported by the inhabitants of
the great cities. After winning the battle of Muhldorf and capturing
Frederick in 1322, and being excommunicated by Pope John XXII in 1324,
Louis sought peace by offering to free Frederick if he would withdraw
his claim to the throne and restore the imperial lands and cities his
supporters had captured in Swabia.* Even though Frederick agreed, his
brother Leopold, duke of Austria, refused, and Frederick was returned
to imprisonment. Louis thereupon suggested that the two should rule
jointly, a plan that was unworkable, and that ended with the death of
Frederick in 1330. By his marriage to Margaret, sister of Count
William of Holland, he secured Holland, Zealand, Friesland, and
Hainaut.* By separating Margaret Maultasch, heiress of Tyrol, from her
husband, a son of John, powerful king of Bohemia, and making her the
wife of his own son Louis to whom he had granted the march+ of
Brandenburg,* Louis created powerful enemies who fomented a new civil
war in 1346 to remove him from the throne. He died suddenly in 1347.
(Bibliog. 68)

Louis the German (804-876), son of the emperor Louis I.* In the first
partition of the empire in 817, he received Bavaria,* Bohemia,
Carinthia, and the subject territories on his eastern frontier.
Angered by the later schemes of division in favor of his half-brother
Charles,* Louis allied himself with his brothers Lothaire and Pepin
against the emperor, their father. After their father's death in 840,
Louis and Charles united against Lothaire whom they defeated in the
battle of Fontenay, and by the Treaty of Verdun,* Louis received the
whole of Germany to the east of the Rhine with Mainz, Spires and Worms
on the left bank. In 858, he invaded West Francia which he hoped to

unite with East Francia, his own state, but Charles the Bald* was stronger that he had realized and he was forced to retreat. Louis expected to obtain the crown after the death of the emperor, but Charles outwitted him, and he died in 876, trying to avenge that wrong. As the first sovereign who ruled over the Germans and over no other Western people, he was considered the founder of the German kingdom. (Bibliog. 68)

Louis V, *le Fainéant* the "Do-nothing" (966-987), son of Lothaire and grandson of Louis IV.* As the last of the Carolingian dynasty, he succeeded Lothaire in March 986 and died in May 987; he was succeeded by Hugh Capet.* His nickname described his effectiveness as a king: "do nothing." (Bibliog. 68)

Louis VI, *le Gros*, "the Fat" (1081-1137), king of France (1108-1137). Son of Philip I* of France and Bertha of Holland he was equally as fat as his father. He waited until he was 35 before marrying Adelaide of Maurienne, and sired one illegitimate daughter, Isabella, whom he married in 1117 to William, son of Osmond de Chaumont in the Vexin. Louis was such a gourmandizer that when he was 46, he was too fat to mount a horse. Further evidence of his greed was shown by examples of his selling his justice to whichever side bid the higher, and by his ordering a young Fleming flogged for refusing to reveal the hiding place of the treasure of Charles the Good, count of Flanders. Yet he was cleverer than his father in his support of the church. He relied on it, he defended it, and he secured its support. He had to spend a good deal of time fighting because he was considered to be both the leader of the army (*dux exercitus*) and defender of the realm (*defensor regni*). His first real taste of fighting occurred at age 16 when in 1097 he fought against William II,* king of England and duke of Normandy. Then he had to fight at the siege of Montmorency in 1101 and campaign against Dreu de Mouchy whose castle he burned. He continued to fight against his counts until in 1109, he had to begin fighting against Henry I* of England. At that time, he summoned his major vassals to serve in the royal army: Robert, count of Flanders; Thibaut IV, count of Blois; William II, count of Nevers; and Hugues II, count of Burgundy. Then he confronted King Henry who challenged him to single combat, but Louis refused. At Bremûle* in 1119, Louis was badly defeated by the English king. He reacted by assaulting Breteuil, but to make that attack, he summoned the bishops with their diocesan militia and then used the *levée en masse*+ to bring troops from Burgundy, Berry, Auvergne, Sens, Paris, Orleans, Vemandois, Beauvaisis, and Laon. Breteuil, however, held out against them. Such a show of resistance by Breteuil made France's greater nobles realize that they needed to devote more time to strengthening their own fiefs, and to live at peace with each other and the king. They further realized that a victory of the Anglo-Norman house over the Capetians would endanger their own interests. Thus they provided no assistance to English King Henry I in his continuing struggles with Louis. Only Thibaut IV, the Great (1093-1152), count of Blois and of Champagne, Louis' only real enemy among the vassals, sided with his uncle, King Henry, but Henry's death in 1135, two years before Louis', plunged his country into a dispute (Stephen* and Matilda* controversy) which benefitted the Capetians. About the same time, William X of Aquitaine died, leaving his daughter, Eleanor,* as his heiress. Whatever the desires of her father may have been, Eleanor married Louis' son, Louis VII,* an event which vastly enlarged the domains of the Capet family. (Bibliog. 74)

Louis VII, *le Jeune*, **"the Young"** (1120-1180), king of France (1137-1180). A tender-hearted, gentle, pious, and bookish man, who chose to live simply, was uniquely just, and was remarkably tolerant, as shown by his acceptance of the Jews in France. Crowned king in 1131 on the death of his older brother, he succeeded to sole rule on the death of his father in 1137. Recognizing the need for an heir to secure the succession of his dynasty, he married Eleanor of Aquitaine* who bore him only two daughters. After their divorce in 1153, Louis married again promptly in his attempt to obtain a male heir for the throne, but his second wife, Constance of Castile, also bore him only daughters. He tried a third time with Alice of Champagne and succeeded in 1167 when she bore him a son, "the Dieudonne" (the Godgiven), Philip II,* Augustus. In 1141, Louis made an unsuccessful attempt to assert his rights over Toulouse, and in 1142 quarreled bitterly with Pope Innocent II over the pontiff's appointment of a nephew to be archbishop of Borges. In his efforts to oust the newly appointed archbishop, Louis, who had been excommunicated, pursued him into Vitry in Champagne, and ordered the town sacked. As a result, the cathedral burned, causing the death of 300 persons who had taken refuge within its walls. Horror-struck at this event, Louis made peace with the clergyman and the pope, but found that nothing less than a pilgrimage to the Holy Land would expiate his crime. Before he could embark on such a trip, however, he learned from a sermon by St. Bernard* in 1444 that Edessa had fallen to the Muslims,* and Christians there had been massacred. Leaving the regency in the hands of Abbé Suger and Raoul, count of Vermandois, Louis set out for the Holy Land with his wife Eleanor, a large company of nobles and 24,000 men. The trip was a fiasco, and he returned a disillusioned man to France. Despite an absence of military victories, his prestige as a French king grew. From his reign, the demesne lands of the Ile de France* remained under the control of the crown. He was a loyal servant of the church, giving refuge and showing deference to Pope Alexander III* who had been driven from Rome by Emperor Frederick I,* Barbarossa. His major internal problem emerged from the growth within his kingdom of a feudal principality of unprecedented strength: the duchy of Aquitaine. Henry Plantagenet, by his marriage to Eleanor, heiress of Aquitaine, in 1152, had added that entire duchy to his inherited fiefs of Normandy and Anjou, and shortly thereafter to his kingdom of England when he ascended the throne. Louis then had to struggle to create a policy to handle this huge suzerainty within his dominions, and under his son, Philip II, Augustus, this policy bore fruit. He died in 1180. (Bibliog. 68, 74)

Louis VIII, the Lion (1187-1226), king of France (1223-1226). Son of Philip II,* Augustus, he had married Blanche* of Castile, granddaughter of Henry II* of England, in 1200. Successfully carrying on the work begun by his father, Philip II Augustus, he burnt himself out in three years of ceaseless activity. Because of marriage he was offered the crown of England in 1216 by the barons+ of England. Accepting that offer, he landed in England in May 1216, but retired early in 1217; he made a second attempt to claim the throne but was unsuccessful, and finally turned his attention to other matters in September 1217. He next took charge of launching the war against the Albigenses+; it continued after his accession to the throne. After that he successfully rounded out that period with the establishment of royal power in Poitou* and Languedoc by annexing Languedoc to the royal demesne.+ He died in Auvergne, probably of pestilence, after the capture of Avignon in 1226; he was succeeded by his son, Louis IX,* still a child. Because his will decreed that each of his sons should receive a portion of his inheritance but the essential unity of the kingdom should not be disrupted, it solidified the concept and system of *appanages*. He decreed that fiefs (*appanages*) should be created for each of his sons, and because his eldest son, Louis IX, was an honorable man, that will was carried out. Thus Louis obtained the kingdom, Robert* received Artois, Alphonse got Poitiers, and Charles was given Anjou. As the boys were only children when their father died, these grants were not given to them until later years. The king had hoped that these grants would prevent the growth of great feudal houses, but the opposite happened: great feudal houses developed which had claims to the throne should the direct line die out. This trouble became apparent by Edward III's* claim to the French throne in the 14th century resulting in the Hundred Years War.* (Bibliog. 68, 74, 124)

Louis IX, Saint Louis (1214-1270), king of France (1226-1270). Ascending the throne at age 12 under the regency of his mother, Blanche of Castile,* this son of Philip II,* Augustus, grew to demonstrate and live by an absolute and uncompromising sense of justice. He was an ideal feudal monarch: a saint on the throne who administered justice to all equally, who tolerated bravado and luxury among others, and who was deeply religious but not obsessed with priests and the priesthood. He transformed the monarchy which had been strong and feared into a monarchy which was loved and respected. Because they had lived under the iron rule of the strong monarch, Philip II, the barons of France saw a golden opportunity to revolt under the rule of a 12-year-old child and his mother. Pierre Mauclerc, count of Dreux, a Breton noble who had ruled Brittany since 1212 by reason of his wife, the sister of Arthur* and daughter of Geoffrey Plantagenet,* organized a coalition against the monarchy. Drawing into this group such foes of the crown as Henry III* of England, Philip Hurepel of Boulogne (a son of Philip II by Agnes de Meran), the duke of Burgundy and others, Pierre's first rebellion in 1226 was formless and haphazard, and was bought off by the queen. His second one shortly thereafter ended with the defection of Count Thibaut of Champagne who had fallen in love with the queen, and abandoned his former allies, and the defeat by Louis of an English invasion planned to coincide with operations of the rebels. Louis increased the holdings of the crown by buying in 1234 the suzerainty of Blois,* Chartres, Sancerre, and Chateaudun from Thibaut of Champagne who desperately needed money. Louis also established the king as the source of justice to whom all men, great and small alike, could turn for remedy of grievances.

The most important single event in his reign was the crusade+ he led to Egypt in 1248, which, with his captivity and sojourn in the Palestine,* kept him in the Near East until 1254. That crusade was made with purely religious motives, for he intended it to be a pious pilgrimage to redeem the holy places. Its failure so rankled in his heart that he felt compelled to repeat the enterprise late in his life, and died on this second crusade in 1270. As a statesman, he did much to make France recognized as a world power because whenever possible he practiced a policy of compromise instead of war with other great states. In 1258, for example, he signed the Treaty of Corbeil with Aragon whereby he gave up all French claims to the old Spanish March that included Roussillon and Catalonia, and King James gave up all the Aragonese claims to Languedoc with the exception of the city of Montpellier. His most famous concession to keep peace was his treaty with England in 1259. Henry III had supported and assisted Pierre Mauclerc in his revolt in 1229 and had been defeated by Louis. Henry again interfered with French affairs in 1241 by supporting the revolt of his stepfather, Hugh of Lusignan. Isabelle of Angoulême, wife of King John* and mother of Henry III, had married Hugh to whom she had been engaged before she married John. Over some slight to her dignity, she convinced her husband to revolt, and persuaded her son to help his stepfather with a small army that invaded Poitou in 1242. Louis met and defeated this army at Taillebourg in 1242 which drove the English out of the country once more. Louis did not take advantage of that position, however, and in 1259, he negotiated with Henry the Treaty of Paris* in which he restored to Henry the districts of Perigord, Quercy and the Limousin on condition that Henry relinquish all claims to Anjou and perform homage to him for all his lands in France. Louis explained this by saying that he would rather have a loyal vassal than an enemy, and pointed out that his children and Henry's were cousins, since both Louis and Henry had married sisters, daughters of the count of Provence, and he wanted perpetual peace between cousins. Ironically, this treaty became one of the remote causes for the Hundred Years War* which broke out many years later. Louis was so respected throughout Europe that he was selected by the English barons as the arbiter for their grievances against Henry III at the time of the Barons' War* in England. The Mise* of Amiens which Louis handed down in 1264 in compliance with that request decided against the barons, and de Montfort* refused to accept it. After his death in 1270, the throne passed to his eldest son Philip III* (1270-1285). (Bibliog. 7, 124)

Louis X, *le Hutin*, "the Headstrong" (1289-1316), king of France. As the eldest son of Philip IV,* the Fair, and Joan of Navarre, he succeeded his mother in the kingdom of Navarre and countships of Champagne and Brie in 1305. He was called the Headstrong probably to commemorate his wild and boisterous youth. He died after an uneventful reign of two years. (Bibliog. 68)

Louis I, of Anjou, king of Naples (1339-1384). Titular king of Naples, he was granted the duchy of Anjou* by his father, King John II* of France. He helped his brother, Charles V,* restore royal authority in France, and simultaneously attempted to enlarge his own holdings. On the death in 1383 of Queen Joanna I of Naples, who had declared him her heir, he claimed the throne. (Bibliog. 98)

Louis de Nevers (fl. 1350), count of Flanders who arrested English merchants in his territory because he stayed stubbornly loyal to King Philip VI of France in the Hundred Years War,* despite the fact that the Flemish were the cloth makers of Europe, and depended on English wool. King Edward III* countered that action by forbidding the export of wool to Flanders; England had an almost total monopoly on wool at that time. Wool was its primary export product and its sovereign merchandise; one unit of wool export, the woolsack, sold for about £10. See maltote.+ By 1339, Count Louis' power had been so greatly reduced by this economic pressure that he and his family fled for their lives. Edward thereupon agreed to allow exports of wool to Flanders, and to transfer the Staple* to Bruges, in return for a military alliance with Jacob van Artevelde, ruthless Flemish captain, and his pikemen. (Bibliog. 203)

Louvain, Godfrey de (d. 1226), younger son of Godfrey III, duke of Brabant and count of Louvain. Godfrey spent most of his life in England under Kings John* and Henry III.* He was made custodian of the castle of Eye* in Suffolk, and married the widow of Ralph de Cornhill, recently deceased, heiress of the Windsor family. Godfrey offered 400 marks to have her in marriage and the lands of her late husband if she could give no reason for refusing him. She, on her part, offered 200 marks, 3 palfreys and 2 hawks for permission not to marry Godfrey, but to marry where and whomever she wished. She ended up by marrying Godfrey, anyway; by her lands Godfrey owed 10 knights' fees+ in London, Middlesex, Essex and Suffolk. (Bibliog. 47)

Louvain, city and county founded in the Low Countries by Louis the Fat in the early 9th century as a fortress against the Normans. Lords of Louvain, vassals of the dukes of Lower Lotharingia, gradually grew in power until they became some of the dukes' chief vassals and were granted the title of count. Only after Godfrey de Bouillon* went on the first crusade+ and the duchy of Lotharingia was split up did the counts of Louvain become direct vassals of the emperor. In 1106, Count Godfrey was granted the ducal title after which it became hereditary. In 1190, the duchy became the basis of the duchy of Brabant; later its capital was established in Brussels. (The English referred to the duke of Brabant as the duke of Louvain.) See also Brabant. (Bibliog. 98, 100)

Lovelich, Henry, member of the London Company of Skinners who wrote two Middle English poems, *Merlin,** and *The Holy Grail* as a compliment to a fellow guildsman of importance, Harry Barton. His original intention seems to have been to turn into English the whole Vulgate *Estoire del Saint Graal*,* *Merlin*,* and *Queste*.* He succeeded in completing the first portion by bringing the story up to the life of King Launcelot, grandfather of Lancelot du Lak,* in his *The Holy Grail*. His *Merlin* was a close translation which suffered from the author's almost total lack of qualifications for the task. He had no talent for writing, and no ear for verse, but so enjoyed the task that he devoted his leisure to it. (Bibliog. 10, 202)

Louvre. See Chateau de Louvre.

Luce, commune in the department of Orne, southeast of Domfront in Maine. It gave its name to the English family of Lucy in Newington. Its real connection with Normandy dated from the occupation in 1092 of Domfront, the castle of Robert de Bellême (see Bellême-Montgomery), by Henry Beauclerc,* then count of the Cotentin, but later Henry I. This connection probably brought the family to the king's notice. (Bibliog. 47)

Lucius Iberius, emperor of Rome in Arthurian legend. He demanded a tribute from and the subjection of Arthur* to Rome. In the war that ensued, he was defeated and slain by Arthur or Gawain.* (Bibliog. 145, 210)

de Lucy, Anthony (c. 1280-1343), soldier and servant of the English crown. He spent all his life in service of the English kings, mainly in the marches of Scotland* and Ireland.* In 1313, he was made warden of the marches of Cumberland, fought at Bannock Burn* (1314), escaped south toward Carlisle after the English defeat, and took refuge with many other refugees at Bothwell castle, but its keeper, a Scot, gave them up to the Bruce.* Lucy was kept prisoner for a long time, and was forced to pay a large ransom. On his release, he was made sheriff of Cumberland and Westmoreland, and the keeper and constable of Carlisle. Summoned to Parliament in 1321, he became Lord Lucy. He was summoned to march to Coventry to fight the adherents of the earl of Cambridge in 1322, but he did not participate in the battle of Boroughbridge* in 1322. For his service, in 1322 the King Edward II made him a banneret.+ On discovering the treason of Andrew Harcla,* Lucy on king's orders arrested him in the hall of Carlisle castle while Harcla was dictating letters. With that, he once again became the chief crown official in the western marches. In 1324 and 1325, he was made warden of the western counties with the express command of resisting the enemy by land or by sea. From then on, he was constantly involved in the border strife with Scotland, raiding with 800 men in March 1333, and raising the siege of Edinburgh castle by the Scottish regent, Moray, with troops from Berwick. He died in 1343. (Bibliog. 47)

de Lucy, Richard, "The Loyal" (d. 1179), chief justiciar+ for 25 years under King Henry II* (1154-1189). He was the son of Count Robert de Meulan,* close friend of King Henry I. His family held land in Norfolk, Suffolk and Kent. He had supported King Stephen* against the cause of Geoffrey of Anjou* in Normandy. After 1140, he was made sheriff of Hertfordshire and Essex, became chief justiciar by 1153 and was made guardian of the Tower of London* and Windsor castle.+ He held the chief justiciarship for 13 years jointly with Robert de Beaumont,* earl of Leicester, and on Beaumont's death in 1168, assumed the sole office. With Henry II at Falaise, he was ordered to use all his powers to procure the elevation of Thomas à Becket* to the archbishopric* of Canterbury, and did so. However, Becket believed that Lucy had drawn up the Constitutions of Clarendon,+ and refused to cooperate with him. Lucy tried in vain to convince Becket to become reconciled with the king.   When the rebellion of young Henry,* the king's eldest son, erupted in 1173, Lucy and Reginald, earl of Cornwall, besieged Leicester which was being held for the rebel earl of Leicester. When Leicester procured a truce until Christmas, Lucy and Humphrey de Bohun* marched against William,* king of Scotland, who had ravaged Durham and entered Yorkshire. Lucy and Bohun burned Berwick, pursued William with fire and sword across the border, and turned southward to meet and defeat a large force of Flemish mercenaries under Leicester's command at Farnham. As King Henry was out of the country at the time, the care of the country rested with Lucy as chief justiciar. At his urging, the king returned to England in 1176, and Lucy resigned to retire to his abbey and die in 1179. (Bibliog. 58, 162)

Ludwig IV, Roman emperor who was brother-in-law to Philippa de Hainault,* queen of Edward III.* In 1337, Edward convinced him to side with the English against Philip VI* for seven years. In that deal, Ludwig appointed Edward to be the vicar-general (or deputy) of the empire with jurisdiction over all imperial fiefs outside Germany. This assignment gave him the theoretical power to summon as his vassals all the lords of the Low Countries and even the counts of Burgundy and Savoy. In reality, he never could exert that power, so that post gave him only a dubious prestige. (Bibliog. 203)

Luxemburg, district in the Roman province of *Belgica prima,* which afterwards formed part of the Frankish kingdom of Austrasia and of the empire of Charlemagne.* About 1057, it came under the rule of Conrad (d. 1086) who took the title of count of Luxemburg from the name of its chief town. His descendants ruled the county, first in male and then female line, until the death in 1437 of the Emperor Sigismund. Its fortunes were advanced by the election in 1308 of Count Henry IV as German king and his coronation as Emperor Henry VII. His son was John, king of Bohemia, who fell at Crécy* in 1346, and John's eldest son was the Emperor Charles IV. (Bibliog. 68)

Lyonel, son of Bors of Gaul and a relative of Lancelot* by whom he was crowned king of France in Arthurian legend. He fought in the Roman war and was slain in London while seeking Lancelot. (Bibliog. 1, 145)

Lyoness, country of Tristan,* probably identified as Lothian or southern Scotland in Arthurian legend. (Bibliog. 1)

M

Macaire, *chanson de geste** from the 13th century, sometimes known as *La Reine Sebile,* this work was written in a Franco-Italian language by a French jongleur who had travelled to northern Italy to earn a better living as a poet than was possible in France. In this story, Macaire, a baron of Charlemagne,* and father of Hervieu de Lyon, but a member of the family of traitors, slandered the queen of France, Blancheflor, because she repulsed his advances. The king, believing Macaire's accusations, sent her into exile in Hungary, accompanied by one of the king's barons, Auberi. There she gave birth to a son marked with a white cross on his shoulder as a sign of his royal birth. (See kingmark.+) Her father, the emperor of Constantinople,* declared war on Charlemagne to avenge her. Her final exoneration was the result of a single combat between Auberi's dog and Macaire in which Macaire lost and was executed. He became a stock traitor in every literary work in which he appeared. (ed. F. Guessard, Paris: APF 9, 1866) (Bibliog. 36, 106, 231)

Maganza, single family from Italy from which all the barons traitorous toward Charlemagne* were said to belong in all the Italian versions and adaptations of the French *chansons de geste.** (Bibliog. 245)

Magyars. See Hungary.

Mahomet, Mohammed, the prophet of Allah; one of the three gods of the Saracens, whose standard was carried by Baligant,* and whose idol was thrown into a ditch and smashed after Marsile's* defeat by Charlemagne* in the *Song of Roland.** (Bibliog. 210)

Maid of Norway. See Alexander III of Scotland.

Maiden castle,+ one of the most famous of European earth fortresses. This Anglo-Saxon site in Dorset was 1,000 yards long and surrounded on three sides by high banks with corresponding ditches, but no English monarch erected even a motte and bailey castle on it. (Bibliog. 247)

maimed kings, in the Grail* legends, King Pellam,* his son, Pelles, and Aleyn, or Alain of the Forain Land, sometimes called the Fisher King or the Rich Fisher, were represented as maimed kings, having been wounded usually through the thighs or the genitals by the Spear of Vengeance. They lived in Corbenic* castle or Carbonek, to await the coming of the successful Grail-seeker. (Bibliog. 1, 54)

Maine, region of northwestern France bordered by Normandy,* Orleanais, Touraine, Anjou* and Brittany.* It became a countship in the 10th century, united with Anjou* through the marriage of its heiress to the count of Anjou in 1126, and became English when Henry II* became the English king in 1154. It was returned to French control when taken from King John* by French King Philip II* in 1204, and thus it passed to the house of Anjou. (Bibliog. 68)

Mainet, fragmentary *chanson de geste** about the youth of Charlemagne,* his *enfances.** Here, Charlemagne, whose pet name was Charlot, was being cheated out of the throne by his illegitimate stepbrothers Heudri and Rainfroi after his father Pippin's (Pepin) death. Sons of a female serf who had impersonated Berta *au gran piés** in the king's bed, they were placed in power by the dying Pepin, and relegated Charles to kitchen duties. Rainfroi plotted with his brother Heudri to kill Charles, but he learned of the plot and fled with some faithful followers to the court of the pagan king, Galafre, in Spain, where he was called Mainet. While in Galafre's service, he vanquished Braimant, won the heart of Galienne, the king's daughter, as well as the hatred and enmity of her brother, Marsile.* From Spain he went to Italy and finally returned to reconquer his own country. Historically, these events happened to Charlemagne's grandfather, Charles Martel,* the illegitimate son of Pepin and his concubine, Alpaide. For his illegitimacy, he had to suffer indignities from Plektrud who wished to have her grandson Theobald become major-domo* instead of Charles. After Pippin's death, she had Charles thrown into prison, but he escaped, and overcame the Neustrian major-domo Raginfred (=Rainfroi) as well as king Chilperic (here called Childeric = Heldri = Heudri) and thereby became master of the empire. (ed. Gaston Paris, *Romania*, IV, 1875, 304ff.) (Bibliog. 106, 231)

major-domo (Middle Latin, *major domus*, "chief of the house"), man having charge of a great household, especially a royal or princely establishment. (Bibliog. 169)

Malmsbury castle,+ fortress erected by Roger, bishop of Salisbury, with misappropriated funds from the Malmsbury Abbey when he was forced to defend himself against King Stephen.* In 1139, it was forced to surrender to King Stephen who intended to destroy it when peace returned to his kingdom. Because it was a royal stronghold right in the midst of the principal areas of fighting between himself and Matilda, it was besieged more than once. Early in 1153, once Henry of Anjou, later Henry II,* gained possession of it through the treachery of one of Stephen's men, no more fighting occurred around it. After the Treaty of Winchester* in 1153, the castle lost its importance, and in 1216, King John* ordered its destruction. (Bibliog. 104)

Malory, Sir Thomas (d. 1471), English author of *Le Morte D'Arthur.*

Man, Isle of, island situated so equally between England and Ireland that long disputes raged as to which country owned it. Finally it was adjudged as belonging to England because snakes from Man survived on English soil whereas others died on Irish soil. In 1065 it became its own country with King Godred, son of Syrric, as its first king, and Fingal, son of Godred, as its second, a year later. (Bibliog. 101)

Manaqib Rashid ad-Din, writer of the Ismailite sect in Syria known as the Assassins.+ He gathered recollections and anecdotes about the Great Master of the sect, Rashid ad-Din Sinan, a contemporary of Saladin,* and the leader of the sect in Syria when Saladin's power was at its height. (S. Guyard, "Un Grand Maître des Assassins au temps de Saladin," *Journal Asiatique,* Series VII, vol. IX, 1877, 324-489) (Bibliog. 83)

Mandeville, Geoffrey de. See Essex.

La Manekine, French romance by Philippe de Beaumanoir.* It treated the theme of a king who wanted to marry his own daughter because she alone resembled his deceased wife. She ran away and became the wife of the king of Scotland. She bore him a child while he was off on a hunting trip, and her wicked mother-in-law wrote to the husband that his wife had borne a beast. He responded that nothing was to be done until his return, but the wicked mother changed the letter to read that the wife was to be abandoned at sea. She was reunited with him only after many ordeals, and the wicked mother-in-law punished.   (ed. H. Suchier, Paris: *SATF*, 1884-1885) (Bibliog. 106, 231)

Manfred of Hohenstaufen (1232-1266), king of Sicily (1258-1266). An illegitimate son of Emperor Frederick II,* he assumed a large role in imperial politics involving the papacy, even assuming control of the imperial army in central Italy in 1246. His father appointed him regent of Sicily in 1250 until his half-brother, Conrad IV,* could arrive to take over two years later.   Conrad's death in 1254 placed Manfred in charge of the imperial army in Italy in its fights against the Guelphs* and Charles of Anjou.* When Conrad's son, Conradin, remained in Germany, Manfred had himself declared king of Sicily in 1258 both by the barons+ of the realm and the Hohenstaufen supporters in Italy. He concluded an alliance with Peter III of Aragon who married his daughter, and then laid claim to his throne of Sicily. He was killed during his army's defeat by the army of Charles of Anjou in the battle of Benevento* in 1266. (Bibliog. 98)

Manny (Mauny), Walter de (c. 1310-1372), English military commander, and soldier of fortune whose Flemish name was Gauthier de Masny. A native of Hainaut,* he entered the service of William I, count of Hainaut, and in 1327 came to England as one of the pages of Philippa* when she married Edward III.* He gained favor rapidly, and distinguished himself in the Scottish wars of King Edward III. Accompanying Edward Baliol* in July 1332, with the king's permission, on his trip to claim the crown of Scotland, and taking a foremost part in the siege of Berwick during the following year, he was knighted for his services and for marvellous feats on the campaign. He was appointed marshal of the King's Marshalsea,+ chose and led men on an expedition into Scotland in 1334, and by 1337 had been made admiral* of the fleet from Thames to Berwick. He was a friend of and patron of Froissart* in whose chronicles his exploits had a conspicuous and exaggerated place. He accompanied Edward III to France in the following year where he proved himself to be one of the boldest and most able of the English commanders. He fought beside the king at Sluys,* and in the three-month siege of Tournai, he captured and burned over 300 towns and killed over 1,000 armed men. He was at Windsor castle* during the banquet when Robert of Artois* made the Vow of the Heron,+ and he took a comparable vow to burn a town held by Godemar de Fay. He prepared for 18 months for an expedition into Brittany to help Joan of Flanders, the valiant countess de Montfort whom Charles of Blois had besieged in the town of Hennebont on the west coast of Brittany.* Her husband was then a war prisoner of the king of France. Bad weather forced a lengthy delay in the sea voyage, so that by the time Manny arrived, the castle was about ready to surrender from the vicious pounding from a great catapult.+ Manny's ships ran the blockade of the harbor, and after dining with the Countess Joan, he led a detachment of troops to destroy the catapult. He continued to fight against Charles of Blois for Brittany, and to receive and keep the castles and towns belonging to the duke of Brittany. Summoned to Parliament he became Lord Manny in 1347; in 1359, he was made Knight of the Garter*; he was one of those charged with the safe custody of King John II* when a prisoner at Calais* in 1360. In 1361 he received 19,000 gold florins from Margaret of Hainaut in settlement of all his claims. He was second in command to John of Gaunt* on his invasion of France in 1369. By 1335 he had married Margaret, daughter and heiress of Thomas Plantagenet,* earl of Norfolk, fifth son of King Edward I.* (Bibliog. 47, 58, 68, 224)

Mansourah, battle of (February 8, 1250). This battle in Egypt was the disastrous end to a poorly planned march into Egypt to capture Cairo. Louis IX* began this advance from Damietta which he had captured in June of the previous year. The Egyptians had fled in panic as the crusaders approached; their leader, Sultan Malek-Saleh, dying of a malignant ulcer on his thigh, hanged 50 of his officers for incompetence before the French arrived. Once there, Louis was delayed for six months by the summer heat and the flooding of the Nile before continuing his advance. This delay allowed the sultan to regroup and reorganize his forces. Even in November, Louis' forces were lethargic. When they reached Mansourah, they faced the Ashmum canal across which they saw the army of the now-dead sultan. To cross this barrier, Louis decided to dam it, and march across rather than attempt a crossing in boats under fire from the Egyptian army. Against the "cats"+ which Louis built to protect his men building the dam, the Egyptians set up 16 military machines: trebuchets,+ mangonels,+ and belfries+ to hurl Greek fire+ and stone missiles. Louis responded with similar machines of his own. As Louis' men got halfway across the canal, the Egyptians cut away the canal bank on their side, being aided by the current. Hoping to catch them by surprise, Louis took a party of men down the canal a distance, crossed at a ford, and came back on the Egyptians' side. Count Robert of Artois and a few knight companions chased a group of Arab horsemen right into the surprised Egyptian camp, but instead of pausing to allow the rest of the army to catch up with them, they charged through the town of Mansourah where they soon were outnumbered, isolated and slaughtered. By the time Louis' cavalry arrived, the surprise element had gone, and the Arabs had regrouped, rallied and pressed hard against the French forces. Seeing the action on the other side of the canal, Louis' forces rushed to complete the dam, throwing anything they could find into the breach so that the infantry could join the beleaguered king. Their arrival broke the Egyptian pressure, and the sultan's forces retired. Louis ordered a halt, for his men were exhausted, and he had lost half of his cavalry and over half of his horses. (Bibliog. 166)

Der Mantel, courtly Middle High German* epic by Heinrich von dem Türlin.* It dealt with a chastity test similar to an episode in Ulrich von Zatzikhoven's *Lanzelet.** Its surviving 900 lines were thought to have been the beginning of a poem about Lancelot.* (ed. O. Warnatsch, *Germanistische Abhandlungen,* II, 1883) (Bibliog. 86)

Mantua, province in northern Italy which in the 11th century belonged to the margrave+ of Canossa, but which became independent in 1115; subsequently, it joined the Lombard League,* and was ruled by the Gonzaga family from 1328 onward. (Bibliog. 200)

Manuel I, Comnenos (c. 1120-1180), Byzantine emperor (1143-1180). The fourth son of John II, he distinguished himself in his father's Turkish war, and thus was nominated emperor in preference to his elder surviving brother. Endowed with a fine physique and great personal courage, he devoted himself to a military career. Endeavoring to restore by force of arms the predominance of the Byzantine Empire in the Mediterranean, he found himself involved in conflicts with his neighbors on all sides. In 1147, he allowed two armies of crusaders,+ those of Louis VII* of France and of Conrad III* of Germany, to pass through his country, but the conflicts and disputes between the crusaders and the native Greeks nearly caused war between Manuel and his guests. In the same year, he warred on Roger of Sicily whose fleet had captured Corfu, but who was defeated in the following year. In 1149, Manuel took the offensive against the Normans in Sicily by invading both Sicily and Apulia. He maintained a foothold in southern Italy, and hence played a role in Italian politics. Back home, he reduced the Serbs to vassalage on his northern border, and made repeated attacks against the Hungarians,* ending in an invasion in 1163. He concluded a truce with them in 1168 by which frontier strips were ceded to him. He died of a fever in 1180. Even though his victories had been balanced by his defeats, his lack of statesmanlike qualities prevented his securing the loyalty of his subjects, which in turn led to the subsequent rapid collapse of the Byzantine Empire. He was succeeded by his son, Alexius II. (Bibliog. 68)

Manzikert, battle of (1071), Romanus Diogenes, colleague and guardian of the young Byzantine emperor, Michael,* marched a huge army of approximately 60,000 to the eastern sections of his dominions to meet the Seljuk Turks head-on and to recover the fortresses of Akhlat and Manzikert. After first capturing Manzikert, he was besieging Akhlat when he was suddenly attacked by a huge army of over 100,000 Seljuk horse-archers under the command of Alp Arslan.* Ignoring the wisdom of the usual Roman tactics of being wary of ambushes and feints, of covering one's flanks and rear, of using infantry for the bulk of the fighting, and of keeping one's army as a unit and not separating it, Romanus ordered his army to advance against the harrying tactics of the Seljuks. They refused to stand and fight, but would scurry, advance, and retreat to frustrate the Greek troops of Romanus. Late in the day, Romanus decided to retreat to his camp, but through mis-understanding, the order was poorly transmitted. As a result, large gaps were left in the Greek lines through which the Seljuks raced to outflank some of the Greeks. In fact, one commander, Andronicus, out of sheer malice, returned to camp instead of turning to confront the attacking Turks, and left the rear exposed. Thus the Turks were able to attack smaller groups and inflict a massive slaughter. In fact, the emperor's horse was killed beneath him, he was captured along with many of his chief officers, and his center line forces were totally annihilated. (Bibliog. 166)

Map, Walter (c. 1140-c. 1208), Latin writer noted for his witty con-versation and good stories. Educated in Paris, he went to England as a clerk in the household of King Henry II,* and served also as an itinerant justice.+ His wit and learning made him a favorite of the king who had him travel with the royal party frequently. Not only did he meet scores of interesting people, but he served as a delegate to the third Lateran Council. At his death, he was archdeacon of Oxford. Only one of his works survived: *De Nugis Curialium* (*Courtier's Trifles*), a collection of stories, historical anecdotes, folklore, witty remarks, amusing incidents, and satire arranged in no logical order; it was composed between 1181 and 1193. (tr. Frederick Tupper and Marbury Ogle, *Master Walter Map's Book,* London: Chatto and Windus, 1924) (Bibliog. 19)

march, mark, boundary or object set up to indicate a boundary or frontier region between two countries or districts. It was found in all languages to mean the same: OE. *mearc*, Du. *merk*, Ger. *Mark*, Fr. *marque*, and Ital. *marca*. In the sense of boundary or a tract of count-ry on or near a boundary or frontier, "mark" gave way to "march." It was used in this sense first in the 8th century to refer to such "mark" or "march" districts on the borders of the Carolingian Empire. Whenever Charlemagne* pushed forward the frontiers of the Frankish realm, he provided for the security of his lands, new and old alike, by establishing mark districts on the border. Their defenses were entrusted to special officers, called margraves,+ or counts+ of the mark who were granted more extensive powers than an ordinary count. These marks were practically obliterated during the reigns of the feeble monarchs who succeeded Charlemagne, but Henry I,* the Fowler, revived the system early in the 10th century with marks set along the German borders. He established Lubeck, Brandenburg, Lusatia and Meissen as marches along his eastern border. In the east, the remnant of the Moravian kingdom, Moravia, became a dependent marchland; Pomerania became a march between Germany and Poland along the Baltic coast; and Croatia or Chrobatia was established on Polish land between Poland and Hungary.

In England in the same connection, the plural of the word, "marches," was used soon after the Norman Conquest in 1066 to refer to the districts along the Welsh border. Lands were granted to lords on the condition that they would defend neighboring counties in England. These areas between England and Wales, being neither town nor county, were considered ground in question lying between the two countries. Englishmen to whom these lands belonged and over which they held great power and jurisdiction were called lords marchers. Among the most powerful was Roger Mortimer* of Wigmore, who was created the earl of March in 1328; he chose March as his dignity rather than Shropshire or Shrewsbury to commemorate his descent from Joan, one of the co-heirs of the counts de la Marche.* (Bibliog. 68, 79, 101)

Marche, Le, region of central France bordered by Toulouse, Berry, Bourbonnais, Auvergne, Limousin, and Poitou. It owed its name to its position as a 10th century march* or border district between the duchy of Aquitaine* and the domains of the kings of France. Sometimes it was called the *Marche Limousin,* and originally was a small district cut partly from its neighbor to the south, Limousin, and partly from Poitou, its neighbor to the west. It became a countship in the 10th century, when William III,* duke of Aquitaine, gave it to one of his vassals named Boso, who took the title of count. In the 12th century it passed to the counts of Limousin, the Lusignan family, where it remained until the death without male issue of Count Hugh in 1303 when it was seized by King Philip IV* of France. In 1316, it was made a duchy for Prince Charles, afterwards King Charles IV,* and a few years later, it passed to the Bourbon* family. (Bibliog. 68, 239)

Marchfeld, battle of the (August 26, 1278), conflict between only mounted warriors which settled the destiny of Austria. It settled whether the eastern regions of the empire should be occupied by a compact Slavonic realm or by the Hapsburg house to preserve the extinct house of Bamberg as a Teutonic state. Ottokar of Bohemia decided to extend his kingdom to the borders of Italy, and to that end had conquered Austria and Carinthia. Beaten back from them by the newly elected Emperor Rudolf, and forced to a disadvantageous peace in 1276, he returned two years later at the head of an army backed by German mercenaries. Rudolf's forces were swelled by Hungarian cavalry under young King Ladislas. These two armies met near the March River; Rudolf was victorious mainly through the efforts of the Hungarians who combined horse-archers with heavily mailed supporting horsemen, and the judicious use of his reserves, not committing them until they were most effective. (Bibliog. 166)

Marhaus, Marhalt. See Morholt.

Marie de France (fl. 1190), earliest known French poetess, author of *lais*,* fables and a work on Saint Patrick. Writing in the third quarter of the 12th century, she called herself "of France" to distinguish herself from such other dominions as Burgundy, Berry, Champagne, Aquitaine, etc. She was well-educated, and moved in high circles of society; she dedicated her *lais* to "a noble king," presumably Henry II* of England, and her story, *Fables*, to a "count William," possibly William Longsword,* natural son of Henry II. Although she was identified as half-sister of King Henry, and abbess of Shaftesbury who died in 1216, more probably Marie meant her dedication of "noble king" to refer to young King Henry, son and heir of Henry II who had been crowned king during his father's lifetime, and "count William" as William Marshal, earl of Pembroke. Twelve of her *lais* have survived: *Bisclavert,* Chaitivel,* Chievrefueil,* Eliduc,* Equitan,* Guigemar,* La Fresne,* Lanval,* Laustic,* Les Deux Amanz,* Milun,* Yonec.** (ed. Alfred Ewert, Oxford, 1969; tr. Eugene Mason, New York: Dutton, 1966) (Bibliog. 106, 147)

Mark, Marc, legendary king of Cornwall, but almost as well known in Wales as well. He was the uncle of Tristan* and the husband of Isolde* in the romance by Gottfried of Strassburg,* *Tristan.** Additionally, one of the famous stories about him concerned a certain secret known only to his dwarf. When curious barons questioned him, the dwarf said that he would confide the information only to a certain hawthorne bush. They could overhear it if they wished, but he would be technically true to his promise to Mark not to reveal it to any person. Thus they listened to the news that Mark had horse's ears; when they told the king about their knowledge, he beheaded the dwarf. As the name Mark in all Celtic languages meant "horse," stories circulated for centuries in Wales and Brittany about King March who murdered his barbers to conceal the embarrassing secret about his ears. (Bibliog. 1, 10, 64, 97, 202)

mark. See march.

Marlborough castle,+ Wiltshire fortress. Some sort of fortification existed on that Wiltshire site from the time of William* the Conqueror, but no castle as such was built until the reign of King Stephen* when John the Marshall, supporter of Matilda FitzEmpress,* erected a fortress to serve as a base for his raids against the king. Henry II* assumed control over it presumably as a protective measure, but Richard I* gave it to Prince John* in 1189. Only after John's rebellion in 1194 did Richard order his justiciar, Hubert Walter,* to reclaim it for the crown. On his accession to the throne, however, John made many visits to the castle, for he had been married there. It was one of those which fell into the hands of the French invaders in 1216, but was recaptured in 1217 and given to William Marshal, son of its former castellan, who put it in order before his death in 1219. Henry III* also visited it frequently and spent heavily on its repair. During the Barons' War,* it was held by a group of marcher* barons loyal to the crown, and after the battle of Evesham* in 1265, King Henry III spent several days at it recovering from that ordeal. Then he gave it to his queen, Eleanor, as part of her dowry. It passed from her possession to Queen Margaret in 1299 and thence to Queen Isabella in 1318 and finally in 1331 to Queen Philippa. (Bibliog. 104)

Marmion, Robert, of Tamworth (d. 1144), fierce cunning baron Warwickshire. In 1143, he expelled the monks of Coventry from their priory to make it a fortress, defending it with an elaborate system of pits and trenches which proved fatal to him. When he rode out to attack the earl of Chester's* forces, his horse stumbled into one of the trenches and threw him. He lay helpless with a broken hip until a common soldier killed him with his knife. His death so rattled his followers who saw it as divine vengeance for his sacrilege that they abandoned the priory without further fighting. His grandson was also Robert Marmion (d. 1218), a justice itinerant and reputedly the king's champion,* because the Marmions were said to have been descended from the Lords of Fontenay le Marmion, who once were the hereditary champions of the dukes of Normandy.* (See Dymoke, Sir John.) (Bibliog. 58, 238)

Marsepia. See Amazonia.

Marsh, William (d. c. 1215), English knight who had been given the Isle of Lundy off the north coast of Devonshire by Prince John* during King Richard I's* absence on the crusade.+ Unfortunately for Marsh, King Henry II* earlier had given the Isle to the Knights Templar.+ Marsh offered 300 marks to Richard I for it in 1194. When John came to the throne he confirmed that it had been a gift to the Templars, and tried to mollify Marsh with a gift of £20. Because Marsh was a hardy, ambitious seaman with piratical desires, Lundy seemed to be ideal as a base of his piratical operations, so he refused to yield it to the Templars. In 1200, the Templars offered 50 marks and a palfrey for Marsh's lands in Somersetshire so long as he held Lundy, and King John granted their request in 1201. Then in 1202, the king gave Alan de Devon, lord of Hartland in Devon, a license to build and garrison a castle to protect his lands from Marsh's raids. In 1204, John pardoned Marsh and granted him a pension, and by 1205, he had become a king's admiral* on one of his war galleys, but he did so without yielding Lundy which remained with him and his heirs. (Bibliog. 171)

Marshal, Earl. See Earl Marshal.

Marshal, William. See Pembroke.

Marsile, Marsille, Marsellon, Saracen king of Saragossa who plotted with Ganelon* to destroy the *douzepeers** of Charlemagne* in the *Song of Roland.** He attacked Charlemagne's forces after choosing twelve Saracens* to offset the twelve peers. In the fight, Roland severed his right hand, and after the defeat of the forces of Baligant* which had come to help defeat the Franks, he died of grief. He appeared in *Prise de Pamplune,** *Gaufrey,** *Anseis de Carthage,** *Galien, Gui de Bourgogne,** among many other *chansons de geste.** (Bibliog. 128, 210)

matière. See matter of romances.

Matilda FitzEmpress (1102-1167), daughter of King Henry I* of England, and claimant for the throne against the usurpation of King Stephen.* She married first the Emperor Henry V* in 1114 at the age of 12, and after his death in 1125, returned to her father. In 1128, she married

Geoffrey Plantagenet,* count of Anjou, and in 1131, bore him a son, Henry, who later became Henry II* of England. In 1135, Henry I named Matilda his heir, but because a large number of barons were opposed to the reign of a woman, their support brought Stephen of Blois* to the throne. That led her to begin a civil war against Stephen which she carried out for almost twenty years until her son Henry was named heir to the throne in 1153, and ascended to it in the following year. Matilda then retired to live out her life in pious activities. (Bibliog. 98)

Matraval, chief city of Montgomeryshire in Powys-land, a section of Wales bestowed by Roderick Mawr on his youngest son in 877. Hence the princes of Powys often were called kings of Matraval. (Bibliog. 101)

matter of romances (matière de Romans), divisions of romances proposed by Jean Bodel* in his *Chansons des Saisnes*:* the matter of France, of Britain, and of Rome. To that division should be added the matter of England. The matter of France contained the stories commonly considered *chanson de geste*;* the matter of Britain included the romances dealing with the Arthurian* legends; the matter of Rome covered the legends of Alexander, the *Roman de Thebes,** the *Roman d'Ænéas,** and the *Roman de Troie**; those of the matter of England were such romances as *King Horn,* Havelock the Dane,* Guy of Warwick,* Bevis of Hampton,* Richard Coeur de Lion,** and *Athelstan.** (Bibliog. 19, 106)

Mauduit, nickname for William, eighth earl of Warwick (1220-1268). It meant "the Dunce;" sometimes it was confused with "Maudit," meaning "Accursed." See Warwick. (Bibliog. 47)

Mauduit family, William Mauduit (d. 1101) probably was a chamberlain+ for English King Henry I* connected with the Winchester treasury, and held lands both in Hampshire and Winchester. His elder son, Ralph (c. 1129), was a chamberlain of the treasury and had some functions in the Norman treasury; his younger son, William Mauduit II, recovered his mother's dowry in England and his father's lands in Normandy, served as a chamberlain and attested Stephen's acts both in England and Normandy, but deserted to Matilda FitzEmpress* who made him her chamberlain. Duke Henry of Anjou (Henry II) granted him in 1153 the chamberlainship with the lands pertaining to that position in England and in Normandy, and in addition, a chamberlainship of the treasury and the lands pertaining to that position, whether in England or Normandy, as his brother Robert had held it on the day of his death. (Bibliog. 130)

Maugis, magician, and thief; son of Beuves of Agremont in the *chanson de geste,* Four Sons of Aymon,** and other French epics.   (Bibliog. 128)

Mauleon, Savari de (d. 1236), French soldier. He was the son of Raoul de Mauleon, *vicomte* de Thouars and lord of Mauleon. Savari sided with Prince Arthur* of Brittany, and was captured at Mirabeau* and imprisoned at Corfe* castle. King John* released him in 1204, enlisted him on his side, and made him seneschal+ of Poitou in 1205. In 1211, Savari assisted Raymond VI, count of Toulouse, as he besieged Simon de Montfort* in Castelnaudary. King Philip II* bought his services, and gave him command of a fleet which was destroyed at the Flemish port of Damme. (See Longespee.) Then Mauleon returned to King John with whom he sided against the barons in 1215. He went to Egypt, was present when Damietta* was captured, and then returned to Poitou for a second time as seneschal for the king of England. He defended Saintonge against Louis VIII* in 1224, but when he was accused of surrendering La Rochelle to the French, the English suspicions drove him once again to the French camp. There, Louis gave him the job of defending La Rochelle and the coast of Saintonge. He died in 1236. (Bibliog. 68)

Mauny, Walter de. See Manny, Walter de.

Mautravers, John (1290-1364), English knight, the son of a Devonshire baron. He was knighted along with Edward,* the Black Prince, in 1306. He was captured at Bannock Burn* in 1314, was sent to Gascony* in the king's service in 1320, sided with Thomas of Lancaster* in his rebellion, and even though he was pardoned in 1321, his goods and lands were seized and he and his brother were arrested. Released and pardoned, he then took part in the burning of Bridgnorth,* and fought beside the earl of Lancaster at Boroughbridge.* He escaped capture at that battle, returned to find his home and lands had been seized again, but he escaped overseas. He returned to England in the entourage of Queen Isabelle* and Roger Mortimer in 1326, and by his special favors for the queen, soon rose to high favor, receiving several manors for his services.   Early in April 1327, he and Thomas de Berkley received the charge of the deposed King Edward II,* then in custody of Henry, earl of Lancaster, at Kenilworth, and took him by night to Corfe* castle and thence to Bristol and on to Berkeley where the king was murdered. Mautravers succeeded in convincing Edmund, the king's brother, that the king still was alive, and so Edmund entrusted Mautravers with letters for the "imprisoned" king which Mautravers delivered instantly to Roger Mortimer. These letters led to the arrest, confession, condemnation, and execution of the Earl Edmund a few weeks later. When Mortimer fell from power soon thereafter, so did Mautravers. He was condemned by Parliament, and sentenced to be handed and beheaded; a reward of 1,000 marks was posted for his capture alive, a price of £500 placed on his head and his lands and offices forfeited. He escaped by way of Cornwall to Germany where he lived obscurely for several years. In 1334, he offered to make a confession to clear his name, and then began to work with Jacob von Arteveldt to bring Flanders on King Edward's side in the impending war with France. For succeeding in that mission, he was awarded an annuity of £100 per year in 1339, and in 1351, for all his work for the king, he was pardoned and his outlawry annulled. He died in 1364. (Bibliog. 47)

Mautravers, William (fl. 1265), English knight who had fought against King Henry III* of England beside Simon de Montfort* at the battle of Lewes* in 1264, but one year later was with the king's forces at the battle of Evesham,* and actually dismembered his former companion, de Montfort, by decapitating his corpse when the battle was over. (Bibliog. 184)

Mayor of London, Lord. See Lords Mayor of London.

mayor of the palace. See major-domo.

Medina Ifrikiya, Kairiwan, sacred city in Tunisia, surnamed the capital of Africa in the early days of Islam*; it was mentioned in the *Song of Roland.** (Bibliog. 210)

Meier Helmbrecht, didactic and satirical Middle High German* poem written between 1250 and 1280 by Wernher der Gartenaere, who named himself in its last line. Helmbrecht was a farmer's son who aped courtly airs, and was determined not to remain a farmer but instead to become a knight. Not being of knightly substance, he robbed and oppressed his neighbors. With nine companions he committed a series of violent crimes. He returned home like a prodigal, and was made welcome, but then he revealed his true purpose: he wished his sister, Gotelind, to marry one of his robber companions. She accompanied him to the wedding feast where the gang was surprised and arrested by officers of the law. The nine were hanged, but Helmbrecht was blinded and mutilated. He returned home, but was rejected by his father. A year later, he was recognized by the farmers as their former oppressor, and hanged. His gruesome fate was caused by his high airs, and by deserting the plow which his father advised him to follow.

(tr. C. H. Bell, *Peasant Life in Old German Epics,* New York, 1931) (Bibliog. 235)

Melbourne castle,+ royal Derbyshire residence during the reigns of Richard I* and John.* During the reign of their father, Henry II,* it had been held by the Beauchamp* family, but in 1194 was assumed by the crown because of the role that family played in John's rebellion against his brother, the king. On John's death it passed to William de Ferrers,* earl of Derby, but subsequently passed to Thomas,* earl of Lancaster, and thus, after the accession of Henry IV to the throne in 1399, to the crown. (Bibliog. 104)

Meleagant, son of Baudemagus* in Arthurian legend. His capture of Guenevere* whom he loved, began his life-long conflict with Lancelot.* (Bibliog. 44, 96, 145, 202)

Meleranz, Middle High German* courtly epic by der Plier,* which re-affirmed the qualities of the Arthurian poetry in a series of adventures all of which ended happily in celebrations at Arthur's court. (ed. Karl Bartsch, Stuttgart, *BLV* 60, 1861) (Bibliog. 86)

Meliador, longest medieval French Arthurian romance written between 1370 and 1388 by Jean Froissart.* A native of Hainaut,* Froissart was attached to the English royal household from 1361 to 1368, and re-garded Edward III* as a second Arthur,* and his queen, Philippa, also from Hainaut, as the greatest queen since Guenevere.* After her death in 1369, Froissart enjoyed at Brussels the patronage of King Wenceslas, duke of Luxemburg,* who commissioned him to write this work. Its story related how Camel, a knight of Northumberland, wooed Hermondine, the daughter of the king of Scotland during the early years of King Arthur's reign. Learning that he walked in his sleep, she put him off by vowing only to marry the knight who showed the greatest valor over a period of five years. Meliador, son of the duke of Cornwall, learned at Arthur's court at Carleon of this unknown maiden's vow, and determined to win her. He met and killed Camel, and then when he saw Hermondine at Aberdeen while he was disguised as a jewel merchant, he became even more inflamed with desire for her. His crowning achievement during the five-year period was to win a tournament at Roxborough against a field of 1,566 knights, and thus he won the hand of the maiden. (ed. Auguste Longnon, Paris: *SATF,* 3 vols., 1895-1899) (Bibliog. 10)

Meliodas, king of Lyoness in Arthurian legend. He was the father of

Tristan by the sister of King Mark.* His second wife was the daughter of Howel, king of Brittany. (Bibliog. 145, 202)

Melion, *lai** of the first half of the 13th century which imitated Marie de France's* *Bisclavert,** but the scene was shifted to Arthur's* court, and the wicked wife changed her husband into a wolf with a magic ring. Including Gawain,* Yvain,* and Ydel (Yder)* as characters, its author also drew heavily on Wace.* (ed. E. M. Grimes, *The Lais of Desire, Graelent, and Melion,* New York: *IFS,* 1928) (Bibliog. 10)

ménestrel de Reims, French storyteller whose *Récits* recounted the famous capture of King Richard I* Coeur de Lion of England by Duke Leopold of Austria whom he had alienated in the Holy Land on the third crusade.+ This minstrel's account of Richard's discovery in a castle belonging to the German Emperor Henry VI* described how Richard and Blondel de Nêsle* in their youth had become fast friends, and how Blondel discovered the whereabouts of the imprisoned Richard by singing a poem known only to the two of them at every castle in Germany he could visit. His account was fictional. (tr. E. N. Stone, *Three Old French Chronicles of the Crusades,* Seattle, WA: University of Washington, 1939) (Bibliog. 27)

Meraugis de Portlesguez, one of the best medieval French Arthurian verse romances, it was written by Raoul de Houdenc early in the 13th century. It concerned the rivalry for the love of Lidoine, daughter of the king of Cavalon, between two friends, Meraugis and Gorvain Cadrut. In telling of this rivalry, Raoul interwove many familiar situations: a tournament+ at Lindesores for which the prize was a sparrow-hawk+; a court of ladies that decided that Meraugis who loved Lidoine for her courtesy was more deserving than Gorvain who loved her for her beauty. Gorvain, in search of the Sword of Strange Hangings, was himself the object of a quest by Meraugis accompanied by a dwarf and Lidoine. At the end the hostility between the two friends was put to rest by a mutual reconciliation. (ed. Mathias Friedwagner, Halle: Niemeyer, 1897) (Bibliog. 10)

Mercia, last and greatest of the Heptarchy,* the seven kingdoms of Britain before the Norman Conquest; it was named Mercia because, being in the middle of the country, it served as a March* on all the others which bordered it. It comprised the counties of Gloucester, Hereford, Worcester, Warwick, Leicester, Rutland, Northampton, Lincoln, Bedford, Nottingham, Buckingham, Oxford, Derby, Stafford, Shropshire, Cheshire, and that part of Hertfordshire not under control of the West Saxons.

Despite its power and size, it fell to the West Saxons. Among its kings were:

542 - Cridda, first king of Mercia
626 - Penda;
656 - Peada, first Christian king
675 - Ethelred, who became a monk after a thirty-year reign
716 - Ethelbald
797 - Kenwolf
819 - St. Kenelm, marty
852 - Burdred, after whose death, the kingdom became a province of the West Saxons.
(Bibliog. 101)

Merciless Parliament (1388). See Lords Appellant.

Meriadeuc. See *Chevalier aux Deux Epées.*

Merlijns Boeck, Dutch version of Robert de Boron's* *Joseph,* written about 1261 by Jacob Van Maerlent. He gave a free rendering of the story up to verse 1,926, where he swung into a close translation of Boron's *Merlin* to verse 10,398 where the work ended abruptly. (ed. J. van Vloten, *Jacob van Maerlents Merlijn,* Leiden, 1880) (Bibliog. 10)

Merlin, poem by Henry Lovelich* of 27,852 lines, translating about 50 percent of the French *Vulgate Merlin.* He was a man of business, a member of the London Company of Skinners. He translated his source as closely as he could, but occasionally made some mistakes through ignorance of a passage in his original. He created a spurious new character of Sir Ambroy Oyselet, for example, out of a French phrase, "oiseau au brai" ("birds in the net"). He made many other similar errors in the translation. (ed. E. A. Kock, Oxford: *EETS ES* #92, #112, #185, 1904-1932) (Bibliog. 10, 202)

Les Merveilles de Rigomer, incomplete lengthy French Arthurian verse romance by Jehan, a *trouvère* of the area of Cambrai and Tournai during the last half of the 13th century. Its title refers to *"un regort de mer"* ("a bay of the sea"), hence the name Rigomer. It recounted the journey of Lancelot* and then of Gauvain (Gawain*) from Caerleon to Ireland to remove the spell from castle Rigomer and its mistress Dionise. Each knight encountered marvels and enchanters along the way. Among them were a polyglot bird, Willeris, which led Gauvain to a castle where his adversaries multiplied as he killed them, the panther of the Male Gaudine (the Evil Wood) which breathed flames, and the falcon which dieted exclusively on human heads. A second quest was made by Arthur,* accompanied by Lancelot to serve as champion for the heiress of Quintefuele. Arthur was successful in killing a usurper in a duel. (ed. Wendlin Forester and H. Breuer, Dresden, 1908-1915) (Bibliog. 10)

metropolitan. See ecclesiastical geographical divisions.

Metz, Mez, Mes, city in Lorraine built on the confluence of the Seille and Moselle rivers. After its destruction by the Huns, it was rebuilt as a Frankish royal residence, and became the capital of Austrasia in the 7th century. It was included in the land awarded to the kingdom of Lotharingia (see Lothaire) with the division of the empire in 843, and a quarter century later was annexed with the rest of the duchy to Germany. It became the battle cry of the Lorrains in the *chansons de geste.** (Bibliog. 67, 128)

Meulan, count of. See Leicester; Warwick; Worcester.

Middle English, vernacular language of England roughly between 1100 and 1500. (Bibliog. 169)

Middle High German, "ideal" poetic language of a single social class—the knights—and of a few non-knightly poets who adopted it between 1100 and 1500; prose was virtually excluded from it. Old High German was used from about 800 to 1100. (Bibliog. 235)

Middleham castle,+ Yorkshire fortress on land granted by William I* to Alan the Red, relative of the duke of Brittany, who erected a simple earthwork fortification on it. Later a simple rectangular keep, 105 by 78 feet, was raised, surrounded by a stone wall 4 1/2 feet thick and 24 feet high, surmounted by a rampart+ and parapet.+ Its main entrance was protected by a drawbridge and a three-story gatehouse. It later belonged to the earls of Warwick.* (Bibliog. 247)

Milan, city in northern Italy. Under the Carolingian emperors and kings of the 9th century, the archbishops of Milan became the feudal lords of the city and its surroundings. Its importance became apparent to the Holy Roman Emperors in the 11th century who attempted to conquer it and impose their dominion over its archbishops and inhabitants. They besieged it several times, but without serious consequences. In the middle of the 12th century, Milan became a provincial center in

Lombardy. To prevent its becoming a principality which would be favorable to Pope Alexander III,* Emperor Frederick I,* Barbarossa besieged, captured and destroyed the city in 1162. It was rebuilt in 1164 and became the center of the Lombard League* which meet and defeated the imperial army at Legnano* in 1176. In 1277, Ottone Visconti* defeated all rivals and proclaimed himself *signore* of the city, and appointed members of his family to key positions in the new administration. This new principality became the most important city in northern Italy, extending its domination over most of Lombardy. (Bibliog. 98, 100)

Milun, French *lai** by Marie de France.* It combined the old folk motif of father and son fighting against each other as in the old Germanic *Hildebrandslied,** and the French *Gormont et Isembart,** with the idea of two lovers communicating with the aid of a swan, an idea with seemingly no medieval parallels. (tr. Eugene Mason, New York: E. P. Dutton, 1966) (Bibliog. 163)

Mirabeau, castle+ on the border of Anjou* and Poitou.* In 1202, Eleanor of Aquitaine* emerged from her retirement at the abbey of Fontevrault* to take up residence at Mirabeau in support of her youngest son, King John* in his conflict with King Philip II,* of France, and the dispute with his nephew, Arthur,* over the throne of England. Being one of John's strongest allies and most sagacious advisors, Eleanor was a prize whom Arthur hoped to capture and bring John to his knees. To that end he besieged Mirabeau. John, nearby outside of Le Mans, raced to his mother's defense. Because the besiegers had already captured the town, and had forced all the castle gates but one, they had driven Eleanor to refuge in the keep+ which they believed they had practically won. They were surprised by the sudden appearance of John's troops, and were slain or captured to a man, the Lusignans* and Arthur himself being among the few prisoners. John immediately sent Arthur to prison at Falaise to prevent his being rescued by Philip, and vented his rage against the town of Tours which he destroyed. This relief of Mirabeau was the only battle John ever fought, and its operation was directed by John's military advisors, and not by John himself. (Bibliog. 162)

mise, a settlement by agreement, particularly a peace treaty. (Bibliog. 169, 184)

Mise of Amiens. See Louis IX.

Mise of Lewes. See Lewes, battle of.

Modena, city northwest of Rome which, in the middle of the 12th century, became the battleground for the feuding forces of the Ghibellines* and the Guelphs*; following its collapse in 1289 under such severe strains, it was taken over and controlled by the Este* family for the next few centuries. (Bibliog. 228)

Monaco, principality in Provence.* In the 9th century, the town of Monaco was included within the county of Nice. Conquered by the Genoese in the middle of the 11th century, it was governed from 1070 by members of the Grimaldi family who established a feudal seignory there. At the end of the 11th century, the Grimaldis became vassals+ of the counts of Provence. In 1297, under Rainerio I, the lords of Monaco took advantage of the wars between the Angevins of Naples, and Genoa and Aragon to proclaim themselves free of feudal ties, and under the protection of the republic of Genoa. Some of its dukes were:

1275 - Rainerio I, Grimaldi
1300 - Rainerio II, Grimaldi
1330 - Carlo I, Grimaldi
1363 - Rainerio III, Grimaldi
1407 - Giovanni Grimaldi.
(Bibliog. 98, 100)

Moniage Guillaume (Fr. "William the monk"), chanson de geste of the Garin de Monglane* cycle that existed in two versions; one, a fragment of 934 verses, was written around 1160 by an author who knew the *Prise d'Orange,* *Charroi de Nîmes,* and the *Chanson de Guillaume.* It recounted how, after his wife of 100 years, Guiborc, died, William of Orange* (Guillaume d'Orange) became inconsolable and entered a monastery in Genoa at the direction of an angel in his dreams. He soon became thoroughly detested by all, for he was a bully, and ate more than his share.   Sending him to the the seacoast to buy fish, the abbot directed him through a woods which the monks know to be infested with dangerous robbers, and admonished him not to strike a blow in his own defense unless he was robbed of his braies+ (linen drawers). To ensure his defense, William bought a valuable braiel (belt), and reached the coast in safety. On his return through the woods, he sang the *Prise d'Orange* so loudly that he disturbed the robbers.   As instructed he kept turning the other cheek until they disturbed his braies, and then he lashed out and killed all 15. He returned to the monastery but had to force his way in. That night an angel in his dream told him to go be a hermit near Montpellier, and the following day he departed.

In the second and complete version of 6,629 lines, Guiborc already had died, and William went at once to Aniane Abbey where also he soon was hated. His adventure to buy fish was similar, except in this version he stopped with a hermit on his way back, and instead of returning to the monastery, he went to Gellone near Montpellier where he wanted to establish a monastery, but the place had too many snakes. He prayed to God for their destruction, and answering with a clap of thunder, God hurled them all into a ravine. An angel told him then to build a monastery there, but a 14-foot giant tried to stop him. William hurled him into the ravine with the snakes, and built his monastery. Then Sinagon, Saracen king of Palermo, captured him and held him in a horrible prison for seven years until he was rescued by King Louis, and was returned to Gellone. Ysoré, Sinagon's nephew, besieged Paris. Louis sent for William because he had no other champion capable of delivering Paris from the evil siege. William killed Ysoré in single combat, delivered the Saracen's head to King Louis and rode back to Gellone. Then he tried to build a bridge across the ravine of the snakes, but the devil prevented its completion by destroying every night the work William had done during the day. Finally William wrestled with the fiend and threw him into the ravine where supposedly he still resides. William then lived in peace for the remainder of his life. The legend of the devil in the ravine remained current for centuries. (ed. W. Cloetta, *Les deux redactions du Moniage Guillaume,* Paris, *SATF,* 2 vols., 1906-1913) (Bibliog. 106)

Moniage Rainouart, chanson de geste* written by Graindor de Brie in Sicily around 1170. It parodied the *chansons de geste* with a plot similar to the *Moniage Guillaume.** (Max Lipke, *Ueber Die Moniage Rainouart,* Halle: Dissertation, 1904) (Bibliog. 21, 106)

Monmouth castle,+ birthplace in Monmouth in its gatehouse in 1387 of the first son and heir of King Henry IV, who became the famous Prince Hal, and later reigned as King Henry V.* (Bibliog. 104)

Mont Dolorous, location of a dangerous knightly adventure set up originally to find only the best knights for King Arthur.* At the command of Uther Pendragon,* Merlin* built at the top of this mountain a magic pillar decorated with 15 crosses: 5 red, 5 white and 5 blue. Only the most valiant of knights could tie their steeds to it, for those who failed or were timorous or weak were driven temporarily insane. In the French verse romance *Fergus,** this mount was identified as

Trimontium or Newstead in Scotland. (Bibliog. 242)

Montacute, name of an ancient and illustrious English family. Its name came from a sharp hill in the southern part of Somersetshire, a place called Biscopeston by the Saxons but Montacute by the earl of Moriton, cousin on his mother's side to William the Conqueror.* It afterwards gave its name to the noble family who were its lords; later they came to be earls of Salisbury.* (Bibliog. 101)

Montferrat, marquisate+ in northwestern Italy that developed from a castle+ built in the late 9th century on the southern bank of the Po River and dominating the road between Milan, Genoa and Turino. Taking advantage of the anarchy prevalent in that section of Italy at the time, the lords of this castle proclaimed themselves counts, and rulers of a vast territory of Italy. Otto I* of Germany made it a march* in 954, and in 967, the hereditary title of margrave+ was granted to the lords as vassals+ of the Holy Roman Empire. In 1147, a count of Montferrat took part in the second crusade,+ but in 1176 the connection of the family with the Holy Land became more intimate when William Longsword, eldest of five sons of Count William III, accepted the invitation of King Baldwin IV to marry the heiress to the kingdom, Sibylla. He died within a few months, but his posthumous son became Baldwin V. Count William himself, uncle of King Philip II* of France, journeyed to the Holy Land to watch over the interests of his grandson, and was captured by Saladin* at the battle of Hattin* in 1187. William's second son, Conrad of Montferrat,* had gone to serve Isaac Angelus,* Byzantine emperor, had married the emperor's sister and had defeated and killed a usurper. His actions were met with suspicion which forced him to flee to the Holy Land. Landing at Tyre, he prevented that city from falling into the hands of Saladin's forces after Hattin. Then he established himself at Tyre, and sent a steady stream of appeals for help to western Europe which strongly influenced a third crusade. Sibylla had married Guy of Lusignan as her second husband, and when Conrad married her younger sister Isabella, now the heiress to the kingdom, he claimed the crown. The struggles of these two for that throne paralyzed the kingdom, and divided the crusaders. King Richard I* supported Guy who came from his own county of Poitou; Philip II of France supported Conrad. After Philip had returned to France, Richard realized that Conrad was the one man capable of ruling the kingdom of Jerusalem, and recognized him as king in 1192. Shortly thereafter, however, Conrad was killed by an Assassin,+ an emissary of the Old Man of the Mountain. Still another son of Count William III, Boniface, Conrad's younger brother, was chosen to lead the fourth crusade on the death of Theobald of Champagne. In the winter of 1201-1202, he visited Philip of Swabia in Germany, and there agreed to divert the fourth crusade from its goal of Cairo to Constantinople, and played a great role in the events up through the assault and capture of that Byzantine city. Expecting to be chosen eastern emperor, he was angered by the selection of Baldwin of Flanders over him. He became king of Thessalonica (1204-1207) and was killed in 1207 during a battle with the Bulgarians. (Bibliog. 68, 98)

Montfort, castle+ in the Holy Land which became the headquarters of the Teutonic Order+ of knights in 1229; it had been named for Montfort l'Amauri near Paris, home of the Montfort* family. It was one of the last crusader fortifications in the Holy Land, and defied attack by the Mameluke sultan Baibars in 1266, but fell to his forces five years later. (Bibliog. 30)

Montfort, Simon V de (c. 1200-1265), earl of Leicester.* This English statesman and soldier was born in France about 1200, the fourth and youngest son of Simon IV de Montfort,* the leader of the Albigensian crusade.+ Simon IV, whose mother was an heiress of the Beaumont* family, claimed in her right and received from King John* the earldom of Leicester in 1207, only to lose it by siding with the French against John. He came to England in 1230, allied himself with Henry III,* and was regranted the earldom of Leicester. In 1238, he married the widow of the younger William Marshal, much to the resentment of Earl Richard of Cornwall,* the king's brother. Differences between him and the crown caused him to return to France in 1239, and to accompany Richard of Cornwall the following year on a crusade+ to the Holy Land where he acquitted himself with distinction, and returned to England to help with Henry III's disastrous French expedition in 1242. He fully supported the king in 1243 and served as mediator in Parliament between the court party and the opposition until 1248. After the king refused permission for him to accompany Louis IX* of France on the crusade, Simon served as governor of Gascony where his harsh methods subjected him to severe criticism. King Henry ordered an investigation which cleared him, but when the king challenged his accounts, Simon again returned to France, angrily. There, the nobles offered him the regency of the French monarchy lately vacated by the death of queen mother Blanche* of Castile, but he chose instead to return to England and make peace with Henry III. With Peter of Savoy* in 1256, he tried to extricate the king from pledges given to the pope about the kingdom of Sicily, but in 1258, he sided with the earl of Gloucester* at the head of the opposition to the crown. He supported the Provisions of

Oxford* strongly, and was one of the Committee of Fifteen chosen to administer them. He left the country in disgust in 1261 after the king rejected the Provisions, but returned two years later at the request of the barons to raise a rebellion and then restore the form of government which the Provisions had called for. He made the mistake of accepting Henry's offer to abide by the arbitration of King Louis IX of France, for at Amiens in 1264, Louis declared that the Provisions were unlawful and invalid. That led to the Barons' War* and Simon's victory at Lewes* in 1264 where the king, Earl Richard and Lord Edward* all fell into his hands. Montfort then set up a government of his own run by a triumvirate of himself, the earl of Gloucester and the bishop of Chichester, and summoned a Parliament in 1265. Opposition from many of the barons, however, led subsequently to his death at Evesham* in 1265 in a second battle against the king's forces, and the end of the rebellion. (Bibliog. 47, 58, 68)

Montfort family, famous French family descended from the counts of Hainaut.* Amauri de Montfort attested charters for King Robert I* of France in 1022. His son, William, living during the 11th century, built a castle+ at Montfort l'Amauri near Paris. A century later Simon III, count of Evreux and Seigneur de Montfort, was a vassal of both the king of France and the king of England as duke of Normandy. He sided with England and gave to Henry II his castles at Montfort, Rochefort and Etampes. He sided with young Henry in the English princes' rebellion of 1173. Until 1209 when Simon IV took the title of count,+ William and his successors were known as barons de Montfort. This Simon IV de Montfort (c. 1160-1218), son of Simon III (d. 1181) played a huge role in the crusade against the Albigenses+ in the south of France. Twice he had gone to Palestine* as a crusader+ before he answered the call of Pope Innocent III* to join the host of Christians marching against the enemies of the church in Languedoc.+ He became the vicomte* of Beziers and Carcassonne, and then the leader of the crusaders. Capturing site after site, he finally defeated Raymond IV, count of Toulouse, at Castelnaudry in 1212, and a year later defeated Raymond's ally, Peter II, king of Aragon. After a lively discussion at the Lateran Council of 1215, the pope reluctantly confirmed him in the greater part of the lands of Count Raymond. Yet in only two more years of warfare, he was killed by a rock hurled by an angry woman defending the walls of Toulouse. Simon's eldest son, Aumari, found himself unable to hold the lands even with help of troops from King Philip II,* Augustus, and abandoned them to the new French king, Louis VIII.* Later he was made constable+ of France in 1230, and in 1239, he went on a crusade to the Holy Land. (See Manny, Walter de.) (Bibliog. 25, 68)

Montgomery castle,+ fortress built on the advice of Henry III's*
advisors in 1223 as a guard for a Severn River crossing. Five years
later the king granted it for life on Hubert de Burgh* with 200 marks
a year for its custody, and the promise of more in case of war. By
1232, however, Hubert had lost the favor of the king, and the castle
as well. In 1254, the king granted it to his son, the Lord Edward.*
After the conquest of Wales, however, it lost its strategic importance
as a frontier post, and as a result little time and money were ex-
pended on its upkeep. After Edward II's* death, Queen Isabelle*
secured it for her lover Roger Mortimer, but he was forced to forfeit
it in 1330. (Bibliog. 104)

Monthermer, Ralph de (d. 1325), knight who became earl of Gloucester*
and Hertford* during the lifetime of his wife, Joan, widow of Gilbert
de Clare,* sixth earl of Gloucester and Hertford, in whose right he
had become earl. In 1307, he was appointed keeper of Cardiff castle,
and later that year when he surrendered the custody of his stepson,
Gilbert de Clare, to the king, he was granted 5,000 marks in lieu of
that custody. Summoned to Parliament in 1309, he became Lord Monthern-
er. He warned Earl Thomas of Lancaster* against leading an armed revolt against King Edward II,* but his advice was ignored. Captured in
the battle of Bannock Burn,* he was released through his friendship
with Bruce* formed at the English court, and was excused from any
ransom. On his return to court, he brought King Edward II's shield
which had been taken at that battle. (Bibliog. 47)

Montjoie, name of Charlemagne's* ensign,+ and his war cry. The name
came from Mount Gaudia, a hill from which weary pilgrims could first
make out Rome in the distance; similar hills existed near Jerusalem
and Santiago de Compostella in Portugal. This exclamation also served
as a pilgrim's outcry after a long journey. See battle cry+; signs of
war.+ It also was mentioned in the *Song of Roland.** (Bibliog. 210)

Montlhery, Tower of, stronghold built about 1000 by Count Thibaut,
fils étoupe ("towhead"), in the Ile de France* on an easily defended
position on the main route between Paris and Orleans. Living by
brigandage, Thibaut attracted the attention of the Capetian kings in
Paris who sought to annex this stronghold. To profit from the
brigandage available from this castle, King Philip I* worked to gain
control of it by marrying a member of his family into the family of
its count. Louis VI, the Fat* made even more certain by entrusting the
castle to one of his closest supporters. See also Philip I.
(Bibliog. 196)

Montlouis, Treaty of. See Falaise, Treaty of.

Montmorency, name of one of the oldest and most distinguished families in France. Its founder was Bouchard I, sire de Montmerency, in the 10th century; it produced numerous important French dignitaries during the centuries. Matthieu I (d. 1160), sire de Montmerency, for example, received the post of constable+ in 1138. His first wife was Aline, illegitimate daughter of Henry I* of England; his second was Alice of Savoy, widow of King Louis VI* and mother of Louis VII.* He shared with Abbé Suger the regency of France during the absence of Louis VII on the second crusade. Seventy-five years later, Matthieu II played an important role in the battle of Bouvines* (1214) and was made constable of France in 1218. On the accession of Louis IX,* he became a chief supporter of queen-regent Blanche* of Castile, and successfully forced all vassals to grant her obedience. (Bibliog. 68)

Montsegur castle,+ French fortress on a peak in the Pyrenees Mountains built in 1204. As the Albigensian+ crusade+ drew to its bloody close, the Cathar heretics took their last refuge in this castle after their defeat by Simon de Montfort.* Besieged in 1243, the garrison under Ramon de Perella surrendered after two months through treachery. In the following year, Montfort burned alive over 200 of the Albigensians who had taken refuge in the castle and who refused to recant their faith in Cathar* religion, and dismantled the castle. (Bibliog. 30)

Moot of Salisbury, judicial council summoned in 1086 by William II Rufus.* Calling all his free tenants who were subject to the obligation of service to the king in case of emergency, regardless of their rank (knight or freeman) and nationality (English or French), William had them take their oath to defend him as their liege+ against all comers. This oath of allegiance to the king by all his free subjects displayed the enormous differences between the English and French monarchies. By this Oath of Salisbury sworn at that Moot,+ the English king established his power independent of the hierarchy of vassals, while at the same time he gained the support of all those beneath him by upholding the Danish and Anglo-Saxon traditions similar to those established by Charlemagne* which had died out as the Carolingian Empire disintegrated. (Bibliog. 178)

mor tuath. See Brehon law.

Morcades. See Morgawse.

Mordred, Modred, officially the son of King Lot,* but actually the incestuously begotten son of King Arthur* by Lot's wife. As a child, he was seized by invading Saxons but was rescued by his kinsmen. When he was grown, he usurped the English throne and Guenevere's* hand in marriage while Arthur was absent on his expeditions against Lancelot,* and was slain by Arthur in the resultant battle. (Bibliog. 1, 145)

Morgan la Fée, Morgain la Fay, Fata Morgana, fairy queen who played a large role in King Arthur's* life. In connection with Arthur in Geoffrey of Monmouth's* *Vita Merlini* written about 1150, she appeared first as Morgen, the fairest of nine enchantresses, skilled in flying through the air and in healing, who lived on an isle of amazing fertility (Avalon*) to which they carried the wounded Arthur after the battle of Camlan. In the *Vulgate Lancelot*, the hero, Lancelot,* twice spurned her proffered love, once when lured by a damsel, and was imprisoned in her castle; the other time, when three enchantresses, Morgain, the Queen of Sorestan, and Sebille, cast a spell on him while he was asleep and had him carried by horse litter and imprisoned in a castle. Morgain claimed him for herself because she maintained she was of higher lineage, and hence he would love her more than either of the other two. She tried to get from him the ring Guenevere* had given him, but he refused to part with it. In the English lay of *Sir Launfal,** an amorous fay, Morgain, offered herself to the hero, and gave him a marvellous steed, but was not rebuffed. Instead, the hero rebuffed the other amorous lady, Guenevere, which revealed the jealous rivalry between them so common in the Arthurian romances. One of her most famous appearances was as the lady behind the whole adventure of *Sir Gawain and the Green Knight.** In that poem, she wanted to test the Round Table,* to humiliate Arthur, and to frighten Guenevere to death. (Bibliog. 80, 141, 206)

Morgawse, Morcades, daughter of Uther Pendragon* and Ygerne,* sister of Arthur,* wife of King Lot* and mother of Gawain,* Agravaine,* Gareth,* Gaheris,* Mordred* and the damsel Clarissant. (Bibliog. 202, 242)

Morholt, Marhalt, Marhaus, huge Irish knight, uncle of Isolde, who when he came to Cornwall to collect from King Mark* the annual tribute of thirty children paid to the Irish by the people of Cornwall, was challenged by Tristan to single combat on an island, and was defeated and slain by Tristan in Gottfried von Strassburg's* *Tristan.** (Bibliog. 1, 97, 202)

Moriaen, Middle Dutch verse romance about the quest of a son for his father. A Christian knight, who later turned out to be Percheval (Perceval*), had a love affair with a black princess, and left her shortly after the birth of his son. As soon as he was grown, the boy, Moriaen, set out to find his father or to avenge his death. His search took him to Arthur's* court, and adventures with Walewein (Gawain*) and Lancelot.* (tr. Jessie L. Weston, London: D. Nutt, 1901) (Bibliog. 10)

Morley, William de, English knight from Norolk summoned to Parliament as a baron in 1299; his son, Robert (d. 1360), was a celebrated warrior largely responsible for the English victory at Sluys,* and contributed much as a fighter in the battle of Crécy.* (Bibliog. 68)

Morligane, city in Spain whose name was used as a rallying cry for Saracens in the *chanson de geste,* *Prise de Pamplune.* (Bibliog. 128)

Mormaership. See Angus.

La Mort Artu, French Arthurian prose romance written between 1215 and 1230 as the concluding portion of the Prose *Lancelot.* After Galahad* and Perceval* had died, Bohort returned to Camelot to tell his story. Lancelot, it seemed, returned to his old ways. Wounded while tourneying at Winchester, he had been nursed by a fair maid of Escalot who fell in love with him. Guenevere's jealousy of this affair was eased when the maid died from her love of Lancelot. Arthur* visited the castle+ where Lancelot had been held captive and saw the scenes Lancelot had painted on the walls while a prisoner. These were described in the *Lancelot proper.* Lancelot saved Guenevere twice: once in a judicial combat to prove her innocence in poisoning a knight, and once as she was about to be burned at the stake for adultery. In that second fight, however, Lancelot accidentally killed Gareth,* Gawain's* brother. Arthur then besieged Joyous Garde* where Lancelot had taken Guenevere, and through the intercession of the pope agreed to take her back. Arthur then pursued Lancelot to his kingdom in France, and in the ensuing fight, Gawain was badly wounded in the head by Lancelot. Arthur returned to England from France on the news that Mordred,* his son begotten in incest, had rebelled. In the ensuing fight in which Mordred died, Arthur was mortally wounded. On the king's death, Lancelot returned to England, killed Mordred's sons in battle, and retired to live out his life as a hermit. (tr. J. Neale Carman, *From Camelot to Joyous Garde,* Lawrence, KN: University of Kansas, 1974) (Bibliog. 42)

Mort Aymeri de Narbonne, *chanson de geste** of the Garin de Monglane* cycle; written probably in the last years of the 12th century, it began with King Louis* in Paris being harassed by his enemy, Hugh Capet,* so he sent for Aymeri to help. Aymeri, ill and bedridden, was expecting death but wanted to see his king and his sons to bid them farewell. On learning about Aymeri's illness, Corsolt of Arabia, a Saracen,* plotted to regain Narbonne. Aimeri, however, was far from dead, and rose from his sickbed to defend his city. Captured by the Saracen forces, Aymeri was saved from execution at the stake by the promises of his wife, Hermenjart, to surrender the city on the promise by the Saracens that they would not abuse it or its citizens. In keeping with their reputation, the Saracens broke their promise and mistreated the citizens, and sent Aymeri into Spain under escort. Hermenjart, however, refused to surrender the main keep+ of Narbonne, and resisted the siege even though she and her women were dangerously short of food. Corsolt then sent Auquaire d'Aumarie to fetch his lady fair, Clarrisant, with her 14,000 attendant maidens, but they were captured by the Franks on their way to relieve Narbonne. After Aymeri was rescued by his sons, the Franks converted Auquaire and enlisted his help in retaking Narbonne. He had Aymeri dress as Clarrisant and his men dress as the attendant maidens. Thus they tricked their way into the city and recaptured it, slaying Corsolt in the battle. Meanwhile, the 14,000 maidens were carried off by the Sajetaires, pagan centaurs who lived in nearby Esclabarie, and thrown into a dismal prison. Aymeri and King Louis led their forces to the rescue and destroyed the Sajetaires. One of them, however, fatally wounded Aymeri and two of his sons with arrows. They were buried with great solemnity at the Church of St. Paul in Narbonne. (ed. J. Couraye du Parc, Paris: *SATF*, 1884) (Bibliog. 106)

Mort Garin le Loherenc, *chanson de geste** supposedly written by Jean de Flagy, centering on the figure of Garin who was the epic nucleus of the entire *Geste des Lorrains.* He allegedly lived at the time of Pepin. He was the eldest son of Hervis de Mes who was famed for his conflicts with the Saracens. Bègue's being made duke of Gascony and his approaching marriage to the daughter of the king of Moriane aroused the envy and hatred of the Bordelese.* During the first encounter between forces of these two areas, Hardré* was killed. His death led to a lengthy war in the area of Cambrai,* Saint-Quentin, and Bar-le-Duc. Bègue overcame Fromont's nephew Isore and killed him. After a short period of peace, the Bordelese renewed the warfare and moved into southern France where their war finally was brought to an end with a decisive peace until Bègue was killed accidentally by a

Bordelese hunter. Garin avenged the death of his brother, but in the end was himself slain. (ed. E. du Meril, Paris, 1846) (Bibliog. 231)

Mortain, district in La Manche which gave its name to a Norman *comté* (county), the holder of which was styled as the earl of Mortain. William the Conqueror,* when he was duke, took this *comté* from his cousin William "the warling" and gave it to his half-brother Robert II,* Curthose, who henceforth was known as the count of Mortain. Robert's son and successor, William, the Clito,* rebelled against Henry I,* and after being captured at the battle of Tinchebrai,* forfeited his possessions. Later, Henry bestowed it on his nephew Stephen* who then was known as the count of Mortain until he became count of Boulogne by marriage, and eventually king of England in 1135. On Stephen's death in 1154, his surviving son (see Warenne) succeeded to the *comté* but because he died childless in 1159, it reverted to the crown. King Richard I* bestowed it upon his younger brother John* who henceforth was known as the count of Mortain until his succession to the throne. Along with the rest of Normandy it reverted to the French crown in 1204. (Bibliog. 47)

Le Morte Arthur, Middle English* romance detailing the triangle relationship in love of Lancelot-Guenevere-Arthur; its manuscript dated from around 1400. It covered two separate episodes of Lancelot's* career: his entanglement with the fair maid of Astolat and his championing of the queen when she was falsely accused of poisoning an Irish knight, and the discovery of the adulterous union of Lancelot and Guenevere* and its tragic sequel—the siege of Benwick and the death of Arthur.* (ed. P. F. Hissiger, The Hague: Mouton, 1975) See also *Mort Artu* and *Morte Arthure.* (Bibliog. 158)

Morte Arthure, alliterative Middle English* verse romance from about 1360. Sometimes identified as the *Gret Gest off Arthure,* this work, sometimes credited to a poet named Huchown, was one of the masterpieces of the English alliterative revival of the 14th century, along with *Sir Gawain and the Green Knight.** It opened with a recapitulation of King Arthur's* conquests taken from the Alexander cycle* and Wace.* Then as the king was about to begin a banquet, messengers arrived from Lucyus, emperor of Rome, and summoned Arthur to do homage.+ His British knights, however, promised Arthur their support and each vowed to perform a deed of valor in battle against the Romans. (See "Vow of the Heron,"+) After hurling oaths of defiance at the emperor, Arthur sent back the messengers and prepared to depart for France. In a dream he saw himself as an eagle defeat a bear,

Lucyus. Once in Brittany, he killed the giant of Mont St. Michel while the emperor gathered his forces; his roster read like a list from the Alexander* cycle. In the battle, Arthur's knights fulfilled their vows and defeated Lucyus, and after Arthur himself killed the emperor, he marched to Rome and accepted the submission of the Romans. Just then, a messenger from England informed him of Mordred's* treason. Returning home speedily, he defeated Mordred's navy at sea, and during the battle to land back on English soil, Gawayne* was killed. Arthur then gave battle to Mordred and slew him, but received a fatal wound, was carried to Glastonbury, died and was buried there with much solemnity. (ed. John Finlayson, Evanston, IL: Northwestern University, 1971) (Bibliog. 159)

Le Morte D'Arthur, famous compilation of the Arthurian legends by Sir Thomas Malory which contained virtually all that was truly significant in the story. To this work, Arthurian romance probably owed its survival in the English-speaking world. In twenty-one books, it covered the birth and crowning of Arthur,* acquisition of Excaliber,* conception and birth of Mordred,* marriage of Arthur to Guenevere,* adventures of Lancelot,* Gawain* and other knights of the Round Table,* the story of Tristram of Lyonesse and Isolde, Lancelot and the birth of his son, Galahad,* the adventures of the search for the Holy Grail,* the split-up of the Round Table caused by the love affair of Lancelot and Guenevere, Mordred's attempts to take the crown of England, the final battle, and death of Arthur and the last days of Lancelot and Guenevere. (ed. E. Vinaver, London: Oxford, repr. 1977) (Bibliog. 145)

Mortimer of Richard's castle, family descended from a lordship with Richard's castle in Hereford* as its *caput,* named for Richard FitzScrub, a Norman favorite of King Edward the Confessor,* who was allowed by Earl Godwine* to remain in England in 1053. The name descended to Robert de Mortimer of Essex who took part in the third crusade+ and probably was a personal attendant of King Richard I.* His son, Robert de Mortimer, was active in court affairs, and served as a lord marcher.* His second wife was Margaret de Say, daughter and heiress of Hugh de Say, lord of barony of Burford and Richard's Castle. Their son, Hugh de Mortimer (b. 1220-1274), served as a lord marcher, allied himself with the king as a royalist in 1264 and 1265, and was rewarded for it afterwards. His son, Roger de Mortimer (d. 1287), served as a lord marcher and was one of the men who slew Llewelyn,* prince of Wales, at Builth* in 1282. His son, Hugh de Mortimer, was a minor in 1287 at his father's death, but came of age

and received livery of his estates in 1295. he was summoned to
Parliament in 1296 whereby he became Lord Mortimer. He married Maud,
niece of William Marshal, and died without male issue in 1304,
apparently accidentally poisoned by his wife, who later was pardoned.
(Bibliog. 47, 70)

Mortimer (Mortemer) of Wigmore, English family descended from Roger
de Mortemer, Seigneur of Mortemer-sur-Elaulne in Normandy* who was one
of the leaders of the Norman troops at the battle of Mortemer in 1054,
but because he assisted the escape of one of the French prisoners,
Ralph, count of Montdidier, to whom he had done homage, his lands were
confiscated and he was exiled. He afterwards was reconciled to Duke
William,* and some of his lands were restored to him, but not Mortemer
which had gone to William de Warenne.* His son, Ralph, was listed as
holding a *DomesdayBook** honour+ with lands in twelve counties and with
its *caput** at Wigmore. His great-grandson, Roger de Mortimer of
Wigmore (d. 1214), was forced to abjure+ the realm for three years in
1191 on a charge of conspiring with the Welsh against the king, but
was back in King Richard I's favor by 1195. He was a strenuous lord
marcher,* but lost to Rhys,* prince of South Wales, near Radnor in
1196. On the loss of Normandy in 1204, he adhered to King John* and
hence was forced to forfeit his Norman lands. His eldest son, Hugh de
Mortimer (d. 1227), was faithful to King John especially during the
trouble with the barons in 1215, and he accompanied the king north and
was with him at his death in 1216. Under Henry III,* he served as a
lord marcher in the west, being one of the great council at Montgomery
who received the promises of Llewelyn and his supporters to make
amends to the English. He died in 1227 without male issue. His brother, Ralph de Mortimer, (d. 1246) succeeded to the family estates, and
served the king as a lord marcher. In 1230, he married Gladys, daughter of Joan, the illegitimate daughter of King John by Llywelyn ap
Iorwerth* ("the Great"). Their son, Roger de Mortimer (d. 1282),
served in Gascony* and between 1255 and 1264 was occupied chiefly with
his duties in the march, opposing the successes of Llewelyn ap
Griffith who was gradually uniting the Welsh chieftains under his
leadership. In 1258, Roger took the barons' side, and was one of the
twelve chosen to act in concert with the twelve chosen by the king. He
attested the king's proclamation for the observance of the Provisions
of Oxford.* These provisions directed, among other things, that Roger
de Mortimer and Philip Basset should accompany the justiciar+ to witness the submission of the French barons to King Louis IX* of France
in their dispute. He fought at Lewes* but fled to Pevensey. He and
others who fled were allowed by Simon de Montfort* to return to their

homes on condition that they should appear at Parliament when summoned and be tried by their peers. In 1265, he contrived the plan by which Prince Edward* escaped from Hereford castle and came to Wigmore where he and Roger de Clifford rode out to meet him and drove off pursuers. That escape plan called for Edward to ride out of Hereford for exercise with Earl Gilbert's brother, Thomas de Clare, and Henry de Montfort. He was to try first one horse and then another, and then quietly ride apart on the one to seem to decide. Then, on a signal from a horseman in the distance, he was to gallop off for Wigamore castle twenty miles away, followed by Thomas de Clare. The escape plan worked, and the prince went first to Wigamore and thence to Ludlow castle where he met with Mortimer and Earl Gilbert* de Clare. At the battle of Evesham* which followed soon therafter, Mortimer commanded the rearguard. After Montfort's* death, his head was sent to Mortimer's wife at Wigmore. Roger was rewarded by the grant of the county and lands of Oxford recently forfeited by Robert de Vere.* Later he was made one of the trustees for the prince's estates on his absence on the crusade. He died in 1282. His second but eldest surviving son, Edmund de Mortimer (d. 1304), had been reared for the church, but on the death of his older brother in 1274, he inherited the estates and the responsibility as a lord marcher. He became Lord Mortimer in 1295. Along with other marcher lords, he had joined the earl of Lancaster against the Despensers,* but surrendered in 1322 and was made prisoner in Tower until he died there in 1326 and all his all possessions forfeited. He married Margaret de Fiennes, cousin of Eleanor, Edward I's queen.

Edmund's son, Roger de Mortimer the Younger (1287-1330), being a minor on the death of his father, came under the wardship of Piers Gaveston* on July 29, 1304. On December 30, 1304, Roger obtained permission to pay off his father's debts at the rate of £20 a year. On April 9, 1306, though still under age, he obtained livery of his father's lands, having satisfied Piers on the debt. He was knighted in 1306 along with Edward, Prince of Wales,* at Westminster. At the coronation of Edward II, he was one of the four bearers of the royal robes and for the next ten years served in Ireland. He was summoned back to England in 1318, and in the dispute between King Edward II and the Despensers on one side, and the earl of Lancaster on the other, Mortimer tried to steer a middle course with the earl of Pembroke. He was appointed justiciar of Ireland from 1319 to 1321. In a private war in 1320 between the earl of Hereford and Despenser about Gower, Roger and his uncle Roger Mortimer of Chirk sided with the earl. Thus, when the king summoned both of them to attend him a year later, they refused because Despenser was there. After the king yielded to pressure from the barons and banished the Despensers, Mortimer was pardoned and returned to the Welsh marches. Early in 1322, he was forced to yield to the king for supporting in Kent a castle which had refused to surrender to the king's forces. He and his father were imprisoned in the Tower of London.

After Lancaster* was defeated at Boroughbridge* in 1322, the Despensers returned to power, and the Mortimers were tried and condemned to death, but the sentence was commuted to perpetual imprisonment. A week later, Roger escaped from the Tower by having someone drug the guards, and fled to France where he was welcomed by King Charles IV.* He repaid the French king by assisting him in his war in Guyenne* against the English king. In the spring of 1325, Queen Isabelle, King Edward's wife and King Charles' sister, crossed to France to arrange a truce about the war in Guyenne. Two months later, in September, Prince Edward crossed the Channel to do homage+ for Aquitaine* and stayed with his mother, with whom Mortimer and other exiles had become closely associated. Mortimer had become the lover of the queen as well as her advisor, and at the end of that year, they went to Hainaut where Prince Edward was affianced to Philippa* of Hainaut, and men and money were obtained for an attack on England. In September 1326, Isabelle, Mortimer, John of Hainaut and their forces landed near Ipswich and were joined by Henry, earl of Lancaster, and other opponents of the Despensers. King Edward fled to Wales with the Despensers; Mortimer followed him. On October 26, the elder Despenser was captured at Bristol, tried by Mortimer, Lancaster, and others the next day, and hanged immediately. On November 16, the king and the younger Despenser were captured at Llantrisant; the next day Mortimer ordered the execution of Arundel,* and on November 24, he, Lancaster, and Kent sat in judgment of the younger Despenser, and hanged him on a gallows 50 feet high.

On January 7, 1327, Parliament deposed Edward II, and made his son king, and a week later, Mortimer with a large company of men visited the city and at the Guildhall promised to maintain the liberties of the citizens. Although he was not present at the king's murder later that year, he was present at the coronation of young Edward III,* and on that same occasion, three of his sons, Edmund, Roger and Geoffrey, were knighted. He soon was pardoned for his escape from the Tower, and for his other delinquencies, and the sentences against him were reversed because he had not been tried by his peers. In 1328, he held one Round Table tournament+ at Bedford, and another on the occasion of the marriage of two of his daughters which the king and the queen mother attended. In October 1328, Roger was created earl of March,* that being the first earldom created in England not of a county. Before that, he had met with little opposition in his goals of self-aggrandizement since his return from exile. He held no offices, but obtained posts for his friends, and secured for himself lucrative grants which gave him great wealth while exercising the almost regal power he had acquired from Queen Isabelle. Discontent grew among his rivals, especially in Henry, earl of Lancaster, who had been appointed guardian of the young king at his accession, but had been ousted gradually by Mortimer from any control of or influence over the young king. Lancaster had refused to attend the Parliament at which Mortimer had been made earl, and he formed in London a coalition among some of the citizens dedicated to destroying Mortimer. Mortimer overran Lancaster's lands, and siezed Leicester on January 4, 1329. As Lancaster marched to oppose Mortimer his allies deserted him, and he was forced to make terms with his enemy, Mortimer.

This success assured Mortimer's rise to power, and he continued to obtain lucrative grants. On May 27, for example, in consideration for his continual attendance on the king, he was granted 500 marks per year from Wales in addition to his annual fee as justice of Wales. In July, he was appointed chief commissioner of array+ and captain of the counties of Hereford, Gloucester, Worcester and Shropshire. This was his last grant, for the universal hatred which his arrogance and greed had inspired came to a head. Early in 1330, he involved Edmund, earl of Kent, uncle of the king, and his own former associate, in a plot to restore Edward II to the throne by persuading Edmund that his half-brother still lived. Edmund's resulting trial for treason, and his execution in March 1330 was a success for Mortimer which soon turned against him. Edward III himself, long unhappy at the restraints imposed on him as king, and at Mortimer's influence over his mother, roused, and headed a conspiracy to get rid of the tyrant. This group decided to seize Mortimer. The governor of Nottingham castle, where Mortimer, Isabelle, and the king lodged, revealed to William de Montagu (later earl of Salisbury*) a secret passage into the castle whereby Mortimer's guards could be evaded. On the night of October 18, the conspirators burst in on Mortimer while he was in conference with the chancellor. Mortimer slew one of his assailants but was overpowered and arrested by order of the king, despite the queen-mother's appeal. He was sent to London with two of his sons, Edmund and Geoffrey, and his chief lay assistants, Simon de Bereford and Oliver Ingham.* On October 28, Edward took the government into his own hands, and at the Parliament which met in London in November, Mortimer was impeached on 14 counts, found guilty without being heard in his own defense, and condemned to be executed; all his honours* were forfeit. He was drawn to execution like a felon and hanged at the Elms, Tyburn, on November 29, 1330; his body was left hanging for two days and two nights.

The earldom of March passed in 1354 to his grandson, Roger de Mortimer (1328-1360), the son of Edmund (d. 1331) who had served King Edward III well. Fighting valiantly beside the Black Prince* at Crécy,* Roger was granted livery of his grandfather's lands in 1346. On his death in 1360, his son, Edmund de Mortimer, "the Good" (1352-1381), became earl of March. He married Philippa, only daughter and heir of Lionel, duke of Clarence, second son of King Edward III. Their son, Roger de Mortimer, earl of March and Ulster, born April 11, 1374, was proclaimed by King Richard II* in 1385 to be heir presumptive* to the crown, for if Richard II died without male issue, the crown would go to the eldest son, Edmund the Good, of the next son of Edward III, Lionel; but Edmund had died, so his son, Roger, became the next in line. Henry of Lancaster, son of John of Gaunt, usurped the throne of England from Roger when he succeeded Richard II in 1399 as King Henry IV. (Bibliog. 47, 70)

Moslem. See Muslim.

Mouskés, Philippe, French author of the *Chronique rimée,* a rhymed chronicle from the fall of Rome to 1241 containing over 30,000 verses. He based the work on Latin chronicles of St. Denis, Orderic Vitalis, Einhard and others, as well as the Pseudo-Turpin (see *Chronique de Turpin).* His information about the Carolingian period was unreliable and untrue, but for the period between 1180 and 1241, his material generally was accurate. Among other fictions, he related details about Eleanor* (of Aquitaine) marrying the count of Aquitaine, and flying out the church window with her children, leaving young Richard, Coeur de Lion, behind when she was forced to remain in church at the elevation of the host. (ed. Reiffenberg, Brussels, 2 vols., 1836-1838, 1845) (Bibliog. 27, 106)

Mowbray, Anglo-Norman barony whose name came from Montbray in Normandy south of St. Lo. This baronial house was founded after the Norman Conquest of 1066 by Geofrey de Montbray, bishop of Coutances. His brother's son, Robert, who rebelled with him against King William II* on the Conqueror's death, was made earl of Northumberland* after their reconciliation, but forfeited the earldom and was imprisoned for life after rebelling again in 1095. Bishop Geoffrey's sister became the mother by Roger d'Aubigny* (of Aubigny in the Cotentin*) of two sons, Nigel and William, who were ardent supporters of Henry I,* and were rewarded by him with great estates in England. William was made the king's butler, and was father of William d'Aubigny (d'Albini), the first earl of Arundel.* Nigel was rewarded with the escheated+ fief of Geoffrey de la Guerche, of which Melton (Mowbray) was the *caput,** and with forfeited lands in Yorkshire. His son, Roger, who took the Anglicized form of the name, Mowbray, was a great lord with 100 knights' fees, was captured with King Stephen* at the battle of Lincoln* in 1141, and joined King Henry II's* sons in rebellion in 1173, but accompanied Richard I* on the third crusade.+ His grandson, William, was one of the leaders in the rising against King John* in 1215, and was selected as one of the twenty-four barons of the *Magna Carta Libertatum,** and was captured fighting against King Henry III* at the second battle of Lincoln in 1217. His grandson, Roger (1266-1298), summoned to Parliament by Edward I,* was the father of John Mowbray (1286-1322) who was knighted in 1306 with the Prince of Wales. He served variously in Scotland between 1308 and 1319, was appointed warden of the Marches,* and captain of Northumberland. Through his marriage to Aline, daughter and co-heiress of Willian de Braose,* he became involved in the dispute with the Despensers,* and this led to his joining the party of Thomas* of Lancaster. When he entered his land at Gower in Wales, the Despensers, who controlled it, prevailed upon the king to dispossess Mowbray. This action led to a confederation of the lords marcher,* headed by the earl of Hereford,* the Mortimers,* and Mowbray against the Despensers who ultimately were banished in 1321. For this, the rebels received a general pardon. Mowbray received a second summons from Lancaster and joined forces with him and besieged Tickhill* castle. He later was captured by Andrew Harcla* at the battle of Boroughbridge* and hanged, and his estates forfeited. (Bibliog. 47, 68)

La Mule sans Frein, (Fr. "Mule without a bridle"), French verse romance from the early 13th century by Paien de Maisières. Called "La Demoiselle a la Mule" by its author, it usually was referred to as the "Mule sans Frein." In it a maiden arrived at Arthur's court seeking a knight who would recover the lost bridle of her mule. She made two assertions: that she would get back her bridle if one of Arthur's knights was willing to undertake the adventure, and that if she came into undisputed possession of the bridle, she would give herself to the knight who had given it back to her. The mule would carry the knight to his destination. Keu (Kay*) volunteered, and clambered on the beast by using the stirrups. After passing safely through a wild forest whose creatures did obeisance to the mule, and reviving himself at a lovely fountain, he returned to the court because he refused to attempt passage across a slender bridge over a fearsome river. Gawain* thereupon leapt on the mule without using the stirrups, and arrived at a revolving castle where he was called upon to undergo the beheading test and vanquish a mysterious knight, lions and serpents before receiving the bridle from the mistress of the castle, the maiden's sister. He returned triumphantly with the bridle. In Heinrich von dem Türlin's romance *Diu Krône** (c. 1215) which told a fuller version of the same story, the bridle served as the patrimony of the two daughters of the knight Laniure.   (ed. R. T. Hill, Baltimore, 1911) (Bibliog. 106, 113)

Muret, battle of (September 12, 1213), battle won by cavalry over an enemy composed of horse and footsoldiers. That was accomplished by a general with exceptional ability who surprised his enemy before he was in proper battle array. After a hard cavalry fight, the footsoldiers were massacred by the victors on horseback. All this occurred at Muret, a small town at the junction of the Garonne and Louge Rivers 20 miles southwest of Toulouse.* Its opponents were Simon de Montfort,* fresh from victories over the Albigenses+ in that bloody crusade, and King Peter II of Aragon. Simon lured Peter into halting his siege of Muret and attacking the town openly. Once Peter's forces were thus committed, Simon's 600 horsemen attacked Peter's 2,000 horsemen and 10,000 to 15,000 footmen. In the mêlée, Peter was slain, and his horsemen were routed; his footsoldiers fled the attacking crusader forces of Simon by dashing into the river or trying to run away. As a result, they were cut to pieces.   Estimates of the Aragonese casualties ranged from 2,000 to 3,000 footsoldiers and horsemen. (Bibliog. 166)

Muslim. Preferred term for a believer in or adherent of Islam.+ In popular usage, the term *Moslem* was used. (Bibliog. 169)

Muslim historians. See Arabic historians.

N

Naimes, Naimon, duke of Bavaria,* and chief private counsellor of Charlemagne* in the *chansons de geste*.* He was the most profoundly German of all Charlemagne's peers. His mother was Seneheult; his father Gasselin; and his uncle was Auberi le Bourgoigne, the half-savage duke of Burgoyne. During his youth, his *enfance*,* after a usurper named Casselle (Tassilon in history) had stolen Gasselin's inheritance, Seneheult died of grief, and Naimes was forced to flee to Romanie. One day, Charlemagne, the great resolver of all injustices, realized that the duke of Bavaria had been wronged, so he brought Naimes from exile, and banished the usurper. From that day on, Naimes, then 100 years old, provided counsel and advice based on his own experience for Charlemagne, and served as the conscience of the king. The emperor, 200 years old, seemed the younger of the two. His qualities were described at length in *Aspremont*.* In the *Song of Roland*,* however, he fought beside his king in the battle against Baligant, was struck and stunned by King Canabeus but was rescued by Charlemagne, and shortly thereafter came to the aid of his king to kill Baligant. He also appeared in almost all other *chansons de geste* in the cycle of the king (see *gestes du roi*). (Bibliog. 88, 210)

Naissance du Chevalier au Cygne, poem by a jongleur+ named Renaut that was grafted to the cycle of the first crusade+ to explain the fairy origins of Godfrey de Bouillon.* Written in the 13th century, this material usually was divided into two sections: *Naissance* and the *Chevalier au Cygne et Enfances Godefroi*.* The *Naissance* recounted how King Lothair of Hungary found a beautiful woman, Elioxe, beside a fountain with a gold fairy chain in her hand. He married her despite the objections of his wicked mother, Matrasilie. When Lothair was away at a war, Elioxe fulfilled a prophecy she had made by giving birth to a daughter and six sons who turned into swans, and then dying. Matrasilie sent the children into the woods to be killed, but instead of obeying those cruel commands, the servant, Manicier, left the infants with a hermit who raised them. Lothair was told on his return that the children had been serpents and had flown away. Years later, Matrasilie recognized the children in the woods by the gold chain each wore, and arranged to have the boys' chains stolen so that they would remain swans; the girl remained in human form. Matrasilie brought the swans to live in a pond near Lothair's castle, and the girl in the castle. Matrasilie used one chain to repair a golden basin. The daughter finally convinced Lothair of the truth of their birth, and he forced his mother to surrender the remaining chains, enabling five of the swans to return to human form; the sixth remained a swan. He was accompanied by one of his brothers who was known as the Swan Knight. (ed. Henry A. Todd, New York: *PMLA* 4, 1889) In a different version, Lothair was known as King Oriant, Elioxe became Beatrice and the swan knight was known as Helyas. (ed. Celestin Hippeau, Paris: PFMA, 1874-1877, 2 vols.) (Bibliog. 36, 106)

Najera, battle of. See Navarette, battle of.

Namur, city and then a province in south central Belgium between Brabant* and Liège* provinces and Hainaut. Originally it belonged to the Francia Media* but later became a part of the kingdom of Lotharingia. In 908 it became a county and its counts became direct vassals of the Holy Roman Emperors. (Bibliog. 98)

Nanteuil, ville and siegnory mentioned in the *chansons de geste** as being located somewhere in L'Est of France, but its exact locality was shadowy. (Bibliog. 128)

Naples, kingdom in southern Italy conquered by the Norman ruler of Sicily to became a part of the kingdom of the Two Sicilies. After 1282 when Sicily became Aragonese, the kingdom of Naples (including Italy south of the Papal States) remained under the control of the house of Anjou* from 1268 to 1435. Some of its important kings were

1282 - Charles I of Anjou
1285 - Charles II
1309 - Robert, brother of Charles II
1343 - Joanna, who married first, Andrew of Hungary, and second, Louis
            of Taranto
1381 - Charles III of Durazzo
(Bibliog. 98, 100)

*Narbonnais, chanson de geste** of the late 12th and early 13th century. In it, the older sons of Aimeri de Narbonne*—Aymer le Chetif (see

Aliscans), Bernart de Brubant (see *Mort Aymeri*), Bueve d'Aigremont (see *Four Sons of Aymon*), Garin d'Anseune (see *Chevalerie Vivien*), Guibert d'Andrenas (see *Mort Aimeri*), Guillaume d'Orange, and Hernaut de Gironde (see *Mort Aymeri*)—were told to leave and seek their own fiefs because Aimeri was reserving Narbonne for his youngest son, Guibelin. The sons were furious, especially when Aimeri struck their mother, Hermenjart, as she tried to interfere, but they left and were as successful as Aimeri had predicted, and then returned to aid their father in his continuing battles with the Saracens. This work united two other works, *Enfances Aimeri* and the *Siege de Narbonne.* (ed Hermann Suchier, Paris: *SATF,* 2 vols., 1898) Andrea da Barberino* also wrote a prose Italian version. (ed. J. G. Isola, Bologna: Coll. di op. ined., LXXXII, 1877) (Bibliog. 21, 106)

Narbonne, Roman city in southern France. Captured by the Arabs in 719, the Franks in 759, it later became the seat of the viscount+ of Narbonne. With Toulouse, it became one of the marts of Languedoc,+ and as such, a real home of southern civilization. During the crusade+ against the Albigenses,+ it was conquered by Simon de Montfort,* and in 1218 it became a possession of the French crown. During the black death+ epidemic in 1348-1349, one quarter of its population perished. (Bibliog. 98, 100, 220)

Navarette, Najera, battle in which Sir John Chandos* overcame Bertrand du Guesclin,* the constable+ of France, in an attempt by Edward,* the Black Prince, to restore Pedro* the Cruel to the throne of Castile* in 1369. (Bibliog. 166, 223, 224)

Navarre, ancient independent kingdom of northern Spain situated between France and Aragon* and Castile.* Under Sancho III (970-1035) it united with Castile and León, but then in 1035 it divided into the three kingdoms of Navarre, Castile and Aragon; it reunited with Aragon between 1076 and 1135, and became an appanage+ of France between 1234 and 1328. Some of its kings were

1194 - Sancho VII
1234 - Thibaut, count of Champagne, nephew of Sancho
1253 - Thibaut III, de Champagne
1270 - Henri
1274 - Jeanne de Champagne and Philippe le Bel,* king of France
1305 - Louis X, King of France
1316 - Philippe V, le Long, king of France
1322 - Charles IV, le Bel, king of France

1328 - Jeanne de France and Philippe d'Evreux
1349 - Charles II, le Mauvais, comte d'Evereux
1387 - Charles III.
(Bibliog. 98, 100)

Nesta, mistress of English King Henry I.* Daughter of Rhys ap Tudor, prince of South Wales, she bore Henry I a son she named Henry who was killed in 1157 fighting on behalf of Henry II* in Angelsey. She also was mistress of Stephen, castellan of Cardigan, to whom she also bore a son, Robert FitzStephen, who was prominent in the Norman invasion of Ireland. She married Gerald of Windsor and bore him four children: William and Maurice FitzGerald, both of whom took active roles in the invasion of Ireland; David who served as bishop of St. David's from 1176 to 1198; and a daughter Angharde who married William of Barry, lord of Manorbier who became the mother of the writer Gerald of Barri (see Giraldus Cambrensis). (Bibliog. 68, 69)

Netherlands. See Frisia.

Neuhaus. See Nouhusius.

Neustria, Frankish province, which between the 6th and 8th centuries, consisted of the northwestern part of the Frankish kingdom between the Somme and Loire rivers with its center at Paris. Developing its own political identity, it had its own Merovingian kings and mayors of the palace. During the 9th and 10th centuries, its frontiers were established between the Seine and Loire rivers. Then it became a duchy within the kingdom of France. After the accession of the line of Hugh Capet* to the throne of France in 987, it ceased to exist as a distinct unit and was divided among feudal counties and seignories. (Bibliog. 98)

Nevers, city in central France on the western border of Burgundy.* In the 11th century, it became the center of a powerful county. Its local dynasty allied themselves with the dukes of Burgundy in the 13th century and the dukes of Bourbon* in the 14th century, making the counts of Nevers members of the highest French aristocracy. (Bibliog. 98, 100)

Neville's Cross, battle of (October 17, 1346). In response to an invasion of the English counties of Northumberland and Durham by Scottish King David Bruce,* an English force was quickly gathered to combat him. Under the nominal leadership of William de la Zouch, archbishop of York, but actually directed by Lords Percy, Neville and Mowbray, and by Gilbert Umphraville, the exiled Scottish earl of Angus,* this English force of horsed archers and hobilars+ attacked the Scots who had taken a position on a hillside among hedges and underbrush. That location proved to be a disastrous one for the Scots, because their three shiltrons+ of pikemen were unable to keep in close touch with each other. Under Neville and Percy, the English outflanked the shiltron of the earl of Moray with swarms of archers who drove off the Scottish light troops, and then continued to pour volley after volley of arrows into the massed pikemen until that formation broke under the deadly fire. Then the English left closed upon the flank of the main Scottish force, while the forces under the archbishop attacked the front. The Scottish king's corps finally gave way, and was badly cut up. As they were losing ground, the left Scottish division under Stuart (later Robert II) hastily left the field. Among the fallen Scots were the earls of Moray and Strathearn, and three great officers of the Scottish crown, David de la Hay the constable,+ Robert Keith the marshal,+ and Thomas Charteris the chancellor.+ Among the prisoners were the Scottish king, badly wounded by an arrow in his face, and scores of noble bannerets+ and knights. That battle was won by the English using their archery against the flanks while the knights and hobilars attacked the front positions of the Scots. (Bibliog. 166)

Newburgh, William of (d. 1198), English chronicler whose *Historia rerum Anglicarum* (1106-1198) served as a valuable authority for the reign of King Henry II,* especially for the years 1154-1174. Considered one of the greatest of the 12th-century historians, he used considerable judgment and impartiality in dealing both with men and events. He was an Augustan canon at Newburgh when he wrote this work in the last decade of the century. (ed. and tr. Joseph Stevenson, *Church Historians*, London: Seeleys, 1876, IV, ii, 297-672) (Bibliog. 99, 174)

Newcastle upon Tyne, important frontier fortress on the Scottish border in Northumberland founded by Robert II,* Curthose, eldest son of William I* on his return from Scotland in 1080. He had been in Newcastle on his return from Scotland, and began building a motte and bailey+ fortress. From him, it went to Robert Mowbray, earl of Northumberland, from whom William II* took it by force in 1095, but lost it to King David* of Scotland. The Scots ruled it until Henry II* regained it in 1157, and spent over £1,000 erecting a fine rectangular keep surrounded by a bailey wall. It was maintained in moderately good repair throughout the next century until in 1296, the threats of increased Scottish attacks led the crown to examine it closely. King Edward I* ordered a brattice+ over the chapel, and the walls strengthened by hanging wooden shields over the battlements. One thousand small jars were purchased to be filled with lime and hurled at the enemy to burn the eyes and skin. Once the danger subsided, however, no money was authorized for its repairs or even simple upkeep, and by 1334, the sheriff of Northumberland complained to the crown that the castle had not one room in which a man could be sheltered nor one gate that could be shut. Orders were issued to keep the townspeople from dumping their rubbish in the moat. Even the few repairs finally authorized were not enough, for in 1357, part of the loft collapsed over the castle's prisons of the Great Pit and the Herron Pit and nearly killed the prisoners. (Bibliog. 104, 247)

Der Nibelunge Nôt, original title of the *Nibelungenlied*; it meant "Need of the Nibelungs." (Bibliog. 235)

Nibelungenlied, anonymous German epic composed around 1200, it was one of the greatest works of medieval German literature. Its hero was Siegfried, a Netherlandish prince, who seized the treasure of the Nibelungs and had become king of the Rhine. That treasure later passed to the Burgundian kings, after which the Nibelungs were called Burgundians.* Divided into two main parts, the story recounted the death of Siegfried first, and then the fall of the Nibelungs. Part 2 had a historical core dating from the period of the great migrations. The Burgundians were an east German tribe from the island of Bornholm in the Baltic Sea who settled on the Rhine in the 4th century. In 437 they were overrun by the Huns under Attila, and their King Gundahari and his nobles were slain. In 453, Attila died of a hemorrhage by the side of a German maiden named Hildico or Hildchen. Later chroniclers changed history by having Hildico kill Attila to avenge the death of her "father," Gundahari, and Burgundy occupied by the Franks. Hildico's name was changed to Grimhild to fit the alliterative scheme of the names for her brothers who were killed treacherously by Attila, not in battle but for the treasure they possessed. These Burgundians came to be called the Nibelungs, and the story of their fall came into the hands of the Bavarians. As the Bavarians were in contact with the Ostrogoths of Italy through the Langobards, and the Gothic-Langobard opinion of Attila was favorable, his reputation had to be cleared. Thus history was changed to fit the needs of the poets who reported that Attila hadn't killed Grimhild's brothers at all. She in fact had done it herself to avenge the death of her first husband, Siegfried.

In this version of the story, Siegfried fell in love with Kriemhild, sister of King Gunther of the Burgundians, and helped Gunther defeat Brunhilde from Iceland for his bride so that he could marry Kriemhild. After marrying Gunther, Brunhilde decided to avenge an insult of Kriemhild by hiring Hagen to murder Siegfried. Years later, the widowed Kriemhild married Etzel (Attila) in hopes of avenging the murder of her first husband. In the final battle, all the Burgundians and Kriemhild are killed.   (tr. H. T. Hatto, London: Penguin, 1965) (Bibliog. 161)

Nicolaa (Nicolla) de la Haye, Dame,+ sheriff+ of Lincolnshire under King John* in 1216. Born in 1150 during one of the worst excesses of King Stephen's* reign, as the eldest daughter of Richard de la Haye, she inherited his English estates after his death sometime during the reign of Henry II.* Included in her inheritance was the castellany+ of Lincoln Castle which was to be her home for almost 80 years, so she knew it well when she defied Longchamps'* siege in 1191, and against the French in 1216. She resigned custody of the castle to her grandson-in-law in 1226, and died four years later in 1230 at the age of 80. (Bibliog. 94, 157)

Niger, Ralph (d. c. 1205), English chronicler and an ardent supporter of Thomas à Becket*; his work *Radulphi Nigri Chronica* (Creation to 1199) contained such bitter invective against Henry II* that he was forced into exile. (ed. Robert Anstruther, London: Caxton Society 13, 1851; repr. New York: Burt Franklin, 1967) (Bibliog. 99)

Niniane, Nimiane, Nimue, Lady of the Lake* who married Pelles* in *Morte D'Arthur** of Malory. In *Arthour and Merlin,** she figured as the woman with whom Merlin* fell in love, and who tricked him into revealing the secrets of his art, and then enclosing him eternally in a tower in the Forest of Broceliand. See also Lancelot. (Bibliog. 1, 117, 221)

ninth, amount granted by the English Parliament to the demands of King Edward III* in 1340 in response to his huge debts in the Low Countries for the war he had been waging against Philip VI.* This grant gave the king a ninth of everything produced for two years: a ninth sheaf of corn, fleece, and lamb from every farm, and the ninth of every townsman's goods. In return, the king had to promise to reduce taxes and make certain governmental reforms. But with this money, he was able to return to Flanders* to redeem his wife and family whom he had pledged as payment of his loans, and was able to renew his war against

Philip. (Bibliog. 203)

Niort, castle on the left bank of the Sèvre Nortaise built to withstand a siege by Henry II* in 1160. After his marriage to Eleanor* of Aquitaine, Henry made Niort one of his capitals. In 1199, after the death of Richard I,* Eleanor resided there. Louis VIII* captured it and held it only for a short time before it fell once again under English control. (Bibliog. 196)

Nobles, Spanish city conquered by Charlemagne's* principal *douzepeer,** Roland, in the *chansons de geste.** (Bibliog. 128)

Nonant, Hugh de (fl. 1190), bishop of Coventry who bought from Richard I* the sheriffdoms of three counties: Leicestershire, Staffordshire, and Warwickshire. William Longchamps,* the chancellor,+ convinced the archbishop of Canterbury* to remonstrate with Hugh about the impropriety of a bishop holding three sheriffdoms, and Hugh gave back two of them, although he managed to get them back when Archbishop Baldwin died in 1190. He worked consistently against King Richard and Longchamps and was the prime mover behind Longchamps' ouster. (Bibliog. 238)

Norfolk, second largest county in England. Originally a portion of the kingdom of the East Angles* from whence it derived its name of northern folk as the southern folk derived Southfolk (Suffolk). Roger Bigod,* a Norman who had amassed considerable holdings in Norfolk, had become one of King William I's* chief barons by 1076, and by 1086 had become sheriff+ of Suffolk and Norfolk, and held great estates in both counties as a tenant-in-chief+ and as a sub-tenant. He continued his power during the reign of William II,* and into the reign of Henry I* whom he served as household steward. His son Hugh was in close attendance on King Henry I, and in 1135 declared under oath before the archbishop* of Canterbury that the Henry I *in extremis* had disinherited his daughter Matilda FitzEmpress* and had nominated his nephew, Stephen of Blois,* as his heir, whereupon the archbishop promptly consecrated Stephen as king. Hugh was created earl of Lincoln in 1141, and that earldom, the old earl of the East Angles, included Suffolk. He was with the king at the battle of Lincoln,* but was one of the first nobles who fled at the first sign of battle. By 1142, he had transferred his allegiance to Matilda, and two years later joined Geoffrey de Mandeville, earl of Essex,* in devastating raids throughout England. In the following year, however, Stephen surprised him and laid waste to his lands. Hugh witnessed the treaty in 1153 by which Stephen recognized Henry of Anjou as his successor, one of the provisions of which recognized Hugh's earldom by both parties. On accession, Henry II* re-created Hugh as earl of Lincoln as a new grant, refusing to recognize Stephen's charter. Even though Hugh supported the rebellion of young Henry* against King Henry II, he retained his earldom until his death in 1177, and was succeeded by his son Roger, but only as one of the barons of England. Not until after Richard I's* coronation+ in 1189 was Roger made earl. He supported the chancellor Longchamps* against Prince John* in 1191, and again in 1193 he was one of the magnates who journeyed to Germany to negotiate Richard I's release. Later he supported King John,* but in 1215 was one of the twenty-four barons chosen to enforce the *Magna Carta Libertatum.*+ He died in 1221, and was succeeded by his son Hugh, who also was one of the twenty-four barons.

Hugh fought against Llewelyn* in 1223, and was present at the proceedings against Faulkes de Breauté.* He married Maud, the eldest daughter of William Marshal,* and was succeeded by his son Roger (1213-1270). In 1258, he was one of the leaders of the baronial opposition to King Henry III,* being on the Committee of Twenty-four to draw up ordinances of reform, and then later became one of the Council of Fifteen. (See Oxford, Provisions of.) Simon de Montfort's* revolt in 1263 drove Hugh back to the king's support. He was summoned to Montfort's* Parliament* in 1264, apparently in opposition, and later after the king had been restored to power, Hugh was appointed as a commissioner in Norfolk and Suffolk to help restore the rebels to the king's peace.+

He was succeeded by his nephew and heir, Roger Bigod, hereditary earl marshal* of England. In 1297, King Edward I* ordered the earls of Hereford and Norfolk, as constable and marshal of England, to proceed with the army to Gascony while the king went to Flanders. Both earls refused the order, but offered to accompany the king in person. Despite all his threats, they refused to go, and thus were removed from their offices. While the king was in Flanders, the two earls appeared before London with a huge army, forcing the king to relent and to restore them to their offices. Later at the battle of Falkirk* in July 1298 with his 50 lances,* Bigod commanded the first division, but he and Hereford refused to participate in any winter campaign and they went home. When he died without issue in 1306, the earldom became extinct. King Edward II* bestowed it next in 1312 on his younger brother, Thomas of Brotherton, son of his father's second wife who had been the daughter of King Philip III* of France. This act gave Thomas the earldom as well as the estates of Roger Bigod which the king earlier had bestowed on him. He joined his brother Edmund in

1321 in the king's campaign against the enemies of the Despensers. Later, in 1326, his name stood first of the temporal lords who elected Prince Edward* as Keeper of the Realm, and in 1329 he joined the barons against the Queen Isabelle and Roger Mortimer, earl of March.* At the coronation of Queen Philippa* (de Hainault) as King Edward's queen in 1330, he and his brother Edmund, dressed as simple grooms, rode on either side of the queen's palfrey+ from London to Westminster, holding her reins. When Thomas died without a son in 1338, the earldom went to his daughter, Margaret, styled countess of Norfolk. (Bibliog. 47)

Norham castle, situated on the River Tweed, this Northumberland fortress belonged to the palatinate+ of Durham, and was maintained by its bishop as one of the most important border castles* in the north of England. Its north and west sides were protected by a steep cliff forming part of the River Tweed's southern bank, and its east side by a deep gully. Built by Bishop Ranulph Flambard in 1121, it was destroyed by the Scots under the leadership of King David* in 1136 and again in 1138 despite the extraordinary efforts of the nine English knights defending it. Later that year peace was declared after the total defeat of the Scots at the battle of the Standard.* King Henry II* ordered Bishop Hugh de Puiset* to rebuild it in stone. Suspecting the loyalty of this bishop, Henry assumed control of it during William the Lion's* invasion of the north of England in 1173-1174, and did not return it to Puiset until 1189. Then, in 1215, Alexander II* of Scotland invaded Northumberland and besieged it, but its constable, Sir Robert Clifford, held out for 40 days. Alexander accepted defeat and raised the siege. A century later, in 1318, Scots under Robert the Bruce* besieged it for nearly a year. At one time, the Scots captured the inner bailey, but three days later the English recaptured it and held out. It repeated the same feat a year later when it held out for seven months. And again in 1322, the Scots besieged it unsuccessfully. Finally in 1327, the Scots successfully captured it by storm, but for naught, because in the following year, peace was signed and the castle was returned to English hands. (Bibliog. 104, 247)

Normandy, duchy in northwest France bounded by Picardy,* the Ile de France,* Maine* and Brittany.* Its early history was obscure. It was invaded by Norsemen from Scandinavia during the 6th through 10th centuries. In those areas, feudalism established itself sooner than elsewhere because allods+ almost entirely disappeared, fiefs+ became hereditary, and were charged with precisely fixed military service, and the rights of relief were subjected to rigorous wardship. For example, Rollo I, first duke of Normandy, forbade the building of castles+ or fortifications without his permisison, a tradition carried on by William I* as he destroyed any castles built without his permission.

In Normandy, the duke of Normandy imposed a peace under which the right of blood feuds, vengeance, and private wars was abolished by the Truce of God which the church imposed. It also forbade anyone from attacking a person working on the land or travelling in reponse to a lord's summons, from carrying arms in a forest, from seeking vengeance on an adversary in war arrayed with banner and horn, from rallying supporters, or from taking prisoners. Its most important power lay in the duke's abilities to enforce the respect for these rules. This strict power ensured peace there more than almost anywhere else in Europe, for it was enforced by the sheriff's official whose job basically was to collect the lord's revenue and to hold local courts. This small principality in the northern area of France dispatched invaders to conquer England in 1066 through the policies established by William the Conqueror, their leader, and his predecessors in the duchy. See Normans. Not until 1361 was Normandy reunited with the French crown. Some of its important dukes were

912 - Rollo
927 - William, I, Long Sword
943 - Richard I
996 - Richard II
1026 - Richard III
1035 - William,* the Bastard, the Conqueror, king of England
1087 - Robert II, Curthose, William's son
1116 - Henry I,* king of England
1135 - Stephen,* king of England
1144 - Geoffrey* of Anjou
1151 - Henry II,* king of England
1189 - Richard I, Coeur de Lion,* king of England
1199 - Arthur,* of Brittany, heir presumptive to the English throne
1199 - John Lackland,* king of England
1204 - Philip Augustus, king of France, who reunited it with the
          French crown
(Bibliog. 72, 100, 178)

Normans (L. *nortmannni*, "men of the north"), common name given by the Carolingian* chroniclers to the Scandinavians. Generally, the name referred to the Norse and Danes whose raids during the 9th century helped to destroy the Carolingian Empire. They expanded their sphere of operations from Scandinavia and Iceland to the eastern shores of Britain and the northern coast of France, leading to Scandinavian principalities in Iceland, the Danelaw* in England and Normandy* in France. These Norsemen raided the waterways of the Carolingian countryside from Germany to Bordeaux. Although the actual damage done by the raiders was small, the terror they caused was considerable, particularly because the Carolingian Empire had no fleet to use against them. In time, the Norsemen established settlements along the mouths of such great rivers as the Seine, Loire, Humber, Elbe, Weser, Rhine, Meuse, Garonne, and Guadalquivir. They frequently were described as a vengeful and cunning race, despising their own inheritance in hopes of winning a greater one elsewhere; eager for gain and power; lavish and greedy; delighting in hunting+ and hawking,+ in horses and accoutrements, yet willing to endure great periods of hunger and cold. They were known as flatterers and clever talkers, and were unbridled unless held in check by justice. They were quick to imitate and assimilate new ideas while keeping their own northern characteristics.

By the 10th century, their name had come to refer to a specific principality in the northern area of France, Normandy. From that base, Normans dispatched invaders to conquer England in 1066 through the policies established by William* the Conqueror, their leader, and his predecessors in the duchy. For example, in the years before the English conquest, bands of Normans had settled in southern Italy and supported themselves by the profits of their brigandage as mercenaries before they established small principalities. At the beginning of the 11th century, Norman knights under the Hauteville family founded a powerful kingdom of Sicily. In 1053, their troops showed their abilities and strength by defeating troops of the papacy. Their leaders, however, were too clever to remain at odds with the papacy for long, because shortly thereafter in 1059 Robert Guiscard did homage to the pope as "duke, by the Grace of God and St. Peter, of Apulia and Calabria and with their aid, of Sicily." By the middle of the 12th century the Normans had established in Sicily one of the strongest and richest states in western Europe. Quite probably they introduced into the kingdom of the Two Sicilies the same principles of authority as the dukes of Normandy had established over their duchy and later applied to England--a territory which combined use of governmental theory with the use of swords. A band of Normans under William invaded England in 1066, and defeated them at the battle of Hastings.* (Bibliog. 72, 98, 178)

Northallerton, battle of. See battle of the Standard.

Northampton, county in the center of England. The earldom of
Northampton was created for William de Bohun,* fifth and youngest son
of Humphrey de Bohun, earl of Hereford* and Essex,* and his second
wife Elizabeth, daughter of Edward I* (1272-1307). Of royal blood,
William came of age six years after Edward III* (1327-1377) became
king, and for thirty years was employed in the service of the crown.
For example, he and his elder brother, Humphrey, were closely
associated with King Edward III's seizure of Roger Mortimer, earl of
March,* in 1330. From then on, he was one of the king's most active
counsellors. He was knighted in 1331, and became earl of Northampton
in 1337. He took a major part in the king's victory in the battle of
Sluys,* and was beside him at the siege of Tournay. He fought at
Crécy* in the first division led by Prince Edward,* and later at
Calais.* He was chosen as one of the first Knights of the Garter,*
took part in the English victory over the Spanish fleet at Winchelsea*
in 1350, and later was a witness to the Treaty of Bretigny* in 1360,
shortly before his death. He died in 1360, and was succeeded by his
son and heir Humphrey, earl of Hereford and Essex, and when he died
without issue, the earldom reverted to the crown. (Bibliog. 47, 66,
101)

Northampton castle, located on one of the main roads to the north,
this castle+ was of great importance to the country in the 12th and
13th centuries, being one of the principal fortresses of the kingdom.
On the death of King Henry I,* Simon de St. Liz took possession of the
castle and kept it until his death in 1153. The following year, Henry
II* claimed it for the crown, and there it remained. In its history,
it resisted sieges by the barons in 1215, and by troops equipped with
French siege-engines+ in the same year. Half a century later, Simon
de Montfort* made it the center of his resistance to King Henry III's*
misgovernment. Later kings apportioned only minor funds for its repair, however, and it deteriorated badly. (Bibliog. 104)

Northumberland, latinized as *Northumbria*, this original Anglian
kingdom stretched north from the Humber River to the Scots border. Its
proximity to Scotland made it a frontier or march* along England's
northern border. A Danish kingdom was established in its southern region, but in the northern section, the Northmen were held at bay.
There, from the early 10th century, seated in the impregnable fortress
of Banborough, its kings and then earls acknowledged the overlordship
of the Saxon kings who were unifying the kingdom of England. Their
territory was diminished, but the old name of Northumberland remained
to the smaller area, though the southern boundary was changed from the

Humber to the Tees River. This pre-Conquest earldom survived the
Norman arrival until it finally was conquered by William II.* As the
Conqueror's marcher earldoms were palatinates,+ so, too, was
Northumberland made a palatinate, but for another reason: its power
had not been delegated by its overlord, but had survived from the uninterrupted practice of its ancient kings. Siward, a Dane, who probably came to England with Cnut,* was its earl before 1041. He had
married the niece of the previous earl, and on or before 1042, the
murder of his wife's uncle, Earl Eadulf, had put him in possession of
the whole of Northumbria from the Humber to the Tweed. He supported
King Edward the Confessor* against Earl Godwine* and his sons, and in
1054 led a force of English and Danes against the Scottish usurper,
MacBeth, which put Malcolm upon his murdered father's throne. He died
in 1055, and was succeeded by Tostig,* a younger son of Earl Godwine,
earl of Wessex. As a favorite of the king, he was made earl of "all
Northumbria." Tostig's violence and extortion caused rebellion, and
his thanes+ assembled at York and in 1065 deposed him as earl, and
elected Morcar, younger son of Alfgar, earl of Mercia, in his place.
After massacring Tostig's soldiers and followers, this group marched
south, ravaging and killing as they went. Harold met them at Oxford,
at Northampton, and on the king's behalf, finally agreed that Morcar
should receive the royal appointment as earl. After his election as
earl was confirmed by King Edward the Confessor, Morcar committed the
northern portion of the earldom to Osulf, younger son of the Earl
Eadulf slain by Siward.* Then his own defense of his earldom against
Tostig and his Norwegian supporters was shattered at Fulford Gate on
September 20, 1066, and York was surrendered to them. Five days later,
Harold defeated Tostig and his Norse allies at Stamford Bridge,+ and
then marched south to confront William I's* invading forces at
Hastings.* Morcar did not march south with him, but after Hastings, he
surrendered his earldom to the Conqueror. He and his brother, Earl
Edwin, fled from William in 1071 and took refuge in the Isle of Ely
with Hereward,* but both finally surrendered and were imprisoned until
their deaths. Tostig's deputy, Copsi, appointed to supersede Morcar's
nominee Osulf north of the Tyne River, was killed on his march north
by Osulf who himself was killed soon thereafter.

William I, in control of the land between the Humber and Tees,
sent Robert de Comines in 1068 to replace Copsi in the north, but he
was opposed by those he was sent to govern, and with 700 of his men,
was slain at Durham on January 28, 1069. Soon after the death of
Comines, Gospatric, grandson both of Malcolm II and of an early earl
of Northumberland, paid William I a large fine to succeed to the
earldom. Soon turning his back on the Norman king, however, Gospatric

joined the Norwegians who sailed up the Humber in September 1069 and took York, massacring the Normans there. When King William in revenge laid waste to the area between York and Durham, Gospatric surrendered and although he begged his king's pardon, he was deprived of the earldom in 1072. William bestowed it on Waltheof, younger son of Siward, earl of Northumberland, but he was executed for treason four years later. (See Huntingdon.) After a few years, the earldom evolved to Robert de Mowbray, siegneur de Bazoches, in 1081, who governed badly and cruelly. In 1095 he rebelled against William II* Rufus in support of a conspiracy to enthrone Stephen, count of Aumale,* son of the Conqueror's sister, Adelaide. Rufus marched north, captured the earl's fortresses at Newcastle, and Tynemouth, besieged Bamborough, recaptured Mowbray, and imprisoned him at Windsor. The earldom was then taken into the king's hands in 1095 and remained with the crown until 1139 when by treaty between King Stephen* and David I* of Scotland, the English king surrendered it and the Scottish king bestowed it on his son, Henry, earl of Huntingdon. It then was held between 1152 and 1157 by William, the Lion,* who later became king of Scotland, when his elder brother Malcolm, king of Scotland, surrendered it to Henry II.* William made numerous attempts to regain it, including accepting the promise of young Henry to restore it to Scotland in return for his support in young Henry's unsuccessful rebellion of 1173. Henry II, however, kept the earldom. Richard I,* on the other hand, sold it to Bishop Hugh le Puiset for 2,000 marks in November 1189 to raise money for his crusade,+ but le Puiset returned it to the king in 1194 on his return to England. It remained in the crown's hands until 1377 when Edward III* bestowed on Henry Percy the earldom in name only, for it no longer was a palatinate, and the earl drew £20 in lieu of the third penny.+ (Bibliog. 47, 101)

North Wales, division of Wales* by Roderick the Great between his three sons, this division fell to his son Anarawd, the eldest. It contained the territory included in the counties of Merioneth, part of Denbigh, Flint, Carnarvon, and the isle of Anglesey. As Aberfraw on Anglesey was the prince's seat, the princes sometimes were called the kings of Aberfraw. The last prince of the blood was Llewelyn ap Gruffyd, who became king in 1246 and died in 1282. (Bibliog. 47)

Norway, country situated along the Atlantic coast of the Scandinavian peninsula. Populated by Germano-Scandinavian tribes, the Norsemen, this country was loosely organized into clans and tribes until intertribal warfare in the 9th century forced some tribes to migrate. These Norsemen settled among other places in the Atlantic islands of

Orkney, Shetland, Faeroe and Iceland, as well as along the shores of Britain and Europe. Tribal confederations in Norway formed the first political unity in the country. King Harold I* formed the first confederation and founded Norway in the 9th century. Civil wars erupted after his death and continued until the end of the 10th century when Olaf I (995-1000) united the realms and introduced Christianity. His capital was Trondheim in the north, for Danes controlled some of ths southern part of the peninsula. After Olaf fell in battle against the Danes in 1000, the country was ruled by the Danes until 1016 when it regained its independence under Olaf II, but in 1028, King Cnut of Denmark and England conquered it. After Cnut's death in 1035, the Norse revolted against the Danes and Magnus I restored its independence and reigned in peace. (Bibliog. 98, 100)

Norwich castle, fortress in Norfolk* which William I* built to protect one of the largest English cities in its exposed position on the flat Norfolk plains. Some 98 properties had to be destroyed to erect this motte and bailey+ bulwark. Its first constable, Ralph de Guader, became involved in a rebellion against King William I* and had to flee. A few years later, Roger Bigod* took the castle+ in another uprising, this time against William II,* who later gave it to Richard de Reviers, earl of Devon.* In the middle of the 12th century, it became the property of William, count of Mortain, King Stephen's* only surviving son. Later, King John* ordered the men of Norwich to fortify it and defend it against the invading forces of Prince Louis* (VIII) of France, but their actions did not prevent that French prince from capturing the castle and garrisoning troops in it. (Bibliog. 247)

Nottingham, city in Nottinghamshire, England. King William I* ordered a castle built there early in his reign, and for most of its existence, it was controlled by the crown. It was captured by Prince John* in 1191, but recaptured by his brother King Richard I* in 1194. In 1212, its walls were decorated with the bodies of twenty-four Welsh hostages. Standing on a sandstone cliff, this castle had a rectangular enclosure with three large corner towers and a Norman keep.+ King John added another outer enclosure with a strong curtain wall+ with towers and a moat. At the southeast of the castle, a secret passageway, later known as Mortimer's Hole, allowed agents of King Edward III* to gain entrance to the castle and capture Roger Mortimer, lover of Edward's mother, Queen Isabelle. He was sent to London, tried and executed. (Bibliog. 101, 247)

Nouhusius, identified in an acrostic reference in the Middle High

German* epic poem, *Lohengrin,** and thought to have been the author of that work; other than a man named Neuhaus who was believed to have been a *ministeriale* in the service of the duke of Bavaria. No Neuhaus or Neuhauser has been otherwise recorded. (Bibliog. 86)

Nubles, Nubians, heathen people of southern Egypt in the *Song of Roland.** (Bibliog. 210)

nuncius, legatus, term throughout the Middle Ages for a message-bearing envoy. Other terms also used were *missus,* and *message* but only for diplomatic envoys. *Nuncius* covered a broad spectrum of envoys, from lackeys and other couriers who merely carried letters, to men who conveyed messsges far more important than mere letters. By delivering a letter orally, a *nuncio* conveyed a much more courteous means of conveying a message than a mere letter on paper. (Bibliog. 206)

O

obligation between king and vassal. When Eudes II, (995-1037), count of Blois, and one of the most undisciplined of the great French vassals, disobeyed a summons to appear at the royal court of King Robert II* in 1023, and hence went to war with the king, he defended those actions successfully in a remarkable document. In part, his document to King Robert II read,

> I am astounded that without having heard me in my own defense, you should hasten to pronounce me unworthy of the fief I hold of you. Consider my ancestry: by dint of it I am entitled to succeed to the counties of Meaux and Troyes. Consider the fief you have bestowed on me: it was not granted out of your royal fisc, but is part of the lands which have come down to me by hereditary right and of your royal grace. And consider the feudal services I have done you: you are well aware that for the favors I have had from you I have served in your household, on your travels and in your wars. And now you have deprived me of your favor, and seek to take away from me the things you have given to me. It may be that in defending myself and my fief, I have committed certain offenses against you. I was driven thereto by necessity and the wrongs I have suffered. By God and my immortal soul, I had rather die defending it than live deprived of it....Wherefore I implore you to show me that clemency which is as a well-spring within you, and which only evil counsel can cause to dry up. And I pray you to cease persecuting me, and let me be reconciled with you. (Bibliog. 74)

That letter to King Robert explained a medieval principle underlying feudalism, a principle which explained the survival of the feeble Capetian dynasty, isolated in the midst of such turbulence: baronial factions pursued vendettas against each other, but never against the king. It also explained the actions of King Henry II* of England in 1159 when Louis VII* came to the rescue of the count of

Toulouse and entered the city of Toulouse.* Henry II also was count of Anjou,* duke of Normandy,* and duke of Aquitaine,* and thus as a vassal of Louis, he decided to abandon his siege for as long as his suzerain should stay in Toulouse. Louis stayed for a long time, and so Henry withdrew. For feeble though he was, the king of France was the Lord's Anointed+, the highest suzerain of all; and directly or indirectly all the barons of the realm were his men. In theory the king of France was the most powerful lord in the kingdom. He remained, nevertheless, subject to the normal customs of feudal landholding and nothing in the Capetian period distinguished his fiefs from those held by other lords. The ancient patrimony of the Roman emperors—the "fisc"—had disappeared almost completely through Merovingian liberality and Carolingian authority. By then, there was no crown "demesne"; the king's lands were the estates he held as a feudal lord. A king could have vassals, but he never could be one. (Bibliog. 74, 98)

obligation, precise definition of feudal, example of a precise definition of feudal obligation occurred in a treaty dated March 10, 1101, between King Henry I* of England and Robert II, count of Flanders.* Count Robert agreed to support Henry in the defense of his kingdom against "all men who live and die," except his fealty to Philip I,* king of France. If Philip wished to invade England, Robert would try to dissuade him but only with words and not with gifts of money or evil counsel. If Philip persisted, Robert as his vassal would accompany him, but with the smallest possible force consistent with avoiding an accusation that might lead to the forfeiture of his lands to his lord. However, if the king of England required aid, he would send letters summoning the count who within forty days would gather 1,000 horsemen (*equites+*) or knights (*milites+*) ready to embark at Gravelines or Wissant in ships sent by Henry I in such a way that each horseman would take three horses. Any such expeditionary force then would equal 3,000 horses and probably 3,000 men, for each horseman had two aids, including one squire (*armiger+*). Robert agreed that he would accompany the force provided he was not too ill to do so, or that he had not been summoned by the French royal host,+ or by the Holy Roman Emperor whose vassal he also was for certain lands. For as long as they remained in England, Henry I would maintain them, even reembursing them for losses just as he was accustomed to do for his own *familia.* (Bibliog. 48)

Octai (Ogotai) Khan, third of four sons of Jenghiz (Genghis) Khan* to whom was left the control of Jenghiz' great khanate*; he was a benevolent and humane ruler of Bokhara* after his father's violent rule. (Bibliog. 68)

Octavian, 13th century *chanson de geste.** When the empress of Rome gave birth to twin sons, she was accused of adultery by her wicked mother-in-law, just as in *Elioxe** and *Lai la Fresne,** and was turned out into the forest with her infants to die. An ape stole one son, and a lion the other. The first, Florent was rescued by a knight, was taken to Paris and grew up as the slave of a butcher named Clement. Florent was impractical in small matters around the butcher shop, but when a Saracen* sultan besieged Paris, Florent defeated him, and married his pretty daughter. Octavian, the other son, was found by his mother who kept both her son and the lion with her under the protection of the king of Jerusalem. When grown, Octavian led the armies of Jerusalem against the Saracens and rescued the king of France, his own father, the emperor of Rome, and his brother Florent, and the family was reunited. (ed. K. Vollmoller, Heilbronn: *AFB,3,* 1883) (Bibliog. 106)

Odo (Eudes) of Bayeux (1036-1097), half-brother of William the Conqueror* who appointed him bishop of Bayeux at age 14. He made a career as a statesman and soldier, however. He fought at the battle of Hastings,* and was made earl of Kent the following year. He served as the king's vicar between 1077 and 1080, but fell into disgrace in 1082 and was imprisoned for planning a military expedition to Italy. He was released on William's death, and returned to Kent where he organized a rebellion against another brother, William II* Rufus, designed to put his oldest brother, Robert II,* Curthose, of Normandy, on the throne. After that plan failed, he returned to Bayeux to devote his efforts to rebuilding the cathedral. He died in 1096 on his way to Palermo to join the crusade.+ (Bibliog. 98, 240)

Ogier le Danois, hero of a 13th-century French saga which originated in the traditions of Charlemagne's* war against the Longobards. The historical figure behind the legends was Autacharius, a Frankish nobleman who in 771 escorted Carloman's widow with her minor children to her father Desiderius, king of the Longobards. Together with Desiderius, he fought Charlemagne in 773 in the mountain passes, but finally surrendered to the victorious emperor in Verona along with Carloman's widow and sons. He was sent into exile, and disappeared. The epic describing Ogier's rebellion against Charlemagne, *Chevalier Ogier de Danemarche,* revised from a lost original by Raimbert de Paris, was dated 1192-1200. His appellation *le Danois* probably was a

corruption of *l'Ardenois*—"from the Ardennes." In this epic, Gaufrey,*
duke of Denmark, grossly insulted four of Charlemagne's messengers.
Charlemagne swore vengeance, which was easy for him to obtain because
Gaufrei's son, Ogier, was a hostage at court. His barons plead for
Ogier's life in vain; Charlemagne insisted that he had to die. Further
action against the young man was postponed when Charles was summoned
to Rome to defend the city against the Saracens. In Italy, Ogier slew
Brunamon de Misor, the Saracen champion, and thereby freed Rome and
won his own knighthood. Charlemagne pardoned him. On their return to
France, Ogier found his small son, Baudouinet, had grown to become a
squire. One day, Charlot, Charlemagne's son, argued with Baudouinet
over a chess game, and killed him with the chess board. Ogier demanded
the life of Charlot in payment for his son's life. Charlemagne refused. Ogier left Charlemagne's court for the court of Desier, king of
the Lombards, swearing unending war until Charlot's life atoned for
the life of his son. After moving around for some time, Ogier finally
was captured by Archbishop Turpin, and taken before Charlemagne who
ordered him to be starved to death. His jailer thwarted the emperor's
command, but circulated the news that Ogier had died. On hearing that,
the Saracens invaded France as far as Laon, and Charlemagne realized
that only Ogier could push them back. Ogier then made known to the emperor that he had not died, and agreed to fight the Saracens only if
Charlemagne would let him avenge his son's death on Charlot.
Charlemagne had no choice and agreed. An angel stayed the falling
sword in Ogier's hand, and the young man received only a slight nick
in satisfaction of Ogier's oath. Then Ogier drove back the enemy.
(ed. Knud Togeby, Copenhagen: Munksgaard, 1967)

Ogier also figured in such other *chansons de geste** as *Song of
Roland,* *Gaydon,** and *Galien.** In many of them, he was the count in
command of the third division of Charlemagne's army, leader of the
Bavarians; he made all the arrangements for the wager of battle+ by
which Ganelon's* guilt or innocence was determined in the *Song of
Roland.* (Bibliog. 106, 210)

Okehampton castle, Devonshire fortress standing on a spur of land extending into the valley of the West Oakment River. This site was
chosen by Baldwin FitzGilbert, whom William I* had appointed sheriff
of Devonshire. By the end of the 13th century, its original wooden
palisade had been replaced with stone as its owner, Hugh II, earl of
Courtenay, modified the defensive aspects of the castle+ to make a
manor for himself. (Bibliog. 247)

Old Sarum castle. See Salisbury castle.

Oléron, Laws of, 12th-century code of maritime laws consisting of a compilation of the customary laws of the sea and the judicial decisions of the maritime court in force on Oléron, an island off the coast of Aquitaine* and forming a peculiar court of the duchy of Aquitaine and embodying the usages of mariners in the Atlantic. They supposedly were published by Eleanor,* duchess of Aquitaine, and were one of the sources for a similar code called the Laws of Wisby, after the town of Wisby or Visby on the island of Gotland, Sweden, which was made the basis of the Ordinances of the Hanseatic League that reflected the customs of the mariners in the North Sea and the Baltic. (See also Admiralty, High court of.) (Bibliog. 68, 169)

Olive and Landres, lost Middle English* romance which was translated into Old Norse for inclusion into the *Karlamagnus Saga** late in the 13th century. Closely resembling the *chanson de geste,** *Doön de la Roche,** this recounted how a falsely accused queen, Olive, the daughter of Pepin, was cast into a dungeon. Her son, Landres, was driven from court, but after various adventures, finally secured the assistance of Charlemagne* in rescuing and vindicating his mother. (tr. Constance B. Hieatt, *Karlamagnus Saga,* Toronto: *PIMS,* Vol. I, Part II, 1975) (Bibliog. 116)

Oliver, one of the *douzepeers,** companion in arms of Roland, brother of Aude, Roland's fiancée; three times he urged Roland to be prudent and sound his horn, Olifant,+ before the final battle at Rencesvals* in *Song of Roland.** He was a fierce fighter in that battle, killing Falsaron and three others, then Climborin and ten other pagans, but finally was mortally wounded by Algalife.* His body was taken back to France for burial at Blaye. (Bibliog. 210)

Orable. See Guiborc.

Orange, principality founded in the middle of the 12th century by a woman, Countess Tiburge. It occupied a strategic location at the junction of the kingdom of France,* the Holy Roman Empire, and Provence,* and was a political reality for over two hundred years. Orange was part of the kingdom of Arles* in the days of the crusades, and when it passed from Count Raimbaud to the house of Les Baux, Frederick I,* Barbarossa, raised it to a principality, and Louis XII* recognized its prince as an independent sovereign. One of its most famous counts was William* (Guillaume), count of Toulouse. (Bibliog. 87)

Ordainers, Lords. See Lords Ordainers.

Order of the Garter. See Garter, Order of.

Orderic Vitalis (1075-1143), Anglo-Norman historian and monk of St. Evroul whose thirteen-book work, *Historia Ecclesiastica,* covered the Christian era up to 1141. Compiled during the years 1123-1141, most of this work provided a contemporary secular and ecclesiastical history of the events in England from 1066 to 1141, and was especially valuable for the reign of Henry I* of England. (tr. Thomas Forester, *The ecclesiastical History of England and Normandy*, London: Bohn's Antiquarian Library, 4 vols., 1853-1865; repr. New York: AMS Press, 1967) (Bibliog. 63, 99)

Orfeo and Heurodis. See *Sir Orfeo*.

Orford castle, fortress in Suffolk.* When Henry II* ascended the throne in 1154, Hugh Bigod,* earl of Norfolk, dominated East Anglia. Henry decided to erect a castle+ near the coast of Norfolk at Orford. Its seven years of construction cost over £1,400. Building the keep occupied the first two years, for it was the strongest and most important portion of the castle. Rising 90 feet high with walls 10 feet thick, the circular keep stood on a splayed plinth.+ In the next five years, the remainder of the castle was built—curtain wall,+ flanking towers,+ and other buildings. Its design was advanced for its time, for it had a number of square towers spaced along its walls which allowed its defenders to discharge their arrows against any attacking troops who had gained the walls. Just as it was completed, the rebellion of Henry's sons broke out in 1173, supported by the 80-year-old Bigod. After Henry suppressed the rebellion, he removed much of Bigod's power, and used Orford castle to maintain control of much of the countryside. Because of its importance, the crown regularly maintained it until 1336 when King Edward III* gave it to Robert de Ufford, and it remained in private hands from then on. (Bibliog. 247)

Orguilleus, Orguillous, giant in the *chansons de geste** of *Auberon,** and *Huon de Faerie*; he was the son of Beugibus, a prince of Hell, and of Murgale, a giant and mother of fourteen other giants, including Agrappant, the giant killed by Huon of Bordeaux. He was the enemy of Auberon,* and lived in the tower of Dunostre, a marvellous city and chateau in fairyland. (Bibliog. 128)

Orkeney, King Lot's* kingdom in Arthurian legend, located vaguely in the north of England, and possibly included all of Scotland.* (Bibliog. 117)

Orlando innamorato. See Boiardo.

Ormond, earl of. James le Boutilliere (or Butler) (1305-1337), was the hereditary chief butler of Ireland. In 1317, he was held hostage in Dublin castle for his father, also the chief butler. King Edward II* took his homage in 1325, though he was underage at the time, and for 2,000 marks gave him license to marry whomever he wished. He was knighted in 1326, and then returned to Ireland where he supported Roger Mortimer; he stayed and fought chiefly in Ireland, and in the following year married Eleanor de Bohun, the king's niece. He obtained a grant of the prisage (custom or duty paid) on wines at Irish ports which he regarded as appurtenant to his hereditary office of butler. As James le Boutilliere of Ireland, he was created earl of Ormond in 1328, and died a few years later "in the flower of his youth." (Bibliog. 47)

Orson et Beauvais, chanson de geste* from the early 13th century. It recounted the story of Orson who accompanied his brother-in-arms,+ the treacherous Ugon de Berri, on a supposed pilgrimage to the Holy Land, but who was sold into slavery by his treacherous companion. Returning to France with the lie that Orson had died, Ugon forced Orson's widow Aceline, to marry him, although she protected her virtue with a magic herb. Orson's son, Milon, escaped from Ugon's castle, and finally found and freed his father from the dungeon of the Saracen Ysore and they returned home. Meanwhile, Ugon had tried to burn his unwilling "wife" at the stake, but she was rescued by Doön de Clermont. When Orson confronted Hugo with his treachery, Ugon lied his way out of his situation so effectively that Charlemagne* believed him. Milon thereupon challenged and defeated Ugon in a trial by combat.+ After that loss which proved him a liar, Ugon was executed by being hanged in his full armor. (ed. Gaston Paris, Paris: *SATF*, 1889) (Bibliog. 106, 231)

Ortenberg, castle+ in Alsace completed near the end of the 13th century. This castle, along the shores of the Rhine, was built into the flank of a mountain. It was a trebly strong fortress with its polygonal donjon offering wide angles from which defenders in its merlons+ could resist attack from almost any angle. (Bibliog. 196)

Ortnit, Middle High German* epic which served as the preliminary portion of the *Wolfdietrich*. Written before 1250, it told of the search for a wife by Ortnit, the young emperor of Lamparten (Lombardy) who ruled all of Italy from the Alps to the Mediterranean. His uncle, King

Ylias of Ruizen (Russia), told him about the beautiful daughter of the heathen King Machorel of Syria who had the unpleasant habit of killing all her suitors. Ortnit decided to take the risk. With the invisible help of Alberich (Auberon) who was his real father, Ortnit won the hand of the bride, and returned to his native land. In revenge the heathen king sent two dragon eggs which a treacherous huntsman secretly brooded in a cave. After they hatched, and began to devastate the countryside, Ortnit set out to slay them. One caught him unawares while sleeping, and killed and devoured him. Both dragons in turn were slain by Wolfdietrich, the ancestor of Dietrich von Bern (see Theoderic the Great). (ed. H. Schneider, *Wolfdietrich,* Halle: *ATB,* 1931) (Bibliog. 235)

De Ortu Walwanii (L. "Birth of Gawain"), Arthurian romance in Latin from the 13th century containing such traditional romance elements as the birth of Gawain,* his parentage and early history; his going under a nickname until his true identity was revealed; his plotting with a woman to obtain a sword with which to slay her abductor, and so on. (ed. J. D. Bruce, *Hesperia,* Baltimore, 1913) (Bibliog. 10)

Othon, sixth son of Doön de Mayence and father of Ivon and Ivoire, two of Charlemagne's* *douzepeers** in the *chansons de geste.** (Bibliog. 128)

Otinel, chanson de geste* from the first quarter of the 13th century that described how Otinel, a young pagan champion, fought with Roland, and was converted to Christianity by the Holy Ghost in the form of a dove sent by God. Then he fought for the Christians, won the hand of Charlemagne's* daughter, Belissant, and the marches of Italy as his fief from the emperor. (ed. M. F. Guessard, and H. Michelant, Paris: *APF* 1, 1859) In an English version, from the mid-14th century, entitled *Otuel a Knight,* a similar duel occurred, and after Otuel felt himself instantly converted by the dove, he lay down his sword, embraced Roland, and became a champion for the Christians. (ed. S. J. Herrtage, London: Oxford University, *EETS ES* #39, 1882) (Bibliog. 106, 202)

Oton, French marquis+ and one of the *douzepeers** in Charlemagne's* army. He was killed at Rencesvals* in the *Song of Roland.** He often was called Haston (in *Galien,** *Four Sons of Aymon,** and others.) (Bibliog. 128, 210)

Otte mit dem Bart. See *Heinrich von Kempten* by Konrad von Wurzburg.

Otto I, the Great (912-973), king of Germany and Holy Roman Emperor. He dreamed of an empire, and modelled his actions on those of Charlemagne.* He also kept a firm hand on the realities of German politics by establishing administrative machinery of government by creating royal chanceries and other royal officials. Throughout his reign, to meet the problems of rebellious dukes, he developed a system of dynastic alliances by placing the great duchies in the hands of relatives and in-laws, and made the counts subordinate to himself rather than through the dukes. At the battle of the Lech in 955, Otto met the Magyars and destroyed their power forever. (Bibliog. 98, 124)

Otto IV (1174-1218), Holy Roman Emperor (1208-1214). Son of Henry the Lion,* duke of Saxony,* he was brought up at the court of his uncle, Richard I* of England. When Emperor Henry VI* died in 1190, Otto was elected to the throne in opposition to the house of Hohenstaufen.* Even though he was supported on the throne by Pope Innocent III,* he still had to contend for it against Philip of Swabia,* and not until after Philip's murder in 1208 was Otto recognized as emperor and crowned the next year. Pausing to marry the daughter of Philip of Swabia to appease the Hohenstaufen* party in Germany, he was delayed in coming to the aid of King John* at the battle of Bouvines* in 1214. As a result of their rout in that battle, he lost his power in Germany, and was compelled by Frederick II,* the ally of the victorious Philip II* of France, to renounce the imperial throne. He was elected as duke of Brunswick in 1215, and died three years later. (Bibliog. 98, 124)

Otuel. See *Otinel.*

Owein, Welsh tale similar in design and story line to the *Yvain** of Chrétien de Troyes.* (Bibliog. 10)

Oxford, town in the county of Oxfordshire, England, famous for its university. Aubrey de Vere,* a Norman from Ver in the Cotentin,* accompanied William the Conqueror* to England in 1066 for which he was granted, besides other lands, the estates of an English thegn+ named Wulfine in Essex,* Suffolk,* and Cambridgeshire. The bulk of his estates lay in northern Essex and southern Suffolk along the valleys of the Colne and Stour rivers. His son, Aubrey II (1090-1141), was sheriff of London and Middlesex in 1121 and 1122, and joint sheriff with Richard Basset of Surrey, Cambridge, Hampshire, Norfolk, Suffolk, Buckinghamshire, and Bedfordshire, and added the counties of Essex, Hertfordshire, Leicester and Northampton after 1130. As a supporter of

King Stephen,* he ended his long career as chief justiciar+ of England, and died in a riot in London in 1141. His son, Aubry de Vere III (1110-1194), married Beatrice, the granddaughter and heiress of the count of Guisnes, and on the death of the grandfather, did homage to Thierry, count of Flanders,* and became count of Guisnes. In 1142, he joined the plot with his brother-in-law, Geoffrey de Mandeville, first earl of Essex,* against King Stephen, and later that same year, Matilda FitzEmpress* granted him the charter as count Aubrey, earl of Cambridgeshire with the third penny,+ unless that county should be held by the king of the Scots, in which case, if she could not obtain it by exchange, Aubrey should be the earl of either Oxfordshire, Berkshire, Wiltshire or Dorsetshire, at his option, an option that was unique in the English earldoms. Because the king of the Scots considered Cambridge as an appanage+ of his earldom of Huntingdon, Aubrey opted for the title of earl of Oxford. As such, he witnessed the treaty between King Stephen and Henry* of Anjou in 1153 which settled the crown on Stephen for his lifetime and then upon Henry. In 1156, Henry II* bestowed the third penny of Oxford upon him. He was present at the coronation of Richard I* in 1189, and was called upon to contribute £30, 2 shillings 6 pence toward that king's ransom. He died in 1194.

The ninth earl, Robert de Vere (1361-1392), hereditary chamberlain+ of England, was knighted by King Edward III* in 1377, and was allowed to exercise his honorary office at the coronation of Richard II* in 1377, in spite of being only 16 at the time. He became the closest friend of the young King Richard over whom he exercised unbounded influence. He was repeatedly appointed commissioner for numerous purposes. In 1381 he went with the king to meet the leaders of the Peasant's Revolt at Mile End. In 1385, when Richard invaded Scotland, de Vere served Richard himself as one of the commanders of the second division leading 140 men-at-arms and 200 archers. He was chosen to become a Knight of the Garter* in 1385. In that same year, in consideration of "his noble blood, strenuous probity, eminent wisdom, and great achievements," he was created marquess of Dublin for life, which granted him the territory and lordship of Ireland.

That title, the first of its kind in England, came from "marchio" or march,* and applied to the holder of an exposed border district, but never had been used as a distinctive English title as the Germans used it in *Markgraf*. This title had no precedent because it was a new peerage dignity, and it gave de Vere precedence over the earls in Parliament. For it, he was to rule and govern Ireland for two years at the king's expense, and then at his own expense, to have lands conquered from the king's enemies, along with the right to

appoint officers and judges and to mint gold and silver coins. In
March 1386, the ransom of John of Blois, 30,000 marks, was assigned to
him in order to provide him with 500 men-at-arms and 1,000 archers for
two years. In 1386, the marquisate was revoked, and de Vere was
created duke of Ireland for life, and was granted Ireland with its
adjacent islands on his liege homage+ only.

He then made a fatal mistake, when in 1387 he deeply offended
the royal dukes by divorcing their niece, Philippe, younger daughter
and co-heiress of Enguerrand de Coucy,* earl of Bedford by Isabel,
daughter of King Edward III. De Vere left her because he had become
infatuated with one of the queen's handmaidens, Agnes Lancecrone, whom
he abducted and took to live with him in Chester. When he returned to
London in November 1387, he was accused of treason by the earls of
Warwick, Gloucester and Arundel, and fled to Chester. At the head of
an army of 6,000 men from Cheshire, Lancashire and Wales, he set out
for London to answer his accusers. On December 20, he found himself
trapped between the armies of Gloucester and Derby at Radcot Bridge.
He deserted his troops, escaped down the riverbank in the fog, and
swam the Thames. Disguised as a groom, he raced to London, saw the
king in a last interview, and fled to the Low Countries. Then he went
to Paris with the earl of Suffolk who died in 1389, leaving de Vere
his wealth. A year later he went to Brabant.* Meanwhile, in England he
had been found guilty of treason, and all his honours+ and property
were forfeited. He died in Louvain from an injury he received in a
boar hunt in 1392. On his death the dukedom of Ireland became extinct,
but the earldom of Oxford was revived in favor of his nephew, Aubrey
de Vere, the tenth earl. (Bibliog. 47, 58, 101)

Oxford, Provisions of, demands for reform presented to English King
Henry III* in June 1258, that called for the appointment of a
Committee of Twenty-four, representing equally the royal and baronial
factions. These men were to form a council to advise the king on all
matters. A Council of Fifteen composed of seven earls,+ three barons,+
and five clergy were to be permanently with the king, and without
their agreement, he could not act. Furthermore, a separate Committee
of Twelve, to be elected entirely by the barons, was to represent the
community of the realm in meetings with the Council three times a year
as a Parliament.+ This group was appointed to draft a resolution and
submit it to the approval of all before delivering it to King Henry
III. It was composed of four bishops to represent the ecclesiastics:
Canterbury, Winchester, Lincoln, and Worcester; four earls to represent the laity: Cornwall,* Norfolk,* Leicester,* Pembroke*; and
two barons to represent the barons: Montficket and Balliol, plus the

abbots of Bury St. Edmunds and Ramsey. This group proposed that four men of power and rank be chosen to be added to the king's council in order to guarantee the king's observance of charters—similar to the plan in Clause 61 of the *Magna Carta Libertatum*.+ If the king or any of his ministers transgressed any charters, the offended parties were to petition for redress. If they did not obtain it, they had the option of resorting to force. A third Committee of Twenty-four was to control all grants of money. This group consisted of twelve chosen by the earls and barons, and twelve chosen by the king who brought the entire administrative system under the joint control of the king and barons. The group chosen to represent the king were Lord Edward, the king's son and heir; the bishop of London; the bishop-elect of Winchester; Henry, son of the king of Germany (Richard of Cornwall); John, earl of Warenne*; Guy of Lusignan*; William de Valence*; John, earl of Warwick*; Sir John Mansel, John of Darlington, Henry of Wingham, and the abbot of Westminster. For their representatives the barons chose the bishop of Worcester; Simon de Montfort,* earl of Leicester; Richard, earl of Gloucester*; Humphrey de Bohun,* earl of Hereford; Roger the marshal; Roger de Mortimer; John FitzGeoffrey; Hugh Bigod*; Richard de Grey; William Bardolf; Peter de Montfort, and Hugh le Despenser.*

These Provisions did not call for the establishment of a permanent government, and they differed considerably from the provisions of the *Magna Carta Libertatum*. In the *Magna Carta*, the barons held that the king was responsible for conforming to a higher law above the crown, and so long as he obeyed this higher law, he was free to do pretty much as he pleased. Under the Provisions, the king's actions were governed and controlled by a committee of the nation, which in fact was a committee of the barons who considered themselves to be the nation. There was no limitation to what the sovereign could do, but the position of sovereign was considered to be not just one man, but a group of men, no part of which could act independently of the others. This document revealed a formal determination for the knights of the shire to associate more closely with local administration and to make them responsible for the first hearing of local complaints. At every meeting of the shire court four knights elected by the shire were "to attend and hear and record all complaints of injuries and trespass." After this group had been elected, they decided to enlarge the scope of their duties: they were to become agents of the new government in a thorough examination of local administration and royal rights. They were to inquire into the monetary demands and practices of every kind of local official—sheriffs, bailiffs, coroners, etc.; into the malpractices of Jews, usurers, exchangers and merchants; and into unauthorized alienation of royal demesne and royal rights. These barons and King Henry III asked King Louis IX* of France to be the judge of these provisions, believing him to share their opinion that the barons' duty of council was not merely an obligation of the vassal+ to his suzerain,+ but was also a right of the nobility,+ a privilege of their class. Louis was of a different opinion. After studying them deeply, he announced in the Mise of Amiens on January 23, 1264, that he agreed with the pope, and declared the Oxford Provisions to be null and void. (Bibliog. 70, 178, 180, 184, 228)

Oyselet, Sir Amboy. See Lovelich, Henry

P

Palais de la cité, castle+ in Paris built mostly by Louis VI,* the Fat (1081-1137). In 1111, Robert, count of Meulan (see Leicester), attacked Paris to settle an old score with the king, and made himself master of the *Ile de la cité.* Louis rushed back to defend his capital, and finding that Robert had destroyed the bridges, had to force his way across the Seine. Once back in power, he reinforced his position by building a new donjon+ or *Grosse Tour,* a great cylinder of stone of 11.73 meters external diameter and 6 meters internal diameter which later was used to house prisoners of distinction. (Bibliog. 104)

Palamèdes, French romance written after the first prose *Tristan* in which the Saracen knight Palamedes first appeared, but before the second version of the *Tristan.* (Bibliog. 10)

Palatinate (Pfalz), county on the Rhine in Germany.* Its name originated in the office of the count palatine,+ an official entrusted with guarding the Roman emperor's palace. By the time of the Carolingian empire, these officials had been given administrative responsibilities, and the territory they controlled was called the Palatinate. Because this area was located in the middle of Germany, it had enormous strategic importance. From the second half of the 12th century, it belonged to the Wittelsbach dynasty, and after 1180 was part of the duchy of Bavaria.* (Bibliog. 98)

pale, district or territory within determined bounds, or subject to a particular jurisdiction, as in the English pale: the confines or dominion of England.* Specifically, the English pale in France* was the territory of Calais*; in Ireland,* it was that section of Ireland over which English jurisdiction was established, and varied geographically in extent at different times, but generally included Dublin at its center. (Bibliog. 169)

Palestine (Holy Land), country on the eastern shore of the Mediterranean which was holy for Christians, Jews, and Muslims.* Rescuing it from the hands of "pagans," unbelievers, and infidels was the motive for the crusades+ which stimulated the hearts and imaginations of Western Europe from the first crusade preached by Pope Urban II in 1095 to the ninth major crusade embarked on by Prince Edward of England late in the 13th century. (Bibliog. 195, 201)

Palomydes, Palomides, son of Saracen King Astlabor, brother of Safere and Segwarides. In *Morte D'Arthur*,* he played a large role. He was in love with Isold, and in a tournament, unhorsed Kay,* Sagramore, and Griflet, but was unhorsed by Tristram, disguised as Tramtris. Later he visited Cornwall* after Mark* and Isold were married, and rescued Brangaine from a tree where two envious ladies had tied her. He fought against Tristram once again, and again was defeated. Isold sent him to Arthur's court to become a knight of the Round Table.* Later he pursued the Questing Beast+ after the death of Pellinore* and experienced many more adventures while at Arthur's court. Despite his Saracen* background, he became one of the best and most courteous knights, an honorable, reliable and excellent champion.   (Bibliog. 117, 145)

Parise la Duchesse, chanson de geste from the early 13th century recounting the story of Parise, daughter of Garnier de Nanteuil and Aye d'Avignon, granddaughter of Doön de Nanteuil, sister of Gui de Nanteuil and wife of Raymond of St. Gilles. When Ganelon's* family falsely accused her of having killed her husband's brother, she was exiled. While in exile, she bore a son, Huon, who was stolen from her and raised in the Hungarian court. He searched for and found his mother at Cologne, and began a war of vengeance against his father for allowing the slander against his mother. Finally, the truth emerged, the traitors were hanged and Huon married the princess of Hungary. (ed. F. Guessard and Loredan Larchey, Paris: *APF,* IV, 1860) (Bibliog. 106)

Partenopeus de Blois, French romance from about 1188 which recounted how Partenopeus, nephew of King Clovis, was led by a boar to the fairy Chief d'Oire Castle where by night he was loved by the fairy mistress, Melior. She agreed to love him, but commanded him never to look on her until she married him publicly. After a year, Partenopeus left for France where he freed his country and king from the Danes, and became engaged to marry his cousin, but he renounced her in favor of his fairy princess. His mother persuaded him to ignore his promise to Melior and to look at her. By that action, she, daughter of the emperor of Constantinople, lost her magical power and renounced Partenopeus forever. Driven mad by that rejection, he returned to France and wandered through the woods where he was found by Melior's sister, Urrake, and restored to sanity. With her help, he participated in the three-day tournament+ in which the knights were competing for the hand of Melior, which he won and with it, the sovereignty of the empire. (ed. Joseph Gildea, Villanova, PA, 1967) It was translated into Middle High German* about 1277 by Konrad von Wurzburg* as *Partenopier und Meliur,* then into Dutch in the middle of the 13th century, and subsequently into Middle English as *Partenope of Blois* (ed. A. Bodtker, London: Oxford, *EETS ES* #109, 1912; repr. New York: AMS Press, 1973), and into Low German, Old Norse, Danish and Spanish. (Bibliog. 10, 106, 202)

Partenopier und Meliur, Middle High German* courtly epic by Konrad von Wurzburg based on the French romance, *Partenopeus de Blois.** Konrad more than doubled the size of his source, and increased the instances of magic and supernatural. (ed. Karl Bartch, Vienna, 1874) (Bibliog. 86)

Parzival, Middle High German* epic poem by Wolfram von Eschenbach based on but freely adapted from Chrétien de Troyes'* *La Conte del Graal* (*Perceval**). This work introduced the legend of the Holy Grail* into German literature, and often was considered to be the most profound work in all German literature. Its first two books concerned the history of Parzival's father, Gahmuret of Anjou, who journeyed on a Crusade+ to the east to seek his fortune. He won the hand of a queen there, but left her in restless search for adventure. At a tournament+ in France, he won the prize of Queen Herzeloyd of Wales. Annulling his marriage to the heathen princess, he married Herzeloyd, but once again restlessly left to seek adventure in the world, and died in a battle in the service of the caliph+ of Bagdad. Shortly after the news of his death reached Herzeloyd, she bore a son, Parzival, and to preserve him from the temptations which had killed his father, she withdrew to the solitude of the forest to bring up her son and to teach him to revere God. One day, the young Parzival met three knights in armor, and learned from them what his mother had sought to keep him from—what knighthood was, and how and where it could be obtained. He could not rest until he visited King Arthur's court to become a knight, and then to sally forth into the world in the full foolishness of childish innocence. He fought and killed the Red Knight, spent time with Gurnemanz who taught him the practical wisdom and the laws of knighthood, he rescued a beautiful young queen, Condiviramurs, spent the night in the castle of Anfortas, King of the Grail, but did not ask the essential questions about the Grail or the bleeding spear. He realized his error only after it was too late to correct it, and spent five years wandering in the world. On Good Friday, he met some pilgrims in the forest who chided him for bearing arms on a holy day, and advised him to seek out a hermit in a nearby forest to free himself of sin. Turning his horse loose to wander because God would guide it appropriately, Parzival ended up at the home of the hermit Treurizent, who was Anfortas' brother and Herzeloyd's and his own uncle. He spent fifteen days with the hermit, learning what he had to do. Then, after winning two battles, one against Gawain,* and the other against his own half-brother, Feirefiz, he was reunited with his wife and two sons, one of whom, Loherangrin (Lohengrin) would succeed him as King of the Grail. This work's main theme was that this world and its aspirations had value in that knightly valor, untarnished by dishonor, was the noblest value on earth, and hence most pleasing to God. (tr. H. Mustard and C. Passage, New York: Vintage Books, 1961; modern German tr. W. Stapel, Munich: 1950, 4th ed.) (Bibliog. 190, 235)

passage of Blanche-taque, sandy-bottomed ford across the River Somme which a peasant showed Edward III* and his forces that allowed the English to continue their march toward Flanders* in 1346. Although the opposite bank was defended by several thousand troops including Genoese crossbowmen, the English forced their way across, despite several volleys from their renowned bowmen. King Philip VI* was close in pursuit, but the river rose and prevented the French forces from crossing. Once across the River Somme, Edward paused, and took stock. His way to Flanders was clear even if things went wrong for him, but nonetheless, he needed to pause to rest his forces. As a result he camped at the small village of Crécy-en-Ponthieu. The following day, the French forces found him and engaged in the famous battle of Crécy.* (Bibliog. 203)

patis, appatis,+ protection racket in France* especially during the Hundred Years War* by which every village and hamlet had to pay the troops from the local stronghold in money, livestock, food and wine not to bother them. If they failed to make these payments, they were punished by arbitrary executions and burnings. Travellers had to pay dearly for safe-conducts+ at the toll-gates and roadblocks set up throughout the countryside. Profits from this extortion were pooled and then the soldiers paid one-third to their garrison commander who sent one third to the king along with one-third of his own profits. In 1359, an average of £41 per parish was collected by garrisons in Brittany. (Bibliog. 203)

Paynel, Ralph, sheriff of Yorkshire in 1088. He took over as tenant-in-chief in the counties of York, Lincoln, Northampton, Gloucester, Devon and Somerset, holding nearly the whole estate of Merlesuen who had been sheriff in Lincoln County in 1066. Paynel also held land in Les Moutiers-Herbert in Calvados, Normandy, and received land in the Cotentin* by William I* on his marriage. After his son William inherited his father's lands, he married twice. By his first wife he had two sons, and by his second, a daughter, Alice. When he died, the problem arose of how to divide the estate. King Stephen* gave the whole of the English barony+ to Richard de Courcy, Paynel's son by his first marriage and the husband of his (Stephen's) daughter; the remainder went to the other son, Fulk, who had remained in Normandy.* After the accession of Henry II,* the eldest son was found to be in possession not only of Les Moutiers-Herbert in Normandy, but also lands in County Lincoln; the second son, Fulk, was in possession of Hambye in Normandy and Drax in County York; while Robert de Gant, who had become the second husband of Alice before Henry's accession to the throne, still held a considerable portion of the English lands including some in Somerset and Lincoln. On the loss of the English lands in France in 1204 (see John, King), Hugh Paynel II, grandson of the eldest son, stayed with King John, losing Les Moutiers-Herbert which went to the king of France. As compensation, Hugh received Drax which had been forfeited by Fulk II, son of Fulk I,* for staying with the king of France and retaining Hambye. (Bibliog. 47)

Peace of Bretigny. See Treaty of Bretigny.

Pedro the Cruel. See Peter IV.

Peerages conferred on the sons of English sovereigns:

Aumale,* earldom: conferred in 1397 upon Edward, earl of Rutland, son and heir of Edmund, duke of York, fifth son of Edward III.* [Thomas of Woodstock,* sixth son of Edward III, who was created duke of Gloucester in 1385, was summoned to Parliament on September 3, 1386, as the duke of Aumale in error, for he never held that title.]

Buckingham,* earldom: conferred in 1377 upon Thomas of Woodstock, sixth son of Edward III.

Cambridge,* earldom: conferred in 1362 upon Edmund of Langley, fifth
    son of Edward III; he was created duke of York in 1385.

Chester,* earldom: conferred in 1254 upon Edward,* son and heir of
    Henry III; he succeeded to the throne as Edward I in 1272, and
    since then the earldom has been granted to none but the heir
    apparent* to the crown.

Clarence,* dukedom: conferred in 1362 upon Lionel,* third son of
    Edward III.

Cork, earldom: conferred in 1396 upon Edward, earl of Rutland, son and
    heir apparent of Edmund, duke of York, the fifth son of Edward
    III; he was created duke of Aumale in 1397, and succeeded as
    duke of York in 1402.

Cornwall,* earldom: conferred in 1227 upon Richard, second son of
    John, In 1328, conferred upon John, second son of Edward II.*

Cornwall, dukedom: conferred in 1337 upon Edward,* earl of Chester
    (the Black Prince), son and heir apparent of Edward III; he
    was created Prince of Wales in 1343.

Derby,* earldom: conferred in 1337 upon Henry of Grosmont,* son and
    heir of Henry, earl of Lancaster, great grandson of Henry III;
    created earl of Lincoln in 1349, and duke of Lancaster in
    1352.

Essex,* earldom: conferred in 1380 upon Thomas of Woodstock, earl of
    Buckingham, sixth son of Edward III; having married Alianore,
    first daughter and co-heiress of Humphrey de Bohun,* earl of
    Hereford and Essex, Thomas was recognized as earl of Essex in
    1386; in 1385 he was created duke of Gloucester.

Gloucester,* earldom: conferred in 1176 upon John,* youngest son of
    Henry II; he succeeded to the throne in 1199.

Gloucester, dukedom: conferred in 1385 upon Thomas of Woodstock, earl
    of Buckingham and Essex, sixth son of Edward III.

Hereford,* dukedom: conferred in 1397 upon Henry, earl of Derby, son
    and heir of John, duke of Lancaster, fourth son of Edward
    III.

Kent,* earldom: conferred in 1321 upon Edmund, sixth son of Edward I.

Lancaster,* earldom: conferred in 1267 upon Edmund, fourth son of Hen-
    ry III. (He was granted the county, castle, and town of
    Lancaster, and was held to have been earl of the county, and
    was so styled, but the grant itself contained no words creat-
    ing him earl.)

Lancaster, dukedom: conferred in 1352 upon Henry, earl of Lancaster,
    grandson of Edmund, fourth son of Henry III.

Lancaster, dukedom: conferred again in 1362 on John (of Gaunt*), earl
    of Richmond, fourth son of Edward III.

Lancaster, dukedom: conferred in 1399 upon Henry, son and heir apparent* of Henry IV; he later ascended the throne as Henry V, and since that time, the dukedom never has been regranted.

Leicester,* earldom: Edmund, fourth son of Henry III, after the fall of Simon de Montfort* in 1265, was granted the honour+ of Leicester, and may have been considered the earl of the county, but rarely was so styled.

Lincoln,* earldom: conferred in 1349 upon Henry, earl of Derby, grandson of Edmund, earl of Leicester, and great-grandson of Henry III.

Norfolk,* earldom: conferred in 1312 upon Thomas of Brotherton, fifth son of Edward I.

Richmond,* earldom: conferred in 1342 upon John (of Gaunt), fourth son of Edward III; he was created duke of Lancaster in 1362.

Rutland,* earldom: conferred in 1390 upon Edward, fifth son of Edmund, duke of York , the fifth son of Edward III; he was created duke of Aumale in 1397.

Ulster,* earldom: conferred in 1352 upon Lionel, second surviving son of Edward III; he was created duke of Clarence in 1362.

York,* dukedom: conferred in 1385 upon Edmund, earl of Cambridge, fifth son of Edward III.

(Bibliog. 47)

Peeresses of England, titled women of England by creation or by descent:

1299 - Margaret Tuston Coke, countess dowager of Leicester, baroness Clifford; bestowed by King Edward I*

1299 - Charlotte Murray, duchess of Athol, baroness Strange, of Knockyn in Shropshire, and lady of Man and adjacent islands; bestowed by King Edward I

1377 - Elizabeth Percy, duchess of Northumberland, baroness Percy; bestowed by King Richard II*

(Bibliog. 101)

Pèlerinage de Charlemagne à Jerusalem et à Constantinople, mock heroic-satiric poem written between 1109 and 1150 to be sung at the Fair at St. Denis.+ It was created as a caricature of the official story that had been forged to explain the existence at St. Denis of some remarkable relics. This humor-filled work detailed how Charlemagne* set out to find out the truth of his wife's remark that the emperor of Constantinople* wore his crown more loftily than he. He told her that he would slay her if she were wrong. Travelling with

1,000 of his knights, including the *douzepeers,** Charlemagne and his entourage arrived first at Jerusalem where the patriarch welcomed them with a large reception and bestowed many relics on them, including the arm of St. Simon, the head of St. Lazarus, some of St. Stephen's blood, a piece of Our Lord's shroud, and the chalice from the Last Supper. Then they travelled on to Constantinople where they found King Hugh plowing with a golden plow. That night the king and the *douzepeers* retired to their bedroom, a noble chamber with twelve beds arranged in a circle around the thirteenth, which Charlemagne was to occupy. After drinking a lot, they began to gab+ (brag) to amuse themselves. Charlemagne, for example, boasted that with one stroke of his famous sword, Joyeuse, he could cleave through Hugh's best knight clad in reinforced armor and mounted on a stalwart steed, and bury his sword into the ground. Others boasted equally preposterous vows. A spy in a pillar in the room noted all the boasting and reported it to Hugh who became furious at what he deemed to be insults. The next day, he told them that they had to fulfill their gabs or die. The knights prayed for God's help, and an angel appeared promising success. Oliver was the first to be put to the test to "know" the emperor's daughter 100 times during the night. Even though God would not aid him in so lusty an adventure, he was saved by the girl lying to her father. Oliver had "known" the girl only 30 times, but she was so delighted by his performance that she willingly lied to her father. After several of the others fulfilled their gabs to the letter, Hugh claimed that he had had enough, and made peace with Charlemagne. Side by side the two wore their crowns with Charlemagne's being a little higher. The Franks then returned with their relics, and the queen was pardoned for her misdemeanor. (tr. Margaret Schlauch, *Medieval Narrative*, New York: Prentice-Hall, 1928, 72-101) (Bibliog. 106)

Pellam, the "Maimed King," king of Lystenoyse (Listeneise), also known as Pelles,* the Fisher King, The Rich Fisher, King of the Waste Lands, and King Pecheour. Because he had been wounded by Balin's* *dolorous stroke,** and unable to be healed, he stayed at Castle Corbenic,* guarding the Holy Grail*; he ultimately was healed by his great-grandson, Galahad.* Queen Amide told another version of the legend of the Dolorous Stroke to Galahad, Perceval* and Bors later on. In her version, the king had been maimed by the Spear of Vengeance for his hardihood in drawing the sword of David on the Mysterious Ship. (Bibliog. 117, 145)

Pellinore, king of the Isles; also known as the Knight with the Strange Beast, for his pursuit of the Questing Beast.+ He was questing after that beast when his horse died and he met young Arthur,* later king, and demanded his horse. He refused Arthur's request to take his place in that quest and promised to accede to Arthur's second request for a fair joust to determine which of them was the better knight. They did meet again, and in the fight, Arthur's sword was broken. Rather than yield, Arthur tried to wrestle Pellinore down. But Pellinore was fearful of Arthur's strength, and managed to unhelm his young adversary and was about to smite off his head when Merlin* arrived to tell Pellinore just who his adversary was. Enraged even further, Pellinore was about to kill Arthur when Merlin cast him into an enchanted sleep. Later he killed King Lot,* whose death was avenged when Gawain* killed Pellinore with his own hands. (Bibliog. 117)

Pembroke, city in Pembrokeshire seated on the forked arm of Milford Haven on the western coast of Wales.* Its earls in its early days were counts-palatine,+ the earldom belonging to a group of half-palatinate+ fiefs in South Wales during the reign of Henry I.* Coming to be known as Pembroke, the tenants of these fiefs, while acknowledging the crown as their superior, exercised practically total sovereign rights over their own territories. These, and their successors in the mid-Welsh areas became known as the Lords Marcher. Early in the 12th century, the lordship of Striguil, a fortress on the Welsh banks of the Wye River later known as Chepstow,* was held by Walter FitzRichard, a border chieftain who had received a grant in Cardigan from King Henry I and upon whom King Stephen* in 1138 had conferred the title of earl of Pembroke. On his death in 1138, he was succeeded by his nephew, Gilbert de Clare,* who made his *caput** at Striguil. De Clare (c. 1100-1148) who may have been known as "Strongbow" (see below), became a great baron+ by obtaining the estates of his paternal uncle Walter, including some in Normandy. He was closely connected by blood and marriage with the greater Norman families in England, being brother-in-law of William de Warenne,* second earl of Surrey, and Walter de Meulan. He married a daughter of Robert de Beaumont (count of Meulan and earl of Leicester), stepdaughter of William de Warenne. During the civil wars between King Stephen and Empress Matilda, the Lords Marcher were in both English camps. Gilbert de Clare fought for Stephen, and was rewarded for his efforts after the battle of the Standard* by being made earl of Pembroke which bestowed on him the jurisdiction of Lord Marcher. He died in 1148, and was succeeded by his son, Richard.

Richard FitzGilbert (1130-1176), earl of Pembroke, also styled "Strongbow"* later, was known as the earl of Striguil. He crossed the Irish Sea in 1168 and fought for Dermot MacMurrough, king of Leinster, married the king's daughter, Eva, and put himself in line for the succession to the Irish throne. He died in 1176, leaving a three-year-old son, Gilbert, who died before he was 17, and a young daughter, Isabel. As a ward of the crown, she was given in marriage almost immediately to William Marshal, younger son of John the Marshal, who served as marshal to both Kings Henry I and Stephen.

King Richard I* bestowed the title of earl of Pembroke (the fourth earl) upon William Marshal in 1189, so he was referred to as earl of Pembroke, earl of Striguil, but most frequently as "the Marshal"; the sword of the earldom was not girded on him, however, until the coronation of King John* in 1199. Immediately after John died, William by common consent became the guardian of the boy King Henry III* and remained so until his death in 1219. He had five sons and five daughters, and all his sons succeeded him to the earldom but all died childless. His eldest son, William (1190-1231), became the fifth earl on his father's death in 1219. He had been active in government affairs during his father's lifetime, joining the baronial opposition to King John that resulted in the *Magna Carta Libertatum*+ in 1215, and being chosen one of the barons to ensure that the king abided by the provisions of that charter. In 1223 he sailed from Ireland with a large force to fight the Welsh, recaptured his castles and defeated and forced Llewelyn to come to terms. Later he was appointed justiciar+ of Ireland. His second wife was the younger daughter of King John, and sister to Henry III,* Eleanor, who later married Simon de Montfort's* second son, Simon. The next son, Richard Marshal, succeeded his brother as sixth earl of Pembroke, and also died childless in 1234; the third son, Gilbert Marshal, the next earl of Pembroke, died without legitimate issue in 1241; then the fourth son, Walter Marshal, became the seventh earl of Pembroke and died without issue in 1245. William's fifth son, Anselm, the ninth earl by inheritance, however, never was invested with earldom, and on his death in 1245, the title reverted to the crown. William I's granddaughter, Joan, lived into the 14th century calling herself "Countess of Pembroke."

She married William of Valence* (or of Lusignan) (d. 1295) who became lord of Pembroke in right of his marriage; he was half-brother of King Henry III; their son, Aymer de Valence,* Lord Valence, became earl of Pembroke in 1307, and died without issue in 1324. William I's daughters, married the richest and most prominent men in the country. The eldest, Maud (d. 1248), married first Hugh Bigod,* earl of Norfolk,* whose son Roger Bigod succeeded her as earl of Pembroke; and second William de Warenne, earl of Surrey.* Isabel (d. 1240) married first Gilbert, earl of Gloucester* whose son and heir, Richard, was earl of Gloucester; and second Richard, earl of Cornwall,* the king's brother, afterward the king of the Romans. Sibyl (d. 1238) married William Ferrers,* earl of Derby.* Eva (d. 1245) married William de Braose,* Welsh Marcher lord. Joan, the youngest, who died before 1234, married William de Munchensy, and left an only daughter, Joan, who afterwards married William de Valence (d. 1295) half-brother to King Henry III. She died in 1307, and the title fell to Laurence de Hastings, descended from the eldest sister of Aymer de Valence, son of William de Valence. (Bibliog. 47, 66, 101)

Pendragon, Uther, king of Britain; son of Constans,* king of Britain. Following Constan's death, several barons put Constan's seneschal,+ Vortiger, on the throne after murdering the eldest of Constan's three sons, Maines. Defeating the Saxons, Uther ascended the throne, adopting his brother's name of Pendragon, and ordered Merlin* to bring the stones of Stonehenge from Ireland to England as a memorial to his dead brother, Pendragon. Then he sent for Duke Gorlois* of Cornwall who had been waging a war against Uther for a long time, ordering him to come to court with his wife, Igerne, for whom Uther had a secret passion. When they learned of Uther's intentions, Gorlois and Igraine departed secretly and suddenly, and prepared for a siege from Uther. In that battle, Gorlois was killed, and Uther with Merlin's magic help, assumed the form of Gorlois and lay with Igerne, begetting Arthur.* Then he married her. On his deathbed, he named Arthur to be his successor. (Bibliog. 117, 145)

Perceval, son of Pellinore*; brother of Aglovale,* Lamorak* and Tor; one of the three Grail knights and a major Arthurian knight who appeared in at least 14 major Arthurian works, including: Chrétien de Troyes', *Li Conte del Graal* (*Perceval**); *Perlesvaus** in French verse; Didot *Perceval* in French prose; Wolfram von Eschenbach's *Parzival* in Middle High German*; *Peredur** in Welsh prose; *Sir Perceval of Galles* in English verse; Manessier wrote a French continuation of Chrétien's *Conte del Graal*; Gerbert de Montreuil also wrote a French continuation of Chrétien's *Conte del Graal*; *Queste del Saint Graal* in French; *Estoire del Saint Graal* in French; *Carduino** in Italian; and three *chansons de geste*: Girart de Roussillon,* Baudouin de Sebourc,* and Bâtard de Bouillon.* See also Chrétien de Troyes. (Bibliog. 243)

Percy, Henry (1272-1314), English knight, grandson of the earl of Surrey* who was summoned in 1294 for military service in Gascony,* but went instead with King Edward I* into Wales.* He was knighted by the king after a valiant role in the capture of Berwick in 1295. He received the submission of the Scottish prelates and nobles including Robert the Bruce* in 1297. He served as regent during the Edward I's absence abroad. Summoned to Parliament in 1298, he became lord Percy. The remainder of his life was spent either fighting in Scotland* or preparing to fight there. He was at Stirling in 1304 with the expedition that ousted Bruce in 1306; he was besieged at Turnberry castle until relieved by the king's forces in 1306. Later, he joined the baronial opposition to the conduct of Edward II* which led to the appointment of the Lords Ordainers.* (Bibliog. 47)

Peredur, Welsh tale similar in design, details and story line to Chrétien's *Perceval*.* (Bibliog. 10)

Perlesvaus, French prose romance of the Grail* written around the end of the 12th century. Its title, another name for Perceval, revealed that it drew on Chrétien's *Perceval*.* and his *Lancelot,*.* as well as Robert de Boron's *Joseph d'Arimathie*.* Three people participated in the quest for the Holy Grail in its eleven "branches." The first began with Josephes telling of a chaste knight and the Grail, and associated it with Arthur's* court. The remaining branches related separate quests of Gawain* and Lancelot* (branches 2-6), Perlesvaus (Perceval) (branches 7-10); branch 11 restored Lancelot to Arthur's favor in a war against Bran des Illes, and ended the story with Perceval's retirement from the world to the equivalent of the 12th century otherworld. (tr. Sebastian Evans, *High History of the Holy Grail,* London: J. M. Dent, 1898, 2 vols.) (Bibliog. 10, 78)

Peter (Pedro) IV, the Cruel (1333-1369), king of Castile from 1350. Son of Alfonso IX, he established an authoritarian regime in the country with the help of Moorish ministers and an army of mercenaries.+ On his father's death in 1350, Peter (or Pedro) sought help from Edward,* the Black Prince, in claiming the throne over the opposition of his illegitimate half-brother, Henry of Trastamara supported by France and Aragon. He had made enemies of the French by abandoning and reputedly murdering his wife who was sister to the queen of France. To court English favor, he gave his daughter, Constance, in marriage to John of Gaunt,* brother of King Edward III.* At first, Peter and the Black Prince were successful, winning at the battle of Navarette* in 1367, but Peter's penchant for murder and inhuman brutalities so disgusted the Black Prince that he withdrew, leaving Henry of Tramastara and Bertrand du Guesclin* with his French mercenaries to overthrow Peter in 1369. (Bibliog. 98, 124)

Peter des Roches (d. 1238), bishop of Winchester.* A native of Poitou,* he served Richard I* as knight and clerk and became one of his chamberlains. He continued as a clerk for King John* of England as well, going abroad for him. John's loss of Normandy,* Poitou and Anjou* in 1204 deprived Peter of his benefices,+ but in 1205 he received the lands of the countess of Perche in England and the custody of the bishoprics of Winchester and Chichester. He stood by King John when Pope Innocent III* threatened to depose him in 1211. When John surrendered to the pope and went to Poitou in 1213, Peter was appointed justiciar+ much to the disgust of the barons who resented an alien in such an important position. In all the barons' anger against the king, Peter stood by him. After Pope Innocent annulled the *Magna Carta Libertatum*,+ Peter urged the excommunication of the barons responsible, and gave the pope the names of the barons to be excommunicated personally. Three years later, he personally crowned young Henry III* with the circlet of gold, and anointed+ him king, and then was appointed the guardian of the underage king. In 1217, he helped relieve the siege of Dame Nicolaa de la Haye* in Lincoln* by entering the castle alone and encouraging her to withstand the assault if at all possible. He was constantly in the forefront of political intrigue and religious controversy until his death. He was friendly with Faulkes de Breauté,* the earls of Chester* and Aumale,* and was involved in a plot to capture the Tower of London and remove the justiciar, his enemy, Hubert de Burgh.* Hubert had denounced him to the king and council as a traitor, and Hubert had the king's ear.

In 1227, Henry III renounced Peter's guardianship, freeing Peter to journey on a crusade+ to the Holy Land where he became influential in diplomacy. On his return trip through France, he mediated a treaty of three years between England and France, and returned in triumph to Winchester. There he gave a huge party and bestowed rich gifts of food, clothes, gold, silver, jewels and horses to increase his popularity. He used that popularity to avenge himself on de Burgh, accusing the chancellor of mismanaging royal funds so that the king was too poor to fight against the Welsh. Hubert and his supporters were replaced and stood trial. Hubert accused Peter of deceit, but Peter withstood the challenges so that when he was back in power, he began to fill vacant positions in the English government with officials from his native Poitou, much to the fury of Richard Marshal, third earl of Pembroke,* and other barons. Soon Peter overreached himself and the king grew weary of him. Finally when he tried to install his own man, Peter le Blount, as archbishop* of Canterbury, the pope refused and chose Edmund Rich instead. At this, the bishops drew up a long list of accusations, but even though Peter withstood the challenge again, he never regained his former standing with the king before he died in 1238. During his life, he had been a warrior, statesman, financial agent, builder, and diplomat, and throughout it all, he was an admirable though arrogant manager. (Bibliog. 58, 184)

Peter, count of Savoy (1213-1268), earl of Richmond,* and marquis of Italy born in Susa, Italy. Over the years, he developed a strong association with England. He was the uncle of Queen Eleanor* of Provence, Henry III's* wife, as well as Sanchia of Provence, wife of Richard* of Cornwall, Henry III's brother; his own brother was Boniface,* who became archbishop of Canterbury. As a young man, he was destined for a career in the church, but he chose not to follow that career, and when he was 21, he resigned and married his cousin Agnes, daughter and heiress of Aymon, count of Faucigny. His marriage provided him with a base on which to build a large area of territory to control. In 1237, he fought and was captured by William, count of Geneva, but was released shortly thereafter. In 1240 he went to England at the invitation of his niece's husband, Henry III, who gave him large estates, made him earl of Richmond, and knighted him in the following year. Fearing the envy of the king's brother, Richard of Cornwall, and other nobles, Peter asked permission to leave England, but the king refused. Instead, he made Peter sheriff of Kent, gave him the castles of Rochester and Dover, and made him a warden of the Cinque Ports.* He served on missions to the continent for the king, and returned in 1247 with a bevy of foreign ladies to be married to the English nobles; two of them married Edmund de Lacy, earl of Leicester,* and Richard, son of Hubert de Burgh.* This angered the people of England, and their anger was aroused even more by Peter being given the wardships of two young nobles: John, earl of Warenne in 1241; Robert Ferrers, earl of Derby, in 1257. He added to his holdings in 1249 by being given the honours* and castles of Hastings* and Tickhill.* He became friends with Simon de Montfort* and joined with him and the other barons to force the king to accept the Committe of Twenty-four as called for by the Provisions of Oxford,* and subsequently at the Parliament of Oxford in June 1258, he was chosen as one of the Council of Fifteen. Always a moderate, he sided with the king as the breach grew between Simon de Montfort and Richard, earl of Clare.* He even was successful in reconciling the king and his son Edward* in 1260. As internal conditions deteriorated and war erupted in 1263, Peter was forced to leave England because he was a foreigner. When his nephew, Boniface, count of Savoy, died in 1263, Peter assumed the title of count of Savoy and marquis of Italy. In 1250, he obtained the ring of St. Maurice which afterwards was used in the investiture of the counts and dukes of Savoy as it had been used for the ancient dukes of Burgundy.* After the battle of Evesham* and the death of Montfort in 1265, Peter's English lands were seized by the barons, but were restored to him shortly before he died in 1268. (Bibliog. 58)

Pevensey castle, one of the early fortresses erected by the Romans to protect the southern coast of England, called the Saxon Shore against raids of the Vikings and Saxons. Known by the Romans as Anderido or Anderita, this installation was taken over by the Normans and enlarged. Near it, William I* landed and fought the battle of Hastings* in 1066. After that battle, William included this castle in the spoils given to his half-brother Robert, count of Mortain.* In 1088, Odo,* bishop of Bayeux and another half-brother of William I, held this castle against his nephew, King William II,* and it had to be captured by siege. In 1147, Gilbert, earl of Pembroke,* held it against King Stephen* but was starved into submission. A century later, a band of King Henry III's* followers who had just been defeated nearby at the battle of Lewes,* took refuge in this castle, and withstood successfully the siege of the soldiers of Simon de Montfort.* (Bibliog. 247)

Pfalzgraf, German count palatine.+ See *Herzog Ernest*; Palatinate.

Philip I (1052-1108), king of France (1060-1108). As the fourth in the Capetian* line of French kings, he was reviled for being a fat and greedy monarch. Pope Gregory VII denounced him as a tyrant possessed by the Devil, a perjurer and a robber. He was criticized for failing to prevent the Norman invasion of England, and the subsequent union of Normandy with England, and for not leading the first crusade.+ Yet, he had to make himself master of his own house, the royal domain, before he could master his kingdom at large. He sowed the seeds of actions which later would have the turbulent barons of the kingdom submit to the king. By marrying his son Philip to Elizabeth, daughter of Guy Troussel, lord of Montlhery, he gained control of a fortress called the Tower of Montlhery.* He cautioned that son, ruling as Louis VI, never to let that tower out of his control, for it had caused Philip untold troubles. Equally, he saw how powerful was his great vassal the duke of Normandy.* Being a minor in 1066, he was helpless to prevent the invasion of England, but he was clever enough to take advantage of quarrels within the Anglo-Norman household. He encouraged and supported Robert II,* Curthose, against his father, William I,* and then against his brother, William II.* (His son Louis cleverly carried on that tradition by fomenting trouble between William the Clito* and

Henry I* of England. Later yet, Philip II,* Augustus, diplomatically used Richard I* against both Henry II* and his brother John.*) Philip I was unable to participate in the first crusade, for he was under sentence of excommunication at the time for his marriage to Bertrada de Montfort, the wife of Fulk V, count of Anjou.* Despite his seeming troubles with the church, Philip maintained a clear policy of cooperation and mutual aid with the papacy. He was reported to have cured the sick with a sign of the cross, and thus, with the pious complicity of churchmen, his actions lead to the legend of the royal healing power, the "royal touch."+ (Bibliog. 74, 178)

Philip II, Augustus (1166-1223), king of France (1180-1223). The great king of the Capetian dynasty, he resembled his grandfather, Louis VI,* with his tendency toward corpulence, his vitality, and his combativeness. King at 14, crusader at 25, he seemingly was afflicted while in the Holy Land with a mystifying sickness which turned him into a cautious, cynical, distrustful, scheming man. Not particularly intelligent, he had a keen practical sense and was capable of making plans on a large scale and of executing them with painstaking care to ensure their success. He was reputed to have told his nine-year-old grandson, Louis IX* (later Saint Louis), that a king should reward his men strictly in proportion to the service they had performed for him, and that no man could become a good king who was not as firm in refusing as he was generous in giving. As a king he was tirelessly active in reorganizing the kingdom, and blessed with some excellent good fortune for his plans. His archenemy, Richard I* of England, had been killed in 1199, ridding him of a dangerous foe. A second potentially dangerous rival, Arthur,* was removed by the greed and savagery of his uncle John,* king of England. That action paved the way for Philip to reclaim to the control of the French monarchy the Plantagenet lands in France. Opposition from Pope Innocent III* prevented Philip from embarking on an extremely risky gamble of invading England, even though he sent his son and troops there in 1217. Innocent's further move to rid northern France of many adventuresome and highly ambitious nobles by encouraging them to venture into its southern region to root out the heresy of the Albigenses+ proved beneficial to Philip in the long run. And on the field of battle, he displayed skill and adroitness at Bouvines.* In his forty-two years on the throne, he came to control a vast royal domain. He was succeeded to the throne by his son, Louis VIII* (1223-1226). (Bibliog. 74)

Philip III, the Bold (1245-1285), king of France (1270-1285). Son of the great Louis IX,* Saint Louis, Philip lived in the shadow of his

father. He was a man of mediocre intelligence who tried to follow in
his father's footsteps. Fortunately, by wisely retaining in their
offices the excellent men with whom his father had surrounded himself,
he did not jeopardize the achievements of his great-grandfather,
Philip II,* Augustus, or of his grandmother, Blanche* of Castile, or
of his father. This move ensured that he reaped the benefits of their
wisdom, and maintained the vast heritage of Alphonse of Poitiers*:
Poitou* and almost all of Languedoc, which was united with the royal
domain in 1271. By marriage, he brought to the throne the counties of
Champagne and Brie. Against the advice of many of his counsellors, but
urged on by his wife, Mary of Brabant, and his uncle, Charles of
Aragon, Philip began a war with Aragon* which made great financial demands on the treasury. He died at Perpignan on October 5, 1285, while
in full retreat from his unsuccessful invasion, and was succeeded by
his son, Philip IV (1285-1314). (Bibliog. 74)

Philip IV, the Fair (1268-1314), king of France (1285-1314). Son of
Philip III* and Isabella of Aragon, Philip was reputed to be the
handsomest man in the world, "but unable to do anything but stare
fixedly at someone without uttering a word." He was a cold, calculating man. During his reign, he brought the papacy under French control,
destroyed the powerful Order of the Templars,+ and laid the
foundations for a national French monarchy. His struggle with Pope
Boniface VIII came to a head after he imposed taxation on the clergy
in direct contradiction to the papal bull+ *Clericis laicos*, which required papal consent before a secular monarch could impose any such
taxation. When Philip retaliated by forbidding the exportation of any
coin from France, the pope yielded; but their strife continued, resulting in the papal bull of 1302, *Unam sanctam*, which asserted the
supreme power of the pope as leader of the church, as well as his duty
to direct secular affairs toward religious goals.   This was the
culmination of a 200-year process which drew together every argument
in favor of papal supremacy raised since the beginning of the papal
reform movement in the middle of the 11th century. Philip ordered the
arrest of the pope on charges of simony, heresy, adultery, and
tyranny, and sent his minister, William de Nogaret, to Rome to arrest
him. Going to his native city of Anagni, de Nogaret found Boniface and
placed him under arrest to be taken to France. However, the angry
townspeople rescued him, forcing de Nogaret to flee, but Boniface died
before he could return to Rome. Boniface's successor, Benedict XI
(1303-1304), absolved Philip, and then died suddenly. His successor
was Bertrand de Got, archbishop of Bordeaux, a protégé of the French
crown. Taking the name of Clement V, he avoided Rome where his enemies

were in power, and by settling the papacy in Avignon, he began the "Babylonian captivity"; it was seventy years before the popes returned to Rome. Clement, completely subservient to Philip, also supported the French king in the disgraceful destruction of the Templars. This Order had turned to international banking after the demise of the kingdom of Jerusalem, and gradually had become creditors of the papacy and of practically all the kings and great lords of Europe, loaning money against future revenues. Philp IV was so deeply in debt to them that the total income of France could not have paid his loans. Their great wealth made them the object of envy and resentment, so accounts of their pride and luxury were distorted with lies about heresy and strange practices. By 1305, Philip was determined to suppress them and claim their assets to erase his huge debt to them; he forced Pope Clement to concur in this action. In 1307, de Nogaret arrested the Templars in France. Under the tortures of the Inquisition,+ they admitted to many crimes and blasphemies which they promptly recanted when removed from torture. At a special tribunal in Paris, fifty-four Templars were burned at the stake. Jacques de Molay, the last Grand Master, imprisoned at Chinon,* was burned at the stake in April 1314, stoutly maintaining the innocence of himself and his order, and pre- dicting that Clement, Philip and de Nogaret would appear before the bar of God's judgment within a year to answer for their crimes. Clement died within a month, de Nogaret soon thereafter, and Philip within six months. His daughter, Isabelle, married Edward II* of England. Three of his sons, Louis X,* Philip V,* and Charles IV* succeeded to the throne of France, but none was survived by a male heir, so the throne passed to Charles V, the first ruler from the house of Valois.* (Bibliog. 15, 68, 124)

Philip V, the Tall (1294-1322), king of France (1316-1322). Second son of Philip IV,* he became king after the death of his brother, Louis X,* and his infant nephew, John I. An assembly of barons and clergy proclaimed his right to reign, denying the right of his niece, Joan, on the grounds that the crown of France could not be transmitted through females. Such a precedent was used against Philip's own daughters after his death in 1322. (Bibliog. 98)

Philip VI, of Valois (1293-1350), king of France (1328-1350). Son of Charles of Valois, he was proclaimed king on the death of Charles IV* (1322-1328), the last Capetian king of France. This necessitated the rejection of the claim of Charles' daughter. His coronation was dis- puted by King Edward III* of England who claimed the crown as the son of Isabelle,* daughter of Philip IV. This dispute degenerated into the

Hundred Years War.* On May 24, 1337, Philip declared that Guyenne had been forfeited by Edward III "because of the many excesses, rebellious and disobedient acts committed by the king of England against Us and Our Royal Majesty," citing in particular his harboring the traitor Robert of Artois.* This generally was considered to have been the beginning of that extended warfare. In October, Edward responded with a formal letter of defiance to "Philip of Valois who calls himself king of France," and laid claim to the French throne. Even though Philip began his reign with a victory over the Flemish at Cassel (1328), he was defeated time and time again in the ensuing years of that war by the English under Edward III and his son, the Black Prince,* including such battles as Crécy,* and Poitiers.* He bought the town of Montpellier from the king of Majorca in 1349, and in that same year, also bought the Dauphine* from its count (or dauphin) in the name of his grandson, the future Charles V. By this acquisition, the borders of France reached the Alps. He died on August 22, 1350, at Nogent-le-roi. On the following Thursday, he was buried at Saint Denis, on the left side of the great altar, his bowels interred at the Jacobins at Paris and his heart at the convent of the Carthusians in Valois. Although he lost badly at Crécy* and at Calais,* he left France a far larger country than he found it. (Bibliog. 203)

Philip (c. 1177-1208), German king and duke of Swabia,* the rival of emperor Otto IV.* He was the fifth and youngest son of Emperor Frederick I,* and brother of Emperor Henry VI.* He became duke of Swabia on the death of his brother Conrad. In May 1197, he married Irene, daughter of the eastern emperor, Isaac Angelus,* and widow of Roger II,* king of Sicily, a lady described by the German poet Walter von der Vogelweide as "a rose without a thorn, a dove without guile." By her he had four daughters. He was murdered in Bamberg in 1208 by the count palatine+ of Bavaria,* Otto of Wittelsbach, to whom he had refused the hand of one of his daughters. (Bibliog. 68)

Philippa of Hainault (Hainaut), queen of England to Edward III.* Daughter of William II,* the Good, count of Hainaut, of Holland and of Zeeland, she married Edward in 1328, and bore him many sons. Edward, the oldest son, later became known as the Black Prince.* Philippa was a tall, beautiful woman with dark brown hair and eyes and a charming nature. Despite her husband's many infidelities, she remained devoted to him all her life. She was shrewd and sensible; her only faults seemed to have been extravagance and overdressing. (Bibliog. 203)

Philippe de Remi, sire de Beaumanoir (c. 1250-1298), French poet who wrote two romances, *Manekine*,* and *Jehan et Blonde** (or *Blonde d'Oxford*). As a youth, he served as page in England and Scotland during the reign of Henry III,* quite possibly serving in the entourage of Simon de Montfort,* count of Leicester, because Simon had much property in and derived income from Remi; Simon's son, Aumeri de Montfort, executed many deeds in Philippe's favor. Both of Philippe's romances revealed an extensive knowledge of England. He served as seneschal+ of Poitou and Saintonge, and as bailiff+ of Touraine and Senlis. He also was an able jurist, composing the famous *Coutumes de Beauvaisis*, an important document for French law. (Bibliog. 106, 127)

Philippe de Thaon, cleric and writer who lived in Thaon, near Caen, Normandy, during the reign of King Henry I* of England (1100-1135). He addressed his works to Adeliz of Louvain, wife of Henry I between 1121 and 1135. Among the oldest works in Anglo-Norman literature which survived, his works, *Bestiare* and *Lapidiare*, contained 37 entries on birds, beasts and gems, with allegorical significance ascribed to each. Some represent Jesus Christ, some represent man, some the Devil, and some the church. (Bibliog. 217)

Picardy, province in northeastern France. One of the last Carolingian centers in France, Picardy was subdivided among several feudal lords, the city of Laon remaining the capital of the kingdom until 987. The most important of its feudal units was the county of Vermandois which was annexed to the royal domain by Philip II* in 1185. (Bibliog. 98)

Picts, people in King Arthur's* time who lived in the highlands of Scotland with their capital at Inverness, and raided the lands south of the Firth of Forth. (Bibliog. 97)

Pinabel of Sorence, friend and peer of Ganelon* who came to Ganelon's trial with twenty-nine other relatives, and fought as Ganelon's champion against Thierry, Charlemagne's champion.* After he lost, he and his relatives were hanged in the *chanson de geste,** *Song of Roland.** (Bibliog. 112, 210)

Pleier, der, minor noble from an area near Scharding on the River Inn, south of Passau, he was a Middle High German* poet who wrote three Arthurian romances between 1250 and 1280: *Garel von dem Blühenden Tal** (ed. M. Walz, Freiburg, 1892); *Meleranz** (ed. Karl Bartsch, Stuttgart: *SLV* 61, 1861); and *Tandareis und Flordibel.* (ed. F. Khull, Graz, 1885). (Bibliog. 235)

podesta, 1) governor of one or more of the Lombard cities, appointed by Emperor Frederick I,* Barbarossa; 2) in medieval Italian republics, one of the chief magistrates with extensive powers. (Bibliog. 169)

Poitiers, Guillaume de (fl. 1075), Norman archdeacon of Lisieux and chaplain for William* the Conqueror. He wrote his *Histoire de Guillaume le Conquérant* about 1073-1074; his description of the battle of Hastings* was the best contemporary account available. (ed. and tr. French by Raymon de Foreville, Paris, 1952) (Bibliog. 99)

Poitiers, city in western France. In the early Middle Ages, Poitiers was one of the most important cultural centers in western Europe where poets, thinkers and theologians gathered. In 732 near Poitiers, Charles Martel defeated an army of invading Moors from Spain in what was described as one of the greatest victories for Christendom for saving Europe from "Moslem barbarism." In the 9th century, it became the capital and cultural center of the duchy of Aquitaine.* Under the leadership of Duke William IX,* Poitiers flourished with the poetry of the troubadours* and Romanesque art. It continued to develop under the presence of the ducal court until 1137 when Eleanor* of Aquitaine married first Louis VII* of France and then later Henry II* of England, and removed the ducal court from the city. In 1356, it was the site of one of the decisive battles of the Hundred Years War* when the Anglo-Gascon army under Edward,* the Black Prince, crushed the French army led by King John II* who was taken captive. It remained under English control until recaptured in 1370 by for France by Bertrand du Guesclin.* Its castle, built by Count William the younger in 1104, became the palace for the counts of Poitou* and dukes of Aquitaine. Its tower the Tour Maubergeon derived its name came from the old word "Mallberg," meaning a Merovingian tribunal. Under Countess Eleanor, it was enlarged by the addition of a grand salon. (Bibliog. 98, 196)

Poitiers, battle of (September 19, 1356), conflict between forces of King John II* of France and the outnumbered invading English forces under Edward,* the Black Prince, whom he had been pursuing. On Sunday, September 18, Edward drew his forces to a rest just below Poitiers, and spotted John's forces not far away. John followed the advice of Cardinal Talleyrand who urged him to keep the Truce of God and not fight on the Sabbath. A French knight, Geoffrey de Charnay, proposed settling the difference by a tourney between 100 knights on each side, but that suggestion was rejected by his companions for it would exclude too many of them from the glory and ransoms they were certain to obtain from combat. Overconfident because of their superiority of numbers, the French charged Edward's position on a hillside. Despite having 19 other knights dressed in armor identical to his—black armor with a white surcoat marked with a fleur-de-lys—King John II was captured in the ensuing battle, and the French lost huge numbers of men and horses. It was one of Edward's finest battles, and one of the worst defeats for French chivalry. (Bibliog. 223)

Poitou, province of west central France. As part of Aquitaine, it came to English control when Eleanor of Aquitaine* married King Henry II* of England, but was recovered for France by King Philip II,* Augustus, in 1204, and in 1241 it was bestowed on Alphonse, brother of Louis IX.* It was reconquered for England by Edward the Black Prince* in 1365, and ceded to England by the Treaty of Bretigny* in 1360; du Guescelin* won it back for France a few years later. Some of its important counts were

932 - Guillaume I, Tête d'Etoupe (Tow-Head)
963 - Guillaume II, Duc d'Aquitaine
990 - Guillaume III
1029 - Guillaume IV
1038 - Eudes, brother, duke of Aquitaine and Gascony
1058 - Gui Geoffroi (called Guillaume VI)
1127 - Guillaume VII
1137 - Eleanor of Aquitaine,* who married Henry II (1152)
1169 - Richard I* of England
1197 - Otto of Brunswick, Richard's nephew
1199 - John Lackland,* Richard's brother
(Bibliog. 98, 100)

Polignac, castle+ built on a volcanic extrusion in the middle of a plain in the Loire valley. Its walls crowned the vertical face of volcanic rock. The viscounts of Polignac used this fortress as a base of operations for brigandage, particularly against their neighbors, the bishops of Puy. After being outlawed, the Lord Pons, *vicomte* Polignac, joined with the *comte* d'Arvene in ravaging the countryside of Brionde in the 12th century. Threatened with excommunication by Pope Alexander III,* Pons journeyed to Clermont-Ferrand to submit. On his return, however, he continued his outlaw ways, as did his successor Heraclius, but on August 21, 1181, he was made to submit to public penance. He was stripped to the waist and flogged by the canons of the church of St. Julien of Brionde. (Bibliog. 196)

Pontefract castle,+ fortress in western Yorkshire built by Ilbert de Lacy late in the 11th century. There King Richard II* was murdered in 1400. (Bibliog. 247)

Ponthieu, ancient region in Picardy* in northern France. It became a countship in the 10th century; it passed to Castile* in 1251 through marriage but was returned to English control through the marriage of Edward I* to Eleanor of Castile in 1272. (Bibliog. 98, 241)

pope, head of the papacy; from 1061, the seat was held by the following:

1061-1073 Alexander II (Anselm, bishop of Lucca) [Milanese]
1073-1085 Gregory VII* (Hildebrand) [Tuscan]
1087-Victor III (Desiderius, abbot of Monte Cassino) [Italian]
1088-1099 Urban II* (Eudes de Lagery, bishop of Ostia) [French]
1099-1118 Paschal II (Ranier, abbot of San Lorenzo) [Italian]
1118-1119 Gelasius II (John of Gaeta) [Italian]
1119-1124 Calixtus II (Guy of Burgundy), archbishop of Vienne
        [Burgundian]
1124-1130 Honorius II (Lambert, bishop of Ostia) [Italian]
1030-1043 Innocent II (Gregory Papi) [Italian]
1043-1044 Celestine II (Guy) [Tuscan]
1144-1145 Lucius II (Gerard of Bologna) [Italian]
1145-1153 Eugenius III (Bernard of Pisa) [Italian]
1153-1154 Anastasius IV (Conrad) [Roman]
1154-1159 Adrian IV (Nicholas Breakspear) [English]
1159-1181 Alexander III (Roland Bandinelli) [Tuscan]
1181-1185 Lucius III (Urbaldo, bishop of Ostia) [Tuscan]
1185-1187 Urban III (Huberto Crivelli, archbishop of Milan) [Lombard]
1187-Gregory VIII (Albert of Morra) [Italian]
1187-1191 Clement III (Paul Scolaro) [Roman]
1191-1198 Celestine III (Hyacinth Bobocard) [Roman]
1198-1216 Innocent III* (Lothaire de Segni) [Roman]
1216-1227 Honorius III (Cencio Savelli) [Roman]
1227-1241 Gregory IX (Ugolino de Segni, bishop of Ostia) [Roman]
1241-Celestine IV (Geoffrey de Castiglione [Lombard]
1243-1254 Innocent IV (Sinibaldo Fieschi) [Genoese]
1254-1261 Alexander IV (Reinald de Segni, bishop of Ostia; nephew of
        Gregory IX) [Roman]
1261-1264 Urban IV (Jacques Pantaleon), [French]
1265-1268 Clement IV (Guy Foulquois) 1265-1268 [French]
1271-1276 Gregory X (Thealdo Visconti) [Lombard]

1276-Innocent V (Pierre de Tarantaise) [French]
1276-Adrian V (Ottoboni Fieschi, nephew of Innocent IV) [Genoese]
1276-1277 John XXI (Peter, archbishop of Braga)[Roman]
1277-1280 Nicholas III (John Gaetani Orsini) [Roman]
1281-1285 Martin IV (Simon de Brion) [French]
1285-1287 Honorius IV (James Savelli) [Roman]
1288-1292 Nicholas IV (Jerome of Ascali) [Italian]
1294-Celestine V (Peter Morrone) [Italian]
1294-1303 Boniface VIII (Benedetto Gaetani) [Roman]
1303-1304 Benedict XI (Nicholas Boccasino) [Italian]
1305-1314 Clement V (Bertrand de Got) [French]
1316-1334 John XXII (Jacques d'Euse) [French]
1334-1342 Benedict XII (Jacques Fournier) [Gascon]
1342-1352 Clement VI (Pierre Rogier) [French]
1352-1362 Innocent VI (Etienne d'Aubert) [French]
1362-1370 Urban V (Guillaume de Grimoard) [French]
1370-1378 Gregory XI (Pierre Rogier, nephew of Clement VI) [French]
    ROMAN LINE
1379-1389 Urban VI (Bartolomeo Prigano) [Neapolitan]
1389-1404 Boniface IX (Pietro Tomacelli) [Neapolitan]
1404-1406 Innocent VII (Cosimo de' Migliorati) [Neapolitan]
1406-1415 Gregory XII (Angelo Cornaro) [Venetian]
    AVIGNON LINE: Antipopes
1378-1394 Clement VII (Robert de Geneva) [French]
1394-1424 Benedict XIII (Pedro de Luna) [Aragonese]
(Bibliog. 124)

Porchester castle, Hampshire fortress built on old Roman ruins on the tip of a long spit of land. As at Pevensey,* so here, William I* strengthened this castle.+ Later, during the rebellion of Robert II,* Curthose, King Henry I* stationed troops there, and came to realize its importance. Once the strife subsided, Henry ordered this simple fortress strengthened by a large one-story keep with walls 12 feet thick, and a curtain wall and corner tower; later other stories were added. Henry II* used this keep as a prison and as a treasure-house. (Bibliog. 247)

Powys, Powys-Land, third part of Wales* which was bestowed by Roderick the Great, king of Wales, on his youngest son, Mervyn. Comprised of the counties of Montgomery and Radnor, with parts of Denbeigh, Brecknock, Merioneth and Shropshire, its principal seat was Matraval in Montgomeryshire; hence princes of Powys were called kings of Matraval. It continued in the family of Mervyn until Meredith ap

Blethyn divided it between Madoc and Griffith, his two sons. When Madoc died in 1160, King Henry II* made Griffith the lord of Powys, setting aside his title of prince. Then, in the reign of King Edward I,* Owen ap Griffith, descended from Griffith, surrendered both his place and title to the king in a Parliament in Shrewsbury, and received them again from the king to be held as a baron. Among its princes and kings were

 877 - Mervyn, third son of Roderick Mawr
 900 - Cadeth, prince of South Wales
 927 - Howel Dha, prince of all Wales
1073 - Meredith ap Blethyn who divided it between his two sons,
           Griffith who was made Lord Powys by Henry II, and Madoc on
           whose death in 1160, the land reverted to North Wales.
(Bibliog. 101)

Prester John, legendary Christian priest and king of a huge wealthy empire in the east. (See Prester John in volume 1.) (Bibliog. 71)

preudhomme, man of prowess. To call a man *preux* or *preudhomme* was to pay him the highest compliment. (Bibliog. 170)

Prince of the Blood, close blood relation to a monarch; usually brother to the king. Robert of Artois,* Alphonse of Poitiers, and Charles of Anjou were Princes of the Blood as younger brothers of King Louis IX* of France. See also *appanage+*; Louis VIII.* (Bibliog. 124, 203)

Princes of Wales, heirs of the royal blood of England to the English throne, and the dates of their elevation to that rank:

1284 - Edward of Carnarvon, son of Edward I*; afterwards King Edward
          II* (1307-1327)
1343 - Edward, the Black Prince,* eldest son of King Edward III* (d.
          1376)
1376 - Richard of Bordeaux, only surviving son of Edward the Black
          Prince; afterwards King Richard II* (1377-1399)
1399 - Henry of Monmouth, eldest son of Henry IV; afterwards Henry V
          (1413-1422) (See volume 1.) (Bibliog. 47)

De principis instructione. See Giraldus Cambrensis.

Prise de Cordres et de Sebille, chanson de geste* of the Garin de Monglane* cycle, related the capture of Cordres and Sebille and began with the wedding of Guibert d'Andrenas* and Agaie at Salerie. Her father (though killed in the Guibert d'Andrenas poem, he had been brought back to life for this work), Saracen King Judas took advantage of the festivities to attack. He captured Hernaut de Gironde (son of Aymeri de Narbonne), Bertrand, Guillaume d'Orange, and Guibert himself. Guibert was taken to Sebille and the remainder of the captives were entrusted to a nameless jailer at Cordres (Cordova). Nubie, the jailer's daughter, fell in love with Bertrand, drugged the entire town, and escaped with the prisoners. Then she helped the Christians capture her father and they finally reached Salerie. Then Cordres surrendered on the pleas of the jailer who had been converted to Christianity. Judas agreed to settle the matter by single combat (see duel+) between Butor and Guibert; the winner was to receive the hand of Agaie and the towns of Salerie and Cordres; if the Saracen champion, Butor, lost, Judas would become a Christian. Butor lost. [Poem ending was lost.] (ed. O. Densusianu, Paris: *SATF,* 1896) (Bibliog. 106, 231)

Prise d'Orange, *chanson de geste** of the Garin de Monglane* cycle; its story followed immediately after the *Charroi de Nîmes,** and explained the capture of the city of Orange and Guillaume's future title taken from it. Guillaume, bored with inactivity at Nîmes, heard a recently freed Christian praise the beauty of the Saracen Princess Orabel of Orange, the virgin wife of the Saracen King Thibaut d'Orange. Deciding to conquer Orange and its pagan Princess Orabel, Guillaume with two companions entered Orange disguised as Saracens, but they were recognized, captured and cast into prison. Orabel rescued them, and gave them arms with which to defend themselves until they were rescued by their comrades from Nîmes. The town was captured and Orabel was christened Guiborc* and married Guillaume. Historically, Guibourc was the real name of Count William of Toulouse's first wife; and Orange was a principal stop along the pilgrimage route, the "via Tolosana."+ (ed. Jean Frappier, Paris: *SEDES,* 1965) (Bibliog. 106, 231)

Prophecies of Merlin, supposedly a translation of prophecies from the Welsh, this work by Geoffrey of Monmouth* was completed by the end of 1135 and dedicated to his superior, Alexander, bishop of Lincoln. He included it later in his *Historia Regum Britanniae.** Geoffrey identified his Merlin as "the Ambrosius who prophesied in the time of King Vortigern." His material fell into three parts with no separations: events which already had taken place, or were supposed to have taken place, at the time he was writing, but which would have been the future. For example, his entry "Lion's cub shall be transformed into fishes of the sea" was a reference to King Henry I's* only son who drowned in the White Ship* disaster in 1120. A second part foretold events in the future for Geoffrey as well as Merlin, such as the coining of round half-pennies which had been discussed but not minted by 1135; and the conquest of Ireland which was easily foretold by anyone who followed national events. He changed the third part to include an astrological nightmare which led to confusion and eccentric interpretations. These prophecies were taken seriously by learned and wise people of many nations. Interestingly enough, Wace did not include them in his translation of Geoffrey's *Historia* but other translators did. (ed. and tr. Sebastian Evans, revised by Charles Dunn, *History of the Kings of Britain*, New York: E. P. Dutton, 1958, 137-152) (Bibliog. 10, 221)

Prose Lancelot, French work written between 1220 and 1230 that contained the *Lancelot,** the *Quest del Saint Graal,** and the *Mort le Roi Artu** (otherwise known as *Mort Artu**). Each of these works appeared to be by an individual author, but the general plan of the work united them. In this prose *Lancelot,* Lancelot, a hero of earthly mundane chivalry, was unworthy to view the marvels of the Holy Grail* because of his sins with Queen Guenevere.* Instead, those high adventures were reserved for his son, Galahad,* knight of perfect purity. Two others, Bohort (Bors) and Percival,* were chosen specially to participate with Galahad in the revelation of the holy mysteries at the castle of Corbenic,* the name used in this work for the Grail Castle of the Fisher Kings.* (ed. H. O. Sommer, *Vulgate Version of Arthurian Romances*, Washington: Carnegie Institute, 1909-1913; repr. New York: AMS, 1979) See also *Lancelot* proper; Vulgate versions. (Bibliog. 10, 78)

Prothesilaus, French romance written between 1174 and 1191 by Hue de Roteland.* This work detailed the theme of a fight between two brothers, Daunus of Apulia and Prothesilaus of Calabria, sons of Ipomedon. Prothesilaus was forced to flee, and after numerous adventures of combat and love in Crete and in Burgundy, he regained his hereditary estates as well as those of his brother, and won a charming wife. (ed. Franz Kluckow, *GrL* 45, I, 1924) (Bibliog. 231, 236)

Provence, province of southeast France bounded by the Rhône River, Mediterranean Sea and Italy. It was invaded by the Visigoths in the 5th century, the Franks in the 6th century, the Arabs in the 8th century, and Charles Martel recovered it for the Franks. It became the kingdom of Arles* in 933, and a part of the Holy Roman Empire in 1033. A major portion of the territory passed from the house of Aragon* to the Angevin* dynasty of Naples in 1246 through marriage. King René of Anjou left Provence to his nephew, Charles of Anjou,* who bequeathed it to King Louis IX* of France. (Bibliog. 98, 124)

Provins, French castle+ at the confluence of the Voulzie and Durtient rivers between Paris and Troyes. Though dating from the time of Theobald II, count of Champagne in the 12th century, its keep was called the Tower of Caesar. It was unique, for the rectangular base of the tower rose to a octagonal structure in the upper floors. Philip IV* (1285-1314) brought it under French control, but the English regained and enlarged it during the Hundred Year's War.* (Bibliog. 30)

Provisions of Oxford. See Oxford, Provisions of.

pseudo-Map Cycle. See *Vulgate Cycle.*

Pseudo-Turpin. See *Chronique de Turpin; Karlamagnus Saga.*

Pseudo-Wachier, first continuation of the *Conte del Graal** of Chrétien de Troyes.

Pulzella Gaia, Italian poem from the 14th century centering on Morgan la Fée.* Pulzella Gaia was Morgan's beautiful daughter, the fairy love of Gawain,* who by complying with her demand that he never tell her name, unspelled her from her serpent shape. She promised to grant his every wish provided that he not reveal her love, but on his boasting of her at a tourney at court, she had to surrender herself to Morgan. Her mother imprisoned her in a tower where she was forced to stand waist-deep in water, and to suffer transformation into a fish shape below the waist. Gawain set out on a quest for her, forced his way into Pela Orso, Morgan's tower where Pulzella was imprisoned, and replaced her with Morgan. Thus transformed by his love, Pulzella rode off with Gawain to Camelot.* (Bibliog. 85, 175)

Pynel, the Savage, kinsman of Lamorak,* he was the poisoner of Patryse at Queen Guenevere's* banquet; Niniane* revealed his guilt. (Bibliog. 145)

Q

Quatre Fils Aymon. See *Four Sons of Aymon.*

Queens of the Kings of England, women who served as consorts and queens for the kings of England:

Matilda of Flanders (1031-1083), consort of William I* (1050-1083), daughter of Baldwin, Count of Flanders
Matilda of Scotland (1079-1118), first consort of Henry I* (1100-1118), daughter of Malcolm III of Scotland
Adeliz (Adelicia) of Louvain (1102-1151), second consort of Henry I (1121-1135), daughter of Godfrey, duke of Brabant
Matilda of Boulogne (d.1151), consort of Stephen* (1128-1151), daughter of Eustace, count of Boulogne
Eleanor of Aquitaine (1122-1204), consort of Henry II* (1152-1189), daughter of the duke of Aquitaine and divorced wife of Louis VII* of France
Berengaria of Navarre (d. 1235?), consort of Richard I* (1191-1199), daughter of Sancho VI, king of Navarre
Iasbelle, (or Hawise, Avisa) (1185-1246), first consort of John* (1191-1200), daughter of William, earl of Gloucester. (Not crowned or acknowledged as queen)
Isabelle of Angoulême (1185-1246), second consort of John (1200-1216), daughter of Aymer, count of Angoulême
Eleanor of Provence (1222-1291), consort of Henry III* (1236-1272), daughter of Raymond, count of Provence
Eleanor of Castile (1244-1290), first consort of Edward I* (1254-1290), daughter of Ferdinand III, king of Castile
Margaret of France (1281-1317), second consort of Edward I (1299-1307), daughter of Philip III,* king of France
Isabelle of France (1295-1358), consort of Edward II* (1308-1327), daughter of Philip IV,* king of France
Philippa of Hainaut (1311-1369), consort of Edward III* (1328-1369), daughter of William, count of Holland and Hainaut

Anne of Bohemia (1366-1394), first consort of Richard II* (1382-1394),
    daughter of Charles IV,* emperor of Germany
Isabelle of Valois (1387-1410), second consort of Richard II
    (1395-1399), daughter of Charles VI,* king of France.
    (Bibliog. 47)

Queensborough castle.+ Also known as the Castle of Sheppey, this Kent
fortress was the only wholly new royal castle built in England during
the period of 1200-1400. Begun in 1361, it also had a unique design of
cylindrical and concentric fortification carried to the logical conclusion of perfect symmetry. Its six towers and leaded roof were not
completed until 1375. (Bibliog. 104, 247)

Quest del Saint Graal, French prose Arthurian romance written between
1215-1230, and considered part of the *Vulgate Cycle.** On Pentecost,
454 years after the Crucifixion, Galaad (Galahad),* already knighted,
was led to Arthur's* court in vermilion arms. He passed the test of
the Siege Perilous,+ thus proving that he was the long-awaited de-
liverer, and the supreme hero of the quest. When knights assembled in
the great hall, the grail floated in, preceded by thunder and lightning, and served each knight with whatever food he desired, and then
vanished. At that, the knights of the Round Table* vowed to search for
it, and departed in separate directions on their quest. Because most
of them did not understand what they sought, they soon met obstacles
and humiliations which forced them to return to court unfulfilled.
Lancelot understood, though, and took heed of his misfortunes, and entered a life of penitence; he visited the Grail castle,* but not to
achieve his quest, before returning to court. Only Galahad, Bohort and
Perceval were the chosen ones. They were welcomed at the castle of
Corbenic* by King Pelles* where eventually Galahad healed the king and
then died. Perceval died a year later; only Bohort survived to return
to Camelot to report his experiences. (ed. H. O. Sommer, *Vulgate
Version of the Arthurian Romances,* Washington: Carnegie Institute,
VII, 1913; repr. New York, AMS Press, 1967) (Bibliog. 10)

Quincy, Saer de (d. 1219), first earl of Winchester.* While a poor
knight, he had married the daughter of Robert III, earl of Leicester*
around 1170, and in 1204 succeeded to his wife's right to half of the
land of Robert IV, earl of Leicester. He was created earl of Winchester in 1207, and sided with the barons in their struggles with King
John.* He was one of the twenty-four* barons set up by Clause 61 of
the *Magna Carta* to exercise control over King John. As a result, John
took a particular dislike to Saer, and confiscated his lands in the

last years of his reign. Saer was captured at the battle of Lincoln*
in 1217, and on his release, went on a crusade+ and died at Acre+
shortly after his arrival in 1219. (Bibliog. 58)

Quinze Vingts, famous hospital built by King Louis IX* near the Saint
Honore gate of Paris for three hundred blind people of Paris.
(Bibliog. 178)

R

Die Rabenslacht, anonymous Middle High German* epic poem written late in the 13th century, and based on the historical battle at Ravenna between Theoderic* and Odovacer. In this poem, Dietrich von Bern (see Theoderic the Great) set out from his haven at Etzel's (Attila's*) court for Italy to fight Eormanrich (Odovacer) who earlier had driven him from his possessions. Accompanying him were his own younger brother and two children of Etzel, for whose safety he pledged his own life. He defeated Ermanrich in battle, but the three young men were killed in a fight with Ermanrich's supporter, Witege. Formerly in the service of Dietrich, Witege had deserted to Ermanrich's court. Recognizing him, the three young boys attacked him impetuously. After only a momentary hesitation, Witege slew all three. Distraught with grief, Dietrich pursued Witege to the sea where one of his kin, a mermaid, rescued him as Dietrich watched incredulously. Sadly, Dietrich returned to Etzel to whom his life was forfeit. Margrave+ Rudiger, however, interceded on his behalf, and effected a forgiveness and reconciliation between the two men. (ed. K. Mullenhoff, E. Martin, et al., *Das deutsche Heldenbuch*, 5 vols., Berlin, 1866-1873) (Bibliog. 235)

Dame Ragnell, hideous damsel whom Gawain* wed, thus achieving her disenchantment in Arthurian legend. This treatment of the Loathly Lady Transformed had appeared in other literatures: Irish, French, Old Norse and others. Three of the six English versions used Arthurian names for the characters: *Wedding of Sir Gawain and Dame Ragnell*, *Marriage of Gawain*, and Chaucer's *Wife of Bath's Tale*. (Bibliog. 1, 10)

Ralph Niger. See Niger, Ralph.

Ralph of Diceto, English chronicler born at Diss in Norfolk, he became dean of St. Paul's in London in 1180. His *Imagines historiarum*, 1148-1202, was based on Robert of Torigni's* *Chronicle* for the material up to 1172, but was original from that time onward; it was especially valuable for King Richard I's* and the early years of King John's* reigns following 1188, for it included many letters, papal bulls,+ and other documents.   (ed. William Stubbs, London: *Rolls Series,* 2 vols., 1876) (Bibliog. 99)

Ramelah (Rames), battles of (September 7, 1101 and May 1102). Saracen* forces based at Ascalon setting out to invade Palestine* were met by the pitifully small band of Christian horsemen and footsoldiers of the kingdom of Jerusalem under their new king, Baldwin I. His little kingdom consisted of nothing more than Jerusalem, and the three seaports of Jaffa, Arsuf and Caesarea. Rash and impetuous, Baldwin resolved to march against the 15,000 Moslem troops with the scanty force he could muster in Jerusalem, and not to wait several weeks for reinforcements to arrive from Antioch or Edessa. These two armies met at Ramelah, halfway between Jerusalem and Jaffa, on September 5. Dividing his 200 knights, 60 sergeants and 900 infantrymen into six corps containing both horse and footsoldiers, Baldwin marched his forces right into the midst of the enemy who had stretched its forces along a front that badly outflanked the Christians. Leaving their infantry a half-mile behind them, the cavalry dashed into the Saracen line that folded its line around them and attacked from all sides. Annihilating the two squadrons to the right, the Moslems concentrated on the three attacking squadrons in their midst when Baldwin with the remaining horse and infantry dashed into the thickest part of the fray, giving much-needed impulse to his hard-pressed forces. At that sudden thrust, the Saracen line broke and fled, along with its victorious left wing who thought the battle had been won. While the cavalry settled the battle in the center, the infantry were beset by the horsemen at the extreme positions of the wings. Success was so much in doubt that the Moslem* forces from its left wing rode up the the walls of Jaffa, displaying shields and helmets of the crusaders, to announce their victory over Baldwin. This group was returning to its base when it met the remainder of the victorious Christian forces, who cut it down almost to a man. In the battle, one-third of Baldwin's cavalry and almost half of his infantry was lost, but the Moslem forces suffered much more heavily; even Saad-ed-Dowleh, the Moslem leader, had fallen from his horse and been killed. The whole battle took less than one hour.

In May of the following year, the Saracens once more marched from Ascalon to Ramelah where they pitched their camp. And once more, Baldwin set out to meet them without waiting for reinforcements from the outlying towns of his tiny kingdom. With only 200 knights, he marched on what he believed to be an army equal to his in size, but found to his dismay as he rode into the center of the line in a repeat of the previous year's tactics, that their numbers were too great, and that he did not have the infantry behind him to relieve the pressure of the enfolding flanks of enemy forces. Only by sheer will, he and a few managed to cut their way out of this mêlée,+ leaving behind over 150 dead knights. He sailed from Arsuf to Jaffa and obtained the much needed reinforcements which would have been his to use had he but waited for their arrival. With that group and others newly arrived from the west, he attacked the Saracens once more in the field. But this time, he followed the lessons he had learned. His 7,000 footsoldiers armed with bow and arbalests+ kept the Moslem horses at bay while the knights rode out to charge and beat back every enemy attack. The enemy finally rode off, deserting their camp and the kingdom of Jerusalem to the Christians. (Bibliog. 166)

Ranulph (Rannulf) de Gernon (d. 1153), earl of Chester and powerful English baron+ who ruled over Chester,* a palatinate+ in western England.* His domain extended over almost one-third of the entire country of England because in addition to the Chester palatinate, he had inherited large estates in Lincolnshire. He was eager to recover the honour+ of Carlisle which his father had held but which he had been forced to yield to King Henry I,* and which subsequently King Stephen* had granted to the son of the king of Scotland* who had married the daughter of Robert of Gloucester.* In 1140, Ranulph seized and occupied the castle of Lincoln. After King Stephen rode to oust him, Ranulph left the city in the hands of his wife and brother, and slipped out to obtain reinforcements. He gathered men from his Chester area, including some Welsh troops, and was joined by his father-in-law, Robert of Gloucester, with his troops which included a group of desperate men who had been forced to forfeit their holdings because they had supported the cause of the Empress Matilda.* On February 2, 1141, the two forces met at the battle of Lincoln.* Stephen's forces lost. Ranulph was poisoned in 1153 by his wife and her lover. (Bibliog. 180)

Raoul de Cambrai, chanson de geste* written possibly by Bertolai de Laon at the end of the 12th century; it usually was classed with the Doön de Mayence* cycle. Three years after the death of Raoul Taillefer, count of Cambrai, his young son Raoul was disinherited by King Louis* so that the fief+ could be awarded to another knight. Both his mother and uncle became outraged but could do little to right that wrong. Raoul grew to manhood, and after he was knighted and was made the king's seneschal,+ his uncle reminded him to demand the return of his rightful fief. King Louis refused his demand, but to placate his anger, promised him the estate of the next count who died. This was Herbert of Vermandois who was survived by four grown sons. Despite his mother's warning about dispossessing others as he himself had been dispossessed, Raoul insisted that the king keep his word. His mother cursed him as she left, and this curse changed him into a cruel and merciless fighter. He invaded the Vermandois and burnt the monastery of Origni with some of the nuns still inside. One of the nuns who perished was the abbess, the mother of Bernier, one of Raoul's vassals+ whose father was Ybert of Ribemont, one of the four sons of Herbert. At this outrage, Bernier renounced his homage to Raoul, and joining his father and uncles in their conflict against Raoul, met his foe in combat and killed him. Raoul's uncle, Guerri le Sor, continued the battle but was defeated. Carrying Raoul's body with him, he returned to Cambrai. Gautier, Raoul's nephew, swore to avenge his uncle's death, and had the opportunity to test Bernier five years later. Their prolonged war finally ended at the court of the king in Paris when Louis directed that their dispute be settled by single combat.* (See duel.+) Half-killing each other, neither man won a decisive victory. Bernier then begged the forgiveness of Raoul's mother which she granted, and then after he married Guerri le Sor's daughter, and the two enemies lived in peace. Bernier and Guerri then journeyed together on a pilgrimage to St. James of Compostella,* and on their return, Bernier was reminded of the fate of Raoul at Origni. This stirred up so angry a memory in Guerri that he attacked and killed Bernier as he bent over a spring to get a drink of water; and the war resumed. Guerri was besieged by his grandsons, Bernier's sons, at Arras, and after they refused his pleas for forgiveness, he rode off into the night to become a hermit. This story was based on the historical Count Herbert of Vermandois who died in 943, leaving four sons against whom Rodolphe de Gouy started a war. After several years, he was killed by Herbert's sons, much to the grief of King Louis. The King Louis in this story was Louis IV d'Outremer.* (tr. Jessie Crosland, London: Chatto and Windus, 1926) (Bibliog. 106, 231)

Raoul de Wanneville, sacristan of the church of Rouen whom King Henry II* of England appointed chancellor+ after the murder of Thomas à Becket.* He left the Chancery for the bishop's throne at Liseux. (Bibliog. 178)

Raymond de Puy (1121-1160), master of the Hospitallers+ who changed the character of that order from one which merely tended the sick and defended hospitals into a military organization, following the example of the Templars.+ Under his leadership the Hospitallers grew to become the main armed force in the Holy Land. (Bibliog. 98)

I Reali di Francia, collection of French epics, amplifying and pseudo-historializing Charlemagne* material based primarily on earlier Italian prose versions of Carolingian stories. These were translated into Italian prose by Andrea de' Magnabotti, who was born in Barberino near Florence in 1370; he was better known as Andrea de Barberino.* This work contained *Fioravante, Buovo d'Antona, Berte, Karleto,* and *Berte e Milone.** (ed. G. Casini, Rome: Collezione I grandi secoli, 1967) (Bibliog. 231)

rebel vassals, one of the series of *chansons de geste** which centered on vassals rebelling against Charlemagne* for one reason or another. Chief among them was Doön de Mayence.* (A *chanson de geste* about him survived only in a late 13th-century form.) Thus, cousins of Ogier and of Huon, and of Gaufrey* and others were said to be brothers of Girart de Roussillon and were designated his kindred, sons Doön de Mayence. Gaufrey, Ogier's father, was the subject of a special epic, based on the old Ogier epic, and included material from the *Huon de Bordeaux.** (Bibliog. 231)

Redvers (Reviers), Baldwin de. See Reviers, Baldwin de

Reginald de Dunstanville, illegitimate son of King Henry I* who was made earl of Cornwall* in 1141. He fortified a small peninsula on the northern shore of Cornwall to which the name Tintagel* was applied. (Bibliog. 188)

regulus. See Brehon law.

Reinfrid von Braunschweig, Middle High German* romance written anonymously around 1300 by a Swiss living in the Lake Constance region. It linked a legend of Heinrich der Löwe (see Henry the Lion), duke of Saxony (1142-1180), with a lion, after the manner of Yvain,* although the lion appeared only in a dream. To the hero's court came a squire to announce that the king of Denmark's daughter, Yrkane, was to hold a Round Table+ tourney.+ The victor in the tourney was to receive a turtledove, and in a sword fight to receive a golden ring and a kiss from the princess. Reinfrid decided to attend, and gathering his knights and a company of minstrels, he went to Linion. He overthrew many knights in the tourney and won the turtledove, and the minstrels sang his praises. On the next day, he won the sword and the kiss.

Later he defended the princess against the slander of a rival lover. He then journeyed to the east for a series of adventures which paralleled those in *Herzog Ernst*,* including the magnetic mountain and the sirens episodes. The work stopped where Reinfrid's return home was interrupted. (ed. Karl Bartsch, Stuttgart: *BLV* 109, 1871) (Bibliog. 86)

Renaud de Dammartin, count of Boulogne. Architect of diplomatic secret negotiations between King John* of England and the German royal court in 1202, he carefully rebuilt the old coalition formed earlier by Richard I* among princes in the Low Countries. Renaud was a cultivated, ambitious, and versatile man who was as much at home with troubadours as with warriors on the battlefield. Philip II,* Augustus, of France had recently quarreled with him and had seized his Norman fiefs+ of Mortain, Domfront, and Aumale, and then had occupied the county of Boulogne itself. With such an incentive to revenge, Renaud focussed all his energy on the ruin of France. Enlisting his kinsman, Count Theobald of Bar,* he communicated with the count of Flanders, the Emperor Otto,* and with Otto's brother, Henry, the count palatine,+ before he left for England early in 1212. There, he and King John bound themselves with a solemn treaty to make no separate peace with the king of France. John told the vicomte de Thouars that these things would be done publicly so that "our friends may rejoice and our enemies be openly confounded." In return for his efforts, Renaud received from John the fiefs in England that formerly belonged to the counts of Boulogne, along with £1,000 a year for three years. His greatest contribution, however, was winning Flanders to John's coalition. He had visited Flanders before going to England, and paved the way for John's message to Ferrand, count of Flanders requesting an alliance. Ferrand, son of Sancho I of Portugal, had recently become count of Flanders by marring the eldest daughter of Baldwin IX, former count of Flanders, who had died a captive in the hands of the Bulgarians. Sancho's natural allegiance with Philip Augustus had been torn asunder when Philip's son, Louis, seized two of his towns near the Flanders border, and refused to relinquish them. Instead of cooperating with Ferrand, King Philip responded to these demands by overrunning Flanders. At this, Sancho threw his lot in with the English. (Bibliog. 180)

Renaut, Jehan (Jean Renart), French author of several romances in the 13th century: *Lai de l'ombre*,* *l'Escoufle*,* *Galeron de Bretayne*,* and *Guillaume de Dôle*.* (Bibliog. 231)

Renaut de Montauban. See *Four Sons of Aymon.*

Renier de Gennes, father of Oliver* and Aude in the *Song of Roland.** (Bibliog. 210)

Rencesvals, (Roncevaux), (Roncesvals), town and mountain pass on the road between Pampelune and St.Jean-Pied-de-Port where the Saracen forces of King Marsile* of Saragossa attacked and killed Charlemagne's* *douzepeers** as they were escorting Charlemagne's baggage train back to France from his seven-year campaign in Spain. It was the scene of the main battle in the *Song of Roland.* (Bibliog. 210)

Reneward (Rainouart) episode, second part of the *Chanson de Guillaume** which relegated Guillaume, the hero, to second place, and elevated Reneward, the kitchen-knave with a club on his shoulder, to be the protagonist. (Bibliog. 106)

Rennewart, Middle High German* epic written in the middle of the 13th century by the Swabian, Ulrich von Türheim. This continuation of Wolfram von Eschenbach's *Willehalm* drew on material from the *chansons de geste.** It was mainly concerned with Rennewart, the son of heathen Prince Terramer and of Rennewart's son, Malefer. (ed. A. Hubner, Berlin: *DTM*, 39, 1938) (Bibliog. 86)

Restormel castle, motte and bailey+ castle+ in Cornwall that had no bailey. Its motte was 125 feet in diameter and was self-contained. Its keep was a simple wooden palisade which was replaced with stone walls early in the 13th century. By then, a stone gatehouse had been erected. Held for Simon de Montfort* by Baldwin FitzTurstin during the Barons' War,* this fortress later was acquired by Richard of Cornwall,* King Henry III's* brother, and passed along to his successor, Earl Edmund. He converted its shell keep into a residence with a hall, chamber and kitchen. Edward,* the Black Prince, was given this castle in 1337 and spent a considerable sum in maintaining it. (Bibliog. 104, 247)

Reviers (Redvers), Baldwin de, earl of Devon. Hearing the rumor of the death of King Henry I* in April 1136, Baldwin, son and heir of Richard de Reviers of Normandy, was the first to revolt. He seized the royal castle+ of Exeter, withstood a long siege by King Stephen,* and ultimately was allowed to withdraw his forces on surrendering the castle. Stephen then chased him to the Isle of Wight* and drove him and his family into exile from it. He took refuge with the count of Anjou,* and soon was conducting raids into Normandy. In spring 1138, he was captured in Normandy by Engurrand de Say, a partisan of Stephen. Regaining his freedom, he returned to England in 1139 shortly before the Empress Matilda,* and landing at Wareham, seized Corfe* castle which he defended successfully against the king, forcing him eventually to lift the siege. For this act, he was created the earl of Devon* by the Empress Matilda. His brother and heir, William de Reviers, also called de Vernon, earl of Devon and lord of the Isle of Wight, took part in the second coronation+ of King Richard I* in 1194, as one of the earls who bore the canopy. He was a consistent supporter of King John,* and died in 1217. His son and heir, Baldwin II (1200-1216), married Margaret, daughter and heir of Warin FitzGerold, the king's chamberlain. On Baldwin's death at age 16, his widow was ed by King John just before his death to marry the notorious Faulkes de Breauté,* at whose downfall she was rescued on the surrender of Bedford castle on August 14, 1224. Directly after this, she demanded that her marriage be annulled because she had been taken prisoner in time of war and had been forced to marry Faulkes without her consent. Faulkes was sentenced to be exiled forever, and her marriage to him was annulled. (Bibliog. 47)

Rhonabwy's Dream, early 13th century Welsh story of Arthurian material. Included in the *Mabinogion*, this tale described how Rhonabwy had been sent to England to hunt down his rebellious brother. Falling asleep in a hovel, he dreamed about meeting someone who bragged about starting the battle of Camlann by distorting messages between Arthur* and Medrawd (Mordred*). Subsequent events involved him with Arthur, now alive again, and troops mustering for the battle of Badon which did not take place, for a truce was agreed on. (tr. Gwyn Jones and Thomas Jones, London: Everyman, 1970) (Bibliog. 10)

Rhys ap Gruffyd (d. 1196), "The Lord Rhys," prince of South Wales of the house of Dynevor, who made his residence at the castle at Cardigan. He rendered homage to Henry II* at Pembroke in 1171, and was appointed royal justiciar+ for all South Wales. When King Richard I* sent Prince John* and William Longchamps,* his chancellor,+ to suppress rebellious Welshmen under Rhys in 1189, the Welsh were impressed and subdued by this display of force. Rhys went to Oxford under a safe conduct+ issued by Prince John to render homage to Richard I as he had done to Henry II. Richard, however, was too busy to receive him. Highly insulted by this slight, Rhys returned to Wales in anger. Although he was an important Welsh prince, he was better remembered for the affair which he held at his castle in 1176, a historic bardic entertainment called an *eisteddfod*, wherein poets and harpists contended in amicable rivalry. (Bibliog. 7, 68)

ri. See Angus; Brehon law.

Richard I (1157-1199), king of England from 1189 to 1199. Third son of Henry II* and Eleanor* of Aquitaine, as his mother's favorite, he was designated the queen's special heir to the county of Poitou* and the duchy of Aquitaine.* Influenced deeply by his mother's love for her homeland, he remained basically a Frenchman all his life. He never learned the English language, and spent most of his time in France, even after his elevation to the throne. Inheriting all the love of warfare, the violent temper and the military genius of his forebears, he was happiest when he was fighting. After he was installed as duke of Aquitaine at the age of 14, his love for that province motivated practically all of his actions. His interest in the art of war led him to learn about military engines, fortress design, tactics, and military strategy. He joined with King Philip II* of France in the third crusade,+ becoming the undisputed leader of the Christian forces after Philip left the Holy Land to return to France. He won resounding victories over the Saracens* under Saladin* at Acre,* and at Arsuf.* Shortly thereafter, on his way back home to counter the threats to his crown by the schemes of his younger brother, Prince John,* and Philip of France, Richard was captured by Leopold* of Austria and held for ransom in the castle at Trifels by the Holy Roman Emperor, Henry VI.* Before obtaining his freedom, Richard was compelled to surrender his kingdom to Henry VI and then to receive it back as a fief+ of the empire. Even though on his deathbed, the emperor released Richard from that obligation, it still had had political significance. The emperor had wanted to break the power of France using Richard as the instrument. On his way back to England after being ransomed for 100,000 marks+ of silver, Richard secured the alliance of many of the leading princes of Germany and the Low Countries by promising annual pensions. Among those who swore homage and fealty to him against the king of France were the dukes of Austria, Swabia, Brabant (or Louvain, as the English recorded his title), and Limburg, the count of Holland, and Baldwin, son of the count of Hainault. Richard returned to England, turned his government over to Hubert Walter* and returned to France to renew his constant battles with Philip II. He died there at Chaluz on April 11, 1199, from a crossbolt wound to the neck, and was buried beside his father at the abbey of Fontevrault* where subsequently he was joined by his mother, Eleanor, in 1204.

A comparison of Richard I of England with Philip II* of France revealed that these two men of similar rank or station could not have been more different. Richard had shown himself to be impulsive, rash, open-hearted and open-handed, recklessly brave, hot-blooded, imaginative and a poet. Philip, on the other hand was cold, sly, cautious, cowardly, and scheming. He deserted the crusade+ in the summer of 1191, which action, in Richard's mind contributed more than anything else to the failure of that expedition. To that cowardly act in Richard's eyes, Philip had done far worse than merely desert his fellow crusaders. He had sneaked back to France, encouraged Richard's scheming younger brother Prince John* in his rebellion and treachery against Richard, tried to persuade the Emperor Henry VI to keep Richard in captivity or to sell him like a slave to the king of France, and then took advantage of Richard's absence to try to steal Normandy from him. On his deathbed, Richard confessed that he had not been able to receive Holy Communion for seven years (an untruth, for he did receive it in 1194) because "in his heart he bore mortal hatred for the king of France." (Bibliog. 7, 27, 92, 163, 180)

Richard I, duke of Normandy whose sister Emma married first King Ethelred* the Unready of England, and upon his death, married King Cnut* (Canute) of Norway who ruled England until 1035. Their son, Edward,* the Confessor, became king of England in 1042, and died in 1066. Richard's grandson, William,* became duke of Normandy, and claimed the English throne on the death of Edward through his relation to Emma, his great-aunt. (Bibliog. 69)

Richard Coeur de Lion, Middle English* metrical romance written about 1240 in rhyming couplets that combined historical and romantic materials. It contained minute details of siege operations and equipment, and made accurate references to geographical localities. At its center lay the superhuman demonic personality of Richard, a beloved and rousing leader. His mother was made to be supernatural; angels and St. George paid him visits; and French monarchs were depicted as cowards, bribe-takers, and braggarts. Its story began with King Henry of England seeking a bride, and encountering Cassodorien, daughter of the king of Antioch. They married, but she insisted that she would not remain in church for the elevation of the Host. When detained forcibly one Sunday, she shook herself loose, and grabbed her daughter and son, John, and flew through the roof to be seen no more; she dropped John back into the church. Richard remained behind, and shortly thereafter succeeded his father to the throne. He tested his knights in a three-day's tournament+ and then made a pilgrimage to the

Holy Land. On his return trip, he was captured by the emperor of Germany, helped by the emperor's daughter with whom he had an affair, killed the emperor's son in a duel of "pluck buffet," tore out and ate the heart of a lion sent to his cell to kill him (hence *Coeur de Lion*, "lion hearted"), and returned to England after being ransomed for half its wealth. After several months, he departed again for the Holy Land on a crusade.+ His experiences there proved him to be a valiant knight and stalwart leader. He fought and won a duel with Saladin,* riding a magical steed given him by that Moslem leader, concluded a truce with him and then returned home to England. (tr. Bradford Broughton, New York: E. P. Dutton, 1966) (Bibliog. 28)

Richard de Templo (fl. 1190-1229), prior of the Augustinian priory of Holy Trinity Church, London, and author of *Itinerarium perigrinorum et Gesta Regis Ricardi*. This account of the third crusade long was ascribed to Geoffrey de Vinsauf,* but now is recognized as having been written by Richard. It incorporated a large amount of material from Ambroise's *Estoire de la Guerre Sainte*. (tr. as "Itinerary of Richard I," London: Bohn's Antiquarian Library, 1848; repr. and ed. Kenneth Fenwick, *The Third Crusade*, London: Folio Society, 1958) (Bibliog. 63, 99)

Richard FitzGilbert de Clare. See Strongbow.

Richard le Pèlerin (the Pilgrim), French poet from Artois reputed to have written two poems about the crusades+: *Chanson d'Antioche** and *Chanson de Jerusalem.** Both originals were lost, and these poems survived only in revisions and redactions made by Graindor de Douai* between 1180 and 1200, who also wrote a totally imaginary poem about the crusades, *les Chetifs.** (Bibliog. 106, 231)

Richard of Devizes. See Devizes, Richard de.

Richard of Ely. See FitzNeal, Richard.

Richmond, English city in Richmondshire, not a county in itself but a portion of Yorkshire lying to the northwest of that county. Richmond, the chief town, was built by Alan I the Red, count of Brittany,* the first earl of that locale after the Norman invasion. Alan's father was Geoffrey, duke of Brittany, who had married Hawise, daughter of Richard I,* duke of Normandy, by whom he had two sons, Alan and Endon. Endon's son, Alan I, the Red, became count of Brittany, and fought at Hastings* along with many other Bretons in the invasion forces. As his reward he received a considerable portion of the forfeited lands of Earl Edwin of Yorkshire. According to the *Domesday*+ survey in 1086, he held over 400 manors. He probably erected the castle at Richmond which became the *caput** of the honour,+ but it was not so listed in the *Domesday* survey; it was, however, the *caput* of the honour which during the 12th and 13th centuries was more often styled the honour of Brittany owing to the tenure of the reigning dukes. Alan stood by King William II* during the rebellion of 1088, and became a suitor for the hand of Matilda, daughter of King Malcolm of Scotland, later queen of Henry I,* but he died unmarried in 1089, and was succeeded by his brother, Alan II, the Black, who also died unmarried five years later. Their youngest brother, Stephen, succeeded his elder brother to the Breton lands and Alan the Black to the honour of Richmond, uniting all the possessions of the family. He died in 1135 and was succeeded in the honour by his second son, Alan III, the Black (1097-1146), who seems to have been the first to be styled earl of Richmond. Alan III married the daughter of Conan III, duke of Brittany. He sided with King Stephen* and was forced to flee from the king's side at the battle of Lincoln* in 1141. Captured by Ranulph, earl of Chester,* he was forced to do homage and to surrender to Reynold de Dunstanville the earldom of Cornwall which King Stephen had granted to him earlier. He died in Brittany in 1145, and was succeeded by his son, Conan IV (d. 1171), duke of Brittany and earl of Richmond.

Although underage, Conan seems to have been recognized as earl of Richmond immediately. About 1155, he went to Brittany where he besieged and captured his stepfather, and became duke of Brittany, and seized the *comté* of Nantes upon the death in 1158 of Geoffrey, brother of King Henry II.* At that, Henry ordered Richmond seized, and crossed the Channel; Conan made peace with him. In 1166, when his daughter, Constance, was betrothed to Geoffrey, third surviving son of Henry II, Conan surrendered Brittany to the king before he died in 1171; his widow married Humphrey de Bohun,* constable+ of England in 1175. Constance was betrothed to Geoffrey when she was 5 years of age in 1166, and when she married him in 1181, he became recognized as duke of Brittany and earl of Richmond. He had left England for Brittany in 1179 and returned only once in 1184. He was killed in a tournament in Paris in August 1186, leaving a posthumous son, Arthur,* born March 29, 1187. In 1190, his uncle, Richard I,* arranged for Arthur's marriage to Ada, daughter of Tancred* of Sicily. Arthur, earl of Richmond, was recognized as heir presumptive* of his uncle Richard, but the Bretons had him educated by the king of France together with his own son. When Richard died in 1199, Arthur was in Brittany. After Arthur's disappearance in 1202, King John committed all the lands of

Richmond, except the castles of Richmond and Bowes, to the earl of Leicester,* and on his death, gave them to the earl of Chester. The rest John took into his own hands. Among its later earls were

1202 - Guy, viscount of Thouars, second husband of Constance
1209 - Randolph of Chester,* surnamed Blundeville, third husband of Constance
1230 - Peter, earl of Dreux, called Meau-clerk, duke of Brittany and earl of Richmond by right of his wife Alice, the eldest daughter and co-heiress of Guy de Thouars and Constance
1231 - Peter of Savoy, uncle to Queen Eleanor,* wife of Henry III*
1286 - John de Dreux, duke of Brittany, who married Beatrice, daughter of King Henry III
1305 - Arthur de Dreux, earl of Richmond
1312 - John de Dreux, son of Arthur, duke of Brittany
1341 - John de Montfort, half-brother of John de Dreux, duke of Brittany
1342 - John of Gaunt,* afterward duke of Lancaster.*
(Bibliog. 47, 66, 101)

Richmond castle, Yorkshire fortress built by Alan the Red, son of the count of Penthièvre, who began building the castle in 1071. A great curtain wall dating from the 11th century formed two sides of a triangular defense, the third side being the River Swale. Its great square keep, over 100 feet high, was built over the gatehouse. Three towers were erected on its wall, one of which, called the Robin Hood Tower, held William the Lion* of Scotland after he was captured in 1174 on a raid near Alnwick. This castle formed the administrative and military center of the great honour+ of Richmond which came into the hands of the crown on the death in 1171 of the fifth earl of Richmond, Conan. King Henry II* thereupon gave it to his son Geoffrey who recently had married Constance, daughter and heir of Conan. (Bibliog. 104, 247)

de Ridder Metter Mouwen, (Dutch, *Knight of the Sleeve*) Middle Dutch romance composed around 1300 about a foundling who attended a monastic school for ten years before going to King Arthur's* court where the queen knighted him. With the sleeve of Clarette, his beloved, fastened on the tip of his lance, he passed through many adventures, conquered knights, giants, a dwarf, a lion, and finally won the hand of Clarette at a tournament at Arthur's court. (ed. B. M. Stempel, Leiden, 1914) (Bibliog. 10)

Rigord (d. c. 1209), monk of St. Denis* who began his career as a physician in Languedoc. His work, *Gesta Philipi Augusti*, was abridged and continued by William of Armorica (Guillaume le Breton), chaplain of King Philip II,* Augustus, of France. These works were valuable for the relations with France of English kings Henry II,* Richard I* and John.* (tr. into French, F. P. Guizot, *Collection des Memoires*: "Vie de Philippe-Auguste," Paris, 1825) (Bibliog. 99)

Rions, Ryons, Rience, king of Ireland, Northgalis and Many Isles in Arthurian legend. He had an interesting hobby of trimming his cloak with the beards of the kings he conquered. He fought his great war against Leodegrance of Cameliard. Shortly after Arthur* acquired Excaliber,* Rions sent him word that his cloak was adorned with the beards which eleven kings had shaved off and presented to him as tokens of their homage to him, and he wanted Arthur's beard to make it an even dozen. However, after he was captured by the two brothers, Balan and Balin,* Rions surrendered to Arthur rather than be killed. (Bibliog. 145)

Der Ritter mit dem Bock. See *Gaurel von Muntabel.*

Rittertreue, anonymous Middle High German* verse story of the 14th century. Willekan von Montauban, a knight on his way to a tournament, spent all his money for an appropriate funeral for a dead knight for whose internment no one had been willing to pay. He then was unable to pay for a horse for the tournament, but finally obtained one on loan from a knight by promising to give him half of any prize he won in the tournament. Unfortunately for Willekan, the prize turned out to be his lady's hand in marriage. After winning the tournament, Willekan reluctantly conceded his share to the knight, and was immediately rewarded; the whole procedure had been a test of his truth to his word. The horse owner proved to be the spirit of the knight whom Willekan had generously buried, and he ascended into heaven leaving Willekan in sole possession of his bride. (Bibliog. 86)

Robert II, joint king of France (996-1031) with his father, Hugh Capet*; crowned on Christmas Day, 979. He was an educated and pious man who was an accomplished warrior as well. His reign, however, was noted for the troubles caused by his marital difficulties. He ruled jointly with his father without any discord until he divorced his first wife, Rosela of Flanders, considerably older than he, and married Bertha of Blois, whom both his father and the pope opposed. Nonetheless, Robert kept her as his wife. After Hugh died in 996, however, Robert succumbed to the pressure of the pope, an old friend, and repudiated Bertha, and then married Constance of Arles, a shrew who made his life miserable. He soon rejected her and summoned back Bertha, but the pressures of the pope became too strong and he submitted to his demands, and once more rejected Bertha and summoned Constance to his bed. She became the mother of his three sons. In 1017, Constance demanded the consecration of her son Hugh as king, while her husband was still alive. Once he had been consecrated as king, however, Hugh fled from his mother's overbearing treatment to live a life of plunder and to die at age 18 in 1025. King Robert then made plans to bestow the crown on his second son, Henry, but because primogeniture+ had not been agreed on as the method used to decide the succession yet, Constance pressed for the crown to be given to the third son, Robert of Burgundy. Nevertheless, Henry I (1031-1060), the second son, was crowned, despite the fury of the queen, and after the death in 1031 of his father, Robert II, she tried every means she could to dethrone him; because he already had been crowned, however, she was unsuccessful, and later, in 1059, Henry secured the coronation of his son, Philip I.* (Bibliog. 124, 178)

Robert II, *"Curthose"* (1054?-1134), duke of Normandy, and eldest son of Duke William II* of Normandy and King William I* of England. Twice the Norman barons swore fealty to him as William's successor, and that was confirmed by the king of France as overlord. He also probably received the homage of Malcolm III of Scotland in 1072 which implied his recognition as heir to the English throne. Robert was called "Curthose" or "Gambaron" as nicknames because of his short fat figure and fat face. Dissatisfied with his position, he revolted in 1078. He was forced to flee from his country, but returned in 1079 and fought against his father, but was forgiven. On the death of his father in 1087, he became Duke Robert II of Normandy, but not king of England, and he took no steps to oust his younger brother, William II,* from the English throne. He was constantly at odds with his brothers. He imprisoned the youngest, Henry,* and in 1089, he and William II dispossessed Henry and seized his lands. In 1094, Robert and William again were fighting, but this time Robert was aided by the King Philip I* of France. It ended in 1096 when Robert embarked on a crusade,+ having pledged Normandy to William for 10,000 marks to raise the money for his trip. He took part in the battles at Dorylaeum* and Antioch* and the siege of Jerusalem where he won fame for his valor and generosity. On his return to Normandy, he learned that his brother William had died, and that Henry had claimed the throne. He crossed to England in 1101 intending to contest Henry's claim, but Henry bought him off. These two still disputed over the next four years until the battle of Tinchebrai* in 1106 at which Henry captured Robert. Taking him to England, Henry kept Robert imprisoned for the remaining twenty-eight years of his life, first at the Tower of London and then at Devizes* and Cardiff castles+; he was not treated with cruelty, however. He died in 1134 leaving a son, William the Clito.* (Bibliog. 58, 68)

Robert de Beaumont. See Leicester, earl of.

Robert de Boron, knight from the village of Boron, eleven miles distant from Montbeliard in east central France, who served Gautier de Montbeliard, and who communicated to him his poem entitled *Joseph d' Arimathie,* sometimes known as *Roman de l'Estoire du Graal,* written about 1215. It was one of the most important Grail romances, next to Chrétien de Troyes' *Perceval.* For Robert, the Grail was a Christian relic, the dish or bowl from which Jesus ate on Holy Thursday with his disciples, and in which Joseph of Arimathia caught the blood from Jesus' side at the Crucifixion. He also wrote a second poem, *Merlin,* intended to connect the early history of the Grail with King Arthur's* court. He may well have been the author of the *Perceval,* a romance from which the Didot *Perceval** was rendered into prose. (Bibliog. 10, 78)

Robert de Courcy, justice and a baron of the Exchequer in Normandy;* one of English King Henry I's* ministers in the duchy next in importance, probably, to Robert de la Haye. He attested Henry's acts as *dapifer* (steward) in England as well as Normandy, and it probably was he who acted as a justice for King Stephen* in England, attested the empress' charters as *dapifer* and justice, and finally Duke Henry as *dapifer.* (Bibliog. 130)

Robert de Monte. See Torigni, Robert of.

Robert Guiscard of Hauteville (c. 1015-1085), duke of Apulia (1054-1085). He undoubtedly was the most remarkable of the Norman adventurers who conquered southern Italy. From 1016 to 1030, the Normans* were purely mercenaries, serving the Byzantines or the Lombards. Then William and Drogo, sons of Tancred of Hauteville,* a petty lord in Coutances,* arrived in 1130 to take Apulia away from the Byzantines; by 1140 they had succeeded. In 1042, William "Iron Arm" had been elected duke, and that dukedom passed in succession through his sons until in 1046 when the youngest, Robert, arrived. In four years he had become the virtual head of the Normans in Calabria and Apulia. In 1053, he captured Benevento, and took Pope Leo IX prisoner, forcing him to recognize Robert's title of duke as a vassal of the papacy. Then he conquered Sicily which he gave to his brother, Roger.* By 1071 the Byzantine possessions in southern Italy came under his control with his capture of Bari, thus allowing him to form it into a Norman state organized as a feudal monarchy. At his death, he was duke of Apulia and Calabria, prince of Salerno and suzerain+ of Sicily. (Bibliog. 68, 98)

Robert of Jumièges (d. 1070), archbishop* of Canterbury. A Norman who became canon of St. Ouen at Rouen and then abbot of Jumièges, he was a close friend of Edward,* the Confessor, and crossed to England with him in 1042 to become the bishop of London. He was the king's closest and most trusted advisor and a leader of the group who were hostile to the influence and power of Earl Godwine.* In 1051, in opposition to the chapter of monks there, the king appointed him archbishop of Canterbury. Sent by Edward on a mission to duke William* of Normandy, he returned just as Godwine returned from exile in 1052. His opposition to Godwine led him to be outlawed and deposed. He fled from England for his life and died at Jumièges in 1070. His mistreatment by Godwine and Godwine's son Harold* was the pretext used by William the Conqueror for invading England. (Bibliog. 68)

Robert le Diable, French romance based on a widespread story about a certain childless duchess of Normandy who asked the Devil to send her a child because God had ignored her prayers to do so. Shortly thereafter, a son with evil instincts was born to her after a particularly painful childbirth. He was so willfully cruel to all as he grew to be large and powerful that his father banished him from his estate and the pope excommunicated him. His cruelty knew no bounds until finally he finally realized the extent of his own wickedness; at that, he forced his mother to reveal the details of his birth. Overcome with grief and remorse at his wicked life, he went on a pilgrimage to Rome, though neither the pope nor a holy hermit was able to give him penance for his evil life. A note from heaven, however, directed him to feign madness, remain mute, take food only from the mouths of dogs, and cause himself to be chased from place to place by an angry populace every day. He accepted that penance, and lived that life for ten years until the Turks invaded Rome. Then he secretly armed himself and saved Rome on three separate occasions. When the grateful emperor promised his daughter to the conquering knight if only he could be found, an evil seneschal+ claimed that he had been the victorious knight. Mute herself, the emperor's daughter knew who the real champion was, and finally recovering her voice, revealed all to her father. Robert refused her hand in marriage, however, because he wished to remain a hermit to save his soul for the earlier life of sin. After his death, his bones were buried in La Puy, Normandy, where he became known as St. Robert. (ed. E. Loseth, Paris: *SATF,* 1903) (Bibliog. 106, 231)

Robert of Artois (fl. 1330), French Prince of the Blood* and brother-in-law to King Philip VI* (1293-1350), and his chief and special companion. Even though he had done a lot to gain the crown for Philip, his own attempts to gain possession of Artois through forged documents was discovered. Two years later his aunt who had inherited Artois, died, supposedly of poison. Found guilty of her murder and condemned to death, Robert was chased from the realm. He fled to England where King Edward III* welcomed him warmly, gave him three castles, and a pension, despite King Philip's warning that he would become the enemy of anyone sheltering Robert. Robert then worked up Edward's anger toward Philip by urging him to defy the French king because he had kept Edward's heritage (the crown) from him wrongfully. In 1338, Robert swore the Vow of the Heron+ at a banquet at Windsor* castle.+ His bravado spurred the entire English court to help their king regain the French crown which three of his uncles had worn. These actions were credited with starting the Hundred Years War.* (Bibliog. 35, 203)

Robert of Bellême. See Bellême-Montgomery.

Robert of Cisyle, Middle English* romance from the later 14th century on the theme of the proud and mighty brought low. King Robert of Sicily, brother of the emperor and pope, had many virtues, but was excessively proud. He thought so much more of his own high estate than of his religious duties that God decided to humble him. After Robert fell asleep in church, an angel assumed his likeness and apparel and left the church with the king's retinue. When Robert awoke, he was in beggar's garb, and was rudely handled when he rushed to the palace protesting that he was the king. After a series of humbling adventures, he realized his own insignificance, and asked for God's forgiveness. The angel revealed that he was God's messenger sent to chasten Robert for his pride, but now that Robert was humble, the angel no longer was needed, and it vanished, and Robert was king once again. (ed. Lillian Hornstein, "King Robert of Sicily," *PMLA,* 78, 1963) (Bibliog. 202)

Robin Hood. See volume 1, pp. 400-401.

Robin Hood Tower. See Richmond castle.

La Roche Derien, battle at (June 27, 1347), conflict in Brittany* between English forces under Sir Thomas Dagworth* and Charles of Blois.* Dagworth had defeated Charles earlier in 1347. To retaliate, Charles besieged Dagworth in the fortress of La Roche Derien for the entire summer. He dug a great series of ditches to protect his men and their horses from the attack he expected by a relieving army. Then he levelled all the hedges and ditches between his forces and the castle+ so that once out of the fortress, Dagworth's archers would have no protection and would have to fire their arrows from bare fields. Dagworth recognized that archers were of little use against men entrenched, so he attacked Charles' encampment before daybreak, launching his men in a column. He sacrificed entirely the advantage of English archery since the fight was entirely in the dark, but he won a hazardous victory. Charles had not expected such a move, and when attacked additionally by forces at his rear, his forces were broken and routed. He was captured, severely wounded, and many of his barons, the flower of the Blois forces, were killed. Archery had not won the battle, but fear of archery had caused the enemy to enclose himself in trenches thereby surrendering the advantage of his superior cavalry. For this victory, Dagworth was granted 25,000 florins *de scuto*, was presented by the earl of Northampton all the castles and lands in Brittany forfeited by the lord of Léon, Hervé VIII, sire de Noylon, and then after being summoned to Parliament in 1347, he was made Lord Dagworth. (Bibliog. 47, 166)

Rochefoucauld, castle+ in Charente, Angoumois, built in the first half of the 11th century by Foucauld de la Roche, and taken by the counts of Angoulême in 1135 and 1147. William IV,* Tallifer, count of Angoulême, rebuilt it soon thereafter. It gave its name to the family living there. (Bibliog. 196)

Rochester castle, fortress in Kent built by Norman kings to control the spot where Watling Street, running from Dover+ to London, crossed the River Medway. This castle+ was one of the most important in southeast England. One of the first English castles to be fortified in stone, it was one of several which were placed under the command of Bishop Odo,* William I's* half-brother.   Disgruntled with the arrangements after William I died, he led dissatisfied barons in a rebellion against the new king, William II, Rufus.* Odo was captured by

William, and imprisoned in Rochester, but he was released by the Rochester garrison. He finally was forced to surrender a second time when the castle surendered to the siege of the new king. Surprisingly, after surrendering, this garrison was allowed to ride their horses out of the castle, carrying their arms. A few years later, after he built the new keep, Henry I* bestowed the castle and its custody on the archbishop of Canterbury* and his successors in 1127, but his namesake successor, Henry II,* did not abide by that gift. One of the causes of the quarrel between Henry II and Archbishop Thomas à Becket* was the king's demand for the return of the custody of this castle. Half a century later, in 1215, when the barons revolted against King John,* Rochester castle saw its first big siege. Seized by the rebels, it was held by 100 to 140 knights as well as other troops. John gathered a mercenary+ army and reached Rochester on October 13, 1215. His army destroyed the bridge so provisions from London could not reach the castle, and for the next two months, John himself led the siege. He ordered five new catapults+ to bombard the castle ceaselessly, had his bowmen send a continuous volley of arrows and crossbow bolts into it, and then mined the outer curtain wall so his men could enter the outer bailey. Its keep was so strong, however, that John's men could not breach it, and he resorted to starvation to force surrender. Upon its final capitulation, John surprisingly ordered only one man hanged. Because of the dispute between the kings and the archbishops of the next few years, this castle was in urgent need of repairs by 1217, and over the next twenty years a lot of money was spent on it. By 1264, it was held for the king by Earl Warenne* and Roger de Leybourne* against the siege of Simon de Montfort* and Gilbert de Clare.* Despite making his way inside the bailey of the castle, Earl Simon was forced to withdraw his troops on the advance of the king's army. Over the next century, it then fell in such a sorry state that builders were purloining material from it to strengthen other buildings. Edward III* took steps to repair the damage, and spent more than £2,000 to rebuild and strengthen it. By 1370, his major work was completed. (Bibliog. 104, 247)

Roger I (1031-1101), count of Sicily (1062-1101). Youngest son of Tancred* of Hauteville in Normandy, he travelled to southern Italy to help his brother, Robert Guiscard,* in 1157. He was made count of Sicily after being placed in charge of conquering that country from the Arabs in 1062. By 1072, he had conquered Palermo and had begun to organize the government of the island. With the death of his brother, Robert, he became the head of the Hauteville house, and his brother's heir to the overlordship of Norman Italy. (Bibliog. 61, 98)

Roger II (1095-1154), king of Sicily (1130-1154). He became count+ of Sicily in 1105 as the successor of Roger I.* Taking advantage of the weaknesses of his Hauteville cousins to get land in southern Italy, he exercised power from his estate in Palermo over a large and powerful state as the duke of Calabria, Apulia and Sicily. He built up a large and powerful army and navy which controlled the Mediterranean, and became so powerful that Pope Innocent II was forced to recognize him officially. His court at Palermo was one of the cultural centers for the 12th century Renaissance. (Bibliog. 98)

Roger, bishop of Salisbury. In 1103 as a priest, he served in King Henry I's* household probably as a seneschal+ and perhaps as chaplain. He was chancellor+ for the king from 1101 to 1102 and subsequently became bishop of Salisbury. His position probably was best described as Henry's "first minister in England." He was interested in architecture, and built the new cathedral at Salisbury which reflected his fondness for architectural display. He continued to hold that position under King Stephen* until 1139, and seems to have held no official functions in Normandy, though he was there with Henry in 1129 or 1130. His nephew, Nigel, was a treasurer in Normandy and witnessed Henry's acts in both countries. He became bishop of Ely in 1133, and early in Henry II's* reign, purchased the office of treasurer for his son, Richard, the author of the *Dialogus*. Another nephew, Alexander, seems to have held no office in the royal administration before he was given the bishopric of Lincoln in 1123, but as such he probably acted as local justice in Lincolnshire. (Bibliog. 120)

Roger FitzOsbern (fl. 1075), earl of Norfolk.* A Norman baron who accompanied William* of Normandy on his English invasion in 1066, he helped to conquer England. For that support and assistance, William created him earl of Norfolk, where his lands were concentrated. He gained so much autonomy in his holdings that he led baronial revolts under William II.* (Bibliog. 98)

Roger de Hoveden (Howden) (d. c. 1201), English chronicler who may have been from Howden in Yorkshire; he was a royal clerk who accompanied King Henry II* to France in 1174 and was an itinerant justice+ of the forest between 1185 and 1190. He accompanied Richard I* on the third crusade+ in 1191 but had returned to England by Christmas of that year. Presumably after that, he settled in Howden to write his *Chronicle*. Its third section covering 1169-1192 was the most valuable for the reigns of Henry II and Richard I, and survived separately as *Gesta Regis Henrici Secundi.** Its fourth portion covering the period 1192-1201 was Hoveden's continuation of his third section and was valuable especially because Hoveden had access to public records and held discussions with the leading men of the time. (tr. Henry T. Riley, *Annals of Roger de Hoveden*, London: Bohn's Antiquarian Library, 1853; repr. New York: AMS Press, 1968) (Bibliog. 99)

Roland, Song of. See *Song of Roland.*

Roland and Vernagu, Middle English* romance detailing the travels of Charlemagne* to Constantinople to help the Emperor Constantius campaign in Spain; in it, Roland fought the giant Ferragus (or Vernagu) in the earliest complete example of the Christian-Saracen duel. (ed. Sidney Herrtage, London: Oxford, *EETS ES* #39, 1882) (Bibliog. 202)

Rolandslied, long Middle High German* poetic version of the *Chanson de Roland,** written about 1170 by a priest, Konrad of Regensburg, in the service of Henry the Lion,* duke of Bavaria and Saxony (d. 1195). Konrad downplayed the French patriotism in his source, and emphasized instead the role played by the Bavarians, and concentrated on the crusading spirit. He made Charlemagne* into an ideal ruler: grim toward his enemies, kind to the poor, victorious in battle, merciful, faithful to God, and a just judge. (ed. F. Maurer, Leipzig: *DLER,* 1940) (Bibliog. 235)

Roman de Rou, history of the Normans written by the Anglo-Norman poet Wace* at the command of King Henry II,* who had been pleased by the success of Wace's earlier work, *Brut.** At verse 24, Wace stopped his work because, as he reminded the king, he was not working for love, and the king was neglecting him financially. To jog the memory of both the king and his queen, Eleanor* of Aquitaine, Wace wrote a 315-line poem which reiterated his purpose in the *Rou,* and as a touch of flattery to remind Henry of his descent from such famous forebears as Matilda and Henry I,* William* the Conqueror, Robert the Devil, William Longsword* and Rollo (Rou), and to urge him to open his purse. A short time later, Wace was appointed canon of Bayeux, so his little trick seemed to work. He resumed work on the poem, and over the next nine years he completed 11,500 more verses in octosyllabic rhymed couplets, bringing his history down to the battle of Tinchebrai* in 1106. King Henry turned to a Maistre Beneëit to rewrite the work. Wace had begun his work with the fall of Troy and included the descent of the Danes from King Danaiis, and the deeds of a pirate named Hastings. After giving the story of Rollo (Rou) which gave the poem its name,

Wace proceeded through dukes William Longsword, Richard the Elder and Richard. Its third division concerned Duke Richard, Robert the Devil, William the Conqueror, William Rufus (William II),* and Henry I, and described the battle of Hastings* in great detail. For his sources, Wace used the chronicles of Dudo of St. Quentin, William of Jumièges, William of Malmsbury, much legendary information and his own vivid poetic imagination. (tr. Edward Taylor, *Master Wace his chronicle of the Norman Conquest from the Roman de Rou,* London, 1837) (Bibliog. 106)

Roman de Thèbes, French romance written around 1150 by an unknown Norman poet. A reworking of the *Thebais* by Statius (A.D. 61-96), this story replaced material which the medieval French audience would have found dull with episodes involving embassies, councils, battles, and scenes from the crusades. It basically reworked the Oedipus story and ended it with the war of the Seven against Thebes. (ed. Leopold Constans, Paris: *SATF,* 2 vols., 1890) (Bibliog. 106)

Roman de tout chevalerie, French romance on Alexander* written in England by Eustache or Thomas of Kent at the end of the 12th century. This was the basis of the other English Alexander poems. Its source was Julius Valerius, *Res gestae Alexandri Macedonis.* (ed. Paul Meyer, *Alexander le Grand dans le littérature française du moyen âge,* Paris, 1886) (Bibliog. 106, 231)

Roman de Tristan de Leonois, French prose romance of the middle of the 13th century by an unknown author. It recounted the adventures of Tristan as a knight-errant+ whose adventures were similar to Lancelot's* (in the *Lancelot* proper*), climaxing in his solemn reception by King Arthur* as a knight of the Round Table.* King Mark* was portrayed as a villain, a traitor, and an enemy of Arthurian knighthood. Tristan was assigned the duty of keeping Mark in check by serving as his rival. In this work, the tragic tale of unlawful love was changed into a romance of chivalry with a simple scale of values, an exaltation of chivalric virtues, and a condemnation of all things lying outside the adventurous kingdom. (last complete edition, Paris, 1536; sections: ed. E. S. Murell, *PMLA,* XLIII, 1928, 343-383; and F. C. Johnson, *MLR,* XXVII, 1933) (Bibliog. 106, 231)

Roman de Troie, romance by Benoît de Sainte-Maure.* Written between 1153 and 1174, it was based mostly on Dares'* story of the siege of Troy. It began with the Argonaut expedition and the previous destruction of Troy by Jason and Hercules. Priam rebuilt Troy, and the

Trojans, seeking revenge for its destruction, abducted Helen. The Greeks set out to rescue her, and besieged the city. More than twenty battles outside the walls were described as though they were episodes in the *chansons de geste*.* Benoît included the wanderings of Odysseus, the death of Agamemnon, the story of Orestes and Andromache and the end of Pyrrhus. (ed. L. Constans, Paris: *SATF,* 5 vols., 1904-1912) (Bibliog. 214, 231)

Roncesvals, Cantar de, 13th-century Spanish ballad of which only 100 lines survived in the Castilian language. Its fragment recounted the discovery by Charlemagne* of the bodies of Bishop Turpin,* Oliver* and then Roland. It differed substantially from the events in the *Chanson de Roland.** See Rencesvals. (ed. J. Horrent, *Roncesvalles,* Paris: 1951) (Bibliog. 237)

Roncesvals. See Rencesvals.

Roncevaux. See Rencesvals.

Ros, Robert de (c. 1169-1226), English knight from Yorkshire with the unexplained nickname of "Furfan" or "Furson." He was a ward of King Henry II* in 1185 while still a minor, and his lands were held by Ranulph de Glanville, but he was given livery of them in 1190. He was made bailiff+ of the royal castellany of Bonneville sur Toques, and in 1196, for the escape of a prisoner in his charge, Richard I* imprisoned him, fined him 1,200 marks and hanged the jailer. He was son-in-law to William the Lion* of Scotland, and went with him to England in 1209. He was one of the twelve barons named as guarantors in King John's* letters to the archbishop of Canterbury in 1213. Though he was a close associate of King John, he was one of the king's most vigorous opponents in the *Magna Carta Libertatum* of 1215; he was one of the twenty-four who were elected to see that its provisions were observed. In 1217, he returned his allegiance to the crown when the new king, Henry III,* ascended the throne, and he was chosen as one of the escorts for Alexander III* of Scotland to England. He married Isabel, illegitimate daughter of William the Lion* of Scotland, and the widow of Robert de Bruce.* (Bibliog. 47)

Rosengarten, Middle High German* heroic epic from about 1260. This work was closely related to and gave a version of the *Biterolf und Dietlieb.** In this story, Kriemhild* owned a rose garden which was surrounded by a silken thread and guarded by twelve warriors. She was eager to see whether Siegfried* or Dietrich* was the better warrior, so she issued a challenge for Dietrich to appear with twelve companions to do battle for a garland of roses and a kiss. Because giants fought on the Burgundian side, Dietrich brought in a doughty monk-warrior, Islan, who had been brought from his cloister just for that occasion. His fellow monks hoped he would not survive this encounter. He won his battle and when Kriemhild presented him with a kiss, his bristly face scratched hers so badly that she bled. Then to each of his fellow monks he brought a garland of roses which he pressed so hard on their shaven heads that they too bled. Rosengarten was the name in the Bavarian and Tyrolese Alps given to various places where the mountains had a reddish glow in the evening sun. (Bibliog. 86, 235)

Round Table, chivalric grouping associated first with King Arthur* by the Anglo-Norman poet Wace* in his *Brut**. In the prose version of the *Merlin* of Robert de Boron,* Merlin persuaded Uther Pendragon* to found the Round Table with 50 knights chosen by Merlin himself and an empty seat corresponding to the place which Judas occupied at the Last Supper. In the Didot *Perceval,* Perceval occupied that seat which resulted in the dire enchantments of Britain. In the continuation of Robert de Boron, the *Huth Merlin,* and followed by Malory in *Morte D'Arthur,** this Round Table passed from Uther* to the father of Guenevere,* King Leodegrance, by whom it was given as his daughter's dowry to Arthur, the number of Uther's knights having been increased inexplicably to 150. *Quest del Saint Graal* added the famous scene of the occupation of the Siege Perilous* by Galahad clad in vermeil arms, of his display of prowess at a tournament, and of the evening meal at the table when all were served by the Grail, veiled in white samite. It appeared also in the most important Italian Arthurian romance, *Tavola ritonda.** King Edward III* was so fascinated by the idea that in 1346 he ordered a special tower built at Windsor* castle,+ 200 feet in diameter, to house such a table around which he expected to seat a group of knights representing King Arthur's band of men. Such a building was never erected, but in the following year, Edward created the Order of the Garter* in honor of his feelings toward King Arthur. (Bibliog. 85, 138)

Roussillon, region of southern France between Languedoc and the Pyrenees Mountains. It maintained itself as a separate locality until it united with Aragon* in 1172. In 1278, it became part of the kingdom of Majorca and its principal city, Perpignan, was the capital of the realm until 1340 when the entire region was returned to the kingdom of Aragon. (Bibliog. 98, 239)

Roxborough castle, one of the strongest Scottish fortresses on the Scottish side of the whole border with England, this castle+ was held by Henry II* from 1175 to 1189. It was seized again by Edward I* in 1296, and was held by the English until the battle of Bannock Burn.* The Scots captured it back in 1342 but lost it again at the battle of Neville's Cross* in 1346. (Bibliog. 104)

Rudolf I, of Hapsburg (1218-1291), king of Germany from 1273. At 13, he became count of Hapsburg, and devoted such faithful service to the Emperors Frederick II* and Conrad IV* that he was rewarded with extensions of his territories. By the Great Interregnum* he became a powerful prince. He was elected emperor in 1272 over attempts of King Ottokar II of Bohemia to secure that royal title. These two fought openly for two years until Rudolf defeated Ottokar and gave his Austrian duchies of Austria, Styria, and Carinthia to his son Albert, thus creating the basis for the Hapsburg fortune. He was the first German king who had not been crowned in Rome, and who concentrated his energies on imposing his authority and the public peace in Germany. (Bibliog. 98, 124)

Rudolf von Ems (c. 1200-1254), knight from Hohenems, Vorarlberg, who also was a Middle High German* poet belonging to the second generation of epic writers of *Blütezeit*.* He was a *ministeriale,* that is, a nobleman in the train of a great noble, the count of Montfort.* His extant works were written between 1220 and 1250. His earliest work was *Der Gute Gerhard** in which his hero was a merchant; *Barlaam und Josephat* was a renunciation of the concept of *minne+* which Gottfried von Strassburg* had exalted; *Willehalm von Orleans* detailed the life of a knight of ideal qualities in a world of harsh realities; *Alexander,* an unfinished work describing an ideal ruler, and *Weltkronik,* an unfinished vast history of the world up to the Hebrew kings. (Bibliog. 235)

Ruodlieb, Old High German verse romance dating from around 1030, it was the first German romance of chivalry. Ruodlieb was a young knight who left his mother's home to enter the service of a foreign king. After serving on an important mission, Ruodlieb obtained permission to return home, and the king gave him twelve bits of advice and two loaves of bread inside which were placed some precious jewels. Only three bits of the advice became sources for adventures. One, "never trust a man with red hair," was the base of Ruodlieb's adventure with a red-haired man who stole his cloak, who rode through crops instead of staying on the road, and who finally was hanged for murdering the old husband of the young wife with whom he lodged. Ruodlieb returned to his mother, and found that the young woman he was pursuing was the mistress of a priest. (tr. E. Zeydel, Chapel Hill, North Carolina: *UNCSRLL*, 1959) (Bibliog. 24, 235)

Rusticiano de Pisa, author of *Meliadus*,* a romance written in 1275 in French, not Italian, drawing on the French *Palamèdes** and *Tristan*. After he was imprisoned by the Genoese in 1298, he wrote down the adventures of a fellow prisoner, Marco Polo, who had travelled extensively throughout the Orient and Africa. (Bibliog. 231)

Rutland, smallest county in England, which was separated from Northamptonshire. Its earldom was bestowed upon Edward, first son and heir apparent* of Edmund,* duke of York,* fifth son of King Edward III.* He was created duke of Aumale* in 1397 during the lifetime of his father, but succeeded to the title of duke of York in 1402 when, according to the terms of its charter, the earldom of Rutland became extinct. As part of the charter, Edward was granted an annuity of 800 marks for the support of the dignity and was granted the castle,+ town and lordship of Oakham and the sheriffdom of Rutland; he held it until he became duke of Aumale when he received an annuity of 40 marks. (Bibliog. 47, 101)

S

Sagramore le Desirus, son of the king of Hungary, kinsman of Brangore, king of Strangore or South Wales in Arthurian legend. He assisted Arthur* at Carmelide and became an important Round Table* knight. (Bibliog. 202)

Saint Denis,+ monastery near Paris founded in the 6th century over the tomb of Saint Denis, bishop of Paris and patron saint of France. It began to gather legends connected with Charlemagne's supposed pilgrimage to the Holy Land, and by the 11th century, these were being cited as the sources for the relics held there. Under the patronage of the kings of France, it became not only the place of royal worship, but also the royal burial place.(Bibliog. 98)

Saint Jacques, Saint James. His tomb in Compostella* in Galicia, Spain, was highly revered and was the destination of many pilgrimages from Europe. The route to his tomb was called the *via Tolosana* or the *via franca.*+ (Bibliog. 128)

Saint-Ulrich, Alsatian castle+ which was the residence of the counts of Ribeaupierre, one of the strongest families in Alsace. Legend recounted that the lord of Ribeaupierre living in Saint-Ulrich decided with his brother who lived in the adjacent chateau, Girsberg, to go hunting one morning. The first one up was to awaken the other by shooting an arrow through his chamber window. The lord of St. Ulrich was up first, but just as he shot his arrow, his brother appeared in the window and was killed by that awakening shaft. (Bibliog. 196)

Saisnes, Chanson de, chanson de geste* of the cycle of the king written about 1200 by Jean Bodel.* Guiteclin, the Saxon, recently married to Sebille, heard about the death at Rencesvals* of Charlemagne's* *douzepeers.** Believing that their demise left France undefended, he attacked and destroyed Cologne. Charlemagne, having just returned to France from the loss of his peers, was anxious to avenge both the death of his beloved men and the loss of Cologne. His barons refused to accompany him unless the Herupois were forced to pay tribute and serve the emperor. These Herupois refused to pay the tribute but agreed to serve Charlemagne if their rights were observed. Charlemagne left for the Rhine River and camped along the left bank. There, Sebille and Roland's brother, Baudouin, fell in love. Finally crossing the Rhine on an improvised bridge, the Franks defeated the Saxons, and slew Guiteclin. Sebille and Baudouin were married and granted the fief of Saxony before Charlemagne departed. To avenge their fallen leader, the Saxons revolted against and slew Baudouin. Charlemagne returned, once more defeated them, and bestowed their kingdom on Dylas, a son of Guiteclin who had been converted to Christianity, and who had taken the name of Guiteclin the convert. Sebille retired to a convent. (ed. F. Mengel, E. Stengel, Marburg: *AA* 99,107, 1906-1909) (Bibliog. 106, 231)

Saladin (Salah al-Din Yussuf) (1138-1193), first Ayyubite sultan of Egypt. A Kurd of Armenia, Saladin was educated in Damascus when his father, a general in the army of Zengi, atabeg of Mosul, was made governor of Damascus. His career fell into three parts: his conquests of Egypt, 1164-1174; his annexation of Syria, 1174-1187; and the destruction of the Latin kingdom and the subsequent campaigns against the Christians, 1187-1192. Nur-ed-din, the caliph,+ feared Egypt because it menaced his empire to the south and was the ally of the Franks. Under Saladin, troops invaded Egypt and fought against the Franks in campaigns in 1164, 1167, 1168, and 1169, resulting in heavy crusader losses and the appointment of Saladin as vizier. On the caliph's death in 1174, Saladin began his conquest of Syria, and by 1175, the caliph declared him sultan. Between 1177 and 1180, he warred on the Christians from Egypt before concentrating his energies on Syria after 1181. By 1186, he had received the homage of the atabeg of Mosul. With this recognition, Saladin had encircled the Latin kingdom of Jerusalem with a hostile empire. In May 1187, he destroyed a small group of the Templars+ and Hospitallers+ at Tiberias, and on July 4, defeated the Christian army totally at Hattin.* He then overran the entire area and besieged Jerusalem, taking it on October 2 and offering its Christian inhabitants chivalric clemency. Only Tyre was left to the Christians. Saladin made a tactical blunder by not taking it before winter stopped warfare, because from Jerusalem the crusaders marched to attack Acre* in 1189. That attacking army was surrounded by Saladin's army for two years. These events prompted a new crusade+ to be led by Henry II* of England and Philip II* of France. The death of Henry and the accession of Richard I to the throne delayed their departure for the Holy Land until 1190. Arriving in June 1191, Richard immediately took over the siege of Acre; it surrendered a month later without Saladin's permission. Richard then marched down the coast to Jaffa and a great victory at Arsouf.* Both sides recognized their stalemate, and despite small victories for each side over the next year and a half, Richard began peace negotiations with Saladin, and signed a treaty with him calling for peace for three years, three months, three weeks, three days and three hours. For it, the coast line was left to the crusaders with free passage to Jerusalem. Richard returned to Europe and Saladin to Damascus where in 1193 he died. He was a generous and hospitable man, who loved children and was gentle to women and the weak. He was not a statesman, for he left no code of law or constitution to the area, and his empire was divided among his relatives on his death, but he had been a leader who stemmed the tide of Western conquest on the East. (Bibliog. 27, 68, 195, 201)

Salisbury, earls of. The title was first conferred in 1142 upon Patrick de Salisbury (d. 1169), descendant of Edward de Salisbury, cited in the *Domesday Book** as *vicecomes* of Wiltshire. Patrick was a supporter of Empress Matilda* who made him her constable.+ He was sheriff of Wiltshire, and later served Henry, duke of Normandy, as a witness to the treaty between King Stephen* and Henry about the succession to the throne in 1153. He continued to serve as sheriff after Henry's accession. Henry II* placed him in command of the royal forces in Poitou in 1167, and he died there, killed in 1168 by Geoffrey de Lusignan on his return from a pilgrimage to Compostella,* Spain. He had married Ela, widow of William de Warenne,* third earl of Surrey,* and the daughter of William Talvas, count of Ponthieu and Alençon. His son William, a dedicated supporter of King Richard I,* serving at his coronation in 1189, died in 1196, leaving a daughter, Ela, as his heiress. She married William Longespee,* an illegitimate son of Henry II by Rosamund Clifford. He died in 1226. His son and heir, William III, died in 1257, leaving a daughter, Margaret. Ela lived until 1261, surviving her husband, and outliving her son and grandson, both called William Longespee, so that on her death in 1261, her great-granddaughter, Margaret (d. 1310), wife of Henry de Lacy, earl of Lincoln,* became countess of Salisbury. She passed the title on to her daughter, Alice, who married Thomas Plantagenet.* On her husband's arrest and conviction for treason in 1322, the countess had to surrender her lands and titles to King Edward II.* In 1337, King Edward III* bestowed the Salisbury title upon William de Montagu, Lord Montagu (Montacute), for his faithful service to the king. His son, William, the seventh earl (1328-1397), served in the Crécy* campaign, being knighted at the landing at La Hogue. He was one of the founding Knights of the Garter,* and was the last survivor of the original twenty-five. He fought against the Spaniards at Winchelsea* in 1350, accompanied Edward,* the Black Prince, on his campaigns in France in 1355 and 1356, being in joint command of the rearguard at Poitiers* in 1356. He then took part in John of Gaunt's* expedition into France in 1369, and was captain of an armada of ships and barges in 1373. At the coronation+ of Richard II* in 1377, he bore one of the ceremonial vestments, and served that monarch in many official capacities. He married Joan, countess of Kent, granddaughter of Edward III. The Montagu family retained the earldom until 1400 when John, eighth earl but third earl of this line, was convicted of treason and his titles forfeited to the crown. (Bibliog. 47, 68, 101)

Salisbury, chief city of Wiltshire in south central England built originally around Old Sarum,* an early fort rebuilt by the Romans, and later moved nearby to the banks of the Avon River near Stonehenge* on the plains of Salisbury. This fortress was built on an ancient site in Wiltshire which the Saxons called Searisbyrig, which the compilers of William I's* *Domesday Book* called Sarisberie; later it was called Old Sarum and then Salisbury. Between 1075 and 1078, the bishopric of Sherburne was transferred to Old Sarum, and the outer fortifications of the old motte and bailey+ castle were increased by order of William I to encompass the entire town. The motte and the four ramparts+ divided the town into quarters. In 1135, it fell into the hands of King Stephen's* enemies, so that when Stephen finally resumed control of it, he ordered Earl Patrick of Salisbury, his sheriff of Wiltshire, to demolish portions of the castle and cathedral; Stephen died before those orders were carried out. Henry II* and his two sons, King Richard I* and John,* kept the castle in good repair. Because the restraint on the earl by the king had caused restrictions imposed on the clergy of the cathedral, the bishop moved his cathedral early in the reign of Henry III* to New Sarum. Nothing new was done to the castle until Edward III* spent a considerable sum to patch up the castle as an obsolete Norman fortification; no contemporary methods of fortification were included. (Bibliog. 66, 104, 247)

Sapaudia, early Middle Ages name for the area known later as Savoy.* (Bibliog. 98)

Saracens, name given to Arabs and Muslims.* Originally it may have signified the Bedouin tribe of Simai, *Banu Sara*. Suggestions for its origin traced it back to mean descendants of Sarah, wife of Abraham.

By extension the term eventually came to refer to all Arabs, then Muslins, or followers of Mohammed, especially to crusaders who used this term to refer to all the enemies peopling the Holy Land. See Sarras. (Bibliog. 98, 169)

Saragossa, city in Aragon on the Ebro River; it was ruled by Marsile in the *chanson de geste,** the *Song of Roland.** (Bibliog. 210)

Sardinia, island in the western Mediterranean conquered by the Vandals in 477, the Byzantines in 534, and the Arabs in 711, who controlled it until 1046 when it was won by competing fleets from Genoa and Pisa. These two Italian cities compromised over the island, giving Genoa the northern and western parts, and Pisa the southern and eastern. In 1239, Emperor Frederick II* made it into a kingdom and gave it to his illegitimate and favorite son, Enzio.* Genoa's naval victory over Pisa in 1284 brought the entire island under Genoese domination. As a result of dynastic claims, the island came under the sovereignty of Aragon* and was placed under the control of Aragonese *cortes,* courts of nobility which controlled it until the middle of the 15th century. (Bibliog. 98)

Sarras, city and realm of King Evelake who was converted by Joseph of Arimathia. Galahad's* quest ended in Sarras, and from it the Holy Grail* was taken into heaven permanently on Galahad's death, according to *Morte D'Arthur.** The name *Saracen* was considered at one time to have come from this locality. At one time Sarras was thought to have been near Jerusalem, but other beliefs placed it in England north of the Humber River. (Bibliog. 117)

Sassanean dynasty. See Bokhara.

Sassoigne, Sessoine, Saxony* in the *chansons de geste,** and the English romances, especially the *Morte D'Arthur.** (Bibliog. 128, 145)

Savoy, Alpine region of southeastern France and northwestern Italy, known in the early Middle Ages as Sapaudia. It became a part of the kingdom of Burgundy in 888, after having been allotted to Lothaire* by the Treaty of Verdun* in 843. When the kingdom of Burgundy was annexed to the Holy Roman Empire in 1032, Umberto (Humbert) I was made count of Savoy, and established his court at Chambery. His granddaughter married Emperor Henry IV* in 1066. At the end of the 11th century, the count of Maurienne (its earliest title), held rights of sovereignty in the Burgundian districts of Maurienne, Savoy (strictly so called), Tarantaise, and Aosta. By the 12th century, the princes of Savoy were hemmed into their own corner of Italy by such princes as Montferrat* at Salauzzo, at Ivrea and at Biandrate. Savoyard extensions began in earnest with Peter of Savoy* in the 13th century. Known as Little Charlemagne,* he enlarged the holdings into a large dominion along the shores of Lake Neufchatel. Through the 12th and 13th centuries, Savoy annexed counties in Piedmont* and in the upper Rhône valley, and through marriages with the royal dynasties of England, France and Cyprus, the house of Savoy acquired much prestige throughout Europe.   After Peter's reign, this land was held for a short time by a separate branch of the Savoyard princes known as the barons of Vaud, and in the middle of the 14th century, their barony passed to the dauphines of Viennois.* (Bibliog. 79, 98, 145)

Saxony, country in northern Germany between the Rhine and Elbe rivers settled by tribes of Saxons who settled there after the 5th century. Some migrated to England where they intermingled with the neighboring tribes of Angles. Under a king, the Saxons resisted attempts to become Christianized through the efforts of St. Boniface. Later he called on the Franks* to continue his mission. After the coronation of Pepin the Short (753), this became a political issue which led to war. The thirty-year conflict between the Saxons and Charlemagne* ended in 802 with the forced conversion of the Saxons. Widukind, the Saxon leader, was captured and exiled to Neustria.* Under Charlemagne and Louis the Pious,* several counts were appointed to administer the conquered Saxon territories, while the frontier along the Elbe was entrusted to the margrave+ of the northern march.* By 843, it was entrusted to Louis the German* who intended it for his son, Louis. By the end of the 9th century, it had become a duchy entrusted by King Henry* the Wrangler of Germany to his son Otto I. In 1125, Duke Lothaire of Supplinburg was elected emperor of the Holy Roman Empire, and enfeoffed Saxony to Henry* the Proud of the Welf dynasty. Under this dynasty, Saxony achieved its greatest heights as it became the base for German colonization eastward. Henry the Lion* was the leader of the *Drang nach Osten* ("drive to the east") policy which led untimately to the colonization for Germany of the area between the Elbe and Oder Rivers. Such an expansion threatened the imperial authority of Frederick I,* Barbarossa, who convicted Henry the Lion of failure to provide his feudal service in 1178. Barbarossa punished him by confiscating the Saxon fief in 1180, by exiling him to England, and by dividing the duchy into a number of units. (Bibliog. 98, 100)

Sayf al-Din, (Saif ad-Din) al-Adil, sultan of Mosul (1145-1176);

youngest son of Zengi, he was appointed sultan of Mosul by his father. Under the influence of Nur-ed-Din, his older brother, he modelled his state after that of Syria. In 1173, he sought the regency of his nephew, but was defeated by Saladin.* (Bibliog. 98)

Scalacronica, chronicle of England and Scotland (1066-1362) written by Thomas Gray* in French. It was begun in Edinburgh in 1355 when its author was a prisoner. Its title, "Ladder Chronicle," pointed to the ladder of the Gray arms, on the rungs of which different sources stood. Although much of this work was based on Bede, Higden* and other well-known writers, it provided much useful information on the reigns of Edward II* and Edward III,* especially on the wars between England and Scotland. Gray was the lord of Heaton manor in Northumberland, and was possibly the first English layman to compose a chronicle. (ed. Joseph Stevenson, Glasgow: Maitland Club #40; repr. New York: AMS, 1976; tr. Sir Hubert Maxwell, Glasgow, 1907) (Bibliog. 99)

Scarborough castle, Yorkshire fortress begun in the reign of King Stephen* by William, count of Aumale* and lord of Hoderness. This castle+ was appropriated by Henry II,* and remained in royal hands from then on. Situated on a rocky promontory overlooking Scarborough harbor, its defenses were concentrated on the accesses from the south and west. Little was done on it for the next few years until King John's* insecurity about the northern frontier led him to spend considerable sums in repairing and strengthening it. During the baronial revolt under Henry III,* a half-century earlier, it was held for the king by Geoffrey de Neville. Its first major action occurred early in the 14th century when discontented barons, led by Thomas, earl of Lancaster,* attacked the castle then held by the hated Piers Gaveston,* favorite of King Edward II.* Despite determined attacks, Piers held out until his garrison was starved into submission. He was promised a safe conduct and a fair trial, but the earl of Warwick* disregarded those promises, and had him beheaded on Blacklow Hill in 1312. Sixty years later, this castle was the prison of a notorious Scottish pirate named Mercer, and in an attempt to rescue him, his son sailed into Scarborough harbor with a fleet of ships. Successfully freeing Mercer from the castle's dungeon, the fleet sailed away but was pursued and recaptured with considerable treasure by a fleet from London. (Bibliog. 104, 247)

Schleswig, duchy comprised of the southern part of the Jutland peninsula, belonging to Denmark in the 9th century. It was conquered by the Germans under Otto II* and became a country within the duchy of

Saxony.* Ceded by the Emperor Conrad II to Canute VI of Denmark in
1202, it became one of the most important principalities of Denmark in
the 11th and 12th centuries.   Henry the Lion* conquered and incorporated it into his duchy of Saxony in 1149. (Bibliog. 98)

Der Schwanritter, Middle High German* verse romance by Konrad von
Wurzburg* which recounted the familiar story of Lohengrin,* although
the knight was not named as such in this work set in the time of
Charlemagne.* In this story, the widow of Duke Godfrey* of Brabant
(Bouillon) sued the duke of Saxony in Charlemagne's court for usurping
her inheritance. These proceedings were interrupted by the appearance
of a swan drawing a boat containing a sleeping knight. This knight of
the Swan became the duchess' champion and asserted her rights by defeating the duke of Saxony. A gap in the manuscript must have included
the knight's marriage to the duchess and the forbidden question: asking him his name, for at the conclusion, he sadly bade farewell to
her. From their children were descended the counts of Gueldres and
Cleves. (ed. E.   Schroder, *Kleinere Dichtung Konrad v. Wurzburg,*
Halle: *ATB,* 1924-1926) (Bibliog. 86)

Scone,+ abbey founded in Scotland by King Alexander I* in 1115 on the
site of a monastery to which King Kenneth was said to have brought
from Dunstaffnage Castle on Loch Etive in 824 the Stone of Destiny on
which Celtic kings were crowned. That stone and its chair were carried
by Edward I* to Westminster Abbey in 1296. See coronation chair.+
(Bibliog. 68, 115)

Scotichronicon. See Fordun, John.

Scotland, kingdom northeast above Hadrian's Wall on the northern portion of the island also containing England and Wales. From the 5th
century, it was inhabited by the Picts, Scots, Angles and Britons who
eventually fused to form the Scottish kingdom. In Arthurian legend, it
was called Escosse and contained nine sub-kingdoms: Benoye or Benwick,
Estrangor, Garloth, L'Isle Estrange, the Long Isles, Lothian, considered to be the territory between the Firth of Forth and the River
Tweed, including part of Northumberland; the North Marches, Orkney and
Pomitain. kings of Scotland from the death of the usurper MacBeth at
the hands of Macduff in 1039 were

1057 - Malcolm III (Cean-Mohr or Canmore), son of Duncan; he was
              killed while besieging Alnwick* castle.
1093 - Donald VII (or Donald Bane), his brother who usurped the throne

but fled to the Hebrides Islands.

1094 - Duncan II, son of Malcolm III.

1094 - Donald Bane, again, but he was deposed, imprisoned and blinded by his nephew, Edgar.

1098 - Edgar, son of Malcolm, and rightful heir; his sister, Matilda, married Henry I* of England.

1107 - Alexander, surnamed "the Fierce," his brother.

1124 - David, another brother who married Matilda, daughter of Waltheof,* earl of Northumberland.

1153 - Malcolm IV,"the Maiden," his grandson.

1165 - William,* surnamed "the Lion," Malcolm IV's brother.

1214 - Alexander II, William's son; married Joan, illegitimate daughter of King John of England.

1249 - Alexander III, son; married Margaret, daughter of Henry III of England

1285 - Margaret, called the "Maiden of Norway," granddaughter of Alexander III, recognized as monarch by the Scots, even though she was a foreigner, a woman, and an infant; she died in 1290 on her way to Scotland. On her death, competition arose for the throne which King Edward I of England decided in favor of

1292 - John Baliol, who surrendered his crown and died in exile, followed by an Interregnum of nine years until

1306 - Robert I Bruce, "Bruce of Bannockburn,"* seized the throne.

1329 - David II Bruce, his son; Edward Baliol disputed the throne with him.

1332 - Edward Baliol, son of John Baliol, resigned.

1324 - David II again, 11 years a prisoner in England.

1371 - Robert II Stewart, nephew.

1390 - Robert III, son of Walter, high steward of Scotland.

(Bibliog. 96, 164, 176)

Scottish Knight, epithet applied to Sir Patryce who was poisoned treacherously by Sir Pynel by an apple at Guenevere's* feast in Arthurian legend in *Morte D'Arthur.** (Bibliog. 145)

Scrope, Richard le (c. 1327-1403), Yorkshire knight who fought at Crécy,* at Neville's Cross* where he was knighted on the field, at the siege of Calais* in 1346-1347, in the sea fight off Winchelsea (Espagnola-sur-Mer*), at the recapture of Berwick in 1356, and at the siege of Paris in 1359-1360. He was commanded to provide 250 archers and to accompany John of Gaunt* to Aquitaine in 1360. He fought next in Edward,* the Black Prince's campaign at the battle of Navarette* in 1367. Summoned to Parliament in 1370, he became Lord Scrope. Following this, he served as a joint warden of the West Marches in 1275, as steward+ of the king's household in 1377-1378. He was lord chancellor in 1378-1379 and 1381-1382. His celebrated controversy with Sir Robert Grosvenor as to the right of bearing arms "azure, a bend gold" was finally decided on May 2, 1389, by the constable, Thomas, duke of Gloucester,* whose judgment was confirmed by the king in 1390. On the conviction and beheading of his first son, the earl of Wiltshire, in 1399, by the first Parliament of King Henry IV,* Scrope implored the king not to disinherit himself or his children, to which the king consented, saying that he had always deemed Scrope to be a loyal knight. (Bibliog. 47)

Sege Perilous. See Siege Perilous.

Segwarides, brother of Palomydes, and enemy of Tristan. He was killed by Lancelot's* men during the abduction of Guenevere* in Malory's *Morte D'Arthur.** (Bibliog. 210)

Seneschal of Anjou, official appointed by Henry II* to help administer the Loire counties. As seneschal+ of Anjou, he was an important official who generally presided in the count's court at Angers in place of the king's court. For much of his reign, Henry was content to leave a somewhat unreliable official, Stephen de Marsai, in that role instead of Maurice de Craon to whom he had entrusted Anjou and Maine. Richard I,* on accession to the throne, threw him into prison and forced him to give back the money he had stolen. In 1200, King John created an hereditary post as seneschal of Anjou, Maine and Touraine. (Bibliog. 161)

Seneschal of Aquitaine, official appointed by Henry II* to oversee the castellans of chateaux and other fortresses in the province of Aquitaine. To control that province, the duke needed chateaux, but to staff such fortifications through feudal service was expensive and unreliable. Thus the duke had to rely on mercenaries+ at considerable expense to the local population. To control these underlings, he installed a new official, the seneschal,+ an important office created by William VII, father of Eleanor* of Aquitaine, who borrowed the idea from his neighbor, the count of Anjou. Nobles of the district held the office first. One of them, Ralph de Faie, Eleanor's uncle, was excommunicated for his money demands on the church. After that, Henry appointed an Englishman, the count of Salisbury on whom he bestowed important powers. After Hugh de Lusignan killed Salisbury with a lance thrust in 1168, Henry returned to the practice of appointing a local man. (Bibliog. 161)

Seneschal of England, title chosen by Simon de Montfort for his new position as head of the government of England in 1264 after the Barons' War.* Because that title had been an ancestral one held by the earls of Leicester, Simon based his authority to rule in its practices. After fifteen months of exercising a protectorate of the throne of Henry III* on June 24, 1264, Simon had summoned a Parliament to which he added four loyal and trustworthy knights for each county elected by the assembly of that county. This group approved the constitution required by Simon which stipulated that Henry III was to remain under guard for the rest of his life, and that during that period, the government was to be run by nine people chosen by three electors: Simon, the new count of Gloucester, Gilbert de Clare,* and the bishop of Chichester. Simon was to be the ruler, a virtual dictator with the title of Seneschal of England. (Bibliog. 161)

Seneschal of France. Under King Louis VI (1081-1137), Etienne de Garland (d. 1150), his chancellor (1108-1137), had become a powerful man in France. Using his high office, he engaged in flagrant nepotism, and accumulated a great number of benefices and offices. He was the archdeacon of Notre Dame de Paris, dean of St. Genèvieve de Paris, dean of Saint Samson and Saint Avit d' Orléans, and dean of the cathedral of Orléans. Louis allowed himself to be dominated by this powerful greedy man, and to appoint him to two of the five chief offices of the crown: chancellor and seneschal. As such he also was given the responsibility for the administration of the army. When reformers prevented his becoming a bishop, he attacked them mercilessly, and instigated the king to impose powerful oppressive measures against them. However, when he tried to transfer this office of seneschal to his son-in-law without consulting the king, he was thwarted and ousted for five years. Yet his influence over the king was so great that he soon was pardoned and reinstated as chancellor. Louis VII* dismissed him as chancellor, but soon found himself saddled with a man, Cahour, equally as insatiable as Etienne. (Bibliog. 178)

Septimania, name for the province of Languedoc between the 5th and 8th centuries while it was under the rule of the Visigoths. (Bibliog. 98)

Sessoine, kingdom of Saxony* in the English romances, especially Malory's *Morte D'Arthur.** (Bibliog. 145)

Shrewsbury, principal town of the English county of Shropshire.

Originally called Scrobbesby Rig by the Saxons, its strong castle overlooking the River Severn was built by its first earl, Roger de Montgomery, comte of Bellême (see Bellême-Montgomery) and Alençon. He was left to administer Normandy while the Conqueror invaded England in 1066. For his service he received from the king the castle of Arundel, the city of Chichester and other Sussex lands. King William II* gave the earldom to Roger's second son, Hugh, assuming that he would make his home in England rather than Normandy and would be free of major continental commitments. Hugh was killed four years later, and the earldom went to his older brother, Robert of Bellême, already in possession of a large Norman fief. For cruelty and treason against King Henry I, he was deprived of all his English fiefs and imprisoned for the remainder of his life. Henry then removed its palatine+ rights, dissolved its earldom, and appointed a royal sheriff to control it. Not until King Richard II* bestowed the earldom on John Talbot (1388-1453) was it revived.

Its castle, built on a peninsula on the river on which the town of Shrewsbury was built, was erected by its first earl Roger of Montgomery, but when his son, Robert of Bellême, fell from power in 1102, it reverted to the hands of Henry I.* It left royal control in 1138 when its sheriff joined King Stephen's enemies, and again in 1215 when Llywelyn ap Iorwerth* captured both town and castle by treachery and cunning, and yet again during the Barons' War.* Then because of his success in the Welsh wars King Edward I* (1272-1307) dramatically reduced the military importance of the castle, and it was allowed to fall into disrepair and decay. (Bibliog. 47, 66, 104)

Sicilian Vespers, revolt in Sicily against the authority of Charles* of Anjou in 1282. Called vespers because it erupted at the hour of vespers service in church, this revolt was a reaction to the conquest of the island sixteen years earlier and to the fall of the house of Hohenstaufen.* (Bibliog. 98)

*Siège de Barbastre, chanson de geste** written in the second half of the 12th century describing how Bueves de Commarchis* and his sons were captured and led as prisoners to Barbastre in Spain. His son Girart fell in love with the emir's+ daughter, and she aided the prisoners. King Louis and William of Orange arrived just in time to help the prisoners win their big battle against the Saracens. The story was reworked by Adenet le Roi* in the 13th century as the *chanson de geste, Bueves de Commarchis.* (ed. J. L. Perrier, Paris: *CFMA* 54, 1926) (Bibliog. 106, 231)

Siege Perilous, (OF. *siège* = seat), seat at Arthur's* Round Table,* described in the *Quest del Saint Graal*.* On Pentecost morning, all the empty seats of the Round Table were found to be inscribed with the names of their rightful occupants. One large empty seat, the Siege Perilous, had the inscription stating that it would be filled that day. Despite Arthur's warning of dire calamity, Perceval* attempted to sit in it but the stone split beneath him, and a voice cried out that Perceval displayed great audacity, and for it he and those of the Round Table would suffer great adversity. Later, at another Pentecost, after Arthur and the others had taken their seats, an old man led in Galahad* (Galaad) attired in vermeil arms, and declared that this young man was the Knight Desired through whom the marvels of that and strange lands would end. Lifting the cloth on the back of the chair, the old man revaled the words on the Siege, "Here is the seat of Galaad," and seated Galahad in the chair. (Bibliog. 139)

Siegfried (Sigurd), Middle High German* hero from Xanten, Netherlands. He was husband of Kriemhild* and was murdered by Hagen.* In the Norse *Edda* sagas, Siegfried or Sigurd belonged to the mythic race of the Volsungs, and was brought up by a dwarf ignorant of his parentage. He killed a dragon, claimed the treasure it was guarding, awakened the sleeping Valkyre Brynhild whom the god Odin had surrounded with a ring of fire on a mountain summit. Leaving his bride, Siegfried went to the land of King Gunnar where a magic potion destroyed his memory so that he would marry Gunnar's sister, Gudrun, and aid Gunnar to marry Brynhild. When Gudrun learned of the deceit used to win her, she swore vengeance. Inciting Gunnar against Sigurd (Siegfried), she successfully had Sigurd murdered, and Brynhild accompanied him on his funeral pyre. Gudrun then married Atli, king of the Huns. In hope of learning the whereabouts of their treasure, Atli invited Gudrun's kinfolk to his court where they all were murdered without revealing the location in the Rhine River of the gold. For that outrage, Gudrun exacted a terrible vengeance against her second husband by giving him the blood of his children to drink, and then by stabbing him to death in his bed. Siegfried also played a large role in the *Nibelungenlied** which described his murder by Hagen, and his wife Kriemhild's revenge for that murder. (Bibliog. 60, 161)

Sigenot, Middle High German* poem written by an unknown poet from the 13th century. In it Dietrich von Bern (see Theoderic the Great) encountered the giant Sigenot who threw him into a cave. Sigenot then encountered Hildebrand, Dietrich's vassal, whom he attacked. Hildebrand killed Sigenot, and with the aid of a dwarf, rescued

Dietrich. (ed. A. C. Schoener, Heidelberg, 1928) (Bibliog. 86)

Sigurd. See Siegfried.

Simon de Pouille, chanson de geste* from the 13th century. It resembled a continuation of the *Pèlerinage de Charlemagne** in that it related how Charlemagne* and his *douzepeers** opposed Simon at Jerusalem, and how their *gabs+* also caused problems for them. (Bibliog. 106)

Simon Frazer. See Frazer, Simon.

single combat, playing important roles in many works, duels+ between two knights included fights between Tristan and the Morholt* in *Tristan und Isolde;* Arthur and Flollo in Geoffrey of Monmouth* and in Wace's *Brut*;* Roland and Oliver in *Girart de Vienne**; Ogier and Charlot in *Ogier le Danois;* Otuel and Roland in *Otuel.** (Bibliog. 231)

Sir Cleges, late 14th-century English romance in which a pious tale, a humorous tale and a minstrel's tale combined to emphasize the qualities of encouraging liberality and punishing greed at the Christmas season. In it Sir Cleges, a knight of Uther Pendragon,* became poor because he was so generous with his largesse.+ Consoled by his wife, he bore his poverty patiently. As he prayed in his garden on Christmas day, he saw cherries growing on the tree over his head. Taking the fruit to the king as a present, he was challenged successively by the porter, the usher and the steward to give them one-third of whatever he received from the king. Delighted with the fruit, the king offered Cleges anything he wished. In response, Cleges asked for twelve blows on anyone he named, and then gave each of the servants his share of the "reward." At Uther's request, Cleges explained his strange conduct. When Uther learned that this stranger was Sir Cleges whom he had thought dead, he made him a steward and gave him the castle of Cardiff and other property. (ed. H. Morley, *Shorter English Poems*, London, 1876) (Bibliog. 202)

Sir Degare, Middle English* metrical romance from the 14th century. It recounted how Degare, a child born to the daughter of the king of England who had been ravished by a knight, was hidden in order to conceal his birth. A hermit found him along with a purse of money, a letter of instructions about rearing him, and a pair of gloves which would designate the lady he was to marry. He grew into a powerful young man who he was about to marry his mother when their relationship was revealed by the gloves. Later he met his father, and the two fought before they recognized each other. (See also *Hildebrandslied*.) (ed. G. Schleich, Heidelberg: *ETB* 19, 1929) (Bibliog. 202)

Sir Degrevant, late 14th-century Middle English* romance describing the motives and manners of the perfect knight. In a realistic treatment of the feudal situation, this romance described a feud and its effects. Sir Degrevant of the Round Table* was summoned home from a crusade+ after a neighboring earl ravaged his hunting grounds. Refusing to make reparations, the earl continued his marauding. Degrevant and his men hunted the earl and his men like deer, but the earl escaped. When the earl refused Degrevant's challenge to joust, his countess appeared on their castle wall with their daughter, Melidor, with whom Degrevant fell instantly in love. They secretly begin a chaste nightly liaison until Degrevant was detected by the earl's steward, and slew his opponents. The earl then permitted the marriage. After thirty years and seven children, Melidor died, and Degrevant went to the Holy Land where he was killed. (ed. Edith Rickert, *Early English Romances in Verse*, New York: Duffield 1908, II) (Bibliog. 202)

Sir Eglamour of Artois, mid-14th century English metrical romance centering on a lovesick knight and his weapons and quests. To win the hand of Christabelle, daughter of the earl of Artois, Eglamour was to perform three feats. With the help of a hound and a magic sword given him by his lady, he killed a famous deer, then a huge boar, then their giant keepers, and returned with the giants' heads on a spear. His final quest was to slay the fiery dragon of Rome, but in the process he was wounded. Meanwhile Christabelle and her son by Eglamour, Degrebelle, were set adrift by her angry father. A griffin+ carried off the baby boy who was rescued by the king of Israel and reared by him as his heir. Christabelle reached Egypt and was brought up by its ruler as his daughter. When Degrebelle was fifteen he was sent to Egypt to marry Christabelle, but before the marriage took place Christabelle recognized him by the cognizance+ on his shield. In a tournament, he was defeated by his father, Eglamour, who also recognized him by a cognizance of a rudderless boat on his shield. Eglamour and Christabelle were married and inherited the realm of the earl of Artois who died when he fell from a tower. (ed. F. Richardson, London: Oxford, *EETS OS* #256, 1965) (Bibliog. 202)

Sir Ferumbras, one of the English Charlemagne* romances* written between 1370 and 1400. At the head of his army, Charlemagne camped close to Morimond when Ferumbras, a giant Saracen knight, appeared and challenged any six French knights to single combat. Charlemagne asked Roland to accept the challenge, but he decided not to. Although he was recovering from a serious wound, Oliver* chose to accept, and overcame the Saracen, forcing him to accept Christianity. Shortly thereafter, Oliver and four other *douzepeers** were captured in a Saracen ambush and thrown into a dungeon in Aigremont. Charlemegne took Ferumbras to his camp and baptized him. Meanwhile, Floripas, daughter of Oliver's captor, promised to help the *douzepeers* escape if they would help her obtain Guy as her husband. They agreed, and she led them through a secret passage to her room. Charlemagne, anxious about his missing peers, sent the remaining peers to search for the five captives. Tricking their way into Aigremont, the seven also were captured and thrown into the same prison as Oliver and the others, but were rescued by Floripas and led to safety in her room. After a series of attacks and counterattacks, the *douzepeers* were rescued by Charlemagne who then routed and captured Floripas' father, Balan, the *emir** of the Saracens. Ogier killed Balan, Floripas was baptized and married to Guy between whom and Ferumbras Spain was divided. Charlemagne returned to Paris and distributed the relics Floripas had given the peers: thorns from Jesus' crown, and nails from the Crucifixion which Ferumbras had carried away from Jerusalem and sent to his father Balan. Ferumbras' name was a corruption of the French "Fierabras," meaning "strong fierce arm." (ed. S. J. Herrtage, London: Oxford, *EETS ES* #34, 1879; repr. 1966) (Bibliog. 202)

Sir Gawain and the Green Knight, greatest Middle English* metrical romance written in the late 14th century in the alliterative tradition. Its principal theme was the beheading game or challenge, and its secondary theme was the temptation. It recounted the story of Gawain's* participating in a challenge game with a huge strange knight dressed all in green at King Arthur's* Christmas court. Challenging Arthur to exchange blows with his huge axe, the Green Knight agreed to Gawain's substituting for his king. After Gawain struck off the giant's head with one blow, the giant picked up his head, and rode off, reminding Gawain of his obligation to meet him at the Green Chapel at the end of a year to receive his blow in return. Departing from court on All Saint's Day (November 1), Gawain searched for the Green Chapel fruitlessly. Finding shelter at a great castle he was entertained lavishly by the host and hostess. His host persuaded him to remain for the three days until his date with the giant, for the Green Chapel was nearby. Then Gawain agreed to exchange with his host whatever each gained throughout the day. His hostess's amorous advances on the first day resulted only in a kiss which Gawain gave to his host in exchange for the deer he had killed. On the second day, Gawain parried her advances with only two kisses which he gave to his host in exchange for a boar. On the third day, Gawain accepted three kisses and some love tokens including a girdle which she told him would protect his life, though he had to conceal it from her husband. He exchanged the three kisses for the fox taken by the husband. On the next morning, Gawain went to the Green Chapel to receive his return blow from the Green Knight. He flinched at the first two blows, but remained firm on the third one, and received only a nick in his neck from the axe blade. As the third blow was over, Gawain sprang to his feet to defend himself, but was told that he had been repaid for the Christmas blow, and that the Green Knight was his host, Sir Bercilak (Bertilak) de Hautdesert* from the nearby castle. That slight wound had been merely Gawain's repayment for concealing the girdle from the host, and all had been a challenge, a testing of Gawain's fidelity, arranged by Morgan la Fay (Morgan la Fée*) to test and shame the knights of the Round Table* and to alarm Guenevere.* (ed. J. R. R. Tolkien and E. V. Gordon, revised Norman Davis, Oxford: Clarendon Press, 1968; tr. Brian Stone, Baltimore: Penguin Classics, 1959) (Bibliog. 206)

Sir Isumbras, English romance written in imitation of *Octavian.** Here, the hero, Isumbras, was a knight blessed with good fortune who forgot to thank God for his blessings. Immediately after an angel warned him of God's displeasure with him for that attitude, his good fortune turned to bad. He made a pilgrimage to Jerusalem to apologize to God. Then he had to serve for seven years before he was restored to his rightful position. (ed. F. S. Ellis, *Sir Isumbras,* London: Kelmscott Press, 1897) (Bibliog. 202)

Sir Landeval, English romance from the first half of the 14th century, this work was similar to the Breton lay.* It was closely copied from the *Lai de Lanval.** (ed. G. L. Kittredge, *AJP* #1, 1889) (Bibliog. 202)

Sir Launfal, English poem by Thomas Chestre in about 1350, influenced by the *Lai de Lanval** and *Graelent** by Marie de France.* Also known by the title *Launfals miles*, the title given the work on its one surviving copy, this work offered an interesting variation on the fairy mistress story. In it a knight of King Arthur's* court was told by two damsels he met that he was to visit the fairy Tryamour. He followed directions and found that she lavished love and riches upon him, and even conferred upon him immunity from harm, but with the stipulation that their love must remain a secret, for if he betrayed it, he would lose everything. At court one day, provoked by a wrongful accusation hurled at him by the queen, he boasted of Tryamour's love. His arrogance caused him to be condemned to death, but he was saved by the timely arrival of his mistress. This tale resembled *Guingamor,** *Partenopeus de Blois,** and *Ogier le Danois.* (ed. A. Bliss, *Thomas Chestre: Sir Launfal,* London, 1960) (Bibliog. 202)

Sir Orfeo, short Middle English* romance written around the beginning of the 13th century; it related the famous classical story of Orfeus and Eurydice. Queen Heurodys was carried off to fairyland despite all human attempts to keep her. Orfeo followed her as a minstrel, and his success as a harper led her back to the haunts of men. (ed. A. J. Bliss, London, 1966). (Bibliog. 202)

Sir Perceval of Galles, Middle English* Arthurian romance composed between 1300 and 1340. This related the basic story of Perceval* and his search for the Grail,* but the Grail itself did not enter the poem. (ed. J. Campion and F. Holthausen, Heidelberg and New York: G. Stechert, 1913) (Bibliog. 202)

Sir Tristrem, Middle English* poem based on the poem by Thomas, who may have been Thomas of Erceldoune or Thomas of Kendale. This was the only English version of the famous Tristan and Isolde love story outside of Malory's *Morte D'Arthur.** The work centered on the disastrous aftereffects of the love potion which the two lovers, Tristrem and Ysolde, had consumed on Tristrem's return to England from Ireland with Ysolde as King Mark's bride. This love was so unquenchable thereafter that Tristrem had to flee from Mark's court. (ed. G. P. McNeill, Edinburgh: *PSTS* 8, 1886) (Bibliog. 202)

Sluys, battle at (June 24, 1340), sea battle off the Dutch coast in which the English decisively defeated the French. In anticipation of an assault by the English, the French ships at Sluys formed into three squadrons fastened to eash other in a line with chains, and protected by planks and small boats loaded with stones. The first French squadron was manned by Flemings and Picards and carried four cannon and crossbowmen. Although the second French squadron was manned by men from Boulogne and Dieppe, and the third by Normans, only a few of their 20,000 men had ever seen battle. Thus, King Philip's Grand Army of the Sea contained fewer than 150 experienced knights and only 400 professional crossbowmen; the rest were frightened untested fishermen and longshoremen who had been pressed into service. On June 23, King Edward III* with his armada of 147 ships of diverse sizes and capacities sailed from Orwell in Suffolk to meet the French fleet at Zeeland. Edward divided his men into three squadrons or groups of three ships each: one filled with men-at-arms flanked by two filled with archers; he kept a fourth squadron entirely of archers in reserve. At 5:00 A.M. when the tide turned, he slipped anchor and steered for Sluys with the tide running with him, and the sun and the wind behind him. The inexperienced French admirals chose to ignore the advice of their experienced Genoese captains to sail out and meet the approaching English. Rather, they stayed at anchor, arrogantly, like a line of castles as the English approached, and allowed English longbow+ arrows and crossbow quarrels+ to rain on them at random, killing thousands. When the two forces of ships finally met and intensified the battle, Englishmen boarded the anchored French ships with swords, axes and pikes, English bowmen continued to rain arrows, and English seamen threw heavy stones, iron bolts and quicklime from their mastheads onto the enemy's vessels. By this opening attack, the English won the battle after such a bloody mêlée.+ The French admiral, Hue Quièret, badly wounded, was beheaded instantly, and Béhuchet was hanged within minutes of being captured. At the sight of their admiral swinging from the yardarm, many of the French leapt overboard without any further resistance. Even though some small contests continued through the night, the main battle was over; the French had been badly defeated, and with the exception of a few ships which had fled, the entire French fleet had been captured or sunk. King Edward commemorated this victory by issuing a new coin the noble+ of six shillings eight pence, which depicted him on board a ship floating on the waves, crowned and bearing a sword and shield which quartered+ the royal arms of England and France. (See coinage in volume 1.) Although he had not won total command of the seas by this victory, Edward certainly had removed the threat of a French invasion of England by it. (Bibliog. 203)

small folk, Scottish chiefs and their retainers as well as independent freemen and townsmen who joined Robert the Bruce* for the battle of Bannock Burn* in 1314 too late to be trained and disciplined with the other army members who were incorporated into his shiltrons.+ These men were held in reserve. After the main encounters between the Scots and the English, these small folk and camp followers descended onto the battlefield with knives and swords and quickly dispatched all the wounded Englishmen they found lying on the ground as they gathered booty. (Bibliog. 20)

Sogdiana. See Bokhara.

Somerset, county in southern England, whose two most famous earls were William Longespee,* illegitimate son of King Henry II* and earl of Salisbury,* appointed earl of Somerset in 1197, and John Beaufort,* eldest son of John of Gaunt* by his third wife, appointed in 1396. (Bibliog. 101)

Sone de Nansai, French romance of adventure written in the second half of the 13th century. Its author from Brabant, drawing heavily on the romances of Chrétien de Troyes,* described its hero's adventures that took place in England, Scotland, Ireland, Norway, Alsace and Lorraine, France, Germany and Italy. In the story, Sone loved Ide de Doncherai, but when she rejected his marriage proposal, he left to seek his fortune in Scotland, and then Norway where he sided with the Norwegians against the invading Irish and Scots. While there, he heard the story about Joseph of Arimathea and his connection with the monastery at Galocke, reputed to be the Grail Castle. The abbot of Galocke told Sone how Joseph drove the pagans out of Norway and married a pagan princess. God was so upset with him for that union that he crippled Joseph, making him the Fisher King.* He became healed, however, before his son Adam died. Then the abbott showed Sone the Holy Grail, the bleeding lance, and relic of the True Cross. When he left Norway, Sone took with him a Norwegian princess, Odee, who loved him. After some adventures in Ireland, they returned to Norway and then went on to Nansai. Ide, who loved Sone after all, angrily left from him in rage when she learned of Odee. In vain people tried to reconcile the two. Not until the king and queen of France sent for Odee and decided that Sone should marry her did the two agree to get together. He and Odee returned to the monastery in Norway where he was crowned king of Norway, and later he became the Holy Roman Emperor. Odee bore him four sons; three became kings of Norway, of Sicily and of Jerusalem; the fourth became pope. The author introduced a "table ronde"+ involving 100 squires at Chalons among the hero's adventures. There, the *amies* of the jousters stood in wooden lodges around a great meadow and handed spears to their squires. If a squire was overthrown, both he and his damsel had to leave the meadow; if he won, then both he and his damsel were crowned in a great tent. (ed. C. Langlois, *La Vie en France au Moyen Âge,* Paris, 1926, pp. 286-319) (Bibliog. 106, 231)

Song of Roland, the oldest and best of the surviving *chansons de gestes.* In it, Roland, the hero,was depicted as the personification of chivalry and knighthood, for he was brave, fearless, and true to his word This epic French poem, written between 1190 and 1135, has been considered one of the most powerful pleas for the crusades. Its story related how Charlemagne* was on his return to France after a seven-year expedition into Spain to reconquer territory from the Moors (Muslims*). Only Saragossa remained in Moorish hands. Based on a historical event which occurred at Rencesvals in the Pyrenees Mountains between France and Spain on August 15, 778, this story detailed the events leading up to and following the deaths in battle of Charlemagne's *douzepeers* at the hands of a huge overwhelming force of Moors led by King Marsile* of Saragossa and Baligant. Scheming to rid Spain of the Christian forces of Charlemagne, Marsile plotted to convince the Frankish ruler to leave Spain by sending Blancandrin to the emperor with lies and false promises. Charlemagne called for a volunteer to carry his reply. Roland, Charlemagne's nephew, volunteered, but the emperor refused to send him. In reaction, Roland suggested and the emperor agreed to send his step-father, Ganelon. At that, and just before he left on the mission Ganelon angrily swore vengeance against his step-son for that nomination. In Spain, he plotted with Marsile against Charlemagne and Roland. As a result, on his way with Blancandrin to the court of Marsile, Ganelon plotted the destruction of the douzepeers whom Charlemagne had placed as the rear guard of his forces.

Ganelon returned to Charlemagne with Marsile's rich gifts and his promises to follow the emperor to France, become his vassal and convert to Christianity. Marsile meanwhile sent an overwhelming force of 400,000 men against the rear guard of only 20,000 men with the douzepeers. When Oliver saw the enemy forces approaching, three times he urged Roland to sound his horn Olifant to summon the assistance of Charlemagne. Each Roland answered that it would disgrace him and his peers to call for help, it would disgrace his country and king to call for help and it would disgrace his God to call for help. So, the battle was joined and after the all the peers except Roland had died, Roland finally blew his horn to summon Charlemagne to avenge the defeat. He blew the horn so loudly and with such force that he burst blood vessels in his head and he died. Hearing the horn, Charlemagne returned to the field to find his peers dead on the field. In response to Charlemagne's plea for help, God made the sun stand still to allow the Franks to defeat the Moors. Then the emperor summoned his council to hear his charges of treason against Ganelon.

Ganelon maintained that he was innocent for he had openly declared his intention to destroy Roland before the fight at Rencesvals, and thus his action had not been treason. Charlemagne countered with the argument that as his appointed agent, Roland was to be considered to be the emperor, and thus Ganelon's actions against the agent were against the emperor himself. Therefore his actions in fact, were treason. That issue was decided by a trial by combat between Thierry, Charlemagne's champion, and Pinabel, Ganelon's champion. After Thierry won, Ganelon's thirty hostages were hanged after Ganelon had been drawn asunder by being tied to four wild horses. The *douzepeers* listed in this work were Roland, Oliver, Gerin, Gerier, Otton, Berengier, Samson, Ivon, Ivoire, Anseis, Girard and Archbishop Turpin. (See *Karlamagnus Saga)* (ed. and tr. Gerald Brault, University Park, PA: Pennsylvania State University Press, 1978) (Bibliog. 210)

Sorence, castle+ of Pinabel,* Ganelon's relative who fought as his champion in the *chanson de geste,** the *Song of Roland.** It probably was Sarrance, three leagues from Oléron on the north slope of the Pyrenees Mountains between France and Spain. (Bibliog. 210)

Stafford, earl of. In 1350, King Edward III* created Ralph Stafford as the first earl of Stafford for his years of valiant service to the king. Born in 1301, Ralph had done homage and received his father's lands in 1323, and entered the king's service in 1325. Being made a banneret+ in 1327, he was summoned to fight in Scotland* in the same year. Five years later, he accompanied Edward Baliol,* son of John de Baliol,* on his invasion of Scotland. He was summoned to Parliament in 1336, served in Scotland in 1336-1337, accompanied the king to France in 1339, and fought beside the king at Sluys.* In 1342, he took part in the siege of Vannes in Brittany, and was captured, but by the truce of Malestroit, he was exchanged for de Clisson.* In 1343, he was sent to Scotland to raise the siege of Lochaber castle, and then to Gascony* with 3 other bannerets, 20 knights, 92 squires, and 90 archers. He fought in a tournament at Hereford in 1344 as one of the challengers of the nobles of the county, and in 1345 was made seneschal of Aquitaine. In 1346, he defended Alguillon successfully against John, son of King Philip VI of France. He served with the king at Calais in 1346-1347. He was chosen as one of the founding Knights of the Garter, and was made earl in 1350. He died in 1372. (Bibliog. 47)

Staple, official depot where England's raw wool was stored and marketed. In 1337, King Edward III* offered to buy the support of the duke of Brabant* by paying him £60,000 and by offering to install the Staple at Antwerp. (Bibliog. 203)

Stephen of Blois (c. 1097-1154), king of England (1135-1154). Third son of Stephen, count of Blois, and Adela,* daughter of William the Conqueror,* he was reared by Henry I,* educated with Henry's son William,* knighted by the king's own hand, and granted lands in England, and the county of Mortain* in Normandy. He was with the royal party in Normandy* in 1120, but became ill so he did not sail on the ill-fated White Ship.* After the death of Prince William in that disaster, Stephen was adopted by Henry into William's place. At Christmas court in 1126, Stephen swore to the king that on Henry's death, he would acknowledge Henry's daughter, Matilda, as the lady of England and Normandy. In 1227, Henry sent him to Flanders to negotiate with the Flemish nobles to prevent William Clito,* son of Henry's older brother, Robert II,* Curthose, duke of Normandy, from obtaining possession of Normandy. Stephen repeated his oath about Matilda in 1333, swearing fealty to her and her infant son, Henry. No sooner was Henry I dead, however, than Stephen went to England and claimed the crown for himself. London welcomed him. His brother, Henry of Blois, had preceded him to Winchester and secured the treasury for him, just as Henry I had done on the death of William II* thirty-five years earlier. Matilda appealed to Pope Innocent III,* but he sided with Stephen. David I* of Scotland invaded England to support Matilda, but Stephen bought him off by granting three earldoms to his son. Stephen suppressed a revolt in 1337, and then went to Normandy which the king of France agreed to let him hold on the same terms: his eldest son to do homage for it. He also made a truce with Matilda's second husband, Geoffrey of Anjou, who was threatening to invade Normandy.

Back in England, he pursued David back across the Scottish border. He chose as his close advisor a Flemish adventurer, William of Ypres and his cohorts, whose influence over him aroused the jealousy of the barons and the old ministers of Henry I. These Flemish advisors were violent and greedy mercenaries whose actions angered the people and the barons. Stephen quarreled with the most influential of all barons, Robert, earl of Gloucester,* Matilda's half-brother, and in 1138, when Robert formally defied the king, the barons in the south and west of England rose with him. Geoffrey Talbot,* a notoriously bitter opponent of the king, seized Hereford* castle, held it for five weeks against the king, but was captured by the bishop of Bath and Wells, who in turn was captured by men from Earl Robert's castle of Bristol. When the bishop obtained his release by surrendering Talbot, King Stephen was furious. Then Stephen summoned Bishop Roger of Salisbury,* the justiciar,+ to Oxford. As both were suspicious, each took armed followers, and soon a disturbance led the king to arrest Bishop Roger, his son Roger the chancellor, and his nephew Alexander,

bishop of Lincoln, and then he took them all with him to besiege
Roger's (the chancellor) castle at Devizes. There he locked the bishop
in a cowshed and threatened to hang the younger Roger if his wife did
not surrender the castle to him. She did. Then the king rode to
capture Roger's two other castles at Sherbourne and Malmsbury. Then he
marched against the bishop of Lincoln, and forced the surrender of his
castle by keeping the owner outside of the castle to starve until he
surrendered. For this, his brother, Henry, the papal legate ordered
him to appear before a church council. Stephen defended his actions by
saying that the castles were private possessions of Bishop Roger and
thus not episcopal possessions, but the council forced him to do public penance for his violence to the bishops.

In 1140, Matilda FitzEmpress* landed in England, joined her
brother Robert, and in a few months was mistress of the western
shires. Then when Earl Ranulph of Chester* seized Lincoln, Stephen
rode to confront him, but in the upcoming battle against overwhelming
numbers, Stephen's men betrayed him and fled. Stephen fought against
them practically alone until he fell. Put into prison, he was deposed,
and Matilda took over, but her harsh government proved to be just as
unacceptable to the people as Stephen's had been. In December 1141,
after she released Stephen in exchange for his brother Robert who also
had been captured at Lincoln, Stephen appealed to the council, and was
reinstated as king. He allowed tournaments to be held, the first
English king to do so, for those military exercises allowed large
groups of armed men to gather, and earlier kings were wary of such
concentrations of power. He suppressed the castles of Matilda's
supporters, and arrested the worst of the troublemakers, Geoffrey de
Mandeville, earl of Essex,* whom he forced to purchase freedom by
surrendering all of his castles. Even though Geoffrey did so, he resumed his lawless ways once he was free of the king's restraints.
Stephen spent most of the rest of his reign fighting the barons. In
1149, Henry of Anjou, Matilda's sixteen-year-old son, came to England
to exert his claim to the throne, but he was unsuccessful. Stephen
wanted it to go to his son Eustace, but the pope refused to support
that succession. Even though the clergy supported the pope, Stephen
tried to frighten them into supporting his position by imprisoning
them, including the archbishop* of Canterbury,* until he could have
his son crowned. When the archbishop escaped, however, no coronation
was possible. In 1153 Henry of Anjou returned to besiege Malmsbury
where his troops met King Stephen's in a stalemate. Over the next few
months, the king's spirit was broken by the deaths of his wife and
then his son. Reluctantly he agreed with Henry that he would remain
king for his lifetime, and then the throne would go to Henry. He died

in 1154. (Bibliog. 58)

Stirling Bridge, battle at (September 11, 1297), battle which taught the English lessons in strategy and tactics. John, earl of Warenne,* had been left as King Edward I's* representative north of the Tweed River. Sixty years old, he seemingly had learned nothing from his numerous battles during a lifetime of service for the crown. At the head of a large army raised in the six northern English counties and Wales, John set out to suppress the Scottish insurgents under Sir William Wallace in the Scottish Lowlands. Determined to stop the English at the Forth River, Wallace massed his small force of 180 mounted knights and squires and hundreds of spearmen in the woods along the winding north bank of the river. In response, Warenne concentrated his men-at-arms and footsoldiers at Stirling, determined to cross Stirling Bridge. This was a long and narrow bridge on which no more than two horsemen could ride abreast. Angered by the insolence of the Scots rejecting his demand to lay down their arms, Warenne arrogantly rejected all advice from his leaders. Sir Richard Lundy pointed out to him that it would take eleven hours for his force to cross the narrow and confining bridge, but that at a ford not far away, they could ride across thirty abreast. Warenne refused to listen, and ordered his men to cross the bridge. Watching this incredible folly from the security of the north shore woods, Wallace let the vanguard under Marmaduke Twenge and Hugh Cressingham the treasurer and a few knights to cross and begin to form up on the north bank, and then he attacked with his whole force as the main English army watched helplessly from the south bank. A special force of Wallace's spearmen held the bridgehead so that Warenne could not move any men across the bridge to help his beleaguered forces. After a short struggle, all the Englishmen who had crossed either had been trampled down or flung into the river. By incredible valor, Twenge managed to fight his way back across the bridge, but he left more than a hundred knights and several thousand English and Welsh footsoldiers dead. In reaction, Warenne, instead of preparing to defend the Forth, garrisoned a force in Stirling* castle and then withdrew the remainder of his forces to Berwick, abandoning the whole of the Scottish Lowlands to the Scots. (Bibliog. 166)

Stirling castle, called appropriately the Key to Scotland, this fortress was one of the slender links between the Highlands in the north, and the Lowlands in the south. Situated on a precipitous rock lying northwest of the town, this promontory had been fortified since the early days by a hill fort which later was replaced by a wooden

castle and palisades. In 1124, King Alexander I* died there and was
succeeded by his brother David.* Stirling later gained prominence when
the Scottish king, William the Lion,* for his support of the rebellion
of Henry II's* sons, was forced to sign the Treaty of Falaise* in
1174. By this, he agreed to have the chief Scottish castles+ staffed
by English soldiers. Not until a century later in 1288 was the first
stone castle erected on this steep-sided rock towering some 300 feet
above the River Forth. It was chiefly remembered for its role in the
Scottish wars for independence from England because it dominated the
passage to the north of Scotland, and thus became the focus of military operations. At first, Edward I* captured it easily because his triumph at Berwick in 1296 so terrified the Scots at Stirling that its
garrison deserted leaving only its porter with its keys. In the
following year the Scots under Wallace* defeated the English at Stirling Bridge,* but in only a year, King Edward recaptured and re-
garrisoned it. When the Scots again assaulted it, its garrison
appealed to the English barons for assistance, but they refused to
leave their comfortable homes for a bitter winter fight in the north,
and so the garrison once again surrendered to the Scots. Edward
besieged it again in 1304 as the last stronghold in Scottish hands.
After he starved it into submission, it remained in English hands for
ten years. Then in 1313, Edward Bruce,* brother of King Robert,
blockaded the fortress, and then agreed that its governor, Sir Philip
Mowbray, would surrender it unless he was relieved before June 24,
1314. King Edward II* sent a detachment of troops for that relief, but
the Scots drove them back and finally won the castle after the battle
of Bannock Burn.* King Robert then destroyed the fortifications to
prevent the English from using them again. However, after the Scots
were defeated at Halidon Hill,* Stirling again was repaired and re-
garrisoned by English soldiers under Sir Thomas de Rokeby. In 1337, it
was besieged again but was relieved by troops under Edward III,* and
heavily provisioned against further attacks. Only five years later, in
1342, the Scots forced it to yield. When the Stewarts came to the
throne, Stirling became a royal residence. In 1373, Robert II's son,
Robert, earl of Mentieth and Fife, and later duke of Albany was made
keeper. (Bibliog. 20, 247)

Stonehenge, circle of blue stones on Salisbury plain. Called "The
Dance of the Giant" by Geoffrey of Monmouth* (VIII, 10), this
structure was named Stonehenge in Henry of Huntingdon's
*Historia Anglorum,** written a few years before Geoffrey's work. Legend
and Geoffrey of Monmouth credited Merlin with magically transporting
these stones from the mountain of Killare in Ireland to the plain at

Salisbury as a long-lasting monument to a group of Britons treacherously slain by Saxons. Wace's *Brut** credited Stonehenge as being the burial place of Uther Pendragon. (Bibliog. 89, 117)

Strathbogie. See Huntley castle.

Der Stricker, Middle High German* poet of the first part of the 13th century. A commoner from Franconia, he lived much of his life in Austria. His two epics were *Karl,* an adaptation of Pfaffe Konrad's* German version of the *Chanson de Roland,** and *Daniel von dem Blühenden Tal,** an Arthurian romance presenting a string of improbable adventures which der Pleier* answered in his work, *Garel von dem Blühenden Tal.* (Bibliog. 235)

Striguil. See Chepstow.

Strongbow, Richard FitzGilbert de Clare, earl of Pembroke. He was son of Gilbert de Clare* upon whom King Stephen* had conferred the title of earl of Pembroke in 1138. In 1166, Diarmait MacMurchada, king of Leinster, was forced into exile and sought military aid from Henry II* to regain his kingdom. His actions led to direct Anglo-Norman intervention into Ireland. Of those Anglo-Normans whom he recruited, the most important was Richard FitzGilbert, to whom Diarmait in the winter of 1166-1167 made a proposal of marriage to his daughter, Aoife, and succession to the kingdom of Leinster after his death in return for military assistance. Late in 1170, Strongbow journeyed to Ireland, a ruined man, out of favor with King Henry who had refused to restore his Welsh holdings. In Ireland, he attacked and captured Waterford town and castle,+ slaughtering 700 citizens in the battle, and capturing the officers of the fortress. A few days later, he married Aoife (Eve), daughter of Dairmait MacMurchada, king of Leinster. Shortly after Diarmait's death in 1171, Richard and his small band of English knights were blockaded in Dublin by an attacking force of Vikings. Breaking the land blockade of Irish forces, Richard surprised the Irish and Vikings and defeated them badly. That resulted in Dairmait's recovery of the kingdom of Leinster and Strongbow's succession to it after his death. Summoned by Henry II to Wales,* he was forgiven his rebellious actions on the condition that he should surrender Dublin and other coast towns absolutely into the king's hands and do him homage+ and fealty+ for the remainder of Leinster. Later Richard served the king well as commandant of the important border fortress of Gisors* in France, following which he was returned to Ireland as its governor in 1175, and died in 1176. (Bibliog. 76, 162) *stupor mundi,* nickname meaning "amazement of the world" applied to Holy Roman Emperor Frederick II.* (Bibliog. 68)

Sucinio, Breton castle+ begun around the beginning of the 13th century by the first duke of Brittany* to came from the house of France, Peter de Dreux. His son, John I, the Red (1237-1286), brashly confiscated church lands on which to build his domain. Four of his children died and were buried beside their mother in the choir of the church at Saint Gildas du Rhuys; his one survivor, John II, built the fortress after 1286. During the war of succession, Sucinio reverberated with the sounds of war, passing from the hands of Blois to Montfort as each man besieged the other until finally French troops of Charles V* under du Guesclin* exterminated the English garrison in 1373. Twenty years later, Arthur de Richemont was born there, the man who in 1425 received the sword as constable of France as the successor to Clisson* and du Guesclin. (Bibliog. 196)

Suddene, home of King Horn in the Middle English* metrical romance. It was variously identified as Surrey, Sussex or Dorestshire, south Cornwall, South Daneland, the Isle of Man and even Westernesse in Ireland. Its true locality remained a mystery. (Bibliog. 63)

Suffolk, ancient portion of the area in England which with Cambridgeshire and Norfolk* made up the kingdom of the East Angles.* Its first earl was Ralph, the Staller, earl of Norfolk and Suffolk (sometimes called East Angles), who died around 1070, and was succeeded by Ralph de Gael, lord of Gael in Brittany. He was one of the leaders of the unsuccessful rebellion against William* the Conqueror in 1075, which led to the forfeiture of all his honours+ and lands. He died on the first crusade.+ His earldom remained with the crown until 1141 when King Stephen* granted it to Hugh Bigod* as the earldom of Norfolk, the title by which he and his successors were known. No separate earldom of Suffolk was created until 1337 when Robert de Ufford, Lord Ufford, was created earl of Suffolk by King Edward III.* He was admiral of the king's fleet northward from the Thames, served with the king at Antwerp, and on many other missions. He served in France from 1344 to 1347, accompanied by a banneret,+ 36 knights, 58 esquires, and 63 archers. He was marshal of the army in 1346 at Crécy and again at Calais,* and was made Knight of the Garter* in 1349. He died in 1368. Because his son and heir, Robert, had predeceased him 1368, the title passed to his grandson, William who also served as king's admiral* for King Richard II.* He was nominated as Knight of the Garter in 1375. He died while walking into the House of

Lords at Westminster in 1381, and because he was childless, the title reverted to the crown. King Richard II bestowed the title on Michael de la Pole, a knight who had served in the retinue of the duke of Lancaster (John of Gaunt*) in his attempts to aid King Charles of Navarre in 1355, and also with Edward,* the Black Prince, in 1359. Continuing his service in the French wars from 1369, he took part in the sieges of Limoges,* under the Black Prince, and of Montfort under the duke of Lancaster. He was created earl of Suffolk in 1385, but his favor with the king made him so unpopular with Parliament that he was impeached, convicted, and heavily fined, and had his lands confiscated. He continued to serve with the king in Wales and the Midlands in 1387, and returned to London with them. But being accused of high treason by the earls of Gloucester, Arundel and Warwick (the Lords Appellant*), he fled the realm in 1387. In his absence he was found guilty, and all his honours were forfeit to the crown. He died in Paris in 1389. (Bibliog. 47)

Suite de Merlin, often called the *Huth Merlin* after the name of the manuscript containing it, this work by Robert de Boron* was a continuation of the Vulgate *Merlin* story, hence the name, "Suite de Merlin." After giving an account of King Arthur's* wars against the rebel kings, this romance continued with an early history of Arthur's reign. It described Mordred's* birth, the revelation of Arthur's parentage, his fight with Pellinore,* his obtaining Excaliber* from the lake, his wars against Rion and Lot,* the tale of Balin, Arthur's marriage to Leodegrance's daughter, the quest of Gauvain (Gawain*), Tor, and Pellinore, the story of Merlin and Niniane, Arthur's wars with the five kings, Morgain's plots to destroy Arthur, and the adventures of Gauvain, Yvain* and the Morholt.* Within the work itself its author named himself. (ed. Gaston Paris and J. Ulrich, Paris: *SATF,* 1886) (Bibliog. 10)

Surrey, portion of land lying south of the Thames River in the early kingdom of the Anglo-Saxons in England; from the Saxon word *Rea,* meaning river, and hence from South-rea, the name Surrey was derived. William de Warenne* I (Varenne in Normandy) was granted generous holdings in Surrey and other counties of England as payment for his service at the battle of Hastings.* Earlier, he had been one of the barons summoned by Duke William I* of Normandy to a council on learning that Harold* had been crowned king of England on the death of Edward* the Confessor. A few years later, he repaid the king for his English estates by joining with Richard de Clare* in the king's absence to put down the rebellion of the earls of Norfolk,*

Northampton-Huntingdon* and Hereford.* After King William I's death, Warenne came out strongly for William II,* and aided him to crush the rebellions of the king's uncles, Odo,* bishop of Bayeux, and Count Robert of Mortain.* In 1188, to secure his loyalty, the king made him earl of Surrey. Later that year, he was mortally wounded at the siege of Pevensey,* and was taken to his castle at Lewes to die, leaving two sons, William II and Rainald. To William II went the English lands and to Rainald those in Flanders. William II supported Duke Robert of Normandy in 1101, so his English fief was forfeit, but the duke himself intervened with his nephew, King Henry I,* and the earldom was restored. He fought beside the king and commanded a royal division at Tinchebrai* (1106) and at Bremûle* in 1119. After the king's death, Warenne remained for some months as governor of Rouen with other barons in Normandy, awaiting the turn of events in England. He appeared at King Stephen's* court in 1139, and was styled as earl of Warenne. He married the daughter of the count of Vermandois (younger son of Henry I) who had married as her first husband, Robert de Beaumont, count of Meulan and had borne him twin sons, Waleran, afterwards count of Meulan, and Robert, earl of Leicester, both of whom were highly respected by King Henry I.

    William de Warenne II died in 1138 leaving his son and heir, William III. This earl deserted Stephen in Normandy and contrived the signing of a truce between Stephen and Geoffrey of Anjou.* On his return he joined the king at the battle of Lincoln* at which the king was captured because Warenne and other barons ignominiously fled just before the first charge. He redeemed himself partially by supporting Stephen's queen during his captivity and then by capturing Earl Robert of Gloucester* whose subsequent exchange for the king set Stephen free. He joined the second crusade+ and was killed on it in 1148, leaving a daughter, Isabel. She married William de Blois, the third but only surviving son and heir of King Stephen; by that marriage he was recognized as earl of Warenne. On the death of his elder brother, Eustace, in 1153, he became count of Boulogne, and then on the death of Stephen, Count of Mortain. These he surrendered to Henry II,* but was reconfirmed in all the holdings which Stephen had held before he became king. He died childless on his way home from Toulouse in 1159. His widow, Isabel, was married to Hamelin Plantagenet,* for whom the king was seeking placement. Hamelin took the name Warenne along with lands of the earldom. He supported Henry II against the rebellious princes in 1173, and died in 1202, leaving a son, William IV. This fourth William supported the barons on the death of King John in inviting the dauphin* of France to invade England, but by 1217, he had made peace with the regent, William Marshal. With the other earls he was responsible for the downfall of Hubert de Burgh* in 1232. He died in 1240 leaving his son, John, then a minor of five years of age. At age 12 in 1247 he had married Alice de Lusignan, half-sister of King Henry III.*

As a young man, this John changed his loyalty from support of the king to support of the Barons' War,* but swung back again to the king. He went on a crusade in 1268 with Prince Edward.* In 1271, in a legal quarrel with Alan la Zouche over the land of the disinherited barons, he forgot his place and his duty to the crown, and attacked and wounded his opponent during the trial at Westminster, and then fled the court. For such a contemptuous action, he was summoned before King Henry III immediately, and wisely submitted himself to the kings' mercy.+ He suffered a huge fine, and did public penance. Afterward, he became one of the staunchest friends of the prince, later King Edward. He died in 1304. As his son and heir had predeceased him by eighteen years, his grandson, John II, de Warenne, born in 1286, became his heir and was granted the lands and title in 1306. As a ward of the crown, he had become a great favorite of King Edward, even marrying the king's granddaughter Joan in 1306. He opposed Gaveston,* acted as an Ordainer,* and supported the throne against the barons. When he died childless in 1347, the title passed to his nephew, Richard FitzAlan, earl of Arundel,* son of John de Warenne's sister, but was forfeited in 1399 by his son, also named Richard, who was beheaded for treason. Thomas de Holland,* earl of Kent,* was made the first duke of Surrey by Parliament of King Richard II* in 1397, but was degraded from that dukedom in 1399 by the first Parliament of King Henry IV,* and beheaded in 1400. (Bibliog. 47, 66)

Sussex, area along the southeast coast of England in the early kingdom of the Anglo-Saxons, from which it took the name South-Sax or Sussex. William d'Aubigny* (de Albeney, d'Albini), son and heir of William d'Aubigny, a Norman from the Cotentin,* and Maud, daughter of Roger Bigod,* had obtained the honour+ of Arundel* by his marriage with the queen dowager, Adeliz, widow of King Henry I.* About 1139, he was created earl of Lincoln,* surrendered that earldom in 1141, and was created earl of Sussex before Christmas of that same year. The title continued in the house of d'Aubigny as a second honour to the family which styled itself earls of Arundel. When Hugh d'Aubigny, fifth earl of Sussex, died childless in 1243, the earldom reverted to the crown. (Bibliog. 47)

Swabia, Suabia, Schwaben, duchy in southwestern Germany whose territory corresponded roughly with the ancient province of Alemania. It began as a kingdom established in 845 by Lothaire* for his son, Charles the Fat.* With the organization of Germany into a kingdom later in that century, Swabia became one of its duchies* and was governed by appointed dukes. In 1180, after Emperor Henry IV* appointed his relative, Frederick of Hohenstaufen* as duke, Swabia became the territorial base of the Hohenstaufen dynasty until the reign of Frederick II* (1212-1250). He granted special privileges to some of its important vassals, among then Rudolf of Hapsburg, who established an important principality in southern Swabia which later became Switzerland. (Bibliog. 98)

Swein, eldest son of Earl Godwine* of England. Through his father's influence, he was appointed earl of Oxford* by King Edward the Confessor* in 1043, but because he seduced an abbess, he was forced to flee to Denmark. He returned to England with the rest of his exiled family in 1051, but again was forced to flee the country because the Witan outlawed him for his outrageous conduct. He died on his return from a trip from the Holy Land in 1052. (Bibliog. 98)

T

Taillebourg, battle of (1242), conflict in Aquitaine* in which English King Henry III* allowed himself to be defeated by French King Louis IX.* With 1,600 knights, 700 bowmen and the general levy+ of the towns in Guyenne (Aquitaine), Henry was situated on one bank of the broad, swiftly flowing Charente River, opposing Louis and his much larger force on the other bank. Relying on guarding the single bridge across the river, Henry did not watch the actions of the French king because he felt his position was secure. Louis, however, simultaneously attacked the bridge and the English with crossbowmen and dismounted knights crossing in large boats. Fearing an attack from both the rear and the front, Henry's bridge guards fled. When he saw that the bridge was lost, Henry immediately asked for a truce, and then fled at night deserting his baggage. He should have attacked the small force of French knights as they disembarked from the boats before others could cross, but his military ignorance cost him the battle. (Bibliog. 166)

tailleor. See Grail.

Talbot, English family descended from a Norman who held land in Normandy* under the counts of Eu,* and had gone to England with William* the Conqueror in 1066. Geoffrey Talbot held lands in Kent from Odo,* bishop of Bayeux, and half-brother of William I. His son, Geoffrey II, was active in Gloucestershire and Herefordshire as a notoriously bitter opponent of King Stephen.* His descendant, Gilbert (1276-1346), was pardoned in 1313 for his role in the death of Piers Gaveston,* but he once again rose against the king by joining the barons against the Despensers.* In 1322 he, with his brother Richard Talbot, and the earl of Hereford,* and others evaded arrest for attacking and burning Bridgnorth, and for attacking the king's subjects in County Warwick. Later that same year, being styled a banneret,+ he was captured in arms against the king at Boroughbridge, but was allowed to pay a fine for his life and his lands, and was discharged from prison. Summoned to Parliament in 1331, he became lord

Talbot for life. He died in 1346, and was succeeded by his son, Richard (1305-1356) who had fought beside him at Boroughbridge* in 1322. Summoned to Parliament in 1332, Richard also became lord Talbot. Through his wife Elizabeth, daughter of Lord Comyn, lord of Badenoch, he claimed large possessions in Scotland in right of his wife, and in defiance of the king's orders, he accompanied Edward Baliol* and the Disinherited* in their invasion of Scotland. He was present at their defeat of the Scots at Dupplin Moor* in 1232. Though wounded early in a campaign near the Seine, he took in the battle of Crécy* in 1346. He went on to serve the king well, dying in 1356. (Bibliog. 47)

Tamerlane, Timur the Lame (1335-1405), Mongol khan* from Samarkand in central Asia (1370-1405). When he was 34, he won control of Tansoxiana, his native territory, and then he turned south and overran Khurusan, Kurdistan, and parts of Afghanistan and Persia. His spoils he took back to Samarkand to make it one of the richest and most beautiful cities in the world. In 1391 and 1395, he defeated Tuktamish, khan of the Golden Horde, and then conquered Kashmir, Delhi, and the northwestern provinces of India in 1398, stretching his empire from the Sea of Aral to the Persian Gulf, from Delhi to Iraq. He was a cruel and merciless man. He massacred children in captured cities, and frequently buried prisoners alive. In 1401 he turned west, overran Anatolia and Syria, captured and destroyed Baghdad, and then turned north into Asia Minor, where on July 28, 1402, on a plain near Angora, his Mongol army of some 200,000 men met the Ottoman force of 120,000 in the greatest battle of centuries. Timur outgeneraled and outmaneuvered the fine Turkish troops who had terrorized Europe, and captured their general, Bayazid. He ravaged Aleppo and Damascus with much slaughter, defeated the forces sent against him from Egypt, and headed east to conquer China, but died on his way there in 1405. (Bibliog. 124)

Tancred (d. 1112), prince of Galilee; member of the Hauteville family of Sicily, and nephew of Bohemond of Taranto whom he accompanied on the first crusade.+ After winning Antioch, he marched on to Jerusalem and joined the army of Godfrey de Bouillon.* As a vassal of Godfrey, he founded the principality of Galilee, and became the main leader of the siege of Haifa after 1100. After the death of Godfrey, he attempted unsuccessfully to ascend the throne of Jerusalem, and when Baldwin I was chosen in his stead, his uncle tactfully appointed him as regent of Antioch which he worked hard to maintain against continuing Moslem hostility. (Bibliog. 98)

Tancred of Hauteville (fl. 1030), Norman baron whose son, Robert Guiscard,* founded the Norman state in southern Italy and the Hauteville* dynasty. Three of his other sons, William Iron-Arm, Drogo, and Humphrey became leaders of the Norman free booters* in the Mediterranean. His youngest son became Roger I,* count of Sicily (1061-1101). (Bibliog. 98, 124)

Tancred of Lecce, king of Sicily between 1190 and 1194. An illegitimate son of Roger II,* duke of Apulia,* he was proclaimed king in 1190 by a party of Norman Sicilians who refused to recognize the claims of his aunt, Constance, fearing that her marriage to the Emperor Henry VI* would bring Sicily under German rule. On their way to the third crusade,+ Richard I* of England and Philip II* of France paused in Sicily in 1190. Richard arrived first, and signed a peace treaty with Tancred, and, according to the chroniclers, such as Roger of Hoveden,* and the *Gesta Henrici*,* made him a present of King Arthur's sword, Excaliber,* which had only recently been unearthed at Glastonbury.* Philip supposedly wrote Tancred a letter accusing the English king of treachery, and asking Tancred's assistance to destroy him. Philip denied the accusation when confronted by Richard, and the two once again agreed on friendship and continued on their crusade. Tancred, however, was unable to maintain his authority, and in 1194, Henry VI conquered the island and enlisted the support of the barons against Tancred. (Bibliog. 27, 98)

tanistry (Irish, *tanaiste*, "second person in rank"), early Irish law of succession by which the heir or successor of a chief or king was appointed during the lifetime of the reigning chief. Not necessarily the eldest son, this man generally was the worthiest and wisest of the male relatives of the chief. Because he was elected by the people from among the eligible families, bloody wars and feuds between families often resulted. (Bibliog. 169)

Taprobane, ancient name for the island of Ceylon. (Bibliog. 146)

Tavola ritonda, most elaborate of the Italian Arthurian prose romances. Composed at the end of the 13th or early 14th century, this work told the stories of Tristan, Lancelot* and other Arthurian knights, combining many Arthurian legends drawn and modified from the prose *Tristan* and other French sources, and adding new episodes. (tr. Anne Shaver, Binghamton, NY: *MRTS* 28, 1984) (Bibliog. 245)

tenants, English word used to refer to the term *tenens* (tenant) meaning servile tenure; *tenens in Capite* (tenant in chief) meant a man who held his land of the king without any intermediary, whether he was a powerful baron or a simple farmer on a demesne. With the exception of the serfs and the outcasts of town or county, all the subjects of the king, rich or poor, bond or free, were tenants. Everyone held tenure of the king or one of his intermediaries, so ultimately, everyone held, directly or indirectly, of the king. This practice was followed in England though the transfer of lands after the Norman Conquest (1066). Its most unfortunate victims were the small Anglo-Saxon farmers of free status whose lands were given to Norman warriors without any compensation. These people were classed as villeins,+ which implied that they had had personal liberty, but by these actions had become tenants bound personally to the lord; thereby they sank to the lowest depths of the social scale alongside the serfs of Anglo-Saxon society. In Capetian France, the word *tenant* continued to denote free peasants. (Bibliog. 178)

Tenlade. See Thanet.

Thanet, island, eight miles long and four miles wide in the northeast of Kent, England, surrounded on three sides by the North Sea, and on the west by the River Stoure. Also called Tenalde, it was the first landing place of the Saxons in England, and also of St. Augustine when he came to Christianize the Britons. (Bibliog. 101)

Theoderic the Great (c. 455-526), king of the Ostrogoths from 474 to 526. In 493, he invaded Italy where he defeated and murdered Odoacer, king of the Heruli at Ravenna. He thereupon became king of Italy and enlarged his kingdom beyond the Alps up to the Rhône River. Known in literature as Dietrich von Bern (Verona) he played an important role in the concluding section of the *Nibelungenlied,** and was the focal figure in such Old High German epics as the *Hildebrandslied.** In the cycle of legends surrounding him, episodes had little relationship to historical fact. Chief among these legends were his thirty years banishment from his rightful inheritance through his wicked rival Odoacer whom later legends replaced with Ermonrich, his stay at the court of Etzel (Attila*), king of the Huns, and his final reconquest of his kingdom in the Rabenslacht* (battle at Ravenna). To this framework were added tales from his youth in which he conquered dragons and giants, and legends about his exemplary personality. He was credited with being brave, chivalrous, a model prince in every respect, but seemingly was pursued and persecuted by a malevolent fate which inflicted one devastating blow after another on him. Despite his enormous strength and skill in combat, however, he was always peacefully inclined and not drawn into fights easily.   Once angry, though, he became invincible. (Bibliog. 235)

Thibaut the Great (1093-1152), count of Blois (as Thibaut IV, 1102-1152) and of Champagne (as Thibaut II, 1125-1152). Between 1108 and 1120, he was one of the strongest allies of Henry I* of England, and strongest adversaries of Louis VI.* However, his attitude was changed dramatically by the drowning of William, only son and heir of Henry I. He suddenly realized the futility of feudal wars, and sought to end them. He became pious and worked to improve and enlarge churches and schools and fairs. He established his courts at Troyes, making Champagne his principality. In 1135, on the death of Henry I, he helped his brother, Stephen* obtain the throne of England. Between 1140 and 1142 conflict arose between him and Louis VII* who invaded Champagne. Thibaut appealed both to Pope Innocent II* and Bernard of Clairvaux.* The peace treaty reached served as peaceful relations between the French king and the house of Blois-Champagne for the remainder of the 12th century. (Bibliog. 98)

Thibaut IV (1201-1253), count of Champagne and king of Navarre (1234-1253). He was one of the most colorful personalities of his era: a feudal lord, a perfect knight, an adventurer, a poet, he helped Queen Blanche* of Castile during her regency for Louis IX* (1228-1232). Simultaneously, he attempted to oppose the royal administration in Champagne where he held his court. He inherited the kingdom of Navarre in 1234, and assumed the title, but was not interested in the area and assigned its administration to his officers. In 1239, he led a crusade+ in the Holy Land and conquered the area between Ascalon and Jerusalem for the realm of Acre. (Bibliog. 98)

Thierry (Terry), brother of Geoffrey of Anjou* and Charlemagne's* champion in the duel with Pinabel* to determine Ganelon's* guilt or innocence of the charge of treason against Charlemagne in the *Song of Roland.** (Bibliog. 210)

Thing, assembly of barons in medieval Sweden that emerged from gatherings of tribal chieftains in the 10th and 11th centuries. Among its prerogatives were the elections of kings and the confirmation of ordinances. Increasing royal power in the 13th century lessened its political importance. (Bibliog. 98)

Thirty, Combat of the (March 27, 1351), one of the most important events of the Hundred Years War* fought when thirty Franco-Breton knights, defeated thirty Anglo-Breton, Gascon and German knights, killing nine of them. It emerged from an attack on the English garrison at Ploermel by a French force under Robert de Beaumanoir. To avoid a siege, Sir Richard Bramborough, the garrison commander, suggested a combat in the open plain before Ploermel between 30 men-at-arms from each side. He told his men (Bretons, Germans and English) to "fight in such a way that people will speak of it in future times in halls, in palaces, in public places and elsewhere throughout the world." These sixty men fought on foot with swords and halberds+ until four of the English and two of the French had been killed and everyone was exhausted. A breathing space was called, but when Beaumanoir, badly wounded, staggered off to find water, an Englishman mocked him with the era's most memorable reply, "Drink thy blood, Beaumanoir, and thy thirst will pass!" and the fight resumed. Although their tight, shoulder-to-shoulder formation made the English seem impregnable, a French knight crept away, mounted his steed and returned at full charge, knocking the English off their feet. At this, the French pounced on the downed knights, killing nine including Bamborough, and capturing the rest, including Croquart,* Hugh Calveley* and Robert Knollys.* (Bibliog. 203, 223)

Thogarmim, name used by the Byzantines to refer to the Turks. See Constantinople. (Bibliog. 50)

Thomas, earl of Lancaster (d. 1322), leader of the English baronial forces against King Edward II* who had fallen under the influences of the two Hugh Despensers,* father and son. These two man quickly grew to occupy with the king the same favored position as had Piers Gaveston* a few years earlier. However, their arrogance and greed un-ited the old nobility against them, and as the greatest and richest noble in England, Thomas was their leader. He summoned northern lords to a meeting in Pontefract* in May 1321 where they formed a league for mutual defense. To strengthen their position, Earl Thomas called the archbishop* of York and his bishops to a meeting in June. The prelates agreed to support all manners of defense against the Scots, but felt that all matters relating to reforming abuses in the realm should be handled in Parliament. Without their expected support, Thomas, a weak and indecisive man anyway, was incapable of taking decisive action, and he let the king crush rebellions at Badlesmere* in Kent, and by the Mortimers* in the west before he took up arms himself. By February 1322, he at last was persuaded by Mowbray, Clifford, and the earl of Hereford* to help them besiege Tickhill* castle. When it held out for over three weeks, he marched to Burton-on-Trent against the king. Royal forces outflanked the rebels on their march, and when they crossed the river unexpectedly, the outnumbered rebels panicked and fled to Lancaster's castle at Pontefract. Learning of their flight, Robert Holand,* Lancaster's treasurer who was bringing reinforcements, deserted and made terms himself with the king at Lancaster's expense. At this both earls of Lancaster and Hereford fled in terror towards the Scots border hoping to obtain help from the neighboring Scottish forces. When they got as far as Boroughbridge on March 16, 1322, they found Sir Andrew Harcla,* warden of Carlisle, holding the bridge. In an effort to take the bridge, Hereford was killed. Discouraged by his death, and unable to cross the bridge because of the volley of arrows from Harcla's archers, Lancaster's men began to waver, but they still were too strong for Harcla to cross the bridge in an attack. They retired for the night, and on their return in the morning, they found that the royal forces had been strengthened by the arrival of the sheriff of Yorkshire with 400 men. This panicked the earl's army, and they fled, abandoning their arms. Lancaster was captured, taken to his own castle of Pontefract, held in a new tower which he had built especially to hold the king. On the next day, he was condemned to die as a traitor. As a member of the royal blood, he was beheaded; the other rebels were hanged. These included Warin de Lisle, William Touchet, Thomas Mauduit,* Henry Bradburn, William FitzWilliam, William Cheney all hanged at Pontefract; John Mowbray* and Roger Clifford* were hanged at York. In May 1322, Parliament met at York and revoked the ordinance previously passed against the Despensers; the elder Hugh was created earl of Winchester*; Sir Andrew Harcla was made earl of Carlisle, and William de Aune, successful defender of Tickhill, was knighted. (Bibliog. 47, 153, 249)

Thomas, of Brotherton (1300-1338), fifth son of King Edward I* of England but the eldest son by his second wife, Margaret, daughter of Philip III* of France, and half-brother of Edward II.* See Norfolk. (Bibliog. 47)

Thomas de Marle (d. 1130), most notorious and savage of the de Coucy* family, called the "ravaging wolf" by Abbé Suger of Saint Denis. He was the son of Enguerrand I* de Coucy and Adele de Marle whom Enguerrand divorced on the grounds of adultery. Bitterly hating his father who had cast his paternity in doubt, Thomas grew up to war ceaselessly against his father. To that end, he kept trying to ruin his father by killing and maiming as many of his peasants as he could, and destroying as many crops, vineyards, tools, barns, and other

possessions as possible, thereby reducing his father's sources of revenue. In this private war, captured men had their eyes gouged out and
their feet cut off. Such private wars were the curse of Europe which
the crusades+ were invented to relieve. Both Thomas and his father
took the cross for the first crusade (1095-1098), and carried on it
their hatred for each other. From this expedition the Coucy
coat-of-arms+ was derived. With five companions, either Thomas or his
father was surprised by a band of Muslims* when out of armor. He took
off his scarlet cloak trimmed with vair+ (squirrel fur), tore it into
six pieces to make banners for recognition, and thus equipped, fell on
the Muslims and destroyed them. In commemoration, their arms were
changed to bear the device of "Barry of six, vair and gules," six
horizontal bands of red on white. (See volume 1, "Heraldry.") Thomas
added his mother's property of Marle and La Fere to the Coucy domains
to which he succeeded in 1116. He continued his career of brigandage,
and directed it against church, town and king. He seized manors from
convents, tortured prisoners by hanging them by their testicles until
they were torn off by the weight of the body, personally cut the
throats of thirty rebellious bourgeois, transformed his castle into a
"nest of dragons and a cave of thieves." The Church excommunicated
him, stripped off his knightly belt, and read an anathema against him
in every parish in Picardy.* King Louis VI* succeeded in recovering
some of the lands he stole. Yet, despite his violent lifestyle, he
died in bed in 1130. (Bibliog. 223)

Tickhill castle,+ typically Norman fortification with a motte over 70
feet high and 80 feet across at the top, this fortress was built by
Roger de Buisli to whom William I* had granted the Yorkshire honour+
of Blythe which extended from Yorkshire into Derbyshire, Lincolnshire,
Nottinghamshire, and Leicestershire. In 1102, its owner, Robert de
Bellême (see Bellême-Montgomery) rebelled against Henry I* and
forfeited his lands. Henry II* gave this castle to Eleanor* of
Aquitaine,* his wife, and subsequently, while Richard I* was absent on
a crusade, Prince John* took it, but it was besieged and recaptured by
Hugh Puiset, bishop of Durham.* When he became king, John reclaimed it
and granted it to the count of Eu,* but by 1244, it was back in royal
hands when in 1254 Henry III* granted it to his son Lord Edward.* It
saw action once again decades later when it was attacked by Thomas* of
Lancaster, King Edward II's* cousin. Despite his use of catapults and
other siege engines, Thomas was unsuccessful in capturing it from its
defender William de Aune and Edward II himself led the column to relieve it. Later, Edward III* granted it to his fourth son, John of
Gaunt* in 1272. (Bibliog. 247)

Timur, the Lame. See Tamerlane.

Tintagel, castle+ stronghold of the duke of Tintagel in Arthurian legend on the northern coast of Cornwall on a headland rising over 250 feet from the water, and projecting a quarter of a mile into the Atlantic Ocean. This was the legendary home of Gorlois, duke of Cornwall, whom Uther Pendragon* impersonated when he impregnated Gorlois' wife, Igerne with Arthur.* Geoffrey of Monmouth's* *Historia Regum Britanniae,*writtenin the middle years of the 12th century, related that Tintagel was the fortress of Gorlois, duke of Cornwall, and the scene of Igerne's seduction by Uther Pendragon. It was the birthplace of King Arthur, as related in Layamon* and Malory's *Morte D'Arthur.* Its Anglo-French name came only with the castle erected by the earls of Cornwall in the 12th and 13th centuries; its original place name was unknown, but might possibly have been Rosnant, an Irish name meaning "Headland by the Valley" and referring to an early school at which such early saints as Enda and Tighernach received their education. This naturally defensible site was fortified by Reginald de Dunstanville,* illegitimate son of Henry I* who was created earl of Cornwall in 1141. This site was called Tintagel because it was similar to a headland on the island of Sark in the English Channel to which the name Tintageu, earlier Tente d'Agel or "Castle of the Devil," was applied. After Reginald became earl of Cornwall, he built a castle there. In 1236, the castle was acquired by Earl Richard,* younger brother of King Henry III,* and king of the Romans from 1257. He held Tintagel until 1272 and carried out massive reconstruction. It subsequently became part of the land granted by Edward II* to Piers Gaveston,* and thence to Edward the Black Prince* in 1337 as part of the duchy of Cornwall. (Bibliog. 104, 180, 247)

Tiois, Thios, Tyois, name used to refer to Germans in such *chansons de geste** as *Song of Roland,** *Berte aus grans piés,** *Prise de Pamplune,* and others. (Bibliog. 128)

Tirant lo Blanc, finest *libro de caballeria* in Catalan. This work was begun in 1360 by Joanot Martorell but finished after his death by Marte Joan de Galba. It was begun as a manual of chivalry but soon became an animated series of adventures, often erotic, that remained remarkably plausible. Tirant was a Breton knight who travelled to England for a royal tournament. Then he went to France and Sicily and helped defend Rhodes against the Turks, before journeying to Constantinople where he witnessed the love affair of the empress and her squire, Hipolit, whom she eventually married. Tirant became a famous general and ended by commanding the entire Byzantine army. (ed. M. de Riquer, Barcelona, 1947) (Bibliog. 237)

Tirel, Walter, lord of Poix, and mercenary+ who had entered the service of William II* (1087-1100) to get the gifts and wages which that English monarch was so lavishly providing his soldiers, and subsequently had married into the illustrious English Clare* family, and had been granted the fief of Langham in Essex. He was the hunter on the fatal hunting expedition in the New Forest who fired the arrow which killed William II in 1100. (Bibliog. 68)

Torfrida, Flemish wife of Hereward the Wake.* (Bibliog. 55)

Torigni, Robert of (fl.1175), also known as Robert de Monte, he was prior of Bec and abbot of Mont St. Michel. Between 1150 and 1186 he added parts 7 and 8 to the *Historia* by Guillaume de Jumièges. This work was valuable for the period around 1150, and particularly for the internal affairs of England in 1153-1154 and for the foreign policy of Henry II.* (trans. Joseph Stevenson, *Church Historians,* London: Seeleys, 1876, IV, part ii) (Bibliog. 99)

Tostig, son of Godwine,* and brother of Harold Godwineson.* A man of nerves and energy, he had obvious natural talent but no one trusted him because he was instinctively cruel and fought constantly with those around him, especially Harold. King Edward the Confessor* exploited this rivalry by making Tostig earl of Northumberland to offset Harold's influence in the south. Undoubtedly the most intelligent of Godwine's sons, Tostig was an authoritative and far-seeing administrator, but he disliked and was disliked by his compatriots and those below him, for he had no patience or common sense. After he married Judith, daughter of Baldwin IV, count of Flanders, Tostig took refuge with his brother-in-law in Bruges along with Godwine and the rest of his family who were exiled in 1051. He returned to England with the rest of Godwine's family a year later, and after his father's death he sought the vacancy of the earldom of East Anglia which Harold had vacated to become earl of Wessex, but he did not get it. In 1065, his thegns+ revolted and forced him out. His housecarls+ were massacred, his supporters killed, his armory and treasury captured and taken to York, and he was outlawed. Morcar, brother of Edwin of Mercia, was appointed to replace him. Tostig fled to Flanders once again for refuge, but in May 1066, raised a fleet to return to England in force. He plundered along the English Channel coast, and finally joined with the Norwegian forces of Harold Hardrada,* king of Norway, on his invasion in September 1066. Both he and Harold Hardrada were killed by the forces of Harold at the battle of Stamford Bridge,+ before Harold had to travel south to meet the invading forces of William the Conqueror at Hastings* in October. (Bibliog. 33)

Toulouse, city in southern France. After being captured from the Visigoths by Clovis, king of the Franks in 507, it declined in importance until it became the center of a large principality including southeastern Aquitaine* and Languedoc under the government of a Frankish count, Bernard of Gothia. In the 10th century, its counts attempted to seize the ducal title to Aquitaine but were defeated by the counts of Poitiers.* As a result, they turned in a different direction and became involved in struggles for power with the counts of Barcelona over Provence* in the 11th and 12th centuries. In 1213, it was conquered by Simon de Montfort* in the Albigensian+ crusade, and became the capital of a principality of Raymond VII in 1218, but lost its control over Languedoc. In 1249, it was inherited by Alphonse de Poitiers, brother of King Louis IX* of France. On Alphonse's death in 1270, it was annexed to the royal domain, and governed by royal officers sent from Paris. (Bibliog. 99, 100)

tournaments, papal opposition to, several popes expressed specific opposition to tournaments. Innocent II at the councils of Clermont (1130) and the Lateran (1139), Eugenius III at the Council of Reims (1148), and Alexander II at the council of the Lateran (1179), in words which passed into the official lawbook of the church, the *Decretals* of Gregory IX, specifically and formally prohibited tournaments. Such disapproval did little to prevent their popularity, however. They had become fashionable among the French early in the 12th century because they gave pleasure to princes and nobles and excited the generous ambition of chivalry. King Richard I* (1189-1199), eager to maintain a class of sturdy and practiced warriors, encouraged their use in England, but placed them under royal control: he charged fixed sums for permission to hold them, laid down rules for the maintenance of public order and the collection of fees, and exacted an oath to maintain the peace from all who wished to tourney. He designated five areas in England as tourney areas: between Salisbury and Wilton, between Warwick and Kenilworth, between Stamford and Wansford, between Brackley and Mixbury (on the borders of the shires of Northampton, Buckingham and Oxford), and between the archepiscopal manor of Blyth and the castle of Tickhill* (on the border between Yorkshire and Nottinghamshire). The last two named were used frequently in later years. As tournaments increased in popularity during the reign of Henry III* (1216-1272), it was impossible for the crown to confine them to particular locations in England. These early tournaments were not fought under the strict rules in confined lists+ as in later times. Rather they were combats of arms and horses in open country much like a battle and almost as dangerous. Lists were placed for participants to withdraw for rest, and weapons were supposed to be blunted, but those niceties were not always observed. At the request of earls, barons and knights of England toward the end of the 13th century, King Edward I* (1272-1307) issued an ordinance which forbade heavy armor, and the use of pointed swords and daggers, staffs and maces in them; only the broadsword was allowed, but no mention was made about the use of the lance, the tournament's chief weapon. (Bibliog. 184)

Tracy, William de (d. 1173), murderer of Thomas à Becket.* Lord of Bradninch in Devon, William had served Becket when he was chancellor. He became one of his foes and one of the conspirators who harkened to the complaint of Henry II about Becket being a troublesome priest whom he wished to be rid of. With three other knights, Tracy entered Canterbury cathedral on Tuesday, December 29, 1170. He was the only one whom the archbishop greeted by name. When the four men attacked the unarmed Becket, Tracy struck him twice, the last blow cleaving his head. After the murder, Tracy confessed to his bishop, and at the insistence of Pope Alexander III, the four men went to the Holy Land to serve the Templars+ for fourteen years in addition to spending the remainder of their lifetimes in fasting and prayer. Tracy got no further than Cosenza in Sicily where he was afflicted with a horrible disease, his flesh decaying while he was yet alive, so that he couldn't refrain from tearing it off with his own hands. He died in agony, praying to St. Thomas, the soul of man he had murdered. (Bibliog. 58)

traitors, characters in the *chansons de geste** and the romances. A traitor usually was a seneschal+ (steward) or some such functionary who stood high in royal confidence. He had the king's ear, was a flatterer, a whisperer, a spy, a tale-bearer who knew well how to have his language serve his own best interests. He hated to see anyone in a position of authority and power which might rival his own. Frequently bishops had similar clerics serving on their staffs—men who watched with evil eye and sought to ruin a personal enemy out of jealousy. Dwarfs frequently were traitors, also. In Béroul's *Tristan,* for example, a dwarf tried deceitfully to trick Tristan; in *Fierabras,** one tried to sneak into Floripas' bed when he was sent by her father to retrieve the magic cincture she had taken. The most notorious of these men usually were associated with the genealogical families of Ganelon,* Roland's step-father, whose treachery caused the slaughter of the *douzepeers** of Charlemagne* at Rencesvals*; or of Hagen,* the liegeman of King Gunther, whose murder of Siegfried* brought about the destructive wrath of his widow, Kriemhild,* as detailed in the *Nibelungenlied.** Macaire was another stock traitor who wormed his way into his king's confidence by means of gifts and then made himself powerful by distributing them. His despicable acts were prompted by his unrequited passion for the emperor's wife whom he tried to compromise by having someone sneak into her bed while the emperor was at mass. Among appearances in other *chansons de geste,* Macaire appeared in *Aiol* where he committed many treacherous acts by getting the law on his side before he set about ruining many noble men. He flattered the king and convinced him not to reward Aiol for loyalty.

Other traitors include Hardré,* his son Fromont, his grandson Fromondin, and Bernart de Naisil. These men were traitors not necessarily for rebellion against their king, but because they had transgressed against the moral code of their time by their conduct against fellow knights. They were traitors because they sought to injure loyal subjects of the king and thereby, like Ganelon, injure the king. They also were motivated by love or gain, jealousy, meanness, unscrupulousness, or some other character trait which made them willing to break their oaths of allegiance if necessary. They were traitors because they harmed their liege lord+ either directly or indirectly through those who served him, and that was a felony. Note that the *Doön de Mayence** cycle of *chansons de geste* frequently was referred to as the "rebellious vassals" cycle, for in each poem commonly grouped under that heading, Charlemagne was forced to pursue and quell some revolting baron who had renounced allegiance, or who had harmed a member of the emperor's immediate household. Chief among the rebels was Doön de Mayence who gave his name to the cycle. (Bibliog. 52, 106)

Tramtris, name assumed by Tristan in Ireland to hide his identity in *Tristan* and Malory's *Morte D'Arthur.** (Bibliog. 97, 145)

Traprian Law, fort (Law = fort) of King Lot* or Loth in the Edinburgh area of Scotland. After the Romans evacuated their walls (Antonnine and Hadrianic), the northernmost of the walls (Antonnine) was manned by chieftains of the Britons at its end in the east at Edinburgh or at the Firth of Forth, and at the Dunbarton Rock on the Firth of Clyde in the west. These tribesmen specifically calling themselves the Men of the North, Gwyr y Gogledd, lived near the ancient hill fort of

Traprian Law in East Lothian. Early in Geoffrey of Monmouth's*
chronicle, their leader was called King Loth (Lott) of Lothian whose
wife was Arthur's* sister, sometimes called Anna, and whose eldest son
was named Gawain.* (Bibliog. 96)

Treaty of Bretigny. See Bretigny, Treaty of.

Treaty of London. See London, Treaty of.

Treaty of Verdun. See Verdun, Treaty of.

Trevet, Nicholas (fl. 1320), Dominican theologian and chronicle writer
who taught at Oxford. His *Annales regum Angliae* covered events between
1135 and 1307. (ed. Thomas Hog, London: English Historical Society,
1845) (Bibliog. 99)

*Tristan de Nanteuil, chanson de geste** describing the adventures of
the son of Gui de Nanteuil. The story included fantastic adventures,
and even changed the sex of Tristan's wife, Blanchandine, to a man
named Blanchandin. (ed. Keith V. Sinclair, Assen, Pay-Bas: Van Gorcum
Co., 1971) (Bibliog. 121, 135)

Tristan legend, one of the most widespread legends in the Middle Ages.
In it, Rivalin, a young nobleman or king, fell in love with and
married Blancheflor, the sister of King Mark* under whom he had come
to Cornwall to serve. Blancheflor died the day their son, Tristan, was
born. The child was brought up by a master and at 14 returned to his
uncle Mark's court and won favor there. He killed the Irish champion
Morholt* who had come to Cornwall demanding the annual tribute of
thirty youths be sent to Ireland. A piece of Tristan's sword remained
imbedded in Morholt's skull, and was preserved by his niece, the
Princess Isolte, who swore to find the slayer of her uncle and to
avenge his death. Later when Tristan arrived in Ireland searching for
a bride for King Mark, he slew a dragon, but was overcome by its noxi-
ous poison. Isolte found him and tended his wounds. As he sat in a
bath, she discovered that he was Morholt's killer by matching the
sword fragment from her uncle's head to the break in Tristan's sword.
She saved Tristan in order to save herself from the seneschal* who
claimed the victory over the dragon and with it the hand of Isolte.
Tristan proved that the seneschal was lying, and thus won Isolte for
his uncle's bride.

On the voyage to Cornwall, Tristan and Isolte inadvertently
were given the love potion intended for Mark and his bride on their

wedding night, and were bound thereby to each other by its spell. Everything was sacrificed for their passion as they used tricks and deceits to avoid detection to be together. Isolte substituted her handmaid, Brangain, in Mark's bed for herself on her wedding night to conceal her loss of virginity; then she plotted Brangain's murder to conceal that fact, but relented and prevented her death.   One of Mark's dwarfs sprinkled flour on the floor of the royal bedchamber to trap the lovers by revealing Tristan's footprints leading to the royal bed.   Tristan outwitted the dwarf by leaping from his bed to Isolte's but in so doing, reopened his wounds from the Morholt fight, and stained the queen's bed with his blood. Those stains convinced Mark of Isolte's guilt, but she offered to endure the ordeal of iron+ to prove her innocence. She arranged for Tristan to meet her at the ordeal disguised so that she could swear to the literal truth of having been in the arms only of the king and the disguised Tristan.   When the iron did not burn her, Mark believed her innocence. Eventually, he banished them, and they fled into the forest of Morois where Mark one day found them asleep with a naked sword between them. Once again convinced of their innocence, he recalled Isolte but sent Tristan into permanent exile. He went to Brittany where he made friends with the ruler's son, Kaherdin, and was persuaded to marry Kaherdin's sister, Isolte of the White Hands, because of her name. He remained true to his beloved Isolte, however, and in time was accused by Kaherdin of neglecting his wife and thereby of insulting his family.   Tristan told Kaherdin of his love for Isolte, and they returned to Cornwall in disguise to verify that fact. Eventually, the two returned to Brittany where Tristan, desperately wounded, sent a messenger to bring Isolde of Ireland to heal him. If the messenger was successful, the ship bearing them would hoist white sails; if not, black sails. Tristan's jealous wife lied that the ship had hoisted black sails, and Tristan died of despair. Isolte, finding that she had arrived too late, died of grief beside him.

Versions include one by Thomas of Britain who wrote in French at the court of King Henry II* of England. Between 1155 and 1185, Gottfried von Strassburg wrote a version (tr. A. T. Hatto, *Gottfried von Strassburg's Tristan,* Baltimore: Penguin 1960). About 1170, Eilhart von Oberg probably translated a French version also in the 12th century (ed. K. Wagner, Bonn: Reinische Beitrage, V, 1924); Béroul, a Norman poet wrote his version late in the 12th century (tr. Alan S. Fedrick, Baltimore: Penguin, 1970); and a 13th-century prose version (ed. S. Löseth, Paris 1891). Other 12th- and 13th-century versions and fragments include the English metrical *Sir Tristrem* * (ed. Sir Walter Scott, Edinburgh, 1804), the only English version except for Malory's *Morte D'Arthur*;* Marie de France's *lai, La Chievrefueil*;* and the Berne *Folie Tristan* (ed. Ernest Hoepffner, Paris, 1949, 2nd ed.) (Bibliog. 10, 97)

Tristano riccardiano, first Arthurian romance written in Italian prose from the end of the 13th century, and based on the French prose *Tristan.* Its author was unknown. It was titled *riccardiano* because the manuscript was preserved in the Riccarciana library in Florence. (Bibliog. 245)

Der Trojankrieg, Middle High German* courtly epic by Konrad von Wurzburg* which he left unfinished; it ended just before the death of Hector. Its source was the *Roman de Troye* by Benoît de Sainte-Maure* which Konrad expanded considerably. Helen's reply to Paris' declaration of love ran for more than 900 lines, and the preparation for the Trojan War occupied 23,000 lines. (ed. A. von Keller and Karl Bartsch, Stuttgart: *BLV* 44, 1858, and 133, 1877). (Bibliog. 86)

tuath. See Brehon law.

Das Turnei von Nantheiz, Middle High German* poem written by Konrad von Wurzburg* in the mid-13th century to describe a tournament purporting to have been held at Nantes between German knights under King Richard of England and French knights under their own king. It contained much detail on coats of arms, weapons, procedures and so on. The character of King Richard was thought to have been Richard of Cornwall who was a candidate for the election as German king and Holy Roman Emperor in 1257. (ed. E. Schroder, *Kleinere Dichtungen Konrads von Wurzburg, ATB,* 1924-1926) (Bibliog. 86)

Turoldus, Latin form of the name Turold, the last redactor of the *chanson de geste** the *Song of Roland** who identified himself in the last stanza of the work; he may have been its original author. (Bibliog. 210)

Turpin, Archbishop, supposed Roman cleric sent by the pope to Charlemagne* who made him his chancellor, and then placed him in the seat at Reims, according to the *Karlamagnus Saga.* Aspremont** related a different story. There Turpin told the pope that he had come from Jumièges in France where he had been since becoming a monk. However, he was born to be a knight and not a monk, for his hands were more fitted to strike with a sword and lance than to bestow benedictions, and his head better suited to wear a helmet than a miter. That first appearance in the *Aspremont* verified that role because he was described as loving arms and horses, not exactly an episcopal attitude. In the story, when Abbé Fromer was too terrified to read to the king a threatening message from the warrior Agolant, Turpin told him petulantly to go chant his matins and read the life of Saint Omer and not ever try such a message as that one; then Turpin laughed. That was not the reaction one expected form an archbishop. He acted similar knightly roles in other *chansons de geste.** When he cleaved the head of the pagan Emaudras in *Gui de Bourgogne,** his companions laughed and praised the nimbleness of his stroke. He fought valiantly to his death beside Roland and the other *douzepeers** in the rearguard against the forces of Marsile* and the other pagans at the battlefield of Rencesvals* in the *chanson de geste*, the *Song of Roland,** dying a warrior's death rather than an archbishop's death. (Bibliog. 88)

Turpin, Chronique de. See *Chronique de Turpin*.

twenty-four barons. Section 61 of the *Magna Carta Libertatum+* (1215) provided for a committee of twenty-four barons who represented the community of the realm. If the king (John) violated any provision of the charter, four of the barons would call upon him to desist and to make restitution. If he refused, the four were to submit the matter to the twenty-four, who then would declare war on the monarch. Thus, the only means the barons could use to guarantee the document was to make rebellion and civil war legal if the king violated it. These twenty-four who signed the orignal document were

Richard, earl of Clare*
William de Fors, earl of Aumale*
Geoffrey de Mandeville, earl of Gloucester*
Saer de Quincy,* earl of Winchester*
Humphrey de Bohun,* earl of Hereford*
Robert de Vere, earl of Oxford*
William Marshal, the younger
Robert FitzWalter, lord of Baynard castle
Gilbert de Clare*
Eustace de Vesci
Hugh Bigod*
William de Mowbray
Robert de Ros*
John de Lacy, constable of Chester*
Richard de Percy
John FitzRobert

William Malet
Geoffrey de Sai
Roger de Montbegon
William de Huntingfield
Richard de Muntfichet
William de Albini of Belvoir
William de Lanvalli
William Hardel, mayor of London
(Bibliog. 107)

Tyre, city in Lebanon which was one of the most important along the eastern coast of the Mediterranean under Byzantine rule. In 1123, when it was conquered by the crusaders+ with naval support from Venice, one-third of its harbor was granted to the Italians. That harbor was second only to Acre in that area of the world. In 1187 after Saladin* defeated Hattin,* Tyre under the leadership of Conrad of Montferrat* became the only city to resist the Saracen attacks of Saladin, and as such served as a base for the third crusade+ led by Richard I* of England and Philip II* of France. After it was conquered by the Mamelukes in 1291, it declined in importance. (Bibliog. 98)

U

Ufford, Robert de. See Suffolk.

Usama ibn Munqidh, *emir** of Shaizar (1095-1188) and one of the most interesting Syrian Muslims* living during the crusades.+ A man of action, a writer, a hunter, a horseman, a lover of books, a courtier, and an unscrupulous political intriguer, he spent most of his life in contact with the Franks, the emirs of Syria and the caliphs+ of Egypt.* He died, however, in obscurity at the height of Saladin's* triumphs. He owed his reputation to his autobiography, *Book of Instruction* with illustrations. It provided a storehouse of information about his Muslim and Frankish contemporaries. (ed. and tr. Philip Hitti, New York, 1925) (Bibliog. 3)

V

Valois, ruling house of France following the demise of the Capetians. On his deathbed in February 1328, Charles IV* of France, the last of the Capetian* dynasty, third son of King Philip IV,* le Bel, named Philip, count of Valois, as his heir. This Philip, count of Valois, Anjou and Maine, was a tall, handsome nobleman, famous for his prowess on the battlefield and tournament field, but he also was a cold, calculating man, quite different from the knight errant of popular tradition. He came to the throne as Philip VI and ruled 1328-1350. (Bibliog. 224)

vassal. See tenants.

Vauxhall. See Reviers; Breauté, Faulkes de.

Verdun, Treaty of, pact drawn up between the three sons of Emperor Louis I in 843. It was intended to put an end to the warfare which erupted on the death of the emperor in 840. Lothaire* received the Francia Media,* Louis the German* received the eastern and Charles the Bald* the western parts of the Carolingian Empire, the areas which subsequently developed into Germany and France. (Bibliog. 98)

de Vere, Robert (1362-1392), ninth earl of Oxford,* marquis+ of Dublin, and duke of Ireland. See Oxford. (Bibliog. 47)

Vexin, the, county in northern France lying west of Paris. In 911, it was divided into the Norman Vexin and the French Vexin. In 1147, Geoffrey of Anjou* gave the Norman Vexin to Louis VII* of France for his help in winning Normandy for Geoffrey. It returned to the Plantagenets* as part of a dowry in 1166. Philip II,* Augustus (1165-1123) reconquered it in 1193, and incorporated it into the

French domains in 1196. (Bibliog. 98)

Vicarius. See Harold II, Godwineson.

viceroy, one who acted as the governor of a country in the name and by the authority of the king. (Bibliog. 169)

vicomte, **viscount,** *vice-comites* or deputies (vicars) of counts, serving as lieutenants of counts. As counts' titles became hereditary, so too did *vicomte* titles, and to this title was added the name of the territory or countship from which they derived their powers. Thus the viscounts of Poitiers* called themselves viscounts of Thouars. In Normandy,* where central power had been strong from the first, *vicomtes* appeared early as deputies of the counts, afterward dukes of the Normans. Immediately after the Norman Conquest of England in 1066, the Normans applied this term to the position which the English called sheriff. In England this man raised the Danegeld+ and "farmed"+ the revenues of the shire which the Normans began to call a county.+ (Bibliog. 68, 178)

Villehardouin, Geoffroi de, marshal of Champagne (1150-1213?), who took part in the fourth crusade,+ and subsequently was made marshal+ of Rumania, and never returned to France. As one of the leaders of this crusade, he wrote his work, *Conquête de Constantinople,* as an old man after 1207, to justify from the point of view of the noble leaders the capture and sacking of Constantinople. (Bibliog. 230)

Vincennes, castle in the Ile de France* which grew from a simple hunting lodge begun by Louis VII* in 1164 to be a favorite of the kings. Under the oak at Vincennes, King Louis IX* used to hold informal tribunals to render justice. His successors, Philip III,* le Hardi, and then Philip IV,* le Bel, followed by his three sons, frequently stayed there. With them the Capetian* line of kings died. It was they who gave this residence its warlike appearance, building walls, enclosing the *enciente*+ and enlarging its tower to a height of 170 feet. (Bibliog. 196)

Visconti, family of the leaders and princes of the duchy of Milan. Claiming descent from the Lombard kings, the Visconti grew strong in the 11th century as supporters of Emperor Henry IV, and emerged as leaders under the guidance of Archbishop Ottone. Before he died in 1295, he ensured the election of his nephew Matteo as "captain of the people," a position which was made official when Emperor Henry VII appointed him as imperial vicar. In that role, he laid the foundations for the duchy of Milan by bringing a number of neighboring towns under his rule. He abdicated in 1322 in favor of his son Galeazzo who defeated the papal army with the assistance of the Emperor Louis the Bavarian in 1324. By 1354, the family was ruling most of northern Italy. His son Galeazzo II, prince of Pavia, married his daughter to the son of King Edward III of England and his son, Gian Galeazzo, to the daughter of King John of France. Gian Galeazzo emerged as the sole ruler of all the Milanese territories, and in 1385 bought the title of duke from Emperor Wenceslas IV for 100,000 florins. (Bibliog. 98)

Viviane. See Lady of the Lake.

vizier, high state official in Muslim* countries. Frequently, he would be invested with vice-regal authority, as a governor or viceroy of a province. (Bibliog. 169)

Vulgate version of Arthurian romances, group of romances containing five branches of the Arthurian cycle in French: *Estoire del Saint Graal, Lestoire de Merlin, Le Livre de Lancelot de Lac, La Quest Del Saint Graal, La Mort le Roi Artu.* This group frequently was referred to by other titles: *Prose Lancelot,** the Lancelot-Grail, and the pseudo-Map cycle. One edition of this cycle also included the *Livre D'Artus* even though its hero was Gawain,* and not Lancelot.* (ed. H. Oskar Sommer, Washington, 1909-1916; repr. New York: AMS Press, 1968.) (Bibliog. 10, 82)

W

Wace (c. 1100-c. 1175), canon of Bayeux, and Anglo-Norman poet whose most famous work, *Brut*,* an Anglo-Norman version of Geoffrey of Monmouth's* *Historia Regum Britanniae,** was completed in 1155. Born on the island of Jersey, he went as a child to Caen in Normandy where he began the study of letters which he continued during his long residence in the Ile de France.* On his return to Caen, he wrote narrative poems in French. In England, he presented Queen Eleanor* with a copy of his *Brut*.* This work considerably enlarged Geoffrey's 6,000 lines to 14,800 French verses, replacing the "facts" of the somber historian with colorful and descriptive scenery. To the Arthurian legends, he added the Round Table* and the idea of Arthur's* survival. By 1160, he again was in Normandy composing his *Roman de Rou** at the request of King Henry II* of England. (Bibliog. 10)

Wala, son of Bernard, a natural son of Charles Martel, and hence a cousin of Charlemagne,* he was reared at the court of Pepin and Charlemagne. In 795 he began service as advisor to King Pepin and from 800 to 814 served as guardian to Pepin's young son and successor, young King Bernard. On his succession to the throne, Louis banished him, and his brothers. Not only were they first cousins to the great Charles, but Wala also was cousin of the famous Count William of Gellone, count of Toulouse, also known as Count Guillaume Court Nez, or William, count of Orange. In fact, Wala married Count William's daughter, Rothlindis, and became a brother-in-law of Bernard of Barcelona. (Bibliog. 6)

Rei Waldelf, Anglo-Norman epic from the early 13th century. It related the story of King Bede, father of Waldelf, whose wicked seneschal,+ Frode, persecuted first the king's sister, and then young Waldelf after Bede's death. Waldelf was saved by his cousin, Florenz, son of the persecuted lady. Later, after Saracens* abducted Waldelf's two sons, they eventually were reared by the emperor of Germany. Waldelf died in a fire in Rochester, but his sons returned to England to avenge his death. (Latin prose version by Johannes Bramis, *Historia regis Waldelf*, ed. R. Immelmann, Bonn, 1912) (Bibliog. 106)

Waleran, count of Meulan. See Worcester.

Wales, area in the west of the island of Britain past the River Severn into which the Britains fled from the pursuing Saxons; the area came to be called Wales and its people Welsh. Among their kings were:

843 - Rodery Mawr, Roderich the Great, who between his three sons
           divided Wales into North Wales, South Wales, and Powys*
1137 - Owen Gwyneth
1169 - David ap Owen
1194 - Llewellen ap Jorweth
1240 - David ap Llewellen
1246 - Llewellen ap Gryffith, last Prince of Wales of the British
           race.

This last king lost his life and his princedom to King Edward I* in 1282. Edward, seeing that the Welsh had no desire to be ruled by a stranger, sent for his queen so that she could deliver on Welsh soil a son who spoke no English. See Prince of Wales.+ (Bibliog. 101)

Wallace, William (1270-1305), famous Scottish outlaw who led the Scots in a spectacular victory over the English at Stirling Bridge* in 1297. This victory led legend makers to credit him with being the hero of a ten-year war against the English, rescuing his own country from their yoke on three occasions by being the hero of battles which never were fought or in which he never participated. Because he was supposed to have been a huge muscular giant, he was said to have killed hundreds of thousands of his enemies. He became the legendary chosen champion of King Philip IV,* le Bel (1285-1314) of France, and supposedly held a parley with the queen of King Edward I* (1272-1307) of England, but she was dead before his "career" began. (See Blind Harry, *Schyr William Wallace,* ed. Moir, Edinburgh: STS, 1889) (Bibliog. 120)

Wallingford castle, Berkshire stronghold which figured prominently in the wars between King Stephen* and the Empress Matilda.* It came into the hands of Henry II* when its lord, Count Brian FitzCount entered a monastery without leaving an heir. In 1215, King John* ordered the castle+ to be strongly fortified against the rebellious barons by or- dering the knights of the honour+ to garrison it, and the men of Berkshire to repair the moats of both town and castle. So strengthened, its garrison held it without incident until peace was restored in 1217. Falling to King Henry III's* brother, Richard,* earl of Cornwall,* in 1231, the castle was kept at its strength until his death in 1272 when it passed to his son, Edmund, earl of Cornwall, who died without issue in 1300. During the reign of Edward II,* it was held by Piers Gaveston* for five years, and then passed into the hands of Queen Isabella on Piers' death. It finally fell into the hands of Edward,* the Black Prince, in 1337 as part of his duchy of Cornwall. (Bibliog. 104)

Walter, Hubert (d. 1205), justiciar* of England and archbishop* of Canterbury (1193-1205). Beginning his career as chaplain to Glanville,* he gained considerable administrative experience. Coupled with his strength of character, ingenuity, and natural propensity for details which had been sharpened by legal training, this administrative experience when joined with his experience on the third crusade+ with King Richard I* led to his being appointed justiciar on his return. With the influence of that king still affecting his career, Hubert was elevated to become archbishop of Canterbury, and on Richard's departure from England to fight against Philip II,* Augustus, in France in 1194, Hubert was entrusted with the government of the realm; he served well and effectively to block the selfish greedy schemes of William Longchamps* during Richard's absence. He was credited with writing the tract on English law frequently attributed to Glanville. (Bibliog. 7, 92, 98, 162)

Walter Tirel. See Tirel, Walter.

Waltheof. See Huntingdon.

Warenne, William de (d. 1138), descendant of a substantial landowner along the River Varenne not far from Dieppe in Normandy* who had two sons, Rudolf, and William; Rudolf inherited his father's estates, leaving William to make his own fortune. He attached himself to Duke William,* and distinguished himself in the Mortemer campaign for which the duke gave him the castle of Mortemer, and Bellencombre which became the center of the Warenne estates in Normandy. He fought at Hastings* for the duke, and under William FitzOsbern* and Bishop Odo* he continued the conquest of England in 1067 while King William was back in Normandy celebrating his victory. Granted an estate in Lewes, he played a large role in suppressing the rebellion of 1075. He transferred his allegiance to King William II* in 1087, probably by being granted the earldom of Surrey.* He died from wounds received in the siege of Pevensey* in 1088. His huge estate in England at his death stretched over thirteen counties but its chief blocks were in Sussex, Yorkshire, and Norfolk. He left two sons, William the elder (called William II) who inherited his father's English estates, and Rainald the younger. William sought to marry Edith (Matilda), daughter of the king of Scots who eventually married King Henry I* of England. He did marry the widow of the earl of Leicester,* who was a granddaughter of King Henry I* of France. He was one of the English king's advisors, judges and generals. He fought at Tinchebrai* in 1107 and at Bremûle* in 1119. On the death of Henry I, because he accepted Stephen* as king, he was put in charge of Rouen and Pays de Caux (where his chief Norman lands lay) while Stephen was establishing himself on the throne in 1136. (See also Surry.) (Bibliog. 130)

Warwick, chief town of Warwickshire, England. Its dukes and earls emerged from a powerful Norman family who held the *comté* of Meulan, Henry de Beaumont* (or de Newburgh). Before the Conquest, Edwin of Warwick, grandson of Leofric,* earl of Mercia and husband of Godiva,* sent no forces to aid King Harold* at Hastings* in 1066, but forfeited his lands by resistance, albeit feeble, to William I* in 1068. In response, William built a castle+ at Warwick in 1088 and entrusted it to Henry de Newburgh, son of Roger de Beaumont, who was created the first earl of Warwick shortly after the date of the *Domesday** survey. Beaumont crossed the Channel soon after the battle of Hastings and was made royal constable+ of the new castle at Warwick. He served William I well, being one of the nobles at Rouen who tried to reconcile William and his eldest son, Duke Robert II,* Curthose. Because he supported William II* against the rebels in 1088, he was rewarded by being created the first earl of Warwick. To support the earldom the king gave him the lands forfeited by Thurkill of Arden, one of the most prominent Anglo-Saxon nobles in Mercia.* Beaumont was with the king when he was killed in the New Forest on August 2, 1100, and took a leading part at Winchester* on August 3 in the selection of Henry I* as William's successor. He was a strong supporter of Henry I. He died in 1119, leaving his son Roger as his heir.

Roger, the second earl, refused to take sides during the controversy between Stephen* and Matilda* for the crown, and so was recognized by both sides. He allowed King Stephen to garrison troops at Warwick castle, and in 1153 was with the king when he heard that the garrison had been tricked by the knights of Henry of Anjou* into surrendering. Although not to blame, he was so overcome with shame and grief that he died suddenly. He had married in 1130 the daughter of William de Warenne,* earl of Surrey,* and was succeeded by his eldest son and heir, William, the third earl of Warwick, who, because he died without issue in 1185, was succceeded by his next youngest brother, Waleran, as the fourth earl. He carried the righthand sword at the coronation of John* in 1199. He married the daughter of Humphrey de Bohun* who bore him a son, Henry, who became the fifth earl in 1203, and during his life adhered strongly to Kings John and Henry III.*

The title passed through Henry's son, Thomas (1229), the sixth earl, to his granddaughter, Margery, countess of Warwick, in 1242, to her husband, John Marshal, marshal of Ireland. He died without issue, as did her second husband, so the earldom passed to William "Mauduit" (a nickname meaning "The Dunce"), Margery's cousin, who succeeded to the title as the eighth earl in 1263. In the Barons' War* he sided with Montfort* at first, but then changed his allegiance to support the king. When Warwick castle was captured by the Kenilworth garrison in April 1264, he and his wife were taken as prisoners to Kenilworth castle, but were released on payment of 1,900 marks ransom. He died in 1269, and was succeeded by his nephew and heir, William de Beauchamp, the ninth earl.   He inherited the office of chamberlain of the Exchequer* from the Mauduit family, and served as Hereditary Pantler at the coronation of King Edward I.* He served at the king's summons against the Welsh for seventeen years, against the Scots for two and overseas for two, and aside from numerous other services performed for the king, served as a member of Prince Edward's Council from 1297 to 1298. He died in 1298 and was succeeded by his son, Guy de Beauchamp, the tenth earl, who also inherited the positions of sheriff of Worcestershire and chamberlain of the Exchequer.

Born about 1271, Guy was knighted by King Edward I at the battle of Falkirk* (1298), receiving for his faithful service to the king a grant of Scottish lands lately belonging to to Geoffrey de Mowbray and others, worth 1,000 marks per year. He served in the division led by the earl of Surrey at the siege of Caerlaverock* (1300), became close friends with Prince Edward (later Edward II*) and served under him at the siege of Stirling castle.* For these and other services to the crown, he was chosen to carry the third sword at Edward II's coronation.+ Arousing the enmity of Piers Gaveston* who called him the "Black Dog of Arden," Guy was prominent in procuring Piers' banishment, and stood alone against his recall in 1309. Then, against the king's orders, he and Thomas of Lancaster* and others entered Parliament armed and were sworn as the Lords Ordainers.* Following Piers' surrender, Warwick took him to Warwick castle from whence, after the arrival of Thomas of Lancaster with the earls of Arundel* and Hereford,* Piers was taken to Blacklow Hill and beheaded on June 19, 1312. These earls remained in arms until peace was proclaimed in

December 1312, but though finally pardoned for their deed, they refused to serve in the Bannock Burn* campaign.

Guy died in 1315 and was succeeded by his son, Thomas de Beauchamp, the eleventh earl and also hereditary sheriff of Worcestershire and chamberlain of the Exchequer. Knighted by the king in 1329, he served in the Scottish campaigns over the next ten years. Then he went overseas with the king, serving in the third division at Vironfosse where both sides were drawn up for battle, but the French withdrew before engaging the English. He served at the siege of Tournai in 1340. Serving as one of the two marshals for the English at the battle of Crécy,* he distinguished himself as one of the two commanders of the Black Prince's* division, and again at the siege of Calais.* He was chosen as one of the founding Knights of the Garter* in 1348. He took part in the king's naval action off Winchelsea* in 1350 and was chosen admiral of the fleet from the mouth of the Thames westward before 1352. He accompanied the Black Prince to Gascony* in 1355, was made constable+ of the army there, and commanded the vanguard at the battle of Poitiers* in 1356. He continued to serve his king loyally, being chosen as a witness for the Treaty of Bretigny* in 1360. He ended his military career by playing a prominent role in John of Gaunt's* expedition into France in 1369, where he personally devastated Caux shortly before dying of the plague at Calais on November 13, 1369.

He was succeeded by his second but first surviving son, Thomas de Beauchamp, the twelfth earl, who had been knighted by the king on his way to France in 1355. Thomas went to Cherbourg with the earl of Suffolk* in 1370 to escort the king of Navarre to England. He was nominated to become a Knight of the Garter* in 1373, and later that same year took part in John of Gaunt's fruitless march from Calais to Bordeaux. He carried the third sword and exercised his hereditary office as Pantler at the coronation of King Richard II* in 1377. He was with the king in the Tower of London during the Peasant's Revolt in 1381, and was sent later with Sir Thomas Percy to protect St. Albans Abbey. In November 1387, he joined the earls of Gloucester and Arundel in "appealing" (accusing) the duke of Ireland (de Vere, earl of Oxford*) and the earl of Suffolk of treason, and with the aid of the earl of Derby,* trapped and defeated de Vere at Radcot Bridge in December. In the "Merciless Parliament" (1388) which followed, these Lords Appellant, including Warwick, impeached de Vere and Suffolk and other leaders of the king's party, some of whom they executed. They further obtained a grant of some 20,000 for themselves, and after introducing some reforms, they remained in power until 1389. In 1397, Thomas was accused of joining the plot of the earls of Gloucester and

Arundel which the king had learned about, and was arrested on a charge of high treason and was committed to the Tower of London. During his trial, he confessed his treason and pleaded guilty. At that plea, his honours and estates were forfeited to the crown and he himself was banished to the Isle of Wight* under the guard of William le Scrope, earl of Wiltshire, who treated him harshly. Liberated on the accession of Henry IV,* he bore the third sword at that monarch's coronation, and then in the following November, 1400, was restored to his estates and honours. He died in 1401. (Bibliog. 47, 238)

Wernher der Gartenaere. See *Meier Helmbrecht.*

Westmoreland, section of England lying west of Yorkshire. Early in its history, the Viponts and then the Cliffords were its hereditary sheriffs; not until 1398 was the title of earl used when King Richard II* conferred it upon Ralph Neville, earl of Raby, the earl marshal. He married first Margaret, the daughter of Hugh Stafford, earl of Stafford,* and second, Joan Beaufort,* only daughter of John of Gaunt,* duke of Lancaster,* by his third wife. (Bibliog. 101)

White Company, large band of mercenary soldiers operating in Italy in the second half of the 14th century under the command of Sir John Hawkwood.* Joining John Paleologus, the marquis of Montferrat, in his war against the Visconti* of Milan, this company of 5-6,000 free lances ravaged Lombardy. Because of the large number of lancers in the group, they introduced the practice of counting cavalry by lances. Five lances formed a company, and five companies a troop; every ten lances had a separate officer. Each "lance" meant a heavily armed knight on a charger, a less heavily armed squire+ also on a charger, and a page+ on a palfrey+; their principal weapon was a long and heavy lance requiring two men to wield, but they also carried swords and daggers, and bows slung across their backs. They fought both on horseback and on foot, but used the lance only on foot in square or circular formations to confront the enemy charge with the points of their lances, or to advance slowly toward their enemy with fierce shouts. The infantry was armed with long bows+ of yew, swords, daggers, and small light ladders with which, by fastening end to end, they were able to scale the highest towers in the country. All in the company were admirably disciplined, and being in the prime of life, they were inured to all kinds of hardships. As a tactic, they usually would burst into a town at night like a flood, massacre the men, rape the women, carry off whatever of value they could find, and then burn the town. Other tactics included exacting contributions under the threat of destroying a town, or capturing and holding for ransom castles and important figures. On one raid into Piedmont, they captured the count of Savoy* and his principal barons, and held them for a ransom of 180,000 florins.+ This group under Hawkwood was called the White Company because the men wore plate armor (*harnois blanc*) not covered by fabric, and hence it glinted in the sun. (See free companies; Hawkwood, Sir John.) (Bibliog. 48, 58)

White Ship disaster, maritime catastrophe on November 25, 1120, in which William, only legitimate son of King Henry I drowned. His death heightened the claim of William Clito,* son of William II, to the English throne, and led to the anarchy in the dispute over the throne after Henry's death in 1135. See also White Ship disaster in volume 1. (Bibliog. 180)

Wight, Isle of, island abutting the English coastline of Hampshire. In the time of William I,* it was taken from the English by William FitzOsbern,* earl of Hereford,* who became its first lord. After his death and the execution of his son Roger for treason, it reverted to the crown. Henry II* bestowed it upon the family of Reviers, earls of Devon.* On the extinction of their line in the reign of Edward I,* it reverted again to the crown. It then was bestowed on men for their lifetimes only. In 1307, Edward III* gave it to Piers Gaveston,* earl of Cornwall.* On his death in 1312, it was given to Edward, earl of Chester* who became Edward III. Richard II* bestowed it upon William Montague, earl of Salisbury,* in 1385. On his death in 1397, the king bestowed it upon Edward, earl of Rutland,* afterwards duke of York, who was killed in 1415. (Bibliog. 47)

Wigmore castle,+ important Hertfordshire fortress on the Welsh border that belonged to the Mortimers,* earls of March. (Bibliog. 104)

The Will, ordinance published by King Philip II* of France (1180-1223) before he left on the third crusade+ in 1190. In it the bailiffs established by the king would hold an assize at which a plaintiff's justice without delay and the king's rights would be safeguarded, and the fines due the king would be listed. In this will, also, he commended his son and heir, Louis* (VIII) of France, to his subjects in France as his heir. (Bibliog. 178)

William I (1028-1087), duke of Normandy,* and conqueror of England to become King William I. He was a stout, bald man with strong arms and a stern face which became awesome in cold rage, for he also was a dis-

agreeable man: masterful, stern, cruel. He loved little besides
politics, war and the chase. He was disciplined and chaste, taciturn
and deliberate, and was capable of working long hours in silence to
accomplish a goal which he had considered long and hard. The son of
Duke Robert I* of Normandy, and born to Herleve, daughter of a tanner
in Falaise, Normandy, he had had a harsh and insecure early life, but
from the age of 20, he had ruled Normandy without rival. His wars
against his kinsman in Normandy had given him excellent training in
managing small bands of cavalry and in improving fortifications; his
wars against the king of France had given him experience in large
warfare against superior numbers. Both types of combat had taught him
the value of discipline. Because of his reputation as a knight and as
a leader of knights, he was well able to attract and unify the dis-
parate groups needed for the Hastings invasion.

He had a far better claim to the English throne than Harold
ever could have had: his grandmother, Emma, widow of Ethelred* the
Unready, had married Cnut and had borne Edward* the Confessor, who was
William's cousin; Edward had promised the throne to him; and Harold
had pledged to support his claim to the throne, a promise wrested when
Harold had been shipwrecked in Normandy in 1064. The English Witan
ignored that promise and placed the crown on Harold's head. William
took the throne and crown from Harold at the battle of Hastings* in
1066. For the next four years, his reign was marked by a series of
Saxon revolts which he finally subdued and was crowned in London in
1070. For the remainder of his reign, he was busy suppressing revolts
by his discontented Norman vassals both in England and on the continent. His greatest task was the fusion of Norman and Saxon institutions to produce the strongest possible monarchy. To accomplish
this, he kept as much power as he could in his own hands, granting his
vassals only a small amount of the freedom that accompanied French
feudalism. Under William, every man was the liegeman of the king, all
private war was outlawed, and all military tenants* were to serve only
in the king's army. Additionally, he maintained the old Saxon fyrd,*
the citizen militia of the Saxon kings. Thus he had a Norman feudal
army to use against the Saxons and a Saxon force to use against his
Norman vassals. Frequently he spent much time in Normandy, leaving
Archbishop Lanfranc* in charge of England in his absences. In August
1087, the forces of the French King Philip I* (1060-1108) left Mantes
and began to pillage Normandy. In retaliation, William fought to regain the Vexin* for Normandy, and to do so, he fought one of the most
brutal campaigns in his history. Through surprise and poor French
generalship, he gained entry into Mantes, and destroyed it in revenge:
he literally left nothing standing, for all its buildings were razed

to the ground. As he rode through its embers, his horse was frightened by fire, and threw him heavily against the high pommel of his saddle, rupturing him lethally. In intense pain, he was carried to a priory outside Rouen to escape the heat and confusion; he died on September 9, 1087, and was buried at the monastery of St. Stephen in Caen which he had founded. Before he died, he worried about his successor. Of his three sons, he recognized that the eldest, Robert, disloyal though he may have been through life, still was the eldest, so by Norman custom of primogeniture,+ he was left the Norman lands; to his second son, William II,* Rufus, he left England; to his third son, Henry Beauclerc, educated to become a priest, he left £5,000 pounds. (Bibliog. 124, 178, 181)

William II, Rufus (1057-1100), king of England (1087-1100); second son but the favorite of William the Conqueror.* Because William I* wished Rufus to become king, he wrote Archbishop Lanfranc* a letter of instructions to assure that the throne went to William instead of to Robert as Norman primogeniture would dictate. Lanfranc was so powerful in England that because no one rose to oppose the dead king's wishes, William II was crowned on September 26, 1087. He was short, stocky, thick-set, overweight, and because of his ruddy complexion, was termed "Rufus." Although he had been educated under Lanfranc, he had no taste for anything but hunting and military exercises. Although he was brave and could act swiftly when circumstances demanded, he basically was a disagreeable man: cynical, blasphemous, capricious, ill-tempered, and vain. He squandered all the money he extorted from his subjects on a mercenary+ army and a licentious court. His court was effeminate, and in all acounts of it, no mention was made of any paramours or illegitimate children; he probably was homosexual. Undoubtedly, he was England's worst king. He died while hunting in the New Forest in southern England on August 2, 1100, when one of his hunting party, Walter Tirel,* lord of Poix, shot him in the back with an arrow. His younger brother, Henry I,* Beauclerc, seized the treasury and had himself crowned within three days of William's death. (Bibliog. 181)

William II, the Good, king of Sicily (1166-1189). He married Joan, daughter of Henry II* of England, and secured peace with the Roman Empire by having his aunt Constance, daughter of Roger II,* marry the son of Frederick I,* the future Emperor Henry VI.* (Bibliog. 98)

William IV, the Great, duke of Aquitaine* (989-1030), and one of the great warriors of his time. Once he had imposed his authority over his vassals by many battles, he obtained the advice of Fulbert, bishop of

Chartres, on the meaning of the feudal oath. His response was the first document to treat homage as a mutual link between lord and vassal. (Bibliog. 98)

William IX (1071-1127), duke of Aquitaine,* and one of the most colorful figures in the medieval period. He was a prince, an adventurer and a poet. Twice he tried to annex Toulouse,* and even though he conquered the city once, he could not maintain his control over it. In 1101, he took part in the crusade of Stephen* of Blois. In 1120, he led a victorious campaign with the king of Aragon against the Moors. His love affair with the beautiful Dangereuse, wife of the viscount of Châtellerault, with whom he lived publicly, brought him papal excommunication, but he continued to write and recite his love poems. He told the bald papal legate that, "The comb will curl the hair on your head before I put aside the Vicomtesse." He was considered the first troubadour,+ and maintained a brilliant center of culture at his court in Poitiers. (tr.   Frederick Goldin, *Lyrics of the Troubadours and Trouvères,* New York: Doubleday, 1973) (Bibliog. 98, 154)

William Aethling (1102-1120), only legitimate son of Henry I* of England. His betrothal in 1113 to Matilda, infant daughter of Fulk V of Anjou,* ended France's attempts to confine Henry's power within Normandy.* As his father's destined successor, he received the homage of the Norman barons in 1115 and of the English in 1116. He went to Normandy in 1119 where he married Matilda and was granted the county of Maine by his father-in-law. In August of that year, he was with his father at the battle of Bremûle.* After the fight, he victoriously returned to his cousin, William Clito,* his horse that had been captured in this war against Henry I which the French king had undertaken on William's behalf. Early in 1120, Henry and Louis made peace, and Louis gave William the duchy of Normandy. Henry also chose him as his deputy in England. His death by drowning in the White Ship* disaster in 1120 fomented the anarchy that followed the death of his father in 1135. (Bibliog. 58, 98, 181)

William, the Clito (1101-1128), son of Duke Robert II* Curthose, duke of Normandy, and grandson of William the Conqueror.* Fearing for his safety because King Henry I* of England was keeping his father in custody, William's aunt placed him with Louis VI's* court in Paris. There he was recognized as the rightful heir to the duchy of Normandy. This led to two rebellions against King Henry, neither of which succeeded. His marriage in 1122 to Sibylle, daughter of Fulk of Anjou,* was declared invalid, at Henry's insistence, because of closeness in degree of consanguinity.+ Subsequently, in 1127, he married Joanna of Montferrat, half-sister of the French queen, and assumed the vacant fief of Flanders.* His stern government caused rebellions, and in the siege of Alost in 1128, William was wounded fatally. He died without issue. After his father, Robert, died six years later, Henry I became undisputed ruler of Normandy. (Bibliog. 68, 124, 180)

William, the Lion (1143-1214), king of Scotland (1165-1214) who spent most of his reign trying to keep Scotland independent. As the second son of Henry of Scotland (1114-1152), he succeeded his brother, Malcolm IV, to the throne. He accompanied English King Henry II* to France and made an alliance with King Louis VII* in 1168. He intervened in the revolt of Henry II's sons against their father in 1173, and was captured when he invaded Northumberland. He won his freedom by signing the Treaty of Falaise* (1174) which assured English suzerainty over Scotland. He successfully separated the church of Scotland from the church of England, making it subject only to the see of Rome. He went on to subdue Moray and to include Caithness* and Sutherland as subject to the Scottish crown. In 1198, Richard I* yielded his claims over Scotland in exchange for 10,000 marks, and twice he averted war with England under King John* by negotiations, but never succeeded in recovering the northern earldoms he had lost earlier. (Bibliog. 58, 98)

William de Aune, defender of Tickhill* castle against the rebels led by Thomas* of Lancaster in 1322; for his valor he was knighted. (Bibliog. 47)

William de Fors (Fortibus) (d. 1260), earl of Aumale.* In 1246, he was appointed by Alexander II* of Scotland to rule one-third of Galloway. On the death of his father, the earl of Aumale (Albemarle) in 1249, he assumed the title because he was a knight of age and had paid £100 in relief.+ He played an active role in Parliament in 1258, was appointed one of the king's standing Committee of Fifteen and later was selected as one of the Twenty-four. (See Henry III.) He actively campaigned against King Henry III's Poitevin brothers-in-law at court, and signed the letter to Pope Alexander IV which complained about them. He had married Isabella, daughter of Baldwin, earl of Devon.* On his death in 1260 and her brother's in 1262, she became the heir to Devon and the Isle of Wight.* Henry III chose her daughter, and heiress, Aveline, to be married to his second son Edmund of Lancaster, but Aveline died at age 15 before she took possession of her mother's lands. A few years later, however, King Edward I* bought her patrimony from Isabella for

20,000 marks, but she kept possession of it until her death in 1293. (Bibliog. 58, 184)

William de Mandeville (fl. 1193), earl of Essex,* count of Aumale,* chief justice with Hugh of Durham* under Richard I.* He married Hawise, heiress of the count of Aumale, and assumed that title in his wife's right. He accompanied Philip of Flanders* on a crusade and helped him win a great victory at Ramelah* in 1177. He became King Henry II's* closest friend, and accompanied him on his last flight from Le Mans to Gisors in 1189. (See Essex.) (Bibliog. 7)

William de Tancarville (d. 1129), chamberlain for English King Henry I.* His son Rabel (d. 1140) also was a chamberlain to the king. William, whose father had been chamberlain for William* the Conqueror while he was duke as well as when king, attested a charter as William FitzRalph as chamberlain in 1082. From 1087, he served Duke Robert* as chamberlain, but after the battle of Tinchebrai* in 1106, he held the same office under Henry, and was succeeded in it by his son Rabel. Both he and his son had property in England and Normandy, with the family seat located at Tancarville in the Seine estuary. (Bibliog. 130)

William des Roches (fl. 1190-1220), one of the important barons of Poitou* and wielded great influence in the reign of Richard I.* On Richard's death in 1199, as a declared enemy of John Lackland,* he was one of the strongest supporters of Arthur's claim to the English throne, and helped Philip II* conquer the Loire valley in 1204. For that service, he was created seneschal+ of Anjou, and served the French government. (Bibliog. 98)

William de Warenne. See Warenne, William de.

William Longchamps. See Longchamps, William.

William of Armorica. See Guillaume le Breton.

William of Hauteville, "Iron Arm" (d. 1046), Norman soldier and adventurer, this eldest of twelve sons of Tancred* of Hauteville, was the first of the family to become a career soldier of fortune in southern Italy. Responding to a call for help, William became captain of the Norman army that allied with the Lombards and conquered Apulia.* By 1042, he called himself count of Apulia. In 1044, he and his overlord, Gaimar of Salerno, invaded Calabria. By that, William became the most powerful leader in southern Italy. He was succeeded on his death by his brother Drogo, and a few years later by another brother, Robert Guiscard.* (Bibliog. 98)

Wiltshire, earl of. Hervé de Léon II, Hervy le Breton (d. 1168), the son and heir of Giomar III, *vicomte* of Léon in Brittany, was so haughty and great a nobleman that he refused Henry I's* repeated invitations to visit England, and accepted only after Stephen* came to the throne. He was with Stephen at Oxford in June 1139 when his men were said to have been attacked by those of the bishop of Salisbury* in the disturbance which led to the arrest of the bishops. Stephen married his illegitimate daughter to Hervé, and shortly thereafter created him earl of Wiltshire. He accepted Stephen's heavy bribes which included the castle of Devizes.* His haughty conduct and arrogant attitude led the people of Wiltshire to besiege the castle in 1141, and force him to surrender and leave England. On his departure his earldom reverted to the crown. It was granted to Sayer (Saer) de Quincy* before he died in 1219, and to Hugh Despenser* by Henry III* late in the 13th century. It was not granted again until 1397 when King Richard II* bestowed the earldom upon William, Lord Scrope, the lord treasurer, but he was beheaded two years later by the new king, Henry IV.* (Bibliog. 101, 184)

Winchelsea, battle of. See Les-Espagnols-sur-Mer.

Winchester, chief city of Hampshire, England, and the royal seat of the West Saxon kings. Bishops of the cathedral there were chancellors+ to the see of Canterbury, and prelates for the Order of the Garter.* Its bishops were considered among the peers+ of England. The earldom of Winchester began with Sayer (Saer) de Quincy,* one of the young knights at the court of Henry II* in attendance on young Henry.* When young Henry left the court to foment rebellion in 1173, Sayer joined him. Sayer had married Margaret, daughter of Simon I de Montfort,* and thereby had obtained a sizeable portion of de Montfort's holdings in Devon* in right of his wife. In 1215, after he joined the barons against King John* who promptly declared his lands forfeited and granted them away, he went to France as the baronial representative to induce Dauphin* Louis to invade England to dethrone and replace John. At Lincoln, the dauphin's forces were decisively beaten and Sayer taken prisoner. The regency for young King Henry III* took the broadest position possible for those barons who had sided with France, and declared an amnesty to allow the rebels to settle accounts with a fine. Sayer and his eldest son Robert had played leading roles in this affair. Robert died in 1217, leaving a daughter who eventually became a co-heiress of Ranulph, earl of Chester* through marriage. Sayer in 1219, took the cross, and journeyed to Palestine* where he died in November of the same year, heavily in debt to the king. The earldom descended through Margaret, daughter of Robert, Sayer's eldest son, to his grandson, Roger de Quincy, on whose death in 1261, the earldom returned to the crown. It lay dormant until it was granted in fee to the elder Hugh Despenser in 1322. Although the lands and titles of both Despensers had been reclaimed by Parliament in 1321, that action was reversed in the following year, and the earldom of Winchester was bestowed on the elder man. Four years later, he was taken by the partisans of Queen Isabella and hanged; his son suffered a similar fate a month later, and the earldom was extinguished by this forfeiture. (Bibliog. 47, 66)

Winchester castle, administrative center of the Norman government of England. There the king kept his treasure, and in the 11th and 12th centuries, the king's treasury was the heart of his government. There the *Domesday Book** was preserved, and there were developed the methods of accounting which subsequently developed into the Exchequer.* It was to Winchester castle+ that Henry FitzEmpress rode immediately to claim the crown on learning of the death of his brother, King William II,* in the New Forest. By the end of the 12th century, both the treasury and Exchequer had been transferred to Westminster in London. Yet Henry III* considered Winchester to be one of his favorite residences. From 1234 onwards, he spent over £10,000 on making Winchester larger and more comfortable for his queen and himself, and for improving the defenses of the castle. For example, the king's chambers had stories from the Old and New Testaments painted in circles on the wainscoting; the queen's chamber was provided with a chimney piece of marble and was rewainscoted in 1252 with Irish wood. During the reign of the Lord Prince,* Edward I,* the castle was frequently repaired. In 1302, the king and queen were asleep in their chambers when a fire broke out, and they were lucky to escape. Even though Edward II* ordered the castle repaired, little seems to have been done, for no major repairs were carried out on the building during his reign. From there on, little was done to restore the edifice to its former glory. (Bibliog. 104)

Windsor castle. The chalk cliffs of Berkshire upon which Windsor castle+ stands was the only strong point in the Thames valley where a fortress could be built between London and Wallingford. There William I* founded a castle which took its name from the ancient royal estate known as Old Windsor. By the reign of Henry I,* if not before, there was within its walls a "king's house." By the Treaty of Winchester* in 1153, Windsor was put into the custody of Richard de Lucy* who remained its constable* until his death in 1179, and its construction continued under his able administration. By the time Henry II* died, the defenses of the upper bailey+ had been completed. In 1193, the castle was handed to Count John,* the king's brother, only to be taken from him during the rebellion the next year. Yet, on his accession to the throne in 1199, King John made certain of the strength of the castle. By 1216, it was strong enough under its castellan, Engelard de Cigogne, to resist the three-month siege of the count of Nevers. John's son, Henry III,* made Windsor one of his principal residences, and began a series of alterations lasting twenty years until about Windsor he could say proudly, "No finer castle exists in the whole of Europe." During his reign, a whole new set of royal apartments was built, consisting of a chamber 60 feet long and 28 feet wide for the king's use near the wall of the castle, and adjoining it, another chamber 40 feet long for the queen. In the half-century between the accession of Edward I and the beginning of Edward III's reign, the castle was maintained by the constable.+ Edward III transformed Windsor into a fortified palace. Unconnected to these fortifications were Edward's efforts on the Round Table* project begun in 1344. In January of 1344, the king commanded that there should be "a most noble house in which the Round Table could be held." Sparing neither labor nor expense, this house was to measure 200 feet in diameter and be built of stone. This idea was abandoned almost as soon as it began, but something of its intention as a center for chivalry in the principal royal castle of the realm was reflected in Edward's subsequent founding of the Order of the Garter.* At the same time Philip VI* of Valois, king of France, stimulated by this action of King Edward, began to build his own Round Table in his own country so that he could attract to his group the knighthood of Germany and Italy before they could hasten to the Table of the English king. Edward's cost of work at Windsor between 1350 and his death in 1377 amounted to over £51,000. So thoroughly had Edward built and strengthened Windsor that his successor, young Richard II,* found no reason to spend any money on its maintenance. It remained England's foremost royal castle. (Bibliog. 104)

Windsor Herald, the oldest English herald* dating from 1338. See heraldry.+

Witenagemot, national assembly of the Witan, the wise men of the land in England before the Norman invasion. This was a formal assembly of the king's counsellors when "all the earls and most distiguished men in the land" were present. It consisted of the archbishops of Canterbury and York, five bishops, five abbots, and earls (or aldermen+). The churchmen's high position throughout Europe in this period was based partly on the recognition of their sacred status, and partly on the need to obtain the counsel of the only fully educated class of society. (Bibliog. 182)

Wolfram von Eschenbach (d. c. 1225), one of the greatest Middle High German poets. Native to a family of petty nobility in Eschenbach, Bavaria, he became a wanderer, but after 1203, he stayed repeatedly at the court of the Landgrave Hermann of Thuringia, attracted by its *minnesingers.*+ He wrote two long poems, *Willehalm,* and greateast and most important work, *Parzival,** which introduced a new theme into German literature, the legend of the Holy Grail. (Bibliog. 235)

women with armies. A general's principal duty was to see that his troops were kept reasonably fit and well-fed and that there were plenty of women with the army to handle the men's sexual needs. Ambroise,* in his description of the third crusade,+ felt that self-imposed chastity was a bigger killer than any of the other diseases crusaders were likely to encounter. On that he said,

> In pilgrims' hearing I declare
> A hundred thousand men died there
> Because from women they abstained
> 'Twas for love they restrained
> Themselves.
> They had not perished thus
> Had they not been abstemious. (Bibliog. 83)

His point was obvious. In Muslim* eyes, however, these necessary activities, whether military or sexual, sometimes took on legendary proportions. Imad ad-Din recorded the following impression of Frankish women arriving at Acre* in 1190.

> There arrived by ship three hundred lovely Frankish women, full of youth and beauty, assembled from beyond the sea and offering themselves for sin. They were expatriates come to help ex-patriates, ready to cheer the fallen and sustained in turn to give support and assistance, and they glowed with ardour for carnal in-tercourse. They were all licentious harlots, proud and scornful,

who took and gave foul-fleshed and sinful, singers and coquettes, appearing proudly in public, ardent and inflamed, tinted and painted, exquisite and graceful, who ripped open and patched up, lacerated and mended, erred and ogled, urged and seduced, consoled and solicited like tipsy adolescents, making love and selling themselves for gold, pink-faced and unblushing. With nasal voices and fleshy thighs, blue-eyed and grey-eyed, broken down little fools. Each one trailed the train of her robe behind her and bewitched the beholder....So they set themselves up each in a pavilion or tent erected for her use, together with other lovely young girls of their age, and opened the gates of pleasure. They dedicated as a holy offering what they kept between their thighs; they plied a brisk trade in their dissoluteness. (Bibliog. 83)

Worcester, one of the ancient and important English boroughs on the banks of the Severn River fortified by a castle during the early years of the Norman Conquest in 1066. This great wooden castle was destroyed by fire in 1113, but soon was rebuilt, and was maintained regularly by all the English kings. In 1216, when the body of King John* was interred in Worcester, the monks of Worcester reminded King Henry III* that earlier monarchs had wrongly erected part of the castle on cathedral burial grounds. Thus that section of the castle containing the "king's houses" was returned to the monks while the tower and motte+ were put under the control of Walter de Beauchamp. Thus dismantled, the castle ceased to have any military value, and so was ignored by the king as valueless as a royal castle.

Its first post-conquest earl was Waleran,* count of Meulan, earl of Warwick (1104-1166), son of Robert de Beaumont, count of Meulan and first earl of Leicester.* He was born as a twin with Robert who later became the second earl of Leicester. When these twins were only 3 or 4 years old, their father decided to divide his estates in England and Normandy between them on his death. He died in 1118 and the boys were reared at the court of Henry I* out of gratitude to their father. Waleran inherited the *comté* of Meulan in the French Vexin,* with the castle and town of Meulan on the Seine. He also received numerous Norman baronies. Although he remained faithful to King Henry I in the rebellion in Normandy in 1118, he was drawn into a conspiracy involving William Clito,* son of Duke Robert II,* Curthose, of Normandy, and had to fight the forces of Henry. In 1124, he charged a royal force at the head of 40 men, but his horse was riddled with arrows and he was captured and imprisoned successively at Rouen, Bridgnorth and Wallingford until 1129 when the king freed him and returned to him all his lands and castles. He was with Henry when the king died in 1135. King Stephen* sought and received his support, and gave him his two-year-old daughter, Maud to marry in 1136, and also gave him the city of Worcester. His child-wife died without issue at age 7 in 1141. Waleran returned to Normandy to join his brother in fighting their common enemy, Roger de Toeny, whom they captured near Vaudreuil. After King Stephen released Toeny, Waleran again had to fight him. In 1138, he was created earl of Worcester for his efforts for the crown in Normandy. That summer, he returned to England and began to oppose the chief justiciar,+ Bishop Roger of Salisbury.* At the battle of Lincoln* in 1141, he was one of the commanders of the royal army who fled when their front was broken by the opening charge, leaving the king to be captured. However, he was one of the three earls faithful to the king during his captivity, but in 1141, he abandoned Stephen and came to terms with Geoffrey Plantagenet* of Anjou. He returned to Normandy and served Geoffrey there as one of his justiciars. In 1146 he went on the second crusade+ but was shipwrecked on his return, saving himself and some companions by clinging to bits of wreckage and drifting to shore. In 1150, when Geoffrey resigned the dukedom of Normandy to his son Henry,* Waleran acted as one of the young duke's justiciars. On Henry's accession to the throne in 1154, Waleran was not re-created as earl of Worcester, despite remaining on good terms with the king. When he died in 1166 as a monk at Preaux, the earldom died with him. (Bibliog. 47, 104)

Wurzburg, Konrad von. See Konrad von Wurzburg.

Y

Yder, French Arthurian verse romance written between 1210 and 1225 in western France. Yder, the illegitimate son of Nuc, left his mother and grandmother at age 17 to seek his fortune. At Carvain, he fell in love with Guenloie, and set out on a life of adventure to prove his love for her. Killing two assailants attacking a single knight who turned out to be King Arthur,* Yder went to the aid of Talac de Rogemont against Arthur's siege when Arthur proved to be ungrateful for his earlier help. Guenloie witnessed his valorous deeds and his prowess, and ordered a physician to tend to the wounds which Quoi (Kay) inflicted treacherously and sneakingly after Yder overthrew him three times in the siege. Seeing that conduct, Arthur convinced him to join the Round Table.* He finally found his father, Nuc, and both went to join Arthur's court. Arthur became violently jealous of him after Queen Guenevere* admitted that she would prefer Yder to Arthur if she were to marry again. After killing two giants and bringing back their huge knives as fulfillment of the feat imposed by Guenloie, they were married, and shortly thereafter, he was legitimized by the marriage of his mother and Nuc. (ed. H. Gelzer, Halle: *GrL,* 1913) (Bibliog. 10)

York, second largest city in England, but the main city of Yorkshire, the largest county in England, being 70 miles in length and 80 miles from east to west. It was divided into three ridings+, or parts, the West Riding, the North Riding, and East Riding; Richmondshire* made the fourth part. Its archbishop was allowed to style himself the Primate of England, but he was secondary to the archbishop* of Canterbury, who titled himself the Primate of all England.

     The earldom of York was said to have been given first to Otto* of Saxony, second son of Henry the Lion,* duke of Saxony and Bavaria; his mother was Matilda, first daughter of Henry II* of England. Born about 1175, he was brought up at the English court. He claimed that in 1190, Richard I* bestowed upon him the county of York, but exchanged it in 1196 for the county of Poitou by which he became count of Poitou. On Otto's election and coronation as king of the Romans in

1198, Richard I resumed the countship of Poitou in his own hands. In 1200, however, Otto was said to have sent his two brothers as ambassadors to his uncle King John,* to claim both York and Poitou, but their trip was unsuccessful. The first actual duke of York was Edmund of Langley, fifth, but fourth surviving, son of Edward III.* Born in Langley, Hertfordshire in 1341, he was created duke of York in 1385 by Richard II,* and lived until 1402. Its dukes and earls were

1190 - Otto of Bavaria, earl of York; emperor of Germany;
1385 - Edmund of Langley, fifth son of King Edward III, earl of
        Cambridge, and duke of York; married 1) Isabel, youngest
        daughter and co-heiress of Peter of Castile and Leon; 2) Joan,
        daughter of Thomas Holland, earl of Kent
1401 - Edward Plantagenet, son of Edmund of Langley, earl of Rutland,
        and duke of York; married Philippa, eldest daughter and
        co-heiress of John, lord Dunster.
(Bibliog. 47, 101)

York castle, even though William I* built two castles+ at York* on his first visit to the city in 1068, both shortly thereafter were burned and had to be rebuilt. One was maintained as a royal castle until the Jewish riots following Richard I's* coronation in 1090, but this replacement also was built of wood, and was destroyed by wind in 1228. In 1244, recognizing its strategic importance to England in the continuing conflict with Scotland, Henry III* had it rebuilt, spending £2,400 over the next thirty years. He placed the work in the hands of two highly experienced craftsmen, Royal Master Mason Henry of Reynes, who was responsible for much of the 13th-century work done on Westminster Abbey, and Master Simon, the carpenter of Northampton.* Basically it was built in the shape of four overlapping circles. Its tower was called the King's Tower until 1322 when the bodies of Sir Robert Clifford and the other Lancastrian leaders were hung from the tower; then it became known as Clifford's Tower. After his defeat at the battle of Bannock Burn,* Edward II* spent a great deal of time at this castle. (Bibliog. 104, 247)

Ysoré l'Esclavon, Christian baron in the *chanson de geste,* *Anseis de Carthage* who became a Moslem because he hated Anseis for impregnating his sister. (Bibliog. 128)

Yvain (Ywain), French Arthurian romance also known as *Knight of the Lion,* it was written late in the 12th century by Chrétien de Troyes.* Yvain was one of King Arthur's* chief knights of the Round Table,* and appeared in most of the romances. He was the son of Urien, nephew of Kings Anguisel and Lot,* and cousin of Gawain* and his brothers. He succeeded his uncle Anguisel as king of Escosse. In this work, King Arthur and Ywain were told by Calogrenant about a beautiful fountain in the Forest of Broceliande.* If a knight looking for adventure poured water from the fountain on a marble slab there, he would find adventures. Calogrenanz had done so, and after a sudden storm, he was unhorsed by an unknown knight who appeared suddenly. Disgraced, Calogrenanz had walked back to Arthur's court. Arthur vowed to visit the fountain, but Yvain planned secretly to arrive there first. He did, defeated and slew the unknown knight, married his widow, and challenged Kay when Arthur and his troop arrived. Then he revealed his identity to Arthur. He obtained his bride's permission to accompany Arthur for a year and a day on the tournament circuit, and when he overstayed his leave, his wife renounced him forever. He went mad, but was healed by the fairy Morgue (Morgan la Fée*), Arthur's sister. He championed a lion as it fought a snake, and out of gratitude the lion followed him as a companion; hence he was called the Knight of the Lion. He fought for Lunette, the maid who had helped him win his wife's hand originally, to save her from the stake. He overcame other difficulties and eventually won back his wife. (tr. W. W. Comfort, London and New York: Everyman, 1955) (Bibliog. 147)

Ywain and Gawain, redaction into English verse of Chrétien de Troyes'* work, *Yvain.** In it, the focus was changed to de-emphasize much of the courtly love and deleted many of the chivalric refinements which stressed deeds of arms. For example, after Arthur's* Whitsunday Feast, the knights and ladies withdrew from the banquet to amuse themselves recounting deeds of arms and venery, not of the anguish, sadness and tribulations of love. Thus the story was one in which deeds of arms prevailed. (ed. Freidman and Harrington, London: *EETS OS* 254, 1964, repr. 1981) (Bibliog. 10)

Z

Zengi, Imad al-Din (1084-1146), atabeg of Mosul. He was a clever leader, for he starved the Frank defenders of Ba'Rin into surrendering and then demanded a ransom of 50,000 dinars. After they had surrendered on the condition that they be allowed to return unharmed to their own domains, they found to their chagrin that relief had been on its way to them, and that they had surrendered too soon. At that same time, he recovered from the Franks the town of Ma'arra. On its recovery by Zengi, the inhabitants begged for the return of their possessions. In response to his request for proof of ownership, the citizens replied that the Franks had taken everything including title proofs. Zengi ordered the registers at Aleppo checked and to anyone who had an entry for land tax on a particular holding, Zengi restored land. (Bibliog. 83)

Appendices

A. Genealogical Charts

Abbreviations used on charts
      b. = born
      bp. = bishop
      br. = brother
      c. = count
      D. = duke
      d. = died
      da. = daughter
      E. = emperor
      e. = earl
      Fr. = France
      H.R.E.= Holy Roman Emperor
      k. = king
      q. = queen

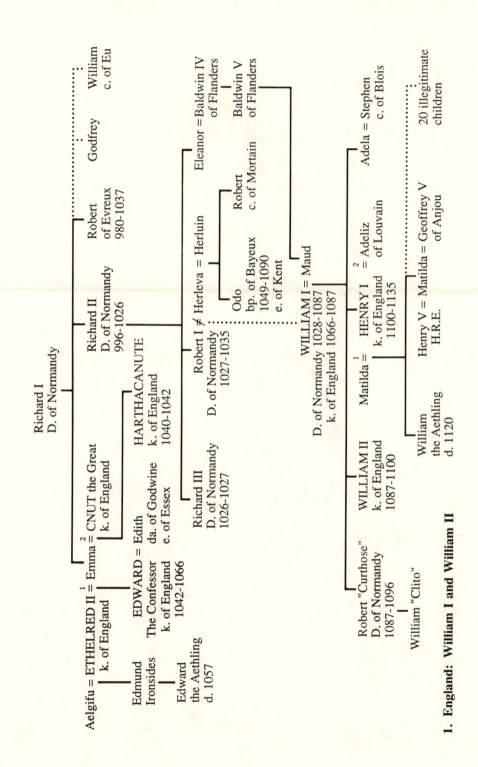

1. England: William I and William II

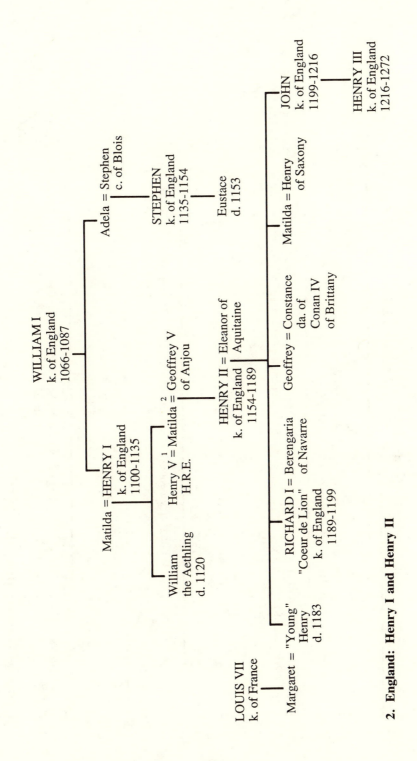

2. England: Henry I and Henry II

Hugh = Isabelle = JOHN ¹= Isabelle
of Lusignan of Angoulême ² k. of England of Gloucester
1199-1216

HENRY III = Eleanor   Richard   Joan = Alexander II   Eleanor = Simon de Montfort
k. of England of Provence e. of Cornwall d. 1238 of Scotland d. 1275 e. of Leicester
1216-1272   (see below)   d. 1272

Eleanor = EDWARD I = Margaret   Margaret = Alexander III   Beatrice = John de Dreux   Edmund "Crouchback"
of Castile k. of England da. of d. 1275 of Scotland d. 1275 D. of Brittany e. of Leicester
1272-1307 PHILIP IV e. of Lancaster
k. of France d. 1296

Edward II
k. of England
1307-1327

William of Valence   Aymer of Valence   Geoffrey of   Guy of
e. of Pembroke   bp. of Winchester   Lusignan   Lusignan

Raymond
of Berenger

Margaret = LOUIS IX   Sanchia = Richard   Beatrice = Charles
k. of France   of Cornwall   of Anjou
br. LOUIS IX

HENRY III = Eleanor
of Provence

3. **England: John and Henry III**

Eleanor $=^1$ EDWARD I $^2=$ Margaret
of Castile | k. of England | s. of PHILIP IV
| 1272-1307 | k. of France

Eleanor
d. 1297

Henry
d. 1274

Joan
"of Acre"

Elizabeth $=^1$ John
c. of Holland

$^2=$ Humphrey
de Bohun
e. of Hereford
e. of Essex

Thomas
of Brotherton
d. 1338
e. of Norfolk

Edmund
d. 1330
e. of Kent

Isabelle $=$ EDWARD II
da. of PHILIP IV | k. of England
k. of France | 1307-1327

EDWARD III $=$ Philippa
k. of England | of Hainaut
1327-1377

John
of Eltham
d. 1336

Eleanor
of Woodstock
d. 1335

Joan $=$ DAVID II
k. of Scotland

Edward $=$ Joan
of Woodstock | of Kent
"Black Prince"

Isabelle $=$ Enguerrand
de Coucy

Lionel
of Clarence

Blanche $=^1$ John $^2=$ Constance
of Lancaster | of Gaunt | of Castile
| $^3=$ Kathryn
| de Swynford

Edmund
e. of
Cambridge
D. of York

Edward
d. 1371

RICHARD II
k. of England
1377-1399

Edmund Mortimer $=$ Philippa
e. of March

Roger Mortimer
e. of March

HENRY IV
k. of England
1399-1413

John Beaufort
e. of Somerset

Henry Beaufort
bp. of Winchester

Thomas
Beaufort
D. of Exeter

Joan
Beaufort

Edward
e. of
Rutland

4. England: Edward I, Edward II, and Edward III

667

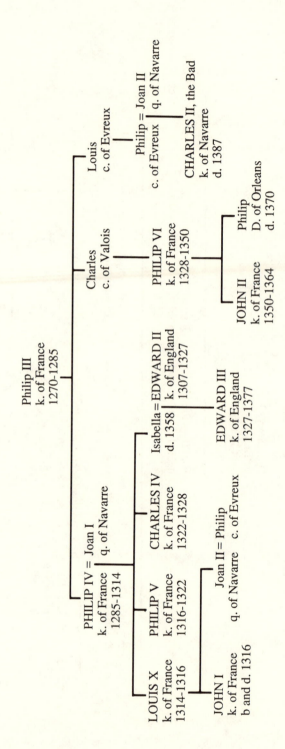

5. England: Edward III's claim to French throne

Philip III
k. of France
1270-1285

Charles
c. of Valois

PHILIP VI
k. of France
1328-1350

JOHN II
k. of France
1350-1364

Philip
D. of Orleans
d. 1370

Louis
c. of Evreux

Philip = Joan II
c. of Evreux q. of Navarre

CHARLES II, the Bad
k. of Navarre
d. 1387

PHILIP IV = Joan I
k. of France q. of Navarre
1285-1314

LOUIS X
k. of France
1314-1316

PHILIP V
k. of France
1316-1322

JOHN I
k. of France
b and d. 1316

CHARLES IV
k. of France
1322-1328

Joan II = Philip
q. of Navarre c. of Evreux

Isabella = EDWARD II
d. 1358 k. of England
1307-1327

EDWARD III
k. of England
1327-1377

668

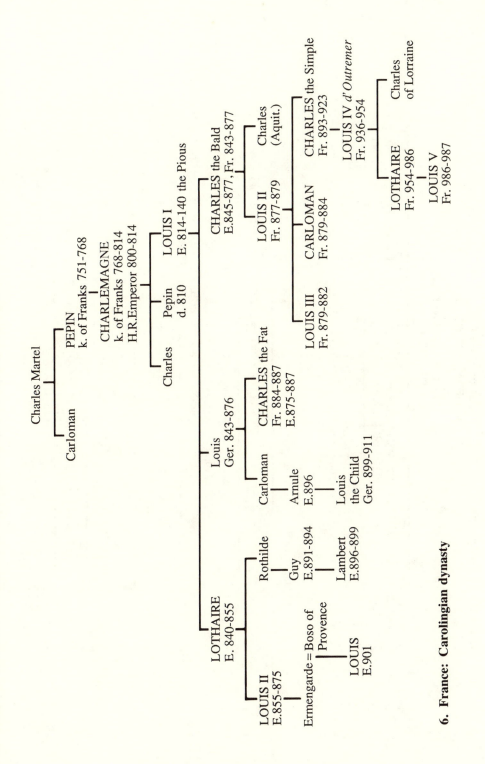

6. France: Carolingian dynasty

7. France: Capetian dynasty

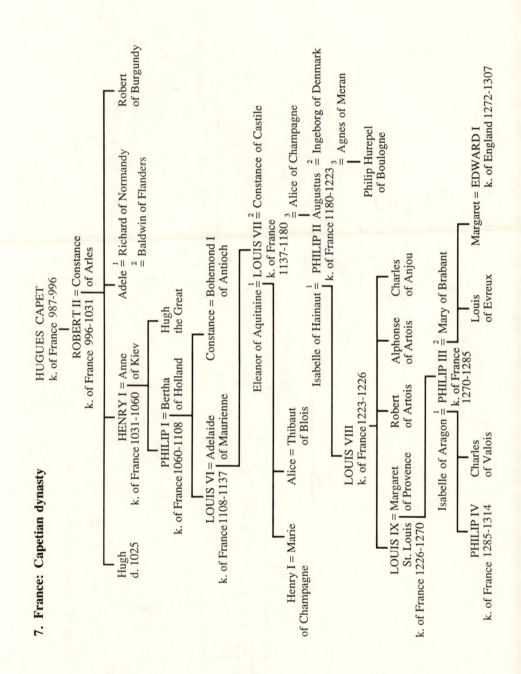

HUGUES CAPET
k. of France 987-996

ROBERT II = Constance
k. of France 996-1031 | of Arles

Hugh
d. 1025

HENRY I = Anne
k. of France 1031-1060 | of Kiev

Robert
of Burgundy

Adele = Richard of Normandy
[1]
= Baldwin of Flanders
[2]

PHILIP I = Bertha
k. of France 1060-1108 | of Holland

Hugh
the Great

LOUIS VI = Adelaide
k. of France 1108-1137 | of Maurienne

Constance = Bohemond I
of Antioch

Henry I
of Champagne

Alice = Thibaut
of Blois

Eleanor of Aquitaine [1] = LOUIS VII [2] = Constance of Castile
k. of France
1137-1180
[3]
= Alice of Champagne

Marie

Isabelle of Hainaut [1] = PHILIP II Augustus [2] = Ingeborg of Denmark
k. of France 1180-1223
[3]
= Agnes of Meran

Philip Hurepel
of Boulogne

LOUIS VIII
k. of France 1223-1226

LOUIS IX = Margaret
St. Louis | of Provence
k. of France 1226-1270

Robert
of Artois

Alphonse
of Artois

Charles
of Anjou

Isabelle of Aragon [1] = PHILIP III [2] = Mary of Brabant
k. of France
1270-1285

Louis
of Evreux

Margaret = EDWARD I
k. of England 1272-1307

Charles
of Valois

PHILIP IV
k. of France 1285-1314

670

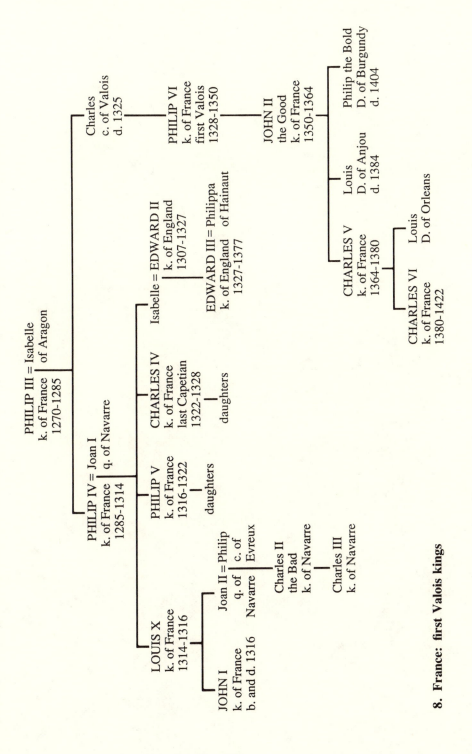

8. **France: first Valois kings**

671

B. Topical List of Entries

Authors

Abu Shama
Abulfeda
Adenet le Roi
Adhemar de Chabannes
Alberich de Pisançon
Ambroise
Amiens, Guy of
Andrea da Barberino
Andreas Capellanus
Anna Comnena
Arabic historians
Ariosto
Baha ad-Din
Baker, Geoffrey le
Barbour, John
Benoît de Saint-Maure
Béroul
Berthold von Holle
Bertrand de Bar-sur-Aube
Bethune, Conan de
Blondel of Nêsle
Boiardo, Matteo Maria
Bracton, Henry of
Brunetto Latini
Chrétien de Troyes
Christine de Pisan
Coggeshall, Ralph of
Coventry, Walter of
Dares
Diceto, Ralph de
Dictys
Eilhart von Oberg
Einhard
Fantôsme, Jordan
Fleck, Konrad
Fordun, John

Froissart, Jean
Gaimar, Geoffrey
Geoffrey of Monmouth
Gervase of Tilbury
Gloucester, Robert of
Gottfried von Strassburg
Graindor de Douai
Guillaume le Breton
Hartmann von Aue
Heinrich von dem Türlin
Heinrich von Veldeke
Henry of Huntingdon
Henry le Duc de Dammartin
Herbert von Fritzlar
Hexham, Richard of
Higden, Ranulph
Hoveden, Roger of
Hue de Roteland
Ibn al-Athir
Ibn al-Qalanisi
Ibn Wasil
'Imad ad-Din
Isidore of Seville
Jakemon Sakesap
John of Salisbury
Joinville, Jehan de
Jumièges, Guillaume de
Kamal ad-Din
Knighton, Henry
Konrad von Wurzburg
Konrad von Stoffeln
Lamprecht, pfaffe
Langtoft, Peter of
Layamon
La Bel, Jean
Limousin astronomer
Lovelich, Henry

Battles

Books

Boniface of Savoy
Canterbury, Gervase of
Champart, Robert
Denis, St.
Durham, bishop of
Gundulf
Hincmar
Hugh, bishop of Lincoln
Hugh of Puiset
Kirkby, John
Lanfranc
metropolitan
Nonant, Hugh de
Odo (Eudes), Bishop of Bayeux
Peter des Roches
Raoul de Wanneville
Robert of Jumièges
Roger, bishop of Salisbury
Turpin, Archbishop
Walter, Hubert

Comtes (counts)
Alençon
Amadeus V
count of Rouen
Dammartin, Renaud de
dauphin
Eu
Eudes II
Hurepel, Philip de
John, bishop of Lisieux
Jourdain, Alphonse
Peter, count of Savoy
Poitou
vicomte
Waleran

Earls and Dukes
Albemarle
Albini
Angus
Arundel
Aumale
Beaumont
Bedevere

Berry, John
Bigod
Buchan
Carlisle
Carrick
Chester
Clare
Cornwall
Desmond
Devon
Dublin
duke
Dunbar
earldoms and barony
earl marshal
Enguerrand de Coucy I
Enguerrand de Coucy III
Enguerrand de Coucy IV
Essex
Este
Ferrers
Gilbert de Clare
Gloucester
Gyrth
Henry of Grosmont
Henry Plantagenet
Hereford
Hertford
Huntingdon
jarl
John of Gaunt
Kent
Kidderminster
Kildare
Lancaster
Leicester
Leofric
Leofwine
Lincoln
Lionel of Antwerp
March
Mauduit
Montfort, Simon de
Norfolk
Northampton
Northumberland

Fictional Characters

Gaheris
Galafers
Galahad
Galeholt
Ganelon
Gareth
Garin d'Anseune
Garnier de Nanteuil
Gawain
Geoffrey (*douzepeer*)
Ginglain
Girart de Roussillon
Gorlois
Green Knight
gregois
Gromer Somer Joure
Guineman
Guinemer
Hagen
Hardré
Haute Prince
Hiaumont
Howel the Hende
Idain
Igerne
Ironsyde
Isolde la Belle
Isolde le Blanche Mains
Joceran
Josephes
Jurfaleu
Karaheut
Kay
Lambors
Lamorak of Wales
Lancelot
Launcelot
Leodegran
Loholt
Lot
Lucius Iberius
Lyonel
Maganza family
maimed kings
Mark, King
Marsile

Maugis
Meleagant
Meliodas
Mordred
Morholt
Naimes, Naimon
Nouhusius
Ogier le Danois
Oliver
Orable
Orguilleus
Othon
Oton
Oyselet, Sir Amboy
Palomydes
Pellam
Pellinore
Pendragon, Uther
Perceval
Pinabel of Sorence
Pynel the Savage
Ragnell, Dame
Sagramore le Desirus
Scottish knight
Segwarides
Siegfried
Sigurd
Tramtris
Turoldus
Ysore l'Esclavon

Individuals
Archpriest
Archpirate
Arnaut de Cervole
Aungervyle
Black Dog of Arden
Brewer, William
Burgh, Hubert de
Chandos herald
Charlot
Chevalier vermeil
Dynas, Sir
Faulkes de Breauté
FitzNeal, Richard
Flambard, Ranulph

free booter
free-lance
Henry le Waleys
herald
Hereward the Wake
Hernaut de Beaulande
Mahomet
Seneschal of Anjou
Seneschal of Aquitaine
Seneschal of England
Seneschal of France
Windsor herald

Knights

Ackerman, Francis
Amr
Badlesmere, Bartolomew of
Baliol, John de
Baliol, John (son)
Banastre, Adam
Basset, Ralph
Basset, Ralph, Lord, of
     Drayton
Beauchamp, John
Beaufort
Beaumanoir, Jean de
Beaumanoir, Philippe de
Bellême-Montgomery
Berkeley
de Bohun
de Braose
Burghersh, Bartholomew
Burnell, Robert
Calveley, Sir Hugh
Campeador
Chandos, Sir John
Charnay, Geoffrey de
Clifford, Robert de
Clifford, Roger de
Clisson, Olivier de
Cobham, Reynald de
Croquart
Dacre, Ranulph
Dagworth, Thomas
Damory, Roger
Darcy, John

D'Eiville, John
de la Warre, Roger
Denis de Morbeque
Despensers
Devereux, John
Douglas, William
Du Guesclin, Bertrand
Dymoke, John
Ednyved, the Little
Edwin of Warwick
Everyingham, Adam de
Felton, John
FitzAlan, Brian
FitzGerald, John FitzThomas
FitzHugh, Henry
FitzJohn, John
FitzOsbern, William
FitzWarin, Fulk I
Florent de Varenne
Frazer, Simon
Gautier d'Arras
Gaveston, Piers
Geoffrey, Plantagenet
Geoffrey (illegitimate son of Henry II)
Geoffrey de Clinton
Geoffrey Ridel
Geoffrey de Preuilli
Gerard de Camville
Giffard, John
Glanville, Ranulph de
Godfrey of Luci
Grailly, Jean de (Captal de Buch)
Grandison, Otes de
Grandison, Piers de
Gray, Thomas
Hamelin Plantagenet
Harcla, Andrew
Hastings, Henry
Havering, John de
Hawkwood, John
Holand, Robert
Holand, Thomas
Ingham, Oliver
Knollys, Robert
Lacy, Richard de
Lacy, Roger de

Legal Terms

Literary Terms

Scotland
Septimania
Shrewsbury
Sogdiana
Somerset
Staple
Stonehenge
Suddene
Suffolk
Surrey
Sussex
Swabia
Taprobane
Tenlade
Thanet
Toulouse
Tyre
Wales
Warwick
Westmoreland
Wight, Isle of
Winchester
Worcester
York

Romances, *Lais*

Alexander (English)
Alexander (German)
Alexander and Dindimus
Alexanderlied
Alexander, Roman d'
Alisaunder
Alpharts Tod
Amadas et Ydoine
Amadas de Gaula
Amys and Amiloun
Appolonius of Tyre
Arme Heinrich, Der
Of Arthour and Merlin
Arthur
Arthur and Gorlagon
Athelstan
Athis und Prophilias
L'Atre Perilleus
Auberon, Roman d'
Aunters of Arthur

Avowing of King Arthur
Beaudous
Le Bel Inconnu
Berte e Milone
Bevis of Hampton
Bisclavret
Biterolf und Dietlieb
Blancandrin et Orgueilleuse
Le Bone Florence
Breton *lais*
Byzantine romances
Caballero Cifar, el
cantare
Carl of Carlisle
Chaitivel
Chastelaine de Vergi
Chatelaine de Coucy
Chevalier a l'épée
Chevalier Assigne
Chevalier au Cygne
Chevalier au Cygne et Enfances
    Godefroi
Chevalier du Papegau
Chevalier aux deux épées
Chievrefueil, La
Cid, Cantar de Mio
Claris et Laris
Cléomadès
Cligés
Comte de Poitiers
Conquete de Constantinople
Crane
Crône, Diu
Culhwch and Olwen
Daniel vom dem Blühenden
    Tal
Dietrich und Wenezlan
Dietrichsage
Dietrich's Flucht
Dieudonne de Hongrie
Doön
Durmart le Gallois
Earl of Toulouse
Eliduc
d'Enéas, Roman
Eneit

Rulers

Abagha, khan of Persia
admiral
Albert I, the Bear,
    of Brandenburg
Alexander I of Scotland
Alexander II, of Scotland
Alexander III, of Scotland
Alexander Nevsky, prince of
    Novgorod
Alexander the Great
Alexius Comnenus, of
    Byzantium
Alfred the Great, of England
algalife
Almoravides, Muslim princes
Alp Arsalan, Seljuk sultan
Apostolic majesty
Arthur, King
Athelstan, king of England
Baldwin of Boulogne
Baldwin II of Jerusalem
Baldwin III of Jerusalem
Baldwin, count of Flanders
Bohemond I of Taranto
Bourbon of France
Bruce family of Scotland
Brutus
Capetian dynasty
Charlemagne, Holy Roman Emperor
Charles the Bald, of France
Charles IV, king of the Romans
Charles IV, the Fair, of France
Charles V, the Wise, of France
Charles of Anjou
Cnut, of Norway and England
Conrad II, Holy Roman Emperor
Conrad III, Holy Roman Emperor
Conrad IV, Holy Roman Emperor
Conrad of Montferrat
Constans, of England
Constantine, of England
Dandolo, Enrico, Doge of Venice
David I, of Scotland
David II, of Scotland
Dietrich von Bern
Edmund Ironside, of England
Edward the Confessor, of England
Edward I, of England
Edward II, of England
Edward III, of England
Edward, the Black Prince,
    of England
emir
emperor of the Eastern Roman
    Empire
Enzio, king of Sardinia
Ermonrich, (Odoacer, king of Italy)
Ethelred the Unready, of England
Fatamid dynasty in the Near East
Ferdinand II of Castile
Frederick I, Barbarossa,
    Holy Roman Emperor
Frederick II, Holy Roman
    Emperor
Fulk I, the Good of Anjou
Fulk III, Nerra of Anjou
Fulk IV of Anjou
Fulk V of Anjou
Galloway, lords of
Geoffrey I of Anjou
Geoffrey II of Anjou
Geoffrey III of Anjou
German duchies
Godfrey de Bouillon
Godfrey of Louvain
Godwine of England
graf
Gregory VII (Hildebrand),
    pope
Gunther, king of Worms
Harold I, Harefoot, of
    England
Harold II, of England
Harold Hardrata of England
Harthacanute of England
Harun al-Rashid
Hengest
Henry I, Beauclerc of England
Henry II, FitzEmpress of
    England
Henry III, of Winchester, of

Bibliography

1. Ackerman, Robert. *Index of the Arthurian Names in Middle English*, Palo Alto, California: Stanford Publications in Language and Literature, X, 1952; repr. New York: AMS, 1967.
2. Ackerman, Robert. "Knighting Ceremonies in Middle English Romances," *Speculum*, XIX (1944), pp. 285-313.
3. *An Arabian-Syrian Gentleman and Warrior in the Period of the Crusades: Memoirs of Usamah Ibn-Munqidh*, tr. by Philip Hitti, New York, 1925.
4. Anderson, William. *Castles of Europe*, London: Elek, 1970.
5. Andreas Capellanus. *The Art of Courtly Love*, ed. and tr. J. J. Parry, Seattle, Washington: University of Washington, 1946.
6. Anonymous. *Son of Charlemagne*, ed. and tr. Allen Cabaniss, Syracuse, New York: Syracuse University Press, 1961.
7. Appleby, John. *England without Richard*, London: G. Bell & Sons, 1965.
8. Ariosto, *Orlando furioso*, tr. Guido Waldman, London: Oxford University, 1974.
9. Armitage-Smith, Sir Sydney. *John of Gaunt*, London: Constable, 1904; repr. 1964.
10. *Arthurian Literature in the Middle Ages*, ed. Roger S. Loomis, London and New York: Oxford University, 1959.
11. Ashdown, Charles. *Armour and Weapons in the Middle Ages*, London, 1925; repr. West Orange, New Jersey: Albert Saifer, 1977.
12. Ashe, Geoffrey. *Discovery of Arthur*, New York: Doubleday, 1985.
13. Ashe, Geoffrey. *Quest for Arthur's Britain*, St. Alban's, England: Paladin, 1971.
14. Ashmole, Elias. *The Institution, Laws, and Ceremonies of the Most Noble Order of the Garter*, London, 1692; repr. Baltimore: Genealogical Publishing, 1971.
15. Barber, Malcolm. *The Trial of the Templars*, London: Cambridge University, 1978.
16. Barber, Richard. *The Knight and Chivalry*, London: Longman, 1970.

17. Barber, Richard. *The Reign of Chivalry*, New York: St. Martin's, 1980.
18. Bartholomew Anglicus. *Medieval Lore*, ed. and tr. by Robert Steele, London, 1869; repr. New York: Cooper Square, 1966.
19. Baugh, Albert C. *Literary History of England*, 2nd ed. Vol I.: *The Middle Ages*, London: Routledge and Kegan Paul, 1967.
20. Becke, Major A. F. "Battle of Bannock Burn," in [Cockayne] *The Complete Peerage*, London: St. Catherine Press, 1957, XI, Appendix B.
21. Bossuat, Robert. *Manuel Bibliographique de la Littérature française du Moyen âge*, Melun: Librairie d'Argences, 1951.
22. Bossuat, Robert. *Supplement I (1949-1953)*, Paris: Librairie d'Argences, 1955.
23. Bossuat, Robert. *Supplement II (1954-1960)*, Paris: Librairie d'Argences, 1961.
24. Bostock, John. *Handbook of Old High German Literature*, London: Oxford University, 1955.
25. Briffault, Robert. *The Troubadours*, Bloomington, Indiana: Indiana State University, 1965.
26. Brook-Little, John P. *An Heraldic Alphabet*, New York: Arco, 1973.
27. Broughton, Bradford. *The Legends of Richard I, Coeur de Lion*, The Hague, The Netherlands: Mouton, 1966.
28. Broughton, Bradford. *Richard the Lion Hearted and Other Medieval English Romances*, New York: E. P. Dutton, 1966.
29. Broughton, Bradford. "Sir Gawain: From Scoundrel to Hero," *English Record* XXXI, #1 (Winter 1980), pp. 9-16.
30. Brown, R. Allen. *Castles: A History and Guide*, New York: Greenwich House, 1982.
31. Brown, R. Allen. *English Castles*, London: Batsford, 1954.
32. Brown, R. Allen. "List of Castles, 1154-1216," *English Literary History*, 74 (1959), pp. 249-280.
33. Brown, R. Allen. *The Normans and the Norman Conquest*, London: Constable, 1969.
34. Bruce, J. D. *Evolution of Arthurian Romance from the Beginnings down to 1300*, Baltimore, Maryland: Johns Hopkins University, 1923.
35. Bryant, Sir Arthur. *Age of Chivalry*, New York: New American Library, 1970.
36. Cabeen, D. C. *Critical Bibliography of French Literature, I: Medieval Period*, ed. U. T. Holmes, Syracuse, New York: Syracuse University, 1947.
37. *Cambridge Medieval History*: V. *Contest of Empire and Papacy*,

ed. J. R. Tanner, C. W. Previte-Orton, Z. N. Brooke,
Cambridge, England: Cambridge University, repr. 1968.

38. *Cambridge Medieval History*: VI. *Victory of the Papacy*, ed. J. R.
Tanner, C. W. Previte-Orton, Z. N. Brooke, Cambridge,
England: Cambridge University, repr. 1968.

39. Cannon, Henry L. "The Battle of Sandwich and Eustace the Monk,"
English Historical Review XXVII (1912), pp. 649-670.

40. Carman, J. Neale. "The Conquests of the Grail Castle and
Dolorous Garde," *PMLA* LXXXV #3 (May 1970), pp. 433-443.

41. Carpenter, D. A. "What Happened in 1258?" *War and Government
in the Middle Ages*, ed. John Gillingham and J. C. Holt, London
and New York: Boydell Press and Barnes and Noble, 1984.

42. Cavendish, Richard. *King Arthur of the Grail: The Arthurian
Legends and Their Meaning*, London, 1978.

43. Caxton, William, ed. and tr. *The Book of the Ordre of Chyvalry*,
Oxford: EETS OS #168, 1926, repr. 1971.

44. Chrétien de Troyes. *Arthurian Romances*, tr. W. W. Comfort, New
York: E. P. Dutton, 1958; repr. 1976.

45. Christine de Pisan. *The Book of Fayttes of Armes and of
Chyvalrye*, tr. William Caxton, ed. A. T. Byles, London: EETS
OS # 189, 1932; repr. New York: Kraus Reprint, 1971.

46. Clephan, Robert. *The Tournament: Its Periods and Phases*, New
York, 1919; repr. New York: Frederick Ungar, 1967.

47. Cockayne, George E. *The Complete Peerage*, rev. ed., London: St.
Catherine's, 1910-1957, 13 vols.

48. Contamine, Philippe. *Warfare in the Middle Ages*, tr. Michael
Jones, Oxford: Blackwell, 1984.

49. Coulson, C. H. "Rendability and castellation in medieval France,"
Chateau Gailliard, VI (September 4-9, 1972), Caen: Centre des
Recherches Archéologiques médiévales, 1973, pp. 59-67.

50. Coulton, George G. *Social Life in Britain from the Conquest to
the Reformation*, Cambridge: Cambridge University, 1918.

51. Cripps-Day, F. H. *History of the Tournament in England and
France*, London, 1918.

52. Crosland, Jessie. *The Old French Epic*, Oxford: Oxford University,
1951.

53. Daniel, Norman. *Heroes and Saracens*, Edinburgh: Edinburgh
University, 1984.

54. Darragh, John. *The Real Camelot*, New York and London: Thames
and Hudson, 1981.

55. Davis, Henry W. C. *England under the Normans and Angevins*,
13th ed., London, 1961.

56. Denholm-Young, N. *History and Heraldry, 1254-1310*, Oxford:

Oxford University, 1965.

57. Denholm-Young, N. "The Tournament in the Thirteenth Century,"
    Studies in Medieval History Presented to Sir Maurice Powicke,
    ed. R. Hunt, R. Southern, Oxford: Oxford University, 1948,
    pp. 240-268.

58. *Dictionary of National Biography*, ed. Sidney Lee, Oxford: Oxford
    University, 1909.

59. Dickinson, Peter. *The Flight of Dragons*, New York: Harper and
    Row, 1979.

60. Dippold, George. *The Great Epics of Medieval Germany*, Boston:
    Roberts Brothers, 1882.

61. Douglas, David C. *The Norman Fate, 1100-1154*, Berkeley, Cali-
    fornia: University of California, 1976.

62. Dunlop, Ian. *Royal Palaces of France*, London: Hamish Hamilton,
    1985.

63. Edwardes, Marion, *Summary of the Literatures of Modern Europe,*
    New York and London: E. P. Dutton, 1907; repr. New York:
    Kraus Reprint, 1968.

64. Eisner, Sigmund. *The Tristan Legend: A Study in Sources,*
    Evanston, Illinois: Northwestern University, 1969.

65. *El Cid, The Epic of*, tr. J. Gerald Markley, Indianapolis,
    Indiana: Bobbs-Merrill. 1961.

66. Ellis, Sir Geoffrey, *Earldoms in Fee: A Study in Peerage Law, and
    History*, London: St. Catherine's, 1963.

67. Elvin, Charles N. *Dictionary of Heraldry*, London, 1889, repr.
    1969.

68. *Encyclopaedia Britannica*, 11th ed., London, 1910-1911.

69. *English Historical Documents, 1042-1189*, ed. by David C. Douglas
    and George Greenaway, London: Oxford University, 1953.

70. *English Historical Documents, 1189-1327*, ed. by Harry Rothwell,
    London: Oxford University, 1975.

71. *English Historical Documents, 1327-1485*, ed. by A. Reginald
    Myers, London: Oxford University, 1969.

72. Evans, Joan. *Life in Medieval France*, London and New York:
    E. P. Dutton, 1969.

73. Farrar, Clarissa, and Austin Evans. *Bibliography of English
    Translations from Medieval Sources*, New York: Columbia
    University Press, 1946; repr. 1964.

74. Fawtier, Robert. *Capetian Kings of France (987-1328)*, London:
    Macmillan, 1962.

75. Ferguson, Mary Anne. *Bibliography of English Translations from
    Medieval Sources*, New York: Columbia University, 1974.

76. Flanagan, Marie Therese. "Strongbow, Henry II and Anglo-Nor-

man Intervention in Ireland," in *War and Government in the Middle Ages*, ed. J. Gillingham and J. C. Holt, Totowa, New Jersey: Barnes and Noble, 1984, pp. 62-87.

77. Fletcher, Robert Huntington. *Arthurian Material in the Chronicles*, Harvard Studies and Notes in Philology and Literature, X, 1906; repr. New York: Burt Franklin, 1958.

78. Frappier, Jean. *Chrétien de Troyes et le Mythe du Graal, (Etude sur Perceval)*, Paris: Société d'Edition d'Enseignement Superior, 1972.

79. Freeman, Edward. *Historical Geography of Europe*, ed. J. Bury, 3rd ed., London: Longman, Green, 1903.

80. Friedman, Albert. "Morgan la Fée in Sir Gawain and the Green Knight," *Speculum* XXXV (1960), pp. 260-274.

81. Froissart, Sir John. *Chronicles of England France and Spain*, tr. Thomas Johnes, New York: E. P. Dutton, 1961.

82. *From Camelot to Joyeuse Garde: The Old French Le Mort le roi Artu*, tr. J. Neale Carmen, ed. Norris Lacy, Lawrence, Kansas: University of Kansas, 1974.

83. Gabrieli, Francesco. *Arab Historians of the Crusades*, tr. E. J. Costello, London: Routledge and Kegan Paul, 1969.

84. Galway, Margaret. "Joan of Kent and the Order of the Garter," *University of Birmingham Historical Journal* I (1947-1948), pp. 13-50.

85. Gardner, E. G. *Arthurian Literature in Italy*, New York and London, 1930.

86. Garland, Henry, and Mary Garland. *Oxford Companion to German Literature*, London: Oxford University, 1976.

87. Gasparri, Francoise. *La Principauté d' Orange au Moyen Age*, Paris: Le Léopard d'Or, 1986.

88. Gautier, Léon. *Les Epopées Françaises*, Paris: Société Générale de Librairie catholique, 4 vols., 1878-1882.

89. Geoffrey de Monmouth. *History of the Kings of Britain*, tr. Charles Dunn, New York: E. P. Dutton, 1958.

90. Gies, Joseph, and Frances Gies. *Life in a Medieval City*, New York: Harper & Row, 1969.

91. Gillingham, John. "Richard I and the Science of War in the Middle Ages," in *War and Government in the Middle Ages*, ed. J. Gillingham and J. C. Holt, Totowa, New Jersey: Barnes and Noble, 1984.

92. Gillingham, John. *Richard the Lion Heart*, New York: New York Times Books, 1978.

93. Gist, Margaret. *Love and War in the Middle English Romances*, Philadelphia: University of Pennsylvania, 1947.

94. Gladwin, Irene. *The Sheriff: The Man and His Office*, London: Routledge and Kegan Paul, 1974.
95. Glover, Richard. "English Warfare in 1066," *English Historical Review* LXVII, 1952.
96. Goodrich, Norma. *King Arthur*, New York and London: Franklin Watts, 1986.
97. Gottfried von Strassburg. *Tristan*, Baltimore, Maryland: Penguin, 1969.
98. Grabois, Aryeh. *Encyclopedia of Medieval Civilization*, London: Octopus Books, 1980.
99. Graves, Edgar B. *Bibliography of English History ito 1485*, London: Oxford University, 1975.
100. Hazlitt, W. C. *The Coinage of the European Continent*, 2 vols., London, 1893-1897; repr. Chicago: Ares Press, 1975.
101. Heylyn, Peter. *A Help to English History*, London: Society of Antiquaries; repr. New York: AMS Press, 1972.
102. Hibbard, Laura. *Medieval Romance in England,* London: Oxford, 1924; repr. New York: Burt Franklin, 1963.
103. Hilton, R. H. *The English Peasantry in the Later Middle Ages*, London: Oxford University, 1975.
104. *History of the King's Works*: I, II *The Middle Ages,* ed. R. Allen Brown, H. M. Colvin, A. J. Taylor, London: Her Majesty's Stationery Office, 1963.
105. Holdsworth, Sir William. *A History of English Law*, 7th ed. (rev. by A. L. Goodhart and H. G. Hanbury), London, I, 1956.
106. Holmes, Urban T. *History of Old French Literature*, New York: Crofts, 1936; repr. New York: Russell and Russell, 1962.
107. Holt, J. C. *Magna Carta*, Cambridge, England: Cambridge University, 1965.
108. Holt, J. C. *The Northerners*, London: Oxford University, 1961.
109. Holt, J. C. *Robin Hood*, London: Thames and Hudson, 1982.
110. Humble, Richard. *The Fall of Saxon England*, London: Arthur Barker, 1975.
111. James, B. S. *Bernard of Clairvaux*, London, 1957; repr. New York: AMS Press, 1979.
112. Jenkins, T. Atkinson. "Why did Ganelon hate Roland?" *PMLA* XXXVI #2 (June 1921), pp. 119-133.
113. Johnston, R. C. and D. R. Owen, *Two Old French Gauvain Romances:* le Chevalier a l'épée and La Mule Sans Frein, Edinburgh: Edinburgh University, 1972.
114. Jones, William. *Credulities Past and Present*, London, 1880; repr. Detroit, Michigan: Gale, 1968.

115. Jones, William. *Crowns and Coronations—A History of Regalia,* London, 1883; repr. Detroit: Gale, 1968.
116. *Karlamagnus Saga,* tr. Constance Hieatt, Toronto: Pontifical Institute of Medieval Studies, I (1975), II (1975), III (1980).
117. Karr, Phyllis, *The King Arthur Companion,* Reston, Virginia: Reston Publishing, 1983.
118. Keen, Maurice. "Brotherhood in Arms," *History* 47 (1962), pp. 1-17.
119. Keen, Maurice. *Chivalry,* New Haven, Connecticut: Yale University, 1984.
120. Keen, Maurice. *The Outlaws of Medieval England,* London, 1961; repr. New York: Penguin, 1969.
121. Kibler, William. *"Bibliography* of 14th and 15th Century French Epics," *Olifant,* XI, No. 1, 1986, pp. 23-50.
122. Kimble, George H. T. *Geography in the Middle Ages,* New York, 1938; repr. New York: Russell and Russell, 1968.
123. LaMonte, John L. *Feudal Monarchy in the Latin Kingdom of Jerusalem, 1100-1291,* Cambridge, Massachusetts: 1932; repr. New York: AMS Press, 1977.
124. LaMonte, John L. *World of the Middle Ages,* New York, 1949; repr. New York: Irvington, 1976.
125. *Lancaster, History of the County of,* ed. W. Farrer and J. Brownbill, London: Arnold Constable, 1908, II.
126. Langlois, Charles V. *La Connaissance de la nature et du monde,* Paris, 1927. [Contains: Philippe de Thaon, *Bestiaire,* pp. 1-43; *Les merveilles de Prêtre Jean,* pp. 44-70; *La mappemonde de Pierre,* pp. 122-134; *L'Image du Monde,* pp. 135-197; Brunetto Latino, *Le livre du trésor,* pp. 335-390.]
127. Langlois, Charles V. *La Vie en France au Moyen Age,* Paris, 1926. [Contains: *Galeron, L'Escoufle, Guillaume de Dôle, Joufrois, Flamenca, Jehan et Blonde, La Chastellaine de Vergi, La Chatelain de Couci, Sone de Nansei.*]
128. Langlois, Ernest. *Table de Noms Propres de Tout Nature Compris dans les Chansons de Geste,* Paris: Librairie Emile Bouillon, 1904; repr. New York: Burt Franklin, 1971.
129. Layamon. "Brut," *Arthurian Chronicles,* London: J. M. Dent, 1912; repr. New York: E. P. Dutton, 1962, pp. 115-264.
130. Le Patourel, John. *Feudal Empires Norman and Plantagenet,* London: Hambledon Press, 1984.
131. Le Patourel, John. "The Plantagenet Dominions," *History* L (1965), pp. 289-308.
132. Lea, Henry C. *Superstition and Force,* Philadelphia: University of Pennsylvania, 1895.

133. Lea, Henry C. *Torture*, Philadelphia: University of Pennsylvania, 1973.

134. Leach, Henry G. *Angevin Britain and Scandinavia*, Cambridge, Massachusetts: Harvard University, 1921.

135. *Lion de Bourges, Poème épique du XIVe siècle*, ed. William Kibler, J. L. Pricherit, T. S. Fenster, 2 vols., Geneva: Droz, 1980.

136. Lloyd, Alan. *King John*, Newton Abbot, England: David and Charles, 1973.

137. *London Encyclopedia*, ed. Ben Weinreb and Christopher Hibbert, London: Macmillan, 1983.

138. Lonigan, Paul R. "Ganelon before Marsile," *Studi Francesci* 41 (1970), pp. 276-280.

139. Loomis, Roger S. *Arthurian Tradition and Chrétien de Troyes*, New York: Columbia University, 1949.

140. Loomis, Roger S. "Edward I, Arthurian Enthusiast," *Speculum* XXVIII (1953), pp. 114-127.

141. Loomis, Roger S. "Morgain la Fée and the Celtic Goddess," *Speculum* XXVIII (1953), pp. 114-127.

142. Loomis, Roger S. *The Grail from Celtic Myth to Christian Symbol*, New York: Columbia University, 1963.

143. Luchaire, Achille. *Social Life in France at the Time of Philip Augustus*, tr. E. B. Krehbiel, 2nd ed., New York: Harper & Row, 1967.

144. Maitland, F. W. *Domesday Book and Beyond*, Cambridge: Cambridge University, 1897; repr. London: Fontana Library, 1969.

145. Malory, Sir Thomas. *Le Morte D'Arthur*, ed. by E. Vinaver, London: Oxford University, repr. 1977.

146. *La Mappemonde de Pierre*, in C. V. Langlois, *La Connaissance de la nature et du monde*, Paris: 1927, pp. 122-134.

147. Marie de France, *Lais*, tr. Eugene Mason, London and New York: E. P. Dutton, 1966.

148. Mathew, G. "Ideals of Knighthood in late fourteenth century England," *Studies in Medieval History Presented to Sir Maurice Powicke*, ed. R. Hunt, R. Southern, Oxford: Oxford University, 1948, pp. 354-362.

149. Matthew, Donald. *Atlas of Medieval Europe*, New York: Facts on File, 1983.

150. MacCulloch, J. A. *Medieval Faith and Fable*, Boston: Marshall Jones, 1932.

151. McFarlane, K. B. "Had Edward I a policy towards the earls?" *History* L (1965), pp. 145-159.

152. McFarlane, K. B. *The Nobility of Later Medieval England,* London: Oxford University, 1973.
153. McKisack, May. *The Fourteenth Century,* London: Oxford University, 1959.
154. Meade, Marion. *Eleanor of Aquitaine,* New York: Hawthorne, 1977.
155. *Medieval Literature of Western Europe, A Review of Research mainly 1930-1960,* ed. John H. Fisher, New York: Modern Language Association, 1966.
156. Morris, W. A. *The Medieval English Sheriff,* Manchester, England: Manchester University, 1927.
157. *Le Morte Arthur: A Critical Edition,* ed. P. F. Hissinger, The Hague, The Netherlands: Mouton, 1975.
159. *Morte Arthure,* ed. John Finlayson, Evanston, Illinois: Northwestern University [York Medieval Texts], 1971.
160. Newton, Arthur P. *Travel and Travellers in the Middle Ages,* London, 1930.
161. *Nibelungenlied,* tr. by A. T. Hatto, London: Penguin, 1965.
162. Norgate, Kate. *England under the Angevin Kings,* London: Macmillan, 1887; repr. New York: Burt Franklin, 1969.
163. Norgate, Kate. *Richard the Lion Heart,* New York: Macmillan, 1924; repr. New York: Russell and Russell, 1969.
164. Ockerby, Horace. *Book of Dignities,* London: W. H. Allen, 1890.
165. *Of Arthour and Merlin,* ed. O. D. Macrae-Gibson, London: EETS OS #279, 1979.
166. Oman, Sir Charles. *A History of the Art of War in the Middle Ages,* 2vols., London: Oxford University, 1924; repr. New York: Burt Franklin, 1959.
167. Owings, Marvin. *The Arts in the Middle English Romances,* New York: Bookman Associates, 1952.
168. *Oxford Companion to English Literature,* London: Oxford University, 1964.
169. *Oxford English Dictionary,* London: Oxford University, 1970.
170. Painter, Sidney. *French Chivalry,* Ithaca, New York: Cornell, 1940; repr. 1979.
171. Painter, Sidney. *The Reign of King John,* Baltimore, Maryland: Johns Hopkins, 1949; repr. 1966.
172. Painter, Sidney. *William Marshall,* Baltimore, Maryland: Johns Hopkins University, 1933; repr. 1967.
173. Paris, Gaston. *Histoire poétique de Charlemagne,* Paris: Libraire Emile Bouillon, 1905.
174. Partner, Nancy F. *Serious Entertainments: Writing of History in 12th Century England,* Chicago: University of Chicago, 1977.

175. Paton, Lucy. *Studies in the Fairy Mythology of the Arthurian Tradition*, New York: Burt Franklin, 1970.

176. Paul, Sir James B. *The Scot's Peerage*, Edinburgh, Scotland: David Douglas, I, 1904.

177. Percy, Bishop Thomas. *Reliques of Ancient English Poetry*, London, 1811; repr. New York: Dover, 1966.

178. Petit-Dutaillis, Charles. *The Feudal Monarchies in France and England from the Tenth to the Thirteenth Centuries*, tr. E. D. Hunt, New York: Harper & Row, 1964.

179. Pohu, M. l'Abbé. *The Royal Abbey of Fontevrault*, tr. Marguerite Gray, Fontevrault, 1961.

180. Poole, A. Lane. *From Domesday Book to Magna Carta, 1087-1216*, 2nd ed., London: Oxford University, 1955.

181. Poole, A. Lane. *Obligations of Society in the XII and XIII Centuries*, London: Oxford University, 1946.

182. Powell, J. Enoch and Keith Wallis. *The House of Lords in the Middle Ages*, London, 1968.

183. Powicke, Frederick M. *The Thirteenth Century,* 2nd ed., London: Oxford University, 1962.

184. Powicke, Frederick M. *King Henry III and the Lord Edward,* London: Oxford University, 1947; repr. 1966.

185. Powicke, Michael R. "Distraint of Knighthood and Military Obligations under Henry III," *Speculum* XXV (1950), pp. 457-470.

186. Prestage, Edgar. *Chivalry: A Series of Studies to Illustrate Its Significance and Civilizing Influence*, London: Knopf, 1928; repr. New York: AMS Press, 1974.

187. Queller, Donald. *Office of the Ambassador in the Middle Ages*, Princeton, New Jersey: Princeton University, 1967.

188. Radford, C. A. Ralegh, and Michael Swanton. *Arthurian Sites in the West*, Exeter, England: University of Exeter English Medieval Studies, 1975.

189. Richardson, H. G., and G. O. Sayles. *The English Parliament in the Middle Ages*, London: Hambledon, 1981.

190. Robertson, John G. *History of German Literature,* 6th ed., Edinburgh: Edinburgh University, 1970.

191. Rogers, J. E. *History of Agriculture and Prices*, I (1265-1400), II (1265-1400), London: Oxford University, 1866.

192. Ross, Susan. *The Castles of Scotland*, London: George Philip, 1973.

193. *Royalty, Peerage, and Aristocracy in the World*, 90, London and New York: International Publication Service, 1967.

194. Rudorff, Raymond. *Knights in the Age of Chivalry*, New York:

Viking, 1974.

195. Runciman, Steven. *History of the Crusades*: I. *The First Crusade*;
II. *The Kingdom of Jerusalem*; III. *The Kingdom of Acre*,
London and Baltimore: Penguin, 1978.

196. Salch, Charles-Laurent. *L'Atlas des Chateaux Forts en France*,
Strassbourg: Editions Publitotal, 1976.

197. Salmon, Paul. *Literature in Medieval Germany*, London: Routlege
and Kegan Paul, 1967.

198. Schramm, Percy E. *History of the Coronation*, London: Constable,
1937.

199. Scott, Martin, *Medieval Europe*, London: Longman Green, 1964.

200. Seltzer, Leon. *Columbia Lippincott Gazeteer of the World*, New
York: Columbia University, 1952.

201. Setton, Kenneth. *A History of the Crusades:* Madison, Wisconsin:
University of Wisconsin, I. *First Hundred Years,* ed. by M. W.
Baldwin, 1969; II. *Later Crusades,* ed. by R. Wolff and H.
Hazard, 1969; III. *Fourteenth and Fifteenth Centuries,* ed. by
H. Hazard, 1975.

202. Severs. J. Burke. *Manual of the Writings in Middle English*:
1050-1500; fascicle 1 - *Romances*, New Haven, Connecticut:
Connecticut Academy of Arts and Sciences, 1967.

203. Seward, Desmond. *The Hundred Years War: The English in
France*: *1337-1453*, New York: Atheneum, 1978.

204. Shaw, William A. *The Knights of England from the Earliest Times*,
London, 1906; repr. Baltimore: Genealogical Publishing, 1976.

205. *Sir Ferumbras,* ed. Sidney Herrtage, Oxford: EETS ES #34, repr.
1966.

206. *Sir Gawain and the Green Knight,* ed. J. R. R. Tolkien and E. V.
Gordon, 2nd ed., London: Oxford University, 1967.

207. *Six Middle English Romances,* ed. Maldwyn Smith, London, 1973.

208. *Six Old English Chronicles*, ed. by J. A. Giles, London, 1885;
repr. Philadelphia: R. West, 1977.

209. Smail, Raymond P. *Crusading Warfare,* Cambridge, England:
Cambridge University, 1956.

210. *Song of Roland: An Analytical Edition,* ed. Gerald Brault,
2 vols., University Park, Pennsylvania: Pennsylvania State
University, 1978.

211. Spence, Lewis. *Dictionary of Medieval Romance and Romance
Writers,* London, 1913; repr. New York: Humanities Press,
1962.

212. Squibb, G. D. *The High Court of Chivalry*, London: Oxford
University, 1959.

213. Stenton, Sir Frank M. *Anglo-Saxon England*, 2nd ed., London:

Oxford University, 1947.

214. *Story of Troilus,* tr. G. K. Gordon, New York: E. P. Dutton, 1964.

215. Strutt, Joseph. *The Sports and Pastimes of the People of England,* London, 1903.

216. Tetlow, Edwin. *The Enigma of Hastings,* London: Peter Owen, 1974.

217. Thaon, Philippe de. "Bestiare," in Charles V. Langlois, *La Connaissance de la nature et du monde,* Paris, 1927, pp. 1-43.

218. Thiebaux, Marcelle. "The Medieval Chase," *Speculum* XXXVII (1962), pp. 260-274.

219. Thrall, William, and Addison Hibbard. *Handbook of Literature,* New York: Odyssey, 1960.

220. Tilley, Arthur. *Medieval France,* New York and London: Hafner, 1964.

221. Tolstoi, Nikolai. *The Quest for Merlin,* Boston: Little, Brown, 1985.

222. Tout, T. F. "Captivity and Death of Edward of Carnarvon," *Bulletin of the John Rylands Library* VI (1921),pp. 69-113.

223. Tuchman, Barbara. *A Distant Mirror,* New York: Knopf, 1978.

224. Turnbull, Stephen. *The Book of the Medieval Knight,* New York: Crown, 1985.

225. Twining, E. F. *European Regalia,* London: Constable, 1967.

226. Uden, Grant. *Dictionary of Chivalry,* Harmondsworth, England: Kestrel, 1977.

227. Ulrich von Zatzikhoven. *Lanzelet,* tr. Kenneth G. T. Webster, ed. Roger S. Loomis, New York: Columbia University, 1951.

228. Vale, Malcolm. *War and Chivalry,* London: Duckworth, 1981.

229. Verbruggen, J. F. *The Art of Warfare in Western Europ during the Middle Ages,* tr. by S. Willard and S. M. Southern, Amsterdam: Elsevier, 1977.

230. Villehardouin and de Joinville. *Memoires of the Crusades,* tr. by Sir Frank Marzials, New York: E. P. Dutton, 1958.

231. Voretzsch, Karl. *Introduction to the Study of Old French Literature,* tr. F. M. Du Mont, 3rd ed., Halle: Max Niemeyer Verlag, 1931.

232. Wace. "Le Roman de Brut," in *Arthurian Chronicles,* London: Everyman, 1928; repr. New York: E. P. Dutton, 1972, pp. 1-115.

233. Wallace-Hadrill, John. *The Long-Haired Kings,* London: Methuen, 1962.

234. Walsh, Clifford, ed. *Dictionary of English Law,* London, 1959.

235. Walshe, Maurice. *Medieval German Literature, A Survey,* Cambridge, Massachusetts: Harvard, 1962

236. Ward, Henry L. D. *Catalog of the Romances in the Department of Manuscripts in the British Museum*, 3 vols., London: British Museum, 1883-1910.
237. Ward, Philip. *Oxford Companion to Spanish Literature*, London: Oxford University, 1978.
238. *Warwick, History of the County of*, II, London: Constable, 1908; VII, London: Oxford University, 1968.
239. *Webster's New Geographical Dictionary*, Springfield, Massachusetts: G. & C. Merriam, 1972.
240. West, Francis. *The Justiciarship in England: 1066-1232*, Cambridge, England: Cambridge University, 1966.
241. West, G. D. *An Index of Proper Names in French Arthurian Prose Romances*, Toronto: Toronto University, 1978.
242. West, G. D. *An Index of Proper Names in French Arthurian Verse Romances, 1150-1300*, Toronto: Toronto University, 1969.
243. Weston, Jessie L. *The Legend of Perceval*, 2 vols., London, 1902.
244. White, Berte. "Battle of Hastings," in [Cockayne] *The Complete Peerage*, London: St. Catherine's, 1957, XI, Appendix L.
245. Wilkins, Ernest. *History of Italian Literature*, rev. T. G. Bergin, Cambridge, Massachusetts: Harvard University, 1974.
246. Wilkinson, Bertie. *The High Middle Ages in England, 1154-1377*, Cambridge, England: Cambridge University, 1978.
247. Wilkinson, Frederick. *The Castles of England*, London: George Philip, 1973.
248. Wright, John L. *Geographical Lore at the Time of the Crusades*, New York: American Geographical Society, 1925.
249. *York*, ed. William Page, in *Victoria History of the Counties of England,II*, London: Constable and Co., 1913.

Index

Bold-face page numbers indicate a major entry; names in parentheses usually indicate the locality of which the entry was sovereign.

About the Author

BRADFORD B. BROUGHTON is Professor of Technical Communications at Clarkson University, Potsdam, New York. In addition to the *Dictionary of Medieval Knighthood and Chivalry: Concepts and Terms* (Greenwood Press, 1986), he is the author of *Legends of Richard I Coeur de Lion, Richard the Lion Hearted & Other English Metrical Romances*, and *Twenty-Seven to 1*.